Applied EXERCISE & SPORT PHYSIOLOGY WITH LABS

FOURTH EDITION

Terry J. Housh
UNIVERSITY OF NEBRASKA–LINCOLN

Dona J. Housh
UNIVERSITY OF NEBRASKA MEDICAL CENTER

Herbert A. deVries

Holcomb Hathaway, Publishers
Scottsdale, Arizona

Library of Congress Cataloging-in-Publication Data

Names: Housh, Terry J., author. | Housh, Dona J., author. | DeVries, Herbert A., author.
Title: Applied exercise & sport physiology with labs / Terry J. Housh, Dona J. Housh, Herbert A. deVries.
Other titles: Applied exercise and sport physiology with labs
Description: Fourth edition. | Scottsdale, Arizona : Holcomb Hathaway, Publishers, [2016] | Includes bibliographical references and index.
Identifiers: LCCN 2016001073 (print) | LCCN 2016001758 (ebook) | ISBN 9781621590491 (print) | ISBN 9781621590507 (ebook)
Subjects: | MESH: Physical Fitness—physiology | Exercise Therapy—methods | Sports—physiology
Classification: LCC QP301 (print) | LCC QP301 (ebook) | NLM WB 541 | DDC 612/.044—dc23
LC record available at http://lccn.loc.gov/2016001073

Photo Credits: *Front cover:* NejroN/123RF. *Back cover:* Alan Poulson/123RF. *Page iii,* Andrii Mertsalov/123RF; *page 1,* tan4ikk/123RF; *page 4,* alicephoto/123RF; *page 19,* Maksim Toome/123RF; *page 39,* John Kropewnicki/123RF; *page 42,* Jakub Hasák/123RF; *page 63,* Jan Novak/123RF; *page 81,* maridav/123RF; *page 109,* Flashon Studio/123RF; *page 135,* sjenner13/123RF; *page 147,* diego cervo/123RF; *page 163,* rido/123RF; *page 193,* Val Thoermer/123RF; *page 227,* alexandralexey/123RF; *page 279,* Wavebreak Media Ltd/123RF; *page 301,* sportgraphic /123RF; *page 313,* tomwang/123RF; *page 333,* marcogovel/123RF; *page 355,* dotshock/123RF; *page 375,* Ann Dudko/123RF; *page 389,* Kostic Dusan/123RF; *page 421,* kzenon/123RF; Andrii Mertsalov

Please note: The authors and publisher have made every effort to provide current website addresses in this book. However, because web addresses change constantly, it is inevitable that some of the URLs listed here will change following publication of this book.

Holcomb Hathaway, Publishers, Inc.
8700 E. Via de Ventura Blvd., Suite 265
Scottsdale, Arizona 85258
480-991-7881
www.hh-pub.com

10 9 8 7 6 5 4 3 2 1

Print ISBN: 978-1-62159-049-1
Ebook ISBN: 978-1-62159-050-7

Printed in the United States of America.

Contents

3 Metabolism and Metabolic Adaptations to Training 39

4 The Nervous System 63

15 Nutrition for Fitness and Athletics 333

16 Ergogenic Aids for Fitness and Athletics 355

Preface

Over the years, we've witnessed dramatic growth in the popularity of physical fitness for all ages and a similar growth in exercise science programs at undergraduate and graduate levels in colleges and universities. As a result, we believe there is a need for an *applied, entry-level* textbook such as *Applied Exercise & Sport Physiology, with Labs,* Fourth Edition, serving students who will become exercise science professionals, physician's assistants, physical therapists, physical educators, and coaches—students who need practical information to apply in hospitals, clinics, schools, and settings such as health clubs, Y's, youth sports, and so forth.

This text, inspired by the classic textbook by Herbert A. deVries titled *Physiology of Exercise for Physical Education, Athletics, and Exercise Science,* is designed as an introduction to exercise and sport physiology. Its applied perspective helps students understand and appreciate the scientific foundations of exercise and sport. As mentioned above, this text is most appropriate for an entry-level course. In some institutions, students receive only limited exposure to the basic sciences such as chemistry, human physiology, and anatomy, and they may take only one course that covers the scientific foundations of exercise and sport. This text was designed for such a situation. If, however, an institution offers an introductory course as well and an advanced or more specialized course in exercise physiology, this book is designed for the first course, serving as a foundational text for the advanced course. It provides an essential introduction to many of the systems of the body, yet it has the breadth to cover the important scientific and applied aspects of exercise and sport physiology. This text is easily adaptable for courses taught under either a quarter or semester system.

A unique aspect of this textbook is that lecture information and laboratory materials are both available in one textbook (no separate lab manual for students to purchase!). In this edition, 18 laboratory experiences accompany the book's chapters (including 7 labs new to this edition). Each lab provides a brief discussion of the theory underlying the test of physical fitness, measurement procedures, example calculations of important parameters, data-recording forms for use in the laboratories, and norms that allow students to compare and classify the results. The laboratories were chosen for several reasons: (1) they complement the topics covered in the text; (2) they are important and useful to exercise professionals, physical educators, and coaches; (3) they provide a demonstration and/or experimental activity for the instructor to use; and (4) they provide an opportunity for hands-on learning.

Special Features of Our Book

- Learning Objectives for each chapter
- Key Concepts listed at the beginning of chapters and highlighted in the page margins for easy reference
- A comprehensive Glossary containing definitions of the book's key concepts for review and study purposes
- Website callouts in page margins to allow readers to further explore relevant topics and locate professional organizations

- Boxes highlighting clinical applications and relevant research in exercise physiology
- Questions for Review at the end of each chapter

New to This Edition

- Integration of the material on female athletes into relevant chapters; for example, the discussion of physical activity and pregnancy and childbirth appears in Chapter 9, and resistance training for female athletes appears in Chapter 11.
- Refocusing of labs to include those that can easily be taught in conjunction with an exercise physiology course without involving sophisticated, expensive equipment.
- Seven new labs (of 18 total) covering topics such as anthropometric measures of health risk, non-exercise-based estimation of the ventilatory threshold, and vertical jump test for measuring muscular power of the legs.
- Incorporation of the FITT-VP principle into discussions of aerobic and resistance exercise prescription.
- Expanded discussion of exercise prescriptions for individuals with various conditions, including overweight/obesity, asthma, and COPD.
- Added research on exercise and managing hypertension, exercise and Parkinson's disease, using EMG and MMG to study muscle function, response of growth and metabolism hormones to exercise, and antioxidant supplements and muscle damage.

About the Student Website

A companion student website is available:

www.hhpcommunities.com/exercisephysiology

Features of this open-access site include:

- Interactive practice quizzes and study guides to help students learn major physiological concepts for test taking, future study, and workplace applications
- A vocabulary review to assist students in learning scientific terminology
- Digital image bank
- Website links allowing students to easily access the sites noted in the book

Instructor Ancillaries

Finally, for instructors, the following aids are available:

- A comprehensive Instructor's Manual including lecture outlines, student assignments, discussion/essay questions, and test questions
- A PowerPoint presentation including key illustrations from the text
- A test bank compatible with learning management systems

We believe this practical textbook is an ideal resource for its target audience, offering access to both theory and application in an appealing, balanced format.

Acknowledgments

We are grateful to the hundreds of scientists around the world who have made this text possible. While it is not possible to acknowledge every contributor to this work, we would like to recognize the following scientists who have been influential in the course of our professional lives: Martha Coryell, Stroudsburg State University; Roger J. Williams, University of Texas; J. Pat Meehan and Aileene Lockhart of the University of Southern California; Glen O. Johnson, University of Nebraska–Lincoln; and William G. Thorland.

We would like to thank the following individuals, who provided feedback as we developed the fourth edition: Janet Barrone-Curry, Arizona State University, Tempe/Polytechnic; Jared W. Coburn, California State University, Fullerton; Shawn Dassie, University of the Incarnate Word; Ann Deblinger, Passaic County Community College; Douglas Herndon, Lorain County Community College; Tom Hood, Doane College; Corey Huck, University of Wisconsin; Joshua Miller, California State University, Bakersfield; Sergej Ostojic, University of Novi Sad; Corey Selland, South Dakota State University; and Bridgette Wilde, Arizona State University, Phoenix.

Our continued thanks also to reviewers of the previous editions, because their contributions are still reflected in this book: Cynthia Allen, Jonathan H. Anning, Jennifer M. Bridges, Lee E. Brown, Shane Callahan, Scott Crouter, Tammy K. Evetovich, Kevin J. Finn, Nancy Gamboian, Roger H. Grant, Matthew S. Hickey, Leta Hicks, Edward M. Heath, John Hjelm, Kathy Howe, Arnold G. Nelson, Richard Newman, Mary Pieklo, Pat Querry, Carole Sloan, Amy Jo Sutterluety, Douglas B. Smith, Lauren Rose Tapp, Mary F. Visser, Aly Williams, and Kerri Winters.

Our sincere thanks go to Loree L. Weir for providing several research boxes, for contributing to the laboratory experiences, and for authoring the Instructor's Manual that goes along with this text. We appreciate her help. We also want to thank Haley Bergstrom for her help in the revision of this text.

We want to thank our many undergraduate students who helped us develop the perspective on exercise science, physical education, and coaching reflected in this text. Most important, we want to say thank you to all of our graduate students who have taught (and continue to teach) us as much as we have taught them. It has been our greatest professional joy to work with you.

About the Authors

Terry J. Housh, Ph.D., FACSM, FNSCA, is a Professor in the Department of Nutrition and Health Sciences, Director of the Exercise Physiology Laboratory, and Co-director of the Center for Youth Fitness and Sports Research at the University of Nebraska–Lincoln (UNL). He received a B.A. degree in Physical Education with teaching endorsements in K–12 Physical Education and Health from Doane College, and an M.P.E. in Exercise Science and a Ph.D. in Exercise Physiology from the University of Nebraska–Lincoln. Dr. Housh taught two years at Portland State University before returning to UNL.

Dr. Housh's primary research interests are growth and development in young athletes and muscle function. He has coauthored over 250 peer-reviewed research articles and eight college textbooks as well as over 250 presentations at annual meetings of professional organizations including the American College of Sports Medicine (ACSM), Society of Health and Physical Educators (SHAPE), National Strength and Conditioning Association (NSCA), and National Athletic Trainers Association (NATA). He was the 1998 recipient of the Outstanding Sport Scientist Award from the National Strength and Conditioning Association.

Dr. Housh is a Senior Associate Editor for the *Journal of Strength and Conditioning Research*, and he reviews for a number of journals including *Medicine and Science in Sports and Exercise, Research Quarterly for Exercise and Sport, Journal of Applied Physiology,* and *Pediatric Exercise Science.*

Dona J. Housh, Ph.D., FACSM, is a Professor in the Oral Biology Department, College of Dentistry, at the University of Nebraska Medical Center, where she teaches Human Physiology to first-year dental students as well as post-doctoral graduate students in various dental specialties. Dr. Housh received a B.S. degree in Physical Education from Portland State University, and an M.P.E. in Exercise Science and a Ph.D. in Exercise Physiology from the University of Nebraska–Lincoln.

Dr. Housh's research interests include muscle function, neuromuscular fatigue, and the hypertrophic responses to resistance training. She has authored numerous peer-reviewed articles in prestigious scholarly journals and given research presentations at annual meetings of the American College of Sports Medicine and the National Strength and Conditioning Association. Dr. Housh is an Associate Editor for the *Journal of Strength and Conditioning Research* and reviews for many other scientific journals including *Medicine and Science in Sports and Exercise* and *Pediatric Exercise Science.*

Herbert A. deVries, Ph.D., FACSM (1918–2009), was Professor Emeritus of the Department of Physical Education at the University of Southern California. He received a B.S. from Pennsylvania State College at East Stroudsburg, an M.Ed. from the University of Texas, and a Ph.D. from the University of Southern California. Dr. deVries was Coordinator of Research and taught in the Department of Physical Education at California State University at Long Beach until 1965. He then taught in the Department of Physical Education at the University of Southern

California until his retirement in 1983. During this time, Dr. deVries was also Preceptor at the USC Gerontology Center and Laboratory Chief of the Physiology of Exercise Laboratory at the Andrus Gerontology Center.

Dr. deVries was world-renown for his research on the physiological adaptations to exercise training in older adults, and throughout his life he remained active in research involving the application of electromyography to various aspects of neuromuscular fatigue. He published extensively in prestigious peer-reviewed journals and was the author of 11 books including five editions of his classic text *Physiology of Exercise for Physical Education, Athletics, and Exercise Science*. For his lifetime of scholarly work, Dr. deVries was honored with the Alumni Honor Award from East Stroudsburg State College, the Silver Anniversary Award by the President's Council on Physical Fitness and Sports, and the Citation Award from the American College of Sports Medicine. In addition, the Council on Aging and Adult Development of AAHPERD named the CAAD Research Award the "Herbert A. deVries Research Award."

1 Why Study Exercise Physiology?

As a result of reading this chapter you will:

Understand why it is important for exercise professionals, physical educators, and coaches to study exercise physiology.

Know that exercise physiology is concerned with both health and athletic performance.

Know the difference between a professional and a layperson in the context of prescribing exercise.

Understand the basics of the scientific method and how a hunch, a hypothesis, a theory, and a principle differ as they relate to the credibility of scientific information.

key concepts

hunch
hypothesis
physiology
physiology of exercise and sport
principle
professional
theory

Undergraduate students in exercise science, physical education, and coaching often regard physiology of exercise and sport as one of the more difficult and rigorous courses in the curriculum. Common questions are, "Do I need an entire course to tell me that exercise is good for me?" or "Is all this scientific preparation really necessary so that I can teach physical education and coach track, swimming, football, and so on?" These are fair questions. In this chapter we answer these questions and give an overview of interesting, provocative, and highly practical material on the physiological basis of human movement, whether performed for work, play, health, physical fitness, or training for athletic competition.

Physiology of exercise and sport is a subdivision of general **physiology** and is concerned largely with the improvement of human functional capacities. This can involve the enhancement of health and physical fitness for the general population or the optimization of performance in the various types and levels of competitive athletics.

physiology of exercise and sport
physiology

WHY PHYSICAL FITNESS?

For many years, discussions about physical fitness frequently evolved into arguments about definition. The discussion often ended with this question: Physical fitness for what? The implication of that question was that we need only be fit enough to meet the physical challenges of our workaday world, with maybe a little bit left over for good measure! Since many of us in this mechanized and industrialized civilization meet very few physical challenges, low levels of functional capacity (fitness) were acceptable. Applying the concept of "pursuit of excellence" to optimizing physical fitness awaited the knowledge boom of the past several decades. We now have enough scientific evidence to answer the question *Physical fitness for what?* with this simple statement: Optimal levels of physical activity and fitness are conducive to lifelong good health. For example, the Society of Health and Physical Educators (SHAPE) America (formerly the American Alliance for Health, Physical Education, Recreation, and Dance, AAHPERD)[1] has concluded:

1. Physical activity is important to the overall health and well-being of everyone, including school-age children.
2. The benefits of physical activity are well documented and include the mitigation of health risks, including those for developing type 2 diabetes, high blood pressure, and high blood cholesterol.
3. Physical activity also contributes to the building and maintenance of healthy bones and muscles, improved health-related fitness, and positive social and mental health.
4. Childhood obesity continues to be a top public health concern throughout the United States, and physical activity is a proven critical tool for preventing and treating obesity and its related risk factors.
5. Healthier students are better learners, and physical activity can improve student academic achievement, as well as attention span, classroom behavior, and attendance.
6. The U.S. Department of Health and Human Services has recommended that children and adolescents should be physically active at least 60 minutes daily and should participate in activities that are moderate to vigorous in intensity and that are muscle- and bone-strengthening.

www

President's Council on Fitness, Sports and Nutrition
www.fitness.gov

National Association for Health and Fitness
www.physicalfitness.org

IMPROVING ATHLETIC AND SPORT PERFORMANCE

In addition to its focus on exercise for health, exercise and sport physiology is also concerned with improving athletic and sport performance. As we seek to help athletes develop the best possible performance, we must recognize that coaching and athletic training are both an art and a science. The art lies in applying sound psychological and sociological principles in motivating and in designing creative training programs that help athletes and clients gain desired ends while avoiding boredom, injury, and unpleasantness. But no matter how good an artist the coach or trainer may be, all is for naught if he or she does not have a sound grounding in exercise and sport physiology, which allows an understanding of the nature of the body's responses to training stimuli, both immediate (acute response) and long term (chronic adaptation).

If a coach or personal trainer has overworked (commonly called *overtrained*) an athlete for a period of time, no amount of art will prevent injury and staleness from setting in. Conversely, a lack of knowledge of the physiological bases of good training practices, such as progressive resistance training for power or interval training for endurance, will prevent the athlete from realizing his or her full potential and will probably result in a poor win–loss record.

Even more important than the win–loss record, however, is the maintenance of good health in athletes. Well-trained professional coaches and personal trainers must know the physiological effects of environmental factors such as heat and cold on their athletes. Every year athletes die on the football field from heat stroke. Most of these deaths could be prevented if all coaches were thoroughly trained in the basics of environmental exercise physiology. Also important to the health of the athlete is good nutritional practice. Too many coaches and athletic trainers, even today, rely on conventional opinions instead of scientific evidence about the diet of athletes. The use of drugs to improve performance is a hazardous practice at best, and it is doubly deplorable because the hazard is rarely accompanied by any significant improvement in performance. With the seeming ease of access for athletes to a variety of drugs, the coach or trainer must not only be aware of the manifestations of these drugs but must also be aware of the health hazards of such drugs. As the list of banned substances grows longer and as drug testing becomes increasingly available and mandated by school athletic organizations, the coach, physical education instructor, exercise scientist, or athletic trainer will have to develop a knowledge base in order to guide and advise athletes.

PROFESSIONALISM IN EXERCISE SCIENCE, PHYSICAL EDUCATION, AND ATHLETICS

During World War II, lay members of the army (enlisted men who had been well-known players in baseball, football, or other sports) were trained to be noncommissioned physical training leaders in six to eight weeks. These soldiers functioned quite well in leading calisthenics programs and athletic competitions. Were these people equivalent to physical education or exercise professionals? Most definitely not! While they knew the "what" of the program, they did not in most cases understand the "why." They had no professional training in basic exercise sciences such as exercise and sport physiology, kinesiology, and motor learning. Thus, they depended on commissioned officers who were professionally trained physical educators to develop the overall training program and to guide its implementation.

Endurance training versus resistance training for health promotion

A study by Grund et al.* highlighted the attributes of endurance-trained, resistance-trained, and untrained individuals. The researchers collected a variety of fitness measures of the 42 men who participated in the study. The results showed clear differences between the groups. In general, endurance-trained men were more active; expended more energy in a 24-hour period; and had lower heart rates, increased heart rate variability (a measure of autonomic nervous system activity), and higher aerobic fitness ($\dot{V}O_2$ max). Resistance-trained individuals had more muscle mass and were stronger than untrained and endurance-trained men. Both the resistance-trained and the endurance-trained individuals were leaner (lower percent fat) than the untrained men. When taken as a whole, the findings of this study show that adaptations are specific to the type of training done and that, in terms of health promotion, endurance training seems to be superior to resistance training.

*Grund, A., Kraus, H., Siewers, M., Rieckert, H., and Muller, M. J. Association between different attributes of physical activity and fat mass in untrained, endurance- and resistance-trained men. *Eur. J. Appl. Physiol.* 84: 310–320, 2001.

WWW

Certification Sites
NSCA
www.nsca.com/Certification/
ACSM
http://certification.acsm.org/

WWW

NASPE Guidelines
www.shapeamerica.org/publications/resources/teachingtools/qualitype/loader.cfm?csModule=security/getfile&pageid=5336

professional

This pattern of utilizing nonprofessional exercise leaders has waned. The public's demand for access to exercise has led health clubs, corporate fitness programs, and clinically supervised conditioning and rehabilitation programs to turn to highly motivated and academically prepared exercise specialists. Many professional organizations require certification or licensure for their individual disciplines or professions. For example, the American College of Sports Medicine (ACSM) offers certifications, including ACSM Group Exercise Instructor, ACSM Certified Personal Trainer, ACSM Certified Health Fitness Specialist, ACSM Certified Clinical Exercise Specialist, and ACSM Certified Clinical Exercise Physiologist. In addition, the National Strength and Conditioning Association (NSCA) certifies individuals as Certified Strength and Conditioning Specialist (CSCS), NSCA-Certified Personal Trainer (CPT), Certified Special Population Specialist (CSPS), and Tactical Strength and Conditioning-Facilitator (TSAC-F). The popularity of these certification programs has been growing. NSCA Certification, for example, offers examinations in many languages and countries and has certified more than 40,000 individuals.[4]

Exercise and sport physiology is an important foundation course for students seeking certification in exercise science, as well as for those preparing for a future in physical education, athletic training, coaching, or the health and fitness industry. The National Association for Sport and Physical Education (NASPE) of SHAPE has recognized this fact by developing a set of guidelines for undergraduate exercise physiology courses.[3]

The difference between a **professional** and a layperson is that the member of a profession has "professed" a commitment to a learned discipline with a well-defined body of knowledge. This profession implies, in turn, the application of the scientific method to the professional body of knowledge, usually within a well-structured college or university curriculum. Thus, the professional exercise scientist and physical educator learn basic principles that are grounded in the scientific method. All practice (to the extent that scientific data are available), then, is based on scientifically derived principles. Untrained laypersons can only practice what has been handed down to them, since they do not understand the underlying principles that should govern their practice. For example, lay coaches can do only what they have seen their coaches (or other athletes) do, whether right or wrong.

While the layperson can function only at the "cookbook" level—that is, follow the instructions of a professionally trained individual—the person trained in the basic sciences, such as exercise and sport physiology, proceeds from scientific principles. We, as members of a learned profession, must always seek out the mechanisms underlying our practice. In doing so, we derive at least four practical advantages: (1) we can better predict results; (2) we can better control the conditioning and training process, thus protecting the health of athletes; (3) we gain better results per unit of time spent; and (4) we may even satisfy our intellectual curiosity with respect to cause-and-effect relationships in our field (this, of course, is research).

WWW

American College of Sports Medicine

www.acsm.org

National Strength and Conditioning Association

www.nsca.com

American Society of Exercise Physiologists

www.asep.org

THE RESPONSIBILITY FOR PRESCRIBING EXERCISE

As an exercise professional, physical educator, or coach, you are likely to be responsible for preparticipation health screening (see **Chapter 1 Lab**), exercise testing, and exercise prescription, whether you are involved in designing a training program for a client at a fitness center, developing unit plans and behavioral objectives for a physical education class, or organizing the fitness component of an athletic practice. Although these occur in different settings and with individuals who have different needs and fitness or performance goals, they all require at least a basic knowledge of the physiology underlying physical activity. Most of us have heard a physician or a well-meaning friend advise: "What you need is some exercise." Implicit in such a prescription is that it makes no difference whether one lifts weights for an hour, walks for 10 minutes, swims a mile, or jogs 3 miles. It is important that the public and the health-related professions, too, understand that the admonition to "get some exercise" is analogous to a physician writing a prescription that simply says, "Take some drugs." Just as there are many drugs to choose from when prescribing an analgesic for a backache, so are there many exercise training and conditioning modalities, each of which can be modified or administered in terms of intensity, frequency, and duration. Exercise science and physical education students must learn what is available from our pharmacopoeia of exercise. We must learn the scientific answers to how much is enough, how much is too much, and how much is best for any given individual.

The future holds great promise for expanding the exercise science and physical education professions to cater to the needs of people of all ages and both genders. Interestingly, the public's acceptance of the need for adult fitness seems to have advanced far more rapidly than our profession's leadership in training the personnel for such programs. Obviously, such personnel must be well grounded in exercise and sport physiology to prevent hazardous situations from arising among middle-aged and older people who may have unrecognized disease, weak muscles and bones, and poor cardiovascular function as a result of sedentary living.

The science of exercise

Over the last 50-plus years the focus of exercise science has gradually narrowed. From the 1960s to the present the focus has changed from studying the effects of acute and chronic exercise on the body at the organ level to studying the cellular and organelle level and, now, the molecular level. Each transition has followed breakthroughs in technologies, such as muscle biopsy techniques in the late 1960s and, subsequently, gene cloning and sequencing technology. Future scientists in the field of exercise science will need the proper academic preparation to compete in this environment.[2]

SCIENTIFIC METHOD

Exercise scientists, physical educators, and coaches who claim membership in the profession must base their practice on the best (most reliable and authoritative) information available. This information comes from the work of researchers who perform controlled experiments as part of the scientific method. The scientific

WWW

The Scientific Method
http://physics.ucr.edu/~wudka/Physics7/Notes_www/node5.html

method involves stating a problem, developing a plausible hypothesis to address the problem, determining an experimental method to test the hypothesis, observing the results of the experiment, and drawing conclusions from the results. Obviously, hearsay evidence is not in the same class as scientific results. The credibility of various sources of evidence can be ordered from poorest to best as follows:

hunch
hypothesis
theory
principle

1. **Hunch** or guess.
2. **Hypothesis:** a tentative supposition (based on prior observations) provisionally adopted to explain certain facts and to guide investigations. A hypothesis is set up to be tested and accepted or rejected on the basis of further observation or experiment.
3. **Theory:** a supposition based on scientific evidence but insufficiently verified to be accepted as fact. Theories provide the basis for developing principles.
4. **Principle:** a settled rule of action based on theories that are well supported by research findings. Principles are the guidelines for making decisions in our professional activities.

True professionals are set apart from lay practitioners in their ability and inclination to challenge the source of information. For example, the lay coach hears that a certain athlete who has broken the world record for the 1,500-meter run is a confirmed vegetarian. Not having been trained in the application of the scientific method and unfamiliar with the available research literature, the coach assumes a cause-and-effect relationship between the outstanding performance and the athlete's vegetarian habits. The coach then attempts to make vegetarians out of all athletes. The professionally trained coach, by contrast, sees this explanation of superior performance for what it is—no better than a hunch or guess, at best. The professional coach goes to the scientific literature, consulting reliable sources in physiology, biochemistry, and nutrition. Finding no support for a cause-and-effect relationship between superior running ability and a vegetarian diet, the coach rejects the hunch that the record performance was causally related to the athlete's vegetarianism.

In the long run, the work of exercise scientists, coaches, and physical educators that is based on scientifically derived principles will be considerably more successful than work based on unproven hunches or personal opinions. For this reason, this text provides the pertinent sources of research information in the hope that you will learn to be a discerning consumer of information about exercise science, physical education, and coaching practices.

summary

Studying exercise and sport physiology can provide the answers to many questions regarding the relationships among exercise, health, physical fitness, and athletic performance. Professional exercise scientists, physical educators, and coaches can then use the scientifically based information to prescribe safe and productive training programs for those interested in improving health-related fitness, to develop appropriate unit plans for students in physical education classes, and to organize effective practice sessions for athletes. This is so because professionals know not only what exercises to recommend and how to perform them, but also why one technique should be used instead of an alternative. The professional exercise scientist, physical educator, or coach understands the physiological mechanisms underlying the various training programs. A basic knowledge of the acute and chronic effects of participation in various forms of exercise can help individuals of all ages benefit from physical activity.

questions for review

1. Why is the study of exercise and sport physiology important to exercise scientists? Physical educators? Coaches?
2. How has the definition of physical fitness evolved over the past several decades?
3. Discuss the advantages of having adequately trained and informed professionals in the fields of exercise science, physical education, and coaching.
4. Describe the scientific method and explain why scientific inquiry is superior to conventional opinions.
5. In terms of health promotion, compare the effects of endurance training to resistance training.

student companion website

For further review of this book's chapters and for test preparation, visit the book's website, **www.hhpcommunities.com/exercisephysiology**, to take practice quizzes, review the vocabulary terms, use the study guide, and view the digital image bank.

references

1. American Alliance for Health, Physical Education, Recreation and Dance. Comprehensive school physical activity programs: Helping all students achieve 60 minutes of physical activity each day. [Position Statement]. Reston, VA: Author, 2013.
2. Baldwin, K. M. Research in the exercise sciences: where do we go from here? *J. Appl. Physiol.* 88: 332–336, 2000.
3. National Association for Sport and Physical Education. *Guidelines for undergraduate exercise physiology in a physical education teacher education program.* [Guidance document]. Reston, VA: Author, 2006.
4. National Strength and Conditioning Association. *NSCA Certification Handbook.* Colorado Springs, CO: Author, 2014.

CHAPTER 1

lab Preparticipation Health Screening, Medical Clearance, and Informed Consent

BACKGROUND

The American College of Sports Medicine recommends that medical supervision during exercise is not necessary for healthy individuals (children, adolescents, men <45 years of age, and women <55 years of age) who have no symptoms or known presence of heart disease or major coronary risk factors.[1] Therefore, the primary purpose of preparticipation health screening is to identify those individuals who should be excluded from exercise due to medical contraindications.

The ACSM has provided recommendations for preparticipation health screening procedures for various populations.[1] The ACSM defines preparticipation health screening as a three-step process that involves (a) risk stratification, (b) exercise testing and participation recommendations based on risk category, and (c) exercise testing and testing supervision recommendations based on risk category.

In addition to the preparticipation health screening, it may be important to have potential participants complete an informed consent document. The primary purpose of the informed consent document is to provide potential participants with clear and exact information about what they will be required to do during the exercise test. When participants fully understand what they must do, they will be instructed to sign the informed consent document, after which they will be allowed to do the exercise test. Page 10 shows an example of an informed consent document for a one-repetition maximum bench press (1-RM strength test).

With the exception of clinical exercise physiology laboratories and cardiac rehabilitation centers, most exercise science laboratories examine typical, healthy individuals. However, some individuals may not be aware of their risk stratification, so it is essential that careful screening procedures be completed. If the results of a preparticipation health screening questionnaire indicate that exercise may present a health risk for an individual, the individual should be encouraged to obtain medical clearance before participating. Determination of whether an individual is actually at risk by exercising can, however, be vague. Thus, the purpose of this laboratory is to describe the procedures used to perform preparticipation health screening.

TERMS & ABBREVIATIONS

- ACSM = American College of Sports Medicine
- 1-RM = one-repetition maximum
- PAR-Q+ = Physical Activity Readiness Questionnaire for Everyone
- risk stratification = categorization of the likelihood of untoward events based on the screening and evaluation of patient health characteristics

PROCEDURES

(see photo 1.1)

An individual's risk during exercise can be assessed with a medical screening instrument such as the Physical Activity Readiness Questionnaire for Everyone (PAR-Q+; see pages 11–14) or a Pre-exercise Testing Health Status Questionnaire (see pages 15–16). The PAR-Q+ is a common medical screening instrument used by many exercise physiology laboratories. The procedures used to determine risk stratification from both the PAR-Q+ and Pre-exercise Testing Health Status Questionnaire are described below.

photo 1.1

Administration of a pre-exercise testing health status questionnaire.

PAR-Q+

1. Begin administering the PAR-Q+ by instructing the individual to complete the first seven questions.
2. If the individual answers "yes" to one or more of the first seven questions, instruct him or her to contact a physician before performing any exercise. Inform the individual that he or she should tell the physician which questions had "yes" answers on the PAR-Q+. The individual should also ask the physician which exercise tests should or should not be performed.
3. If the individual answers "no" to all of the first seven questions, he or she should be allowed to perform the exercise test.

Pre-exercise Testing Health Status Questionnaire

1. Begin the Pre-exercise Testing Health Status Questionnaire by instructing the individual to complete the general information at the top of the questionnaire and sections A through G.
2. Examine the completed questionnaire and determine whether the individual can safely perform the exercise test that you are asking him or her to do. If you feel that the individual may be at a health risk during the exercise test, instruct him or her to contact a physician and receive medical clearance before performing the test.

REFERENCE

1. American College of Sports Medicine. *ACSM's Guidelines for Exercise Testing and Prescription,* 9th edition. Baltimore: Wolters Kluwer/Lippincott Williams & Wilkins, 2014.

INFORMED CONSENT FOR A BENCH PRESS 1-RM TEST

1. Purpose and Explanation of the Test

You will perform a one-repetition maximum (1-RM) bench press strength test using an Olympic barbell, weight plates, and a standard free weight bench. To begin the test, you will perform a warm-up with just the barbell. For each warm-up repetition, you will be required to lower the weight to your chest and then press it upward until your forearms are fully extended. Following the warm-up repetitions, additional weight will be added to the bar, and you will be asked to perform one repetition. If you can successfully complete the repetition, you will be allowed to rest for two minutes while additional weights are added to the bar. You will then be asked to perform one repetition with the new weight. Weights will be continually added to the bar until you are no longer able to complete the movement throughout the full range of motion. The heaviest weight that you were able to lift once will be your bench press 1-RM.

2. Attendant Risks and Discomforts

There is a slight possibility of straining or tearing a muscle during the bench press 1-RM test. Elevations in blood pressure and lightheadedness immediately after the strength test may occur. You may experience muscle soreness for a few days after the test. Every effort will be made to minimize potential risks by allowing for a thorough warm-up prior to the 1-RM test.

3. Responsibilities of the Participant

Information you present about your health status and previous experiences of muscle or joint injuries (e.g., muscle strains, tears, joint dislocations) may affect the safety of your strength test. Your prompt reporting of these conditions is very important to ensure that you are not injured during the 1-RM test. In addition, you will be asked several times during the strength test if you feel any joint or muscle pain.

4. Benefits to Be Expected

The results obtained from your test will provide information regarding your upper-body strength. This information may be helpful for you in the design of future training programs.

5. Inquiries

You are encouraged to ask any questions about the procedures used in the exercise test or the results of your test. If you have any concerns or questions, please ask us for further explanations.

6. Use of Medical Records

The information that is obtained during exercise testing will be treated as privileged and confidential as described in the Health Insurance Portability and Accountability Act of 1996. It is not to be released or revealed to any person except your referring physician without your written consent. However, the information obtained may be used for statistical analysis or scientific purposes with your right to privacy retained.

7. Freedom of Consent

I hereby consent to engage voluntarily in an exercise test to determine my upper-body strength. My permission to perform this test is given voluntarily. I understand that I am free to stop the test at any point if I so desire.

I have read this form, and I understand the test procedures that I will perform and the attendant risks and discomforts. Knowing these risks and discomforts, and having had an opportunity to ask questions that have been answered to my satisfaction, I consent to participate in this test.

Date *Signature of Participant*

Date *Signature of Witness*

Date *Signature of Person Conducting the Test*

2015 PAR-Q+

The Physical Activity Readiness Questionnaire for Everyone

The health benefits of regular physical activity are clear; more people should engage in physical activity every day of the week. Participating in physical activity is very safe for MOST people. This questionnaire will tell you whether it is necessary for you to seek further advice from your doctor OR a qualified exercise professional before becoming more physically active.

GENERAL HEALTH QUESTIONS

Please read the 7 questions below carefully and answer each one honestly: check YES or NO.	**YES**	**NO**
1) Has your doctor ever said that you have a heart condition ☐ OR high blood pressure ☐?	☐	☐
2) Do you feel pain in your chest at rest, during your daily activities of living, **OR** when you do physical activity?	☐	☐
3) Do you lose balance because of dizziness **OR** have you lost consciousness in the last 12 months? Please answer **NO** if your dizziness was associated with over-breathing (including during vigorous exercise).	☐	☐
4) Have you ever been diagnosed with another chronic medical condition (other than heart disease or high blood pressure)? **PLEASE LIST CONDITION(S) HERE:** ______	☐	☐
5) Are you currently taking prescribed medications for a chronic medical condition? **PLEASE LIST CONDITION(S) AND MEDICATIONS HERE:** ______	☐	☐
6) Do you currently have (or have had within the past 12 months) a bone, joint, or soft tissue (muscle, ligament, or tendon) problem that could be made worse by becoming more physically active? Please answer **NO** if you had a problem in the past, but it ***does not limit your current ability*** to be physically active. **PLEASE LIST CONDITION(S) HERE:** ______	☐	☐
7) Has your doctor ever said that you should only do medically supervised physical activity?	☐	☐

If you answered NO to all of the questions above, you are cleared for physical activity. Go to Page 4 to sign the PARTICIPANT DECLARATION. You do not need to complete Pages 2 and 3.

- Start becoming much more physically active – start slowly and build up gradually.
- Follow International Physical Activity Guidelines for your age (www.who.int/dietphysicalactivity/en/).
- You may take part in a health and fitness appraisal.
- If you are over the age of 45 yr and **NOT** accustomed to regular vigorous to maximal effort exercise, consult a qualified exercise professional before engaging in this intensity of exercise.
- If you have any further questions, contact a qualified exercise professional.

If you answered YES to one or more of the questions above, COMPLETE PAGES 2 AND 3.

Delay becoming more active if:

- You have a temporary illness such as a cold or fever; it is best to wait until you feel better.
- You are pregnant - talk to your health care practitioner, your physician, a qualified exercise professional, and/or complete the ePARmed-X+ at **www.eparmedx.com** before becoming more physically active.
- Your health changes - answer the questions on Pages 2 and 3 of this document and/or talk to your doctor or a qualified exercise professional before continuing with any physical activity program.

OSHF Ontario Society for Health and Fitness

 1 / 4
01-01-2015

2015 PAR-Q+

FOLLOW-UP QUESTIONS ABOUT YOUR MEDICAL CONDITION(S)

1. Do you have Arthritis, Osteoporosis, or Back Problems?

If the above condition(s) is/are present, answer questions 1a-1c If **NO** ☐ go to question 2

1a.	Do you have difficulty controlling your condition with medications or other physician-prescribed therapies? (Answer **NO** if you are not currently taking medications or other treatments)	**YES** ☐ **NO** ☐
1b.	Do you have joint problems causing pain, a recent fracture or fracture caused by osteoporosis or cancer, displaced vertebra (e.g., spondylolisthesis), and/or spondylolysis/pars defect (a crack in the bony ring on the back of the spinal column)?	**YES** ☐ **NO** ☐
1c.	Have you had steroid injections or taken steroid tablets regularly for more than 3 months?	**YES** ☐ **NO** ☐

2. Do you have Cancer of any kind?

If the above condition(s) is/are present, answer questions 2a-2b If **NO** ☐ go to question 3

2a.	Does your cancer diagnosis include any of the following types: lung/bronchogenic, multiple myeloma (cancer of plasma cells), head, and neck?	**YES** ☐ **NO** ☐
2b.	Are you currently receiving cancer therapy (such as chemotheraphy or radiotherapy)?	**YES** ☐ **NO** ☐

3. Do you have a Heart or Cardiovascular Condition? *This includes Coronary Artery Disease, Heart Failure, Diagnosed Abnormality of Heart Rhythm*

If the above condition(s) is/are present, answer questions 3a-3d If **NO** ☐ go to question 4

3a.	Do you have difficulty controlling your condition with medications or other physician-prescribed therapies? (Answer **NO** if you are not currently taking medications or other treatments)	**YES** ☐ **NO** ☐
3b.	Do you have an irregular heart beat that requires medical management? (e.g., atrial fibrillation, premature ventricular contraction)	**YES** ☐ **NO** ☐
3c.	Do you have chronic heart failure?	**YES** ☐ **NO** ☐
3d.	Do you have diagnosed coronary artery (cardiovascular) disease and have not participated in regular physical activity in the last 2 months?	**YES** ☐ **NO** ☐

4. Do you have High Blood Pressure?

If the above condition(s) is/are present, answer questions 4a-4b If **NO** ☐ go to question 5

4a.	Do you have difficulty controlling your condition with medications or other physician-prescribed therapies? (Answer **NO** if you are not currently taking medications or other treatments)	**YES** ☐ **NO** ☐
4b.	Do you have a resting blood pressure equal to or greater than 160/90 mmHg with or without medication? (Answer **YES** if you do not know your resting blood pressure)	**YES** ☐ **NO** ☐

5. Do you have any Metabolic Conditions? *This includes Type 1 Diabetes, Type 2 Diabetes, Pre-Diabetes*

If the above condition(s) is/are present, answer questions 5a-5e If **NO** ☐ go to question 6

5a.	Do you often have difficulty controlling your blood sugar levels with foods, medications, or other physician-prescribed therapies?	**YES** ☐ **NO** ☐
5b.	Do you often suffer from signs and symptoms of low blood sugar (hypoglycemia) following exercise and/or during activities of daily living? Signs of hypoglycemia may include shakiness, nervousness, unusual irritability, abnormal sweating, dizziness or light-headedness, mental confusion, difficulty speaking, weakness, or sleepiness.	**YES** ☐ **NO** ☐
5c.	Do you have any signs or symptoms of diabetes complications such as heart or vascular disease and/or complications affecting your eyes, kidneys, **OR** the sensation in your toes and feet?	**YES** ☐ **NO** ☐
5d.	Do you have other metabolic conditions (such as current pregnancy-related diabetes, chronic kidney disease, or liver problems)?	**YES** ☐ **NO** ☐
5e.	Are you planning to engage in what for you is unusually high (or vigorous) intensity exercise in the near future?	**YES** ☐ **NO** ☐

OSHF Ontario Society for Health and Fitness

01-01-2015

2015 PAR-Q+

6. Do you have any Mental Health Problems or Learning Difficulties? *This includes Alzheimer's, Dementia, Depression, Anxiety Disorder, Eating Disorder, Psychotic Disorder, Intellectual Disability, Down Syndrome*

If the above condition(s) is/are present, answer questions 6a-6b — If **NO** ☐ go to question 7

6a.	Do you have difficulty controlling your condition with medications or other physician-prescribed therapies? (Answer **NO** if you are not currently taking medications or other treatments)	YES ☐ NO ☐
6b.	Do you **ALSO** have back problems affecting nerves or muscles?	YES ☐ NO ☐

7. Do you have a Respiratory Disease? *This includes Chronic Obstructive Pulmonary Disease, Asthma, Pulmonary High Blood Pressure*

If the above condition(s) is/are present, answer questions 7a-7d — If **NO** ☐ go to question 8

7a.	Do you have difficulty controlling your condition with medications or other physician-prescribed therapies? (Answer **NO** if you are not currently taking medications or other treatments)	YES ☐ NO ☐
7b.	Has your doctor ever said your blood oxygen level is low at rest or during exercise and/or that you require supplemental oxygen therapy?	YES ☐ NO ☐
7c.	If asthmatic, do you currently have symptoms of chest tightness, wheezing, laboured breathing, consistent cough (more than 2 days/week), or have you used your rescue medication more than twice in the last week?	YES ☐ NO ☐
7d.	Has your doctor ever said you have high blood pressure in the blood vessels of your lungs?	YES ☐ NO ☐

8. Do you have a Spinal Cord Injury? *This includes Tetraplegia and Paraplegia*

If the above condition(s) is/are present, answer questions 8a-8c — If **NO** ☐ go to question 9

8a.	Do you have difficulty controlling your condition with medications or other physician-prescribed therapies? (Answer **NO** if you are not currently taking medications or other treatments)	YES ☐ NO ☐
8b.	Do you commonly exhibit low resting blood pressure significant enough to cause dizziness, light-headedness, and/or fainting?	YES ☐ NO ☐
8c.	Has your physician indicated that you exhibit sudden bouts of high blood pressure (known as Autonomic Dysreflexia)?	YES ☐ NO ☐

9. Have you had a Stroke? *This includes Transient Ischemic Attack (TIA) or Cerebrovascular Event*

If the above condition(s) is/are present, answer questions 9a-9c — If **NO** ☐ go to question 10

9a.	Do you have difficulty controlling your condition with medications or other physician-prescribed therapies? (Answer **NO** if you are not currently taking medications or other treatments)	YES ☐ NO ☐
9b.	Do you have any impairment in walking or mobility?	YES ☐ NO ☐
9c.	Have you experienced a stroke or impairment in nerves or muscles in the past 6 months?	YES ☐ NO ☐

10. Do you have any other medical condition not listed above or do you have two or more medical conditions?

If you have other medical conditions, answer questions 10a-10c — If **NO** ☐ read the Page 4 recommendations

10a.	Have you experienced a blackout, fainted, or lost consciousness as a result of a head injury within the last 12 months **OR** have you had a diagnosed concussion within the last 12 months?	YES ☐ NO ☐
10b.	Do you have a medical condition that is not listed (such as epilepsy, neurological conditions, kidney problems)?	YES ☐ NO ☐
10c.	Do you currently live with two or more medical conditions?	YES ☐ NO ☐

PLEASE LIST YOUR MEDICAL CONDITION(S) AND ANY RELATED MEDICATIONS HERE: ______________________

____

GO to Page 4 for recommendations about your current medical condition(s) and sign the PARTICIPANT DECLARATION.

OSHF Ontario Society for Health and Fitness

01-01-2015

2015 PAR-Q+

If you answered NO to all of the follow-up questions about your medical condition, you are ready to become more physically active - sign the PARTICIPANT DECLARATION below:

- It is advised that you consult a qualified exercise professional to help you develop a safe and effective physical activity plan to meet your health needs.
- You are encouraged to start slowly and build up gradually - 20 to 60 minutes of low to moderate intensity exercise, 3-5 days per week including aerobic and muscle strengthening exercises.
- As you progress, you should aim to accumulate 150 minutes or more of moderate intensity physical activity per week.
- If you are over the age of 45 yr and **NOT** accustomed to regular vigorous to maximal effort exercise, consult a qualified exercise professional before engaging in this intensity of exercise.

If you answered **YES** to **one or more of the follow-up questions** about your medical condition:

You should seek further information before becoming more physically active or engaging in a fitness appraisal. You should complete the specially designed online screening and exercise recommendations program - the **ePARmed-X+ at www.eparmedx.com** and/or visit a qualified exercise professional to work through the ePARmed-X+ and for further information.

Delay becoming more active if:

- You have a temporary illness such as a cold or fever; it is best to wait until you feel better.
- You are pregnant - talk to your health care practitioner, your physician, a qualified exercise professional, and/or complete the ePARmed-X+ **at www.eparmedx.com** before becoming more physically active.
- Your health changes - talk to your doctor or qualified exercise professional before continuing with any physical activity program.

- You are encouraged to photocopy the PAR-Q+. You must use the entire questionnaire and NO changes are permitted.
- The authors, the PAR-Q+ Collaboration, partner organizations, and their agents assume no liability for persons who undertake physical activity and/or make use of the PAR-Q+ or ePARmed-X+. If in doubt after completing the questionnaire, consult your doctor prior to physical activity.

PARTICIPANT DECLARATION

- All persons who have completed the PAR-Q+ please read and sign the declaration below.
- If you are less than the legal age required for consent or require the assent of a care provider, your parent, guardian or care provider must also sign this form.

I, the undersigned, have read, understood to my full satisfaction and completed this questionnaire. I acknowledge that this physical activity clearance is valid for a maximum of 12 months from the date it is completed and becomes invalid if my condition changes. I also acknowledge that a Trustee (such as my employer, community/fitness centre, health care provider, or other designate) may retain a copy of this form for their records. In these instances, the Trustee will be required to adhere to local, national, and international guidelines regarding the storage of personal health information ensuring that the Trustee maintains the privacy of the information and does not misuse or wrongfully disclose such information.

NAME ______________________________ DATE ______________________

SIGNATURE ______________________________ WITNESS ______________________

SIGNATURE OF PARENT/GUARDIAN/CARE PROVIDER ______________________________

For more information, please contact
www.eparmedx.com
Email: eparmedx@gmail.com

Citation for PAR-Q+
Warburton DER, Jamnik VK, Bredin SSD, and Gledhill N on behalf of the PAR-Q+ Collaboration. The Physical Activity Readiness Questionnaire for Everyone (PAR-Q+) and Electronic Physical Activity Readiness Medical Examination (ePARmed-X+). Health & Fitness Journal of Canada 4(2):3-23, 2011.

The PAR-Q+ was created using the evidence-based AGREE process (1) by the PAR-Q+ Collaboration chaired by Dr. Darren E. R. Warburton with Dr. Norman Gledhill, Dr. Veronica Jamnik, and Dr. Donald C. McKenzie (2). Production of this document has been made possible through financial contributions from the Public Health Agency of Canada and the BC Ministry of Health Services. The views expressed herein do not necessarily represent the views of the Public Health Agency of Canada or the BC Ministry of Health Services.

Key References

1. Jamnik VK, Warburton DER, Makarski J, McKenzie DC, Shephard RJ, Stone J, and Gledhill N. Enhancing the effectiveness of clearance for physical activity participation; background and overall process. APNM 36(S1):S3-S13, 2011.
2. Warburton DER, Gledhill N, Jamnik VK, Bredin SSD, McKenzie DC, Stone J, Charlesworth S, and Shephard RJ. Evidence-based risk assessment and recommendations for physical activity clearance; Consensus Document. APNM 36(S1):S266-s298, 2011.

OSHF Ontario Society for Health and Fitness

 4 / 4
01-01-2015

PRE-EXERCISE TESTING HEALTH STATUS QUESTIONNAIRE

Name ____________________ Date ____________________

ID# ____________________ Birthdate (mm/dd/yy) ____________________

Home Address ____________________

Work Phone ____________________ Home Phone ____________________

E-mail Address ____________________

Person to contact in case of emergency ____________________

Emergency Contact Phone ____________________

Personal Physician ____________________ Physician's Phone ____________________

Gender ____________________ Age (yrs) ____________________

Height (ft) (in) ____________________ Weight (lbs) ____________________

Does the above weight indicate: ◯ *a gain* ◯ *a loss* ◯ *no change* in the past year?

If a change, how many pounds? ____________ (lbs)

A. JOINT-MUSCLE STATUS (*✔ Check areas where you currently have problems.*)

JOINT AREAS

- ◯ Wrists
- ◯ Elbows
- ◯ Shoulders
- ◯ Upper spine & neck
- ◯ Lower spine
- ◯ Hips
- ◯ Knees
- ◯ Ankles
- ◯ Feet
- ◯ Other

MUSCLE AREAS

- ◯ Arms
- ◯ Shoulders
- ◯ Chest
- ◯ Upper back & neck
- ◯ Abdominal regions
- ◯ Lower back
- ◯ Buttocks
- ◯ Thighs
- ◯ Lower leg
- ◯ Feet

B. HEALTH STATUS (*✔ Check if you previously had or currently have any of the following conditions.*)

- ◯ High blood pressure
- ◯ Heart disease or dysfunction
- ◯ Peripheral circulatory disorder
- ◯ Lung disease or dysfunction
- ◯ Arthritis or gout
- ◯ Edema
- ◯ Epilepsy
- ◯ Multiple sclerosis
- ◯ High blood cholesterol or triglyceride levels
- ◯ Loss of consciousness
- ◯ Other conditions that you feel we should know about ____________________
- ◯ Pregnant
- ◯ Acute infection
- ◯ Diabetes or blood sugar level abnormality
- ◯ Anemia
- ◯ Hernia
- ◯ Thyroid dysfunction
- ◯ Pancreas dysfunction
- ◯ Liver dysfunction
- ◯ Kidney dysfunction
- ◯ Phenylketonuria (PKU)
- ◯ Allergic reactions to medication
  Please describe: ____________________
- ◯ Allergic reactions to any other substance
  Please describe: ____________________

QUESTIONNAIRE, page 2

C. PHYSICAL EXAMINATION HISTORY

Approximate date of your last physical examination ____________________

Physical problems noted at that time ____________________

____

Has a physician ever made any recommendations relative to limiting your level of physical exertion? *YES* *NO*

If YES, what limitations were recommended? ____________________

____

Have you ever had an abnormal resting electrocardiogram (ECG)? *YES* *NO*

D. CURRENT MEDICATION USAGE (List the drug name and the condition being managed.)

MEDICATION	CONDITION

E. PHYSICAL PERCEPTIONS *(Indicate any unusual sensations or perceptions. ✔ Check if you have recently experienced any of the following during or soon after physical activity (PA) or during sedentary periods (SED).*

PA	SED		PA	SED	
○	○	Chest pain	○	○	Nausea
○	○	Heart palpitations ("fast irregular heartbeats")	○	○	Lightheadedness
○	○	Unusually rapid breathing	○	○	Loss of consciousness
○	○	Overheating	○	○	Loss of balance
○	○	Muscle cramping	○	○	Loss of coordination
○	○	Muscle pain	○	○	Extreme weakness
○	○	Joint pain	○	○	Numbness
○	○	Other	○	○	Mental confusion

F. FAMILY HISTORY *(✔ Check if any of your blood relatives—parents, brothers, sisters, aunts, uncles, and/or grandparents—have or had any of the following.)*

- ○ Heart disease
- ○ Heart attacks or strokes (prior to age 50)
- ○ Elevated blood cholesterol or triglyceride levels
- ○ High blood pressure
- ○ Diabetes
- ○ Sudden death (other than accidental)

G. CURRENT HABITS *(✔ Check any of the following if they are characteristic of your current habits.)*

- ○ Smoking. If so, how many per day? ________
- ○ Regularly does manual gardening or yardwork.
- ○ Regularly goes for long walks.
- ○ Frequently rides a bicycle.
- ○ Frequently runs/jogs for exercise.
- ○ Regularly participates in a weight training exercise program.
- ○ Engages in a sports program more than once per week. If so, what does the program consist of?

____

____

EXTENSION ACTIVITIES

worksheet **1.1**

NAME DATE

1. Administer the PAR-Q+ and Pre-exercise Testing Health Status Questionnaire to someone in your class. Based on the results from the questionnaires, could the individual safely perform the following exercise tests? Circle the appropriate answer next to each exercise test.

   YES NO Bench Press One-Repetition Maximum (1-RM) Strength Test

   YES NO Leg Extension One-Repetition Maximum (1-RM) Strength Test

   YES NO Submaximal Cycle Ergometer Test

   YES NO Maximal Cycle Ergometer Test

   YES NO Maximal Treadmill Test

   YES NO Flexibility Test

   YES NO Test for Anaerobic Power

2. Complete the PAR-Q+ and Pre-exercise Testing Health Status Questionnaire for yourself. Based on the results, determine whether you would be able to safely perform the exercise tests listed in question 1.

As a result of reading this chapter you will:

Be able to describe differences among smooth, skeletal, and cardiac muscle.

Understand the basic structure of skeletal muscle.

Know the characteristics that differentiate fast-twitch from slow-twitch muscle fibers.

Be familiar with the sliding filament model of muscle contraction.

Structure of Muscle Tissue and Muscle Contraction

2

key concepts

A band
acetylcholine (ACH)
actin
action potential
adenosine diphosphate (ADP)
adenosine triphosphate (ATP)
cardiac muscle
cross-bridge recycling
end bulb
endomysium
epimysium
fascia
fasciculus
fast-twitch glycolytic (FG) fibers
fast-twitch oxidative glycolytic (FOG) fibers
H band
I band
mitochondria
motor neuron
motor unit

TYPES OF MUSCLE

All physical activity of humans, including exercise and sport, depends ultimately on the contraction of muscle tissue. Three types of muscle tissue are present in the human body:

1. *Smooth, nonstriated* (which means it does not have a striped appearance) *muscle* is found in the walls of the hollow viscera and blood vessels.
2. *Skeletal striated muscle* is attached to the skeleton and provides the force for movement of the bony leverage system.
3. *Cardiac striated muscle* is found only in the heart.

Smooth muscle is innervated by the autonomic nervous system and ordinarily contracts independently of voluntary control. The fibers of smooth muscle are usually long, spindle-shaped bodies, but their external shape may change somewhat to conform to the surrounding elements. Each fiber usually has only one nucleus.

Skeletal muscle, which is innervated by the voluntary or somatic nervous system, consists of long, cylindrical muscle fibers. Each fiber is a large cell with as many as several hundred nuclei and is structurally independent of its neighboring fiber or cell. Skeletal, or striated, muscle, as the name implies, is most easily distinguished by its cross-striations of alternating light and dark bands (Figure 2.1).

Cardiac muscle (also called the myocardium; *myo* = muscle, *cardium* = heart) in all vertebrates is a network of striated muscle fibers. It differs structurally from the other two types of muscle tissue mainly in the interweaving of its fibers to form a network, called a **syncytium.** This network differentiates it from skeletal muscle, which is also striated. It further differs from smooth muscle in that it has cross-striations, which smooth muscle does not have. Cardiac muscle contracts rhythmically and automatically, without outside stimulation. Whereas skeletal muscle is made up of discrete fibers that can contract individually (but with other members of its motor unit), cardiac muscle is composed of a network of fibers that responds to innervation with a wavelike contraction that passes through the entire muscle.

fascia
epimysium
fasciculus
perimysium

GROSS STRUCTURE OF SKELETAL MUSCLE

If we dissected the upper arm and removed the skin, subcutaneous adipose tissue, and superficial fascia, we would see the biceps brachii muscle and note that it is completely covered by a deep layer of **fascia** (connective tissue) that binds the muscle into one functional unit. This outermost sheath of connective tissue is called the **epimysium,** and it merges at the ends of the muscle with the connective tissue of the tendon. Thus, the force of muscular contraction is transmitted through the connective tissues binding the muscle to the tendon, then through the tendon to the bone, to bring about movement. Disruption of the fascial tissues due to trauma or disease can lead to a substantial reduction in muscle strength.

In cross-section, we can see that the interior of the muscle is subdivided into bundles of muscle fibers (Figure 2.2). Each bundle contains upward of a dozen, possibly as many as several hundred, fibers. Each bundle is called a **fasciculus** and is surrounded by a connective tissue sheath called the **perimysium.** The structures discussed so far are visible to the naked eye.

figure 2.1

Skeletal muscle fibers showing cross-striations.

MICROSCOPIC STRUCTURE OF SKELETAL MUSCLE

A microscope is needed to see the structure of an individual muscle fiber and how the fibers form fasciculi (Figure 2.2). Each fiber is surrounded by a flimsy sheath called the **endomysium.** You may better understand the need for these connective tissue sheaths—endomysium around the single fiber, perimysium around the fasciculus, and epimysium about the whole muscle—by realizing that one fiber may not run through the whole length of a muscle, or even through a fasciculus. Therefore, it becomes necessary to transmit the force of contraction from fiber to fiber to fasciculus, and from fasciculus to fasciculus (since these sometimes do not run through the length of a large muscle either) to the tendons, which act upon the bones. This is a function of the connective tissue sheaths described above.

The dimensions of individual fibers vary in diameter from approximately 10 to 100 microns (1,000 microns = 1 mm) and in length from 1 mm to the length of the whole muscle. Thus, the thickness of a large fiber is roughly comparable to that of a fine human hair, while the smaller fibers cannot be seen without a microscope. Each fiber constitutes one muscle cell. Each muscle has fibers of characteristic size, and the thickness of each fiber is related to the forces involved in the function of the muscle. For example, the fibers of the extrinsic ocular muscles are small in diameter, in part because they do not have to produce much force. On the other hand, the fibers of the quadriceps femoris are large and produce great force.

STRUCTURE OF THE MUSCLE FIBER

The cell membrane of the muscle fiber is called the **sarcolemma.** This membrane is extremely thin and seems almost structureless, even under the electron microscope (Figure 2.2). Inside the sarcolemma are the many nuclei, mainly situated peripherally, close to the sarcolemma. Corresponding to the cytoplasm of other cells is the **sarcoplasm,** which is the fluid part of the cell. Running longitudinally within the sarcoplasm are slender columnlike structures called **myofibrils,** which have alternating segments of light and dark color. The presence of the myofibrils imparts to the fiber as a whole the appearance of lengthwise striations. The cross-striations, however, are far more obvious because the dark segments of the many myofibrils are arranged in lateral alignment. All light segments are likewise aligned with one another.

MUSCLE FIBER TYPES

For many years, anatomists and histologists classified muscle fibers as red or white. In this classification, the red fibers were considered better suited to long-term, slow contractions, as required of postural, antigravity muscles, while the white fibers were considered differentiated for speed of contraction.

With the advent of modern histochemical techniques, examination of chemical constituents at the cellular level became possible and provided the means to correlate the structure and function of individual fibers. Thus, identifying skeletal muscle fiber types has become more sophisticated and at the same time has provided information that helps us understand why one person may be better suited to endurance activities, while another excels in sprint-type activities.

Based on laboratory techniques, two to as many as eight different muscle fiber types have been identified. The disparity in the number of types named has resulted in part from the fact that some investigators have used human muscle while others have used laboratory animal muscle. In addition, nomenclature was based on at least four different approaches: (1) the anatomical appearance: red

key concepts

- muscle action potential (MAP)
- myofibril
- myofilament
- myoneural junction
- myosin
- myosin ATPase
- myosin cross-bridge
- neuromuscular junction
- perimysium
- sarcolemma
- sarcomere
- sarcoplasm
- sarcoplasmic reticulum
- skeletal muscle
- sliding filament model
- slow-twitch oxidative (SO) fibers
- smooth muscle
- synapse
- syncytium
- transverse tubules
- troponin
- tropomyosin
- Z-line

- endomysium
- sarcolemma
- sarcoplasm
- myofibrils

www

Muscles
http://users.rcn.com/jkimball.ma.ultranet/BiologyPages/M/Muscles.html

Muscle Physiology—Myofilament Structure
http://muscle.ucsd.edu/musintro/fibril.shtml

figure 2.2 Muscle fibers and connective tissue sheaths.

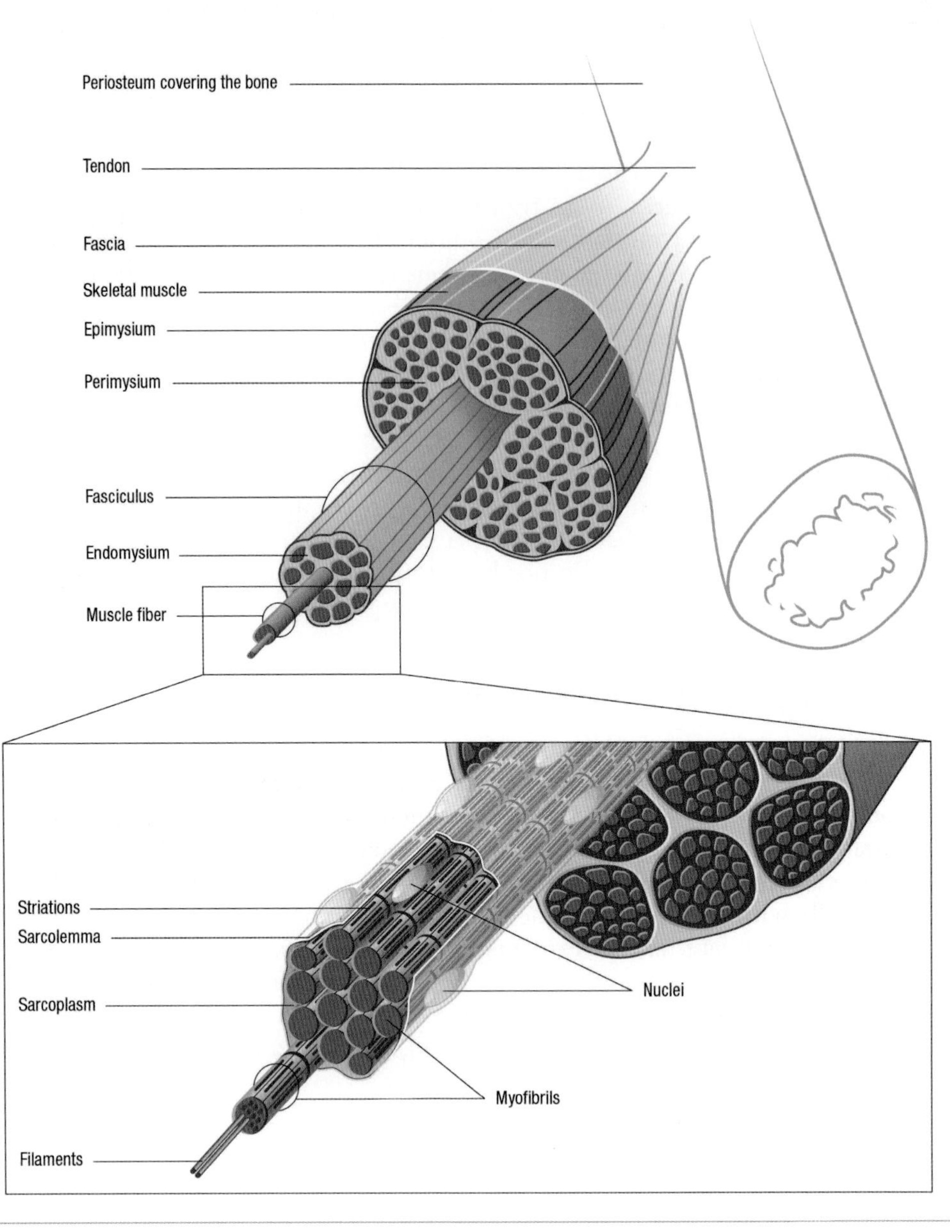

From J.W. Hole, Jr., *Human Anatomy and Physiology*, 5th Edition. Copyright © 1990 Wm. C. Brown Communications, Inc., Dubuque, Iowa. Reprinted with permission of The McGraw-Hill Companies.

versus white; (2) muscle function: fast–slow or fatigable versus fatigue resistant; (3) biochemical properties, such as high or low aerobic capacity; and (4) histochemical properties, such as the enzyme profile of the fiber.

The nomenclature proposed by Peter et al.[9] is especially useful for describing the differences between muscle fiber types (Table 2.1). The older muscle fiber–type classification system, fast-twitch (white) versus slow-twitch (red), has become inadequate because there are two primary subtypes of fast-twitch fibers, with both physiological and histochemical differences. Most important, they respond differently to training. The three primary fiber types in human skeletal muscle are **slow-twitch oxidative (SO), fast-twitch oxidative glycolytic (FOG),** and **fast-twitch glycolytic (FG).**[9] These fiber types have also been called type I, type IIa, and type IIb,[4] or Beta/slow, type

slow-twitch oxidative (SO)

fast-twitch oxidative glycolytic (FOG)

fast-twitch glycolytic (FG)

Characteristics of muscle fiber types. **table 2.1**

A. NOMENCLATURE			
1. Older systems	Red slow-twitch (ST)	White fast-twitch (FT)	
2. Dubowitz and Brooke[4]	Type I	Type IIa	Type IIb
3. Smerdu et al.[11]	Beta/slow	Type IIa	Type IIx
4. Peter et al.[9]	Slow, oxidative (SO)	Fast, oxidative, glycolytic (FOG)	Fast, glycolytic (FG)
B. CHARACTERISTICS			
1. Speed of contraction	Slow	Fast	Fast
2. Strength of contraction	Low	High	High
3. Fatigability	Fatigue resistant	Fatigable	Most fatigable
4. Aerobic capacity	High	Medium	Low
5. Anaerobic capacity	Low	Medium	High
6. Size	Small	Large	Large
7. Capillary density	High	High	Low

IIa, and type IIx, respectively.[11] The names SO, FOG, and FG, however, provide descriptive information about the characteristics and functioning of the various fiber types, while types I, IIa, and IIb do not. For example, from the names, we know that SO fibers are slow-twitch and favor oxidative (aerobic) energy production, while FG fibers are fast-twitch and favor glycolytic (anaerobic) energy production.

A **motor unit** is made up of a motor neuron (nerve) and all of the fibers that it innervates. A motor unit may include only a few fibers (perhaps even only one) in small muscles such as those of the eye, while there may be several hundred fibers in a motor unit scattered throughout a large muscle of the quadriceps.[8] All muscle fibers within a motor unit are the same type.

motor unit

The percentages of the three fiber types in the various muscles of one individual may be quite different. Postural muscles, such as the soleus, which help us stand for long periods of time, need to be fatigue resistant and, therefore, tend to be composed mostly of SO fibers. On the other hand, some of the ocular muscles are largely fast-twitch. Most other muscles fall somewhere in between, depending on their function. Furthermore, there is no difference between men and women with regard to fiber type distribution patterns.

Although a limited number of studies[2] have reported training-induced fiber type conversions from fast- to slow-twitch fibers, the percentage change is typically small ($\leq$6%) and not sufficient to affect performance. Thus, it is generally accepted that an individual's fiber type pattern is genetically determined and that training does not affect the relative proportions of slow- and fast-twitch fibers within a muscle. Training can, however, bring about substantial improvements in the performance capabilities of all three fiber types, and there are training-induced conversions within fast-twitch fibers. For example, endurance and resistance training result in a shift from FG to FOG fibers.[5,6]

The significance of the fiber-type composition for athletics becomes readily apparent from a review of Table 2.1. The individual endowed with a high percentage of SO fibers, which contract slowly but are highly fatigue-resistant, would be a good candidate for distance running or other endurance events. On the other

The adaptable muscle

Muscle is a very adaptable tissue. Depending on the type of stress applied, muscle tissue can undergo extensive remodeling of its contractile and calcium-cycling machinery, show an increase in the number and size of **mitochondria,** exhibit an increase in the number of capillaries and increased blood flow, and also develop an increased ability to utilize oxygen. You may think that all of this would take months to accomplish. However, depending on the specific type of exercise, these changes begin to take place and can be measured within days of the exercise.[1]

hand, a person whose genetic makeup produced high percentages of fast-twitch (FT) fibers would be predisposed toward success in power and sprint events. Typically, the thigh and leg muscles of elite endurance athletes have a high percentage (greater than 75%) of SO fibers, while elite sprinters tend to have far more fast-twitch fibers. Individuals in the general population of non-athletes usually have a fairly even mixture of slow-twitch and fast-twitch fibers in these muscles.

With respect to fiber type, our genetic endowment determines to a large extent whether we are likely to excel in endurance-type sports or sports that demand sprint or power in their performance. In either case, ultimate success depends on many other factors, such as training, skill, and dedication.

STRUCTURE OF THE MYOFIBRIL AND THE CONTRACTILE MECHANISM

The advent of the electron microscope has provided insight into both the structure and function of the myofibril within the muscle fiber.

sarcomere · Z-line · myofilaments · myosin · A band · actin · H band · I band

The **sarcomere** is the functional unit of the myofibril, and it extends from Z-line to Z-line, as shown in Figure 2.3. The **Z-line** is the membrane that separates sarcomeres. Each sarcomere is composed of interdigitating (interlocking) parallel filaments (called **myofilaments**). One myofilament, **myosin,** is about twice as thick as the other, and its length is equal to the length of the **A band** (the dark band seen as part of the striation effect). The second and thinner myofilament, **actin,** is longer and extends inward from both Z-lines, almost to the center of the sarcomere (Figure 2.4). The amount by which the two ends of the actin molecules fail to meet constitutes a lighter band within the dark A band that is called the **H band.** The area between the ends of the myosin molecules is also less dense, thereby creating the light band of the striation effect, which is known as the **I band.** The I band is a part of two adjacent sarcomeres and is divided down the middle by the Z-line. Thus, the light and dark striped effect of striated muscle is due to bands of greater and lesser optical density.

figure 2.3 A sarcomere extends from Z-line to Z-line. Also shown are the A, H, and I bands that give skeletal muscle its striated appearance.

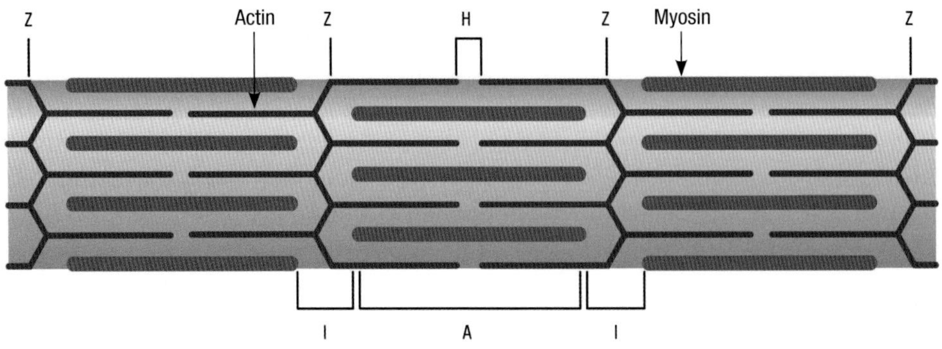

Contractile proteins actin, myosin, troponin, and tropomyosin. **figure 2.4**

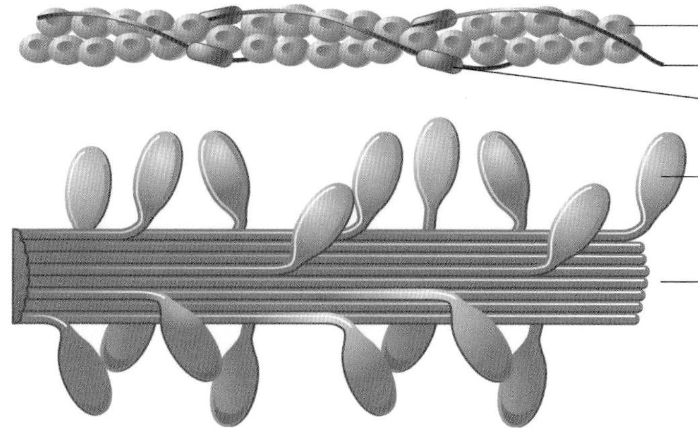

MUSCLE CONTRACTION AND THE SLIDING FILAMENT MODEL

Contraction of skeletal muscle underlies all voluntary human movement. Exercise professionals, physical educators, and coaches can, therefore, benefit from a basic understanding of the physiological processes that allow us to perform physical activity. For example, the mechanisms of muscle contraction are central to understanding many diverse aspects of physical performance, such as the acquisition of motor and sports skills as taught by physical educators and coaches, the development of muscle size and strength through resistance training, ways to delay the onset and reduce the effects of fatigue through training program design, and making informed decisions about the use of anabolic steroids or growth hormone. Without a solid foundation in the cellular processes of muscle contraction, it is difficult, if not impossible, to provide valid, scientifically based answers to the many questions asked of exercise professionals, physical educators, and coaches.

WWW
Sliding Filament Model
http://users.rcn.com/jkimball.ma.ultranet/BiologyPages/M/Muscles.html

Although debate continues,[10] the **sliding filament model** is widely accepted as the most complete explanation of the mechanism of muscle contraction. The sliding filament model describes the series of events that lead to muscle contraction[7] (Figure 2.5).

- sliding filament model

1. An electrical impulse passes along a **motor neuron.** When the impulse reaches the end of the neuron (called the **end bulb**) it causes the release of the stimulatory neurotransmitter **acetylcholine (ACH)** from storage vesicles. The intersection of a motor neuron and muscle fiber is called the **myoneural junction** or **neuromuscular junction.**

- motor neuron
- end bulb
- acetylcholine (ACH)
- myoneural junction
- neuromuscular junction

2. The ACH is released into a small gap between the motor neuron and muscle fiber called a **synapse.** The ACH then binds to receptor sites on a specialized area of the muscle fiber membrane called the *motor end plate.*

- synapse

3. If enough ACH binds to the receptors, an electrical current called a **muscle action potential (MAP)** or, more simply, **action potential** will spread along the sarcolemma (cell membrane) of the muscle fiber.

- muscle action potential (MAP)
- action potential

4. As the action potential passes along the sarcolemma it moves into the interior of the fiber by traveling down channels called **transverse tubules** or *t-tubules.* Transverse tubules are extensions of the sarcolemma that allow the action

- transverse tubules

figure 2.5 Aspects of the sliding filament model of muscle contraction.

At Rest

1. Tropomyosin inhibits actin–myosin binding.
2. Calcium is stored in the sarcoplasmic reticulum.

Contraction

1. Neural stimulation causes the sarcoplasmic reticulum to release calcium.
2. Calcium binds to troponin, which removes the inhibitory effect of tropomyosin and actin–myosin bind.
3. Myosin cross-bridges swivel, pulling the actin and Z-lines.
4. Fresh ATP binds to the myosin cross-bridges, leading to cross-bridge recycling.
5. Neural stimulation ceases and relaxation occurs.

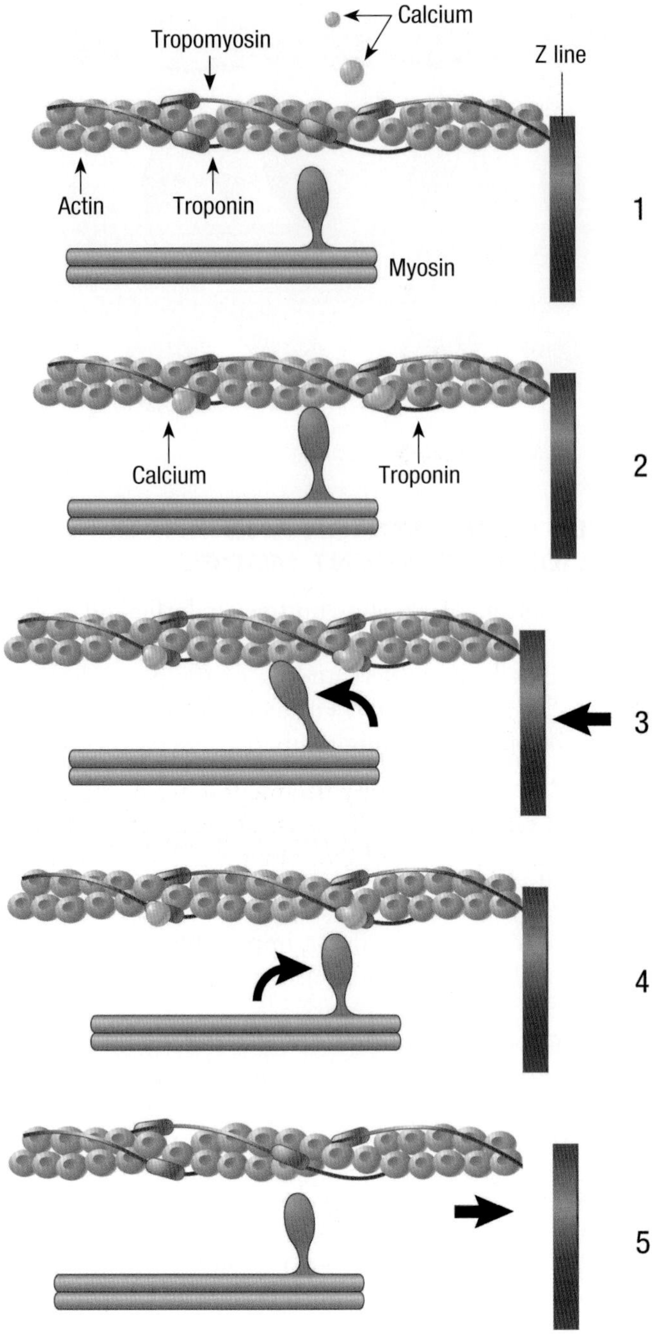

potential to move from the outside to the inside of the fiber, where contraction actually occurs.

sarcoplasmic reticulum

5. The action potential travels down the t-tubules and intersects a cell organelle called the **sarcoplasmic reticulum.** The action potential causes the sarcoplasmic reticulum to release calcium into the sarcoplasm (fluid part) of the fiber.

troponin

tropomyosin

6. The calcium then binds to the protein molecule **troponin,** which is bound to a **tropomyosin** molecule (Figure 2.4). The binding of calcium to troponin causes

Muscle contraction at the molecular level

Although the critical role of calcium in muscle contraction has been recognized for nearly 40 years, its effect on the protein molecules that interact to produce muscle contraction is still unclear. Skeletal muscle tissue is made up of thick (myosin) and thin (actin with troponin and tropomyosin) filaments. These filaments slide past each other during muscle contraction with the "heads" of the myosin filaments pulling on the actin filaments. This whole process is mediated through changes in intracellular calcium concentration.

Narita et al.,* using a technique called electron cryo-microscopy, have studied the way in which the troponin, tropomyosin, and actin molecules compose a calcium-sensitive switch that controls muscle contraction. The authors wanted to develop detailed models of the molecular movements and structures involved. During contraction, calcium levels in the muscle cells rise. The calcium binds to troponin, causing a change in the position of tropomyosin and actin, regulating the interaction of actin with the myosin heads. The results of this study showed that when calcium was high, troponin had a very different shape and position on actin compared with its shape and position under low calcium conditions. Tropomyosin moves away from the active sites on actin, allowing the myosin heads to attach under high calcium concentrations, whereas when calcium is low, one end of the tropomyosin molecule shifts, blocking most of the active sites.

Narita et al. have contributed to our understanding of the precise way in which the movements of the various components of the thin filaments regulate contraction and have given detailed models of the positions of tropomyosin when intracellular calcium is low (muscle at rest) and high (muscle contraction).

* Narita, A., Yasunaga, T., Ishikawa, T., Mayanagi, K., and Wakabayashi, T. Ca^{2+}-induced switching of troponin and tropomyosin on actin filaments as revealed by electron cryo-microscopy. *J. Molecular Biology* 308: 241–261, 2001.

a change in the shape of the tropomyosin molecule. Under resting conditions, the contractile proteins (myofilaments) actin and myosin are separated by the presence of tropomyosin. That is, at rest, actin and myosin are inhibited from binding by the presence of tropomyosin. The change in the shape of tropomyosin, following the binding of calcium to troponin, uncovers the binding sites on the actin molecule.

7. The **myosin cross-bridge** (also called the *myosin head*) is then free to bind with the binding site on the actin molecule (Figure 2.4).

- myosin cross-bridge

8. Muscle contraction depends on the presence of **adenosine triphosphate (ATP)** and its breakdown to **adenosine diphosphate (ADP)** and inorganic phosphate. The breakdown of ATP provides large amounts of energy. There are two primary theories regarding the way in which the energy from the breakdown of ATP is used in muscle contraction.

- adenosine triphosphate (ATP)
- adenosine diphosphate (ADP)

Theory 1. The process of actin–myosin binding activates an enzyme called **myosin ATPase**. The function of myosin ATPase is to break down an ATP molecule, which is bound to the myosin cross-bridge, and liberate energy.

- myosin ATPase

The energy liberated from the breakdown of ATP is used to cause the myosin cross-bridge to swivel inward toward the center of the sarcomere. Because myosin molecules are bound to actin molecules, which are bound to the Z-lines of the sarcomere, as the myosin cross-bridges swivel, they pull the Z-lines closer together, thus shortening the sarcomere. This is what we call muscle contraction.[7]

The shortening of the sarcomere associated with the swiveling of any one or group of myosin cross-bridges is not sufficient to cause complete contraction of a muscle fiber. Therefore, after swiveling, a fresh ATP molecule binds to the myosin cross-bridge, causing it to release from the actin molecule. The myosin cross-bridge then stands back up and binds to a different actin binding site farther down the molecule. The binding again activates myosin ATPase to break down the new ATP molecule bound to the myosin cross-bridge, which then swivels and pulls the Z-lines even closer together.

This process of a myosin cross-bridge swiveling inward, being released from the actin molecule, standing back up, rebinding to the actin molecule, and swiveling

cross-bridge recycling

again is called **cross-bridge recycling** or *cross-bridge recharging*.

Theory 2. In a resting state, the myosin cross-bridge is energized and bound to ADP and inorganic phosphate (Pi). The energized cross-bridge stores the energy liberated from the breakdown of ATP by the enzyme myosin ATPase. The binding of actin and the myosin cross-bridge releases the stored energy, causing the myosin cross-bridge to swivel and resulting in muscle contraction. During the swiveling action, ADP and Pi are released from the myosin cross-bridge. As in Theory 1, fresh ATP must bind to the myosin cross-bridge to release it from actin during cross-bridge recycling. Unlike in Theory 1, however, after actin and myosin dissociate, the fresh ATP is broken down and the liberated energy is used to reenergize the myosin cross-bridge, which is then available to repeat the cross-bridge cycle.[3,10]

9. When the electrical impulse ceases, relaxation occurs because the calcium no longer binds to the troponin molecule and the tropomyosin molecule returns to its normal shape, which physically inhibits actin–myosin binding.

summary

The human body has three types of muscle tissue: smooth, skeletal, and cardiac. In skeletal muscle, muscle fibers (or cells) are oriented in bundles called fasciculi. Each fiber, fasciculus, and whole muscle is surrounded by connective tissue sheaths called the endomysium, perimysium, and epimysium, respectively. These sheaths transfer force production from the muscle fiber to the tendon and then to the bone to cause movement.

Three primary muscle fiber types are present in humans: slow-twitch oxidative (SO), fast-twitch oxidative glycolytic (FOG), and fast-twitch glycolytic (FG). The proportions of these fiber types in the various muscles of the human body are determined by genetics.

The sliding filament model is the generally accepted theory of muscle contraction. This model describes the series of events from excitation to the binding of actin and myosin, which leads to force production.

questions for review

1. Draw a cross-section of muscle and label all connective tissue layers with related structures.
2. What are the characteristics that differentiate fast-twitch from slow-twitch muscle fibers?
3. Discuss the effect of endurance training and resistance training on muscle fiber type.
4. What is the significance of fiber-type composition for athletes?
5. Draw a diagram of a sarcomere. Include and label all relevant structures.
6. Describe the sliding filament model.

student companion website

For further review of this book's chapters and for test preparation, visit the book's website, **www.hhpcommunities.com/exercisephysiology**, to take practice quizzes, review the vocabulary terms, use the study guide, and view the digital image bank.

references

1. Baldwin, K. M. Research in the exercise sciences: where do we go from here? *J. Appl. Physiol.* 88: 332–336, 2000.
2. Baumann, H., Jäggi, M., Soland, F., Howald, H., and Schaub, M. C. Exercise training induces transitions of myosin isoform subunits within histochemically typed human muscle fibres. *Pflugers Arch.* 409: 349–360, 1987.
3. Brooks, G. A., Fahey, T. D., White, T. P., and Baldwin, K. M. *Exercise Physiology. Human Bioenergetics and Its Application,* 3rd edition. Mountain View, CA: Mayfield Publishing Company, 2000, pp. 350–352.
4. Dubowitz, V., and Brooke, M. H. *Muscle Biopsy: A Modern Approach.* Philadelphia: W. B. Saunders Company, 1973.
5. Fleck, S. J., and Kraemer, W. J. *Designing Resistance Training Programs,* 3rd edition. Champaign, IL: Human Kinetics, 2004, pp. 135–137.
6. Henriksson, J. Cellular metabolism and endurance. In *Endurance in Sport,* eds. R. J. Shepard and P. O. Astrand. London: Blackwell Scientific, 1992, pp. 46–60.
7. Huxley, H. The mechanism of muscular contraction. *Science* 164: 1356–1366, 1969.
8. Kernell, D. Muscle regionalization. *Can. J. Appl. Physiol.* 23: 1–22, 1998.
9. Peter, J., Barnard, R., Edgerton, V., Gillespie, C., and Stempel, K. Metabolic profiles of three fiber types of skeletal muscle in guinea pigs and rabbits. *Biochemistry* 11: 2627–2633, 1972.
10. Pollack, G. H. *Muscles and Molecules: Uncovering the Principles of Biological Motion.* Seattle: Ebner and Sons Publishers, 1990.
11. Smerdu, V., Karsh-Mizrachi, I., Campione, M., Leinwand, L., and Schiaffino, S. Type IIx myosin heavy chain transcripts are expressed in type IIb fibers of human skeletal muscle. *Am. J. Physiol.* 267: C1723–C1728, 1994.

lab Determination of One-Repetition Maximum Bench Press and Leg Press Strength

BACKGROUND

The one-repetition maximum, or 1-RM, refers to the maximum amount of weight that can be lifted one time. The 1-RM is a standard index to quantify muscle strength. A 1-RM determination can be made for any dynamic constant external resistance (DCER; formerly known as isotonic) strength exercise, such as the bench press, leg extension and flexion, leg press, squat, or power clean. In addition, 1-RM testing can be performed using free weights or machine exercises. The procedure is a trial-and-error method where, after a warm-up period, progressively heavier weights are lifted one time until the subject cannot successfully complete the lift of a given weight.[1] The weight is then reduced until the heaviest successful weight is determined.

In performing 1-RM testing for a given exercise it is helpful (but not required) to have subjects with some minimal level of weightlifting experience, because strength exercises are a motor skill that improves with practice. Therefore, a 1-RM value is affected not only by the subject's strength but also by the subject's skill in performing the task. In addition, prior experience allows subjects to estimate their strength more accurately prior to testing. This estimate helps eliminate unnecessary lifts that are either too easy or too hard, so that the testing is efficient and the effects of fatigue are minimized.

In this laboratory you will learn to perform 1-RM strength testing for bench press and leg press exercises. You will also compare the 1-RM strength values to age- and gender-specific norms. Percentile rank norms for strength relative to body weight (1-RM strength in lbs/body weight in lbs) are provided in Tables L2.1 through L2.4 for the bench press and leg press exercises for males and females.

photo 2.1

Bench press with spotter. The subject should lower the weight slowly until the barbell touches the mid-chest.

photo 2.2

Bench press with spotter. During ascent and descent the forearms should be vertical to the floor and parallel to each other.

Bench Press

The bench press is a common exercise in both training and testing (see photos 2.1 and 2.2). The motion of the bench press is analogous to a push-up, except the subject lies on his or her back and the resistance is supplied by a barbell or a bench press machine. The pectoral muscles, triceps brachii, and anterior deltoid muscles are the primary muscles involved in the lift. Because the use of a barbell requires that the subject balance the resistance in addition to lifting the weight, the 1-RM from a free weight bench press may be quite different from the 1-RM determined on a machine. Further, because the mechanics of the different machines vary, the 1-RM from the same subject on different machines may also differ substantially. These factors should be kept in mind when interpreting the results relative to the normative values provided in Tables L2.1 and L2.2.

When using free weights, a failed attempt to lift a weight may result in injury if the bar becomes out of control. Therefore, an experienced "spotter" should be ready to help the subject lift the weight when the attempt is clearly going to fail.[2] Most bench press machines do not require the use of a spotter.

For the free weight bench press, the subject should lie supine on the bench with both feet flat on the floor with the buttocks and shoulders in contact with the bench. The subject should grip the barbell with a closed grip. That is, the thumb should wrap around the barbell so that it cannot roll out of the hand. Grip width should be slightly wider than the shoulders and evenly spaced so that the load is the same on each arm. The barbell should then be removed from the bench press racks. The spotter may help the subject by assisting the "liftoff." After the liftoff, the subject should lower the weight slowly until the barbell touches the mid-chest.[2] This should take

table L2.1 Percentile rank norms for bench press 1-RM relative to body weight by age for males.[3]

PERCENTILE RANK	20-29	30-39	40-49	50-59	60-69
90	1.48	1.24	1.10	0.97	0.89
80	1.32	1.12	1.00	0.90	0.82
70	1.22	1.04	0.93	0.84	0.77
60	1.14	0.98	0.88	0.79	0.72
50	1.06	0.93	0.84	0.75	0.68
40	0.99	0.88	0.80	0.71	0.66
30	0.93	0.83	0.76	0.68	0.63
20	0.88	0.78	0.72	0.63	0.57
10	0.80	0.71	0.65	0.57	0.53

Note: Values are bench press 1-RM in lbs/body weight in lbs.

table L2.2 Percentile rank norms for bench press 1-RM relative to body weight by age for females.[3]

PERCENTILE RANK	20-29	30-39	40-49	50-59	60-69
90	0.54	0.49	0.46	0.40	0.41
80	0.49	0.45	0.40	0.37	0.38
70	0.42	0.42	0.38	0.35	0.36
60	0.41	0.41	0.37	0.33	0.32
50	0.40	0.38	0.34	0.31	0.30
40	0.37	0.37	0.32	0.28	0.29
30	0.35	0.34	0.30	0.26	0.28
20	0.33	0.32	0.27	0.23	0.26
10	0.30	0.27	0.23	0.19	0.25

Note: Values are bench press 1-RM in lbs/body weight in lbs.

one to two seconds. As soon as the barbell touches the chest, the subject should lift it upward until the elbows are locked. During the descent and ascent, the forearms should be parallel to each other and oriented vertical to the floor.[2] After the lift, the spotter may help the subject place the barbell on the racks. Lifts are not acceptable if the barbell bounces off the chest or if the buttocks come off the bench.

Leg Press

(see photos 2.3 and 2.4)

The leg press is a machine-based exercise that primarily involves the simultaneous activation of the leg extensors (quadriceps) and hip extensors (gluteal muscles and hamstrings). There are several different types of machines, and the body position can vary considerably from machine to machine, which will affect the amount of weight that can be lifted. Therefore, as with the bench press, caution should be used when interpreting the normative leg press values in Tables L2.3 and L2.4. Most machines allow you to alter the angle between the torso and thigh, and, if possible, this should be set to about 90 degrees.[2]

At the start of the lift, the feet should be about shoulder-width apart and the toes pointed up or in a slightly "toe out" position. The shoulders and buttocks should be firmly braced against the machine.[2] Most leg press machines have hand grips that the subject can use to help stabilize the torso during the lift. Once positioned, the subject will unrack the weight so that the legs are fully extended (although the legs should not be hyperextended at the start of the lift). From full extension, the subject lowers the weight slowly until the angle at the knee joint reaches approximately 90 degrees (photo 2.3), and then extends the legs and hips until the legs are again fully extended (photo 2.4). The subject should keep the legs in line with the hips and ankles, so that the legs do not track in (knock-kneed) or out.[2]

TERMS & ABBREVIATIONS

- DCER = dynamic constant external resistance
- 1-RM = one-repetition maximum, a standard index to quantify muscle strength that refers to the maximum amount of weight that can be lifted one time

photo 2.3

Leg press. The subject lowers the weight slowly until the angle at the knee reaches approximately 90 degrees.

photo 2.4

Leg press. The subject should keep the legs in line with the hips and ankles.

Percentile rank norms for leg press 1-RM relative to body weight by age for males.[3] **table L2.3**

PERCENTILE RANK	20-29	30-39	40-49	50-59	60-69
90	2.27	2.07	1.92	1.80	1.73
80	2.13	1.93	1.82	1.71	1.62
70	2.05	1.85	1.74	1.64	1.56
60	1.97	1.77	1.68	1.58	1.49
50	1.91	1.71	1.62	1.52	1.43
40	1.83	1.65	1.57	1.46	1.38
30	1.74	1.59	1.51	1.39	1.30
20	1.63	1.52	1.44	1.32	1.25
10	1.51	1.43	1.35	1.22	1.16

Note: Values are leg press 1-RM in lbs/body weight in lbs.

Percentile rank norms for leg press 1-RM relative to body weight by age for females.[3] **table L2.4**

PERCENTILE RANK	20-29	30-39	40-49	50-59	60-69
90	2.05	1.73	1.63	1.51	1.40
80	1.66	1.50	1.46	1.30	1.25
70	1.42	1.47	1.35	1.24	1.18
60	1.36	1.32	1.26	1.18	1.15
50	1.32	1.26	1.19	1.09	1.08
40	1.25	1.21	1.12	1.03	1.04
30	1.23	1.16	1.03	0.95	0.98
20	1.13	1.09	0.94	0.86	0.94
10	1.02	0.94	0.76	0.75	0.84

Note: Values are leg press 1-RM in lbs/body weight in lbs.

- ☐ leg extensors = the quadriceps, made up of the rectus femoris, vastus lateralis, vastus intermedius, and vastus medialis
- ☐ hip extensors = the gluteal muscles (gluteus maximus and gluteus medius) and the hamstrings (biceps femoris, semitendinosus, and semimembranosus)
- ☐ hyperextension = extension of a joint beyond the normal range of motion

PROCEDURES (see photos L2.1 to L2.4)

1. Have the subject estimate his or her 1-RM strength and record it on Worksheet 2.1.
2. Have the subject perform a general warm-up (three to five minutes) of the body area to be tested.
3. Continue the warm-up by performing eight repetitions at a weight equal to 50% of the estimated 1-RM and three repetitions at 70% of the estimated 1-RM.

4. To determine the 1-RM, perform a single repetition at a heavier weight than that used during the warm-up. The increase in weight should be based on the relative ease or difficulty of the set in the warm-up.
5. Repeat performing single repetitions using progressively heavier weights until a weight is reached that cannot be successfully lifted. Adjust the increases in weight so that increments are approximately evenly spaced and so that at least two single lifts are performed between the weight used in the warm-up and the estimated 1-RM.
6. At failure, decrease the weight to a level approximately midway between the last successful lift and the weight at failure.
7. Repeat using heavier or lighter weights until the desired level of precision is achieved (usually within about 5 lbs) and record the 1-RM weight on Worksheet 2.1.
8. Rest intervals between single lifts should be between one and five minutes.[4,5]
9. Try to determine the 1-RM in about three to five single lifts, excluding warm-up lifts.[1]
10. To increase time efficiency, more than one subject can be tested at a given station, so that one person is performing lifts while the others are resting.

SAMPLE CALCULATIONS

Gender: male

Body weight: 180 lbs

Age: 21 years

Mode of lift: Bench press

Estimated 1-RM: 200 lbs

WARM-UP

1. 8 repetitions at 100 lbs (approximately 50% of estimated 1-RM)
2. 3 repetitions at 140 lbs (approximately 70% of estimated 1-RM)

1-RM TESTING

1. *Circle:* (success) failure at 170 lbs
2. *Circle:* (success) failure at 185 lbs
3. *Circle:* success (failure) at 200 lbs
4. *Circle:* (success) failure at 195 lbs
5. *Circle:* success failure at ______ lbs
6. *Circle:* success failure at ______ lbs
7. *Circle:* success failure at ______ lbs

1-RM/body weight: 195 lbs/180 lbs = 1.08

Percentile rank classification for 1-RM in lbs/body weight in lbs
= 52nd percentile (see Tables L2.1–L2.4)

DETERMINATION OF ONE-REPETITION MAXIMUM STRENGTH — worksheet 2.1

NAME ______________________________ DATE ______________

Gender: ______________

Body weight: ______________ lbs

Age: ______________

Mode of lift: ______________

Estimated 1-RM: ______________ lbs

WARM-UP

1. _______ repetitions at _______ lbs (approximately 50% of estimated 1-RM)
2. _______ repetitions at _______ lbs (approximately 70% of estimated 1-RM)

1-RM TESTING

1. *Circle:* success failure at ____________ lbs
2. *Circle:* success failure at ____________ lbs
3. *Circle:* success failure at ____________ lbs
4. *Circle:* success failure at ____________ lbs
5. *Circle:* success failure at ____________ lbs
6. *Circle:* success failure at ____________ lbs
7. *Circle:* success failure at ____________ lbs

1-RM/body weight: ______________

Percentile rank classification for 1-RM in lbs/body weight in lbs = ____________
(see Tables L2.1–L2.4)

worksheet 2.2 EXTENSION ACTIVITIES

NAME ______________________________ DATE ______________

1. Given the following data, fill in the blanks below.

   Gender: female

   Age: 22 years

   Bench press 1-RM: 70 lbs

   Body weight: 150 lbs

   Bench press 1-RM in lbs/body weight in lbs: ______________

   Percentile rank = ______________ (see Table L2.2)

2. Given the following data, fill in the blanks below.

   Gender: male

   Age: 44 years

   Leg press 1-RM: 275 lbs

   Body weight: 180 lbs

   Leg press 1-RM in lbs/body weight in lbs: ______________

   Percentile rank = ______________ (see Table L2.3)

EXTENSION QUESTIONS

1. What are some common mistakes that may occur in administering this lab?

2. Identify possible sources of error in this lab.

3. Assess the practicality of using this lab in the field.

4. Research the reliability and/or validity of this lab using online resources, journal articles, and other credible sources.

REFERENCES

1. Brown, L. E., and Weir, J. P. ASEP Procedures Recommendation I: Accurate assessment of muscular strength and power. *J. Exercise Phys. Online* 4: 1–21, 2001.
2. Graham, J. F. Resistance exercise techniques and spotting. In *Conditioning for Strength and Human Performance,* eds. T. J. Chandler and L. E. Brown. Baltimore: Lippincott Williams & Wilkins, 2008, pp. 182–236.
3. Hoffman, J. *Norms for Fitness, Performance, and Health.* Champaign, IL: Human Kinetics, 2006.
4. Matuszak, M. E., Fry, A. C., Weiss, L. W., Ireland, T. R., and McNight, M. M. Effect of rest interval length on repeated 1 repetition maximum back squats. *J. Strength Cond. Res.* 17: 634–637, 2003.
5. Weir, J. P., Wagner, L. L., and Housh, T. J. The effect of rest interval length on repeated maximal bench presses. *J. Strength Cond. Res.* 8: 58–60, 1994.

3 Metabolism and Metabolic Adaptations to Training

As a result of reading this chapter you will:

- Understand why exercise scientists, physical educators, and coaches need a basic understanding of metabolism.
- Have a basic knowledge of aerobic and anaerobic metabolism.
- Be able to differentiate between activities that are primarily aerobic or anaerobic.
- Be able to identify the metabolic adaptations to endurance, sprint, and resistance training.

key concepts

adenosine triphosphate–phosphocreatine (ATP–PC) system
aerobic
allosteric inhibition
anabolism
anaerobic
anaerobic glycolysis
beta oxidation
carbohydrate sparing effect
catabolism
coenzyme
cofactor
dehydrogenase enzymes
electron transport system (ETS)
enzyme
glycogen
glycogenolysis
glycolysis
Krebs cycle
lactate
Law of Mass Action
lock-and-key method
metabolism
myoglobin
phosphagen
phosphatase
phosphocreatine (PC)
phosphofructokinase (PFK)
polypeptide
power
reactant
substrate
triglyceride

DEFINING METABOLISM

Metabolism is the foundation of all voluntary human movement. Simply stated, **metabolism** involves utilizing the food that we eat to store energy in the form of adenosine triphosphate (ATP). We then break down the ATP, liberate the energy, and use it to cause muscles to contract. Metabolism means "to change" and includes the processes of anabolism and catabolism. **Anabolism** means "to build up"; the term refers to processes in which structures are created, such as the use of amino acids to make proteins that contribute to muscle mass. **Catabolism** means "to break down"; it refers to processes such as breaking down glycogen (stored glucose) to glucose molecules, or glucose to pyruvate for ATP production.

Exercise scientists, physical educators, and coaches should have a basic understanding of metabolism for a number of reasons. For example:

1. ATP is the only source of energy that we can use directly for muscle contraction. Since all forms of exercise and sport rely on muscle contraction, producing enough ATP is essential to our ability to perform physical activity.

2. Many important adaptations to exercise training involve aspects of metabolism, as discussed later in this chapter.

3. An important consideration when designing training programs for athletes or prescribing exercise programs for non-athletes is the metabolic demands of the sport or activity. The benefits of the program will be specific to the metabolic demands of the training. For example, endurance training results in improved aerobic capabilities, while sprint training improves anaerobic capabilities.

OVERVIEW OF ATP PRODUCTION

The ATP required for muscle contraction can be produced aerobically or anaerobically. **Aerobic** means "with oxygen"; therefore, aerobic ATP production requires sufficient oxygen in the cellular environment. **Anaerobic** means "without oxygen." When there is insufficient oxygen in the cell, ATP can be produced anaerobically. Most physical activities involve ATP production from both aerobic and anaerobic sources, ranging from being almost totally aerobic (such as distance running) to almost totally anaerobic (such as weight lifting). Most activities, however, fall somewhere in between; for example, boxing and the 800-meter run are roughly 50 percent aerobic and 50 percent anaerobic. Table 3.1 lists some popular activities and their approximate aerobic and anaerobic contributions.[30]

The information in Table 3.1 is particularly valuable to coaches and athletes for organizing practice times and designing optimal training programs. Knowing the relative importance of aerobic versus anaerobic ATP production to a sport can guide you in selecting the types of conditioning to be used and how much time to dedicate to each. For example, football is largely anaerobic, and conditioning sessions should, therefore, involve activities such as sprints, plyometrics, and resistance training. A large volume of aerobic training is not likely to benefit football performance. On the other hand, because boxing is roughly 50 percent aerobic and 50 percent anaerobic, conditioning for boxing needs to include both anaerobic and aerobic phases. This, of course, is typical of conditioning programs for boxers, who not only spar and use the heavy bag and medicine ball (anaerobic training) but also perform distance running (aerobic training), which is often referred to as "road work." Thus, in general, over the years, trainers for boxers have learned that conditioning that is consistent with

aerobic
anaerobic

table 3.1 Approximate percentages of aerobic and anaerobic contributions to ATP production for various physical activities.

ACTIVITY	% AEROBIC	% ANAEROBIC
Resistance training (low repetitions, high resistance)	0	100
Circuit weight lifting (high repetitions, low to moderate resistance)	15	85
100-meter run	0	100
200-meter run	5	95
400-meter run	15	85
800-meter run	50	50
1,500-meter run	65	35
3,000-meter run	80	20
10,000-meter run	98	2
Marathon	100	0
Triathlon	100	0
100-meter swim	20	80
200-meter swim	50	50
800-meter swim	80	20
Football	5	95
Basketball	10	90
Tennis	25	75
Baseball	10	90
Gymnastics	5	95
Field hockey	30	70
Speed skating	15	85
Boxing	50	50

the metabolic demands of the activity pays off in better performance. A basic knowledge of metabolism can help you to design efficient and effective practice and training sessions.

This information also has application for personal trainers and physical educators. Knowing aerobic and anaerobic ATP contributions can help with the selection of activities to meet the goals of a particular client or lesson plan. For example, if an improvement in cardiorespiratory fitness is the goal, the personal trainer or physical educator can select from a variety of activities that are predominantly aerobic. On the other hand, if the goal involves increasing muscular strength and power, activities that are largely anaerobic, such as resistance training or circuit weight lifting, should be used.

www

Biological Energy Conversion, Review of Anaerobic Metabolism
www.life.uiuc.edu/crofts/bioph354/lect2.html

Glycolysis and Krebs Cycle
www.uic.edu/classes/bios/bios100/lecturesf04am/lect12.htm

Anaerobic Metabolism

The metabolic pathways involved in anaerobic ATP production include the **adenosine triphosphate–phosphocreatine (ATP–PC) system** and anaerobic glycolysis,

- adenosine triphosphate–phosphocreatine (ATP–PC) system

Professional knowledge and expertise

Exercise scientists, physical educators, coaches, and athletic trainers are often and rightfully viewed as experts regarding issues related to exercise and diet. Frequently athletes, students, clients, or patients are curious about the potential positive and negative effects of the latest dietary supplement or training fad. An accurate response will be based, in part, on the metabolic effects of the supplement or activity.

phosphagen
phosphocreatine (PC)
anaerobic glycolysis

which will be discussed later in the chapter (refer to Figure 3.2). The fuels (metabolic substrates) associated with these systems are the **phosphagens** for the ATP–PC system and carbohydrates (glucose) for anaerobic glycolysis. The phosphagens include ATP and **phosphocreatine (PC),** also called *creatine phosphate.* **Anaerobic glycolysis** occurs in the sarcoplasm of the muscle fiber and involves the metabolism of carbohydrates in the form of the six-carbon sugar glucose to an end product of lactate. When we are exercising too hard to supply and utilize enough oxygen to meet our ATP needs aerobically, and available oxygen in the cellular environment is, therefore, insufficient, we anaerobically metabolize the phosphagens and glucose to supply the ATP for muscle contractions.

Aerobic Metabolism

Krebs cycle
electron transport system (ETS)

Aerobic metabolism involves the use of oxygen in the breakdown of carbohydrates, fats, or proteins to produce ATP (Figure 3.1). Aerobic metabolism of carbohydrates (carbohydrate oxidation) involves converting glucose to pyruvate through the same glycolytic processes involved in anaerobic glycolysis. Pyruvate then enters the mitochondria of the cell, is converted to acetyl coenzyme A, and continues to be metabolized through the **Krebs cycle** (named for Sir Hans Krebs, Nobel Prize winner in 1953; also called the *citric acid cycle* or *tricarboxylic acid cycle*) and the **electron transport system (ETS),** also sometimes called the *respiratory chain,* where large amounts of ATP are produced and oxygen is utilized. Thus, during the aerobic metabolism of carbohydrates, anaerobic glycolysis precedes the aerobic phases of ATP production.

beta oxidation

Aerobic metabolism of fats (fatty acid oxidation) first involves the liberation of fatty acids from their storage location as a part of triglycerides. The long carbon chain fatty acids are then metabolized through a process called **beta oxidation** into two carbon aceytl coenzyme A molecules. These enter the Krebs cycle and proceed through the ETS for ATP production (Figure 3.1).

Protein metabolism involves the conversion of amino acids into keto acids by the liver or muscle. Keto acids can then form substances that produce ATP through the Krebs cycle and ETS (Figure 3.1).

ENZYMES

reactant
substrate
enzyme

The production of ATP involves anaerobic and aerobic pathways. Each pathway includes a number of enzymatic steps. Each enzymatic step involves the conversion of a **reactant** (also sometimes called a **substrate**) to a product by a specific enzyme. To understand ATP production you need to have a basic knowledge of the functioning of enzymes.

Enzymes are proteins that have specific properties and functions. Three primary aspects of the actions of enzymes are:[10]

figure 3.1 Fat, carbohydrate, and protein can be used to produce ATP aerobically.

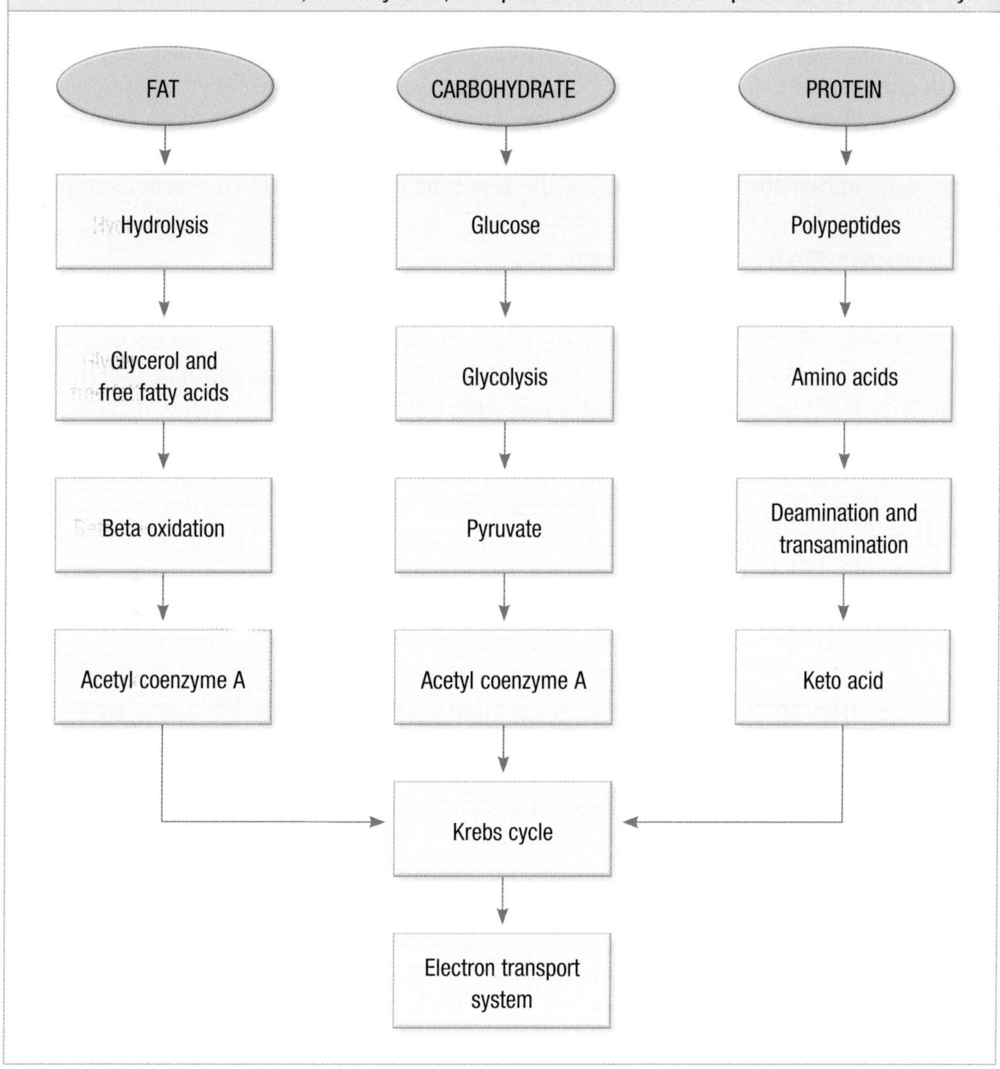

1. An enzyme speeds up or catalyzes a reaction. A reactant will convert to a product naturally without an enzyme, but the process will take considerably longer. During exercise, when ATP is used continuously, enzymes are required to convert reactants to products at the accelerated rate necessary to meet the demands of the activity.

2. An enzyme is not changed when it catalyzes a reaction. Thus, enzymes can function repeatedly to convert many molecules of reactants to products.

3. An enzyme does not change the result of the reaction. With or without an enzyme, the reactant will be converted to the same product.

Activation Energy

For a reaction to occur, there must be sufficient activation energy or energy of activation to catalyze a reaction. In a laboratory, we can heat the solution in a test tube. Obviously, this is not possible in living cells. To meet the requirement for activation energy during metabolism, enzymes reduce the amount of activation energy required for a reaction to occur.[10]

Lock-and-Key Work Method of Enzymes

lock-and-key method

Enzymes work by a **lock-and-key method.**[10] That is, enzymes (the key) are very specific to the reactant (the lock) with which they bind. An enzyme must fit precisely with the reactant to catalyze the reaction. As discussed above, enzymes are proteins and, therefore, have a three-dimensional shape. The specific location on the enzyme that actually catalyzes the reaction is called the *active site.* The shape of the active site must match the *binding site* on the reactant for a reaction to be catalyzed.

Turnover Rate of Enzymes

phosphofructokinase (PFK)

The efficiency and effectiveness with which an enzyme can convert a reactant to a product is determined by its *turnover rate.* The turnover rate of an enzyme is defined as the number of molecules of reactant converted to product per minute. Enzymes vary greatly in turnover rate, and within a metabolic pathway such as glycolysis, one specific enzyme will therefore have the lowest turnover rate. This enzyme is called the *rate-limiting enzyme,* and for glycolysis it is **phosphofructokinase (PFK).** The rate-limiting enzyme can be thought of as the weak link in the chain for a metabolic pathway. The rate of conversion of the initial reactant to the final product through a series of enzymatic steps will proceed no faster than the rate-limiting enzyme will allow.

A number of factors can affect the turnover rate of an enzyme.[10]

The temperature and level of acidity (pH) of the cellular environment. The turnover rate of an enzyme rises and then falls as temperature or pH increases. At low or high temperatures or pH, enzymes are least effective, and there is a rather narrow range of temperature and pH values where enzymes have the highest turnover rates.

The relationship between temperature and turnover rate probably plays a minor role in metabolism, since normally only small changes take place in body temperature during exercise. Nevertheless, warming up prior to competition may affect this relationship and provide for optimal enzyme efficiency.

lactate

On the other hand, vigorous exercise results in substantial changes in cellular pH. For example, anaerobic glycolysis can result in the production of **lactate,** which can decrease cellular pH. The increase in acidity affects the turnover rate of the enzymes in the glycolytic pathway and reduces the rate of ATP production.

Law of Mass Action

The concentration and activity of reactants and enzymes. The conversion of a reactant to a product is determined in part by the concentration of reactant as well as the amount of enzyme available to catalyze the reaction. The ability of a reversible reaction to be driven from an area of high concentration to an area of low concentration is known as the **Law of Mass Action.** Two of the beneficial metabolic adaptations to exercise training are the increases in the concentrations of reactants and enzymes. Thus, based on the Law of Mass Action, exercise training can increase the rate of ATP production by increasing the availability of reactants and enzymes in a metabolic pathway.

allosteric inhibition

End product inhibition. End product inhibition means that the final product of a series of enzymatic steps inhibits the activity (reduces the turnover rate) of a specific enzyme or enzymes in the pathway. This takes place through a process called **allosteric inhibition.** Allosteric (which means "other site") inhibition describes the way in which the end product inhibits the activity of the enzyme. The allosteric inhibitor (end product) binds to the enzyme at a site other than the active site, which changes its shape and thereby reduces the binding affinity of the

RESEARCH

Heart rate and $\dot{V}O_2$ during high-speed racing

Some believe that automobile racing is not a "real" sport and that the drivers are not "true" athletes. However, Jacobs and Olvey* assessed physiological responses during simulated high-speed racing to measure heart rate (HR) and oxygen consumption rate ($\dot{V}O_2$) and to compare these values with laboratory assessments of peak $\dot{V}O_2$ and HR during leg and arm ergometry tests. HR and $\dot{V}O_2$ values were related to lap time, with values increasing dramatically at paces under 1 minute per lap. Peak HR and $\dot{V}O_2$ values during simulated race driving at competitive speeds ranged from 158 to 182 bpm and 2.90 to 3.35 L • min^{-1}, respectively, or over 75 percent of $\dot{V}O_2$ peak measured during leg ergometry. In competition, the physical work and psychological stress would demand even more of the drivers, and it would seem prudent to tailor the training methods of these athletes to the requirements of their sport. Specifically, aerobic training programs designed to increase peak $\dot{V}O_2$ would help protect the athlete from fatigue during competitive racing conditions.

* Jacobs, P. L., and Olvey, S. E. Metabolic and heart rate responses to open-wheel automobile road racing: a single-subject study. *J. Strength Cond. Res.* 14: 157–161, 2000.

enzyme for its reactant. This reduced binding affinity results in decreased turnover rate and prevents the end product from building up too much. For example, ATP is an allosteric inhibitor of the glycolytic enzyme PFK. If there is sufficient ATP in the cellular environment, such as at the end of exercise, allosteric inhibition will slow glycolysis through its effect on the turnover rate of PFK.

The availability and concentrations of cofactors and coenzymes. **Cofactors** are metals such as calcium, magnesium, zinc, and others. In some cases, for its active site to be properly shaped, the enzyme must be bound to a cofactor. When the enzyme and cofactor are attached to each other, the active site will be properly shaped to bind with the reactant. The lack of an appropriate cofactor will decrease the turnover rate of the enzyme.

cofactors

Coenzymes are derivatives of vitamins. One of the primary functions of coenzymes is to transport hydrogen within the cell. With regard to metabolism, primary coenzymes include flavin adenine dinucleotide (FAD), nicotinamide adenine dinucleotide (NAD), coenzyme A, and coenzyme Q, which are derived from the vitamins riboflavin (B_2), niacin (B_3), pantothenic acid, and vitamin E, respectively. FAD and NAD are involved in a variety of enzymatic reactions in glycolysis, the Krebs cycle, and the electron transport system. Coenzyme A and coenzyme Q are associated with the Krebs cycle and the ETS, respectively (see Table 3.2). The turnover rates of specific enzymes in these metabolic pathways are influenced by the availability of coenzymes. Thus, exercise performance can be affected by vitamin or mineral deficiencies.

coenzymes

ANAEROBIC ATP PRODUCTION

As mentioned previously, ATP can be produced anaerobically, that is, without oxygen, through two pathways: the ATP–PC system and anaerobic glycolysis.

ATP–PC System

Three primary enzymatic reactions occur in the ATP–PC system.

1. $\text{ATP} \xrightarrow[\text{ATPase}]{\text{Myosin}} \text{ADP} + \text{inorganic phosphate (Pi)} + \text{energy}$

table 3.2 Selected coenzymes in metabolism.

		METABOLIC SYSTEM		
Coenzyme	**Vitamin**	**Glycolysis**	**Krebs cycle**	**ETS**
FAD	Riboflavin (B_2)		✓	✓
NAD	Niacin (B_3)	✓	✓	✓
Coenzyme A	Pantothenic acid		✓	
Coenzyme Q	Vitamin E			✓

2. $PC + ADP \xrightarrow[\text{Kinase (CK)}]{\text{Creatine}} ATP + C$

3. $2ADP \xrightarrow[\text{Kinase (AK)}]{\text{Adenylate}} ATP + AMP$

In reaction 1, the ATP molecule, which is bound to the myosin head, is broken down by the enzyme myosin ATPase (also called actomyosin ATPase or just ATPase). The products of this reaction are ADP (adenosine diphosphate) plus Pi plus energy. Thus, a phosphate is cleaved off from ATP, which liberates the energy from the high-energy phosphate bond. The energy is then used to cause the myosin head to swivel inward toward the center of the sarcomere, pulling the actin molecule and Z-line with it, and resulting in shortening of the sarcomere (i.e., muscle contraction).

Because we can store only a very small amount of ATP (probably enough for only a few seconds of exercise), it is necessary to resynthesize it rapidly to continue to exercise. This resynthesis of ATP is accomplished very effectively by reaction 2, which is catalyzed by the enzyme creatine kinase (CK). Creatine kinase is so effective at resynthesizing ATP that there is little change in the level of ATP in muscle during exercise. The stores of PC in muscle, however, are sufficient to fuel the resynthesis of ATP for only approximately 15–20 seconds during maximal exercise. During high-intensity exercise ATP is broken down at such a rate that ADP concentration can increase substantially within the muscle fiber.

Reaction 3 describes how two ADP molecules produce ATP and adenosine monophosphate (AMP). This reaction is catalyzed by the enzyme adenylate kinase (AK) (which is also called myokinase) and not only helps with ATP availability but also keeps ADP from building up excessively within the muscle fiber.

Anaerobic Glycolysis

Anaerobic glycolysis is the primary system for ATP production during activities that can be maintained from approximately 20 to 30 seconds to two to three minutes. This range of values reflects, in part, an individual's level of conditioning. Examples of activities that rely predominantly on anaerobic glycolysis include the 400- to 800-meter runs, 100- to 200-meter swims, gymnastics, field hockey, and speed skating. Many sporting activities, however, involve ATP production from more than one energy production system simultaneously. That is, some of the ATP production during a 400-meter race comes from the ATP–PC system and from anaerobic glycolysis, while during a 1,500-meter race both anaerobic glycolysis and the aerobic metabolism of carbohydrates contribute to ATP production.

As discussed earlier, anaerobic means "without oxygen." Glycolysis involves the breakdown of sugar (*glyco* means "sugar" and *lysis* means "to break"). Thus, anaerobic glycolysis involves the breakdown of sugar (in the form of glucose) without the use of oxygen.

The final products of carbohydrate digestion in the digestive tract are the monosaccharides (six-carbon-atom sugars): glucose, fructose, and galactose. These are the results of the breakdown of such larger carbohydrate molecules as starch and the usual sugars included in the diet (disaccharides). The three monosaccharides are interconvertible, and as they pass through the liver they are converted almost entirely to glucose for transport in the blood to the muscle fibers and other tissues of the body.

As the glucose molecule enters the muscle cell through the sarcolemma, a process greatly aided by the presence of the pancreatic hormone insulin, it is immediately *phosphorylated.* That is to say, the six-carbon-atom monosaccharide picks up a phosphate radical on its number 6 carbon and becomes glucose-6-phosphate. Note in Figure 3.2 that this process of phosphorylation requires the presence of the enzyme hexokinase, as well as the breakdown of one ATP to form ADP + Pi. Since our discussion has to do with formation of ATP, this first step would seem to be in the wrong direction, but as we will see later, we recoup this ATP (and more) later in glycolysis.

Once phosphorylated, the glucose molecule is trapped in the muscle cell because it requires the enzyme **phosphatase** to dephosphorylate the glucose. The muscle cell has no phosphatase, although the liver cells and some other tissues do. This is important from a practical standpoint because energy stored away in one muscle is not available to another that may be in the process of exhausting its energy in locally heavy work.

phosphatase

The glucose-6-phosphate can be either utilized directly for energy, by continuing through glycolysis as shown in Figure 3.2, or stored, depending on the level of activity of the muscle fiber. To be stored it must be converted to **glycogen,** which is a large chain or network of glucose molecules called a *polymer.* The polymerization process involves several steps and requires a number of enzymes. The glycogen is deposited as granules in glycogen columns within the muscle fiber. (Storage in the form of large polymerized molecules is necessary so that the intracellular osmotic pressure is not unduly raised, which it would be if carbohydrate were stored as glucose units.) The breakdown products of protein and fat digestion and lactate can also be converted to glucose and then to glycogen for storage.

glycogen

Figure 3.2 illustrates the process of anaerobic metabolism of carbohydrates. Glucose becomes available as an energy substrate either by the **glycogenolysis** (conversion of glycogen to glucose) of glycogen stored in the muscle fiber or by the transport of blood glucose into the muscle fiber. Through **glycolysis,** the glucose molecule is broken down into two pyruvate molecules. As discussed earlier, the enzyme hexokinase is necessary to add a phosphate (P) radical to make glucose-6-phosphate. This process costs the breakdown of one ATP to ADP + Pi. Each of the further steps of glycolysis is also catalyzed by at least one enzyme specific to that step, and one more ATP is broken down to add the second P to form fructose-1,6-bisphosphate (the 1,6 means that there are two phosphates in the molecule, one at the number 1 carbon atom and one at the number 6 carbon). Note, however, that the cost of breaking down two ATPs is recouped with a net total gain of two ATP molecules during the process of anaerobic glycolysis, which results in the formation of two molecules of pyruvate. In the absence of sufficient oxygen in the cellular environment, the end product of glycolysis is lactate. This last step is important because if lactate accumulates, the muscle fiber becomes acidic and fatigue occurs (Figure 3.2).

glycogenolysis

glycolysis

figure 3.2 Anaerobic glycolysis involves the breakdown of glucose to lactate.

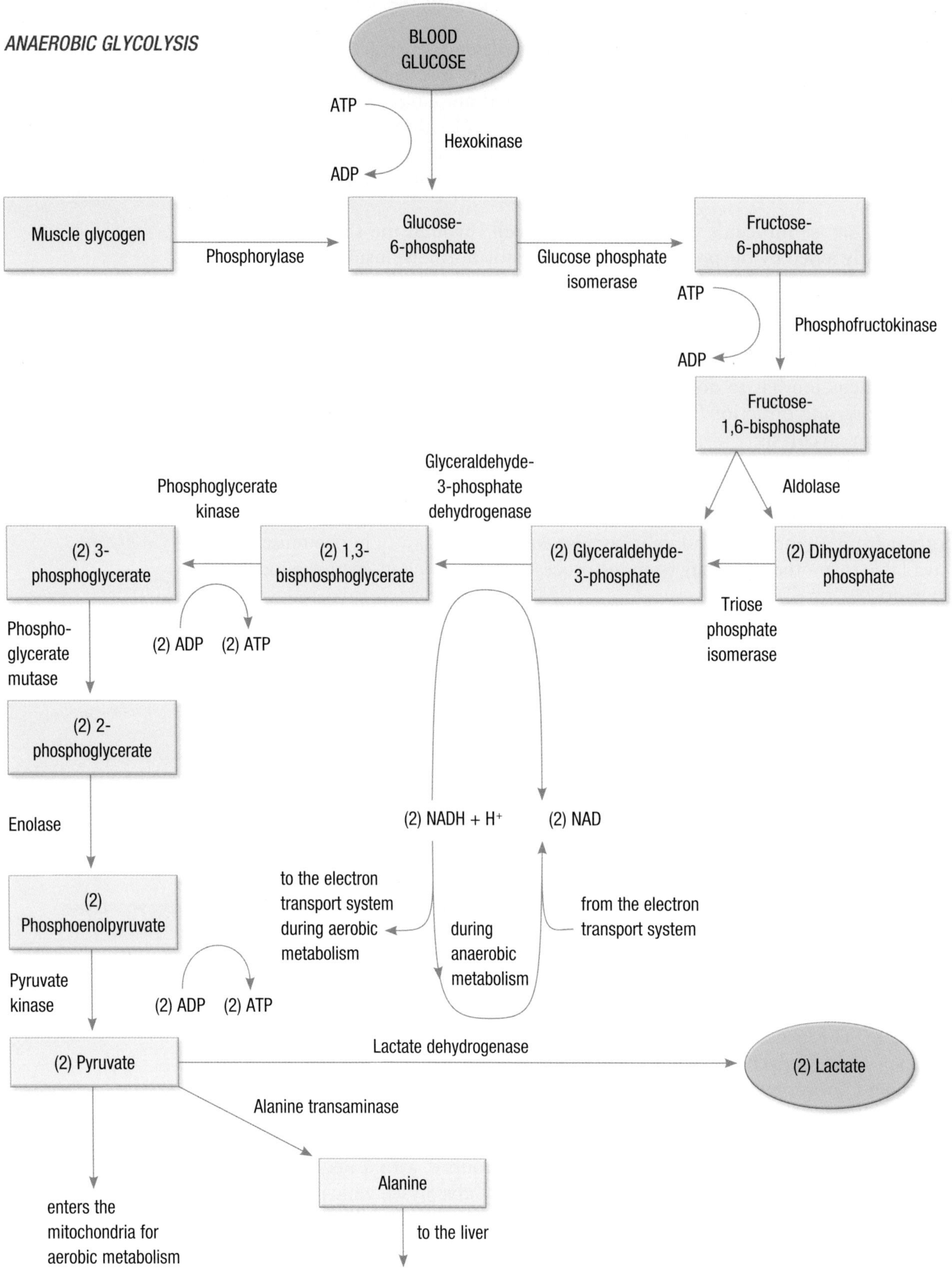

AEROBIC (OXIDATIVE) METABOLISM OF CARBOHYDRATES

In the presence of sufficient oxygen, pyruvate from anaerobic glycolysis enters mitochondria of the muscle fiber, where ATP is produced aerobically in the Krebs cycle and ETS (Figures 3.3 and 3.4).[14,16] Aerobic metabolism of carbohydrates is much more advantageous, because anaerobic glycolysis nets us only two ATP molecules from one molecule of glucose. The complete aerobic breakdown of carbohydrates provides 38 molecules of ATP per molecule of glucose (Figure 3.5).

The Krebs cycle occurs within the mitochondria of the muscle fiber. **figure 3.3**

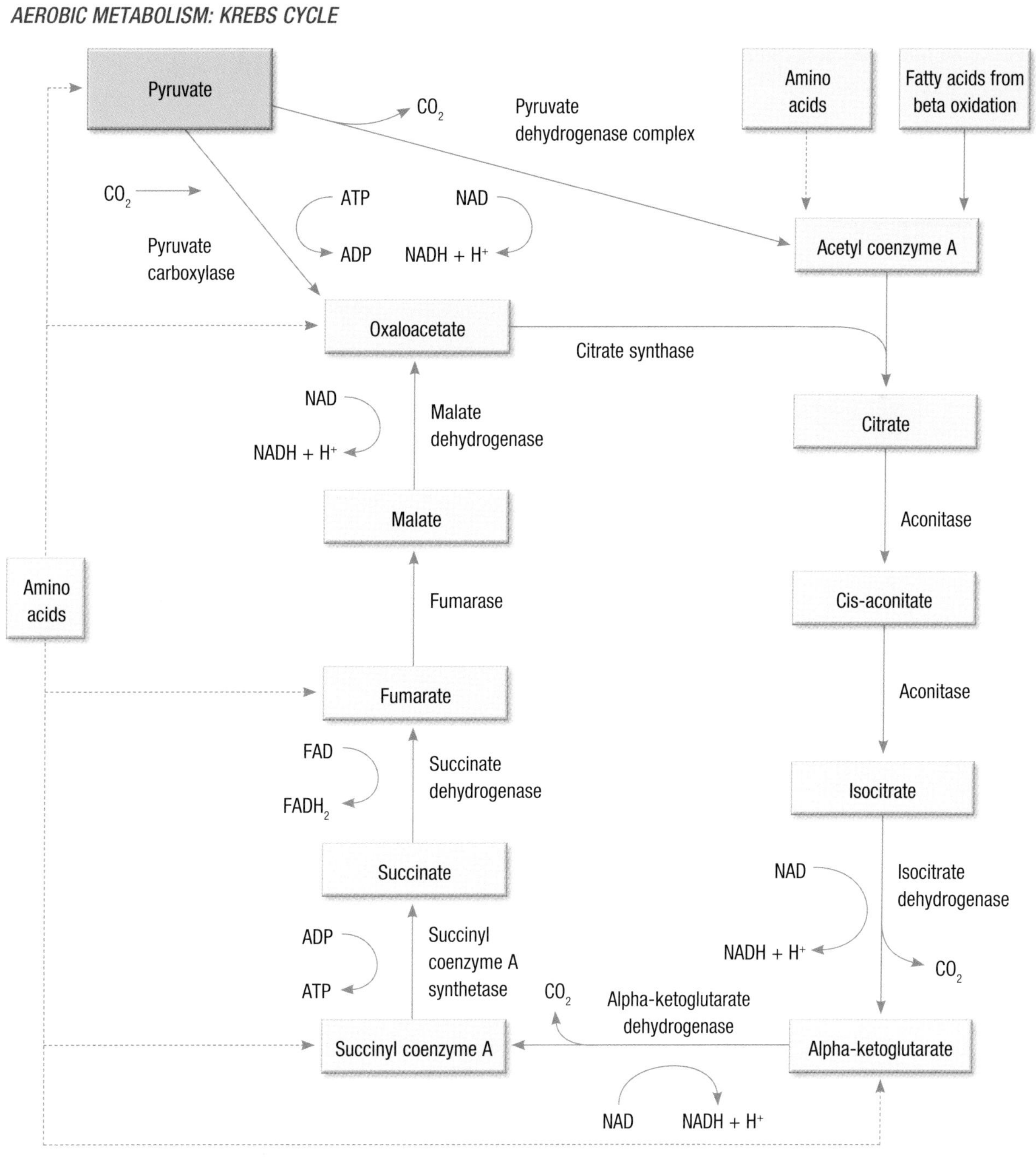

figure 3.4 Most ATP is produced in the electron transport system.

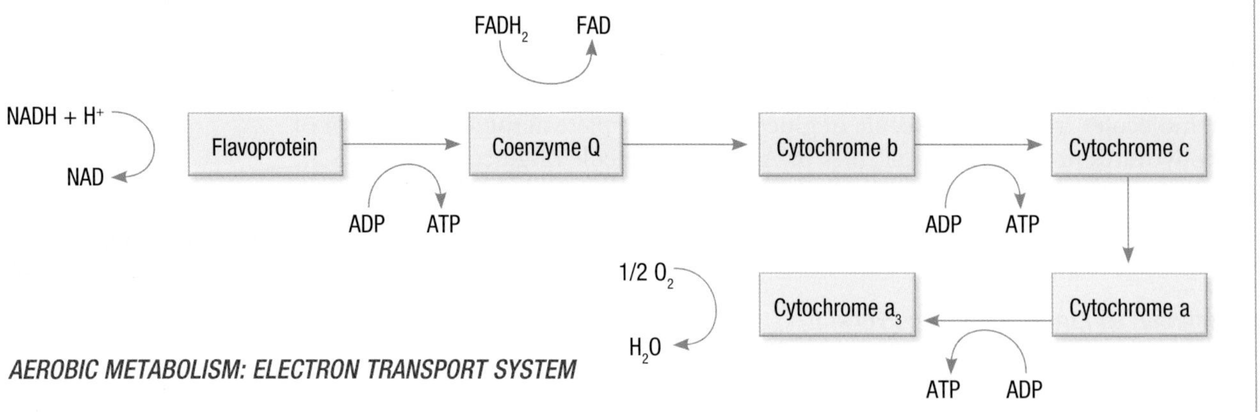

figure 3.5 Anaerobic breakdown of glucose results in the net production of only 2 ATP, while aerobic metabolism nets 38 ATP.

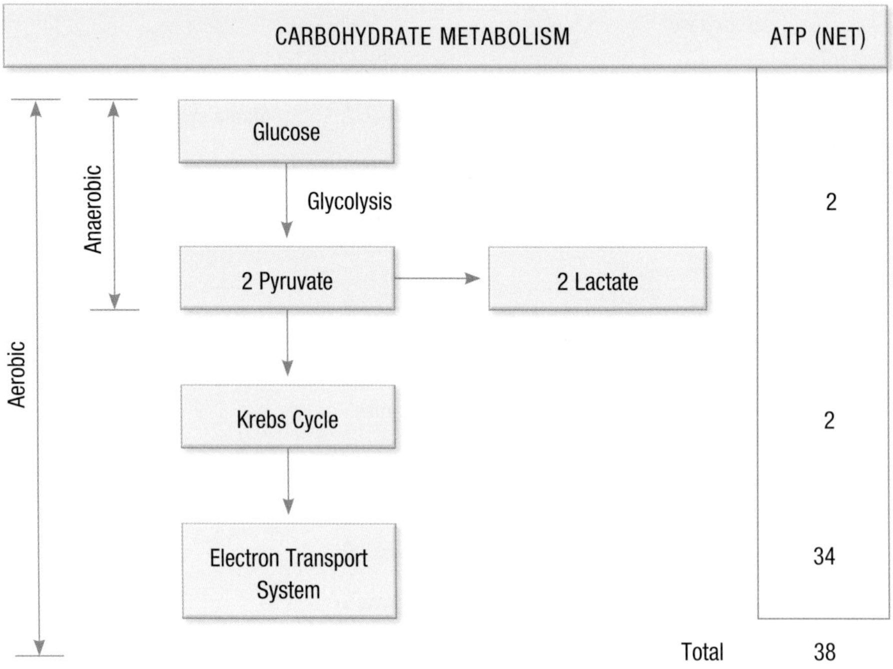

The next stage in glucose breakdown requires the conversion of the two pyruvate molecules into two molecules of acetyl coenzyme A (acetyl CoA) (Figure 3.3). Acetyl CoA combines with the oxaloacetate to become citrate, and the Krebs cycle is under way. Within glycolysis and the Krebs cycle are six reactions catalyzed by **dehydrogenase enzymes** (Figures 3.2 and 3.3). At each of these steps, oxidation–reduction reactions transfer two hydrogen atoms to the coenzyme NAD or FAD. Accepting the hydrogen causes the coenzymes to become reduced, and now they are written as NADH + H^+ and $FADH_2$. The metabolism of one molecule of glucose through glycolysis and the Krebs cycle results in the formation of 10 NADH + H^+ and 2 $FADH_2$ (Figures 3.2 and 3.3). These reduced

dehydrogenase enzymes

coenzymes are then used to produce ATP in the ETS (Figure 3.4). Note, however, that only two ATP molecules are regenerated from one molecule of glucose directly in the Krebs cycle (Figure 3.5).

ELECTRON TRANSPORT SYSTEM

As shown in Figure 3.5, the ETS is where most of the ATP is produced during aerobic metabolism. Of the 38 ATP produced from the aerobic metabolism of one molecule of glucose, 34 ATP are produced in the ETS. In the ETS (Figure 3.4) each NADH + H^+ produces 3 ATP, and each $FADH_2$ produces 2 ATP. It should be noted that there are differences of opinion regarding the number of ATP produced from each NADH + H^+ and $FADH_2$ in the ETS. For example, according to the chemiosmotic hypothesis,[25] each NADH + H^+ produces an actual yield of only 2.5 ATP, and each $FADH_2$ produces 1.5 ATP in the ETS (instead of the theoretical yield of 3 and 2 ATP, respectively, as described in this text). Thus, the number of usable ATP produced from NADH + H^+ and $FADH_2$ in the ETS is still being debated, and various sources therefore present different numbers of total ATP production for the aerobic metabolism of carbohydrates, fats, and proteins.

Electron Transport System
http://faculty.nl.edu/jste/electron_transport_system.htm

At the end of the ETS, one half of an oxygen molecule accepts the two hydrogens passed through the ETS and produces water (H_2O). Thus, oxygen is called the *final electron acceptor*. It is at the end of the ETS that the oxygen we consume during exercise is used to help produce ATP. **Chapter 3 Lab** provides a means of estimating maximal oxygen consumption rate ($\dot{V}O_2$ max). The more oxygen we are able to supply to the muscle and utilize at the end of the ETS, the more ATP we can produce and the more aerobic exercise we can perform. Therefore, typically, an athlete with a high $\dot{V}O_2$ max excels in endurance activities that rely primarily on aerobic ATP production.

The net chemical reaction for the aerobic metabolism of glucose is:

$$C_6H_{12}O_6 + 6O_2 + 38ADP + 38P \longrightarrow 6CO_2 + 6H_2O + 38ATP$$

Since each high-energy phosphate bond represents about eight kilocalories and each gram molecular weight of glucose (180 gm) has an ultimate energy value of about four kilocalories per gram, the efficiency of this process of storing glucose energy as ATP is about:

$$\frac{38 \times 8}{180 \times 4} = \frac{304}{720} = 42\%$$

This demonstrates that while the aerobic metabolism of glucose can produce substantial ATP, less than one half of the potential energy from glucose is ultimately available for muscle contraction.

FAT AND PROTEIN METABOLISM

Low- to moderate-intensity exercise (up to about 60–70% of maximum) proceeds largely by way of ATP gained from fat metabolism. Thus, ATP production from fatty acid sources is quite important in many forms of exercise. Protein metabolism can also provide ATP. This becomes especially important in a state of negative energy balance (starvation or the semistarvation of rigorous weight reduction). Generally, however, protein metabolism accounts for less than 15–18 percent of total ATP production during exercise.

Use of Fat for ATP Production

triglyceride

Fat is a combination of three fatty acids, each of which is attached to one of the three carbon atoms of a glycerol molecule. Chemically this combination of fatty acids and glycerol is called a **triglyceride.**[20]

The first step in utilizing fat for energy is the hydrolysis into the original components, glycerol plus three fatty acids. The fatty acids undergo beta oxidation, which involves a stepwise breakdown of the long-chain fatty acid molecule into acetyl CoA molecules. These molecules enter the Krebs cycle and proceed, just as the acetyl CoA from carbohydrates, through the ETS (Figure 3.1).[3,33]

Use of Protein for ATP Production

polypeptide

Proteins are very large, complex molecules that consist of from 20 to 100,000 amino acids, which are the basic building blocks of all proteins. The digestive enzymes of the stomach start the breakdown of protein. In the small intestine the breakdown is carried to the **polypeptide** (combination of several amino acids) level, and breakdown is completed to the amino acid level when the polypeptides pass through the wall of the small intestine into the blood. The amino acids are *deaminated* (the nitrogenous portion is removed) in the liver or muscle, becoming keto acids. These resulting keto acids are then converted into substances that can enter the Krebs cycle and proceed through the ETS (Figure 3.1).[20,27] The primary amino acids metabolized in skeletal muscle are the branched chain amino acids leucine, isoleucine, and valine, although others may also be utilized for ATP production.[6,12]

POWER AND CAPACITY OF ATP PRODUCTION SYSTEMS

power

In mechanical terms, **power** is defined as work divided by time. Thus, when we consider power, time is an important factor. The same is true when we consider an ATP production system. *Power* describes the amount of ATP a system can produce per unit of time. When we are sprinting or performing an explosive movement, we need to produce a lot of ATP very quickly. For example, when we explode out of the blocks at the beginning of a 100-meter dash or jump to spike a volleyball, we need ATP for muscle contraction immediately. Thus, to perform these activities we need to use a very powerful ATP production system such as the ATP–PC system. On the other hand, some activities, such as jogging or walking, do not require high-intensity, explosive movements. The ATP demands of these activities can be met by less powerful systems such as carbohydrate or fatty acid oxidation, since not as much ATP is utilized per unit of time. The power of an ATP production system is, in part, determined by the number of enzymatic reactions and the availability of the fuel source. The most powerful system is the ATP–PC system because it requires few enzymatic steps and the phosphagens are readily available. Fatty acid oxidation, however, is the least powerful system because of the large number of enzymatic steps and the need to liberate fatty acids from storage prior to ATP production.

The *capacity* of an ATP production system is the total amount of ATP that can be produced. In this regard, the capacity of a system would be analogous to mechanical work, while the power of a system would be analogous to mechanical power. When considering the capacity of an ATP production system, time is not

The working muscle

Blood flow patterns change during exercise so that oxygen is available to the working muscle. However, the amount of blood going to a muscle varies according to fiber type, with fast-twitch fibers getting as little as 60 mL • min^{-1} and slow-twitch fibers as much as 400 mL • min^{-1} of blood. This reflects the metabolic capabilities of the muscle and is influenced by training.[15]

a factor. For example, during an explosive activity such as blocking by a football lineman, there is a need for a large amount of ATP in a short period of time (supplied by the powerful ATP–PC system), but the activity lasts, at most, only a few seconds. Therefore, the total amount of ATP needed by the lineman is small, and the ATP production system does not have to have great capacity (also the ATP–PC system). On the other hand, recreational bicycling at a leisurely pace for a long period of time requires a lot of total ATP production from a system with great capacity (such as fatty acid oxidation) but not very much ATP per unit of time. The capacities of the ATP–PC system and of carbohydrate and fatty acid oxidation are determined by the amount of stored phosphagens, glycogen, and fats, respectively. Because there is a limited store of phosphagens available, the ATP–PC system has low capacity. Although there are substantial glycogen stores in skeletal muscle and the liver, the capacity for carbohydrate oxidation is limited by glycogen depletion, such as that occurring during a marathon race or distance cycling. Fatty acid metabolism has the greatest capacity because even the thinnest person has an essentially inexhaustible supply of energy in the form of energy-rich fats. A healthy individual cannot exercise long enough to exhaust the stores of fats.

It should now be clear that there is an inverse relationship between the power and the capacity of ATP production systems (Figure 3.6). That is, a powerful system has little capacity for total ATP production and vice versa. The differences in power and capacity between ATP production systems allow us to be very versatile in the activities we can perform. We can participate in short-term, explosive movements, as well as low-intensity, long-duration activities. Although the success with which we can perform anaerobic and aerobic activities differs substantially among individuals, the great variety of power and capacity characteristics of our ATP production systems allows for participation in very diverse physical activities.

METABOLIC ADAPTATIONS TO TRAINING

The principle of *metabolic specificity* indicates that metabolic adaptations to training are specific to the type of training we do. That is, endurance training (see Chapter 10) results in metabolic and cellular changes that are asso-

There is an inverse relationship between the power and capacity of ATP production systems.

figure 3.6

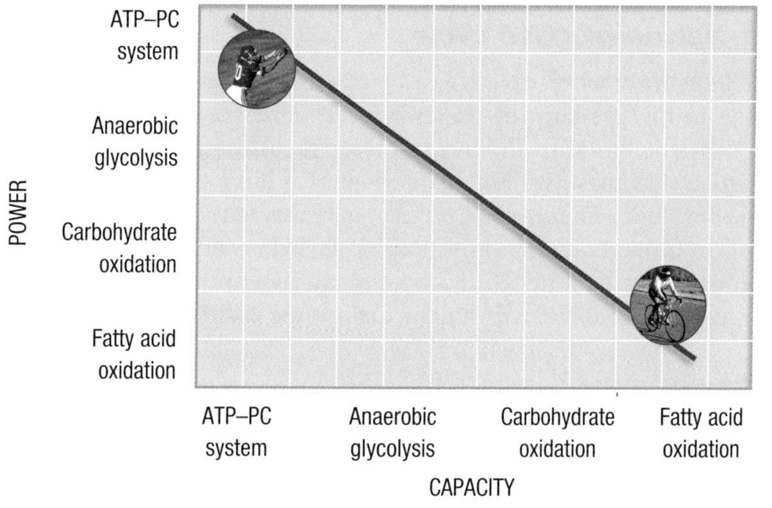

ciated with aerobic metabolism, sprint training (see Chapter 13) tends to improve our ability to use anaerobic metabolism, and resistance training (see Chapter 11) increases maximal force production, as well as our anaerobic capabilities.

Therefore, we shall discuss metabolic adaptations in three different areas: (1) endurance training (aerobic metabolism), (2) sprint training (anaerobic metabolism), and (3) resistance training. The metabolic adaptations described here are training-induced changes in humans.

Endurance Training (Aerobic Metabolism)

Endurance training results in adaptations in skeletal muscle and in the cardiovascular system. These adaptations help to explain the improvement shown with training in the capacity for prolonged exercise.

Myoglobin

myoglobin

Myoglobin is an iron-containing structure that transports oxygen from the sarcolemma to the mitochondria of the skeletal muscle fiber, where it is used for aerobic metabolism. Endurance training tends to increase myoglobin in skeletal muscle by as much as 90 percent,[18] which increases the amount of oxygen available as the final electron acceptor at the end of the ETS and, therefore, enhances aerobic ATP production.

Mitochondrial size, number, and enzymes

The mitochondrion is the location of aerobic ATP production within the cell. Thus, the more mitochondria within a muscle fiber and the larger the mitochondria are, the greater the ability to produce ATP aerobically. Endurance training increases both the number and size of mitochondria within skeletal muscle by up to 120 percent.[21] Within the mitochondria are the aerobic enzymes associated with the Krebs cycle, ETS, and beta oxidation of fatty acids. Krebs cycle enzymes, including citrate synthase,[31] succinate dehydrogenase,[11] and malate dehydrogenase,[29] increase up to approximately 95 percent following endurance training, while ETS enzymes increase by up to about 39 percent.[2] There are also major increases in the levels of enzymes involved in the activation, transport, and beta oxidation of long-chain fatty acids, up to 24 percent,[26] improving our ability to utilize fat as an energy source. As expected, endurance training–induced increases in mitochondrial size and number, as well as these enzymatic changes, greatly improve the capacity of trained muscles to metabolize a variety of substrates.

Glucose–alanine–glucose cycle

Figure 3.2 indicates that pyruvate can be converted in muscle tissue to the amino acid alanine in the presence of the enzyme alanine transaminase. The alanine is transported by the blood to the liver, where its carbon skeleton is reconverted to glucose, which becomes available as energy at a later time in the form of blood sugar (glucose). Since endurance exercise increases alanine transaminase by up to 80 percent[19] in trained muscles, it is possible that this adaptation could result in the conversion of a greater proportion of pyruvate to alanine and less to lactate, thus creating a more favorable environment for muscle contraction.

Glycolytic enzymes

Although endurance exercise results in changes to some glycolytic enzymes by up to 83 percent,[7] the glycolytic process is probably not limiting in endurance exercise. The limits to endurance performance are likely set at the level of the Krebs cycle and ETS.

Preferential use of free fatty acids as energy substrate

Endurance-trained individuals tend to use fatty acids preferentially over carbohydrates for ATP production.[8] This provides a **carbohydrate sparing effect**[17] and increases muscular endurance. Therefore, at any submaximal exercise intensity, a greater proportion of total ATP production comes from fatty acids than from carbohydrates in trained compared with untrained individuals.

carbohydrate sparing effect

Sprint Training (Anaerobic Metabolism)

The effects of sprint training on anaerobic metabolism are less well defined than the well-documented effects of endurance training on aerobic metabolism. In short-term, high-intensity exercise, the only significant energy pools available are (1) the breakdown of the phosphagens ATP and PC and (2) anaerobic glycolysis, the breakdown of glucose to pyruvate and then lactate as described in Figure 3.2.

Limiting factors

Sprinting performance is limited by the depletion of phosphagens (particularly phosphocreatine) and/or the buildup of metabolic byproducts (i.e., lactate, inorganic phosphate, and/or ammonia), depending on the duration of the maximal or near maximal intensity exercise. Activities that can be continued maximally for up to approximately 15 or 20 seconds are fueled largely from ATP and PC sources. Depletion of the small PC stores then forces a reduction in the intensity of exercise. Sprinting activities that last from approximately 20 or 30 seconds to two or three minutes rely predominantly on anaerobic glycolysis for ATP production, and fatigue occurs due to the buildup of metabolic byproducts (see Chapter 14) within the muscle fiber.

Metabolic effects of sprint training

There are fewer data available regarding the metabolic adaptations to sprint training than those regarding endurance training. Sprint training, however, has been shown to increase the glycolytic enzymes phosphorylase,[22,23] hexokinase (HK),[4] phosphofructokinase (PFK),[28,29] pyruvate kinase,[32] and lactate dehydrogenase (LDH)[29] by up to 106 percent, as well as enzymes of the ATP–PC system, including myosin ATPase,[32] creatine kinase (CK),[29] and adenylate kinase (AK),[22] by up to 44 percent. Increases in the cellular concentrations of these key anaerobic enzymes can improve sprinting performance by increasing the rate of ATP production. Furthermore, sprint training can also increase ATP and phosphocreatine stores within the muscle by up to 18 percent.[16,24] This increase would allow very high-intensity exercise to be maintained for a longer period of time, before depletion and the onset of fatigue.

WWW

Cycling Performance Tips, Basic Physiology, Cell Energy Metabolism
www.cptips.com

Resistance Training

Resistance training results in increases in the strength and size of the exercised muscle. In addition, metabolic adaptations contribute to increases in force production capabilities.

The metabolic effects of resistance training are specific to the type of program. That is, there are differences in metabolic adaptations between traditional high-resistance, low-repetition programs, designed primarily to increase strength, and moderate-resistance, high-repetition programs, designed for increased strength, muscle size, and muscle endurance.[9] Resistance training has been shown to increase myosin ATPase and CK by up to 45 percent,[1,5] as well as the glycolytic enzymes phosphorylase,[5,13] HK,[13] PFK,[5,13] and LDH[13] by up to 28 percent. Furthermore, resistance training tends to increase ATP and phosphocreatine stores within the muscle by up to 39 percent,[24] whereas immobilization tends to decrease intramuscular phosphocreatine levels.[24] The combination of training-induced increases in anaerobic enzyme concentrations and stored energy sources within the muscle fiber can improve ATP availability and lead to greater maximal muscle strength and an enhanced ability to perform repeated muscle contractions.

summary

The ATP for muscle contraction can be produced aerobically or anaerobically. The anaerobic ATP systems include the ATP–PC system and anaerobic glycolysis. The ATP–PC system utilizes the phosphagens, while anaerobic glycolysis involves the breakdown of glucose to lactate. Carbohydrate, fat, and protein can all be used to produce ATP aerobically.

Most exercise and sporting activities include a combination of both anaerobic and aerobic ATP production, although some activities, such as the marathon, are almost totally aerobic, while weight lifting, for example, is overwhelmingly anaerobic. A basic understanding of metabolism is important in designing effective training programs for athletes in various sports.

Endurance training improves aerobic capacity mainly through increased myoglobin concentrations, mitochondrial size and number, and aerobic enzyme activity. Sprint training and resistance training increase enzymes of the ATP-PC system and anaerobic glycolysis as well as stores of ATP and PC.

questions for review

1. Why is understanding metabolism important for exercise scientists, physical educators, and coaches? How might they use this knowledge in preparing lesson plans or training programs?
2. Define anaerobic metabolism and aerobic metabolism.
3. Describe the specific properties and functions of enzymes.
4. What factors affect the turnover rate of enzymes?
5. What are the three primary enzymatic reactions in the ATP–PC system?
6. What is anaerobic glycolysis?
7. What is the Krebs cycle?
8. Describe the electron transport system.
9. Discuss the differences between the power and capacity of the various ATP production systems.
10. Identify the metabolic adaptations to endurance, sprint, and resistance training.

student companion website

For further review of this book's chapters and for test preparation, visit the book's website, **www.hhpcommunities.com/exercisephysiology**, to take practice quizzes, review the vocabulary terms, use the study guide, and view the digital image bank.

references

1. Barnard, R. J., Edgerton, V. R., and Peter, J. B. Effect of exercise on skeletal muscle. Biochemical and histochemical properties. *J. Appl. Physiol.* 28: 762–766, 1970.
2. Benzi, G., Panceri, P., de Bernardi, M., Villa, R., Arcelli, E., D'Angelo, L., Arrigoni, E., and Berte, F. Mitochondrial enzymatic adaptation of skeletal muscle to endurance training. *J. Appl. Physiol.* 38: 565–569, 1975.
3. Bulow, J. Lipid mobilization and utilization. In *Principles of Exercise Biochemistry,* 2nd revised edition, ed. J. R. Poortmans. Basel: Karger, 1993, pp. 158–185.
4. Coggan, A. R., Spina, R. J., Kohrt, W. M., and Holloszy, J. O. Effect of prolonged exercise on muscle citrate concentration before and after endurance training in men. *Am. J. Physiol-Endocrinol. Metab.* 264: 215–220, 1993.
5. Costill, D. L., Coyle, E. F., Fink, W. F., Lesmes, G. R., and Witzmann, F. A. Adaptation in skeletal muscle following strength training. *J. Appl. Physiol.* 46: 96–99, 1979.
6. Cramer, J. T. Bioenergetics of exercise and training. In *Essentials of Strength and Conditioning,* 3rd edition, eds. T. R. Baechle and R. W. Earle. Champaign, IL: Human Kinetics, 2008, pp. 21–40.
7. Eriksson, B. O., Gollnick, P. D., and Saltin, B. Muscle metabolism and enzyme activities after training in boys 11–13 years old. *Acta Physiol. Scand.* 87: 485–497, 1973.
8. Evans, W. J., Bennett, A. S., Costill, D. L., and Fink, W. J. Leg muscle metabolism in trained and untrained men. *Res. Q.* 5: 350–359, 1979.
9. Fleck, S. J., and Kraemer, W. J. *Designing Resistance Training Programs,* 2nd edition. Champaign, IL: Human Kinetics, 1997.
10. Fox, S. I. *Human Physiology,* 3rd edition. Dubuque, IA: Wm. C. Brown, 1990, pp. 89–136.
11. Gollnick, P. D., Armstrong, R. B., Saltin, B., Saubert, C. W., Sembrowich, W. L., and Shepherd, R. E. Effect of training on enzyme activity and fiber composition of human skeletal muscle. *J. Appl. Physiol.* 34: 107–111, 1973.
12. Graham, T. E., Rush, J. W. E., and MacLean, D. A. Skeletal muscle amino acid metabolism and ammonia production during exercise. In *Exercise Metabolism,* ed. M. Hargreaves. Champaign, IL: Human Kinetics, 1995, pp. 131–175.
13. Green, H., Dahly, A., Shoemaker, K., Goreham, C., Bombardier, E., and Ball, B. Serial effects of high-resistance and prolonged endurance training on Na+–K+ pump concentration and enzymatic activities in human vastus lateralis. *Acta Physiol. Scand.* 165: 177–184, 1999.
14. Greenhaff, P. L, Hultman, E., and Harris, R. C. Carbohydrate metabolism. In *Principles of Exercise Biochemistry,* 2nd revised edition, ed. J. R. Poortmans. Basel: Karger, 1993, pp. 89–136.
15. Hamilton, M. T., and Booth, F. W. Skeletal muscle adaptation to exercise: a century of progress. *J. Appl. Physiol.* 88: 327–331, 2000.
16. Hargreaves, M. Skeletal muscle carbohydrate metabolism during exercise. In *Exercise Metabolism,* ed. M. Hargreaves. Champaign, IL: Human Kinetics, 1995, pp. 41–72.
17. Havel, R. J. Influence of intensity and duration of exercise on supply and use of fuels. In *Muscle Metabolism During Exercise,* eds. B. Pernow and B. Saltin. New York: Plenum Press, 1971, pp. 315–325.
18. Holloszy, J. O. Adaptation of skeletal muscle to endurance exercise. *Med. Sci. Sports.* 7: 155–164, 1975.
19. Hood, D. A., and Terjung, R. L. Effect of alpha-ketoacid dehydrogenase phosphorylation on branched-chain amino acid metabolism in muscle. *Am. J. Physiol.* 261: 628–634, 1991.
20. Houston, M. E. *Biochemistry Primer for Exercise Science.* Champaign, IL: Human Kinetics, 1995.
21. Kiessling, K. H., Piehl, K., and Lundquist, C. G. Effect of physical training on ultrastructural features in human skeletal muscle: muscle metabolism during exercise. *Adv. Exp. Med. Biol.* 11: 97–101, 1971.
22. Linossier, M. T., Dormois, D., Perier, C., Frey, J., Geyssant, A., and Denis, C. Enzyme adaptations of human skeletal muscle during bicycle short-sprint training and detraining. *Acta Physiol. Scand.* 161: 439–445, 1997.
23. MacDougall, J. D., Hicks, A. L., MacDonald, J. R., McKelvie, R. S., Green, H. J., and Smith, K. M. Muscle performance and enzymatic adaptations to sprint interval training. *J. Appl. Physiol.* 84: 2138–2142, 1998.
24. MacDougall, J. D., Ward, G. R., Sale, D. G., and Sutton, J. R. Biochemical adaptation to human skeletal muscle to heavy resistance training and immobilization. *J. Appl. Physiol.* 43: 700–703, 1977.
25. Mougios, V. *Exercise Biochemistry.* Champaign, IL: Human Kinetics, 2006, pp. 159–160.
26. Phillips, S. M., Green, H. J., Tarnopolsky, M. A., Heigenhauser, G. J., and Grant, S. M. Progressive effect of endurance training on metabolic adaptations in working skeletal muscle. *Am. J. Physiol.* 270: 265–272, 1996.
27. Poortman, J. R. Protein metabolism. In *Principles of Exercise Biochemistry,* 2nd revised edition, ed. J. R. Poortmans. Basel: Karger, 1993, pp. 186–229.
28. Roberts, A. D., Billeter, R., and Howald, H. Anaerobic muscle enzyme changes after interval training. *Int. J. Sports Med.* 3: 18–21, 1982.
29. Rodas, G., Ventura, J. L., Cadefau, J. A., Cusso, R., and Parra, J. A short training programme for the rapid improvement of both aerobic and anaerobic metabolism. *Eur. J. Appl. Physiol.* 82: 480–486, 2000.
30. Strauss, R. H. *Sports Medicine.* Philadelphia: W. B. Saunders, 1984, p. 387.
31. Taylor, A. W., and Bachman, L. The effects of endurance training on muscle fibre types and enzyme activities. *Can. J. Appl. Physiol.* 24: 41–53, 1999.
32. Thorstensson, A., Sjodin, B., and Karlsson, J. Enzyme activities and muscle strength after sprint training in man. *Acta Physiol. Scand.* 94: 313–318, 1975.
33. Tucotte, L. P., Richter, E. A., and Kiens, B. Lipid metabolism during exercise. In *Exercise Metabolism,* ed. M. Hargreaves. Champaign, IL: Human Kinetics, 1995, pp. 99–130.

CHAPTER 3

lab Non-Exercise-Based Estimation of Maximal Oxygen Consumption Rate ($\dot{V}O_2$ max)

BACKGROUND

The determination of maximal oxygen consumption rate ($\dot{V}O_2$ max) provides information related to an individual's level of cardiorespiratory fitness and is a valuable predictor of endurance exercise and sports performance. In Chapter 19 Lab, the Astrand–Rhyming submaximal cycle ergometer test utilizes the relationship between heart rate and power output to estimate $\dot{V}O_2$ max. In the present laboratory, regression equations for males and females are used to estimate $\dot{V}O_2$ max without the need for subjects to exercise. The equations in this laboratory utilize demographic variables such as age, height, and body weight, as well as descriptive variables related to exercise habits, including the duration of exercise, intensity of exercise, and years of training. Typically, the errors associated with these equations (±10 to 15%) are approximately the same as those for exercise-based estimates of $\dot{V}O_2$ max.[1,2,3] The accuracy of the equations, however, is influenced by the level of fitness of the subject, and in this laboratory equations are therefore provided that can be used for both untrained and aerobically trained individuals.

TERMS & ABBREVIATIONS

- R = multiple correlation coefficient; a numerical measure of how well a dependent variable can be predicted from a combination of independent variables (a number between –1 and 1)
- regression equations = statistical methods that are developed and used to relate two or more variables
- SEE = standard error of estimate; a measure of the accuracy of the predictions made using a regression equation
- $\dot{V}O_2$ max = maximal oxygen consumption rate

PROCEDURES

Record the following information on Worksheet 3.1.

1. Your height in cm, body weight in kg, and age in years.
2. Refer to the Borg Rating of Perceived Exertion Scale (refer to Figure 10.1 on p. 205) to estimate the typical intensity of training, answering the following statement:[2,3] "Indicate, in general, the intensity at which you perform your exercise regimen."
3. Indicate the duration of training, answering the following question:[2,3] "How many hours per week do you exercise?"
4. Record the years of training, answering the following question:[2,3] "How long have you consistently, no more than one month without exercise, been exercising?"
5. Determine the natural log of years of training. That is, enter the client's years of training and then hit "LN," or natural log function, on a handheld calculator. You may also search online for "What is the natural log of ______?" In the blank insert the years of training.

6. Determine $\dot{V}O_2$ max in L • min^{-1} or mL • min^{-1}.
7. Calculate $\dot{V}O_2$ max in mL • kg^{-1} • min^{-1} using the relevant equation below.
8. Identify fitness category from Table L3.1.

Equations

Untrained males[1]

$\dot{V}O_2$ max (L • min^{-1}) = (0.046 × height in cm) – (0.021 × age in years) – 4.31
R (multiple correlation coefficient) = 0.87
SEE = 0.458 L • min^{-1}

Untrained females[1]

$\dot{V}O_2$ max (L • min^{-1}) = (0.046 × height in cm) – (0.021 × age in years) – 4.93
R = 0.87
SEE = 0.458 L • min^{-1}

**Aerobically trained males*[3]

$\dot{V}O_2$ max (mL • min^{-1}) = (27.387 × body weight in kg) + (26.634 × height in cm) – (27.572 × age in years) + (26.161 × duration of training in hours per week) + (114.904 × intensity of training using the Borg Scale) + (506.752 × natural log of years of training) – 4609.791
R = 0.82
SEE = 378 mL • min^{-1}

**Aerobically trained females*[2]

$\dot{V}O_2$ max (mL • min^{-1}) = (18.528 × body weight in kg) + (11.993 × height in cm) – (17.197 × age in years) + (23.522 × duration of training in hours per week) + (62.118 × intensity of training using the Borg Scale) + (278.262 × natural log of years of training) – 1375.878
R = 0.83
SEE = 247 mL • min^{-1}

*Aerobically trained is defined as having participated in continuous aerobic exercise three or more sessions per week for a minimum of one hour per session, for at least the past 18 months.[2,3]

SAMPLE CALCULATIONS

AEROBICALLY TRAINED MALE[3]

Height: 180 cm
Body weight: 80 kg
Age: 25 years
Intensity of training: 15
Duration of training: 6 h • wk^{-1}
Years of training: 8 yr: natural log of 8 = 2.08

Equation: 27.387 × 80 = 2190.96
plus 26.634 × 180 = 6985.08
minus 27.572 × 25 = 6295.78
plus 26.161 × 6 = 6452.75
plus 114.904 × 15 = 8176.31

plus 506.752 × 2.08 = 9230.35

minus 4609.791 = $\dot{V}O_2$ max (mL • min^{-1}) = 4620.56 mL • min^{-1}

$\dot{V}O_2$ max (mL • kg^{-1} • min^{-1}) = 4620.56 / 80 = 57.76 mL • kg^{-1} • min^{-1}

Fitness category from Table L3.1 = Superior

UNTRAINED FEMALE[1]

Height: 166 cm

Body weight: 59 kg

Age: 22 years

Equation: 0.046 × 166 = 7.64

minus 0.021 × 22 = 7.18

minus 4.93 = $\dot{V}O_2$ max (L • min^{-1}) = 2.25 L • min^{-1}

$\dot{V}O_2$ max (mL • min^{-1}) = 2.25 × 1000 = 2250 mL • min^{-1}

$\dot{V}O_2$ max (mL • kg^{-1} • min^{-1}) = 2250 / 59 = 38.14 mL • kg^{-1} • min^{-1}

Fitness category from Table L3.1 = Excellent

table L3.1 Men's and women's aerobic fitness classification (predicted).

MEN		AGE (YEARS)					
CATEGORY	MEASURE	13–19	20–29	30–39	40–49	50–59	60+
I. Very Poor	$\dot{V}O_2$ max (mL • kg^{-1} • min^{-1})	<35.0	<33.0	<31.5	<30.2	<26.1	<20.5
II. Poor	$\dot{V}O_2$ max (mL • kg^{-1} • min^{-1})	35.0–38.3	33.0–36.4	31.5–35.4	30.2–33.5	26.1–30.9	20.5–26.0
III. Fair	$\dot{V}O_2$ max (mL • kg^{-1} • min^{-1})	38.4–45.1	36.5–42.4	35.5–40.9	33.6–38.9	31.0–35.7	26.1–32.2
IV. Good	$\dot{V}O_2$ max (mL • kg^{-1} • min^{-1})	45.2–50.9	42.5–46.4	41.0–44.9	39.0–43.7	35.8–40.9	32.2–36.4
V. Excellent	$\dot{V}O_2$ max (mL • kg^{-1} • min^{-1})	51.0–55.9	46.5–52.4	45.0–49.4	43.8–48.0	41.0–45.3	36.5–44.2
VI. Superior	$\dot{V}O_2$ max (mL • kg^{-1} • min^{-1})	>56.0	>52.5	>49.5	>48.1	>45.4	>44.3

WOMEN		AGE (YEARS)					
CATEGORY	MEASURE	13–19	20–29	30–39	40–49	50–59	60+
I. Very Poor	$\dot{V}O_2$ max (mL • kg^{-1} • min^{-1})	<25.0	<23.6	<22.8	<21.0	<20.2	<17.5
II. Poor	$\dot{V}O_2$ max (mL • kg^{-1} • min^{-1})	25.0–30.9	23.6–28.9	22.8–26.9	21.0–24.4	20.2–22.7	17.5–20.1
III. Fair	$\dot{V}O_2$ max (mL • kg^{-1} • min^{-1})	31.0–34.9	29.0–32.9	27.0–31.4	24.5–28.9	22.8–26.9	20.2–24.4
IV. Good	$\dot{V}O_2$ max (mL • kg^{-1} • min^{-1})	35.0–38.9	33.0–36.9	31.50–35.6	29.0–32.8	27.0–31.4	24.5–30.2
V. Excellent	$\dot{V}O_2$ max (mL • kg^{-1} • min^{-1})	39.0–41.9	37.0–40.9	35.7–40.0	32.9–36.9	31.5–35.7	30.3–31.4
VI. Superior	$\dot{V}O_2$ max (mL • kg^{-1} • min^{-1})	>42.0	>41.0	>40.1	>37.0	>35.8	>31.5

Source: Cooper, Kenneth H. *The Aerobics Way.* Toronto: Bantam Books, 1977, pp. 280–281. Printed with permission of Kenneth H. Cooper, MD, MPH, www.cooperaerobics.com.

NON-EXERCISE-BASED ESTIMATION OF $\dot{V}O_2$ MAX

worksheet 3.1

NAME ______________________ DATE ______________

height = ____ cm
intensity of training (from Borg Scale) = ____
years of training = ____ yr
body weight = ____ kg
duration of training = ____ $hr \cdot wk^{-1}$
age = ____ yr
natural log of years of training = ____

Equations

Untrained male

0.046 × height = __________
minus 0.021 × age = __________
minus 4.31 = $\dot{V}O_2$ max ($L \cdot min^{-1}$) = __________ $L \cdot min^{-1}$

$\dot{V}O_2$ max ($mL \cdot min^{-1}$) = __________ × 1000 = __________ $mL \cdot min^{-1}$
$\dot{V}O_2$ max ($mL \cdot kg^{-1} \cdot min^{-1}$) = __________ / body weight = __________ $mL \cdot kg^{-1} \cdot min^{-1}$
Fitness category (Table L3.1, page 60) = __________

Untrained female

0.046 × height = __________
minus 0.021 × age = __________
minus 4.93 = $\dot{V}O_2$ max ($L \cdot min^{-1}$) = __________ $L \cdot min^{-1}$

$\dot{V}O_2$ max ($mL \cdot min^{-1}$) = __________ × 1000 = __________ $mL \cdot min^{-1}$
$\dot{V}O_2$ max ($mL \cdot kg^{-1} \cdot min^{-1}$) = __________ / body weight = __________ $mL \cdot kg^{-1} \cdot min^{-1}$
Fitness category (Table L3.1) = __________

Aerobically trained male

27.387 × body weight = __________
plus 26.634 × height = __________
minus 27.572 × age = __________
plus 26.161 × duration of training = __________
plus 114.904 × intensity of training = __________
plus 506.752 × natural log of years of training = __________
minus 4609.791 = $\dot{V}O_2$ max ($mL \cdot min^{-1}$) = __________ $mL \cdot min^{-1}$

$\dot{V}O_2$ max ($mL \cdot kg^{-1} \cdot min^{-1}$) = __________ / body weight = __________ $mL \cdot kg^{-1} \cdot min^{-1}$
Fitness category (Table L3.1) = __________

Aerobically trained female

18.528 × body weight = __________
plus 11.993 × height = __________
minus 17.197 × age = __________
plus 23.522 × duration of training = __________
plus 62.118 × intensity of training = __________
plus 278.262 × natural log of years of training = __________
minus 1375.878 = $\dot{V}O_2$ max ($mL \cdot min^{-1}$) = __________ $mL \cdot min^{-1}$

$\dot{V}O_2$ max ($mL \cdot kg^{-1} \cdot min^{-1}$) = __________ / body weight = __________ $mL \cdot kg^{-1} \cdot min^{-1}$
Fitness category (Table L3.1) = __________

worksheet 3.2 EXTENSION ACTIVITIES

NAME ______________________________ DATE ______________

1. Given the following data, (a) calculate $\dot{V}O_2$max in L • min^{-1}, mL • min^{-1}, and mL • kg^{-1} • min^{-1}, and (b) determine the individual's fitness category from Table L3.1 (page 60).

   untrained male

   height = 175 cm

   body weight = 78 kg

   age = 30 yr

   $\dot{V}O_2$max (L • min^{-1}) = __________ L • min^{-1}

   $\dot{V}O_2$max (mL • min^{-1}) = __________ mL • min^{-1}

   $\dot{V}O_2$max (mL • kg^{-1} • min^{-1}) = __________ mL • kg^{-1} • min^{-1}

   Fitness category (Table L3.1) = __________

2. Given the following data, (a) calculate $\dot{V}O_2$max in mL • min^{-1} and mL • kg^{-1} • min^{-1}, and (b) determine the individual's fitness category from Table L3.1.

   aerobically trained female

   height = 169 cm

   body weight = 65 kg

   age = 27 yr

   intensity of training = 14

   duration of training = 9 h • wk^{-1}

   years of training = 6 yr

   $\dot{V}O_2$max (mL • min^{-1}) = __________ mL • min^{-1}

   $\dot{V}O_2$max (mL • kg^{-1} • min^{-1}) = __________ mL • kg^{-1} • min^{-1}

   Fitness category (Table L3.1) = __________

EXTENSION QUESTIONS

1. What are some common mistakes that may occur in administering this lab?
2. Identify possible sources of error in this lab.
3. Assess the practicality of using this lab in the field.
4. Research the reliability and/or validity of this lab using online resources, journal articles, and other credible sources.

REFERENCES

1. Jones, N. L., Makrides, L., Hitchcock, C., Chypchar, T., and McCartney, N. Normal standards for an incremental progressive cycle ergometer test. *Am. Rev. Respir. Dis.* 131: 700–708, 1985.
2. Malek, M. H., Housh, T. J., Berger, D. E., Coburn, J. W., and Beck, T. W. A new non-exercise based $\dot{V}O_2$max equation for aerobically trained females. *Med. Sci. Sports Exerc.* 36: 1804–1810, 2004.
3. Malek, M. H., Housh, T. J., Berger, D. E., Coburn, J. W., and Beck, T. W. A new non-exercise based $\dot{V}O_2$max prediction equation for aerobically trained men. *J. Strength Cond. Res.* 19: 559–565, 2005.

4 The Nervous System

As a result of reading this chapter you will:

Know how the nervous system is organized.

Know how motor neurons innervate muscle fibers.

Understand the role of the nervous system in simple reflexes.

Understand proprioception and kinesthesis.

Understand the involvement of higher brain centers during voluntary movement.

Understand the role of the nervous system in maintaining posture and balance.

Know the effects of exercise on several neurological disorders.

key concepts

afferent neuron
alpha motor neuron
autonomic nervous system
axon
basal ganglia
Betz cells
central nervous system
crossed extensor reflex
dendrite
efferent neuron
electromyography
electronic integrators
endolymph
extrafusal (EF) muscle fibers
extrapyramidal system
flexion reflex
frequency domain
gamma motor neuron
Golgi tendon organs
integration
internuncial neuron
intrafusal (IF) muscle fibers
kinesthesis
lower motor neuron
motor cortex
motor neuron
muscle action potential (MAP)
muscle spindle
myotatic reflex
neuron
parasympathetic branch
peripheral nervous system
planimetry
power density spectrum (PDS)
premotor cortex
proprioception
pyramidal system
pyramidal tracts
qualitative electromyography
quantitative electromyography
reciprocal inhibition
reflex
righting reflex
sensory neuron
somatic nervous system
spinal reflex
sympathetic branch
time domain
upper motor neuron
vestibular receptor

ORGANIZATION OF THE NERVOUS SYSTEM AND ITS CONTROL OF BODY MOVEMENT

central nervous system
peripheral nervous system
autonomic nervous system
sympathetic branch
parasympathetic branch
somatic nervous system

The nervous system can be divided in two ways. First, it can be divided anatomically into central and peripheral components. The **central nervous system** consists of the brain and spinal cord, whereas the **peripheral nervous system** consists of the nerve fibers that lie outside the brain and spinal cord (Figure 4.1). Second, it can be divided functionally into autonomic and somatic systems, both of which have central as well as peripheral components (Figure 4.2). The **autonomic nervous system** innervates organs and tissues that are not usually under voluntary control, such as cardiac muscle, smooth muscle, and glands. The autonomic nervous system has two divisions: (1) the sympathetic division, which originates in the thoracic and lumbar regions of the spinal cord, and (2) the parasympathetic division, which originates in the brain and in the sacral region of the spinal cord. Generally, the **sympathetic branch** is activated in emergency or stressful situations. Because of this, it is sometimes referred to as the "fight or flight" branch of the autonomic nervous system. The **parasympathetic branch,** on the other hand, is activated during times of inactivity and is responsible for encouraging all of those processes leading to the digestion of nutrients. Therefore, it is sometimes referred to as the "rest and digest" branch of the autonomic nervous system.

The **somatic nervous system** consists of the central and peripheral components of the nervous system that deal with the sensory impulses and motor responses of skeletal muscle. Therefore, the somatic system is involved with voluntary control of muscular activity. This chapter will concentrate on the somatic system and its relation to movement. It will begin by describing the cells of the nervous system, then move on to discuss some simple reflexes. After that, more complicated integration of neural impulses in the production of complex motor activity will be described.

www

The Peripheral Nervous System, Neuromuscular Junction and Muscle
http://users.rcn.com/jkimball.ma.ultranet/BiologyPages/P/PNS.html

THE CELLS OF THE NERVOUS SYSTEM

neuron
dendrites
axon

A single nerve cell is called a **neuron** and is the basic structural unit of the nervous system. Neurons differ in size and shape more than cells from any other tissue in the body. However, all neurons have certain features in common: they usually have dendrites, a cell body, and an axon (see Figure 4.3). The **dendrites** receive impulses and conduct them to the cell body, and the **axon** conducts the impulses away from the cell body. Although neurons are microscopic in width, one cell may extend in length from the cerebral cortex almost to the caudal (tail) end of the spinal column or from the spinal cord to a muscle in the foot. Although the neurons are microscopic when alone, when they join other neurons to make a nerve they are easy to see with the naked eye. There are billions of neurons in the nervous system, connected by synapses (junctions between cells) to form pathways for the conduction of nervous impulses. The neurons that conduct sensory impulses from the periphery to the central nervous system are called **sensory** or **afferent neurons,** and the neurons that conduct impulses from the central nervous system to the muscles and other effectors are called **motor** or **efferent neurons.**

A motor unit is a motor neuron and all of the muscle fibers it innervates. The cell body of a motor neuron that innervates skeletal muscle lies in the gray matter in the ventral horn of the spinal cord, and its axon joins other axons to form a spinal nerve. After entering a muscle through the epimysium, one axon branches into many twigs, each of which innervates one muscle fiber. Therefore, a single motor neuron usually innervates many muscle fibers, but each muscle fiber is innervated by only one motor neuron (see Chapter 2).

figure 4.1

Diagram of the peripheral nerves, depicting the extensive nature of the nervous system.

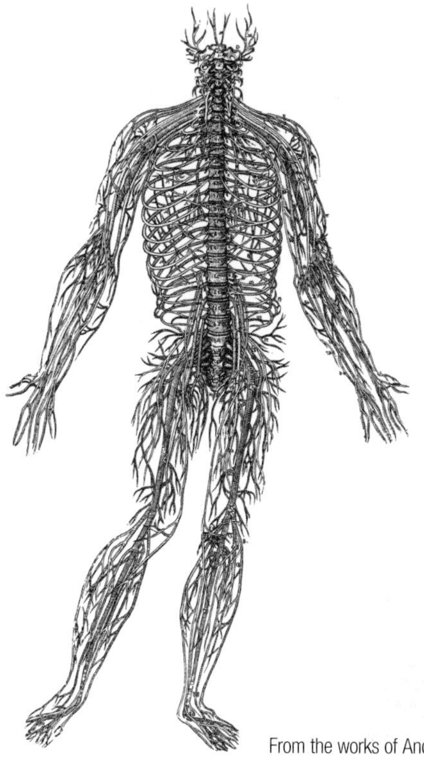

From the works of Andreas Vesalius.

REFLEXES

Simple Reflexes and Involuntary Movement

A **reflex** is an involuntary motor response to a sensory stimulus. Some reflexes are very complex and can involve the higher centers of the brain, whereas other reflexes are very simple. The simplest reflex is the **spinal reflex,** which involves a minimum of two neurons. The sensory (afferent) neuron receives a stimulus and carries an

- afferent neuron
- efferent neuron
- reflex
- spinal reflex

Functional divisions of the nervous system. **figure 4.2**

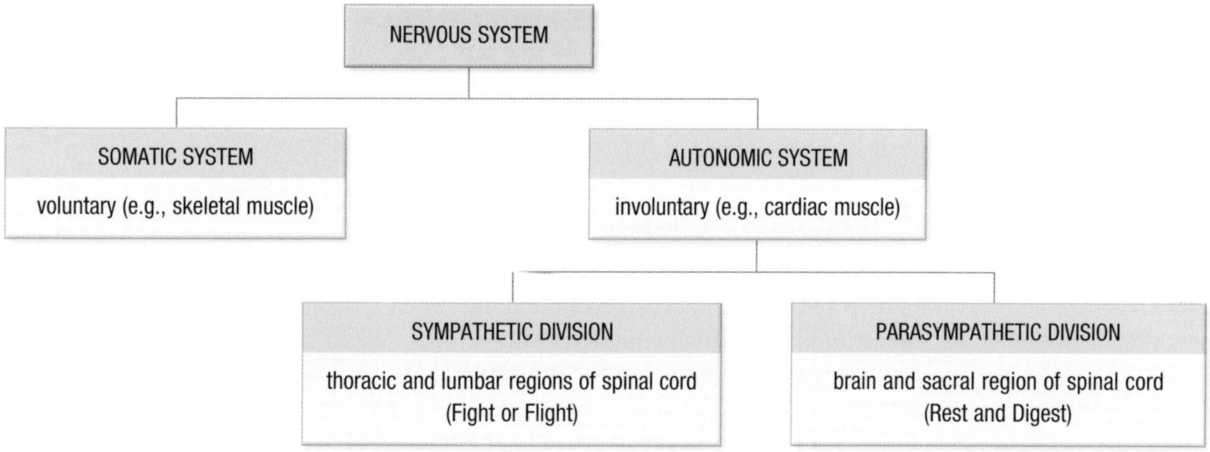

figure 4.3

The neuron and its components.

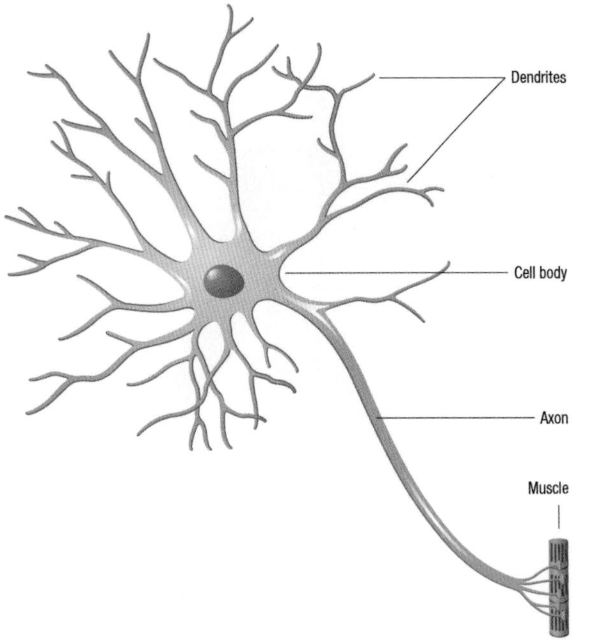

figure 4.4

Diagram of a two-neuron reflex, from a spindle in a muscle back to the muscle fibers of the same muscle.

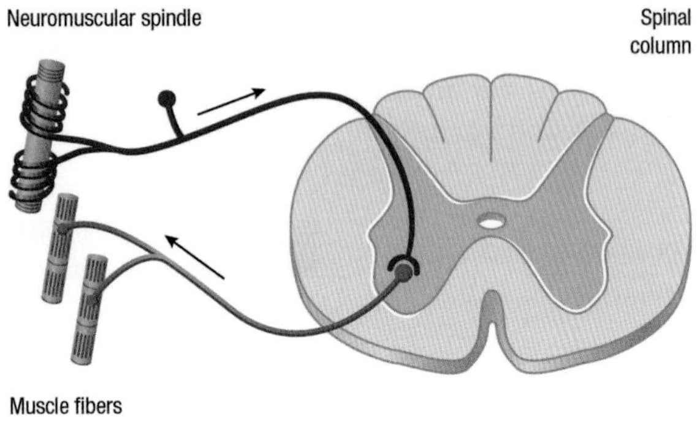

Adapted from E. Gardner, *Fundamentals of Neurology,* 2d ed. © 1958.

impulse to the spinal cord, where the impulse is transmitted across a synapse to a motor (efferent) neuron, which carries the impulse to a muscle or gland. The **myotatic** (or stretch) **reflex** is an example of a simple, two-neuron reflex. The myotatic reflex occurs when a physician taps on the patellar ligament with a rubber mallet, triggering a knee-jerk response (see Figure 4.4). The myotatic reflex will be discussed further in the section on kinesthesis.

Even the most simple reflexes are not usually this simple. Most involve a third neuron, called an **internuncial neuron,** which lies in the gray matter of the spinal cord, between the sensory and motor neurons. An example of a simple reflex, called the **flexion reflex,** that involves an internuncial neuron is when you "automatically" move your hand away from a hot surface. Sensory nerve endings in your hand detect the heat and generate an impulse that travels along the sensory neuron to the spinal cord. There, it synapses with an internuncial neuron, which acts as an intermediary between the sensory neuron and the motor neuron to the forearm flexor muscle (the effector, in this case). When the impulse arrives at the forearm flexor, your forearm flexes and pulls your hand from the hot surface (Figure 4.5).

Reciprocal Inhibition

The preceding discussion regarding simple reflexes is an oversimplification of what actually occurs. For example, the flexion reflex also involves another motor neuron that inhibits the antagonistic extensor muscles, preventing them from contracting. This is called **reciprocal inhibition.**

Crossed Extensor Reflex

When you step on a sharp object, the flexion reflex results not only in withdrawing the foot and the concomitant reciprocal inhibition of the extensor muscles of the same leg but also in causing the extension of the contralateral (opposite) leg to support the body during the flexion reflex. This is called the **crossed extensor reflex.**

Conditioned Reflexes

Although reflexes occur quickly and seemingly automatically, it is incorrect to assume that all reflexes are developed prenatally. In fact, most are learned responses to various stimuli and involve higher brain centers. When we are initially presented with a novel task, for example, our movements are very deliberate. As time goes on, we begin to perform the task "automatically." The same is true when we learn a new sport or activity, such as tennis. Playing tennis is a very complex set of tasks. Many of the movements are reflexive, but at first they require quite a bit of conscious modi-

myotatic reflex
internuncial neuron
flexion reflex
reciprocal inhibition
crossed extensor reflex

fication. As practice proceeds and the learner becomes more adept at modifying these reflexes to meet the demands of the changing environment, the deliberate movements of the beginner become the smooth, subconscious moves of the experienced athlete.

figure 4.5

Diagram illustrating how impulses from a cutaneous receptor reach an effector (skeletal muscle) by a three-neuron arc at the level of entrance.

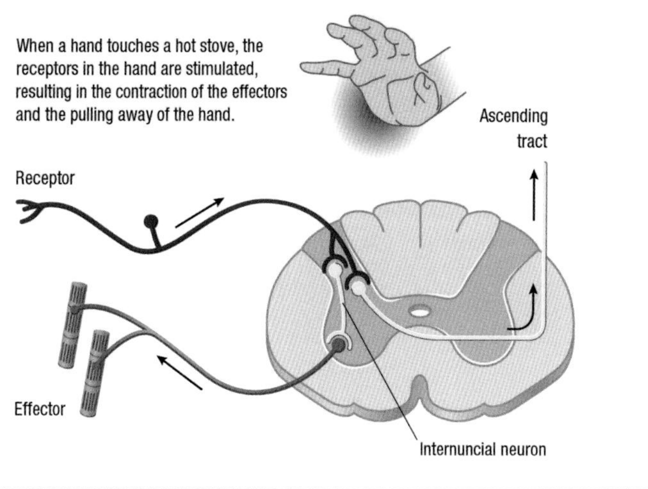

Adapted from E. Gardner, *Fundamentals of Neurology,* 2d ed. © 1958.

PROPRIOCEPTION AND KINESTHESIS

The nervous components involved in proprioception and kinesthesis are of even greater interest. Because of receptors located throughout the body, it is easy to tell your body position and what your limbs or body segments are doing at any given time without looking. For the optimal coordination of motor patterns to take place in the brain and spinal cord, a constant supply of sensory information must be available to feed back the results of movement as it progresses.[2] This feedback of sensory information about movement and body position is termed **proprioception.** The receptors for proprioception are of two types: vestibular and kinesthetic.

The **vestibular receptors** are found in the nonauditory labyrinths of the inner ear. Each of these two labyrinths, one on each side in the temporal bone of the skull, consists of a small chamber, the *vestibule,* which communicates with three small canals (superior, lateral, and posterior) known as the *semicircular canals* (see Figure 4.6). Within the semicircular canals is a fluid called **endolymph.**

- proprioception
- vestibular receptors
- endolymph

Structural relations of innervation of the human labyrinth. figure 4.6

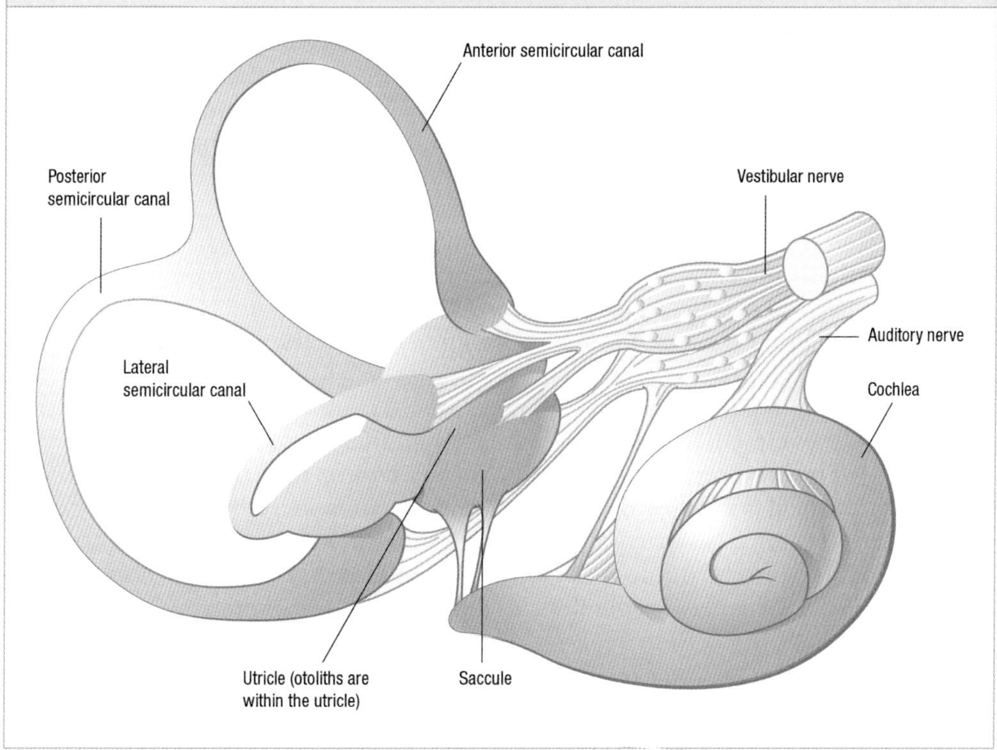

RESEARCH

Exercise and managing hypertension

Exercise is often recommended as an important part of the management of hypertension in adults. Ghadieh and Saab* performed an extensive review of the literature and found many studies indicating that exercise exerts direct effects on blood pressure by way of two primary mechanisms: the sympathetic nervous system and the hypothalamic–pituitary–adrenal axis. The effects of these mechanisms are classified as acute, post-exercise, and chronic. Acute effects are those that occur for only a short time and post-exercise effects are those that occur immediately following an exercise bout. Chronic effects are those that occur for a long period of time, and these appear to be most prevalent following more long-term exercise. Physical activity has been shown to have effects on blood pressure in all three classifications. The current treatment guidelines for the management of mild to moderate hypertension include physical activity. Moderate-intensity aerobic exercise utilizes the sympathetic nervous system to lower both systolic and diastolic blood pressure. Therefore, this mode of exercise induces sympathetic nervous system adaptations, which allow for a more healthy blood pressure.

*Ghadieh, A. S., and Saab, B. Evidence for exercise training in the management of hypertension in adults. *Can. Fam. Physician* 61 (3): 233–239, 2015.

www

The Nervous System
www2.estrellamountain.edu/faculty/farabee/biobk/biobooknerv.html

The Autonomic Nervous System
www.ndrf.org/ans.html

Neurons
http://users.rcn.com/jkimball.ma.ultranet/BiologyPages/N/Neurons.html

The inertia of the endolymph, which results in its remaining stationary at the first part of a movement of the body, and also its continued movement when the body has returned to a resting position, disturbs a sensory receptor organ, the *crista.* This disturbance is transmitted to the brain by way of the vestibular branch of the eighth cranial nerve. Thus the sensory information from the cristae of the semicircular canals provides data regarding movement, more specifically, rotational acceleration or deceleration as in twisting or tumbling. Movement in itself is not recognized. For example, moving at almost the speed of sound in an airliner produces no sensation unless a change of direction or velocity occurs.

Along with the semicircular canals, the *saccule* and *utricle* of the vestibule complete the vestibular system. Apparently, the saccule has little if any function in equilibrium or position sense; it seems to be involved only in sensory perception of vibration. The utricle, however, is the sense organ that provides the data for positional sense. The *otolith organ* in the utricle responds to linear acceleration and to tilting, and thus seems to be the source of data that inform us of our posture in space.

Although no sensation of movement is produced in the body of a passenger in an airliner (in smooth air), the orientation of the body in space, as in standing upright or lying down, is clearly recognized, even with the eyes closed. This recognition of spatial orientation is the result of the interpretation of sensory information received from the otolith organ in the utricle.

kinesthesis

Kinesthesis (or *kinesthesia*) is defined as the sense of movement and position of the body parts in space. The receptors involved are of several types and include muscle spindles, Golgi tendon organs, Pacinian corpuscles, Ruffini receptors, and free nerve endings.

Kinesthetic awareness plays an important role in such simple tasks as standing with one's eyes closed, as well as in more complicated sports activities. The perceptions sensed by the receptors are relayed to higher brain centers, although the process of motor learning may allow these perceptions to go unnoticed by the consciousness. All of the receptor types listed above are important in kinesthesis; however, two of these serve such essential roles in muscle function that they need to be examined in detail. These are the muscle spindles and the Golgi tendon organs.

Muscle Spindles and Kinesthesis

muscle spindles

Muscle spindles are widely distributed throughout the muscle tissue, but distribution varies from muscle to muscle. In general, the muscles used for complex movements (such as finger muscles) are abundantly supplied with up to 30 spindles per gram of muscle, whereas muscles such as the latissimus dorsi, which are involved in only very gross movements, may have only one or two per gram. In some of the cranial muscles no spindles have been found.[1,6]

Each spindle is large enough to be seen with the naked eye and is *fusiform,* which means it is wider in the middle and tapered at the ends. It consists of a connective tissue sheath 4 to 10 mm long that contains from five to nine **intrafusal (IF) muscle fibers** (see Figure 4.7) that are quite different from typical skeletal muscle fibers, **extrafusal (EF) muscle fibers.** The contractile elements, composed of striated myofibrils, are located at each end of an IF fiber. Because spindles are always oriented parallel to the EF fibers, whenever the EF fibers are stretched, the IF fibers stretch. This stretching of the IF fibers results in a deformation of the sensory nerve endings attached to the IF fibers, which initiates an impulse that travels to the spinal cord, resulting in a motor response: contraction of the muscle that was stretched. This is a stretch or myotatic reflex (the type of reflex that occurs when a physician taps on the patellar tendon). This action stretches the quadriceps, which stretches the IF fibers within the spindles, which sends impulses to the spinal cord via a sensory neuron that synapses with an **alpha motor neuron,** which causes the quadriceps muscle to contract. The stretch reflex that originates in the muscle spindles is the basis for unconscious muscular adjustments of posture, where, for instance, a slight stretching of the extensor muscles at the knee is immediately corrected by a reflex shortening to prevent collapse.

Exercise and blood pressure

The change in blood pressure as a result of moderate-intensity aerobic exercise can be as great as the change from pharmaceutical control of blood pressure. High blood pressure is a common problem in our sedentary society. Moderate-intensity aerobic exercise, such as jogging, swimming, or bicycling, can be a very cost-effective and healthy method of lowering blood pressure without the use of medication.[3]

- intrafusal muscle fibers
- extrafusal muscle fibers
- alpha motor neuron
- gamma motor neuron

The muscle spindles also have their own motor nerve system, which constitutes about one-third of the total efferent fibers that enter skeletal muscle.[5] Rather than *alpha* motor neurons, the IF fibers in the muscle spindles are innervated by **gamma motor neurons.** The nerves of the gamma motor system, which when stimulated cause contraction of the contractile portions at the ends (polar regions) of the IF fibers, have two possible roles: (1) they may provide a mechanism by which the spindle's sensitivity is maintained during a muscle contraction, and (2) contraction of the polar regions of the IF fibers, which causes stretch of the middle (equatorial regions) of the IF fibers, which in turn deforms the sensory nerve endings and may help to maintain a muscle contraction (Figure 4.7).

figure 4.7

Muscle spindle.

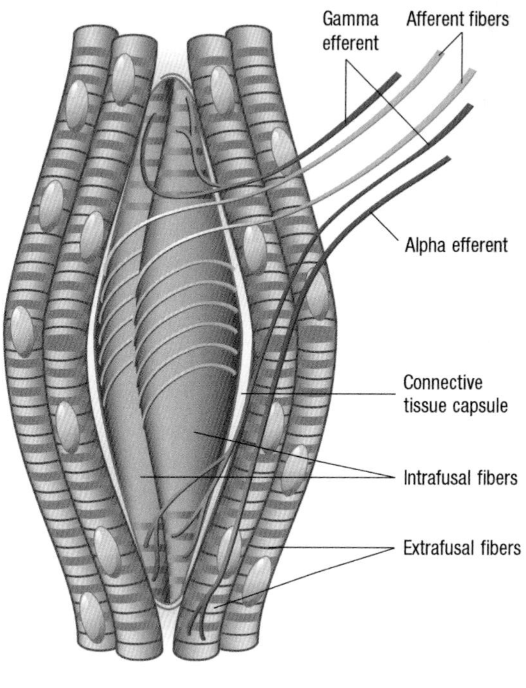

Golgi Tendon Organs and Kinesthesis

- Golgi tendon organs

Golgi tendon organs are also fusiform in shape, but rather than lying within a muscle, they are located at the junction between a muscle and its tendon. They lie in series with the skeletal muscle fibers (as opposed to in parallel as in muscle spindles) and therefore are deformed by tension in the tendon, whether by passive

figure 4.8

Golgi tendon organ.

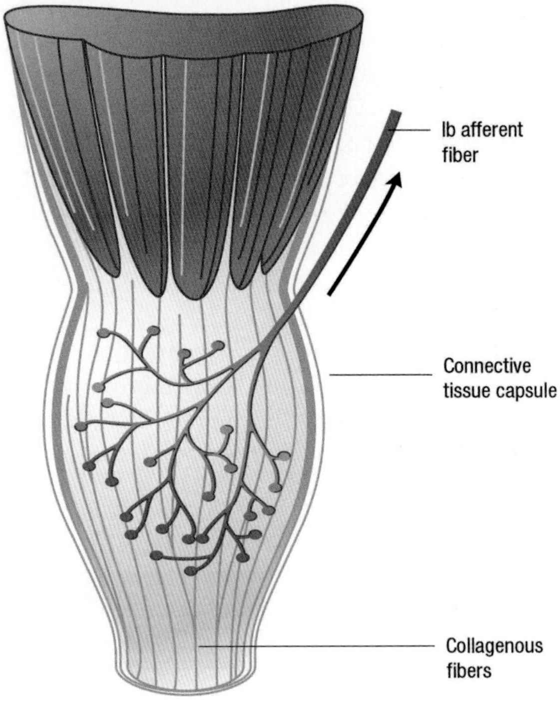

stretching or active shortening of the muscle. Each is innervated by a single large-diameter group Ib afferent (sensory) fiber. Therefore, Golgi tendon organs provide only sensory information (Figure 4.8).

Although these tendon organs respond to both the stretch and the contraction of the adjacent muscle, the response is much stronger when the muscle is contracting, and it results in the inhibition of further contraction and the stimulation of the muscle's antagonist. Therefore, the tendon organ seems to be a protective device, preventing damage to a muscle or joint by excessive contraction of a muscle. From a practical standpoint, it is important not to perform bouncing or jerking movements in stretching, as this will cause many spindles to discharge at once, initiating the myotatic reflex and causing the muscle to contract. Obviously, this would not be desirable either in warming up cold muscles for athletic participation or in stretching exercises that are designed to improve flexibility. The physical educator and coach should apply known physiological principles and use sustained stretching in order to eliminate mass muscle spindle response and allow the muscle to be loosened or relaxed. A slow, sustained force also triggers the Golgi tendon organs to inhibit the muscle and thus further aids in stretching the muscle.

HIGHER NERVE CENTERS AND MUSCULAR CONTROL

So far the discussion of muscular control has centered on the involuntary reflex systems. Now we will consider the voluntary control of muscular activity by the brain. It will be convenient to consider this in three parts: (1) the pyramidal system, (2) the extrapyramidal system, and (3) the proprioceptive–cerebellar system. Although much is known about the function of the brain in controlling muscular activity, a much greater portion awaits further research. Furthermore, a complete discussion of what is known of the motor functions of the brain is beyond the scope of this text and unnecessary for its purposes. Therefore, the following discussion is somewhat brief and is confined to those aspects that are of interest to physical educators, coaches, and exercise professionals.

The Pyramidal System

The cerebral cortex has been mapped out in fair detail, over a period of time, by two methods: (1) by relating clinically observed motor defects with the lesions seen in surgery and autopsies, and (2) by electrically stimulating the cortex of experimental animals and observing the resulting motor effects. This research has resulted in cytoarchitectural maps of the human cortex. The most commonly used map is that of Brodmann. Our areas of interest are shown in Figure 4.9.

pyramidal system

pyramidal tracts

Betz cells

The **pyramidal system** originates in large nerve cells, shaped like pyramids, that lie mainly in area 4 of the cortex. The axons from these cell bodies form large descending motor pathways, called **pyramidal tracts,** that go directly (in most cases) to synapses with the motor neurons in the ventral horn of the spinal cord. (It was once thought that the giant **Betz cells** in area 4 were the entire source of the pyramidal tracts, but research has indicated that they are only about 2 percent of the total motor neurons of the pyramidal system.) The neurons whose cell bodies are in the brain are commonly called **upper motor neurons,** and those in the spinal cord are called **lower motor neurons.** Eighty-five percent or more of the nerve fibers of the pyramidal tract cross from one side to the other, some at the level of the medulla, others at the lower motor neuron level.[7]

Area 4 of the cortex is also referred to as the **motor cortex** or, because of its central location in the brain, as the *precentral gyrus.* The mapping of the motor cortex clearly demonstrates a neat, orderly arrangement of stimulable areas. The area of cortex devoted to a given body part is not proportional to the amount of tissue served but rather to the complexity of the movement potential of the body part. For example, it has been shown that the hands and the muscles of vocalization involve a disproportionate share of motor neurons.

It should be pointed out that the motor cortex is oriented by movement, not by muscle. That is, stimulation of the motor cortex results not in a twitch of one muscle but in a smooth, synergistic movement of a group of muscles.

figure 4.9

The areas of the human cerebral cortex involved in the pyramidal and extrapyramidal systems. In the frontal lobe are areas 4, 6, and 8. In the post central region are areas 1, 2, 3, and 5. Down in the temporal lobe, area 22 is concerned with the extrapyramidal pathways.

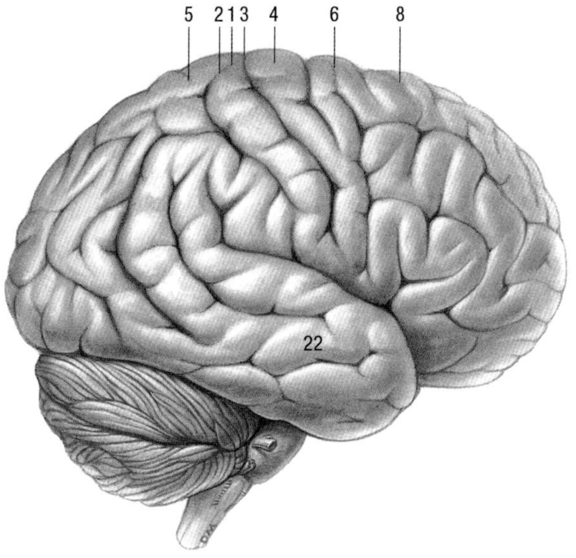

The Extrapyramidal System

The **extrapyramidal system** has its origin mainly in area 6, according to Brodmann's nomenclature. This area is anterior to area 4, the motor area, and is sometimes called the **premotor cortex.** Evidence, however, indicates that some of the fibers descending in the extrapyramidal tracts also originate from cell bodies in other areas, notably areas 8 and 5, and also areas 3, 1, and 2, which are usually considered the sensory areas.

- upper motor neurons
- lower motor neurons
- motor cortex
- extrapyramidal system
- premotor cortex

The descending tracts that are composed of the axons from the neurons of the premotor cortex are considerably more complex than those of the extrapyramidal tracts. These fibers do not go directly to synapses with the lower motor neurons but by way of relay stations, which are called *motor nuclei.* The most important nuclei are the corpus striatum, substantia nigra, and red nucleus. These nuclei are part of the **basal ganglia,** paired masses of gray matter in each cerebral hemisphere. Some fibers also go by way of the *pons,* a prominent white mass at the base of the brain, to the cerebellum. The pons serves as a bridge-like structure that connects the spinal cord with the brain and parts of the brain with each other.

- basal ganglia

For the coach or physical educator, the most important differences between the pyramidal and extrapyramidal systems are the functional differences. Whereas electrical stimulation of area 4 produces specific movements, stimulation of area 6 produces only large, general movement patterns. Consequently, it is believed that learning a new skill in which conscious attention must be devoted to the movements (as in learning a new dance step, where every movement is contemplated) involves area 4. As skill progresses, the origin of the movement is thought to shift to area 6 (dancers no longer concentrate on their feet but rather on very general patterns of movement, so that they can interpret the music better). However, area 4 still participates as a relay station, with fibers connecting area 6 to area 4.

The Proprioceptive-Cerebellar System

We have already dealt with some of the sensory functions of the proprioceptive–cerebellar system, namely, the kinesthesis and vestibular function in proprioception. In general, the pathway of vestibular proprioception leads to the cerebellum, either directly or by way of the vestibular nucleus in the medulla. Of the fibers that conduct kinesthetic information, some go to the thalamus and cortex to provide sensory knowledge of movement at the conscious level. Others go to the cerebellum. The confluence of sensory data for position, balance, and movement in the cerebellum is indicative of the importance of this organ to movement.

The cerebellum rivals the cerebral cortex in complexity, but unfortunately it is not as well understood. Removing the cerebellum of experimental animals results in a loss of function that has three distinct components: (1) impairment of volitional movements, (2) disturbances of posture, and (3) impaired balance control. Consequently, its functions may be deduced. Without entering into anatomical detail we can say that the cerebellum receives constant sensory information from receptors in muscles, joints, tendons, and skin, and also from visual, auditory, and vestibular end organs.

Despite all of this sensory reception, however, no conscious sensation is aroused in the cerebellum. This function is served by the sensory cortex of the cerebral hemispheres. The cerebellum is intimately connected with the motor centers, from the motor cortex all the way to the spinal cord, and may be considered a modifier of muscular activity from the beginning to the end of a movement pattern.

POSTURE, BALANCE, AND VOLUNTARY MOVEMENT

It is now appropriate to consider how all of the foregoing discussion relates to a better understanding of human muscular activity, which is the purpose of this text.

Posture

Human upright posture is mainly brought about through reflexes. The major part of these reflexes is the basic stretch, or myotatic, reflex, which has been described. Let us therefore direct our attention to the postural mechanism that occurs about the knee joint. If the joint starts to collapse (flex), immediately as the muscle spindles of the quadriceps are stretched, an impulse is generated that is propagated over large afferents to the cord, where a synapse is made with a motor neuron. This motor neuron innervates fibers in the quadriceps and causes the quadriceps muscle to contract and thus reextend the joint into its proper position. This reflex, however, occurs only in the presence of facilitation by the vestibular nucleus in the medulla, whose fibers in the cord tend to maintain a state of excitation of the motor neurons innervating the muscles, so that a relatively small afferent impulse can cause the motor neuron to respond. Furthermore, postural reflexes also depend on effects of the extrapyramidal system to bring about smoothly coordinated contraction of the proper strength.

Balance

righting reflex

This aspect of muscular activity is best discussed by referring to the **righting reflex,** which illustrates the underlying principles rather well. If one drops a cat from a small height in supine position (upside down), one can observe the sequential events that invariably lead to its righting itself and landing on all four feet. The first reaction is a turning of the head toward the floor in an attempt to normalize the sensations coming from the otolith organs, which inform the cat it is not oriented in space as it would wish to be. This turning of the head innervates muscle spindles, tendon organs, and other nerve endings in the neck muscles that initiate kinesthetic impulses and reflexively bring about the execution of a half twist, usually long before the cat hits the ground.

Exercise and Parkinson's disease

Parkinson's disease is a neurological disorder that has debilitating effects on an individual's ability to function physically, psychologically, socially, and functionally as the disease progresses. Without treatment, Parkinson's patients will deteriorate over time to the point where many are dependent on others to accomplish the daily tasks of living. Exercise can be utilized to improve both physical fitness and cognitive abilities in individuals battling this disease. Exercise not only improves the ability of the brain to self-repair, but it also has been shown to have protective benefits with regard to impeding the onset of Parkinson's disease symptoms. Exercise appears to accomplish these benefits in two primary ways: by (1) inducing the release of neurotrophic factors and (2) increasing the oxygenation of the brain. These two mechanisms work together to promote new cell growth and cell survival.

A review of the effectiveness of exercise for people with Parkinson's disease analyzed 14 randomized controlled trials that examined the effectiveness of exercise on physical, psychological, and social functioning and on quality of life.[4] The majority of the evidence suggests that exercise is beneficial in the improvement of physical functioning, health-related quality of life, strength, balance, and gait speed in people with Parkinson's disease. Although dopamine release, which was reported as having positive emotional consequences, and improved strength and balance, which would tend to improve a person's ability to walk, are both consequences of exercise, further research is necessary to hone in on the method of exercise most likely to manage depression and to prevent falls in this population.

As the cat turns right side up, its visual receptors bring the necessary sensory data to the cerebellum for organization of muscle activity in the extensors to bring about a gradual absorption of the force involved in landing. As the cat lands, the force that flexes the legs invokes the stretch reflex in the extensors. If the cat was an unwilling subject, the muscles of propulsion also would already be under way. These principles apply equally well in diving, gymnastics, and all other activities in which balance is a factor. In the human, as in the cat, sensations from the otolith organs inform the athlete of his orientation in space. The degree of stretch of the muscles is sensed by the muscle spindles and Golgi tendon organs, informing the athlete of the position of his body parts in space. In addition, it is the stretch of the intrafusal fibers within the muscle spindles, as a gymnast makes contact with the floor, that initiates extrafusal muscle fiber contraction and therefore movement such as leg extension upon landing in a flexed position. Thus, it is the coordination of the otolith system and the muscle and tendon receptors that provides the athlete with the perception of his orientation and the position of his body parts in space for optimum performance.

Voluntary Movement

Let us now take a very simple voluntary movement and analyze the neural activity involved in bringing it about. Assume the right arm is at the side-horizontal position and the desired movement is to bring the right index fingertip to the end of the nose. Since this is not a usual movement, neural activity will probably originate in the arm section of area 4 of the motor cortex and proceed by way of the pyramidal tracts to synapse with the lower motor neuron in the cord and out to the appropriate muscles by way of the brachial plexus, the network of nerves in the axilla (armpit). At the same time, kinesthetic impulses traverse the afferent pathways to the cerebellum and bring about the proper control and coordination so that the shoulder muscles are activated to support the arm as it is moved through horizontal flexion adduction.

Furthermore, the same kinesthetic impulses act reflexively to relax the antagonists through reciprocal inhibition. The gamma efferent system is busy all the while innervating the muscle spindles so that constant measurements of the movement's progress can be fed back. As the movement accelerates, more and more motor units are activated, and the rate of impulse transmission to each motor unit increases, with each motor unit participating at the proper time in the sequential development of the movement.[2] Finally, the movement has to be decelerated in reverse fashion.

ELECTROMYOGRAPHY AND NEUROMUSCULAR FUNCTION

Basic Concepts of Electromyography

As discussed earlier in this chapter and in Chapter 2 in the section entitled "Muscle Contraction and the Sliding Filament Model," electrical stimulation from the motor cortex of the brain travels through the pyramidal tracts to the lower motor neurons and activates motor units, causing contraction of the muscle fibers. Muscle contraction results from a **muscle action potential (MAP)** passing along the sarcolemma of the muscle fiber, which leads to the cascade of events in the sliding filament theory.

muscle action potential (MAP)

We have known at least since the middle of the 19th century that the contraction of muscle tissue is accompanied by MAPs that can be recorded and measured. The recording of MAPs (or their currents) is called **electromyography** (EMG), which reflects the interaction between the functioning of the nervous system and muscle contraction. Thus, EMG is often used to examine aspects of neuromuscular function.

electromyography

The MAP arises at the muscle cell membrane (or sarcolemma) and passes lengthwise through the fiber in wavelike form as the fiber is stimulated to contract. The science of recording and analyzing MAPs probably received its greatest impetus in the related technique of electrocardiography, in which the events of the cardiac cycle are recorded on *electrocardiograms* (ECGs) and examined for abnormality. Physicians also use electromyography clinically in the diagnosis of various types of muscular diseases such as spasticity and paralysis.

WWW

Electromyography Fundamentals
http://moon.ouhsc.edu/dthompso/pk/emg/emg.htm

Qualitative Electromyography

EMG instrumentation and procedures have been developed for use by physicians in diagnosing abnormal neuromuscular function. These techniques may be thought of as **qualitative electromyography** since the greatest concern is with the recording and analysis of the wave form of the MAP from single discrete motor units.

qualitative electromyography

Quantitative Electromyography

Quantitative electromyography is the study of the amount of electrical activity present in a given muscle under varying conditions. Obviously it is not electrical activity per se that is of interest here; rather it is the fact that EMG recordings accurately reflect muscle activation.

quantitative electromyography

Investigators in exercise physiology, kinesiology, physical therapy, and physical medicine are concerned mainly with events in the whole muscle rather than in isolated motor units. For this reason, they often use surface electrodes on the skin over the belly of the muscle. Thus they can observe the firing of many motor units simultaneously and obtain a better statistical sampling than by the use of needle electrodes. This results, however, in a wave form that is a summation of the random activity of the many motor units observed, and it tells nothing about any one motor unit. Also, the MAPs, in passing through the muscle tissue, fascia, subcutaneous fat, and skin, are severely attenuated (decreased in magnitude). Therefore, if we wish to know what is going on in a resting or relatively inactive muscle, we need recordings of extremely high sensitivity. The difference between recordings of individual motor units with needle electrodes and recordings of summated potentials from many motor units with surface electrodes is shown in Figure 4.10. Quantitative EMG includes information in both the time (also called the amplitude) and frequency domains.

figure 4.10

Differences between recordings of single motor-unit potentials with needle electrodes (left) and summated potentials from many motor units with surface electrodes (right).

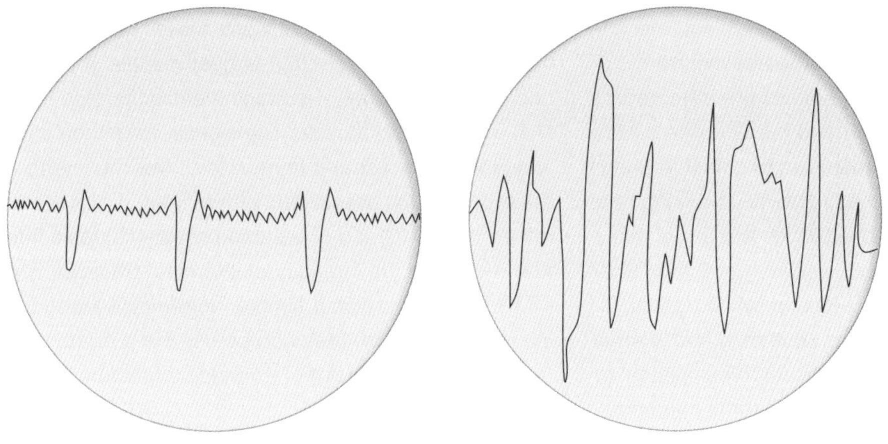

Frequency domain

The frequency domain of the EMG signal is often used to examine various aspects of neuromuscular fatigue (see the section in Chapter 14, "Myoelectric Manifestations of Fatigue"). The **frequency domain** of the EMG signal is the rate at which the wave form fluctuates above and below the baseline, and it is expressed in hertz (Hz). One Hz is equal to one cycle per second. The frequency domain of the EMG signal is usually characterized by the **power density spectrum (PDS),** which displays the amount of power (volts squared per Hz = V^2/Hz) in the EMG signal at each frequency (Figure 4.11).

- frequency domain
- power density spectrum (PDS)
- time domain

The most common variables used to describe the characteristics of the PDS of the surface EMG signal are the mean power frequency (MPF) and median power frequency (MDPF). (See Figure 4.11.) The MPF refers to the average frequency value of the PDS, and the MDPF separates the PDS into two equal halves. The frequency content (MPF and MDPF) is influenced by the MAP conduction velocity along the sarcolemmas of the active muscle fibers and by the shape of the MAP wave form.

figure 4.11

Diagrammatic depiction of the power density spectrum (PDS) of a surface EMG signal.

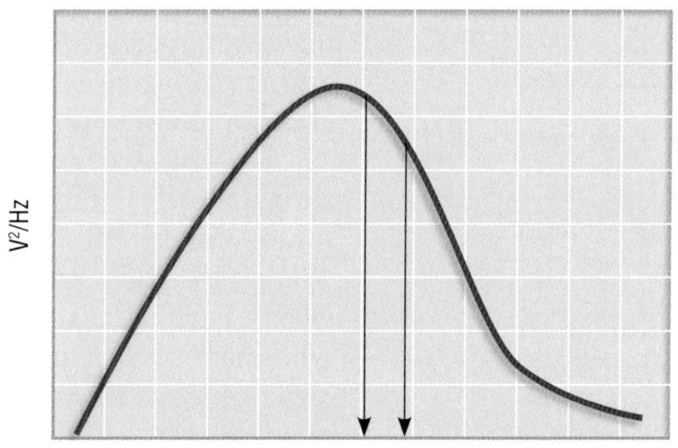

Time domain

The time domain of the EMG signal has many applications related to muscle function and exercise, including providing information regarding muscle relaxation, motor unit activation strategies, and neuromuscular fatigue, as well as the magnitude and sequence of activation of specific muscles during activities such as walking, sit-ups, and various weight-lifting exercises.

The **time domain** involves determining the amplitude (voltage) of electrical current that exists during a specific period of time. It is important to realize that when many motor units fire randomly, some will, by chance, fire simultaneously, and the size of the wave form recorded at that point will be larger. Furthermore, as a muscle is required to produce more tension, ever greater numbers of motor units are recruited; by the law of chance, more will fire

RESEARCH

Using EMG and MMG to study muscle function

Muscles at work generate both electrical signals and mechanical signals. Electrical signals are detected by electromyography (EMG), whereas mechanical signals are detected by mechanomyography (MMG). EMG and MMG utilize a non-invasive technique that allows researchers to gather important information regarding the recruitment patterns and firing rates of muscles during various types of activities and under many types of conditions.

Zuniga et al.* examined the EMG and MMG signals, in addition to other parameters, of nine adult men and women during an incremental cycle ergometry test to exhaustion in order to determine the physiological mechanisms that underlie fatigue. EMG and MMG signals were obtained from the vastus lateralis muscle (the largest muscle in the quadriceps group) by way of surface electrodes placed on the skin overlying the muscle. The signals were then utilized to examine the motor unit firing rate of this muscle to analyze the mechanisms associated with fatigue. It was also determined that EMG and MMG can provide valuable information regarding the intensity of exercise. Because EMG and MMG signals provide a simple, non-invasive way to examine muscle activity, they can be used in a number of ways to provide further insight into muscle function during various types of activities.

*Zuniga, J. M., Housh, T. J., Camic, C. L., Hendrix, C. R., Schmidt, R. J., Mielke, M., and Johnson, G. O. A mechanomyographic fatigue threshold test for cycling. *Int. J. Sports Med.* 31: 636–643, 2010.

simultaneously, and the wave form will grow larger in amplitude as more tension is produced.

The information to be gained from the pattern of motor unit spikes shown in the left-hand side of Figure 4.10 is immediately obvious. We can count the spikes and measure the amplitude, but we have absolutely no quantitative knowledge of what the whole muscle is doing. We know only what is going on in one motor unit. In the time domain, the physiological significance of the electrical activity in the whole muscle rests on the average amplitude of the summated MAPs. The problem here can be immediately recognized by posing the question: What is the average amplitude of the summated MAPs shown in the right side of Figure 4.10? How do we get a true average (mean) value for a function that varies constantly and randomly over time as does the interference pattern (so-called from electronics parlance) of Figure 4.10? To do this requires mathematical integration, part of calculus.

integration

This concept of **integration** is simply depicted in Figure 4.12. First, the integration process can be applied only to either the electrically positive or negative halves of the spikes (both halves are shown in Figure 4.12A). Otherwise the end result would be zero, with the positive being balanced out by the negative aspects of the wave form. Thus, as shown in Figure 4.12B, we have eliminated the negative part of the spikes (a process called rectification). Next, we must think of the spikes as having area, as in Figure 4.12C. The dimensions of this area are, vertically, microvolts of electrical activity (μV) and, horizontally, time in fractions of a second.

planimetry

The next step is to convert the area under the random spikes into a neat geometric figure such as a rectangle whose area equals height times length (or in this case μV times seconds). This conversion to the rectangle can be accomplished by **planimetry** (tracing the curve with an engineering instrument that provides the area under any curve). Figure 4.12D shows that now we have the area in an approximate rectangle whose dimensions are a height of 1.0 μV and a time of 0.40 seconds, yielding an area of 1.0 x 0.40, or 0.40 μV seconds. This is the reading we would obtain from the planimeter. To get the mean μV level, then, we need only divide as follows:

$$(\mu V \times sec) / sec$$

or

$$(1.0\ \mu V \times 0.40\ sec) / 0.40\ sec = 1.0\ \mu V$$

Integration of muscle action potentials to get true mean value of their amplitude. **figure 4.12**

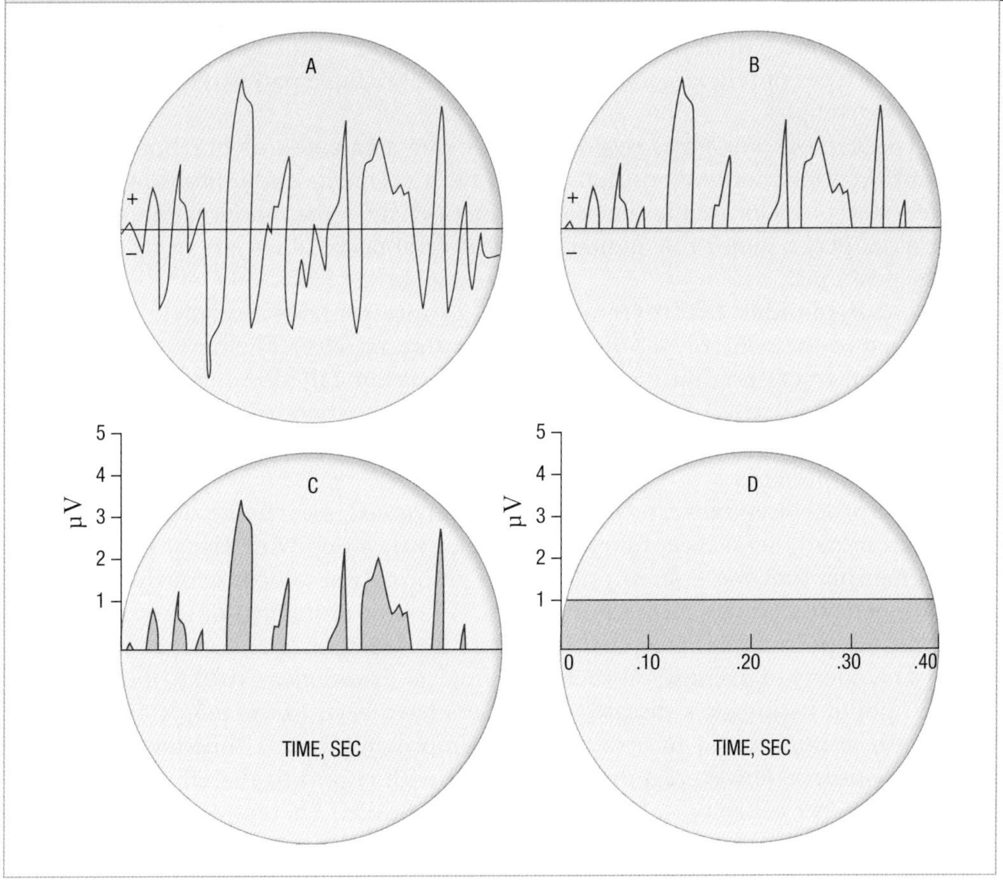

Now we can say that over the 0.40-second observation period the mean amplitude of the MAPs was 1.0 μV. This value is called the time-averaged, integrated EMG amplitude. Fortunately, **electronic integrators** are available that accomplish the whole procedure without resorting to planimetry.

electronic integrators

Through integration we can accurately evaluate data regarding the physiological importance of the electrical activity in the muscle. Even such a tedious process as measuring spike amplitudes is of little value for precise data, because the amplitude varies constantly and randomly. To get a true mean, one must know over what period of time the spike has acted. A fat spike is more important than a thin spike of equal amplitude in determining the true mean value.

In addition to the time-averaged, integrated EMG value, the amplitude of the EMG signal is often expressed as the root mean square (RMS) value. The RMS value is calculated as the standard deviation of the individual EMG voltages over a selected period of time. The information contained in the RMS and time-averaged, integrated EMG amplitude values is very similar. Although the absolute μV values differ for RMS and time-averaged, integrated values, they are very highly correlated, and either can be used to express EMG amplitude.

summary

The nervous system is a highly organized, multidimensional system. Motor neurons conduct nervous impulses from the brain and spinal cord (central nervous system) out to structures in the periphery, and sensory neurons conduct nervous impulses from peripheral structures to the brain and spinal cord. A reflex is the simplest nervous system mechanism involving both sensory and motor neuron activity. There are many types of reflexes. Some involve relatively simple pathways, whereas others are more complex.

The nervous system is responsible for our awareness of our body positions (proprioception) and the positions of our body segments and limbs (kinesthesis) in space. Receptors located in the inner ear, as well as in the muscles, joints, tendons, and skin, play a major role in making the central nervous system aware of various body positions.

The pyramidal, extrapyramidal, and proprioceptive–cerebellar systems are involved in the control of voluntary muscular activity. The nerve fibers of the pyramidal tracts originate in the area of the brain called the motor cortex and are involved in specific movements, whereas the fibers of the extrapyramidal tracts originate primarily in the premotor cortex and are involved in general movement patterns.

The proprioceptive–cerebellar system is involved in receiving sensory information from peripheral receptors and the inner ear, along with visual and auditory information, and the system utilizes this information subconsciously to modify motor activity during a movement pattern. All of the aforementioned systems allow for proper posture, balance, and voluntary movement.

The effects of exercise on such neurological disorders as stroke, multiple sclerosis, polio, Parkinson's disease, and others have been examined. It appears that strength training has a positive effect on improving muscle function in many of these disorders; however, no research exists with regard to the effects of exercise on many other neurological disorders and conditions. Therefore, more research is needed in this area in order to gain a better understanding of the effect of exercise on these conditions.

questions for review

1. Discuss the organization of the nervous system.
2. Describe the following: myotatic reflex, flexion reflex, reciprocal inhibition, crossed extensor reflex, and conditioned reflexes.
3. Define proprioception and kinesthesis.
4. Describe the parts of the brain involved in voluntary control of muscular activity.
5. How does the human body maintain posture, achieve balance, and move voluntarily?
6. Discuss the effects of exercise on disorders or injuries of the nervous system.
7. What can coaches and exercise professionals learn from studying EMG curves?

student companion website

For further review of this book's chapters and for test preparation, visit the book's website, **www.hhpcommunities.com/exercisephysiology**, to take practice quizzes, review the vocabulary terms, use the study guide, and view the digital image bank.

references

1. Bourne, G. A. *The Structure and Function of Muscle,* vol. 1. New York: Academic Press, 1960.
2. Buchanan, J. J. Perceptual estimates of motor skill proficiency are constrained by the stability of coordination patterns. *J. Motor Beh.* Published online: 12 Mar 2015.
3. Ghadieh, A. S., and Saab, B. Evidence for exercise training in the management of hypertension in adults. *Can. Fam. Physician* 61 (3): 233–239, 2015.
4. Goodwin, V. A., Richards, S. H., Taylor, R. S., Taylor, A. H., and Campbell, J. The effectiveness of exercise interventions for pe ople with Parkinson's disease: a systematic review and meta-analysis. *Move. Disord.* 23: 631–640, 2008.
5. Hunt, C. C. The effect of stretch receptors from muscle on the discharge of motorneurons. *J. Physiol.* 117: 359–379, 1952.
6. Voss, H. Tabelle der absoluten und relativen muskelspindelzahlen der menschlichen skelettmaskulatur. *Anat. Anz.* 129: 562–572, 1971.
7. Zhou, S. Chronic neural adaptations to unilateral exercise: mechanisms of cross education. *Exerc. Sport Sci. Rev.* 28: 177–184, 2000.

The Cardiovascular System 5

As a result of reading this chapter you will:

Know the components of the cardiovascular system.

Know the basic, general anatomy and physiology of the cardiovascular system.

Understand the responses of the cardiovascular system during exercise.

Understand the responses of the cardiovascular system to exercise training.

key concepts

arteriole
arteriovenous anastomose (AV shunt)
artery
atrioventricular (AV) node
atrium
autorhythmicity
blood flow
blood pressure
capacitance vessels
capillary
cardiac contractility
cardiac cycle
cardiac output (CO)
cardiac reserve
diastole
diastolic pressure
dynamic exercise
end diastolic volume (EDV)
end systolic volume (ESV)
ephaptic conduction
exercise intensity
Fick method
Frank–Starling law of the heart
gap junction
heart murmur
hypertrophy

The cardiovascular system, composed of the heart and the blood vessels, moves blood to and from the various tissues of the body. The primary function of the heart is to pump the blood to the lungs and to the systemic circulation. The blood vessels serve as a dynamic pipeline for carrying the blood to and from the tissues. Tissues require the oxygen, nutrients, and hormones that blood carries. Blood also transports carbon dioxide and other waste products away from the tissues.

FUNCTIONS OF THE CARDIOVASCULAR SYSTEM

The heart is a muscular organ that serves as two pumps: one (the right heart) pumps blood to the lungs, where the blood is oxygenated, and the other (the left heart) pumps the oxygenated blood to the systemic circulation, where the blood provides oxygen and nutrients to the tissues of the body.

The blood vessels carry the blood from the heart to the tissues and then back to the heart. There are several types of blood vessels. **Arteries,** as a general rule, carry blood away from the heart and toward the tissues. **Veins,** on the other hand, usually carry blood from the tissues back to the heart. The exceptions to this rule are the **pulmonary veins,** which carry oxygenated blood from the lungs to the left heart so that the oxygenated blood can then be pumped out of the left heart into the systemic circulation. The arteries and veins are connected to each other by smaller vessels called arterioles, capillaries, and venules. **Arterioles** are very muscular vessels that have the primary responsibility of keeping the pressure low in the capillaries. The **capillaries** are very thin-walled (one cell thick) vessels through which gases (such as oxygen and carbon dioxide), nutrients (such as glucose), and waste products (such as lactic acid) are exchanged. **Venules** are very small vessels that connect the capillaries to the veins.

(margin: arteries · veins · pulmonary veins · arterioles · capillaries · venules)

THE HEART

Anatomy

The heart contains four chambers: the right and left **atria** (singular: atrium), which receive blood from the veins, and the right and left **ventricles,** which pump blood into the arteries (Figure 5.1). The heart is able to pump blood because it is a muscular organ. In many ways, heart (or cardiac) muscle is like skeletal muscle: it is striated; the contractile proteins of cardiac and skeletal muscle are of the same types (actin, myosin, troponin, and tropomyosin); and cardiac muscle fibers, like skeletal muscle fibers, are stimulated by the nervous system, which triggers contractions.

There are also some important distinctions between cardiac muscle and skeletal muscle. Between the cardiac muscle cells are connective tissue structures called **intercalated disks,** which allow one cell to pull on the surrounding cells. Within the intercalated disks are **gap junctions,** which are like passageways between cells, allowing for ion exchanges between the cytosol of adjacent cells. Intercalated disks and gap junctions allow cardiac muscle to function as a **syncytium,** or network of cells. This means that not every cardiac cell requires its own innervation. Therefore, the stimulation of one cardiac cell to contract stimulates an adjacent cell, and so on, until the impulse has been transmitted to all cells of the heart. This transmission of an electrical impulse from cell to cell is called **ephaptic conduction.**

(margin: atria · ventricles · intercalated disks · gap junctions · syncytium · ephaptic conduction)

Origin and Conduction of Electrical Activity

(margin: autorhythmicity)

The muscle tissue of the heart is capable of self-excitation (**autorhythmicity**), which means that it does not require a stimulus or innervation to produce a contraction. If

Basic anatomy of the heart. **figure 5.1**

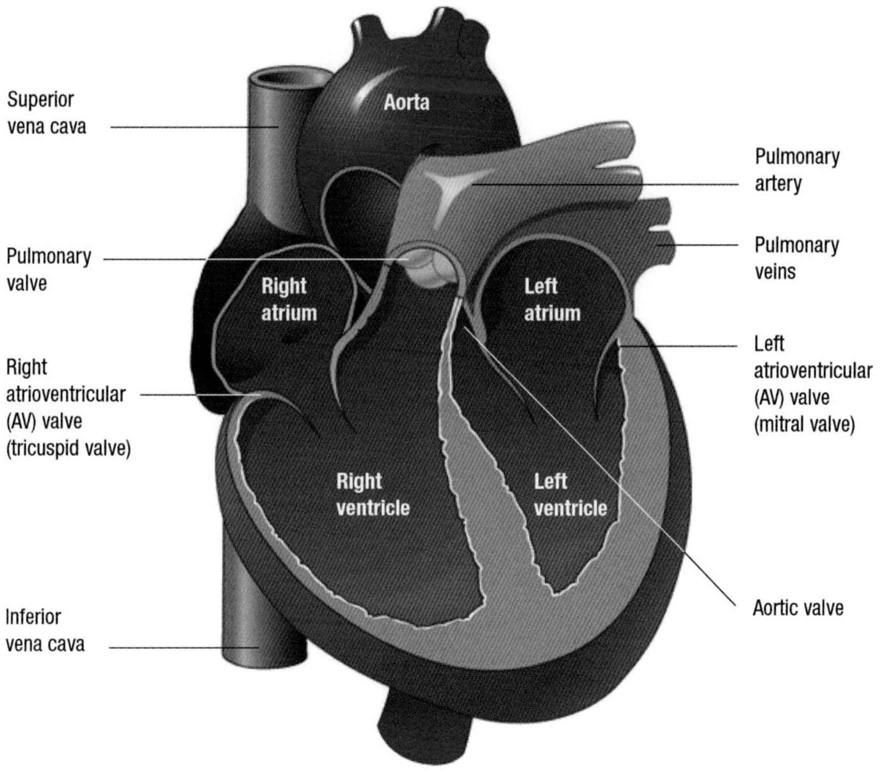

key concepts

- indicator dilution method
- intercalated disk
- maximum heart rate (HR_{max})
- metarteriole
- myocardium
- non-pathologic cardiac hypertrophy
- pathologic cardiac hypertrophy
- pressure gradient
- pulmonary vein
- Purkinje fibers
- reserve of heart rate
- resistance
- resistance vessels
- resting heart rate
- sinoatrial (SA) node
- sphygmomanometer
- static exercise
- stroke volume (SV)
- stroke volume reserve
- syncytium
- systole
- systolic pressure
- vagus nerve
- vein
- ventricle
- venule
- viscosity

you were to place a piece of heart tissue alone in a dish, that tissue would contract. Under normal conditions, in an intact heart, however, a wave of excitation begins at the **sinoatrial (SA) node** (Figure 5.2) and travels throughout the heart. The reason for the SA node's leadership role in the initiation of the impulse is the frequency with which it generates its impulses. All other parts of the heart can initiate impulses too, but they do so less frequently. If, under abnormal conditions, such as heart disease, infection, drug use, or congenital lesions, the SA node slows its impulse frequency, another area of the **myocardium** (heart muscle) that has a faster inherent rate may assume the role of pacemaker, resulting in an abnormal rhythm. It is the SA node's inherent rate of 60 to 100 impulses per minute, in conjunction with sympathetic and parasympathetic influences (described below), that results in an average heart rate between 70 and 80 beats per minute.

Figure 5.2 illustrates the transmission of the wave of excitation from the SA node, by way of ephaptic conduction in the atria, to the **atrioventricular (AV) node,** at the base of the atria in the interatrial septum (wall). From there the impulse travels through the atrioventricular bundle (bundle of His), bundle branches, and **Purkinje fibers,** specialized conducting cells of the heart that conduct the impulses throughout the ventricular myocardium.

- sinoatrial (SA) node
- myocardium
- atrioventricular (AV) node
- Purkinje fibers

Under normal circumstances, the heart, although capable of self-excitation, is influenced by both the sympathetic and the parasympathetic branches of the autonomic nervous system. Sympathetic stimulation of the SA node results in an increased heart rate, whereas parasympathetic stimulation results in a decreased heart rate. Both branches are tonically active at all times, which allows either branch to increase or decrease the heart rate as needed. This will be discussed in more detail in the section "Control of heart rate and stroke volume" (pp. 86–87).

figure 5.2 The conducting system of the heart. The impulse is initiated at the SA node and travels to the AV node, bundle of His, bundle branches, and Purkinje fibers.

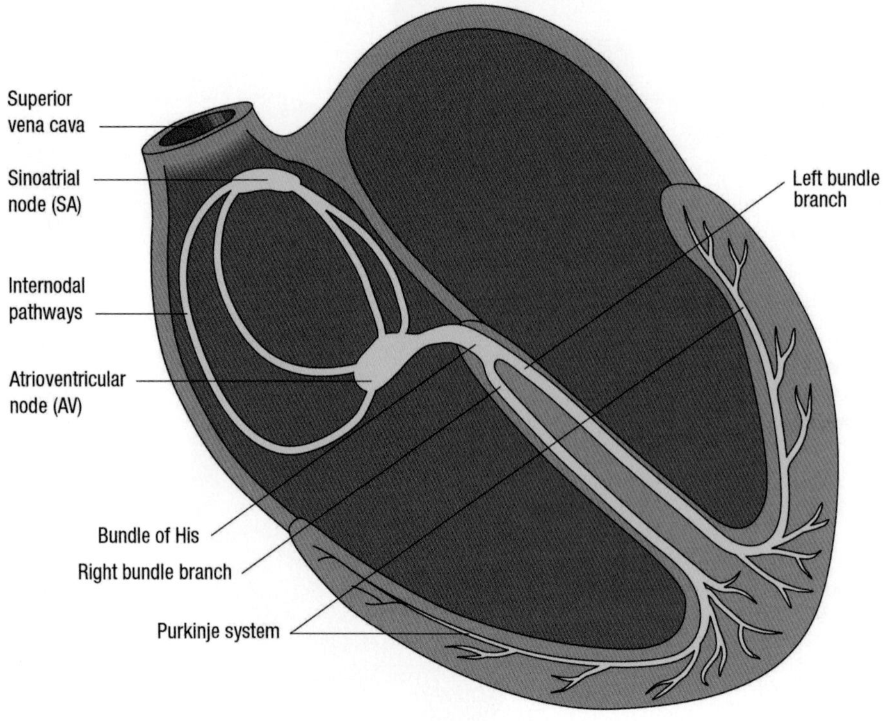

The Cardiac Cycle

cardiac cycle
diastole
systole

The cyclic pattern of contraction and relaxation of the heart is referred to as the **cardiac cycle.** The relaxation phase of the cycle is called **diastole** and the contraction phase is called **systole** (see Figure 5.3). Valves located between the atria and the ventricles and between the ventricles and the vessels leading out of the heart (pulmonary artery on the right and aorta on the left) are constructed in such a way as to allow for unidirectional blood flow. Therefore, after the blood passes through the valves, they close, preventing the backflow of blood. It is the closure of the valves that is responsible for the heart's sounds. This will be discussed in greater detail in the box on heart murmurs (see p. 90). Structurally sound valves not only are critical for allowing forward flow and preventing backflow of blood but also are necessary in order for the pressure within the ventricles to build up to the point that blood can be ejected out of the heart with enough force to get it to its destination.

Atrial contraction is responsible for the completion of ventricular filling but accounts for only approximately 20 to 30 percent of the filling of the ventricles. The remainder of ventricular filling occurs because of gravity. Atrial contraction, therefore, is not necessary, and under abnormal circumstances in which the atria are not contracting well, a person can survive without significant complications. Ventricular contraction, on the other hand, is required to pump the blood to the pulmonary circulation and to the tissues of the body and therefore is required for life. Thus, even though the atria do contract and relax, because of the greater importance of ventricular contraction compared with atrial contraction, when the terms "diastole" and "systole" are used without reference to specific chambers, they refer to contraction and relaxation of the ventricles. During diastole the ventricles fill with blood, and during systole the ventricular muscle contracts to force

www

Cardiovascular System
www.innerbody.com/image/cardov.html

American Heart Association
www.heart.org

figure 5.3 The events of the cardiac cycle, depicting the changes in pressure, volume, electrocardiogram, and phonocardiogram for the left ventricle.

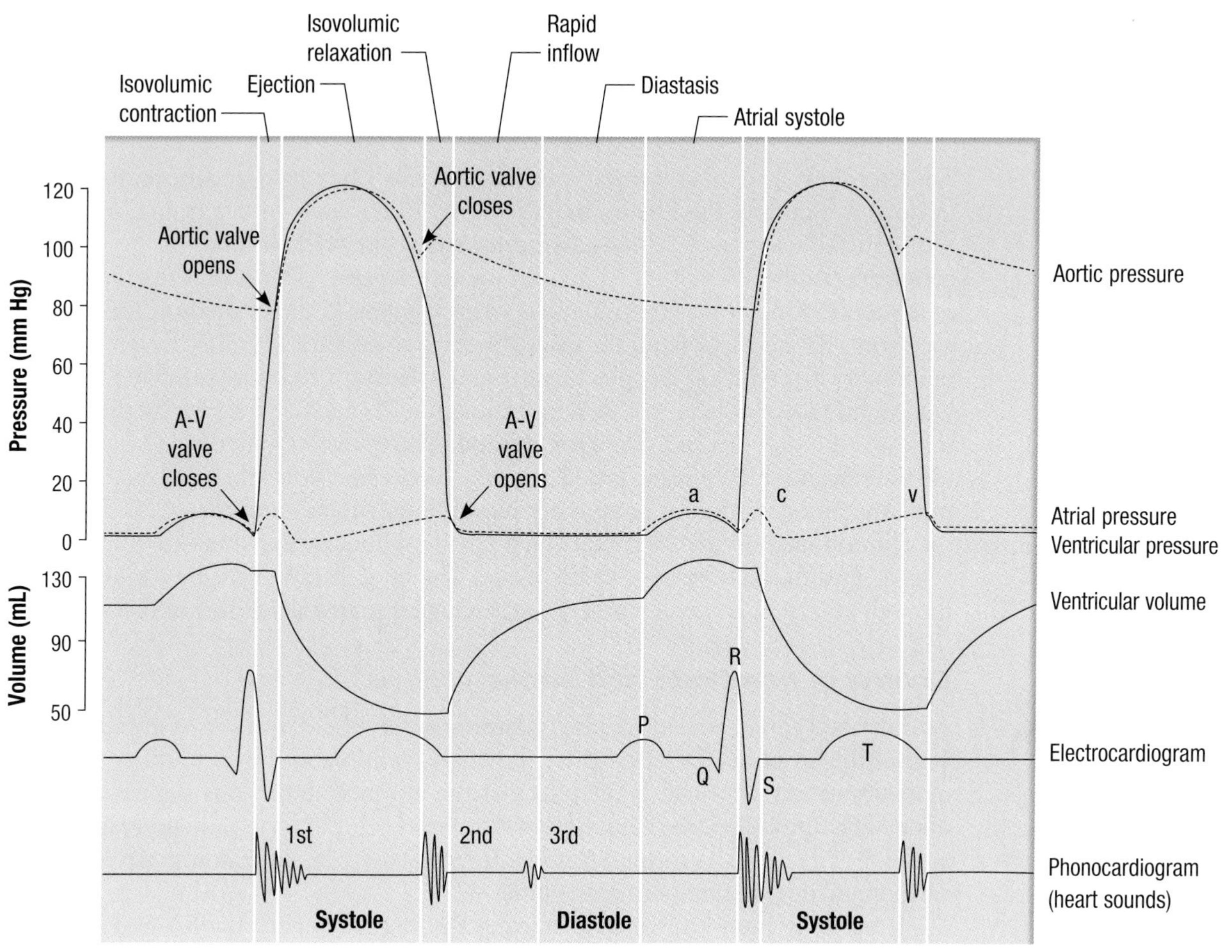

blood out of the chambers of the ventricles. The amount of blood in each ventricle at the end of diastole is called the **end diastolic volume (EDV)** and is equal, on average, to approximately 135 mL. The amount of blood that remains in each ventricle at the end of systole is called the **end systolic volume (ESV)** and is approximately 65 mL. The difference between EDV and ESV (70 mL on average) is called the **stroke volume (SV),** which is the amount of blood ejected out of each ventricle with each cardiac contraction. During systole, even a healthy heart ejects only 50 to 60 percent of the EDV. A heart that is compromised as a result of disease or inactivity ejects an even smaller percentage of its EDV.

- end diastolic volume (EDV)
- end systolic volume (ESV)
- stroke volume (SV)

Figure 5.3 shows the pressure changes, volume changes, electrocardiogram, and phonocardiogram (recording of heart sounds) during the normal cardiac cycle.

Cardiac Output

The **cardiac output** (CO) is the amount of blood ejected by the heart each minute. At rest, the average cardiac output is approximately 5 liters per minute; it can increase to over 40 liters per minute in a well-trained athlete. The ability to increase cardiac output maximally is one important limiting factor in athletic performance. Therefore, an athlete who is more highly trained and has a higher CO would have an advantage

- cardiac output (CO)

WWW

The Heart.Org Cardiology Online
www.theheart.org

over an athlete whose CO is not as great. The cardiac output is determined by two factors: the heart rate and the stroke volume.

$$CO = HR \times SV$$

Therefore, the CO can be altered by changing the HR and/or the SV.

Measurement of cardiac output

To determine a person's cardiac output, it seems obvious that all one would have to do is to multiply the HR by the SV. Heart rate is easy to determine: merely find a superficial artery such as the carotid (in the neck) or the radial (in the wrist) and count the number of pulsations in each minute. Stroke volume, on the other hand, is much more difficult to determine in a living person. A direct method for obtaining a person's SV and CO would involve inserting a catheter into the person's aorta or pulmonary artery. Most people, however, are reluctant to undergo such a procedure (and rightly so!). Indirect methods for estimating CO include the Fick method and the indicator dilution method. The **Fick method** involves estimating the CO by determining the rate at which oxygen is added to the blood as it flows through the lungs. This results in an estimation of pulmonary blood flow, which is equal to CO. The **indicator dilution method** involves injecting a small amount of dye (indicator) into a large vein or into the right atrium of the heart. The concentration of the dye as it passes through an artery is then recorded, and CO is estimated using this information.

Fick method

indicator dilution method

Control of heart rate and stroke volume

As described earlier, the heart rate is determined by the frequency of impulses generated at the SA node. This frequency, however, is influenced by a number of factors, most important of which is the effect of the autonomic nervous system on the SA node. The autonomic nervous system supplies both parasympathetic (**vagus nerve**) and sympathetic fibers to the SA node. In both cases the innervation arises from the cardioregulatory centers of the medulla.

vagus nerve

It has long been known that severing the vagus fibers to the SA node results in an immediate increase in the heart rate. Therefore, these fibers have an inhibitory influence on the SA node. On the other hand, severing the sympathetic fibers to the SA node results in an immediate decrease in the heart rate. Therefore, these fibers have a stimulatory influence on the SA node. Under normal circumstances both branches of the autonomic nervous system exhibit *tone*—that is, they are continually active. This means that there is some inhibitory and some stimulatory nervous influence on the heart rate at all times. If one were to block both the parasympathetic and sympathetic influences to the SA node, the heart rate would speed up from its average resting rate of 70 to 80 beats per minute to approximately 100 beats per minute. This seems to indicate that vagal tone is greater than sympathetic tone. Various bodily activities require varying amounts of oxygen, nutrients, and waste product removal. Therefore, whenever the activity level changes, the heart rate is adjusted to meet the demands of the activity.

Cardiac output during exercise

Cardiac output (CO) increases from four- to eightfold from rest to maximal exercise. The amount of blood pumped by the heart at rest is 5 L • min^{-1}. During exercise this increases to about 20 L • min^{-1} for young sedentary individuals and up to 40 L • min^{-1} for elite athletes. Maximum heart rates do not increase with training, which means that the enormous increases in CO observed in elite athletes are due entirely to an increase in stroke volume.

The stroke volume of the heart involves many factors; however, it is simplest to remember that SV is a direct function of the EDV of the ventricle. This idea is based on the classic work of Otto Frank and Ernest Starling, who studied denervated (nerves removed) heart–lung preparations and discovered that if they increased the amount of blood returning to the heart, stroke volume would increase proportionately. Therefore, ventricular contraction force is proportional to EDV. These observations became known as the **Frank–Starling law of the heart,** which states that contraction force during systole is dependent on the length of the cardiac muscle fibers at the end of diastole (i.e., EDV).

Frank–Starling law of the heart

The method by which the Frank–Starling law works is related to the fact that prior to ventricular filling, the cardiac sarcomeres are kept at a length that is shorter than the optimum length for tension production. However, as blood fills the ventricles, the sarcomeres are stretched, improving the amount of actin–myosin overlap and resulting in a more forceful contraction. It seems obvious that it would be beneficial for the EDV to increase during exercise in order to bring the stroke volume to a sufficient level for supplying the working muscles with adequate blood flow. This appears to be the case in submaximal aerobic exercise; however, during maximal anaerobic exertion there appears to be no rise in stroke volume. The increased sympathetic drive that accompanies such heavy exercise results in the shortening of diastole. This shorter diastole limits the time for ventricular filling, most likely limiting stroke volume.[3]

Cardiac contractility refers to the heart's ability to produce force per unit of time or, in other words, power. Whenever sympathetic stimulation is increased, the contractility of the heart increases, causing systolic pressures to rise faster and reach higher levels. This means that in addition to the obvious advantage of a more forceful contraction, there is more time for ventricular filling in diastole because systole is completed more rapidly in each cardiac cycle. Therefore, during exercise, increases in both heart rate and contractility are important factors enabling the heart to meet the demands of the activity.

cardiac contractility

Factors affecting heart rate

The heart rate at rest varies widely from individual to individual and also within the same individual under varying circumstances. Therefore, it is almost meaningless to speak of a "normal" heart rate. We may, however, say that the average **resting heart rate** is between 70 and 80 beats per minute (bpm) without implying that a rate of 40 (observed in highly trained endurance athletes) or 100 is necessarily "abnormal." Although the heart rate during the stress of exercise or during the recovery period after exercise is a very valuable source of information for the exercise physiologist, the resting rate is affected by so many variables that it has very little meaning for the prediction of physical performance. Variables that affect the resting heart rate include age, gender, size, posture, ingestion of food, smoking, emotion, body temperature, and environmental factors.

resting heart rate

Age. The heart rate at birth is approximately 130 bpm, and it slows down with each succeeding year until adolescence. The average resting heart rate in an adult male who is standing is usually between 70 and 80 bpm. The **maximum heart rate** (**HR_{max}**) a person can attain decreases with age and can be estimated with the simple equation 220 minus the person's age. Thus, at age 20, the HR_{max} is about 200 bpm. It will decrease to about 160 bpm at age 60.

maximum heart rate (HR_{max})

Gender. The resting heart rate in adult females averages 5 to 10 beats faster than in adult males under any given set of conditions.

WWW

AACVPR—American Association of Cardiovascular and Pulmonary Rehabilitation

www.aacvpr.org

Size. In the animal world it seems to be a general, biological rule that the heart rate varies inversely with the size of the species. For example, the canary has a heart rate of approximately 1,000 bpm, whereas an elephant's is about 25 bpm. No consistent relationship between size and heart rate in adult humans has been demonstrated.

Posture. Posture has a very definite effect on heart rate. Although the results of different investigations vary, the typical response to the change from a lying down to a standing position seems to be an increase of about 10 to 12 bpm.

Ingestion of food. The resting heart rate is higher for the first few hours following a meal. This is caused by the increase in metabolism required to digest the food. The heart rate is also higher for a given exercise load following a meal. Therefore, it is a good idea to avoid heavy exercise immediately after a meal because the body is busy digesting.

Smoking. Smoking produces a significant increase in heart rate. Masson and Gilbert[6] found this increase to be approximately 13 bpm after smoking one cigarette, with a moderate nicotine content, in women who were regular cigarette smokers.

Emotion. Emotional stress or anxiety causes a cardiovascular response that is very similar to the response to exercise. Even before an exercise bout begins, the heart rate increases in response to an increase in anxiety level. This occurs through both a decrease in the parasympathetic influence of the SA node and an increase in the sympathetic influence of the SA node. Psychological pressure in anticipation of an activity can augment this increase in heart rate, and it has been shown that the higher the perceived level of pressure, the greater the elevation in heart rate.[1] Interestingly, in very precise, accuracy-based activities that demand a calm and steady hand, such as sharpshooting and golf putting, the more highly skilled performers tend to acquire the ability to calm themselves. This calming is indicated by a decrease in heart rate immediately prior to performing, to prevent the emotional stress from inhibiting the performance. Evidence of this calming ability is the greater reduction in heart rate in expert versus novice performers.[2]

Body temperature. As the body temperature increases above normal, the heart rate also increases. Conversely, with decreases in the body temperature, the heart rate decreases. A body temperature of about 78°F or below will result in abnormal electrocardiograms, indicating a danger of heart failure.

Heat and humidity. When the environmental temperature is high, sweat gland activity increases. This is good, because a great deal of body heat can be lost as the sweat evaporates. The negative aspect of this process is that in a hot environment, one can become dehydrated from the water lost during sweating. This water loss results in a decrease in the plasma portion of the blood and, therefore, a decrease in the amount of blood carrying oxygen to the tissues. To ensure that the body gets enough oxygen, the heart rate increases.

Humidity also affects the heart rate. When the environment is humid, the evaporation process slows. This results in the use of alternate heat loss mechanisms such as radiation. Radiation of body heat involves pumping the blood to the subcutaneous vessels to allow the heat to radiate through the skin and out into the environment. The heart rate increases so that more blood reaches the subcutaneous vessels.

Factors affecting stroke volume

As described earlier in this chapter, the amount of blood the heart pumps is profoundly affected by the amount of blood the heart receives and by the contractile capabilities of the heart muscle itself. Therefore, the most influential factors affecting stroke volume are those that can alter venous return and cardiac contractility. These include gravity, muscular activity, heart size, and nervous influences.

Gravity. Gravitational forces can have a tremendous effect on venous return. If a person stands still for an extended period of time, gravity causes the blood to pool in the lower extremities, decreasing venous return and therefore stroke volume. It is not uncommon for soldiers who stand at attention for long periods of time to pass out because of the reduction in cardiac output caused by blood pooling in the lower extremities. Contracting the muscles of the lower extremities is an effective method for combating this pooling effect.

Muscular activity. The blood vessels, especially the veins, can store a great deal of blood. At any given time, approximately 60 percent of the body's total blood volume of 5.2 L is in the veins of the systemic circulation. In other words, more than 3 L of blood is sitting in your systemic veins at this very moment! The veins do have a layer of smooth muscle that can contract in response to sympathetic stimulation to shunt blood toward the heart in times of emergencies, but for the most part the veins rely on the contractions of the skeletal muscles surrounding them to compress the vessels and squeeze the blood toward the heart. The mechanism by which the blood is sent toward the heart, rather than away from it, consists of valves that prevent the backflow of blood (Figure 5.4). Figure 5.4 shows how the contracting muscles surrounding a vein bulge inward toward the vein, causing blood to be shunted toward the heart. It also shows the valves, which prevent the backflow of blood.

The one-way valves of the veins. Contraction of the surrounding skeletal muscle aids in the movement of blood toward the heart, and the valves prevent blood from moving away from the heart.

figure 5.4

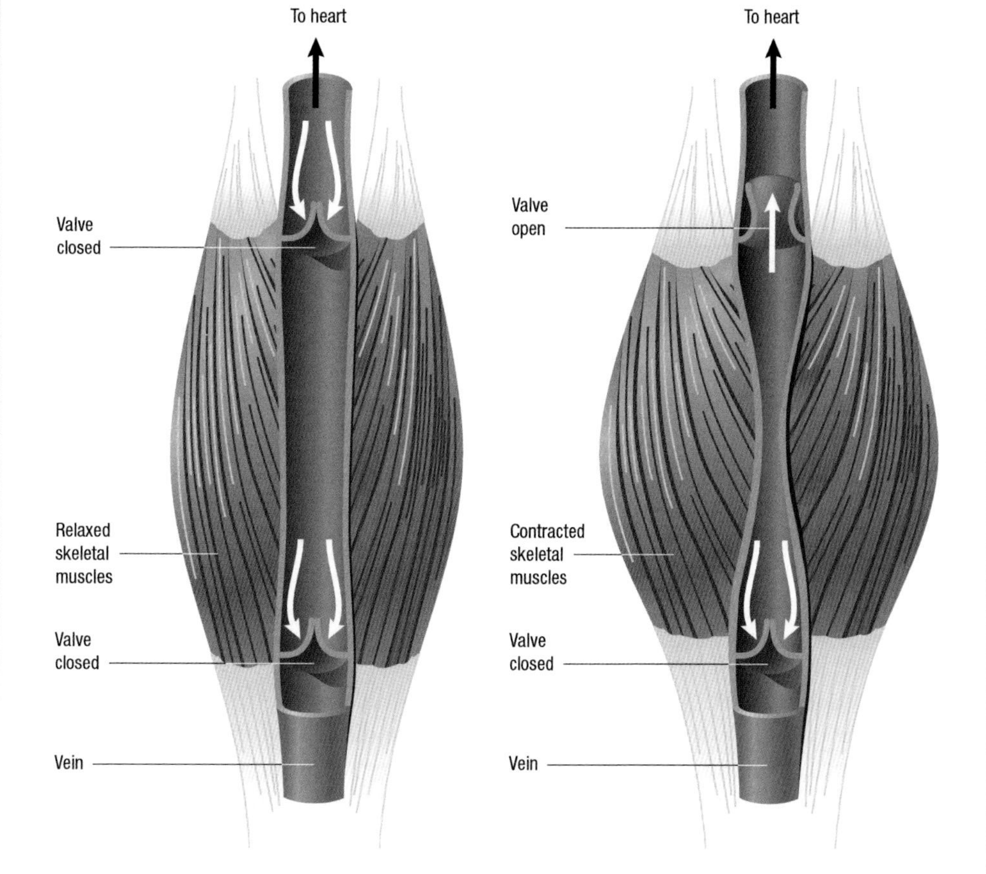

CLINICAL APPLICATIONS

Heart murmurs

A **heart murmur** is a sound created by blood that is not flowing smoothly. Blood that is moving smoothly is described as having *laminar flow,* whereas blood that has developed swirls, or eddy currents, is described as having *turbulent flow.* Eddy currents are prone to occur wherever there are irregularities (such as atherosclerotic plaques) in the vessel walls or abrupt changes in the dimensions of the vessels. There are some areas, such as at the base (roots) of the aorta and pulmonary artery, where the fast flow during systole and the relatively small openings leading into these large vessels cause turbulent flow. These are normal sounds, which have no pathological significance, and are called *functional murmurs.*

On the other hand, cardiac valves are sometimes malformed at birth (congenital valve defects) or become damaged by disease. The murmurs caused by the regurgitation (backflow) of blood through an insufficient valve (one that doesn't close completely) or by the restricted outflow of blood through a stenotic valve (one that doesn't open properly) are valuable diagnostic signs to the physician. Exercise professionals, physical educators, and coaches should understand the significance of these murmurs.

Heart valve insufficiencies causing either regurgitation or restricted outflow of blood cause the heart to work harder than a heart that is free of these problems. When a valve allows for regurgitation of blood or when a valve does not open sufficiently, not allowing blood to leave a chamber freely, the heart compensates for the increase in blood volume it has retained by increasing its contraction force. As contraction force increases, more oxygen is consumed. Therefore, a heart with murmurs caused by valve defects is less efficient. This decreased efficiency may be so slight in some cases as to be a limiting factor only in very strenuous exercise, but in other cases it may severely limit exercise tolerance. Individuals with heart murmurs should consult a physician before participating in strenuous exercise or athletics. Physicians and cardiologists recognize the advantages that can be gained from appropriate exercise programs. Therefore, physical educators, exercise scientists, and physicians should communicate with one another to develop training protocols that meet the needs and address the limitations of their patients.

heart murmur

This is why rhythmic activities such as running, cycling, and swimming result in greater blood flow and venous return than activities requiring isometric contractions. During an activity that has repeating cycles of skeletal muscle contraction and relaxation, blood is squeezed toward the heart during the contraction, and blood comes into the previously occupied space in the vessels during relaxation. During an isometric contraction, the continuous squeezing of the vessels doesn't allow for blood to come in and replace the blood that was just squeezed out. Not only does this reduce the amount of venous return to the heart, but the constant contraction also increases the pressure on the arterial side of the heart, causing the heart to work harder in order to pump against the increased resistance.

The muscles of the extremities are not the only ones responsible for the pumping of blood back to the heart. The muscles involved in respiration also play a key role in this process during the breathing cycle. During expiration, when the pressure in the abdominal cavity is low, blood fills the large abdominal veins. During inspiration, when the pressure in the abdominal veins is high and the pressure in the thoracic (chest) cavity is low, the blood moves from the abdomen to the thorax. This repeating cycle of expiration and inspiration has a tremendous impact on increasing venous return and therefore stroke volume.

Size of the heart. In any muscle, the more contractile proteins there are, the greater the capability for a strong contraction (see discussion in Chapter 2). Cardiac muscle is no exception. In general, larger hearts contract more forcefully than smaller ones. Under some circumstances, however, an increase in the size of the heart reflects not only an increase in contractile tissue but also a change in the size of the chambers of the heart. This condition is termed cardiac **hypertrophy.**

hypertrophy

There are two general categories of cardiac hypertrophy: non-pathologic and pathologic. **Non-pathologic cardiac hypertrophy** is an exercise-induced hypertrophy that results in an increase in the thickness of the heart walls (primarily the left heart), as well as an increase in the diameter of the left ventricle. This is advantageous to the athlete who, as a result of training, has developed a heart that is much more efficient. During exercise, the endurance-trained heart has a lower heart rate, longer diastole, faster diastolic relaxation, improved diastolic filling, and generally reduced cardiac work.[3] **Pathologic cardiac hypertrophy,** on the other hand, results when the heart is subjected to chronic increases in arterial pressure (which is the case in hypertension) or faulty valves that do not allow the blood to be freely ejected out of the heart. These types of stressors tend to result in an increase in the thickness of the walls of the heart with either no change, or a decrease, in the size of the ventricular chamber. From a practical standpoint, it doesn't do much good to increase the contractile capabilities of the heart if the amount of blood available to pump out of the heart (EDV) is reduced, as would be the case if the size of the ventricular chamber were decreased.

non-pathologic cardiac hypertrophy

pathologic cardiac hypertrophy

Nervous influences. Because the ventricles are innervated primarily by the sympathetic branch of the autonomic nervous system, with very little innervation by the parasympathetic nerves, the sympathetic nerves play a large role in contraction force and, therefore, stroke volume. The increase in stroke volume that is observed during exercise is greater in the athlete's heart than in the untrained heart and is a function of the degree of sympathetic activity involved. Through regular exercise training, an athlete "trains" her nervous system to respond more efficiently to the demands of the exercise.

Heart Rate During and After Exercise

The exercise load that the body can tolerate is largely determined by the rate at which the heart can supply the necessary blood to the working tissues. We have already seen that this rate of blood flow, the cardiac output, is the result of two components: heart rate and stroke volume. Since heart rate is easily measured, it is fortunate that research has shown heart rate to be more important than stroke volume in responding to the demands of aerobic exercise. The heart rate is more important for at least three reasons:

1. Stroke volume probably increases very little with an increase in metabolism until a metabolic level approximately eight times the resting level is reached.
2. Heart rate is proportional to the workload imposed.
3. Heart rate is proportional to oxygen consumption during exercise.

The typical heart rate response to exercise

As exercise begins, the heart rate rises rapidly. If the exercise is light or moderate, a *plateau* (leveling off) is seen within the first minute. The actual rate during the plateau, or *steady state,* is proportional to the workload. If the workload is heavy (10 or more times the resting metabolic level), the heart rate increases until exhaustion (Figure 5.5). For the first two or three minutes after the end of exercise, the heart rate decreases almost as rapidly as it increased. After this initial decrease, the heart rate declines more slowly, at a rate that is roughly related to the intensity and duration of the work.

Responses of the heart rate to differences in exercise

Static versus dynamic exercise. During **static exercises,** which involve holding a position (such as isometric contractions), only a slight increase in heart rate is observed. At the other end of the continuum are **dynamic exercises,** which

static exercise

dynamic exercise

figure 5.5 Heart rate changes in a moderately conditioned, middle-aged subject at workloads of 100 and 150 watts on a bicycle ergometer.

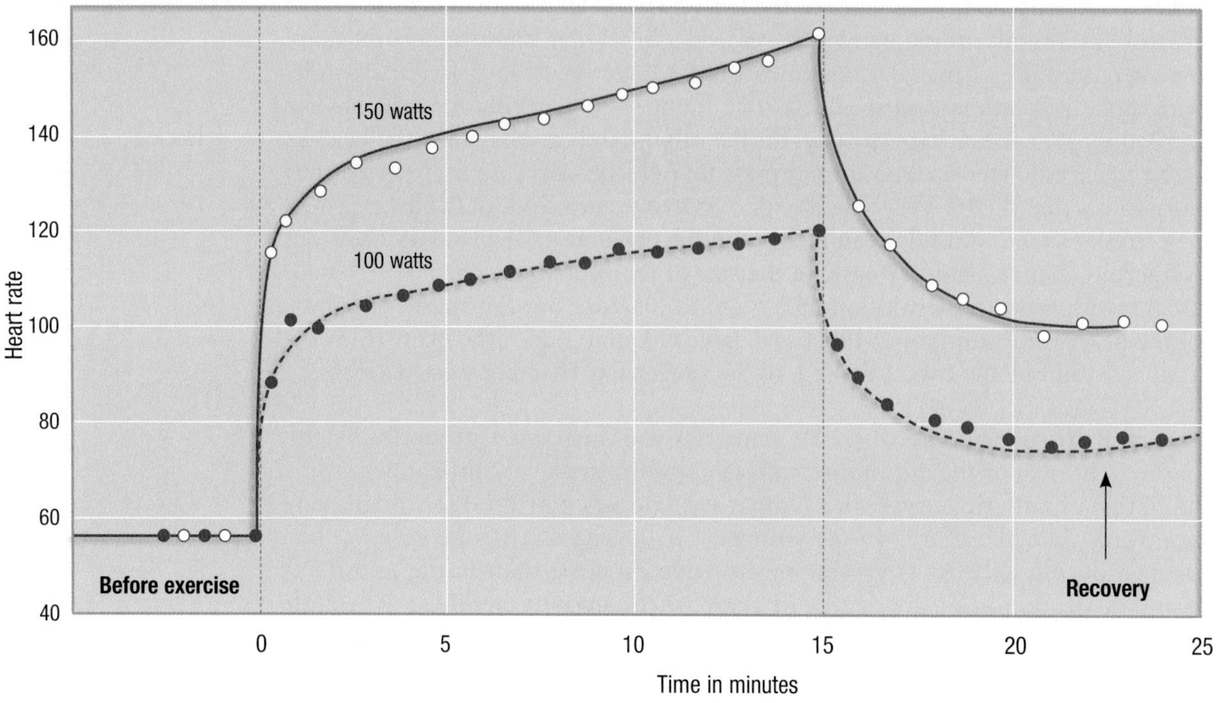

involve rapid contractions alternating with relaxations (such as running or cycling). During dynamic exercise, large increases in heart rate may occur. These different heart rate responses occur for two reasons:

1. As discussed earlier in this chapter, venous return to the heart is largely dependent on the pumping action of the muscles and on the decrease in intrathoracic pressure that occurs during the inspiration portion of the breathing cycle. Static exercises, when compared with dynamic ones, decrease venous return by eliminating the pumping action of the working muscles and increasing the intrathoracic pressure.
2. The heart rate is proportional to the workload per unit of time, and slow, sustained contractions usually do not result in a workload that is sufficient to cause a large increase in heart rate.

exercise intensity

Intensity of the exercise. The intensity of exercise is the most important factor affecting the heart rate during that exercise. **Exercise intensity** refers to the workload of an exercise—in other words, how strenuous an exercise is. It is described as the number of foot-pounds (or kilogram-meters) of work per minute expended in an exercise. Since Work = Force x Distance, in a simple exercise such as bench-stepping, the workload (or intensity) may be increased by increasing the height of the bench, increasing the rate of stepping, or increasing both. Increasing the height and/or rate of stepping increases the distance per unit of time. The force could be increased by having the subject carry a weight. All of these factors increase the intensity of the exercise.

Duration of the exercise. If a moderate workload is maintained over a considerable period of time, a secondary increase in heart rate takes place after the plateau has been attained and held. This increase can best be explained in terms of fatigue of the skeletal musculature. As a muscle tires and fatigue progresses, more motor units are recruited, which results in a greater metabolic demand for the same workload. The heart rate must then increase in order to meet these demands. This secondary increase is usually progressive and continues until exhaustion ends the exercise.

Effects of Training on the Heart

Heart rate

As a result of training, both the resting heart rate and the heart rate for a given submaximal exercise load decrease (Table 5.1).[8,9] The slower resting heart rate appears to be a result of an increase in the parasympathetic (vagal) inhibition of the SA node, whereas the slower exercise heart rate more likely results from a decrease in the sympathetic drive.[5,7]

Stroke volume

A preponderance of evidence indicates that the increased maximum cardiac output in athletes is due largely to an increase in stroke volume. This is not to say that the immediate adjustment to exercise, which was discussed earlier, is the result of an increased stroke volume. During continuous, moderate-intensity exercise, heart rate increases and stroke volume decreases, which results in a stable cardiac output (Figure 5.6). The maximum stroke volume increase seems to be a long-term effect caused by the increased contractility of the trained heart.[4]

As discussed above, exercise-induced hypertrophy of the heart may result in greater stroke volume. The increased stroke volume may result from either an increased EDV or an increased cardiac muscle mass, or both, depending on the type of exercise. Both an increased EDV and an increased cardiac muscle mass would have the effect of increasing the stroke volume. Generally speaking, sports requiring dynamic endurance effort (such as running, swimming, and cycling) tend to produce left ventricular dilation without marked left ventricular hypertrophy, whereas activities requiring heavy isometric effort (such as weight lifting) increase left ventricular wall thickness and mass. Many sports, such as football, wrestling, and skiing, have both an endurance component and an isometric component and therefore have the potential to increase both EDV and cardiac muscle mass.

The cardiac reserve capacity

During intense exercise, when the demands of the tissues are greatly increased, the heart utilizes three main mechanisms in order to meet those demands: the reserve of

Changes in cardiovascular function following endurance training. **table 5.1**

	AT REST	DURING SUBMAXIMAL EXERCISE	DURING MAXIMAL EXERCISE
Heart rate	↓	↓	slight ↓
Stroke volume	↑	↑	↑
Cardiac output	no Δ	no Δ or slight ↓	↑
Heart size	↑	↑	↑
Blood volume	↑	↑	↑
Total hemoglobin	↑	↑	↑
Skeletal muscle capillary density	↑	↑	↑

figure 5.6 Graphic representation of the short-term changes in heart rate, stroke volume, and cardiac output during continuous, moderate-intensity exercise.

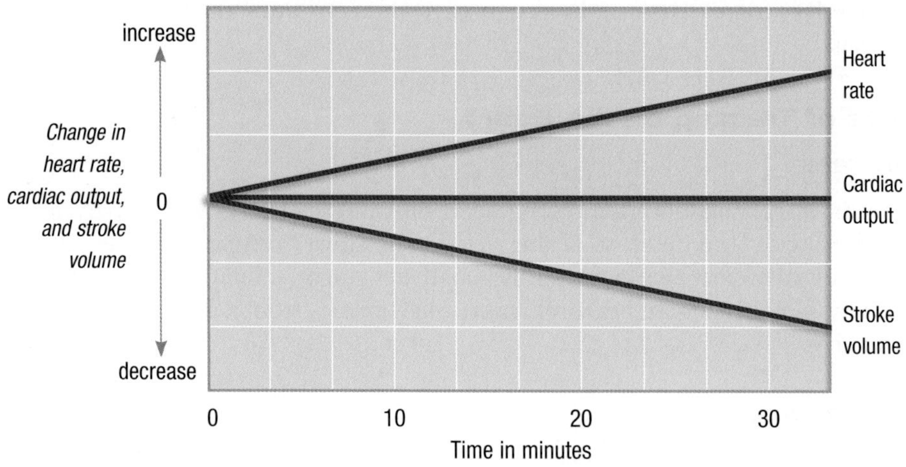

heart rate, the stroke volume reserve, and the oxygen level in the blood. Together, the first two mechanisms are referred to as the **cardiac reserve.**

cardiac reserve

Reserve of heart rate. The first mechanism is the **reserve of heart rate,** which allows the heart rate to increase from its resting value of approximately 70 to 80 bpm to a rate of 170 to 180 bpm, resulting in a cardiac output 2 to 2.5 times the resting value. Although the heart rate can exceed 180 bpm, the cardiac output does not increase at these rates, because the stroke volume begins to decline as a result of the decreased diastolic filling time.

reserve of heart rate

Stroke volume reserve. The second mechanism is the **stroke volume reserve,** which comes into play only at very high exercise intensities. It involves two methods for increasing the stroke volume:

stroke volume reserve

1. Increasing the strength of the cardiac contraction
2. Increasing the filling pressure and possibly the distensibility of the ventricles

Oxygen level in the blood. The third mechanism for supplying the working tissues with the additional oxygen they require during extreme exercise is the greater extraction of oxygen from the blood that occurs during strenuous exercise. The level of oxygen in the blood supplying the muscles is approximately 19 mL per 100 mL of blood. At rest, only about 5 to 6 mL per 100 mL of blood is extracted, whereas during extreme exercise 16 to 17 mL of oxygen per 100 mL of blood may be extracted. This increased ability for the working muscle to extract oxygen provides a mechanism other than increase in cardiac output for the body to meet the demands of intense exercise.

THE BLOOD VESSELS

Anatomy

The anatomical differences among the various types of blood vessels (aorta, arteries, arterioles, capillaries, venules, veins), like those of most tissues, reflect their roles within the system. The aorta and the large arteries contain a large number of elastic fibers so that the vessels can distend during systole and recoil during diastole. This is important in preventing extreme changes in blood pressure during the cardiac cycle and helps to keep the blood flowing toward the periphery. The arterioles are very muscular and serve as **resistance vessels.** This means that their muscularity allows them to resist the pressure of the blood as it flows through them, resulting in a rather precipitous drop in blood pressure and damping of the pressure pulsations that are so noticeable in the arteries. This drop in pressure and damping of pressure pulsations is critical for the protection of the capillaries, which are very thin walled (one cell thick) and therefore extremely fragile. Too much pressure in a capillary can have devastating consequences, especially in the brain, where a ruptured capillary can result in a stroke.

resistance vessels

The venules and the veins serve as the collecting vessels, draining the various tissues of the body. Systemic veins are very distensible and therefore act as adjustable reservoirs for blood. The smooth muscle within the walls of veins contracts in response to nervous and hormonal stimulation, reducing the amount of blood held in these vessels and shunting it toward the heart for redistribution. During exercise, for example, blood is shunted from the large veins of the abdomen toward the heart and then to the capillaries of the working skeletal muscle.

Hemodynamics: Principles Governing Blood Flow

Pressure

Blood flows through the vessels of the circulatory system because of differences in pressure. It flows from a point of high pressure (the left ventricle of the heart) to a point of low pressure (the right atrium of the heart). The difference in pressure between the two points is called the **pressure gradient.** This pressure gradient serves as the driving force for blood flow through the circulatory system.

pressure gradient

Flow

The amount of blood flowing to the various organs each minute is referred to as **blood flow.** The distribution of blood flowing to individual tissues is related to (1) the weight of the tissue, (2) the activity level of the tissue, and (3) the amount of heat dissipation required in certain tissues such as the skin. The approximate blood flow values for individual tissues during rest and exercise are given in Table 5.2.

blood flow

table 5.2 Distribution of blood to systemic tissues at rest and during heavy exercise.

	REST		EXERCISE	
	$L \cdot min^{-1}$	% of total	$L \cdot min^{-1}$	% of total
Brain	0.70	14.0	0.70	2.8
Cardiac muscle	0.25	5.0	0.75	3.0
Kidney	1.00	20.0	0.60	2.4
Liver	1.25	25.0	0.75	3.0
Skeletal muscle	1.00	20.0	20.00	80.0
Skin	0.50	10.0	2.00	8.0
Other	0.30	6.0	0.20	0.8
Total flow	5.00	100.0	25.00	100.0

Obviously, larger tissues, as well as tissues with greater metabolic activity, require greater blood flow. During exercise, the blood flow requirements of the heart and skeletal muscles increase as their metabolism increases. Muscle tissue has the greatest range of metabolic activity of any tissue. During heavy exercise the metabolic activity level is 40 to 50 times that of the resting level. The skin also receives greater blood flow during exercise so that the heat produced by the working muscles can be dissipated.

Resistance

resistance

viscosity

Resistance may be thought of as the sum of the forces that oppose blood flow. Factors such as the viscosity of the fluid (blood), the length of the vessel, and the diameter of the vessel affect resistance and, in turn, affect flow. **Viscosity** refers to the stickiness and thickness of the blood. The more viscous the blood, the slower the flow. For example, molasses, which is very viscous, flows much slower than water. The same is true for blood with an increased hematocrit, or number of red blood cells.

The length of the vessel affects flow because flow is slowest along the vessel wall, where there is the greatest frictional resistance, and the longer the vessel, the more vessel wall there is. This is a variable that ordinarily doesn't change, but it helps explain the differences in resistance to flow among various areas of the body. For example, the resistance through the pulmonary circulation is much less than that of the systemic circulation, because the pulmonary vessels are so much shorter.

The most practically relevant factor affecting resistance and flow is vessel diameter. Small changes in vessel diameter have profound effects on blood flow, and vessel diameter can be altered to meet the needs of the body. Both sympathetic nerves, which innervate the smooth muscle within the vessel walls, and circulating factors such as hormones and blood gases control the diameter of vessels, thereby controlling the blood flow to the tissues.

figure 5.7 The microcirculation.

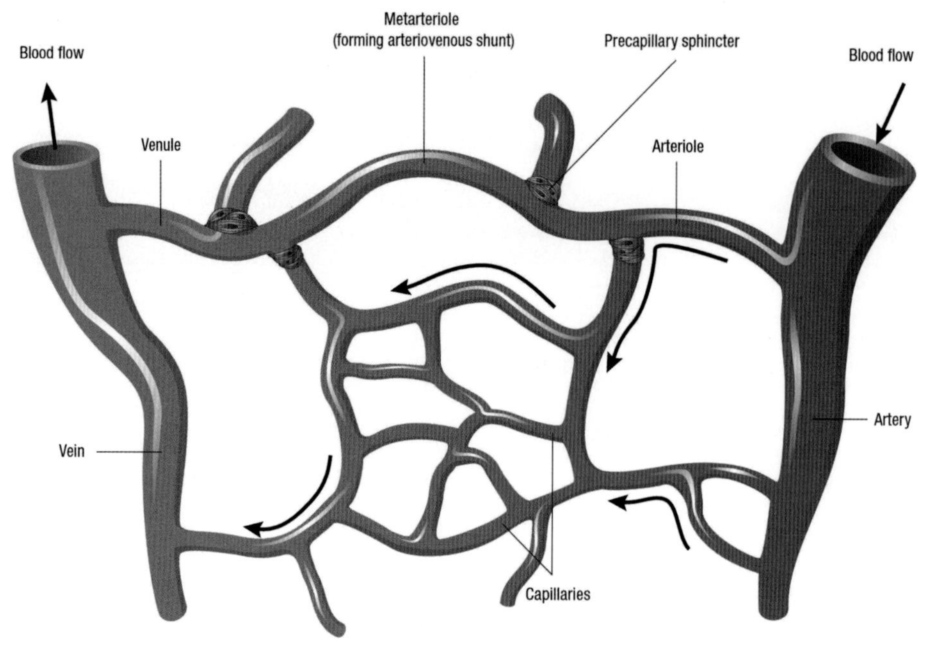

Microcirculation

The *microcirculation* is a well-organized network in which the arterioles give rise to the **metarterioles** (Figure 5.7). The metarterioles act as major thoroughfares or preferential channels through tissues, and they remain open even during resting conditions. Eventually they join a collecting venule. The true capillaries are tubes made of a single layer of endothelium. Therefore, they have no smooth muscle. True capillaries arise from metarterioles via a precapillary sphincter that closes down the true capillaries during resting conditions and relaxes to open them during muscle activity to allow for an increase in circulation. The greater a tissue's potential for high metabolic activity, the greater the ratio of true capillaries, which nourish the tissue, to metarterioles.

metarterioles

Another alternative route for blood flow is by way of **arteriovenous anastomoses (AV shunts)** that form a short and direct connection between (1) small arteries and veins, (2) arterioles and venules, and (3) metarterioles and venules. These "shunts" are prevalent in the extremities, where they function as part of a heat-loss mechanism during exercise or when the environmental temperature rises. They contain smooth muscle that is under sympathetic nervous control and can dilate to allow more blood to collect in the veins, which are closer to the surface than the arteries.

arteriovenous anastomoses (AV shunts)

Blood Distribution

Blood flow to the tissues is controlled by changes in the diameter of the small arteries and arterioles. These changes in diameter occur by way of two mechanisms: nervous regulation and chemical regulation. Since the main function of the small arteries and arterioles is to dilate or constrict to control the resistance to flow, they are properly referred to as the resistance vessels. The walls of the veins, although much thinner, also contain smooth muscle and, therefore, can also actively change their diameters. Changes in the venous wall tension do not have any great effect on resistance to flow, but they are important in altering the capacity of the postcapillary system. Thus, veins are important in determining the rate of return flow to the heart and may be referred to as **capacitance vessels.**

capacitance vessels

Nervous regulation

The sympathetic nervous system governs all blood flow to the skeletal muscles. Two types of sympathetic nerves are involved: (1) sympathetic adrenergic, which cause vasoconstriction, and (2) sympathetic cholinergic, which cause vasodilation. Normally, the vessels supplying the skeletal muscles exhibit sympathetic tone. This tone means that there is a certain degree of vasoconstriction. The amount of blood flow to the muscles can be increased either by decreasing the degree of sympathetic adrenergic activity or by increasing the sympathetic cholinergic activity of the nerves controlling the smooth muscle of the vessels supplying the skeletal muscles. The sympathetic cholinergics appear to be most important in increasing blood flow to the muscles in emotional situations and immediately before an exercise bout, in anticipation of skeletal muscle activity. During exercise, however, changes in blood flow appear to be a result of decreased sympathetic adrenergic activity. The release of vasoconstrictor tone in the active tissues, with concomitant vasoconstriction in less active tissues, such as the skin and viscera, results in greater blood flow to the working muscles. The arterioles and venules, which have nerves supplying stimuli, play an important role in regulating the amount of blood flowing through the tissues. Other vessels of the microcirculation, such as the metarterioles and precapillary sphincters, are not innervated and, therefore, rely on chemical changes to alter their diameters.

RESEARCH

Exercise and endothelium function

The layer of epithelial cells that lines the blood vessels is called the endothelium. This layer of cells plays a major role in the control of vascular homeostasis. Normal endothelial function is critical in maintaining the balance between vasodilation and vasoconstriction, and any upset in this balance can result in damage to vessel walls. Endothelial dysfunction is correlated with arterial stiffness and appears to be a key contributor to atherosclerotic disease.

Gerasimos et al.* investigated the acute effects of continuous moderate-intensity aerobic exercise and high-intensity interval aerobic exercise on the function of the endothelium, as well as stiffness of central and peripheral arteries. Twenty healthy males (average age: 23 years) were subjects for the study. The subjects performed two exercise sessions: (1) 30 minutes of cycle ergometry at 50 percent of aerobic max and (2) a total of 30 minutes of interval cycle ergometry at aerobic max. Flow-mediated dilation of the brachial artery was utilized to determine endothelial function, carotid femoral pulse wave velocity was utilized to determine central aortic stiffness, and femoral tibial pulse wave velocity was utilized to determine peripheral arterial stiffness. Each measurement was done both before and immediately after each exercise session. Although no significant differences between these two modes of exercise were found for any of the parameters measured, both modes of exercise resulted in significant improvements in both flow-mediated dilation of the brachial artery and peripheral artery stiffness. The authors concluded that both continuous moderate-intensity aerobic exercise and high-intensity interval aerobic exercise significantly improved endothelial function, and this may explain the cardioprotective effects of exercise in deterring the progression of atherosclerosis in peripheral arteries.

*Gerasimos, S., Athanasiou, D., Gerasimos, T., Stasinaki, A., Tourikis, P., Dimitropoulos, E., Tsouroulas, S., Gouliopoulos, N., Oikonomou, E., Zaromitidou, M., Mourouzis, K., Tsalamandris, S., Kokkou, E., Stefanadis, C. I., and Tousoulis, D. The impact of different types of aerobic exercise on endothelial function and arterial stiffness. *J. Am. Coll. Cardiol.* 65 (10S): 1199–1208, 2015.

Chemical regulation

Chemical changes that result from an increase in metabolic activity also play a role in increasing blood flow to the active tissues. The rise in lactate and CO_2 levels and the fall in oxygen level that occur during metabolic activity cause vasodilation of the vessels of the microcirculation. Because they are not innervated, the metarterioles and precapillary sphincters rely on this type of chemical regulation to adjust the resistance. This local mechanism can have a potent effect on the flow through the microcirculation, overriding more centrally mediated vasoconstrictor stimuli. During exercise, nervous regulation seems to close down, to a large extent, the circulation to inactive tissues, while the chemical regulatory mechanism opens the precapillary sphincters of the microcirculation so that greater flow is provided through the true capillaries, which serve the metabolic needs of the active muscle tissue.

Blood Pressure

It is important to study blood pressure (BP) because it is the driving force for the movement of blood through the circulatory system. It is also important to consider the dangers of hypertension (high BP) as a determinant in such serious health problems as heart attacks, strokes, and kidney disease. Several factors, including age (Figure 5.8), gender, emotional state, time of day, and body position, affect blood pressure.

Measurement of blood pressure

blood pressure
systolic pressure
diastolic pressure

Blood pressure is defined as the pressure during systole (**systolic pressure**) over the pressure during diastole (**diastolic pressure**). The most common method of measur-

Range of systemic arterial BP as a function of age. figure 5.8

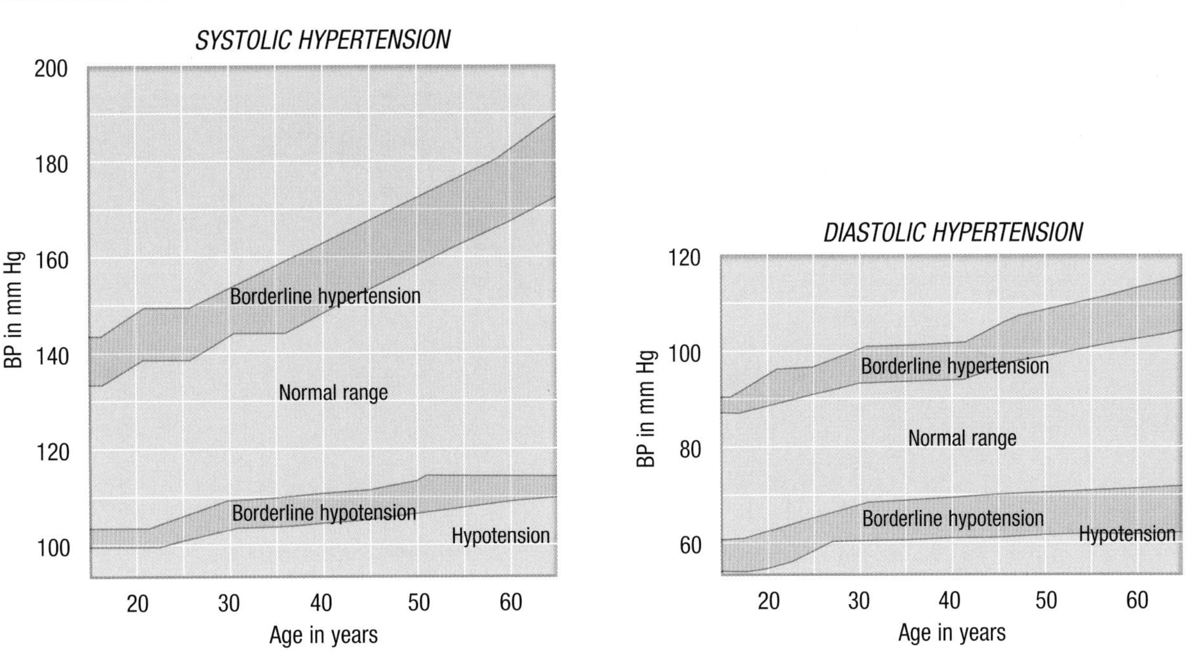

ing BP involves using a **sphygmomanometer,** which is a pressure cuff and mercury or aneroid manometer. The sphygmomanometer cuff is applied to the upper arm, as the subject sits comfortably, so that the cuff is approximately at heart level. First, the cuff is inflated, compressing the brachial artery to the point that blood flow is pinched off and there is no sound. Next, a valve is turned to allow the cuff to deflate slowly, reducing the pressure on the brachial artery. When the cuff pressure equals the systolic pressure, turbulent blood flow can be heard, and the pressure at which this occurs is recorded as the systolic pressure. When the cuff pressure equals the diastolic pressure, the turbulent flow ceases, and the pressure at which the silence occurs is recorded as the diastolic pressure. See **Chapter 5 Lab** on measuring BP.

sphygmomanometer

Blood pressure changes during exercise

During exercise, blood flow increases due to the increased cardiac output, and the peripheral resistance is reduced by the vasodilation of the microcirculation. The balance between these two factors results in the BP change during exercise. Clearly, the resulting arterial BP is considerably influenced by the type and intensity of the exercise and by the physical condition of the subject.

In rhythmic exercise that involves moderate to strenuous workloads, the typical response is an elevation in systolic pressure with little, if any, elevation in diastolic pressure. Figure 5.9 shows a typical response for a young male. In static, or isometric, exercise, where the glottis (the structure that closes the top of the trachea) is closed to prevent expiration, the situation is quite different. The intrathoracic pressure increases from 80 to 200 mm Hg or more. This dramatic increase in intrathoracic pressure decreases the venous return to the right atrium and puts a greater load on the heart. The resultant increase in BP can be dangerous in certain populations. Therefore, isometric contractions should be avoided in any exercise situation in which high cardiac workloads are undesirable, as in cardiac rehabilitation exercise or in conditioning programs for older adults.

figure 5.9 The typical time course of the arterial BP response to rest–exercise–recovery in a healthy young male.

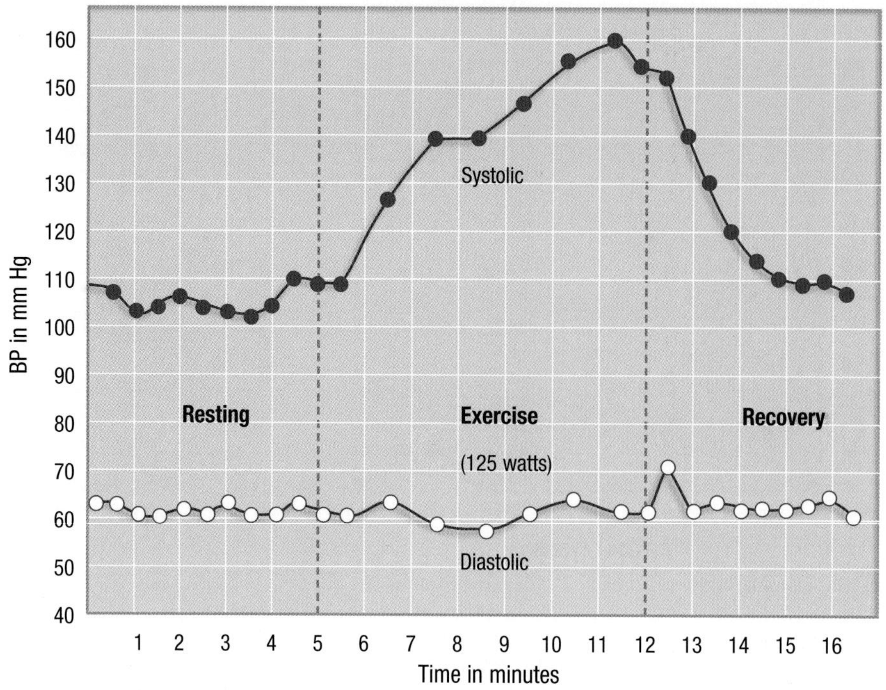

summary

The cardiovascular system includes the heart and the blood vessels, which work in concert to supply blood to all parts of the body. The heart serves as a pump, whereas the vessels serve as a dynamic pipeline. Both the heart and the blood vessels are affected by the autonomic nervous system. Generally speaking, the heart rate speeds up in response to sympathetic stimulation and slows down in response to parasympathetic stimulation. The stroke volume of the heart is affected by many factors, the most important of which is the end diastolic volume, or amount of blood in the ventricles at the end of diastole. The greater the venous return to the heart, the greater the stroke volume. The size of the heart also affects its contractile strength. In general, there are two types of cardiac hypertrophy, non-pathologic and pathologic, which affect cardiac function in different ways.

The blood vessels have anatomical differences that reflect their roles within the cardiovascular system. The arteries are more muscular to withstand the high pressure created by the left ventricle, whereas the veins are thin walled and serve as adjustable reservoirs for blood. The principles governing the movement of blood through the vessels include pressure, flow, and resistance. Changes in these factors determine how much blood gets from one area of the body to another.

Exercise affects the cardiovascular system in different ways, depending on the type, intensity, and duration of the exercise. Long-term exercise training generally results in a slower heart rate and a greater stroke volume, especially exercise with a strong endurance component. The blood pressure is also affected by exercise and should be monitored carefully in older individuals or those undergoing cardiac rehabilitation.

questions for review

1. Where does a wave of excitation originate in the heart and how is it transmitted through the heart?
2. Describe the changes in atrial and ventricular pressure during a normal cardiac cycle.
3. What is cardiac output and how is it measured?
4. Discuss the effect of the parasympathetic and sympathetic fibers on heart rate.
5. Discuss the Frank–Starling law of the heart and its implications for exercise.
6. What factors affect stroke volume? Why?
7. What is a heart murmur? What effect does it have on a person's capacity for exercise?
8. How does heart rate respond to static exercise? Dynamic exercise?
9. What are the effects of training on heart rate? Stroke volume? Cardiac reserve capacity?
10. How is blood pressure affected by exercise?
11. What causes the increase in cardiac output in elite athletes?

student companion website

For further review of this book's chapters and for test preparation, visit the book's website, **www.hhpcommunities.com/exercisephysiology**, to take practice quizzes, review the vocabulary terms, use the study guide, and view the digital image bank.

references

1. Cooke, A., Kavussanu, M., McIntyre, D., and Ring, C. Psychological, muscular and kinematic factors mediate performance under pressure. *Psychophysiology* 47: 1109–1118, 2010.
2. Cooke, A., Kavussanu, M., Gallicchio, G., Willoughby, A., McIntyre, D., and Ring, C. Preparation for action: psychophysiological activity preceding a motor skill as a function of expertise, performance outcome, and psychological pressure. *Psychophysiology* 51: 374–384, 2014.
3. Huonker, M., Konig, D., and Keul, J. Assessment of left ventricular dimensions and functions in athletes and sedentary subjects at rest and during exercise using echocardiography, Doppler sonography and radionuclide ventriculography. *Int. J. Sports Med.* 3: S173–179, 1996.
4. Jensen-Urstad, M., Bouvier, F., Nejat, M., Saltin, B., and Brodin, L. A. Left ventricular function in endurance runners during exercise. *Acta Physiol. Scand.* 164: 167–172, 1998.
5. Lucini, D., Vigo, C., Tosi, F., Toninelli, G., Badilini, F., and Pagani, M. Assessing autonomic response to repeated bouts of exercise below and above respiratory threshold: insight from dynamic analysis of RR variability. *Eur. J. Appl. Physiol.* 114: 1269–1279, 2014.
6. Masson, C. L., and Gilbert, D. G. Cardiovascular and mood responses to quantified doses of cigarette smoke in oral contraceptive users and nonusers. *J. Behav. Med.* 22: 589–604, 1999.
7. Mizuno, M., Kawada, T., Kamiya, A., Miyamoto, T., Shimizu, S., Shishido, T., Smith, S. A., and Sugimachi, M. Exercise training augments the dynamic heart rate response to vagal but not sympathetic stimulation in rats. *Am. J. Physiol. Regul. Integr. Comp. Physiol.* 300: R969–R977, 2011.
8. Munisekhar, K., Muralidhar, M. V., Venkatachalam, M., and Hemalatha, D. Comparison of heart rate and blood pressure changes during walking and running before and after training in healthy adult women. *Int. J. Physiother. Res.* 2: 537–541, 2014.
9. Ozdal, M., Daglioglu, O., and Demir, T. Effect of aerobic training program on some circulatory and respiratory parameters of field hockey players. *Int. J. Acad. Res.* 5: 97–103, 2013.

Measuring Blood Pressure

BACKGROUND

In addition to measuring heart rate, physical fitness assessments may involve the measurement of another basic vital sign: blood pressure (BP). BP is commonly defined as a measurement of the force of the blood acting against the vessel walls during and between heartbeats.[2] The pressure exerted against the vessels during a heartbeat (systole) is called the *systolic blood pressure,* while the pressure recorded between heartbeats (diastole) is called the *diastolic blood pressure.* The BP measurement is a combination of both the systolic and diastolic pressure and is usually written as "systolic/diastolic" (e.g., 120/80). BP is usually measured in units of millimeters of mercury (mm Hg). A common and normal BP measurement would be written as 120/80 mm Hg.

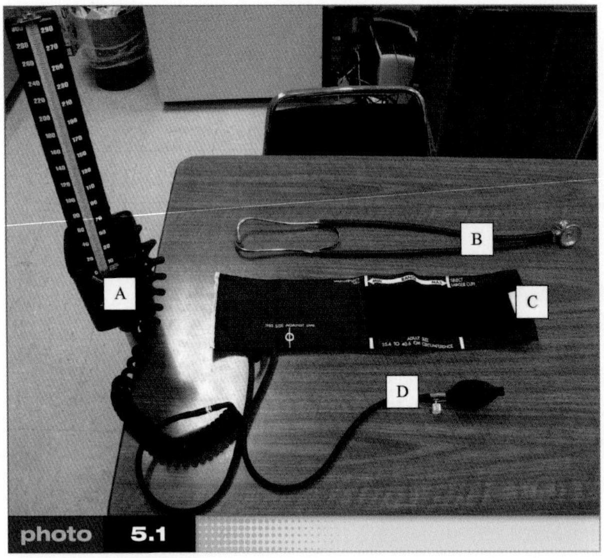

photo 5.1

A mercury sphygmomanometer. (A) Mercury column with pressure gradients listed from 0 to 300 mm Hg, (B) stethoscope, (C) cuff, (D) air bulb and pressure release valve for inflating and deflating the cuff.

photo 5.2

An automated sphygmomanometer.

Sounds are emitted as a result of the pressure exerted against the vessel walls, and these sounds are called Korotkoff sounds. The detection and disappearance of Korotkoff sounds when external pressure is applied provides the basis of traditional BP assessments. Sphygmomanometry is the most common and clinically acceptable technique to measure BP.[3] The American Heart Association regards the mercury sphygmomanometer (photo 5.1) as the gold standard measurement device for clinical BP assessment.[3] However, other devices, such as aneroid (pressure gauge) and automated (photo 5.2) sphygmomanometers, are increasingly common, but these may be more prone to errors than mercury sphygmomanometers.[3] Nevertheless, with either mercury or aneroid sphygmomanometry, auscultation with a stethoscope placed over the brachial artery is necessary to hear the Korotkoff sounds. Therefore, sphygmomanometry is commonly called the "cuff," "auscultation," or "Korotkoff" technique.[3]

The premise of sphygmomanometry with auscultation is that the brachial artery is occluded with an air-inflated cuff placed around the arm (just distal to the shoulder). The amount of pressure used to inflate the cuff to occlude brachial artery blood flow should be greater than the individual's systolic BP.[3] As the cuff is deflated slowly, blood will eventually squeeze past the occlusion point (cuff) at a pressure that is equal to the systolic BP. A stethoscope is placed over the brachial artery distal to the cuff to auscultate the sounds made by the blood (i.e., Korotkoff sounds).

The cuff pressure at which the first audible Korotkoff sounds occur while the cuff is deflating is denoted as the systolic BP, and the cuff pressure of the last audible Korotkoff sounds is recorded as the diastolic BP.

BP assessments are important for detecting hypertension (Table L5.1) and monitoring the antihypertensive effects of an exercise program or dietary changes.[4] BP measurements are most often performed at rest (before exercise). BP can be assessed during and after exercise; however, these techniques require advanced skills for measurement and interpretation and will not be covered in this context.[1] The BP measurement technique described in this laboratory focuses on resting BP to evaluate the presence of hypertension and, consequently, the readiness of individuals to undergo other physical fitness tests. For example, if successive BP measurements indicate the possibility of hypertension (Table L5.1) in an individual, then physical fitness testing may have to be postponed until medical clearance is granted by a physician. For more information on pre-exercise health status evaluations, see the Chapter 1 Lab.

TERMS & ABBREVIATIONS

- ☐ auscultation = listening to sounds arising from organs to aid in diagnosis and treatment
- ☐ BP = blood pressure, measured in millimeters of mercury (mm Hg). BP is defined as a measurement of the force of the blood acting against the vessel walls during and between heartbeats.
- ☐ systolic blood pressure = the pressure exerted against the vessels during a heartbeat (systole)
- ☐ diastolic blood pressure = the pressure recorded between heartbeats (diastole)
- ☐ Korotkoff sounds = the sounds emitted as a result of the pressure exerted against the vessel walls; these sounds provide the basis of traditional BP assessments.
- ☐ sphygmomanometer = the instrument used to measure BP in an artery, consisting of a pressure gauge and a rubber cuff, used with a stethoscope. Mercury and aneroid sphygmomanometers are available.
- ☐ hypertension = an abnormally high BP reading (≥140/90)

Classification of hypertension (JNC*–7). **table L5.1**

BP CLASSIFICATION	SYSTOLIC BP (mm Hg)	DIASTOLIC BP (mm Hg)
Normal	< 120	< 80
Prehypertensive	120–139	80–89
Stage 1 hypertension	140–159	90–99
Stage 2 hypertension	≥ 160	≥ 100

*Joint National Committee on Prevention, Evaluation, and Treatment of High Blood Pressure.

Source: JNC 7: A. V. Chobanian, G. L. Bakris, H. R. Black, et al. Seventh Report of the Joint National Committee on prevention, detection, evaluation, and treatment of high blood pressure. *Hypertension* 42: 1206–1252, 2003.

PROCEDURES

Mercury Sphygmomanometry (Auscultation Technique)[3,4]

1. To prepare for a resting BP assessment, have the subject relax and comfortably sit upright with the legs uncrossed and the back and arms supported (photo 5.3). All clothing that covers the location of the cuff should be removed. The room temperature should be comfortable (not hot or cold), the environment should be free from distracting background noises, the subject's bladder should be relieved prior to the test, and no talking should be allowed by the subject or the tester during the test. Resting BP should always be taken prior to exercise, and caffeine, alcohol, and nicotine should be avoided for at least 30 minutes prior to any BP measurement.
2. Since various cuff sizes are available, determine the appropriate cuff size by measuring the arm circumference with a tape measure (photo 5.4) at 50 percent of the distance from the shoulder to the elbow. Once the arm circumference has been recorded, determine the appropriate BP cuff size using Table L5.2.[3]
3. Place the cuff around the left or right arm so that the cuff is level with the heart. To do this, it is important to position the subject so that the arm is resting in the same horizontal plane as the heart. BP measurements taken with the arm hanging below or raised above the heart level will be inaccurate.[3] In addition, most cuffs have an identification line that is to be placed over the brachial artery. This feature allows the air bladder within the cuff to be positioned directly over the brachial artery. This is important for the occlusion of the artery during cuff inflation. Position the cuff so that the bottom edge of the cuff is approximately one inch (2.5 cm) above the antecubital space (elbow crease).
4. Once seated and relaxed, allow the subject to rest for at least five minutes prior to the first BP measurement.
5. With the subject's palm facing up, place the stethoscope head in the antecubital space firmly but not hard enough to indent the skin. It is recommended that the tester use his or her dominant hand to control the air bulb and the inflation/deflation of the cuff, while the nondominant hand should be used to hold the stethoscope (see photo 5.3; the tester is right-handed).
6. Ensure that the mercury column (or aneroid pressure gauge) is easily readable by the tester. In photo 5.3, the mercury column is visible and at eye level for the tester. For aneroid pressure gauges, it is recommended to place the gauge in the tester's lap or clip it to the cuff to enable a quick and accurate pressure reading.
7. It is important to avoid contacting the stethoscope head with the air tubes connected to the mercury sphygmomanometer. If the air tubes contact the stethoscope head, the sound may be mistaken for a Korotkoff sound and may result in erroneous BP measurements. Therefore, position the air tubes away from the stethoscope head as much as possible.

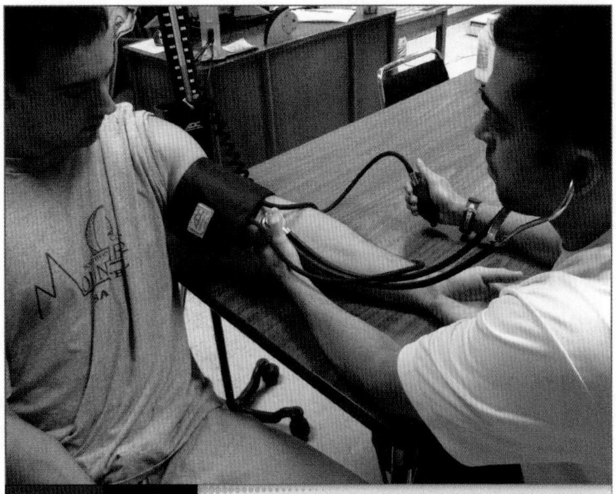

photo 5.3

Example of mercury sphygmomanometry with auscultation by the tester (right) controlling the air bulb for inflation/deflation of the cuff while monitoring the mercury column (upper left).

photo 5.4

A Gullick tape.

Determining cuff dimension using arm circumference. **table L5.2**

SIZE	MEASURED CUFF DIMENSIONS	MEASURED ARM CIRCUMFERENCE
Small adult	12 x 22 cm	22–26 cm
Adult	16 x 30 cm	27–34 cm
Large adult	16 x 36 cm	35–44 cm

8. Once the cuff, stethoscope, and sphygmomanometer have been properly placed, make sure the air release valve is closed on the air bulb and then quickly inflate the cuff either to 160 mm Hg or to 20 mm Hg above the anticipated systolic BP.
9. Upon reaching the maximum inflation pressure, carefully turn the air release valve counterclockwise to release the cuff pressure. The rate of pressure release should be approximately 2 to 3 mm Hg per second.
10. While the cuff is deflating, listen carefully for the Korotkoff sounds. Record the systolic BP as an even number to the nearest 2 mm Hg where the first Korotkoff sound is heard. Record the diastolic BP as an even number to the nearest 2 mm Hg where the last Korotkoff sound is heard. Usually, Korotkoff sounds are described as sharp tapping noises that are similar to tapping the stethoscope head (bell) gently with a finger. After the Korotkoff sounds have disappeared, observe the mercury column for another 10 to 20 mm Hg of deflation to confirm the absence of sounds.
11. When it is confirmed that no more Korotkoff sounds are audible, rapidly deflate and remove the cuff.
12. After a minimum of two minutes of rest, measure BP again using the same technique described above. If the two consecutive measurements of either systolic BP or diastolic BP differ by more than 5 mm Hg, take a third BP measurement. After either two or three consecutive BP measurements, calculate the average systolic and diastolic BP. The average systolic and diastolic BP values should be used as the final scores.

Automated Sphygmomanometry

The American Heart Association recommends that any BP measurement technique other than mercury sphygmomanometry (including automated systems) should be validated prior to being used in practice.[3] Substantial errors in BP measurements and erroneous values may occur in both validated and unvalidated devices, but the probability of errors is reduced with validation.[3]

Most automated sphygmomanometers operate very similarly to the regular auscultation technique described above, except that a stethoscope is not required. Subject positioning and cuff placement are usually the same. Therefore, steps 1–4 and step 12 (above) may be applied. Because individual manufacturers may have different procedures, the manufacturer's directions should be carefully followed for any automated BP assessments. Photo 5.5 shows an automated sphygmomanometer BP assessment.

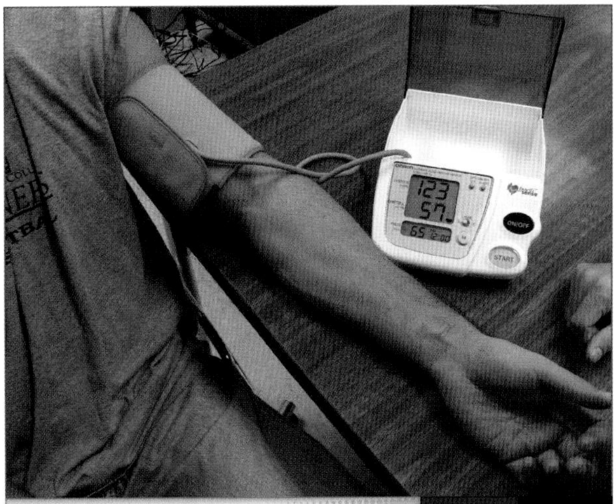

photo 5.5

An automated sphygmomanometer BP measurement.

SAMPLE CALCULATIONS

Gender: Male

Age: 19 years

BLOOD PRESSURE	TRIAL 1	TRIAL 2	TRIAL 3
systolic (mm Hg) =	124	118	118
diastolic (mm Hg) =	72	66	70

Step 1: Calculate the average systolic and diastolic BP values.

systolic: (124 + 118 + 118) ÷ 3 = 120

diastolic: (72 + 66 + 70) ÷ 3 = 69.3

final BP = 120/69.3 mm Hg

Step 2: Classify the final BP measurement using Table L5.1.

A score of 120/69.3 mm Hg would be classified as normal in Table L5.1.

BLOOD PRESSURE FORM — worksheet 5.1

NAME ____________________ DATE ____________

Gender: ____________

Age: ____________

BLOOD PRESSURE:	TRIAL 1	TRIAL 2	TRIAL 3
Systolic (mm Hg)			
Diastolic (mm Hg)			

1. Final resting BP (mm Hg) = ____________
2. Resting BP classification = ____________ (see Table L5.1)

EXTENSION ACTIVITIES — worksheet 5.2

NAME ____________________ DATE ____________

Use the following data with Table L5.1 to answer the questions below.

Gender: Female

Age: 32 years

BLOOD PRESSURE:	TRIAL 1	TRIAL 2	TRIAL 3
Systolic (mm Hg)	136	130	132
Diastolic (mm Hg)	78	84	82

1. Calculate the subject's BP.

   Final resting BP (mm Hg) = ____________

2. Classify the subject's BP based on Table L5.1.

   Resting BP classification = ____________

REFERENCES

1. American College of Sports Medicine. *ACSM's Guidelines for Exercise Testing and Prescription,* 9th edition. Baltimore: Wolters Kluwer/Lippincott Williams & Wilkins, 2014.
2. Beam, W. C., and Adams, G. M. *Exercise Physiology Laboratory Manual,* 7th edition. New York: McGraw-Hill, 2014.
3. Pickering, T. G., Hall, J. E., Appel, L. J., Falkner, B. E., Graves, J., Hill, M. N., Jones, D. W., Kurtz, T., Sheps, S. G., and Roccella, E. J. Recommendations for blood pressure measurement in humans and experimental animals. Part 1: Blood pressure measurement in humans: A statement for professionals from the subcommittee of professional and public education of the American Heart Association Council on high blood pressure research. *Circulation* 111: 697–716, 2005.
4. Ryan, E. D., and Cramer, J. T. Fitness testing protocols and norms. In *NSCA's Essentials of Personal Training,* eds. R. W. Earle and T. R. Baechle, 2nd edition. Champaign, IL: Human Kinetics, 2012, pp. 201–250.

As a result of reading this chapter you will:

Know the structures and functions associated with external respiration.

Understand the factors that control breathing during exercise.

Know the effects of exercise training on pulmonary function.

Understand the basics of gas transport in the blood.

Be aware of factors related to the regulation of acid–base balance.

Understand the primary concepts related to internal respiration.

Respiration 6

key concepts

acid
alkaline reserve
alveolar duct
alveolar ventilation rate
alveolus
anatomical dead space
base
Boyle's law
bronchioles
bronchi
buffer system
coefficient of oxygen utilization
diffusion gradient
dyspnea
erythrocyte
esophagus
eupnea
exercise-induced asthma (EIA)
exercise-induced broncho-spasm (EIB)
exercise-related transient abdominal pain (ETAP)
expiration phase
expiratory reserve volume
external respiration
functional residual capacity
Gay-Lussac's law
globin
glottis

Each cell of every tissue in the human body depends on oxidative metabolism for energy. A specialized respiratory system is necessary to provide the oxygen for metabolism. The respiratory process can be broken down into three component functions:

1. Gas exchange in the lungs, in which the blood in the lung capillaries takes up oxygen and gives up much of its carbon dioxide.
2. Gas transport and distribution from the lungs to the various tissues by the blood.
3. Gas exchange between the blood and cells (such as muscle fibers).

The first process is also referred to as **external respiration** or **pulmonary ventilation;** the third process is referred to as **internal** (or **tissue**) **respiration;** and the second process, gas transport, is the function of the cardiovascular system.

EXTERNAL RESPIRATION

The flow of air proceeds through the nose (or mouth) into the nasal cavity, where it is warmed, humidified, and agitated by striking shell-shaped structures called concha nasalis or **turbinates.** The air then flows through an area of the throat called the **nasopharynx** and past the **glottis,** where the **pharynx** separates into the **trachea** for air conduction and the **esophagus** for the passage of food. The trachea splits into the two chief **bronchi** (singular: bronchus), one going to the left lung and the other to the right lung (Figure 6.1).

The lungs can be considered a system of branching tubes that perform two major functions: conduction of air and external respiration. The conductive portion of the system proceeds from the chief bronchi that branch in the lung root. Subsequent branching of the conductive pathway occurs within the lungs and results in smaller bronchi, which in turn branch into smaller tubes called **bronchioles.** Throughout the repeated branchings, each branching results in a larger total cross-sectional area, as was also the case in the circulatory system. The bronchioles eventually branch into the terminal bronchioles, the last units of the conductive system, which are from 0.5 to 1.0 mm in diameter.

Each terminal bronchiole divides into two respiratory bronchioles, which in turn may divide once more (or even twice). These divisions form **alveolar ducts.** The alveolar ducts may or may not branch, but they eventually terminate in thin-walled sacs called **alveoli** (singular: alveolus). These alveoli, with their supporting structures, are highly vascularized. Thus, the lung unit is considered to consist of the alveolar duct and its subdivisions (alveoli), together with the blood and lymph vessels and the nerve supply. Within the lung unit, only two very thin endothelial layers separate the air in the system from the blood in the capillaries, thus allowing for very efficient diffusion of gases. The total cross-sectional area available for diffusion has been estimated to be between 500 and 1,000 square feet.

turbinates
nasopharynx
glottis
pharynx
trachea
esophagus
bronchi
bronchioles
alveolar ducts
alveoli

Mechanics of Lung Ventilation

The flow of respiratory gas depends on a pressure gradient between the air in the lungs and the ambient (outside) air. For air to flow into the lungs, the pressure within must be lower than atmospheric pressure. This lowering of pressure in the lungs occurs when the diaphragm descends (the muscle fibers contract) and the external and anterior internal intercostal muscles raise the ribs. The diaphragm descends approximately 1.5 cm in normal, quiet respiration and as much as 6 to 10 cm during maximal breathing. Thus, the volume of the lungs is considerably increased during inspiration, largely by virtue of elongation. This increase

The respiratory system, showing the respiratory passages and the function of the alveolus to oxygenate the blood and to remove carbon dioxide. **figure 6.1**

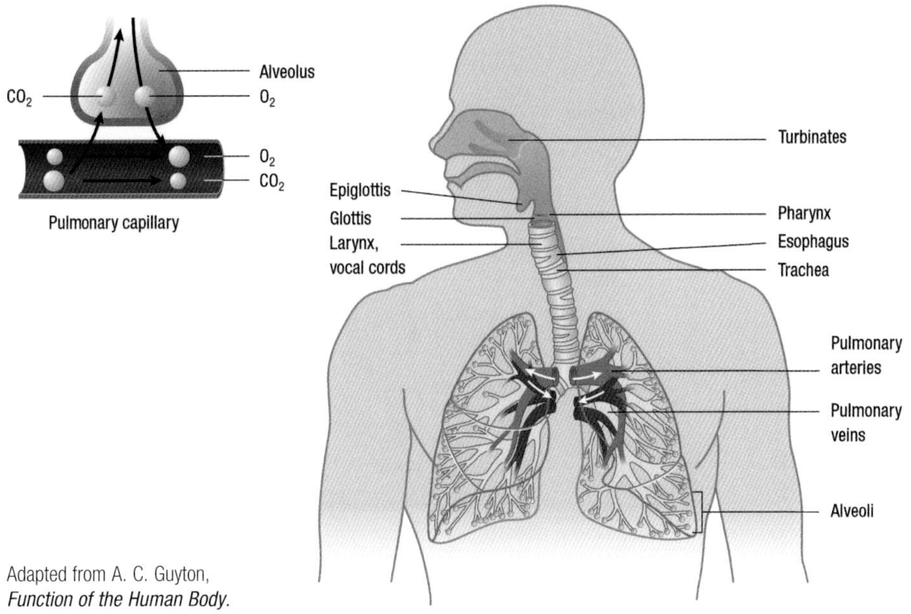

Adapted from A. C. Guyton, *Function of the Human Body.*

in volume results in a temporary lowering of pressure within the lungs so that a pressure gradient exists. The ambient air has the higher pressure and thus moves into the lungs during inspiration.

In the respiratory cycle, the **inspiration phase** is the active phase and is brought about by the active contraction of the primary muscles of respiration (the diaphragm and the intercostals). The **expiration phase** under resting conditions results largely from the elastic recoil of these muscles and associated structures as they snap back to their resting length (see Figure 6.2). Thus the elastic recoil creates a higher-than-atmospheric pressure within the lung, which results in the pressure gradient that moves the air out during expiration.

Ventilation of the alveoli, where the greatest part of the diffusion process occurs, has been attributed to the enlargement of the alveolar ducts (in length and width) without a concomitant enlargement of the alveoli themselves. However, it appears more likely that the alveoli participate proportionately in the overall enlargement during inspiration. This enlargement is about twofold for the alveolar duct and the alveolus. This doubling in volume can result in a 70 percent increase in alveolar area for diffusion.

The description so far holds only for normal resting breathing conditions. During exercise, metabolic demands are greater, and rate and depth of breathing increase. The increased depth of respiration is brought about by the accessory muscles of breathing. In inspiration, greater volume is provided by the scalene and the sternocleidomastoid muscles, which help lift the ribs. In the expiration phase of heavy exercise, the passive elastic recoil of the primary muscles of breathing is greatly aided by the active contraction of the abdominal muscles. The abdominal muscles serve two important mechanical functions: (1) raising the intra-abdominal pressure, which results in greater intrathoracic pressure to aid in expiration, and (2) drawing the lower ribs downward and medially, which helps to push air from the lungs.

key concepts

- heme
- hemoglobin
- Henry's law
- hyperventilation
- hypocapnia
- hypoventilation
- inspiration phase
- inspiratory capacity
- inspiratory reserve volume
- internal respiration
- ischemia
- law of partial pressures
- lung ventilation rate
- nasopharynx
- oxygenation
- oxygen cost of breathing
- oxygen dissociation curve
- pharynx
- pulmonary ventilation
- residual volume
- respiratory center
- second wind
- stitch in the side
- tidal volume
- tissue respiration
- total lung capacity
- trachea
- turbinate
- ventilation equivalent
- vital capacity

www

AACVPR—American Association of Cardiovascular and Pulmonary Rehabilitation
www.aacvpr.org

National Jewish Health
www.nationaljewish.org

figure 6.2 Diagram of inspiration and expiration.

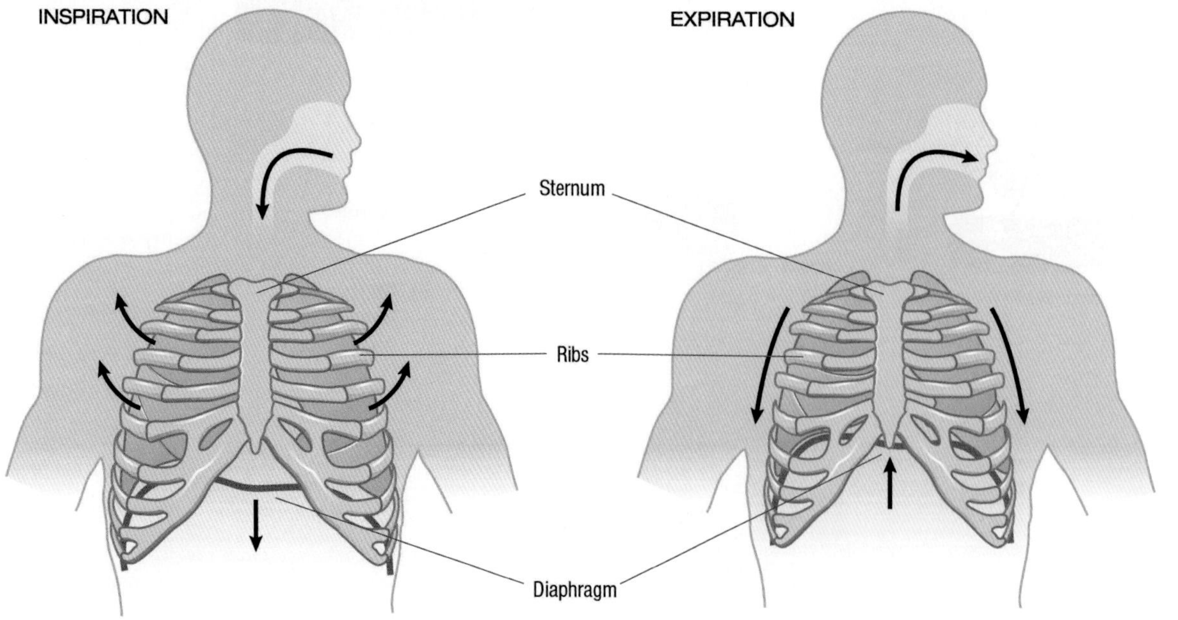

Lung Volumes and Capacities

Lung volumes

Four primary lung volumes are measured. They are independent of each other.

tidal volume

1. **Tidal volume** (approximately 500 mL at rest) reflects the depth of breathing. It is the volume of gas inspired or expired during each respiratory cycle.

inspiratory reserve volume

2. **Inspiratory reserve volume** (approximately 1900–3100 mL) is the maximum amount of gas that can be inspired from the end-tidal (the end of a breath) inspiratory level.

expiratory reserve volume

3. **Expiratory reserve volume** (approximately 800–1200 mL) is the maximum volume of gas that can be expired from the end-tidal expiratory level.

residual volume

4. **Residual volume** (approximately 1000–1200 mL) is the volume of gas remaining in the lungs after a maximal expiration.

Do individuals with large lung volumes perform better during exercise? In general, as long as lung function values are within a normal range, the answer is no! Only in elite athletes is lung function a possible limiting factor to exercise performance. Highly trained endurance athletes have such high cardiac outputs that the lung's ability to oxygenate the blood during maximal exercise may become an important limiting factor.

www
American Lung Association
www.lungusa.org

Lung capacities

Four lung capacities are measured. Each includes at least two of the primary lung volumes.

total lung capacity

1. **Total lung capacity** (approximately 4200–6000 mL) is the amount of gas in the lung after a maximal inspiration. It includes the tidal volume, inspiratory reserve volume, expiratory reserve volume, and residual volume.

2. **Vital capacity** (approximately 3200–4800 mL) is the maximum amount of gas that can be expired with a forceful effort following a maximal inspiration. It includes the tidal volume, inspiratory reserve volume, and expiratory reserve volume.
3. **Inspiratory capacity** (approximately 2400–3600 mL) is the maximum amount of gas that can be inspired from the resting expiratory level. It includes the tidal volume and inspiratory reserve volume.
4. **Functional residual capacity** (approximately 1800–2400 mL) is the amount of gas remaining in the lungs at the resting expiratory level. It includes the expiratory reserve volume and residual volume.

vital capacity

inspiratory capacity

functional residual capacity

Respiratory Control

The rate and depth of respiration must be controlled to maintain homeostasis during varying metabolic demands, ranging from rest to the very vigorous exercise of competitive athletics.

The nerve cells responsible for the automatic and rhythmic innervation of the muscles of respiration lie in the lower brain below the thalamus in the pons and medulla.[1] As a group, these nerve cells are called the **respiratory center.**

respiratory center

The frequency and depth (tidal volume) of breathing adjust to the metabolic demands for oxygen through input to the respiratory center from many sources, including neural input within the brain, neural input from muscles and joints, and humoral (bloodborne) input.[1,3,4,10,20]

Neural input within the brain

Neural input from the motor cortex to the respiratory center is primarily responsible for the elevated ventilation during exercise. The control of ventilation by the motor cortex is sometimes called the "central command" of breathing.[1,4] Neural communication between the motor cortex and respiratory center is also responsible for the unique breathing patterns used during various sports, such as in swimming, and the temporary holding of the breath during sprint running and weight lifting.[1]

In addition to the motor cortex, secondary control of breathing comes from:[1] (1) the hypothalamus, which is sensitive to exercise-induced changes in body temperature; (2) the cerebellum, which passes along feedback from contracting muscles to the respiratory center; and (3) the reticular formation, which is sensitive to central nervous system arousal and facilitates ventilation during exercise.

WWW

National Heart, Lung, and Blood Institute
www.nhlbi.nih.gov.htm

Neural input from muscles and joints

The metabolic state of the muscle fiber affects respiration.[1,20] For example, during heavy exercise, the buildup of lactic acid within the muscle fiber may result in neural input to the respiratory center to increase respiration. In addition, the activation of mechanoreceptors such as muscle spindles, Golgi tendon organs, and joint receptors may respond to expansion of the lungs and chest and send nervous impulses to the respiratory center to increase respiration.

Humoral input

Humoral factors involve chemical activation from substances in the blood that provide input to the respiratory center. For example, specialized cells of the medulla may respond to changes in hydrogen ion concentrations in the medullary interstitial fluid, as well as the effects of acidity (pH) and partial pressure of arterial carbon dioxide changes in the cerebral spinal fluid.

Carotid bodies (located at the bifurcation of the common carotid artery in the neck) also provide neural signals to the respiratory center in response to humoral stimulation.[1] The carotid bodies are stimulated by the effects of changes in the partial pressures of arterial oxygen and carbon dioxide and also by changes in pH. In addition, other peripheral receptors that are sensitive to humoral stimulation and provide input to the respiratory center may exist in the aorta, brachiocephalic artery, right heart, pulmonary artery, and lungs.

Breathing Patterns

Rate and depth

lung ventilation rate

Lung ventilation rate (volume of breathing per minute) is the result of two variable factors: frequency (rate of breathing) and tidal volume (depth of breathing). At rest, the breathing frequency is typically less than 10 breaths • min^{-1}, but it may increase to 30–35 breaths • min^{-1} during maximal exercise. Tidal volume at rest is usually around 500 mL and increases to a maximum of about 2,500 mL. Total lung ventilation averages 7 L • min^{-1} at rest, but it may increase to 150 L • min^{-1} or more during very intense exercise.

alveolar ventilation rate

anatomical dead space

During exercise, it is more efficient to increase tidal volume than breathing frequency to provide the optimal rate of air flow to the alveoli (**alveolar ventilation rate**). This is due to the **anatomical dead space,** which is defined as the volume of the conducting portion of the airways of the lung where no gas exchange occurs. Each breath must fill the anatomical dead space. Thus, fewer breaths with large tidal volumes result in greater alveolar ventilation rates.

Effect of type of exercise on breathing pattern

Sporting activities result in considerably different respiratory responses. The rhythm of exercise affects the rhythm of breathing. In some sports, such as the crawl stroke in swimming, the rate of breathing and possibly the tidal volume are dictated by the stroke rhythm, because breathing can occur only intermittently when the swimmer's face is out of the water. During such activities as pedaling a cycle ergometer or walking, the rate of breathing is influenced by the rate of limb movement through feedback to the respiratory center from muscles and joints.[4]

Diaphragmatic versus costal breathing

At rest, no major differences exist with respect to either gender or age in the relative contribution of the diaphragm and the intercostal muscles to tidal volume. In moderate and heavy exercise, tidal volume increases in both inspiratory and expiratory directions.[7] Virtually all of the inspiratory increase is produced by the rib cage and most of the expiratory increase by the abdomen (diaphragm).

Oral versus nasal breathing

There is considerable variation among individuals in breathing patterns. For most adults, however, the shift from nasal to oral breathing occurs at about 35–40 L • min^{-1} of ventilation. This shift facilitates greater air flow to the lungs as the need for oxygen by the working muscles increases.

Efficiency of Breathing and Respiratory Phenomena

Lung ventilation and oxygen consumption in exercise

Between resting and a moderate exercise intensity (approximately 2.0 liters of oxygen consumption), a very constant ratio of ventilation rate to oxygen consumption is maintained. This ratio is usually termed the **ventilation equivalent** and is defined as the number of liters of air breathed for every 100 mL of oxygen consumed. Thus, at rest, the ventilation equivalent is:

ventilation equivalent

$$\frac{7.0 \text{ L of air breathed per minute}}{275 \text{ mL of oxygen consumed per minute}}$$

$$\frac{7.0}{2.75 \text{ (hundred mL)}} = 2.54$$

This ratio also indicates that 25.4 liters of air must be inspired for a person to consume 1 liter of oxygen:

$$\frac{7.0 \text{ L}}{0.275 \text{ L}} = 25.4 \text{ L}$$

This ratio holds until the exercise intensity demands more than about 2 liters of oxygen per minute, at which point the ratio grows higher. The reason for the higher ventilation equivalent at higher exercise intensities is that the steady state is no longer maintained: lactic acid accumulates that acts upon the respiratory center through lowering the pH, thereby increasing respiration.

Oxygen cost of breathing

Under resting conditions, the muscular work done in breathing (**oxygen cost of breathing**) is relatively small. Probably not much more than 1 percent of the resting metabolism is devoted to this function. As exercise becomes vigorous, however, the oxygen cost of breathing increases disproportionately. Probably at a point between 150 and 250 L of ventilation, the cost of moving the air takes all of the additional oxygen provided. However, this range of ventilation is seldom achieved in the normal ventilation, even during maximal exercise.

oxygen cost of breathing

Stitch in the side

What is commonly referred to as a **stitch in the side** is a phenomenon called **exercise-related transient abdominal pain (ETAP)** that occurs in approximately one in five running event participants. It is commonly noted during the period of respiratory adjustment to more intense exercise, but it can also be experienced during repetitive movements such as horseback riding. It is unclear whether the pain is a result of the changes involved in adjustments for increased respiration, if it is a result of the repetitive movement of the activity, or both. ETAP is most commonly felt in the lateral aspects of the mid-abdomen, along the costal border, and has been described as cramping, aching, or pulling when it is less intense, as well as sharp or stabbing when the pain is more severe. The condition appears to be exacerbated by pre-exercise food and/or drink intake.

stitch in the side

exercise-related transient abdominal pain (ETAP)

There is no scientific evidence to explain this pain; however, researchers have presented **ischemia** (insufficient blood flow) of the diaphragm, stress on the ligaments that connect the diaphragm to the viscera, gastrointestinal ischemia, cramping of the abdominal muscles, and irritation of the parietal peritoneum, as well as a number of other possible reasons for ETAP. Because the etiology of the pain is still unknown, it is difficult to recommend strategies for preventing its occurrence; however, some recommendations that appear to be effective are to avoid eating or drinking large quantities for at least two hours prior to exercise, improve thoracic posture during exercise, and improve core strength. Further research is necessary to better understand the etiology of ETAP so that recommendations for the prevention of this unwanted phenomenon can be made.[15]

ischemia

CLINICAL APPLICATIONS

Exercise-induced asthma (EIA)

Exercise can induce bronchoconstriction (asthma attack or **exercise-induced asthma [EIA]**) in asthmatics.[13] The nature of the exercise is important in reducing the frequency and severity of EIA. Swimming is well tolerated by asthmatics, possibly due to the usually higher ambient temperature and humidity. Furthermore, intermittent exercise may be preferable to continuous, and continuous running may be the activity most likely to cause EIA.[14]

The **exercise-induced bronchospasm (EIB)** associated with asthma can be effectively managed and should not limit participation in vigorous physical activity or sports participation.[12,16] Eichenberger et al.[5] performed a systematic review and meta-analysis of training studies in asthmatic subjects and recently recommended that physical activity should be utilized as a supplementary therapy to medication for managing asthmatics. The National Athletic Trainer's Association[12] and National Institutes of Health[16] recommend the following treatments for managing EIB:

1. $Beta_2$-agonists will prevent EIB in more than 80 percent of patients. Short-acting inhaled $beta_2$-agonists used as close to exercise as possible may be helpful for two to three hours. Salmeterol can prevent EIB for up to 12 hours. In addition, Cromolyn and Nedocromil can help to prevent EIB.
2. A lengthy warm-up may benefit patients who can tolerate continuous exercise with minimal symptoms. The warm-up may preclude a need for repeated medications.
3. Long-term control of asthma with anti-inflammatory medications will reduce airway responsiveness, which is related to a reduction in the frequency and severity of EIB.
4. Teachers and coaches need to be notified that a child has EIB, should be able to participate in activities, and may need inhaled medication before activity.
5. Competitive athletes should be aware that their medication use should be disclosed and should adhere to the standards of athletic governing bodies such as the U. S. and International Olympic Committees.

Second wind

second wind

dyspnea

eupnea

"Second wind," familiar to most endurance athletes, is typified by the feeling of relief upon making the necessary metabolic adjustments to a heavy exercise intensity. The major manifestation is the changeover from **dyspnea** (labored breathing, shortness of breath) to **eupnea** (normal breathing).

The respiratory adjustment, however, is probably only a reflection (an effect rather than a cause) of metabolic adjustment to the exercise intensity. The most likely explanation for the second wind is a change in skeletal muscular efficiency such as might be brought about by increasing muscle temperature.

Hypoventilation

hypoventilation

If lung ventilation is decreased, either voluntarily or involuntarily, without a corresponding decrease in metabolic rate, the reduction is called **hypoventilation.** It occurs only in abnormal situations, such as those involving airway obstruction. Because metabolism continues at a faster rate than lung ventilation, carbon dioxide accumulates and the arterial carbon dioxide increases *(hypercapnia),* which stimulates the respiratory center to increase respiration.

Hyperventilation

hyperventilation

hypocapnia

The converse of hypoventilation is **hyperventilation,** in which the lung ventilation rate is greater than is needed for the existing metabolic rate. In this case, carbon dioxide is blown off faster than it is produced. Thus, hyperventilation results in decreasing quantities of carbon dioxide in the circulorespiratory system, but it has no effect on oxygen values in the blood (since blood is virtually saturated with oxygen when it leaves the lungs). This lowering of blood carbon dioxide is called **hypocapnia.** Hyperventilation and hypocapnia are very interesting, as they occur accidentally as the result of emotional excitement, particularly in the inexperienced athlete, or are brought about intentionally to increase breath-holding ability. Hypocapnia decreases the urge to breathe, and hyperventilation can therefore provide a significant advantage in competitive athletics whenever breath-holding time is a factor in overall performance. In swimming the crawl stroke, for example, turning the head away from the midline to breathe slows the sprint swimmer's time. Hyperventilation immediately before an event enables the swimmer to go farther before breathing becomes necessary.

The physiology of breath-holding involves respiratory, circulatory, and cardiac changes. The most obvious changes when the breath is held are the increasing level of carbon dioxide and the decreasing level of oxygen in the alveolar air. These changes reflect the changes in the level of respiratory gases in the blood—the result of the continuing metabolism. The rising carbon dioxide level is more important in determining the length of time the breath can be held.

WWW

Chronic Obstructive Pulmonary Disease (COPD)

www.nlm.nih.gov/medlineplus/copd.html

The maximum duration of a voluntary breath-hold is longer at high lung volumes than at low volumes. This is probably due to the inhibitory effect of lung inflation on respiratory motor neuron activity. The longest breath-hold is probably found at volumes close to total lung capacity.

Effects of Air Pollution on Respiration

Many different chemical entities pollute our urban environments. The major contaminants are:

1. Particulate matter (dusts, fumes, and mists of solid particles)
2. Carbon monoxide resulting from incomplete combustion of hydrocarbons such as gasoline
3. Hydrocarbons from industrial plants and so on
4. Sulfur oxides resulting from burning of fossil fuels such as coal
5. Nitrogen oxides forming when most combustibles are burned, because of the large fraction of nitrogen in air
6. Ozone resulting from the sun's action on nitrogen dioxide and certain hydrocarbons

Many other contaminants become important under certain specified and unusual circumstances.

Ozone is of great importance to us because it is such a common constituent of the upper atmosphere and because it is a toxic contaminant predominant in the smog of numerous urban areas. It can seriously disrupt biochemical and physiological functions through lesions in the respiratory tissues and blood.

Until fairly recently, most experimentation with air pollutants had been carried out with exposure to varying levels of contaminant only at rest or during light exercise. But the total exposure to ozone, for example, is related not only to its concentration in the air breathed but also to ventilation, which may increase by 20 times in heavy work or exercise. Thus, the important question for us is: What is the effect of smog, as measured by ozone concentration, on the exercising human?

Exposure to ozone can have substantial negative effects on performance, including decreased distance running ability and reduced $\dot{V}O_2$ max and maximum ventilation rate. During submaximal exercise, ozone exposure can cause shallow, more frequent breathing and a reduction in tidal volume.

On the basis of the available evidence, physical educators, coaches, school administrators, and exercise scientists in urban areas exposed to smog would be well advised to monitor ozone levels. Exercise classes, athletic practices, and competitions should be discontinued, or activities should be made less vigorous, when ozone levels approach 0.3 parts per million.

Exercise and COPD

People with chronic obstructive pulmonary disease (COPD) are not able to force the air out of their lungs as quickly as normal subjects, and up to twice as much air remains in their lungs following forced expiration. This makes breathing difficult and unpleasant; therefore, most people with COPD are not as active as the general population, and COPD patients tend to exhibit skeletal muscle dysfunction because of the deconditioning from physical inactivity.[6,21] Exercise training appears to be an effective method for improving muscle function in these patients.[19] Guzun et al.[9] have shown that training at mild exercise intensities can have beneficial effects on muscle energy metabolism in COPD patients, by improving mitochondrial oxidative phosphorylation through the creatine kinase system. The practical significance of these changes is that even low-intensity exercise training can increase muscular endurance in these patients, improving their ability to perform daily tasks of living and making it possible for these patients to increase their activity levels.

Smoking, which may be considered self-induced air pollution, has long been indicated as a cause of respiratory problems in athletes. Smoking substantially reduces airway conductance, which may lead to a 5 to 10 percent decrease in total lung air supply during intense exercise.

Respiratory Muscle Fatigue and the Effects of Training on Pulmonary Function

Exercise training and pulmonary function

The ventilation equivalent for oxygen (the number of liters of air breathed for every 100 mL of oxygen consumed) decreases as the result of training. This improved efficiency in breathing, however, is not the result of improvement in the lung tissue per se but rather of reduced metabolic acidosis during exercise and thus a lower drive to increase ventilation. Endurance training also increases the oxidative capacity of respiratory muscles.[17]

Endurance training brings about important changes in the lung volumes and capacities, including decreased functional residual capacity, decreased residual volume, a decrease in the ratio of residual volume/total lung capacity, and increased vital capacity. These changes provide better alveolar ventilation and consequently weigh in favor of improved athletic performance.

Respiratory muscle fatigue

Respiratory muscle fatigue may limit exercise performance because of a lack of sufficient blood flow to provide an adequate oxygen supply or to remove metabolic byproducts.[11] It is also possible that the excessive requirements for oxygen and blood flow to the respiratory muscles during intense exercise limit blood flow to the locomotor muscles.[2]

GAS TRANSPORT

Three processes intervene between lung ventilation and actual tissue respiration: (1) diffusion of oxygen across two very thin membranes: the wall of the alveolus and the wall of the capillary; (2) transport of oxygen in the blood to the capillary bed of the active muscles; and (3) diffusion of oxygen across the capillary wall to the active muscle fibers. As the blood unloads oxygen, it takes on carbon dioxide for the return trip to the right heart and back to the lungs.

At this point we must consider the nature of the diffusion process and some of the laws that govern it. Recall that fluids flow from point to point only because of differences in pressure called pressure gradients. This is equally true for gases. For this reason physiologists usually refer to respiratory gases in terms of pressure rather than in terms of concentration (percentage and so on).

Table 6.1 gives percentages and approximate pressures of oxygen exerted in a standard atmosphere. Note that the percentage concentration of oxygen is the same at 40,000 feet as it is at sea level. However, since one becomes unconscious in a matter of seconds at 40,000-feet altitude due to lack of oxygen, it is obvious that percentage has little meaning in this situation. The atmospheric pressure of oxygen, on the other hand, tells the story rather well.

Properties of Gases Versus Liquids

Basic to all gas laws is the molecular theory that all gases are composed of molecules that are constantly in motion at very high velocities. A gas has no definite shape or volume and conforms to the shape and volume of its container. Its pressure is the result of the constant impact of its many molecules upon the walls of the container. Obviously, one can increase the pressure of a gas by confining it in a smaller volume or by increasing the activity of each molecule. Because a rise in temperature increases the velocity of molecular movement, heat increases pressure.

Liquids, on the other hand, are composed of molecules that are much closer together. This closeness results in their having a definite, independent volume that varies little with temperature or with the size and shape of the container.

Composition of Respiratory Gases

The atmospheric air is composed mainly of nitrogen, oxygen, and carbon dioxide. It also contains rare gases (argon, krypton, etc.), but these are ordinarily lumped together and included with the nitrogen fraction.

Table 6.2 illustrates some important features of respiratory gas exchange. The partial pressures of dry atmospheric air are proportional to the percentages as per the law of partial pressures. However, the alveolar air is saturated with water vapor, which contributes a partial pressure of 47 mm Hg at body temperature. The partial pressure of oxygen in the lungs, then, would be 20.93 percent of 713 (760 – 47) mm Hg, or approximately 149 mm Hg, if we could completely exchange the air in the lungs. This, of course, is impossible because alveolar air in the lungs is a mixture of atmospheric air with air that has already participated in the respiratory exchange. For this reason, note in Table 6.2 that the actual partial pressure of oxygen in the alveolar air is 100 mm Hg instead of the 149 mm Hg that would

Percentages and partial pressures of O_2 by altitude. **table 6.1**

ALTITUDE (FEET)	ATMOSPHERIC PRESSURE (MM HG)	PERCENT O_2	APPROXIMATE PRESSURE EXERTED BY O_2 IN THE ATMOSPHERE (MM HG)
Sea level	760	20.93	159
10,000	523	20.93	109
20,000	349	20.93	73
30,000	226	20.93	47
40,000	141	20.93	29

mm Hg = millimeters of mercury

table 6.2 Composition of atmospheric air and the consequent partial pressures of respiratory gases.

GAS	PERCENT IN DRY ATMOSPHERE	PARTIAL PRESSURE IN DRY ATMOSPHERE (MM HG)	PARTIAL PRESSURE IN ALVEOLAR AIR (MM HG)	PARTIAL PRESSURE IN MIXED VENOUS BLOOD (MM HG)	DIFFUSION GRADIENT
Total	100	760	760	705	
H_2O	0	0	47	47	
O_2	20.93	159	100	40	60
CO_2	0.03	0.2	40	45	5
N_2	79.04	600.8	573	573	

be present if there were no dead space and if the lung collapsed to empty itself completely at each breath.

diffusion gradient

The importance of all this lies in the diffusion gradients for oxygen and carbon dioxide that ultimately determine the amount of gaseous exchange taking place. The **diffusion gradient** describes the movement of gases from an area of high concentration to an area of lower concentration. The diffusion gradient for oxygen is some 60 mm Hg, for carbon dioxide only 5 to 6 mm Hg. Since these figures are based on typical, healthy individuals, the diffusion gradient for carbon dioxide is obviously sufficient to maintain the necessary homeostatic relations for carbon dioxide levels. This can be explained by the fact that diffusion of gases across a membrane depends not only on the gradient but also on the ease with which a particular gas can penetrate the membrane. This, in turn, depends on the solubility of the gas in the membrane (largely water). The fact that the solubility of carbon dioxide in water is some 20 or more times that of oxygen explains the need for a greater diffusion gradient of oxygen.

Basics of the laws governing gases

To understand the influence of respiratory physiology on exercise performance, it is necessary to have a basic understanding of the laws that govern the behavior of gases.

Boyle's Law: This law states that if temperature remains constant, the pressure of a gas varies inversely with its volume. If, for example, we decrease the volume by one half, the pressure will be doubled.

Gay-Lussac's Law: If its volume remains constant, the pressure of a gas increases directly in proportion to its (absolute) temperature.

Law of Partial Pressures: In a mixture of gases, each gas exerts a partial pressure, proportional to its concentration. Thus, in atmospheric air with a total pressure of 760 mm Hg, oxygen, which makes up 20.93 percent, has a partial pressure of 159 mm Hg: 20.93 / 100 x 760 mm Hg = 159 mm Hg.

Henry's Law: The quantity of a gas that will dissolve in a liquid is directly proportional to its partial pressure, if temperature remains constant.

Gas Transport by the Blood

Oxygen

Blood is capable of carrying only about 0.2 volume percent of oxygen (0.2 mL of oxygen per 100 mL of blood) in solution at normal atmospheric pressures. In reality, however, it transports 20 volume percent of oxygen, 100 times as much as will dissolve in physical solution.

erythrocytes
hemoglobin
heme
globin
oxygenation

The reason for this great discrepancy is the presence of hemoglobin in the **erythrocytes** (red blood cells). **Hemoglobin** is an iron-bearing pigment, consisting of **heme** (which contains iron) and **globin** (which is a protein). Hemoglobin has the unique characteristic of combining with oxygen quickly and reversibly and without requiring help from enzymes. The term **oxygenation** refers to this process. The reaction can be described thus:

$$\text{hemoglobin} + \text{oxygen} \leftrightharpoons \text{oxyhemoglobin}$$

Carbon dioxide

Carbon dioxide, a byproduct of metabolism in the cell, diffuses across the cell membrane into the tissue fluid, and then across the capillary wall into the blood plasma, where a small portion of it is transported. The larger proportion, probably 90 to 95 percent, diffuses from the plasma into red blood cells. The red blood cells transport the carbon dioxide in three forms: (1) in combination with hemoglobin as carbamino-hemoglobin; (2) as bicarbonate, HCO_3; and (3) as dissolved carbon dioxide, a portion of which ionizes into carbonic acid, H_2CO_3.

The exchange of carbon dioxide, at the lungs and at the tissues, involves the following reversible reaction:

$$HCO_3^- + H^+ \leftrightharpoons H_2CO_3 \leftrightharpoons \text{water } (H_2O) + \text{carbon dioxide } (CO_2)$$

This is ordinarily a slow reaction. However, an enzyme, carbonic anhydrase, catalyzes these reactions so that they can be completed before the blood leaves the lung or tissue capillaries.

INTERNAL RESPIRATION

Much of the story concerning internal respiration, or gas exchange in the tissues, has already been told. Two other factors, however, are basic to an understanding of the respiratory exchange: (1) oxygen dissociation and utilization and (2) regulation of acid–base balance.

Oxygen Dissociation and Utilization

Oxygen dissociation curve

It is an interesting biochemical fact that the loading of carbon dioxide into the blood at the tissues considerably aids the unloading of oxygen from blood to tissues. The reverse is also true in the lungs: the unloading of carbon dioxide in the lungs aids the loading of oxygen into the blood.

oxygen dissociation curve

These facts are best illustrated by the **oxygen dissociation curve,** a graphic indication of the amount of oxygen released from hemoglobin as a result of changing carbon dioxide levels in the tissues (Figure 6.3). If one places a straightedge vertically along the line representing a partial pressure of oxygen of 30 mm Hg (that of the tissues), the difference in hemoglobin saturation level between the points where the 40 mm Hg carbon dioxide curve (blood carbon dioxide level) and the 80 mm Hg carbon dioxide curve (active tissue level) cross this vertical line represents the difference in percentages of oxygen that the hemoglobin can hold.

This amount of oxygen, in this case from approximately 58 percent to approximately 42 percent (i.e., 16 percent), is released from the hemoglobin by changing carbon dioxide levels in the tissues. In other words, increasing the carbon dioxide level of the blood from its arterialized level of 40 mm Hg to 80 mm Hg, which probably represents the temporary local changes in blood level at the tissues, results in driving off 16 percent of the total oxygen load.

Another point regarding the oxygen dissociation curve is of very practical interest with respect to the effect of altitude on human respiration. Note that the curve for 40 mm Hg of carbon dioxide, which represents the mixed venous blood (typical of the body as a whole but not of any localized tissue site), is not very steep from 100 mm Hg to approximately 60 mm Hg of oxygen partial pressure. The upper figure is typical of alveolar oxygen partial pressure at sea level. The lower figure represents alveolar oxygen partial pressure at about 15,000 to 16,000

figure 6.3 The oxygen dissociation curve for human blood.

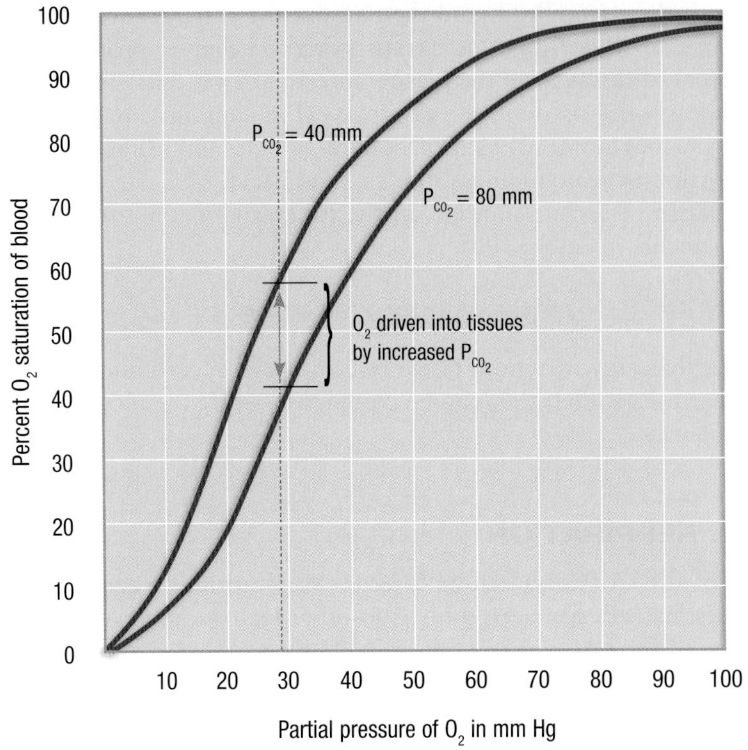

feet above sea level, the level at which resting humans (pilots and others) begin showing serious symptoms due to the lack of oxygen. (Military regulations require the use of oxygen above 10,000 feet to provide a safety margin that allows for individual variance.) If this oxygen dissociation curve were a straight diagonal line, physical impairment would probably commence at about 90 mm Hg of oxygen partial pressure, an altitude of about 6,000 feet, instead of at 60 mm Hg.

Another important feature of the oxygen dissociation curve is that it is steep (close to vertical) when the partial pressures of oxygen are low. This means, of course, that small changes in partial pressure of oxygen in this part of the curve make large changes in the amount of oxygen the hemoglobin can hold, thus making large exchanges of respiratory gas efficient when the need is greatest.

Coefficient of oxygen utilization

coefficient of oxygen utilization

The **coefficient of oxygen utilization** can be defined as the proportion of oxygen transported by the blood that is given off to the tissues. Since 99 percent of the transported oxygen is bound to hemoglobin, this story also can be related in terms of the oxygen dissociation curve. During resting conditions at sea level, the hemoglobin leaving the lungs is at least 95 percent saturated with oxygen. After leaving the capillary bed of resting tissue, it is still at least 70 percent saturated. (In Figure 6.3, use the 40 mm Hg carbon dioxide curve and note its intersections at the 100 mm Hg and 40 mm Hg oxygen partial pressure lines.) Thus the hemoglobin has given off 23/98 of its oxygen, or approximately 23 percent, in resting conditions.

In exercise, this situation becomes much more favorable. The hemoglobin leaving the lungs is still approximately 95 percent saturated, but after leaving active muscle tissue it may approach zero saturation. Thus the coefficient of oxygen utilization may increase from three to four times in exercise. It should be repeated that this increase is facilitated by the steepness of the oxygen dissociation curve at the lower oxygen partial pressures (as was mentioned before).

At this point it may be well to note the combination of factors that contribute to supplying the increased oxygen demands of exercising muscle tissue. First, cardiac output can increase about six times its resting value. Second, in combination with an increased utilization coefficient of three to four times, this means a possible increase of at least 18 times the resting value. Third, with respect to the local situation at any given active muscle, this may be multiplied by another factor of two, due to the approximate doubling of the number of open capillaries. Thus a total increase of at least 36 times the resting oxygen supply is possible at any active muscle group.

Regulation of Acid–Base Balance

acids

bases

Acids can be defined as compounds that yield positively charged hydrogen ions (H^+) in solution. Conversely, **bases** can be defined as compounds that yield negatively charged hydroxyl ions (OH^-) in solution. A very convenient yardstick for measuring and describing degrees of acidity or alkalinity has been set up: pH, which is the negative logarithm of the hydrogen ion concentration in gram molecular weight. This may be visualized as follows:

←	Strongest acid Increasing acidity					Neutrality					Strongest base Increasing alkalinity		→
pH = 1	2	3	4	5	6	7	8	9	10	11	12	13	14

Since this is a logarithmic scale, a very small change in pH makes a considerable change in acidity or alkalinity. Therefore pH is given to at least one and usually two decimal places. For example, the extreme fluctuations of the pH of normal blood lie within pH values of 7.30 to 7.50. The extreme values in illness have been known to go as low as 6.95 and as high as 7.80. However, in healthy subjects, surprisingly low values (down to 6.80) can result from heavy anaerobic exercise. The short-term pH changes such as those associated with very intense exercise are well tolerated in healthy subjects.

Even under resting conditions, the acid–base equilibrium of body fluids is constantly challenged by the formation of carbon dioxide as the end product of cellular metabolism. Furthermore, when exercise intensities become severe, lactic acid is also formed, constituting an additional influence that tends to drive pH downward. Illness brings about other acidifying or alkalinizing influences. Because long-term pH changes beyond the range of 7.30 to 7.50 are inconsistent with good health, it is obvious that the human organism must be able to control acid–base balance.

Two processes are involved in the control of acid–base balance. The first line of defense against pH changes is the combination of three buffer systems that serve to deal with sudden changes. Ultimately, however, physiological changes have to be brought about to maintain the organism in homeostasis over the longer period of time. These physiological changes involve mainly the lungs and the kidneys.

Buffer systems

buffer system

A **buffer system** consists of a weak acid and a salt of that acid. The system functions as follows:

HL		$NaHCO_3$		NaL		H_2CO_3
Lactic acid	+	Sodium bicarbonate	→	Sodium lactate	+	Carbonic acid

In this case, lactic acid (a relatively strong acid) combines with sodium bicarbonate (salt of a weak acid) to form sodium lactate (which no longer has acid tendencies) and carbonic acid (which is a very weak acid). Thus a strong acid has been exchanged for a weak acid, and the tendency for the lactic acid to lower the pH of the blood has been greatly lessened by the buffering action of the carbonic acid bicarbonate system.

Blood must be considered as two fluids that need buffering: the plasma and the fluid within the erythrocytes. In the plasma, the acids to be buffered are largely *fixed acids,* so called because they are not subject to rapid excretion. They are, in general, stronger acids, such as hydrochloric, phosphoric, sulfuric, and lactic acids (the stronger acids occur in very small quantities). The most important buffers in the plasma are:

$$\frac{H_2CO_3}{NaHCO_3} \quad \text{and} \quad \frac{\text{H protein}}{\text{Na proteinate}}$$

The blood proteins can act as buffer systems because, at the pH of blood, they behave as weak acids and react with the base to form a salt. In the intracellular fluids of the erythrocytes, on the other hand, the major acid to be buffered is the carbonic acid that results from the respiratory exchange. The buffer systems mainly responsible for this are hemoglobin and oxyhemoglobin, each of which can act as a weak acid or as a potassium salt, as follows:

$$\underset{\text{Oxyhemoglobin System}}{\frac{\text{H Hb }O_2}{\text{K Hb }O_2}} \quad \text{and} \quad \underset{\text{Hemoglobin System}}{\frac{\text{H Hb}}{\text{K Hb}}}$$

Both plasma and cells also contain other, less important buffer systems, such as the acid and basic sodium and potassium phosphates.

Physiological regulation of acid–base balance

Although the buffering systems can resist fast changes in pH, a change does occur with the addition of an acid (or base) to the body fluids. These changes are corrected by two physiological mechanisms for excretion of the acid (or base): changes in respiratory function and changes in kidney function.

The lungs are important in regulating acid–base balance. For example, if the breath is held, the carbon dioxide resulting from metabolism accumulates. This has the effect of pouring acid into the tissue fluids and blood: $CO_2 + H_2O = H_2CO_3$. This decrease in pH is interpreted as the "error signal" by the respiratory center in the medulla, which corrects the situation by increasing the rate and depth of ventilation (if possible). When the breath is held, the error signal simply grows larger and larger, until the urge to breathe overcomes the willpower to hold the breath. The rate and depth will then be greater than normal until equilibrium has been reestablished by expiring more carbon dioxide than is being formed: $H_2CO_3 = CO_2 + H_2O$. Thus the importance of the respiratory function in acid–base regulation lies in the fact that the decomposition products of carbonic acid are volatile and can be readily expired by the lungs.

In hyperventilation, on the other hand, more carbon dioxide is expired than is formed, bringing about a change in the ratio of H_2CO_3 to $NaHCO_3$. The normal ratio is 1:20. If H_2CO_3 and $NaHCO_3$ are increased or decreased proportionately, the ratio does not change, and consequently there is no change in pH. In the case of hyperventilation, however, the H_2CO_3 decreases disproportionately because the $NaHCO_3$ remains the same. Thus a relative increase in the base occurs, with a rise in pH.

If the hyperventilation is of short duration, as in preparing for an athletic event, the increased production of carbon dioxide during the event corrects the situation. But if hyperventilation is long-term (one hour or more), as in fever, a secondary adjustment must be made to excrete some of the bicarbonate to keep the ratio close to 1:20. This excretion of bicarbonate is done through the kidney.

The last line of defense, and the one concerned with long-term changes in acid–base equilibrium, is the excretion of abnormal amounts of acid or base by the kidney to maintain all the buffer systems at the proper acid–salt ratio for maintaining normal pH. When it is no longer possible to maintain these ratios, acidosis or alkalosis ensues. In severe acidosis, death ensues as a result of coma. In severe alkalosis, death may be brought about by rigid contractions and the resulting muscle spasm of respiratory muscles.

Acid-base balance as a factor-limiting performance

Metabolism in general provides a constant acidifying influence. When the metabolic rate increases to seven or eight times that of the resting level, the increase in carbon dioxide is proportional, but ventilation can usually keep pace to maintain acid–base equilibrium. However, when the exercise intensity goes beyond aerobic capacity, lactic acid becomes the end product of metabolism, instead of carbon dioxide. This is a much stronger acid, and it cannot be excreted quickly by respiration as can carbon dioxide. It has already been pointed out that under conditions of extremely intense anaerobic exercise the pH can drop as low as 6.80.

Therefore, the body's ability to buffer fixed acids (such as lactic acid) plays a large part in determining the end point of anaerobic activity. Because these fixed acids are largely buffered by the bicarbonate system, the combining power of the plasma bicarbonate has been referred to as the **alkaline reserve.** Although this concept rests on a reasonably sound rationale, it is an oversimplification of the complex biochemical interactions involved in acid–base regulation.

alkaline reserve

Changes in Lung Diffusion in Exercise

The diffusion of oxygen from the alveoli to the pulmonary capillaries increases in virtually direct proportion to the intensity of exercise. It is likely that the intensity-related increase in pulmonary diffusion is the result of increased pulmonary capillary blood volume during exercise, brought about by the opening of previously unopened capillaries. In the absence of disease, it is not likely that pulmonary diffusion capacity for oxygen is a limiting factor in exercise.

In addition, highly trained athletes demonstrate better pulmonary diffusion during maximal and submaximal exercise than do non-athletes. This may be either an innate, inherited characteristic of champion athletes or the result of rigorous training.

Use of Oxygen to Improve Performance

Athletes sometimes breathe oxygen-enriched gas before or after an event in an attempt to improve performance or aid in recovery. For example, it has become commonplace to see football players breathing oxygen on the sidelines. Does oxygen supplementation before, during, or after an athletic event improve performance?

Breathing oxygen before a competitive event does not improve performance, because the oxygen would have to be stored to benefit performance. Unfortunately, we cannot store substantial amounts of oxygen in the body.

Oxygen supplementation after exercise does not hasten recovery. The hemoglobin in arterial blood is almost fully saturated (95–98%) with oxygen when it leaves the lungs, and therefore, an increase in oxygen concentration in inspired air does not improve oxygen transport to any meaningful degree or enhance recovery.

Inspiring oxygen-enriched gas during aerobic exercise may improve performance by increasing oxygen delivery to the muscle[1] and/or reducing the work of the respiratory muscles.[18] To gain these benefits, however, the athlete would have to carry a supply of oxygen and breathe through a mask during the event.[8] This, of course, is not practical and has no real utility in athletics.

From a physiological perspective, oxygen supplementation is not useful for improving athletic performance. Its psychological effects, however, should not be discounted. Perhaps, if the athlete believes that the oxygen is helpful, performance or recovery will be enhanced.

What Limits Maximal Oxygen Consumption Rate ($\dot{V}O_2$ max)?

Maximal oxygen consumption rate ($\dot{V}O_2$ max) is influenced by oxygen transport to the working muscles and oxygen utilization to produce ATP within the active muscle fibers.[18] Therefore, the determination of $\dot{V}O_2$ max provides information relative to an individual's level of cardiorespiratory fitness and is a valuable predictor of endurance exercise and sport performance. See **Chapter 6 Lab** for the 1.5-mile run test to estimate $\dot{V}O_2$ max.

Oxygen transport is associated with cardiac output and the hemoglobin concentration in the blood, while oxygen utilization for energy production is affected by such factors as myoglobin level, mitochondrial size and number, and enzyme characteristics. The relative contribution of oxygen transport and oxygen utilization to $\dot{V}O_2$ max is open to debate. It is possible that in activities involving large muscle masses (such as running), $\dot{V}O_2$ max is limited by cardiac output, but in sports that involve only arms or only legs, peripheral factors such as muscle blood flow and oxygen utilization set the limit. In any case, aerobic exercise training can improve factors related to both oxygen transport and oxygen utilization.

summary

In the present chapter, respiration includes external respiration, gas transport, and internal respiration. External respiration (also called pulmonary ventilation) involves gas exchange in the lungs, in which the blood in the capillaries of the lungs takes up oxygen and gives up much of its carbon dioxide. Gas transport is the function of the cardiovascular system. Internal respiration (also called tissue respiration) involves gas exchange between the blood and cells (such as muscle fibers).

The respiratory center in the pons and medulla controls the frequency and depth of breathing. Input to the respiratory center comes from many sources, including neural input from within the brain, neural input from muscles and joints, and humoral or bloodborne input.

Exercise training can have positive effects on pulmonary function. For example, aerobic training decreases the ventilation equivalent for oxygen, functional residual capacity, and residual volume, and it increases the oxidative capacity of respiratory muscles and vital capacity. These changes provide improved alveolar ventilation and probably contribute to better performance in endurance activities.

Gas transport involves the transport of oxygen in the blood from the lungs to the capillary beds of the active muscles and carbon dioxide from the muscles back to the lungs for expiration. Most oxygen is transported bound to hemoglobin in erythrocytes (red blood cells), although a small portion is dissolved in the blood. Carbon dioxide is transported primarily by erythrocytes in three forms: (1) carbamino-hemoglobin, (2) bicarbonate, and (3) dissolved carbon dioxide.

Internal respiration involves gas exchange at the tissue level. It includes factors related to unloading oxygen from the blood into the cell (such as a muscle fiber) and the removal of carbon dioxide from the cell into the blood.

questions for review

1. Discuss the sequence of the flow of air through the ventilation system during external respiration.
2. Define the four primary lung volumes and the four lung capacities.
3. Describe the respiratory cycle during normal resting breathing conditions. How does it change during exercise?
4. How does the respiratory center control respiration?
5. Explain the oxygen cost of breathing. Explain stitch in the side. Explain second wind.
6. What type of exercise is appropriate for someone with exercise-induced asthma?
7. What are the effects of pollution on athletic performance?
8. What effects does exercise training have on pulmonary function?
9. How is acid–base balance regulated?
10. Explain the oxygen dissociation curve. What does it tell us about the effect of altitude on human respiration?
11. What factors contribute to supplying the increased oxygen demands of exercising muscle tissue?
12. What effect does the body's ability to buffer fixed acids have on performance? Why?
13. Should oxygen be used to improve performance? Why or why not?
14. What limits $\dot{V}O_2$ max?

student companion website

For further review of this book's chapters and for test preparation, visit the book's website, **www.hhpcommunities.com/exercisephysiology**, to take practice quizzes, review the vocabulary terms, use the study guide, and view the digital image bank.

references

1. Brooks, G. A., Fahey, T. D., and Baldwin, K. M. *Exercise Physiology: Human Bioenergetics and Its Applications*, 4th edition. Boston: McGraw-Hill, 2005.
2. Dempsey, J. A., Harms, C. A., and Ainsworth, D. M. Respiratory muscle perfusion and energetics during exercise. *Med. Sci. Sports Exerc.* 28: 1123–1128, 1996.
3. Dempsey, J. A., and Smith, C. A. Do carotid chemoreceptors inhibit the hyperventilatory response to heavy exercise? *Can. J. Appl. Physiol.* 19: 350–359, 1994.
4. Duffin, J. Neural drives to breathing during exercise. *Can. J. Appl. Physiol.* 19: 289–304, 1994.
5. Eichenberger, P. A., Diener, S. N., Kofmehl, R., and Spengler, C. M. Effects of exercise training on airway hyperreactivity in asthma: a systematic review and meta-analysis. *Sports Med.* 43: 1157–1170, 2013.
6. Eisner, M. D., Iribarren, C., Blanc, P. D., Yelin, E. H., Ackerson, L., Byl, N., Omachi, T. A., Sidney, S., and Katz, P. P. Development of disability in chronic obstruc-

tive pulmonary disease: beyond lung function. *Thorax* 66: 108–114, 2011.

7. Farkas, G. A., Cerny, F. J., and Rochester, D. F. Contractility of the ventilatory pump muscles. *Med. Sci. Sports Exerc.* 28: 1106–1114, 1996.
8. Foss, M. L., and Keteyian, S. J. *Fox's Physiological Basis for Exercise and Sport,* 6th edition. Boston: WCB McGraw-Hill, 1998.
9. Guzun, R., Aguilaniu, B., Wuyam, B., Mezin, P., Koechlin-Ramonatxo, C., Auffray, C., Saks, V., and Pison, C. Effects of training at mild exercise intensities on quadriceps muscle energy metabolism in patients with chronic obstructive pulmonary disease. *Acta Physiol.* 205: 236–246, 2012.
10. Jennings, D. B. Respiratory control during exercise: Hormones, osmolarity, strong ions, and $PaCO_2$. *Can. J. Appl. Physiol.* 19: 334–349, 1994.
11. Johnson, B. D., Aaron, E. A., Babcock, M. A., and Dempsey, J. A. Respiratory muscle fatigue during exercise: Implications for performance. *Med. Sci. Sports Exerc.* 28: 1129–1137, 1996.
12. Miller, M. G., Weiler, J. M., Baker, R., Collins, J., and D'Alonzo, G. National Athletic Trainer's Association position statement: Management of asthma in athletes. *J. Athl. Train.* 40: 224–245, 2005.
13. Morton, A. R., Fitch, K. D., and Hahn, A. G. Physical activity and the asthmatic. *Phys. and Sportsmed.* 9: 51–64, 1981.
14. Morton, A. R., Hahn, A. G., and Fitch, K. D. Continuous and intermittent running in the provocation of asthma. *Ann. Allergy* 48: 123–129, 1982.
15. Morton, D., and Callister, R. Exercise-related transient abdominal pain (ETAP). *Sports Med.* 45: 23–25, 2015.
16. National Asthma Education and Prevention Program. *Expert panel report 3: Guidelines for the diagnosis and management of asthma.* Bethesda, MD: National Institutes of Health., 1–3, 2007.
17. Powers, S. K., and Criswell, D. Adaptive strategies of respiratory muscles in response to endurance exercise. *Med. Sci. Sports Exerc.* 28: 1115–1122, 1996.
18. Powers, S. K., and Howley, E. T. *Exercise Physiology: Theory and Application to Fitness and Performance,* 8th edition. Boston: McGraw-Hill, 2012.
19. Seymour, J. M., Spruit, M. A., Hopkinson, N. S., Natanek, S. A., Man, W. D-C., Jackson, A., Gosker, H. R., Schols, A. M. W. J., Moxham, J., Polkey, M. I., and Wouters, E. F. M. The prevalence of quadriceps weakness in COPD and the relationship with disease severity. *Eur. Respir. J.* 36: 81–88, 2010.
20. Ward, S. A. Peripheral and central chemoreceptor control of ventilation during exercise in humans. *Can. J. Appl. Physiol.* 19: 305–333, 1994.
21. Watz, H., Waschki, B., Meyer, T., and Magnussen, H. Physical activity in patients with COPD. *Eur. Respir. J.* 33: 262–272, 2009.

1.5-Mile Run Test

BACKGROUND

The 1.5-mile run test provides a simple method for estimating a person's maximal oxygen consumption rate ($\dot{V}O_2$ max) by measuring the elapsed time during 1.5 miles of running (or walking). Walking is allowed during this test; however, the objective is to complete the 1.5-mile distance as quickly as possible. A faster pace (speed) during the test will result in a lower time to complete the 1.5 miles, and, therefore, a higher predicted $\dot{V}O_2$ max. The following gender-specific regression equations have been developed[1] to predict $\dot{V}O_2$ max using body weight (kg) and the 1.5-mile run time (min):

MEN

$\dot{V}O_2$ max (mL • kg^{-1} • min^{-1}) = 91.736 – (0.1656 × body weight in kg) – (2.767 × 1.5-mile run time in min)

R (multiple correlation coefficient) = 0.90

SEE (standard error of estimate) = 2.8 mL • kg^{-1} • min^{-1}

WOMEN

$\dot{V}O_2$ max (mL • kg^{-1} • min^{-1}) = 88.020 – (0.1656 × body weight in kg) – (2.767 × 1.5-mile run time in min)

R = 0.90

SEE = 2.8 mL • kg^{-1} • min^{-1}

The standard error of estimate values associated with these equations represent approximately 6.0% of $\dot{V}O_2$ max.

TERMS & ABBREVIATIONS

- ☐ R = multiple correlation coefficient; a numerical measure of how well a dependent variable can be predicted from a combination of independent variables (a number between –1 and 1)
- ☐ SEE = standard error of estimate; a measure of the accuracy of the predictions made using a regression equation
- ☐ $\dot{V}O_2$ max = maximal oxygen consumption rate

PROCEDURES[2]

1. Measure body weight (in kg) on a scale.
2. Have the subject warm up by walking and/or jogging for 5 minutes prior to the test.
3. Instruct the subject to run (or walk if necessary) as fast as possible for 1.5 miles (2.4 kilometers). Emphasize that a faster speed will result in a higher predicted $\dot{V}O_2$ max.

4. Measure the time it takes to complete the 1.5 miles and record it (in minutes) on Worksheet 6.1.
5. Use one of the regression equations below to predict $\dot{V}O_2$ max.
6. Compare the estimated $\dot{V}O_2$ max score to the norms listed in Table L6.1.

Equations

MEN

$\dot{V}O_2$ max ($mL \cdot kg^{-1} \cdot min^{-1}$) = 91.736 – (0.1656 × body mass in kg) – (2.767 × 1.5-mile run time in min)

WOMEN

$\dot{V}O_2$ max ($mL \cdot kg^{-1} \cdot min^{-1}$) = 88.020 – (0.1656 × body mass in kg) – (2.767 × 1.5-mile run time in min)

SAMPLE CALCULATIONS

Gender: Female

Age: 28 years

Body weight: 54 kg

1.5-mile run time: 12:24 min:sec

Step 1: Convert time to minutes.

24 sec ÷ 60 sec = 0.4 min

Therefore,

12:24 min:sec = 12.4 min

Step 2: Calculate the predicted $\dot{V}O_2$ max.

$\dot{V}O_2$ max = 88.020 – (0.1656 × 54 kg) – (2.767 × 12.4 min)

= 44.8 $mL \cdot kg^{-1} \cdot min^{-1}$

Step 3: Compare the predicted $\dot{V}O_2$ max score from the 1.5-mile run to the norms in Table L6.1.

A score of 44.8 $mL \cdot kg^{-1} \cdot min^{-1}$ would be classified as "superior" for a 20- to 29-year-old woman in Table L6.1.

Men's and women's aerobic fitness classifications (predicted). **table L6.1**

MEN		AGE (YEARS)					
CATEGORY	MEASURE	13-19	20-29	30-39	40-49	50-59	60+
I. Very Poor	$\dot{V}O_2$ max (mL • kg^{-1} • min^{-1})	<35.0	<33.0	<31.5	<30.2	<26.1	<20.5
II. Poor	$\dot{V}O_2$ max (mL • kg^{-1} • min^{-1})	35.0–38.3	33.0–36.4	31.5–35.4	30.2–33.5	26.1–30.9	20.5–26.0
III. Fair	$\dot{V}O_2$ max (mL • kg^{-1} • min^{-1})	38.4–45.1	36.5–42.4	35.5–40.9	33.6–38.9	31.0–35.7	26.1–32.2
IV. Good	$\dot{V}O_2$ max (mL • kg^{-1} • min^{-1})	45.2–50.9	42.5–46.4	41.0–44.9	39.0–43.7	35.8–40.9	32.3–36.4
V. Excellent	$\dot{V}O_2$ max (mL • kg^{-1} • min^{-1})	51.0–55.9	46.5–52.4	45.0–49.4	43.8–48.0	41.0–45.3	36.5–44.2
VI. Superior	$\dot{V}O_2$ max (mL • kg^{-1} • min^{-1})	>56.0	>52.5	>49.5	>48.1	>45.4	>44.3

WOMEN		AGE (YEARS)					
CATEGORY	MEASURE	13-19	20-29	30-39	40-49	50-59	60+
I. Very Poor	$\dot{V}O_2$ max (mL • kg^{-1} • min^{-1})	<25.0	<23.6	<22.8	<21.0	<20.2	<17.5
II. Poor	$\dot{V}O_2$ max (mL • kg^{-1} • min^{-1})	25.0–30.9	23.6–28.9	22.8–26.9	21.0–24.4	20.2–22.7	17.5–20.1
III. Fair	$\dot{V}O_2$ max (mL • kg^{-1} • min^{-1})	31.0–34.9	29.0–32.9	27.0–31.4	24.5–28.9	22.8–26.9	20.2–24.4
IV. Good	$\dot{V}O_2$ max (mL • kg^{-1} • min^{-1})	35.0–38.9	33.0–36.9	31.5–35.6	29.0–32.8	27.0–31.4	24.5–30.2
V. Excellent	$\dot{V}O_2$ max (mL • kg^{-1} • min^{-1})	39.0–41.9	37.0–40.9	35.7–40.0	32.9–36.9	31.5–35.7	30.3–31.4
VI. Superior	$\dot{V}O_2$ max (mL • kg^{-1} • min^{-1})	>42.0	>41.0	>40.1	>37.0	>35.8	>31.5

Source: Cooper, Kenneth H. *The Aerobics Way.* Toronto: Bantam Books, 1977, pp. 280–281. Printed with permission of Kenneth H. Cooper, MD, MPH, www.cooper-aerobics.com.

worksheet 6.1 1.5-MILE RUN TEST FORM

NAME ______________________________ DATE ______________

Gender: ______________

Age (years): ______________

Body weight (kg): ______________

1. Time (in min:sec) to complete the 1.5-mile run = ______________ min
2. Equation for men: $\dot{V}O_2$ max ($mL \bullet kg^{-1} \bullet min^{-1}$) = 91.736 – (0.1656 × body weight in kg)
   – (2.767 × 1.5-mile run time in min) = ______________________________

   Equation for women: $\dot{V}O_2$ max ($mL \bullet kg^{-1} \bullet min^{-1}$) = 88.020 – (0.1656 × body weight in kg)
   – (2.767 × 1.5-mile run time in min) = ______________________________
3. Classification = ______________________________ (see Table L6.1)

EXTENSION ACTIVITIES

worksheet **6.2**

NAME ______________________ DATE ______________________

Use the following data and Table L6.1 to answer the questions below.

Gender: Male

Age: 18 years

Body weight: 82 kg

1.5-mile run time: 13:45 min:sec

1. Calculate the subject's predicted $\dot{V}O_2$ max from the 1.5-mile run test.

   $\dot{V}O_2$ max = ______________________ $mL \cdot kg^{-1} \cdot min^{-1}$

2. Classify the subject's predicted $\dot{V}O_2$ max from the 1.5-mile run test (see Table L6.1).

   Classification = ______________________

3. On the graph below, draw the expected relationship between 1.5-mile run times and $\dot{V}O_2$ max.

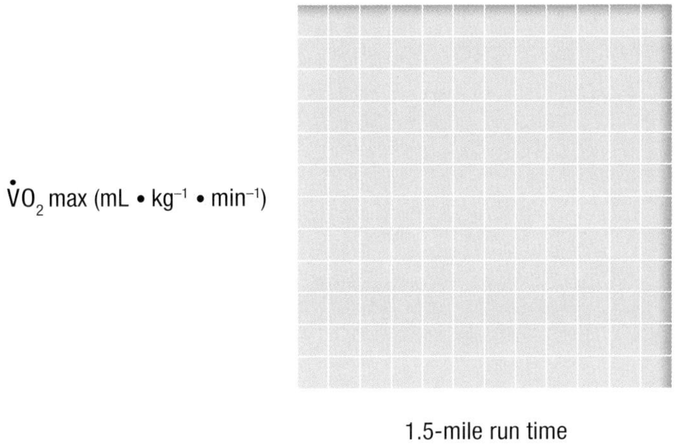

EXTENSION QUESTIONS

1. What are some common mistakes that may occur in administering this lab?

2. Identify possible sources of error in this lab.

3. Assess the practicality of using this lab in the field.

4. Research the reliability and/or validity of this lab using online resources, journal articles, and other credible sources.

REFERENCES

1. George, J. D., Vehrs, P. R., Allsen, P. E., Fellingham, G. W., and Fisher, A. G. VO_2max estimation from a submaximal 1-mile track jog for fit college-age individuals. *Med. Sci. Sports Exerc.* 81: 401–406, 1993.
2. Heyward, V. H. *Advanced Fitness Assessment and Exercise Prescription,* 7th edition. Champaign, IL: Human Kinetics, 2014.
3. Ryan, E. D., and Cramer, J. T. Fitness testing protocols and norms. In *NSCA's Essentials of Personal Training,* eds. R. W. Earle and T. R. Baechle, 2nd edition. Champaign, IL: Human Kinetics, 2012, pp. 201–250.

As a result of reading this chapter you will:

Understand the general functions of the endocrine system.

Be able to define the terms *endocrine* and *hormone.*

Know the three basic chemical structures of hormones.

Know the general mechanisms by which hormones alter cellular activity.

Know the effects of exercise on hormone secretion.

7 The Endocrine System

key concepts

amenorrhea
anovulation
catecholamine
cyclic AMP (cAMP)
endocrine
epinephrine
estrogen
exocrine
glucagon
gonads
growth hormone
hormone
insulin
menarche
norepinephrine
parathyroid hormone (PTH)
phenolic amine hormone
progesterone
protein hormone
steroid hormone
testosterone

For the human organism to meet the demands of exercise that may increase the metabolic rate by as much as twentyfold requires coordination of many physiological systems. It would be futile for the lungs to operate at maximum capacity if the heart did not cooperate by pumping blood at a rate necessary to move the blood gases and nutrients needed by the muscle tissues involved. In fact, most of the systems of the body become involved in the adjustments necessary to support all-out athletic efforts. Obviously, the various physiological systems must be properly coordinated to bring about the appropriate responses to the imposed demand.

Two systems exist for coordinating the physiological functions of the human organism: the nervous system, discussed in Chapter 4, provides the mechanism for bringing about short-term (quick) homeostatic responses; and the endocrine system may be thought of as functioning in the long-term (slower) control of the systems involved. The functions of the two systems are highly interrelated. Each affects the function of the other.

endocrine
exocrine

The term **endocrine** describes the system of ductless glands that secretes its products, called hormones, into the blood, which carries them to "target" organs or systems where they have their effects. The organs or systems may be quite distant. This is in distinction to **exocrine** glands (such as sweat glands), which secrete their products through ducts to the exterior. Figure 7.1 shows the locations of the major endocrine glands. Table 7.1 is a partial listing of the major endocrine glands, hormones they secrete, target tissues, and resultant effects.

figure 7.1 Locations of major endocrine glands.

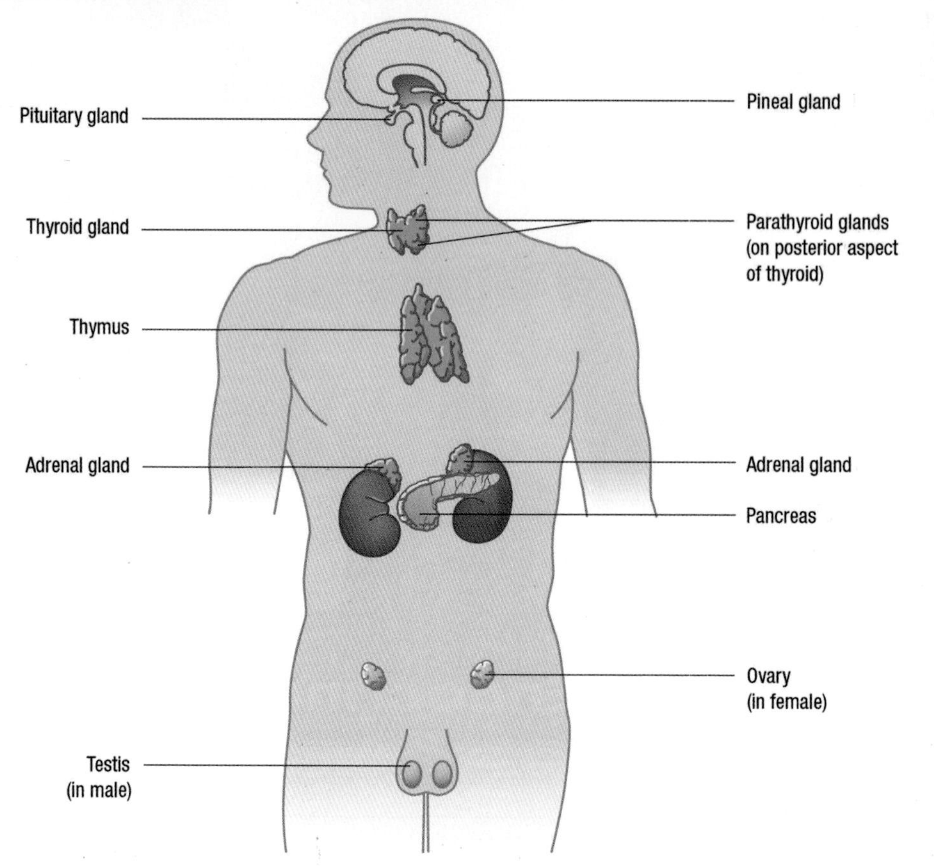

Adapted from J.W. Hole, Jr., *Human Anatomy and Physiology,* 5th Edition. Copyright © 1990 Wm. C. Brown Communications, Inc., Dubuque, Iowa. Adapted with permission of The McGraw-Hill Companies.

table 7.1

Major endocrine glands, hormones, chemical natures of the hormones, and the general functions elicited in the target tissues.

GLAND	HORMONE	CHEMICAL NATURE	GENERAL FUNCTION
Anterior pituitary	Growth (Somatotropin)	Protein	Tissue growth and metabolism
Thyroid	Thyroxine and Triiodothyronine	Phenolic amine	Tissue growth and metabolism
Pancreas	Insulin	Protein	Nutrient metabolism
Pancreas	Glucagon	Protein	Nutrient metabolism
Adrenal cortex	Cortisol	Steroid	Nutrient metabolism
Adrenal medulla	Epinephrine	Phenolic amine	Nutrient metabolism
Adrenal medulla	Norepinephrine	Phenolic amine	Nutrient metabolism
Parathyroid	Parathormone	Protein	Mineral metabolism
Thyroid	Calcitonin	Protein	Mineral metabolism
Kidney	Vitamin D	Steroid	Mineral metabolism
Posterior pituitary	Antidiuretic	Protein	Fluid balance
Adrenal cortex	Aldosterone	Steroid	Fluid balance
Ovary/placenta	Estrogen	Steroid	Reproductive function
Ovary/placenta	Progesterone	Steroid	Reproductive function
Testes	Testosterone	Steroid	Reproductive function
Ovary/testes	Inhibin	Protein	Reproductive function
Posterior pituitary	Oxytocin	Protein	Reproductive function
Placenta	Somatomammotropin	Protein	Reproductive function
Anterior pituitary	Thyrotropin	Protein	Tropic (stimulate other glands)
Anterior pituitary	Adrenocorticotropin	Protein	Tropic (stimulate other glands)
Anterior pituitary	Luteinizing	Protein	Tropic (stimulate other glands)
Anterior pituitary	Follicle stimulating	Protein	Tropic (stimulate other glands)
Anterior pituitary	Prolactin	Protein	Tropic (stimulate other glands)
Placenta	Chorionic gonadotropin	Protein	Tropic (stimulate other glands)

HORMONES

A **hormone** is a biological chemical that is secreted by an endocrine gland. All hormones fall into one of three categories, according to their basic structure: steroid hormones, protein hormones, and phenolic amine hormones (Figure 7.2). **Steroid hormones** are derived from cholesterol and therefore exhibit a classic four-ring structure, whereas **protein hormones** are chains of amino acids, and **phenolic amine hormones** contain a phenol group attached to an amine.

The action of a hormone on its target cell or tissue is usually a control function that accelerates or decelerates normal cellular processes. Figure 7.3 illustrates

- hormone
- steroid hormones
- protein hormones
- phenolic amine hormones

www

Endocrine System Topics
www.nlm.nih.gov/medlineplus/endocrinesystem.html

the process by which steroid hormones gain entry into a cell's internal machinery. Since both the steroid hormone and cell membrane are lipid, the steroid hormone enters easily through the cell membrane. Once inside, this type of hormone combines with specific protein molecules called *receptors*. The hormone and its receptor are analogous to a key and lock, in that both hormone and receptor are specific for each other. This steroid–receptor complex enters the nucleus and activates the synthesis of messenger RNA (mRNA), which proceeds to the ribosome to provide a template for the manufacture of new proteins. The type of protein produced depends on the type of target cell the hormone has entered. For example, one of the target cells of the steroid hormone testosterone is the muscle cell (fiber). Testosterone enters the muscle cell, binds with a receptor, travels to the nucleus, and initiates mRNA production and eventually the production of the contractile proteins (actin, myosin, troponin, and tropomyosin). It is the accumulation of contractile proteins that results in larger and stronger muscles.

figure 7.2

The three basic hormone structures.

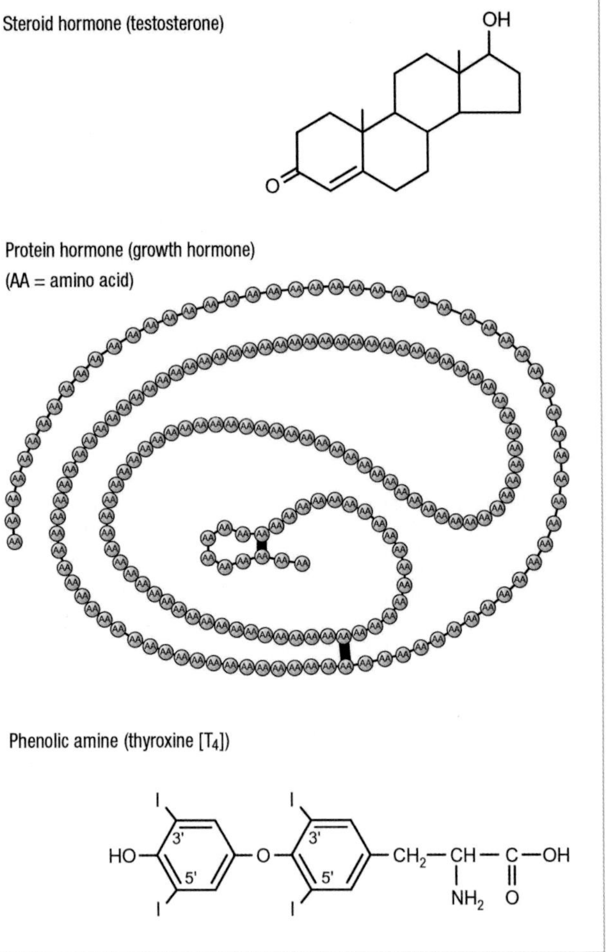

Protein hormones, on the other hand, are not lipid soluble and therefore cannot diffuse through the cell membrane. Figure 7.4 illustrates the general mechanism of action of protein hormones. The hormone binds with a receptor located on the cell membrane, which activates a cyclizing enzyme, which in turn initiates the production of a cyclic nucleotide such as **cyclic AMP (cAMP)** or cyclic GMP (cGMP). These cyclic nucleotides are called *second messengers* and, when activated, induce the phosphorylation (addition of a phosphate group) of specific proteins, thereby activating those proteins. The protein hormone insulin, for example, binds to extracellular receptors located on the cells of many tissues, and its actions are specific to the type of cell with which it interacts. In the liver, one of the activities resulting from insulin–receptor binding is cAMP production and the subsequent activation of the enzyme glycogen synthetase, which acts in the conversion of glucose to its storage form, glycogen.

cyclic AMP

The location of the receptor for a phenolic amine depends on the specific hormone. Receptors for the thyroid hormones triiodothyronine (T_3) and thyroxine (T_4), for example, are located within the cell, whereas the catecholamines (epinephrine and norepinephrine), which are produced by the adrenal medulla, bind to receptors that are located on the cell membrane. Therefore, some phenolic amine hormones (thyroid hormones) possess a mechanism of action similar to that of steroid hormones, and other phenolic amine hormones (catecholamines) exhibit a mechanism of action similar to that of protein hormones.

www

Endocrine System
www2.estrellamountain.edu/faculty/farabee/Biobk/BioBookENDOCR.html

Control of Hormone Secretion

Three primary types of stimuli may initiate the secretion of a hormone: neural, hormonal, or the concentration of a substance in the blood. For example, during pregnancy, as the fetus grows, the uterus is stretched. This stretching stimulates receptors in the uterus and, through a nervous reflex, results in the release of oxytocin from the posterior pituitary. The oxytocin travels to receptors located on the cells of the uterine myometrium, causing the contraction of those muscle cells. The thyroid gland, on the other hand, secretes T_3 and T_4 primarily in response to levels of thyroid-stimulating hormone (TSH) in the blood, whereas the pancreas responds to glucose levels by secreting either insulin or glucagon, depending on whether blood glucose levels are high or low, respectively. On a long-term basis, secretion rates are usually maintained by a negative feedback mechanism in which high levels of a hormone, or a substance secreted in response to a hormone, feed back on the gland to inhibit further secretion of the hormone.

EXERCISE AND ENDOCRINE FUNCTION

Our knowledge of the hormone response to exercise, and conversely the effects of the level of secretion of various hormones on health and performance, is still far from complete. Methods have now become available, however, for measuring many of the hormones in blood during exercise. Previously, many of the important hormones, such as those produced by the adrenal cortex, had to be estimated from breakdown products that appear in the urine after the completion of an exercise bout. Obviously, urinalyses could not provide a very accurate time relation between physical exercise and the hormonal response elicited.

As a result of newer methods, such as radio enzymatic techniques, investigators have made measurements of much improved sensitivity, specificity, precision, and accuracy. Although our body of knowledge is still fragmentary, the emerging evidence indicates that the effects of hormones on exercise performance are of considerable importance and likewise that the effects of exercise on endocrine function are considerable.

The Pancreas and Exercise

The ability of the body to supply the working tissues with fuel is one of the most significant factors determining exercise and athletic performance. The hormones glucagon and insulin, secreted by the pancreas, play especially important roles in the control of the fuel supply. **Glucagon**, synthesized and secreted by the alpha cells of the pancreas, acts mainly to raise blood glucose levels by promoting the release of glucose from the liver. It also stimu-

figure 7.3

(A) A steroid hormone passes through a cell membrane and (B) combines with a protein receptor in the cytoplasm. (C) The hormone–receptor complex enters the nucleus and (D) activates the synthesis of messenger RNA. (E) The messenger RNA leaves the nucleus and (F) functions in the manufacture of protein molecules.

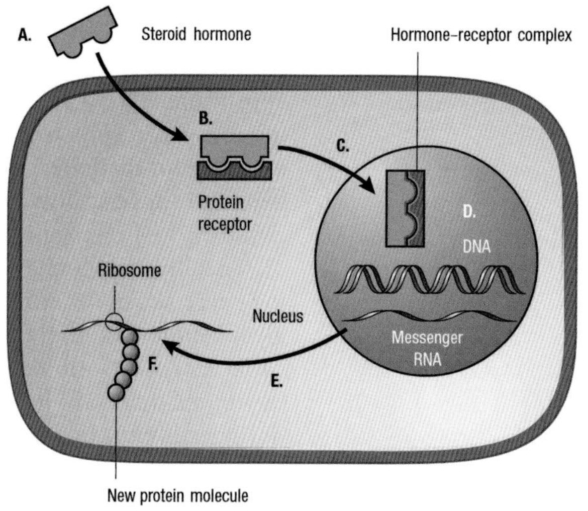

figure 7.4

(A) The protein hormone reaches its target cell via the blood and (B) combines with a receptor located on the cell membrane. (C) As a result, molecules of an enzyme such as adenyl cyclase are activated and (D) cause the activation of a second messenger such as cyclic AMP, which (E) brings about various cellular changes.

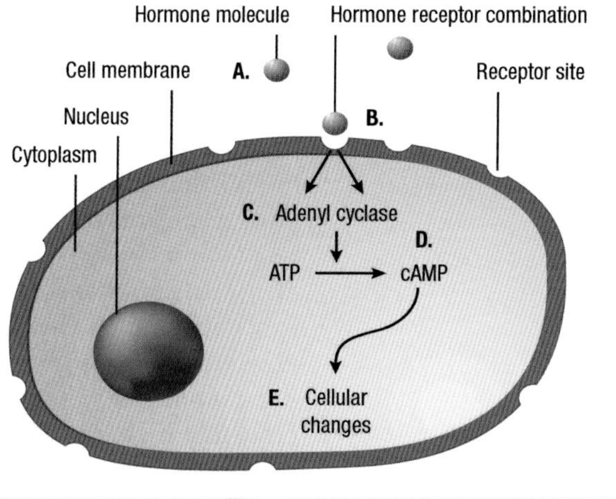

glucagon
insulin

www
The Pituitary Foundation
www.pituitary.org.uk/

lates glycogenolysis (conversion of glycogen to glucose) and gluconeogenesis (formation of glucose from non-carbohydrate sources), both of which result in higher blood glucose levels. **Insulin,** on the other hand, lowers blood glucose levels by facilitating glucose transport through cell membranes. It also activates the enzyme glycogen synthetase, which converts glucose to its storage form, glycogen. In addition to its role in glucose uptake and storage, insulin is a potent inhibitor of lipolysis (fat breakdown for use as an energy source).[15]

Blood glucagon levels tend to rise with strenuous exercise, but the response is slow and does not appear to occur in a linear fashion in accordance with either the duration or the intensity of the exercise.[7,10,12] Insulin levels in the blood, on the other hand, decrease in direct proportion to the increases in workload above approximately 50 percent of $\dot{V}O_2$ max.[10] The rapid uptake of glucose by the working muscles results from both insulin-dependent increases in receptor number and non–insulin-mediated glucose uptake by the working muscles. There is some evidence to suggest, however, that even non–insulin-mediated uptake of glucose still requires the presence of at least some insulin.[7]

In subjects who have undergone training, the rise in blood glucagon levels during exercise appears to be less than in untrained subjects, resulting in a reduction in glycogenolysis and gluconeogenesis.[5] Training also appears to decrease the body's capacity for insulin secretion. Both resting insulin levels and insulin production during exercise are lower following training. This reduction in insulin secretion during activity, however, appears to be counterbalanced by the training-induced increase in insulin receptor sensitivity. Therefore, following training, less insulin is required to handle a given carbohydrate load.[21] Furthermore, Smutok et al.[22] found that strength training and aerobic training were equally effective in improving the body's ability to handle glucose.

The Adrenal Medulla and Exercise

Although the pancreatic hormones, glucagon and insulin, play key roles in maintaining the appropriate glucose level to meet the needs of the body during rest and exercise, the catecholamines, epinephrine and norepinephrine, produced and secreted by the adrenal medulla (middle portion of the adrenal gland), also serve to increase the availability of fuel to the active muscles.[11] The **catecholamines** are involved not only in maintaining a constant fuel supply to active tissues but also in helping to regulate heart rate and blood flow. All of the **epinephrine** in the blood is secreted by the adrenal gland. **Norepinephrine,** on the other hand, is released from both the adrenal gland and sympathetic nerve endings.

catecholamines
epinephrine
norepinephrine

During exercise, blood levels of both epinephrine and norepinephrine rise, resulting in increases in glycogenolysis, lipolysis, heart rate, stroke volume, and the redistribution of blood flow to the working muscles and the skin (for heat loss). It has also been suggested that during exercise, mental performance may be improved. This too is thought to be a function of the catecholamines.[7]

Training results in a reduction in the catecholamine response to the same absolute intensity of exercise, but it appears to increase the adrenal medulla's response to stimuli such as hypoglycemia, hypoxia, hypercapnia, glucagon, caffeine, and maximum exercise.[21] Although it appears that catecholamine levels do not change substantially in response to acute exercise, resting catecholamine levels are significantly higher in trained individuals. Because the catecholamines are, at least in part, responsible for some very important aspects of physical performance (heart rate, stroke volume, blood flow to skeletal muscle and skin, and the enhancement of mental performance), it is logical that an increased capacity for catecholamine secretion would serve as an advantage in athletics.[7,21]

Diabetes therapy

Diabetes mellitus is a broad term used to describe a group of metabolic diseases characterized by high blood glucose levels. Diabetes is caused by an inability of the pancreas to produce enough insulin or by a decrease in the sensitivity (or increase in the resistance) of the body tissues to insulin. Type 1 diabetes is caused by the failure of the pancreas to produce enough insulin and is often referred to as "insulin dependent" diabetes. Type 2 diabetes typically begins with insulin resistance and, if not managed, can result in chronically high blood glucose levels that can damage the pancreas and reduce its ability to produce insulin. Almost 400 million people in the world have diabetes, and approximately 90 percent of those cases are of the type 2 classification. Prevention and treatment of type 2 diabetes involve maintaining a healthy diet and body weight, as well as regular physical exercise.

Joint recommendations by the American College of Sports Medicine (ACSM) and American Diabetes Association (ADA) describe the quantity and quality of exercise to help manage glucose levels in people with diabetes.[6] Both aerobic and resistance training improve the action of insulin and are effective in managing blood glucose levels. Individuals with diabetes should perform moderate-intensity aerobic activity (50–70% maximum heart rate) at least 150 minutes per week. Because progressive resistance exercise improves insulin sensitivity in older men with type 2 diabetes, the ADA also recommends a progressive (progressing to three sets of 8 to 12 repetitions) resistance training program three times per week for these individuals. Because the changes in blood glucose management that occur with exercise are considered acute (lasting less than 72 hours) rather than chronic, exercise should be done on a regular basis—every other day—in order to maintain the beneficial effects.

The Thyroid and Exercise

Because the thyroid hormones triiodothyronine (T_3) and thyroxine (T_4) are important regulators of metabolism, it seems likely that they would be called upon to help regulate metabolic processes during exercise. In general, however, either no change[17] or small increases[3,8] in the levels of these hormones have been shown to occur with acute exercise. Training-induced changes in thyroid function, on the other hand, have been shown to result in increased levels of both T_3 and T_4.[8] This may explain, at least in part, the higher metabolic rate in chronic exercisers and athletes.[14]

The Parathyroid and Exercise

Parathyroid hormone (PTH, parathormone) is involved in calcium regulation. PTH increases calcium levels in the blood by: (1) promoting intestinal calcium absorption, (2) enhancing renal calcium reabsorption, and (3) mobilizing calcium from the bone (bone resorption).[29] It is generally accepted that regular exercise plays an important role in producing and maintaining a healthy skeleton; however, the mechanism by which this occurs is not completely understood. Tsai et al.[23] and Zerath et al.[30] have shown that both moderate and severe aerobic exercise result in increases in both PTH and blood calcium levels, whereas Ashizawa et al.[1] found decreases in both PTH and blood calcium levels following one bout of moderate resistance exercise. Endurance training, however, has been shown[4] to result in decreased PTH levels, but increased blood Ca^{++}, suggesting that the Ca^{++} response to exercise may not be associated with PTH. Clearly, a complex mechanism exists to regulate levels of Ca^{++} in the blood.

parathyroid hormone (PTH)

The Gonads and Exercise

The sperm- and egg-producing reproductive organs of the male and female are the **gonads**—the testes in the male and the ovaries in the female. The gonads not only produce the components that will eventually become offspring, they also are

gonads

RESEARCH

Response of growth and metabolism hormones to exercise

Several hormones that play significant roles in growth and metabolism are released in response to exercise. Stokes et al.* studied the changes in the levels of growth hormone (GH), cortisol, testosterone, prolactin, and insulin in response to resistance, sprint, and endurance exercise to see whether changes in hormone secretion were specific to the type of exercise performed. Eight healthy male adults were subjects for this investigation. The subjects were studied on four separate occasions, separated by at least seven days, in which they performed, in random order, a 30-minute resistance exercise bout, a 30-second cycle ergometer sprint, a 30-minute cycle at 70 percent $\dot{V}O_2$ max, and a seated rest period. Blood was drawn and analyzed for hormone content before exercise; immediately post-exercise; and 20, 40, and 60 minutes post-exercise. The results showed that:

1. GH concentrations were significantly different between trials and over time. There was a significant increase in GH from pre-exercise to post-exercise for both the sprint and endurance work bouts, and GH concentration was significantly greater in the endurance trial than in either the resistance or the rest trial.
2. Cortisol concentrations were significantly different between trials and over time. There was also a different pattern of cortisol secretion between trials, a significant difference between pre- and post-exercise for the sprint and endurance work bouts, a significant difference between the endurance bout and both the resistance and rest trials, and a significant difference between the sprint bout and the rest bout.
3. Testosterone concentrations were significantly different over time for all trials (except rest), but there was no difference between trials.
4. Prolactin concentrations were significantly different between the trials, but there was no significant change in concentration from pre- to post-exercise. There was, however, a different pattern of prolactin secretion between trials and a significantly greater prolactin concentration following the sprint trial than either the resistance or the rest trial.
5. Insulin concentrations were significantly different between trials and over time. Both the resistance and sprint exercises resulted in significant increases in insulin secretion, and insulin concentration decreased significantly in the endurance work bout.

The results show that there is not a global hormonal secretion in response to exercise, but rather that specific hormone secretion is dependent on the mode of exercise. Each of the hormones studied in this investigation plays a specific role in the metabolic processes that are required during resistance, sprint, and endurance exercises. The type and magnitude of hormone secretion may reflect the roles the hormones play in meeting the demands of the exercise.

*Stokes, K. A., Gilbert, K. L., Hall, G. M., Andrews, R. C., and Thompson, D. Different responses of selected hormones to three types of exercise in young men. *Eur. J. Appl. Physiol.* *113:* 775–783, 2013.

testosterone
estrogen
progesterone

responsible for the production of the gonadal hormones. **Testosterone** is the major hormone secreted by the gonads of the male, whereas **estrogen** and **progesterone** are the major female gonadal hormones. These hormones perform a number of anabolic functions that result in the growth and development of many different tissues in the body.

Serum testosterone levels increase following both high-intensity aerobic and anaerobic exercise bouts, with increases ranging from 13 to 185 percent. These increases in testosterone appear to be independent of changes in pituitary luteinizing hormone (LH), which normally stimulates the testes to produce testosterone, but dependent on the intensity and duration of the activity and the fitness level of the individual. Acute submaximal exercise, however, has been shown to result in an initial increase in testosterone, followed by a decrease to or below baseline values. This decline in testosterone associated with submaximal exercise is also evident in endurance-trained athletes, who generally exhibit lower testosterone levels. More severe aerobic training, however, appears to be associated with an increase in serum testosterone,[6] as does weight training.[18,24]

The effects of heavy exercise on the female reproductive system have become relatively well known. Delayed **menarche, amenorrhea,** and **anovulation** are probably the most commonly known effects. As in the male, plasma levels of the gonadal hormones (estrogen and progesterone in the female) tend to rise following exercise of sufficient intensity. Unlike their male counterparts, however, female athletes who exhibit reproductive disturbances also exhibit consistent reductions in LH levels following exercise training.[13] Menstrual cycles that are accompanied by an ovulatory phase and that occur regularly are dependent on a certain level of LH. Therefore, the reductions in LH levels that occur with training may provide at least a partial explanation for the reproductive disturbances mentioned previously.

- menarche
- amenorrhea
- anovulation

Growth Hormone and Exercise

Growth hormone, secreted by the anterior pituitary, is involved in regulating the growth and metabolism of many tissues of the body. Serum growth hormone levels increase during strenuous exercise and tend to reflect an increasing workload in prolonged exercise until a maximum load is reached.[16,19,26,27,28] The effects of training on the exercise-induced increase in growth hormone level have not been established; some studies report a diminished response,[25] while others report an enhanced response,[2,9,18] and still others report no change[2,16,20] in the growth hormone response to exercise. As with many hormonal responses to exercise, these differences may be due to differences in the intensity, duration, and type of exercise; the fitness level of the subjects; the hormone sampling methods; and a number of other variables.

- growth hormone

WWW

Growth Hormone

http://arbl.cvmbs.colostate.edu/hbooks/pathphys/endocrine/hypopit/gh.html

summary

Essentially, two systems coordinate the physiological functions of the human organism: the nervous system and the endocrine system. The endocrine system functions in the long-term control of these functions. Endocrine glands are ductless glands that secrete hormones into the blood, which carries the hormones to their "target" tissues where the hormones have their effects. By acting in a key-and-lock fashion, hormones bind to receptors and regulate the cellular processes of their target tissues.

The various hormones play a variety of roles both at rest and during exercise. Some hormones, such as those of the pancreas and the adrenal medulla, help to supply working tissues with energy, while others, such as the gonadal steroids, stimulate the process of making new contractile proteins in skeletal muscle. It is evident that a complex interplay among exercise, hormone secretion, and tissue function exists; however, our knowledge of the hormonal response to exercise and the effects of hormones on health and performance is incomplete. With continuing advances in laboratory techniques, it becomes easier to measure bloodborne substances accurately, making a clearer definition of some of these effects possible.

questions for review

1. What are the locations of the major endocrine glands?
2. What are the three categories of hormones and the characteristics of each?
3. Describe the process by which steroid hormones gain entry into a cell.
4. Describe the process by which protein hormones gain entry into a cell.

5. What role do glucagon and insulin play in exercise? How does training affect the role of these hormones?
6. What role do the catecholamines play in exercise? How does training affect the role of these hormones?
7. What role does parathyroid hormone play in exercise? How does training affect the role of this hormone?
8. What role do the gonadal hormones play in exercise? How does training affect the role of these hormones?
9. What role does growth hormone play in exercise? How does training affect the role of this hormone?

student companion website

For further review of this book's chapters and for test preparation, visit the book's website, **www.hhpcommunities.com/exercisephysiology**, to take practice quizzes, review the vocabulary terms, use the study guide, and view the digital image bank.

references

1. Ashizawa, N., Fujimura, R., Tokuyama, K., and Suzuki, M. A bout of resistance exercise increases urinary calcium independent of osteoclastic activation in men. *J. Appl. Physiol.* 83: 1159–1163, 1997.
2. Bosco, C., Colli, R., Bonomi, R., vonDuvillard, S. P., and Viru, A. Monitoring strength training: neuromuscular and hormonal profile. *Med. Sci. Sports Exerc.* 32: 202–208, 2000.
3. Bosco, C., Tihanyl, J., Rivalta, L., Parlato, G., Tranquilli, C., Pulvirenti, G., Foti, C., Viru, M., and Viru, A. Hormonal responses to strenuous jumping effort. *Jpn. J. Physiol.* 46: 93–98, 1996.
4. Brahm, H., Strom, H., Piehl-Aulin, K., Mallmin, H., and Ljunghall, S. Bone metabolism in endurance trained athletes: a comparison to population-based controls based on DXA, SXA, quantitative ultrasound, and biochemical markers. *Calcif. Tissue Int.* 61: 448–454, 1997.
5. Coggan, A. R., Swanson, S. C., Mendenhall, L. A., Habash, D. L., and Kien, C. L. Effect of endurance training on hepatic glycogenolysis and gluconeogenesis during prolonged exercise in men. *Am. J. Physiol.* 268: E375–E383, 1995.
6. Colberg, S. R., Sigal, R. J., Fernhall, B., Regensteiner, J. G., Blissmer, B. J., Rubin, R. R., Chasan-Tabar, L., Albright, A. L., and Braun, B. Exercise and type 2 diabetes: the American College of Sports Medicine and the American Diabetes Association joint position statement executive summary. *Diabetes Care* 33: 2692–2696, 2010.
7. Cumming, D. C. Hormones and athletic performance. In *Endocrinology and Metabolism,* eds. P. Felig, J. D. Baxter, and L. A. Frohman. New York: McGraw-Hill, 1995.
8. Duma, E., Orbai, P., and Derevenco, P. Blood levels of some electrolytes and hormones during exercise in athletes. *Rom. J. Physiol.* 35: 55–60, 1998.
9. Eijnde, B. O., and Hespel, P. Short-term creatine supplement ation does not alter the hormonal response to resistance training. *Med. Sci. Sports Exerc.* 33: 449–453, 2001.
10. Galbo, H. *Hormonal and Metabolic Adaptation to Exercise.* New York: Thieme–Stratton, 1983.
11. Ganong, W. F. *Review of Medical Physiology.* San Francisco: Appleton & Lange, 1997.
12. Gyntelberg, F., Rennie, M. J., Hickson, R. C., and Holloszy, J. O. Effect of training on the response of plasma glucagon to exercise. *J. Appl. Physiol.* 43: 302–305, 1977.
13. Harber, V. J. Menstrual dysfunction in athletes: an energetic challenge. *Exerc. Sport Sci. Rev.* 28: 19–23, 2000.
14. Harber, V. J., Peterson, S. R., and Chilibeck, P. D. Thyroid hormone concentrations and muscle metabolism in amenorrheic and eumenorrheic athletes. *Can. J. Appl. Physiol.* 23: 293–306, 1998.
15. Horowitz, J. F. Regulation of lipid mobilization and oxidation during exercise in obesity. *Exerc. Sport Sci. Rev.* 29: 42–46, 2001.
16. Kanaley, J. A., Weatherup-Dentes, M. M., Jaynes, E. B., and Hartman, M. L. Obesity attenuates the growth hormone response to exercise. *J. Clin. Endocrinol. Metab.* 84: 3156–3161, 1999.
17. Kraemer, R. R., Blair, M. S., McCaferty, R., and Castracane, V. D. Running-induced alterations in growth hormone, prolactin, triiodothyronine, and thyroxine

concentrations in trained and untrained men and women. *Res. Q. Exerc. Sport* 64: 69–74, 1993.

18. Kraemer, W. J., Hakkinen, K., Newton, R. U., Nindl, B. C., Volek, J. S., McCormick, M., Gotshalk, L. A., Gordon, S. E., Fleck, S. J., Campbell, W. W., Putukian, M., and Evans, W. J. Effects of heavy-resistance training on hormonal response patterns in younger vs. older men. *J. Appl. Physiol.* 87: 982–992, 1999.
19. Maas, H. C. M., deVries, W. R., Maitimu, I., Bol, E., Bowers, C. Y., and Koppeschaar, P. F. Growth hormone responses during strenuous exercise: the role of GH-releasing hormone and GH-releasing peptide-2. *Med. Sci. Sports Exerc.* 32: 1226–1232, 2000.
20. Marx, J. O., Ratamess, N. A., Nindl, B. C., Gotshalk, L. A., Volek, J. S., Dohi, K., Bush, J. A., Gomez, A. L., Mazzetti, S. A., Fleck, S. J., Hakkinen, K., Newton, R. U., and Kraemer, W. J. Low-volume circuit versus high-volume periodized resistance training in women. *Med. Sci. Sports Exerc.* 33: 635–643, 2001.
21. Shephard, R. J., and Astrand, P. O. Endurance in sport. In *The Encyclopedia of Sports Medicine*. Boston: Blackwell Scientific Publications, 1992.
22. Smutok, M. A., Reece, C., Kokkinos, P. F., Former, C. M., Dawson, P. K., DeVane, J., Patterson, J., Goldberg, A. P., and Hurley, B. F. Effects of exercise training modality on glucose tolerance in men with abnormal glucose regulation. *Int. J. Sports Med.* 15: 283–289, 1994.
23. Tsai, K. S., Lin, J. C., Chen, C. K., Cheng, W. C., and Yang, C. H. Effect of exercise and exogenous glucocorticoid on serum level of intact parathyroid hormone. *Int. J. Sports Med.* 18: 583–587, 1997.
24. Tsolakis, C., Messinis, D., Stergioulas, A., and Dessypris, A. Hormonal responses after strength training and detraining in prepubertal and pubertal boys. *J. Strength Cond. Res.* 14: 399–404, 2000.
25. Urhausen, A., Gabriel, H. H., and Kindermann, W. Impaired pituitary hormonal response to exhaustive exercise in overtrained endurance athletes. *Med. Sci. Sports Exerc.* 30: 407–414, 1998.
26. Wallace, J. D., Cuneo, R. C., Baxter, R., Orskov, H., Keay, N., Pentecost, C., Dall, R., Rosen, T., Jorgensen, J. O., Cittadini, A., Longobardi, S., Sacca, L., Christiansen, J. S., Bengtsson, B. A., and Sonksen, P. H. Responses of the growth hormone and insulin-like growth factor axis to exercise, GH administration and GH withdrawal in trained adult males: a potential test for GH abuse in sport. *J. Clin. Endocrinol. Metab.* 84: 3591–3601, 1999.
27. Wallace, J. D., Cuneo, R. C., Bidlingmaier, M., Lundberg, P. A., Carlsson, L., Boguszewski, C. L., Hay, J., Healy, M. L., Napoli, R., Dall, R., Rosen, T., and Strasburger, C. J. The response of molecular isoforms of growth hormone to acute exercise in trained adult males. *J. Clin. Endocrinol. Metab.* 86: 200–206, 2001.
28. Waters, D. L., Qualls, C. R., Dorin, R., Veldhuis, J. D., and Baumgartner, R. N. Increased pulsality, process irregularity, and nocturnal trough concentrations of growth hormone in amenorrheic compared to eumenorrheic athletes. *J. Clin. Endocrinol. Metab.* 86: 1013–1019, 2001.
29. Widmaier, E. P., Raff, H., and Strang, K. T. *Vander's Human Physiology: The Mechanisms of Body Function*, 13th edition. New York: McGraw-Hill, 2014.
30. Zerath, E., Holy, X., Douce, P., Guezennec, C. Y., and Chatard, J. C. Effect of endurance training on postexercise parathyroid hormone levels in elderly men. *Med. Sci. Sports Exerc.* 29: 1139–1145, 1997.

As a result of reading this chapter you will:

Understand the basic organization and function of the immune system.

Know the relationships among the cells of the immune system.

Be able to describe the effects of acute and chronic exercise on leukocytosis and lymphocytosis.

Be able to discuss the effects of exercise intensity and duration on the risk of developing upper respiratory infection.

Know the risks associated with exercise during infection.

The Immune System 8

key concepts

acquired immune deficiency syndrome (AIDS)
antibody
antibody-dependent cell-mediated cytotoxicity (ADCC)
antigen
B cell
cell-mediated immunity
cluster designation (CD)
complement protein
helper T cell
human immunodeficiency virus (HIV)
humoral immunity
immune
immunoglobulin
interferon
killer T cell
leukocyte
leukocytosis

There is a popular belief that chronic exercise and improved physical fitness make an individual "healthier." Much research has been conducted with regard to chronic illnesses such as coronary heart disease and obesity, but relatively little is known about the effect of exercise on infectious diseases. Anecdotal evidence from athletes and non-athletes suggests that exercise enhances an individual's resistance to infection. However, coaches often express concerns about an increase in the number of infectious episodes in their athletes, particularly near the end of the competitive season. These conflicting testimonials indicate a need for systematic investigations to answer important questions regarding the interactions between exercise and immune function such as:

1. Does an acute bout of exercise affect immune function?
2. Does chronic exercise affect immune function?
3. Are the effects of exercise on immune function related to the metabolic characteristics (aerobic or anaerobic) of the activity?
4. What are the relationships among intensity, duration, and frequency of exercise and immune function?
5. What are the clinical implications of the interactions between exercise and immune function?

IMMUNE SYSTEM

The term **immune** is derived from the Latin word *immunis,* meaning "free." As this root suggests, the function of the immune system is to keep us free from invading organisms such as bacteria and viruses that may cause diseases. The immune system can be divided into two general classifications, depending on whether they provide a defense against a specific pathogen: non-specific mechanisms and specific mechanisms. The estimated one trillion cells of the immune system generally function within one of these two classifications but are, in some cases, involved in both non-specific and specific immunity. The cells of the immune system display surface proteins called **cluster designations** (CD) that researchers use to identify, classify, and study these cells.[21] Thus, in some sources, you will find the various immune cells named by the prefix CD and then a number, such as CD3 for helper T cells. This nomenclature, however, is not very descriptive for an introductory chapter on the immune system, and we will therefore use the traditional names for the cells of the immune system, as shown in Figure 8.1.

immune
cluster designations

The general term for cells of the immune system is **leukocytes.** Leukocytes (white blood cells) are formed from undifferentiated stem cells in bone marrow and can be classified as granular or agranular. The population of granular leukocytes can be further classified into neutrophils, eosinophils, and basophils. **Neutrophils** are the most abundant of the granular leukocytes and make up approximately 50 to 75 percent of all blood leukocytes.

leukocytes
neutrophils

There are two major classifications of agranular leukocytes: lymphocytes and monocytes. **Lymphocytes** make up approximately 20 to 40 percent of blood leukocytes. The population of lymphocytes includes **T cells, B cells,** and **natural killer (NK) cells.** There are four subclassifications of T cells (killer, helper, suppressor, and memory T cells) and two of B cells (plasma cells and memory B cells) (see Figure 8.1). **Monocytes,** which constitute about 5 percent of blood leukocytes, can be transformed into **macrophages,** large ameboid mononuclear cells capable of ingesting foreign particles and other cells.

lymphocytes
T cells
B cells
natural killer (NK) cells
monocytes
macrophages

Relationships among cells of the immune system. **figure 8.1**

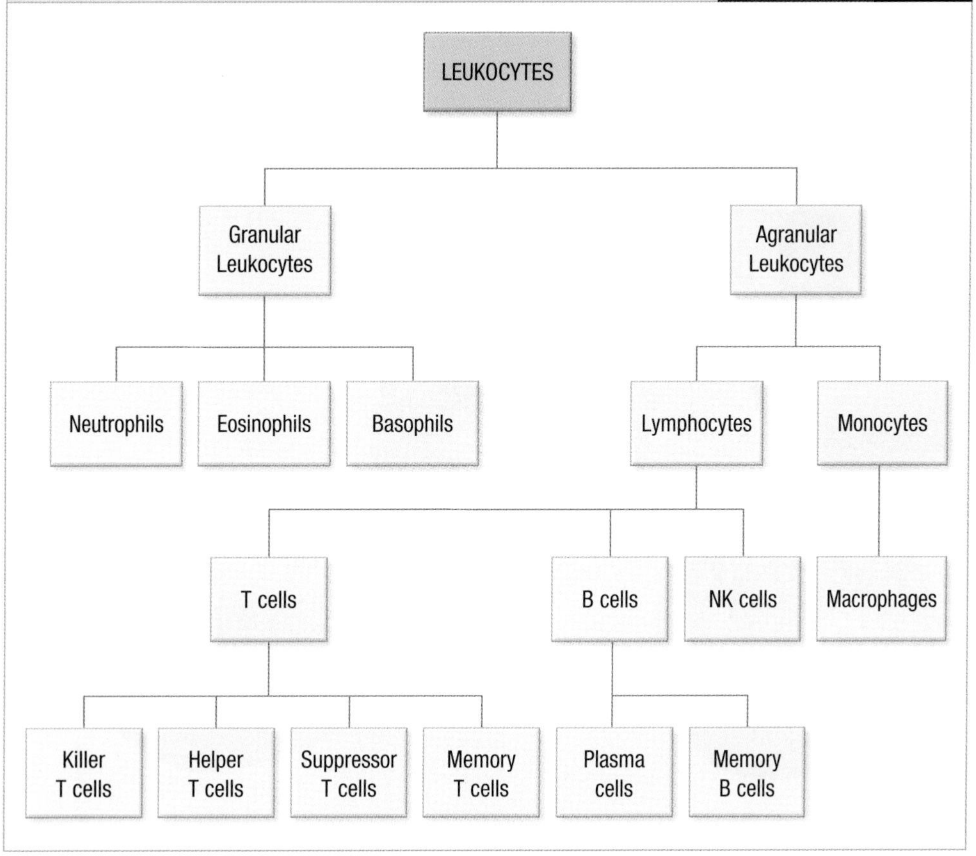

NON-SPECIFIC IMMUNE MECHANISMS

The non-specific immune mechanisms are the first lines of defense against potentially pathogenic (disease-causing) organisms. Non-specific immunity involves two mechanisms: external and internal. The external mechanisms include structures such as the skin, digestive tract, respiratory tract, and urinary tract. These barriers are effective in protecting the body from most invading organisms. They are reinforced by internal mechanisms designed to destroy those pathogens that penetrate the first (external) lines of defense. The internal mechanisms associated with non-specific immunity include the actions of phagocytic cells, NK cells, complement proteins, and interferons.

Phagocytosis. Two major groups of cells are involved in the non-specific phagocytic process: neutrophils and mononuclear phagocytes such as monocytes, macrophages, and tissue-specific phagocytes in the liver, spleen, lymph nodes, lungs, and central nervous system. **Phagocytosis** is a process by which unwanted particles are engulfed and destroyed by digestive enzymes (Figure 8.2). An extension of the phagocytic cell membrane (called a *pseudopod*) "reaches" for the particle and surrounds it. Once the particle is engulfed, it binds to a cell organelle called the *lysosome,* which contains digestive enzymes, and is destroyed.

Natural killer cells. NK cells are non-T and non-B lymphocytes that are thought to be involved with immune surveillance against cancer by destroying certain cells before they can produce tumors. The exact association between NK cell activity and

key concepts

- lymphocyte
- lymphocytosis
- lymphotoxin
- macrophage
- macrophage activating factor
- macrophage chemotactic factor
- macrophage migration inhibiting factor
- memory B cell
- memory T cell
- monocyte
- natural killer (NK) cell
- neutrophil
- phagocytosis
- plasma cell
- suppressor T cell
- T cell
- upper respiratory infection (URI)

www

The Immune System
www.niaid.nih.gov/topics/immunesystem/Pages/default.aspx

- phagocytosis

figure 8.2 Phagocytosis by a neutrophil or macrophage.

Phagocytic cell extends pseudopods around object to be engulfed (such as a bacterium). Dots represent lysosomal enzymes. If the pseudopods fuse to form a complete food vacuole (1), lysosomal enzymes are restricted to the organelle formed by the lysosome and food vacuole. If the lysosome fuses with the vacuole before fusion of the pseudopods is complete (2), lysosomal enzymes are released into the infected area of the tissue.

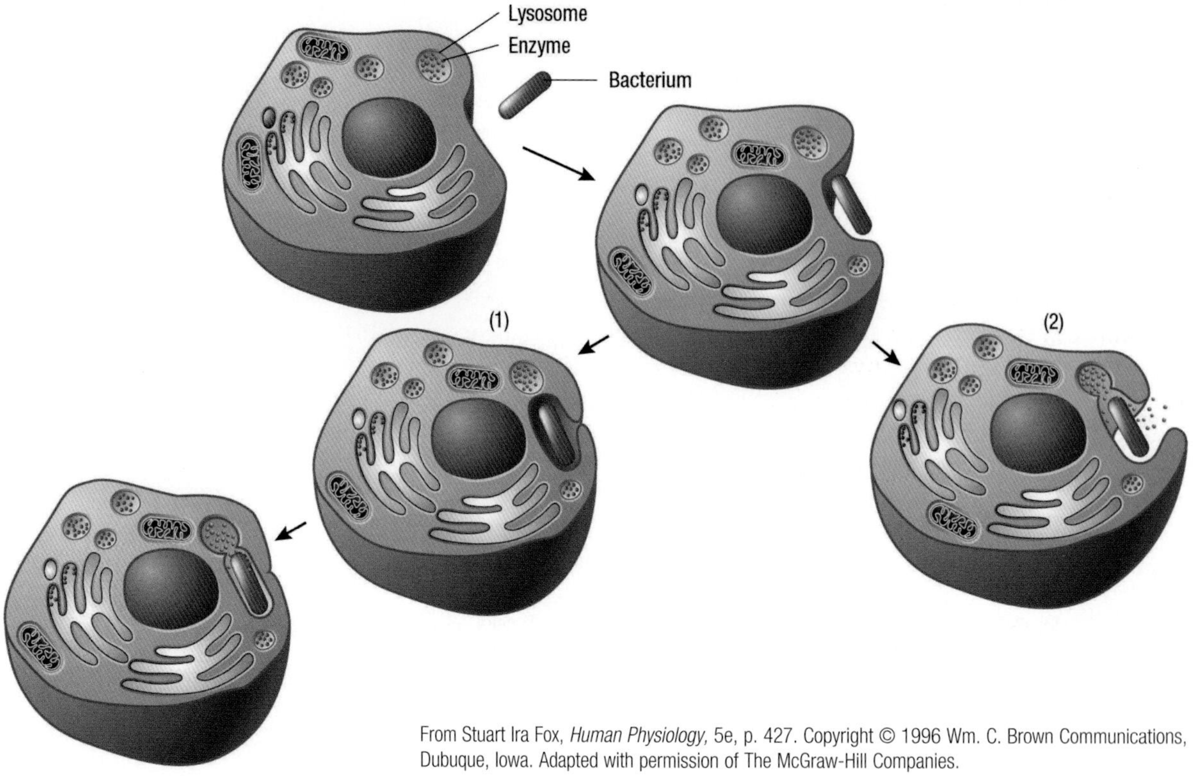

From Stuart Ira Fox, *Human Physiology,* 5e, p. 427. Copyright © 1996 Wm. C. Brown Communications, Inc., Dubuque, Iowa. Adapted with permission of The McGraw-Hill Companies.

the risk of developing cancer in humans is unclear. In addition, the precise method by which NK cells destroy virally infected and tumor cells is currently unknown.

complement protein

Complement proteins. The **complement protein** system consists of nine protein components (C1 through C9), which exist in an inactive state in blood and other bodily fluids. The complement system destroys cells that have been "marked" for elimination by **antibodies** (substances produced by plasma cells, discussed later in this chapter). Activation of the complement protein system occurs when antibodies bind with specific chemical substances on the membrane of the invading cells, called **antigens** (also discussed later in this chapter). Following activation, the complement system proceeds through a series of events including binding to the cell membrane (a process called *fixation*) and destroying the cell. Destruction of the cell is accomplished by proteins C5 through C9, which puncture the cell membrane. This allows water to enter, which eventually causes the cell to burst.

antibodies

antigens

Interferons. The name *interferon* is appropriate because these polypeptides "interfere" with the ability of viruses to replicate. **Interferons** are produced by cells infected with viruses and act on neighboring cells to prevent infection. The antiviral effects of interferons can be identified within hours following infection and may continue for several days.[37] The association with virally infected cells has

interferons

implicated interferons in immune surveillance against cancer. Many types of cells produce interferons, including leukocytes, fibroblasts, and lymphocytes, which release alpha, beta, and gamma interferon, respectively. The mechanism of interferon action is both direct and indirect. The direct action involves the production of cellular enzymes that prevent viral protein synthesis and the destruction of viral messenger RNA. Interferons destroy infected cells indirectly by stimulating NK and killer T cell activity, as well as antibody production in plasma cells.

WWW

The Anatomy of the Immune System: Nonspecific Inflammatory Response

www.sumanasinc.com/webcontent/animations/content/inflammatory.html

SPECIFIC IMMUNE MECHANISMS

While the non-specific immune mechanisms are often successful in preventing disease, a second system of specific immune mechanisms provides additional defenses against invading pathogens. The specific immune mechanisms involve the production of cells or substances (called *antibodies*) to provide defense against a specific pathogen (called an *antigen*).

The specific immune mechanisms can be divided into two general classifications: *humoral* and *cell-mediated* immunity. Both target the antigen molecules located on the cellular membranes of invading organisms. Antigen molecules exhibit two unique characteristics: (1) they stimulate antibody production, and (2) they combine with the specific antibody. Most antigens are proteins, but some are large polysaccharides. If the body is exposed to a particular antigen, it will provide defenses specifically targeting that antigen.

Humoral Immunity

In Latin, the term *humor* means "liquid." Thus, **humoral immunity** exists within the liquid components of the body such as blood and lymph.

humoral immunity

B cells

Humoral immunity is mediated by B cells. The letter *B* was originally applied to these cells because they were found in the bursa of Fabricius of chickens. The name *B cell* is used in association with humoral immunity in humans even though mammals do not have a bursa and the location of B cell development is unknown. Fully developed B cells reside in lymph nodes, spleen, and other lymphoid tissues throughout the body.

B cells respond to antigens presented by macrophages. The exact process by which the macrophages orient the antigen so that B cells will respond has not been fully identified. Once the B cell has been exposed to the antigen, it enlarges and divides into two subclassifications: plasma cells and memory B cells (Figure 8.3).

Plasma cells

Plasma cells secrete into circulation antibodies that are specific to the antigen presented by the macrophage. Each plasma cell is capable of producing approximately 2,000 antibody molecules per second for the four- to seven-day lifespan of the cell. Thus, a plasma cell can produce more than one trillion antibody molecules in its short lifetime.

plasma cell

Antibodies

Antibodies (also known as **immunoglobulins**) are glycoproteins produced and secreted by plasma cells. The total number of antibody molecules within the human body is staggering, at an estimated 100 million trillion. These antibodies are specific to millions of different antigens. There are five subclassifications of antibodies:

immunoglobulin

figure 8.3 Role of B cells in humoral immunity.

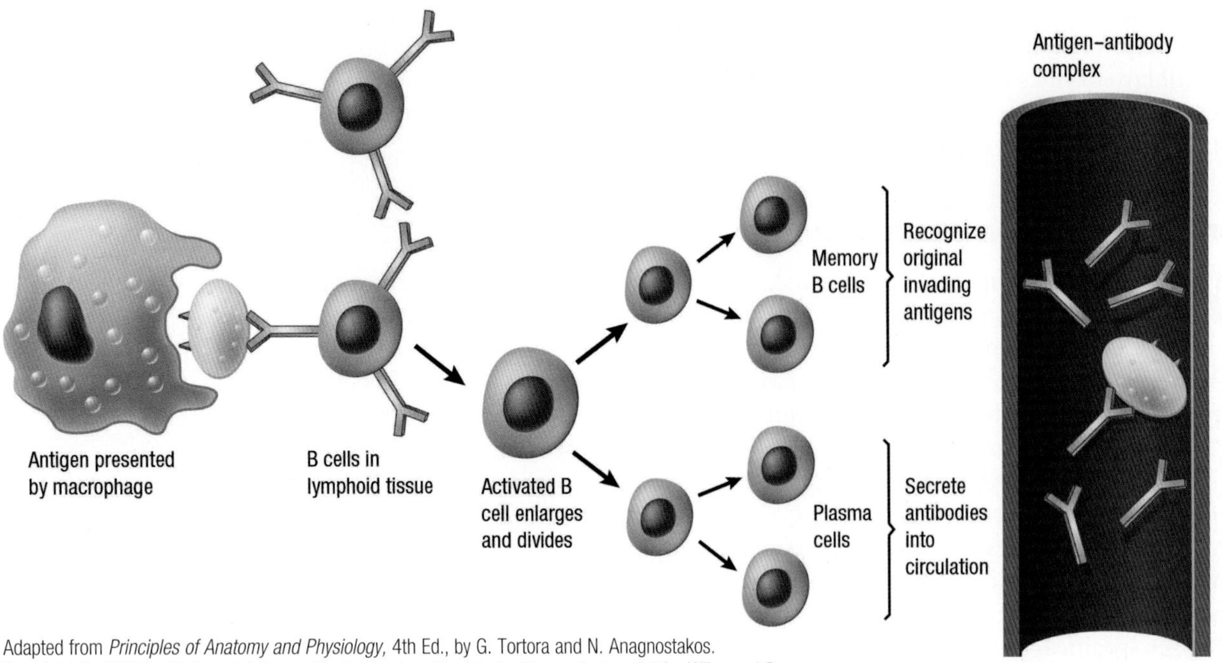

Adapted from *Principles of Anatomy and Physiology,* 4th Ed., by G. Tortora and N. Anagnostakos.

immunoglobulin G (IgG), IgA, IgM, IgD, and IgE. The immunoglobulin subclasses are uniquely involved in the humoral defense mechanisms. For example, IgG and IgA are the most common antibodies found in serum and saliva, respectively, while IgM and IgD function as antigen receptors on the surface of lymphocytes prior to immunization. The IgE antibody subclass is involved in allergic reactions.

www
Antibody Production
www.cellsalive.com/antibody.htm

Antibodies are known to function in many ways, although all of the mechanisms are not completely understood. It is important to recognize, however, that the antibody itself does not directly destroy cells but rather activates non-specific immune mechanisms. One of the primary mechanisms of antibody action involves the activation of the complement protein system. The antibody serves to identify the invading cell by binding with an antigen, which directs the complement system to destroy the invader.

In addition to activation of the complement system, antibodies can stimulate phagocytosis by binding with an antigen and macrophages through *opsonization,* the process of making foreign cells more susceptible to the actions of the phagocytes. As discussed earlier in this chapter, phagocytosis involves engulfing the invading organism and destroying it with lysosomal enzymes.

antibody-dependent cell-mediated cytotoxicity

Antibodies are also involved in the destruction of cells through a process called **antibody-dependent cell-mediated cytotoxicity** (ADCC). ADCC involves the binding of an antibody to an antigen on the cell surface, targeting the invader for destruction. The targeted cell is then lysed by certain lymphocytes, macrophages, neutrophils, and eosinophils. The mechanisms associated with the lysing of the targeted cells are not well understood but do not involve phagocytosis.

In addition to the more common mechanisms of antibody action discussed above, specific antibodies work in diverse ways. For example, particular antibodies neutralize pathogenic chemicals called *toxins,* prevent colonization by reducing the adherence of invading organisms to mucosal surfaces of the upper respiratory tract, and block antiphagocytic properties of some organisms.

Memory B cells

Memory B cells remember a previous invader and act quickly to eliminate it. They are indistinguishable from the original B cells that enlarged and divided in response to an antigen. Memory B cells are available to respond quickly and decisively to future exposure to the same antigen.

memory B cell

Cell-Mediated Immunity

The second classification of the specific immune system—**cell-mediated immunity**—refers to a class of lymphocytes called *T cells* that also provides defenses against specific antigens. Unlike B cells, however, the T cells provide immunity that does not involve the production and secretion of antibodies. When a macrophage presents an antigen to T cells located in lymphoid tissue that are programmed specifically for that antigen, the T cells become activated or sensitized. Sensitized T cells enlarge and divide into four subclassifications: *killer T cells, helper T cells, suppressor T cells,* and *memory T cells* (Figure 8.4). Each subclass has a unique function in cell-mediated immunity.

cell-mediated immunity

Killer T cells

Unlike B cells, which secrete antibodies into circulation through the blood or lymph, **killer T cells** must be near or in contact with the cell targeted for destruction. Killer T cells provide both direct and indirect mechanisms for defense against invading organisms. The direct mechanisms include the production of cytotoxic polypeptides called **lymphotoxins.** Killer T cells migrate from the lymphoid tissues in which they are stored to the location of the invaders, attach to the targeted cells,

killer T cells

lymphotoxins

Role of T cells in cellular immunity. **figure 8.4**

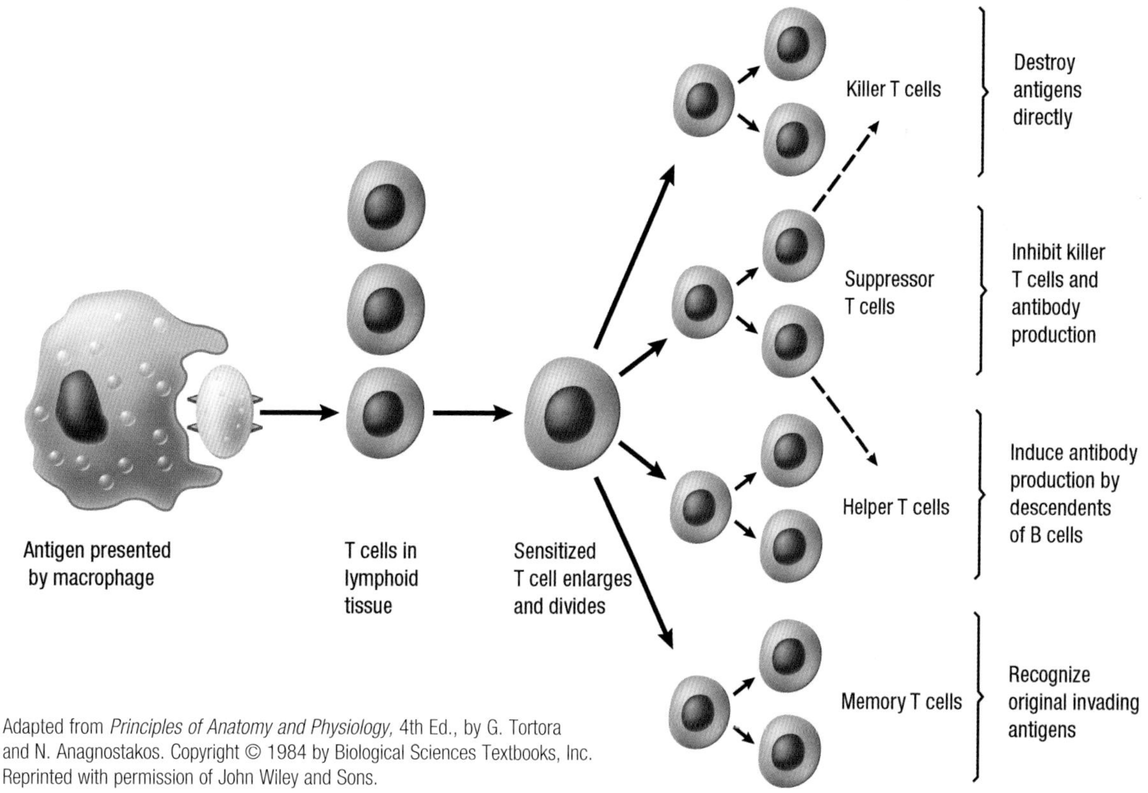

Adapted from *Principles of Anatomy and Physiology,* 4th Ed., by G. Tortora and N. Anagnostakos. Copyright © 1984 by Biological Sciences Textbooks, Inc. Reprinted with permission of John Wiley and Sons.

macrophage chemotactic factor

macrophage activating factor

macrophage migration inhibiting factor

and release lymphotoxins. Lymphotoxins are probably lysosomal enzymes that destroy the invading cell.

The indirect mechanisms of killer T cell action include the release of interferons and of substances that enhance phagocytosis called **macrophage chemotactic factor, macrophage activating factor,** and **macrophage migration inhibiting factor.** As the names imply, these substances respectively attract macrophages to the site of the invaders (chemotaxis), stimulate phagocytosis by macrophages (activation), and prevent macrophages from exiting the area (migration inhibiting).

Helper T cells

helper T cell

Helper T cells have two main functions in cell-mediated immunity. Following activation by the macrophage–antigen complex, helper T cells stimulate the cytotoxic action of killer T cells and increase antibody production by plasma cells. Thus, there is an interaction between cell-mediated immunity and humoral immunity through the action of helper T cells.

Suppressor T cells

suppressor T cell

Suppressor T cells regulate the action of killer T cells and the development of B cells into plasma cells. Thus, suppressor T cells modulate humoral immunity by inhibiting antibody production. The action of suppressor T cells helps to keep the immune defense from exceeding the limits necessary for destruction of the invading organism.

Memory T cells

memory T cell

Memory T cells are capable of recognizing an antigen from a previous exposure. The ability to identify potentially pathogenic invaders precisely enables a more rapid cell-mediated response. Usually the invading organism is destroyed before any outward symptoms of the disease appear.

EXERCISE AND IMMUNE FUNCTION

Interest in the effects of exercise on immune function dates back at least to the 1920s, when several studies were conducted to assess the impact of fatigue on susceptibility to infection.[2,21,30,33] Even with this history of controlled investigations, we know relatively little about the impact of exercise on immune function in humans. It is likely, however, that advances in technology such as the electron microscope and sensitive assay techniques will lead to more conclusive research in this area.

Exercise and Leukocytosis

leukocytosis

Leukocytosis refers to an increase in the number of circulating white blood cells (leukocytes). The majority of the currently available evidence indicates that exercise results in leukocytosis.[1,3,5,9,13,21,27,34,39] It appears, however, that the effect is transient and the leukocyte number returns to normal within 24 hours after an acute bout of exercise.[13,24] The exercise-induced leukocytosis may be related to the intensity of exercise. Mackinnon and Tomasi[24] have stated, "Maximal exercise in trained or untrained subjects and submaximal exercise in untrained subjects cause leukocytosis, whereas submaximal exercise in trained individuals does not."

The exercise-induced leukocytosis often exhibits a biphasic response.[9,24,34] That is, an immediate increase in leukocyte number is followed by a period of normal values usually lasting approximately two hours, and then a second increase occurs two to three hours following the exercise bout.

The mechanisms responsible for leukocytosis as a result of exercise have not been fully identified. It has been suggested that the immediate leukocyte response may be mediated by an increase in plasma levels of specific hormones called *catecholamines* (see Chapter 7), which are known to induce leukocytosis.[24] The mechanism underlying the delayed response to exercise is unknown.

Furthermore, Mackinnon and Tomasi[24] have suggested that exercise causes a release of leukocytes into circulation from storage areas of high blood flow, such as the lungs. It is also likely that during exercise, leukocytes from the lymph vessels are redistributed into the bloodstream. It does not appear that changes in hemoconcentration or newly synthesized lymphoid cells account for the increase in circulating leukocytes as a result of exercise.[24]

Exercise and Lymphocytosis

Most research studies have found that maximal and submaximal exercise results in **lymphocytosis,** a temporary increase (usually lasting less than 45 minutes) in circulating lymphocytes that ranges from approximately 35 to 180 percent.[1,16,18,24,34,38,39] The disparity among investigations in the magnitude of the lymphocytosis is likely due to differences in the intensity and duration of exercise as well as the fitness level of the subjects. In addition, physical training affects the extent of the post-exercise lymphocytosis.[38] In general, the increase in the number of circulating lymphocytes as a result of a single bout of exercise following a training program is less than the increase found prior to the training program. That is, the lymphocyte response to physical activity is diminished as a result of exercise training. This may be due to a decrease in the catecholamine response (a potent stimulator of lymphocytosis) to exercise in a trained state compared with an untrained state.[24]

lymphocytosis

Acute exercise affects the subclassifications of lymphocytes in a differential manner. Generally, total T cell numbers are only slightly affected by exercise or remain unchanged, while the numbers of circulating B cells and NK cells increase.[18,20,24,38,43] Within the total T cell population, however, exercise results in a redistribution in the number of circulating T suppressor cells and T helper cells such that the ratio of T suppressor to T helper cells increases.[6,8,18,20,34]

Exercise and Antibodies (Immunoglobulins)

It is generally accepted that exercise has little or no effect on serum immunoglobulin levels.[7,12,13,22,27,32,37] Cross-sectional studies have found that endurance athletes have levels within the normal range.[12,13] In addition, it is likely that the increases in serum immunoglobulin levels that have been reported following acute bouts of exercise can be explained by a decrease in plasma volume.[28] Nehlsen-Cannarella et al.[28] reported a modest 20 percent increase in serum immunoglobulin levels following 15 weeks of brisk walking in mildly obese females. This change was not greater than that of the control group, and the authors concluded that "exercise training has a minimal effect on serum immunoglobulin levels."

Secretory immunoglobulins are found in mucosal fluids such as saliva and provide a valuable line of defense against pathogens by preventing attachment and colonization. For example, the level of secretory immunoglobulin A is related to the occurrence of upper respiratory infection.[23] Several studies have found that intense and prolonged bouts of acute exercise temporarily (1 to 24 hours) reduce salivary immunoglobulin A (sIgA) levels[10,22,23,35,40–42] and, thus, may increase susceptibility to upper respiratory infection. In addition, Tomasi et al.[41] reported that cross-country skiers involved in high volumes of exercise training have depressed resting levels of sIgA. Tharp and Barnes[40] reported a significant decrease in resting sIgA levels across a competitive season in collegiate swimmers. Interestingly, in a subsequent study,

The effects of high-volume exercise on the immune system

It is generally accepted that exercise elicits changes in the immune system that may be beneficial or detrimental, depending on the intensity and duration of the exercise. While chronic, moderate-intensity exercise may be beneficial to the immune system, acute, high-intensity/high-volume exercise is immunosuppressive.

To study the effects of high-volume exercise throughout a lifetime on the immune system, Moro-Garcia et al.* compared several immunological indicators, including blood leukocyte, lymphocyte, and natural killer cell quantities and functionalities in 95 subjects. The subjects in the study were divided into four groups based on age and activity level: (1) young non-athletes, (2) young athletes, (3) older adult non-athletes, and (4) older adult athletes. Physical activity level was estimated using an extensive questionnaire, and cardiorespiratory fitness was estimated from the questionnaire. Subjects were excluded from participation in the study if they had any condition that might influence the immune system. Blood was collected from all of the subjects and analyzed for immunological markers.

The results of the study indicated that there were significantly lower quantities of leukocytes and lymphocytes in both the young and older adult athlete groups. These numbers appeared to be more pronounced with age, and the authors concluded that frequent participation in high-volume exercise throughout the lifespan contributes to the maintenance of these changes. The results also indicated that the quantity and level of activation of NK cells were significantly higher in the young athletes than in the young non-athletes. The authors postulated that the increase in the number and activity of the NK cells might represent a compensatory mechanism for the lower quantities of leukocytes and lymphocytes in order to maintain the immune health of athletes.

*Moro-Garcia, M. A., Fernandez-Garcia, B., Echeverria, A., Rodrigues-Alonso, M., Suarez-Garcia, F. M., Solano-Jaurrieta, J. J., Lopez-Larrea, C., and Alonso-Arias, R. Frequent participation in high volume exercise throughout life is associated with a more differentiated adaptive immune response. *Brain, Behavior & Immunity* 39: 61–74, 2014.

Tharp[39] found an increase in resting levels of sIgA in prepubescent and high school basketball players across a season. Perhaps the effect of exercise on sIgA is a function of the metabolic demands (aerobic versus anaerobic) of the sporting event.

It should be noted, however, that in studies with non-athletes, moderate-intensity (60–80% of maximal capacity) bouts of exercise for durations up to 45 minutes had no effect on sIgA.[25] This was also true for 30 minutes of running at 80 percent of maximal capacity at ambient temperatures between 6° and 35°C.[19] In addition, 10 weeks of moderate- or high-intensity endurance training performed three times per week for 20 minutes per session had no effect on resting sIgA levels.[26] Thus, the preponderance of the currently available evidence suggests that high-intensity, long-duration bouts of exercise such as those performed by endurance athletes during practice or competition result in a transient decrease in sIgA that lasts less than 24 hours. Repeated high-intensity endurance-exercise sessions throughout a season may also result in depressed resting levels of sIgA. In general, however, acute bouts of submaximal exercise or moderate-intensity endurance training have no effect on sIgA.[19,25,26]

Few studies have examined the effect of exercise on secretory levels of immunoglobulins other than IgA. Mackinnon et al.[22] reported that a two-hour maximal bicycle test resulted in reduced sIgA and sIgM but not sIgG levels. Additional research is needed to examine further if there is a differential response of the secretory immunoglobulin subclassifications to exercise.

Exercise and Complement Proteins

Few studies have examined the effect of exercise on complement proteins. Eberhardt[7] reported that 20 minutes of high-intensity cycle ergometry resulted in a small increase (14%) in certain complement proteins in untrained subjects, while Hanson and Flaherty[13] found no change in C3 or C4 following a 12.8-km run in trained subjects.

Nieman et al.,[32] however, found 15.3 and 11.3 percent increases in C3 and C4, respectively, in marathon runners following a maximal treadmill test. Interestingly, Nieman et al.[32] also reported depressed resting levels of C3 and C4 in marathoners compared with age-matched sedentary controls, while Green et al.[12] found normal resting levels. Although much additional research is needed before conclusive evidence will be available, Simon[36] has stated that "it seems unlikely that exercise induces functionally important alterations in the complement system of athletes."

Exercise and Interferons

Viti et al.[42] found a small but statistically significant increase in plasma interferon (3 IU pre-exercise versus 7 IU post-exercise) following 60 minutes of cycle ergometry at 70 percent $\dot{V}O_2$ max in untrained males. The increase was transient, lasting less than two hours. Simon[36] has concluded, "There is little evidence that exercise produces functionally important changes in circulating interferon levels."

CLINICAL IMPLICATIONS OF EXERCISE AND IMMUNE FUNCTION

Few studies have examined the clinical implications of the effect of exercise on immune function. Mackinnon and Tomasi[24] have stated, "Although many studies show that exercise alters several parameters central to immunity, it has not been shown conclusively that exercise influences resistance to disease." To address this issue fully would require long-term, controlled investigations, which are expensive and difficult to conduct. A limited number of studies, however, do support the anecdotal evidence of a clinically important relationship between exercise and immune function.

Epidemiological Studies of Exercise and Upper Respiratory Infection

Recent epidemiological studies have examined the relationship between exercise and the incidence of **upper respiratory infection (URI),** runny nose, sore throat, or cough on two consecutive days. Several studies have found that the risk of URI increases with exercise. For example, Heath et al.[15] reported that subjects who ran more than 485 km per year (average of 9.3 km per week) had a risk of developing URI that was 2.0 to 3.5 times greater than those subjects who ran fewer than 485 km per year. Nieman et al.[31] found that the risk of developing URI during the two-month period prior to competing in a marathon race was 2.0 times greater in those competitors whose training distance was more than 97 km per week compared with those who ran fewer than 32 km per week. In addition, the risk of developing URI during the week following the marathon was 5.9 times greater in participants than in subjects who had trained for, but chose not to run in, the race.

upper respiratory infection (URI)

WWW

Upper Respiratory Infection

www.ncbi.nlm.nih.gov/pmc/articles/PMC1320353/pdf/jathtrain00016-0058.pdf

Interestingly, Mackinnon et al.[23] found that episodes of URI in squash and hockey players were preceded (within two days) by exercise-induced decreases in sIgA of 22 to 27 percent. Those athletes who did not develop URI exhibited markedly less change (±10%) in sIgA following exercise. The authors concluded that there is a temporal relationship between exercise-induced decreases in sIgA and the subsequent appearance of URI and stated that "large changes in mucosal IgA occurring during exercise may be related to an increased incidence of URI in elite athletes."

These findings have implications for both coaches and athletes who are concerned with "overtraining." Excessive training and highly demanding competitive events are likely to increase the risk of developing URI and adversely affect the health and performance of athletes. Thus, extremely high volumes of training may result in illness and be counterproductive to performance. The combined effect of multiple stressors such as excessive training, caloric restriction, dehydration, and the psychological stress of competition may exacerbate the problem. This may be especially problematic for athletes such as wrestlers, gymnasts, boxers, and bodybuilders.

Exercise, HIV, and AIDS

human immunodeficiency virus (HIV)

acquired immune deficiency syndrome (AIDS)

Human immunodeficiency virus (HIV) cripples the immune system by decreasing the number of helper T cells.[4] Infection with HIV progresses through three stages.[4] During stage 1, relatively few helper T cells are affected, and individuals are generally asymptomatic. Stage 1 can last up to 10 years. Stage 2 is characterized by some loss of T cells and by increased viral replication and results in fatigue, intermittent fever, weight loss, and diarrhea. Stage 3 includes severe depletion of helper T cells with major complications such as cancer or an opportunistic infection and is defined as **acquired immune deficiency syndrome (AIDS).** The fatality rate is 90 percent for those diagnosed with AIDS for more than two years.

Exercise does not exacerbate the progression of HIV and may actually slow progression through the three stages and delay the onset of AIDS.[4] Both aerobic and resistance training can help HIV-infected individuals maintain health. Moderate aerobic exercise training sufficient to increase maximal oxygen consumption rate ($\dot{V}O_2$ max), such as 30 minutes or more three days per week, can increase helper T cell and NK cell counts.[4] Resistance training that includes 10 to 15 repetitions of each exercise can help to maintain or increase muscle mass and, thereby, diminish the weight loss characteristic of stages 2 and 3 of HIV infection.[4]

WWW

Comprehensive AIDS and HIV Information
www.thebody.com

Strategies for Reducing the Risk of Illness

Gleeson[11] recommends the following strategies to help athletes minimize the risk of becoming ill:

1. Allow sufficient time between training sessions for recovery. Include one or two days' resting recovery in the weekly training program; more training is not always better.
2. Avoid extremely long training sessions. Restrict continuous activity to less than two hours per session. For example, a three-hour session might be better performed as two 1.5-hour sessions, one in the morning and one in the evening.
3. Use periodization of training (see Chapter 11) to avoid becoming stale.
4. Avoid training monotony by ensuring variation in the day-to-day training load. Ensure that a hard training day is followed by a day of light training.
5. When increasing the training load, increase the load on the hard days. Do not eliminate the recovery days.
6. When recovering from overtraining or illness, begin with very light training and build gradually.
7. Monitor and record mood, feelings of fatigue, and muscle soreness during training; decrease the training load if the normal session feels harder than usual.
8. Keep other life/social/psychological stresses to a minimum.
9. Get regular and adequate sleep (at least six hours per night).

Stress and the immune system

Traditionally, it has been accepted that stress has a negative impact on the immune system. However, it appears that the stress of exercise may be an exception. Although intense, exhaustive exercise has been shown to be an immunosuppressor, moderate-intensity exercise can enhance immune function and has been associated with significant disease protection through its beneficial effect on many of the cells of the immune system.[29]

CLINICAL APPLICATIONS

Exercise during infection

When athletes are experiencing common illnesses, the question of whether or not to exercise often arises. There is currently no definitive evidence regarding the effects of exercise during common illnesses; however, it is generally accepted that exercise restriction during minor upper respiratory infections such as the common cold is not necessary. In fact, there is a widely accepted belief that if the symptoms are limited to "above the neck," a moderate-intensity exercise bout may even improve symptoms such as runny nose, sneezing, or sore throat. "Below the neck" symptoms such as muscle aches, chest cough, fever, diarrhea, and vomiting are viewed somewhat differently and are often linked with infection-associated fatigue, which, according to Harris,[14] can lead to problems associated with overtraining and predisposition to other injuries.

10. If necessary, get more rest after travel across time zones to allow circadian rhythms to adjust.
11. Pay attention to diet. Diet is important, and many vitamins and minerals are associated with the ability to fight infection, particularly vitamin C, vitamin A, and zinc. A well-balanced diet should provide all the necessary vitamins and minerals, but if fresh fruit and vegetables are not readily available, consider using multivitamin supplements.
12. Ensure adequate total dietary energy, carbohydrate, and protein intake. Be aware that periods of carbohydrate depletion are associated with immunosuppression.
13. Consider drinking carbohydrate "sports" drinks before, during, and after prolonged workouts. These beverages appear to reduce some of the adverse effects of exercise on immune function.
14. Consider discussing vaccination with your coach or doctor. Influenza vaccines require five to seven weeks to take effect, and intra-muscular vaccines may have a few small side effects, so it is advisable to vaccinate out of season. Do not vaccinate pre-competition or if symptoms of illness are present.

Guidelines for Exercise During Infection

Simon[36] states that "mild upper respiratory infections generally do not require interruption of exercise schedules. In fact, some individuals report relief of symptoms, probably because of the increased mucus flow associated with exercise." In addition, Gleeson[11] has provided the following advice for athletes and coaches regarding exercise during infection:

1. Exercise tolerance may be reduced when an infection is present.
2. Exercising with an infection may increase the severity and duration of the illness, although light exercise during convalescence may enhance recovery.
3. Iron supplements should not be taken during periods of infection, to limit bacterial infection.
4. Training should be stopped if fever or systemic symptoms including aching joints and muscles are present. Continuing training (though at a reduced load) is probably appropriate if the symptoms are all above the neck.
5. Training should be resumed gradually.
6. Team members with infection should be isolated as much as possible from the rest of the team.

These suggestions provide useful guidelines for considering the appropriateness of training and competition during infection.

summary

The function of the immune system is to keep us free from potentially pathogenic (disease-causing) organisms. The cells of the immune system (leukocytes) are formed in the bone marrow and can be classified as granular (neutrophils, eosinophils, and basophils) or agranular (lymphocytes and monocytes). Monocytes can be transformed into macrophages, and lymphocytes include three primary subclassifications: T cells, B cells, and natural killer (NK) cells.

Generally, exercise results in leukocytosis (increased number of leukocytes) and lymphocytosis (increased number of lymphocytes), but high-intensity exercise for a long duration may increase an individual's susceptibility to upper respiratory infection (URI) due to decreased salivary levels of the antibody immunoglobulin A. Mild URI generally does not require interruption of exercise schedules, but vigorous exercise should be avoided in the presence of fever, myalgia, and other symptoms of systemic infection.

questions for review

1. What are the two classifications of the immune system and the characteristics of each?
2. What are the two classifications of the specific immune mechanisms and the cells associated with each?
3. What effect does exercise have on leukocytosis? Lymphocytosis? Antibodies? Complement proteins? Interferons?
4. What do current studies indicate about the relationship of exercise and upper respiratory infection?
5. What effect does exercise have on patients with HIV and AIDS?
6. What strategies might a coach recommend to athletes to minimize the risk of becoming ill?
7. As a coach or physical educator, what recommendations might you make regarding exercise during infections?

student companion website

For further review of this book's chapters and for test preparation, visit the book's website, **www.hhpcommunities.com/exercisephysiology**, to take practice quizzes, review the vocabulary terms, use the study guide, and view the digital image bank.

references

1. Ahlborg, B., and Ahlborg, G. Exercise leukocytosis with and without beta-adrenergic blockade. *Acta Med. Scand.* 187: 241–246, 1970.
2. Bailey, G. H. The effect of fatigue upon the susceptibility of rabbits to intratracheal injections of type I pneumococcus. *Am. J. Hygiene* 5: 175–195, 1925.
3. Berk, L. S., Nieman, D., Tan, S. A., Nehlsen-Cannarella, S., Kramer, J., Eby, W. C., and Owens, M. Lymphocyte subset changes during acute maximal exercise. *Med. Sci. Sports Exerc.* 18: 706, 1986.
4. Birk, T. J. HIV and exercise. *Exerc. Immunol. Rev.* 2: 84–95, 1996.

5. Busse, W. W., Anderson, O. L., Hanson, P. G., and Fots, J. D. The effect of exercise on the granulocyte response to isoproterenol in the trained athlete and unconditioned individual. *J. Allergy Clin. Immunol.* 65: 358–364, 1980.
6. Calabrese, L. H. Exercise, immunity, cancer, and infection. In *Exercise, Fitness, and Health*, eds. C. Bouchard, R. J. Shephard, T. Stephens, J. R. Sutton, and B. D. McPherson. Champaign, IL: Human Kinetics, 1990.
7. Eberhardt, A. Influence of motor activity on serum serologic mechanisms of nonspecific immunity of the organism. II. Effect of strenuous physical effort. *Acta Physiol. Pol.* 22: 185–194, 1971.
8. Edwards, A. J., Bacon, T. H., Elms, C. A., Verardi, R., Felder, M., and Knight, S. C. Changes in the population of lymphoid cells in human peripheral blood following physical exercise. *Clin. Exp. Immunol.* 58: 420–427, 1984.
9. Eskola, J., Ruuskanen, O., Soppi, E., Viljaner, M. K., Jarvinen, M., Toivoren, H., and Kouvalainen, K. Effect of stress on lymphocyte transformation and antibody formation. *Clin. Exp. Immunol.* 32: 339–345, 1978.
10. Gleeson, M. Mucosal immune responses and risk of respiratory illness in elite athletes. *Exerc. Immunol. Rev.* 6: 5–42, 2000.
11. Gleeson, M. The scientific basis of practical strategies to maintain immunocompetence in elite athletes. *Exerc. Immunol. Rev.* 6: 75–101, 2000.
12. Green, R. L., Kaplan, S. S., Rabin, B. S., Stanitski, C. L., and Zdziarski, U. Immune function in marathon runners. *Ann. Allergy* 47: 73–75, 1981.
13. Hanson, P. G., and Flaherty, D. K. Immunological responses to training in conditioned runners. *Clin. Sci.* 60: 225–228, 1981.
14. Harris, M. Infectious disease in athletes. *ACSM Current Sports Medi. Rep.* 10: 84–89, 2011.
15. Heath, G. W., Ford, E. S., Craven, T. E., Macera, C. A., Jackson, K. L., and Pate, R. R. Exercise and the incidence of upper respiratory tract infections. *Med. Sci. Sports Exerc.* 23: 152–157, 1991.
16. Hedfors, E., Biberfeld, P., and Wahren, J. Mobilization of the blood of human non-T and K lymphocytes during physical exercise. *J. Clin. Lab. Immunol.* 1: 159–162, 1978.
17. Hedfors, E., Holm, G., Ivansen, M., and Wahren, J. Physiological variation of blood lymphocyte reactivity: T-cell subsets, immunoglobulin production, and mixed lymphocyte reactivity. *Clin. Immunol. Immunopath.* 27: 9–14, 1983.
18. Hedfors, E., Holm, G., and Ohnell, B. Variations of blood lymphocytes during work studied by cell surface markers, DNA synthesis and cytotoxicity. *Clin. Exp. Immunol.* 24: 328–335, 1976.
19. Housh, T. J., Johnson, G. O., Housh, D. J., Evans, S. A., and Tharp, G. D. The effect of exercise at various temperatures on salivary levels of immunoglobulin A. *Int. J. Sports Med.* 12: 498–500, 1991.
20. Landmann, R. M. A., Muller, F. B., Perini, C. H., Wesp, M., Erne, P., and Buhler, F. R. Changes of immunoregulatory cell induced by psychological and physical stress: Relationship to plasma catecholamines. *Clin. Exp. Immunol.* 58: 127–135, 1984.
21. Mackinnon, L. T. *Exercise and Immunology*. Champaign, IL: Human Kinetics, 1992.
22. Mackinnon, L. T., Chick, T. W., van As, A., and Tomasi, T. B. The effect of exercise on secretory and natural immunity. *Adv. Exp. Med. Biol.* 216: 869–876, 1987.
23. Mackinnon, L. T., Ginn, E., and Seymour, G. Temporal relationship between exercise-induced decreases in salivary IgA concentration and subsequent appearance of upper respiratory illness in elite athletes. *Med. Sci. Sports Exerc.* 23 (Suppl.): S45, 1991.
24. Mackinnon, L. T., and Tomasi, T. B. Immunology of exercise. In *Sports Medicine, Fitness, Training, Injuries*, ed. O. Appenzeller. Baltimore: Urban and Schwarzenberg, 1988.
25. McDowell, S. L., Chaloa, K., Housh, T. J., Tharp, G. D., and Johnson, G. O. The effect of exercise intensity and duration on salivary immunoglobulin A. *Eur. J. Appl. Physiol.* 63: 108–111, 1991.
26. McDowell, S. L., Hughes, R. A., Hughes, R. J., Housh, T. J., and Johnson, G. O. The effect of exercise training on salivary immunoglobulin A and cortisol responses to maximal exercise. *Int. J. Sports Med.* 13: 577–580, 1992.
27. Moorthy, A. V., and Zimmerman, S. W. Human leukocyte response to an endurance race. *Eur. J. Appl. Physiol.* 38: 271–276, 1978.
28. Nehlsen-Cannarella, S. L., Nieman, D. C., Balk-Lamberton, A. J., Markoff, P. A., Chritton, D. B., Gusewitch, G., and Lee, J. W. The effect of moderate exercise training on immune response. *Med. Sci. Sports Exerc.* 23: 64–70, 1991.
29. Neto, R., Lira, F., Mello, M., and Santos, R. Importance of exercise immunology in health promotion. *Amino Acids* 41, 1165–1172, 2011.
30. Nicholls, E. E., and Spaeth, R. A. The relation between fatigue and the susceptibility of guinea pigs to infections of type I pneumococcus. *Am. J. Hygiene* 2: 527–535, 1922.
31. Nieman, D. C., Johanssen, L. M., Lee, J. W., and Arabatzis, K. Infectious episodes in runners before and after the Los Angeles Marathon. *J. Sports Med. Phys. Fitness* 30: 316–328, 1990.
32. Nieman, D. C., Tan, S. A., Lee, J. W., and Berk, L. S. Complement and immunoglobulin levels in athletes and sedentary controls. *Int. J. Sports Med.* 10: 124–128, 1989.
33. Oppenheimer, E. H., and Spaeth, R. A. The relation between fatigue and the susceptibility of rats towards a toxin and an infection. *Am. J. Hygiene* 2: 51–66, 1922.
34. Robertson, A. J., Ramesar, K. C. R. B., Potts, R. C., Gibbs, J. H., Browning, M. C. K., Brown, R. A., Hayes, P. C., and Beck, J. S. The effect of strenuous physical exercise on circulating blood lymphocytes and serum cortisol levels. *J. Clin. Lab. Immunol.* 5: 53–57, 1981.

35. Schouten, W. J., Verschuur, R., and Kemper, H. C. G. Habitual physical activity, strenuous exercise, and salivary immunoglobulin A levels in young adults: The Amsterdam growth and health study. *Int. J. Sports Med.* 9: 289–293, 1988.
36. Simon, H. B. Exercise and infection. *Phys. Sportsmed.* 15: 135–141, 1987.
37. Soppi, E., Varjo, P., Eskola, J., and Laitinen, L. A. Effect of strenuous physical stress on circulating lymphocyte number and function before and after training. *J. Clin. Lab. Immunol.* 8: 43–46, 1982.
38. Steel, C. M., and Evans, J. Physiological variation in circulating B cell: T cell ratio in man. *Nature* 247: 387–389, 1974.
39. Tharp, G. D. Basketball exercise and secretory immunoglobulin-A. *Med. Sci. Sports Exerc.* 22: S125, 1990.
40. Tharp, G. D., and Barnes, M. W. Reduction of saliva immunoglobulin levels by swim training. *Eur. J. Appl. Physiol.* 60: 61–64, 1990.
41. Tomasi, T. B., Trudeau, F. B., Czerwinski, D., and Erredge, S. Immune parameters in athletes before and after strenuous exercise. *J. Clin. Immunol.* 2: 173–178, 1982.
42. Viti, A., Muscettola, M., Paulesu, L., Cocci, V., and Almi, A. Effect of exercise on plasma interferon levels. *J. Appl. Physiol.* 59: 426–428, 1985.
43. Yu, D. T. Y., Clements, P. J., and Pearson, C. M. Effects of corticosteroids on exercise-induced lymphocytosis. *Clin. Exp. Immunol.* 28: 326–331, 1977.

9 Health Benefits of Physical Activity

As a result of reading this chapter you will:

Be familiar with the health benefits of physical activity for children, adolescents, and adults as identified by the U.S. Dept. of Health and Human Services.

Know the relationships among physical activity, fitness, and all-cause mortality.

Be able to describe the relationships between body weight and the likelihood of developing various diseases.

Understand the associations among physical activity and various health conditions.

Understand the benefits of and contraindications to physical activity during pregnancy.

key concepts

angina pectoris
asthma
atherosclerosis
basal metabolic rate
body mass index (BMI)
cardiovascular disease
chronic obstructive pulmonary disease (COPD)
chylomicron
claudication
collateral circulation
coronary heart disease (CHD)
degenerative disease
diabetes mellitus
dyslipidemia
embolus
hemorrhagic stroke
high-density lipoprotein
hyperglycemia
hyperlipidemia
hyperplastic obesity
hypertension
hypertrophic obesity
hypoglycemia
intermediate-density lipoprotein
isocaloric state
law of energy balance
lipoprotein
low-density lipoprotein
myocardial infarction
negative caloric balance
obesity
osteoporosis
peripheral artery disease (PAD)
positive caloric balance
spot reducing
state anxiety
stroke
thromboembolic stroke
thrombus
trait anxiety
type 1 diabetes mellitus
type 2 diabetes mellitus
very-low-density lipoprotein

During the twentieth century, the nature of the illnesses that beset the American population underwent a transition from a predominance of infectious diseases to the present predominance of degenerative diseases. Today, we live longer only to fall prey to **degenerative diseases** such as cardiovascular disease (heart attacks and strokes), hypertension, and cancer. It is clear that the increase in degenerative diseases has been influenced by lifestyle choices. As a society:

1. We participate in work and leisure activities that are far less active than in the past.
2. We produce and eat more food than we need.
3. We control our environment with very little expenditure of physical energy.
4. We subject ourselves to more stress and to unusual stressors.

In the nineteenth century, our forebears labored long and hard physically in the home, in agriculture, or in industry. Today, exercise, sport, and physically active recreation must replace the hard work that kept our ancestors physically fit. Here is the challenge for physicians, exercise professionals, physical educators, and allied health professionals, and we have much work to do. For example, the Centers for Disease Control and Prevention (www.cdc.gov) has reported that:

1. Obesity among U.S. adults has risen significantly over the last two to three decades.
2. Approximately 35.1 percent of U.S. adults 20 years of age or older are obese.
3. The percentage of young people who are overweight has tripled since 1980.
4. Approximately 20.5 percent of children and adolescents age 12 to 19 years are considered obese.
5. More than 50 percent of U.S. adults do not get enough physical activity to provide health benefits.
6. More than 30 percent of young people in grades 9 to 12 do not regularly engage in vigorous physical activity.
7. Unhealthy diet and physical inactivity can cause or aggravate many chronic diseases and conditions, including type 2 diabetes, hypertension, heart disease, stroke, and some forms of cancer.

The U.S. Department of Health and Human Services has identified the health benefits of physical activity, including those shown in Table 9.1.

PHYSICAL ACTIVITY, FITNESS, ALL-CAUSE MORTALITY, AND PREMATURE DEATH

In general, physical activity and cardiorespiratory fitness are inversely related to overall mortality (Figure 9.1).[9,23] That is, the more active you are and the better your cardiorespiratory fitness, the less likely you are to die prematurely. This is true independent of age or gender,[9] which supports the benefits of regular physical activity across the lifespan. Improvements in cardiorespiratory fitness reduce overall mortality risk, particularly in low-fit individuals.[9,23] Thus, a modest increase in physical activity, particularly in sedentary individuals, can have a substantial, positive effect on health. The reduction in risk of overall mortality from improving cardiorespiratory fitness from low to moderately fit is approximately the same as, or maybe even greater than, from smoking cessation.[9]

CARDIOVASCULAR DISEASES

Cardiovascular diseases are the number one cause of death in the Western world and account for over 25 percent of all deaths in the United States.

table 9.1 Health benefits of physical activity for children, adolescents, and adults.[24]

CHILDREN AND ADOLESCENTS	
1.	Increased cardiorespiratory fitness
2.	Increased muscular fitness
3.	Improved bone health
4.	Favorable changes in body composition
5.	Improved mood and mental health
ADULTS	
1.	Reduced risk of premature death
2.	Reduced risk of cardiovascular risk factors and diseases (coronary heart disease, stroke, hyperlipidemia, hypertension, peripheral artery disease, diabetes mellitus, metabolic syndrome, obesity)
3.	Potential for reduced risk of some forms of cancer (colon, breast, reproductive system, lung)
4.	Improved bone health
5.	Increased muscular fitness
6.	Improved mood and mental health
7.	Enhanced weight management

figure 9.1 The relationship between physical activity and cardiorespiratory fitness versus all-cause mortality is inverse.

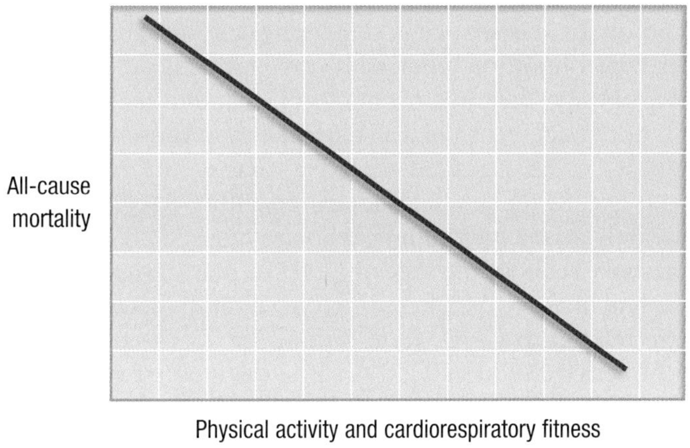

The primary **cardiovascular diseases** are coronary heart disease, stroke, hypertension, and peripheral artery disease. Physical activity is inversely related to the risk of developing cardiovascular diseases (Figure 9.2).

cardiovascular disease

Physical Activity and Coronary Heart Disease

Coronary heart disease (CHD) has its origin very early in childhood and is usually manifested much later in life as a heart attack (also called a **myocardial infarction;** myocardial = heart muscle, infarction = necrosis or death of tissue). Most heart attacks result from atherosclerosis, which over a period of many years can block blood flow and reduce oxygen transport through coronary arteries. **Atherosclerosis**

coronary heart disease
myocardial infarction
atherosclerosis

figure 9.2 Increases in physical activity reduce the risk of cardiovascular diseases (coronary heart disease, stroke, hypertension, and peripheral artery disease), and increases in physical fitness provide even greater benefits.

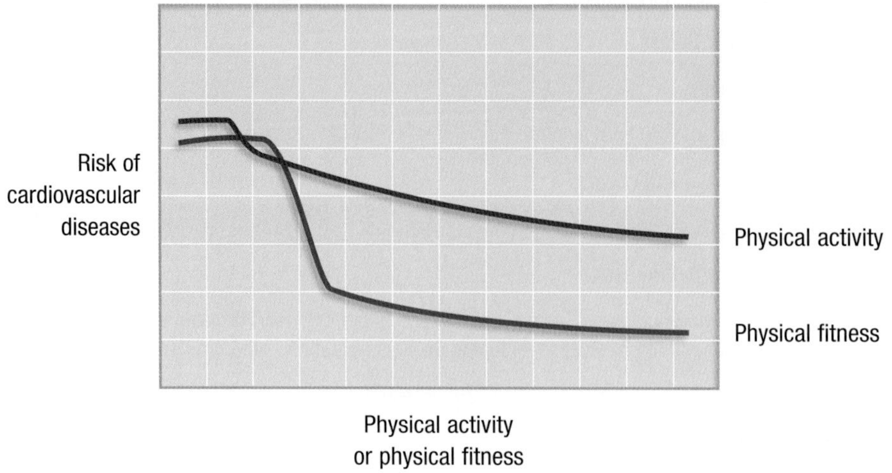

begins with an injury to the interior wall of a coronary artery. This is followed by the attachment of cells of the immune system to the injured area, and eventually a fibrous plaque, made up primarily of smooth muscle cells, forms at this site. As the years pass, lipids or fats are deposited in the plaque, and it enlarges, sometimes to the point where the artery is totally blocked. A common symptom of blocked coronary arteries is **angina pectoris,** which causes pain and a choking feeling in the chest due to a lack of oxygen in the heart.

angina pectoris

WWW

Physical Activity and Health, Women
www.cdc.gov/nccdphp/sgr/women.htm

The epidemiological evidence is clear: physical inactivity is a CHD risk factor. Even after controlling for other CHD risk factors such as age, race, elevated blood pressure, obesity, diet, socioeconomics, diabetes mellitus, and so on, inactive adults are more likely to have heart attacks than those who are highly active.[9] There also appears to be a graded response; that is, the risk of CHD is less the more active you are. Sedentary individuals are more likely to have heart attacks than are moderately active individuals, who are more likely than the highly active.

Physical activity reduces the risk of CHD in many ways. For example, active individuals are less likely to be obese or to develop diabetes mellitus or hypertension, which are related to CHD. In addition, one of the primary ways in which regular physical activity reduces CHD risk is through its effects on blood lipids. Elevation of lipids in the blood is called **hyperlipidemia,** which is strongly related to CHD. The lipids of greatest concern are triglycerides and cholesterol, which are found in atherosclerotic plaque in coronary arteries. Triglycerides are composed of a glycerol backbone with three fatty acids attached, while cholesterol has the typical four-ring steroid structure. Cholesterol is transported in the blood in combination with special proteins to form **lipoproteins.**[12] A number of lipoproteins are responsible for this transport, and they are differentiated by their densities: (1) **high-density lipoprotein** (HDL with subclasses HDL_2 and HDL_3), (2) **low-density lipoprotein** (LDL with subclass lipoprotein a), (3) **intermediate-density lipoprotein** (IDL), (4) **very-low-density lipoprotein** (VLDL), and (5) **chylomicrons.**

hyperlipidemia

lipoprotein

high-density lipoprotein

low-density lipoprotein

intermediate-density lipoprotein

very-low-density lipoprotein

chylomicron

High levels of total cholesterol ($\geq$240 mg • dL^{-1}), chylomicrons, VLDL, LDL (>160 mg • dL^{-1}), IDL, lipoprotein a (>25 mg • dL^{-1}), and triglycerides (>200 mg • dL^{-1}) increase the risk of CHD (Figure 9.3).[2,12] High levels of HDL ($\geq$60 mg • dL^{-1}), especially HDL_2, however, reduce the risk of CHD (Figure 9.4). LDL and VLDL

Elevated levels of certain blood lipids (total cholesterol, chylomicrons, VLDL, LDL, IDL, lipoprotein a, and triglycerides) are positively related to the risk of coronary heart disease.

figure 9.3

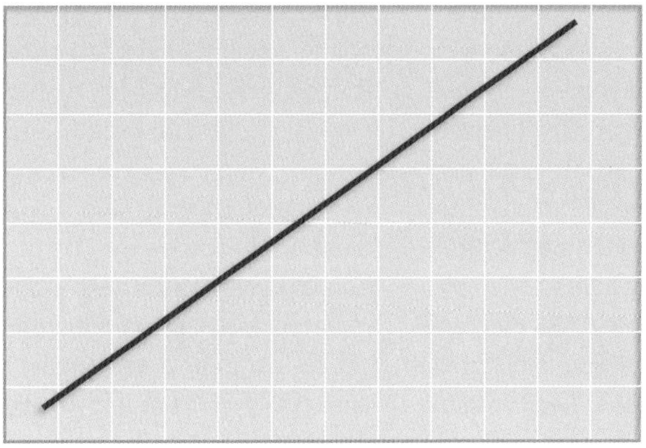

High levels of high-density lipoproteins (HDLs) protect against the development of coronary heart disease.

figure 9.4

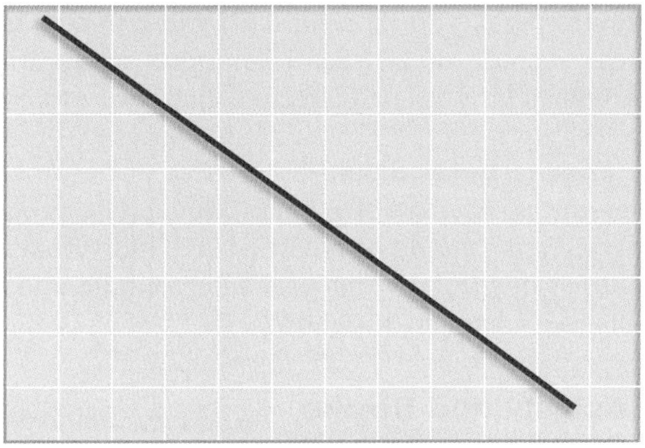

transport cholesterol and triglycerides from the liver throughout the body. On the other hand, HDL transports cholesterol from LDL molecules to the liver. In any event, with respect to CHD, HDLs are the "good guys" and LDLs and VLDLs are the "bad guys." **Dyslipidemia** refers to an elevation of LDL or triglycerides, or a reduction in HDL, and is a major, modifiable risk factor for CHD.[2]

Regular aerobic physical activity can improve blood lipid profiles and thereby reduce the risk of CHD. There is conflicting evidence regarding the effects of physical activity on circulating levels of total cholesterol, chylomicrons, LDL, and lipoprotein a. The training-induced decreases in these parameters reported in some studies[12] may be primarily due to decreases in body fat and body weight. Perhaps the most consistent and important training-induced change in blood lipids involves an increase in HDL, particularly HDL_2. The ACSM's[2] recommended exercise prescription for individuals with dyslipidemia includes:

Frequency: Greater than or equal to five days per week.

- dyslipidemia

www

Your Guide to Physical Activity and Your Heart

www.nhlbi.nih.gov/health/resources/heart/obesity-physical-active-guide

RESEARCH

Healthy lifestyle behaviors and optimal health

Heart disease, cancer, and diabetes mellitus are major causes of death in the United States. Interestingly, many of the risk factors associated with the development of these diseases are modifiable, including physical activity level, dietary habits, obesity, cigarette smoking, stress levels, and alcohol consumption. A study by Burke et al.* highlights the importance of controlling these factors for the maintenance of optimal health. The authors were interested in the factors associated with remaining healthy in 5,888 men and women over 65 years of age. The subjects were monitored over the course of seven years for changes in health status. The behavioral factors that were significantly related to health maintenance of interest to people in the field of exercise science were (1) low-fat, high-carbohydrate diet, (2) being overweight, and (3) exercise—particularly the intensity of exercise. Subjects were asked about both their frequency and type of exercise, and it appears that in this population, intensity of exercise may be more closely related to health than is weekly caloric expenditure. This study stresses the importance of lifelong adherence to healthy lifestyle behaviors so that people can remain healthy and able to enjoy a high quality of life at each stage of life.

* Burke, G. L., Arnold, A. M., Bild, D. E., Cushman, M., Fried, L. P., Newman, A., Nunn, C., and Robbins, J. Factors associated with healthy aging: the cardiovascular health study. *J. Am. Geriatr. Soc.* 49: 254–262, 2001.

Intensity: 40 to 75% $\dot{V}O_2$ reserve or heart rate reserve.

Time: 30 to 60 minutes per day. However, to promote or maintain weight loss, 50 to 60 minutes per day or more of daily exercise is recommended. Performance of intermittent exercise of at least 10 minutes in duration to accumulate these duration recommendations is an effective alternative to continuous exercise.

Type: The primary mode should be aerobic physical activities that involve the large muscle groups. As part of a balanced exercise program, resistance training and flexibility exercise should be incorporated. Individuals with dyslipidemia without comorbidities may follow the resistance training and flexibility guidelines for healthy adults (see Chapters 11 and 12).

Physical Activity and Stroke

stroke

thromboembolic stroke

thrombus

embolus

hemorrhagic stroke

Stroke is classified as a cardiovascular disease and affects blood flow to the brain. Strokes are responsible for approximately 5 percent of all deaths in the United States. There are two major types of stroke: (1) thromboembolic and (2) hemorrhagic. Like CHD, atherosclerosis underlies thromboembolic stroke, while hypertension is the major determinant of hemorrhagic stroke.[1] As the name implies, a **thromboembolic stroke** occurs when a **thrombus** (blood clot) forms or an **embolus** (blood clot or other mass) breaks loose from elsewhere in the body and blocks an artery in the brain that is already partially occluded from atherosclerosis. The blockage interferes with oxygen availability to part of the brain, which may then die. A **hemorrhagic stroke** results from a ruptured vessel in the brain, often at the site of an aneurysm or weak spot in the vessel that balloons from being filled with blood. This too can cause the death of brain tissue. The scientific evidence regarding the effects of physical activity or fitness on the risk of stroke is equivocal.[1] There is clearly a need for additional research in this area. The common association of atherosclerosis with both CHD and stroke, however, suggests that physical activity may reduce the risk of stroke by slowing the development of atherosclerosis. Physical activity may also indirectly influence the risk of stroke through its favorable effect on hypertension, the major cause of hemorrhagic strokes.

An individual who is limited by the effects of a stroke may need to begin an aerobic exercise program at an intensity of approximately 40 to 50 percent $\dot{V}O_2$

max, performed three to five times per week. The initial duration should be about 20 minutes per session (or two 10-minute sessions). As fitness increases, the duration can be increased to accomplish a caloric expenditure of 300 kilocalories per session.[1]

Physical Activity and Hypertension

hypertension

Blood pressure (BP) is the pressure that blood exerts against artery walls. **Hypertension** is elevated BP and affects approximately 65 million Americans (25% of U.S. adults). About one-half of those with hypertension don't know they have it. BP is measured during contraction (systolic) and relaxation (diastolic) of the heart. Normal BP is less than or equal to 120/80 mm Hg (systolic/diastolic). Hypertension has been defined as resting systolic BP greater than 140 mm Hg or resting diastolic BP greater than 90 mm Hg.[2]

Most epidemiological evidence suggests that physical activity is inversely related to BP as well as to the risk of later development of hypertension. Typically, aerobic training programs result in less than a 10 percent (approximately 5–7 mm Hg) decrease in systolic and diastolic BP, with a greater response in hypertension patients than normotensive individuals.[2] According to the ACSM,[2] aerobic exercise should be emphasized over resistance training, but the precise mechanism by which aerobic exercise training leads to reduced BP is unknown. Some of the potential contributors include decreased vascular resistance to blood flow, hormonal factors, baroreflex sensitivity, reduced body fat, and changes in insulin resistance.

The ACSM's[2] recommended exercise prescription for individuals with hypertension includes:

Frequency: Aerobic exercise on most, preferably all, days of the week; resistance exercise two to three days per week.

Intensity: Moderate-intensity aerobic exercise (e.g., 40 to less than 60% $\dot{V}O_2$ reserve or heart rate reserve; rating of perceived exertion of 11 to 13 on a 6 to 20 scale) supplemented by resistance training at 60 to 80 percent 1-RM.

Time: 30 to 60 minutes per day of continuous or intermittent aerobic exercise. If intermittent, use a minimum of 10-minute bouts, accumulated to total 30 to 60 minutes per day of exercise. Resistance training should consist of at least one set of 8 to 12 repetitions for each of the major muscle groups.

Type: Emphasis should be placed on aerobic activities such as walking, jogging, cycling, and swimming. Resistance training using either machine weights or free weights may supplement aerobic training. Such training programs should consist of 8 to 10 different exercises targeting the major muscle groups (see Chapter 11).

Physical Activity and Peripheral Artery Disease

peripheral artery disease

claudication

Peripheral artery disease (PAD) is much like CHD except that it occurs in the vessels of the lower extremities instead of the heart.[7] As in CHD, atherosclerotic lesions form and reduce blood supply to the leg muscles. The decreased blood flow leads to intermittent **claudication,** which is analogous to angina pectoris in CHD and is characterized by leg pain due to inadequate oxygen supply. Peripheral artery disease and CHD share common risk factors, including hyperlipidemia, smoking, hypertension, and diabetes mellitus.

Regular aerobic exercise can improve work capacity and reduce the symptoms of peripheral artery disease. Because the lower extremities are the locations for peripheral artery disease, walking and jogging are, typically, the exercises of choice. The increased oxygen demand from walking or jogging may stimulate the develop-

collateral circulation

ment of new arteries and capillaries (called **collateral circulation**) in the thigh and calf muscles to compensate for blocked arteries.[7]

The ACSM's[2] recommended exercise prescription for individuals with peripheral artery disease includes:

Frequency: Weight-bearing aerobic exercise three to five days per week; resistance exercise at least two days per week.

Intensity: Moderate intensity (i.e., 40% to less than 60% $\dot{V}O_2$ reserve) that allows the patient to walk until he or she reaches a pain score of 3 (i.e., intense pain) on the 4-point pain scale. Between bouts of activity, individuals should be given time to allow ischemic pain to subside before resuming exercise.

Time: 30 to 60 minutes per day, but some patients may need to start with 10-minute bouts and exercise intermittently to accumulate a total of 30 to 60 minutes per day. Many patients may need to begin the program by accumulating only 15 minutes per day, gradually increasing time by 5 minutes per day biweekly.

Type: Weight-bearing aerobic exercise, such as walking, and non–weight-bearing exercise, such as arm and leg ergometry. Cycling may be used as a warm-up but should not be the primary type of activity. Resistance training is recommended to enhance and maintain muscular strength and endurance (see Chapter 11).

Physical Activity and Metabolic Syndrome[2]

Metabolic syndrome includes a group of cardiovascular disease risk factors. Typically, metabolic syndrome is diagnosed when an individual has at least three of the gender-specific risk factors listed in Table 9.2. (See **Chapter 9 Lab** for anthropometric measures of health risk, including waist circumference, body mass index, and waist-to-hip ratio.) It has been estimated that approximately 27 percent of adults in the United States meet the criteria for metabolic syndrome.

The ACSM's[2] recommended exercise prescription for individuals with metabolic syndrome includes:

1. Initial exercise training should be performed at a moderate intensity (40–60% of $\dot{V}O_2$ reserve or heart rate reserve) and, when appropriate, progress to more vigorous intensity (greater than or equal to 60% of $\dot{V}O_2$ reserve or heart rate reserve) to allow for optimal health/fitness improvements.

2. Because of the high likelihood of overweightness and obesity, most individuals with metabolic syndrome may benefit by gradually increasing their physical

table 9.2 Metabolic syndrome is diagnosed when an individual has at least three of the gender-specific cardiovascular disease risk factors.[2]

CARDIOVASCULAR RISK FACTOR	MEN	WOMEN
1. Abdominal obesity (waist circumference)	>102 cm (>40 in)	>88 cm (>35 in)
2. Triglycerides	$\geq$150 mg • dL^{-1}	$\geq$150 mg • dL^{-1}
3. High-density lipoprotein cholesterol (HDL)	<40 mg • dL^{-1}	<50 mg • dL^{-1}
4. Blood pressure	$\geq$130 mm Hg systolic and/or $\geq$85 mm Hg diastolic	$\geq$130 mm Hg systolic and/or $\geq$85 mm Hg diastolic
5. Fasting glucose	$\geq$110 mg • dL^{-1}	$\geq$110 mg • dL^{-1}

activity levels to approximately 300 minutes per week or 50 to 60 minutes five days per week. This level of physical activity may be accumulated in multiple daily bouts of at least 10 minutes in duration or through increases in other forms of moderate-intensity lifestyle activities. For some individuals to promote or maintain weight loss, progression to 60 to 90 minutes per day may be necessary.

BODY WEIGHT AND OBESITY

"Overweight" and "underweight" are widely used terms and imply that we know what constitutes normal body weight for a given individual. Frequently, "normal" body weight is predicted from height–weight charts that have been developed by insurance companies to provide minimum, average, and maximum body weights for any given age, height, and gender. Do these height–weight charts really tell us one's proper body weight? We could answer "yes" only if the data from which the charts were calculated were taken from a population of people whose body weights were normal. This, however, is not the case. It is not uncommon for such height–weight charts to result in gross errors in predicting normal body weight. For example, a man six feet tall with a very slight skeletal framework might be 30 to 40 pounds overweight at 200 pounds, whereas an extremely muscular man might be at his best weight for athletic competition at six feet and 200 pounds. The use of height–weight charts to determine the true association between body weight and health is questionable.

WWW

Physical Activity and Weight Control

www.niddk.nih.gov/health-information/health-topics/weight-control/better-health/Pages/better-health-and-you-tips-for-adults.aspx

Obesity Society

www.obesity.org

Body Weight and Health

Andres[6] has provided some interesting data regarding the concept of an ideal (healthy) body weight. Figure 9.5 describes the relationships for the ratio of actual to expected mortality (percent) with respect to **body mass index** (BMI = body weight divided by height squared: kg/m^2) for a variety of diseases and causes of death. It is clear that the relationships are disease specific (see **Chapter 9 Lab**). For example, with respect to CHD and diabetes mellitus, a low body weight (at a given height) is beneficial. For other diseases, however, such as hypertension and kidney disease, the greatest risks of death are associated with both low and high body weights. Interestingly, death from pneumonia, influenza, or suicide is more likely to occur with a low body weight. These data should provide much food for thought for professionals who routinely counsel individuals with respect to body weight goals in an attempt to improve health and increase longevity.

body mass index

Fat Cell Development and Obesity

Obesity is a disease characterized by excessive body fatness.[23] For both males and females, greater than or equal to 30 percent body fat constitutes obesity. A number of laboratory and field techniques are available for determining percent body fat and other body composition characteristics; these include underwater weighing and skinfold assessments (see Chapter 15 Lab). It has been estimated that more than 100 million Americans are over-fat and that the prevalence of obesity has increased at an alarming rate in both genders and in all ethnic groups.[13,19] The incidence of severe obesity (BMI >40) more than tripled between 1960 and 2010.[14,16] Obesity is an independent risk factor for coronary heart disease even when adjusted for the confounding influences of other risk factors including age, cholesterol, systolic blood pressure, smoking, left ventricular hypertrophy, and glucose intolerance.[18] Furthermore, inactivity is one—but not the only—factor that contributes to obesity.[23]

obesity

Obesity can be classified as hypertrophic (also sometimes called adult-onset) or hyperplastic (juvenile-onset). **Hypertrophic obesity** is characterized by a normal number of fat cells (about 25 billion), which are about twice as large as those of

hypertrophic obesity

figure 9.5 Ratio of actual to predicted mortality with respect to body mass index for causes of death.

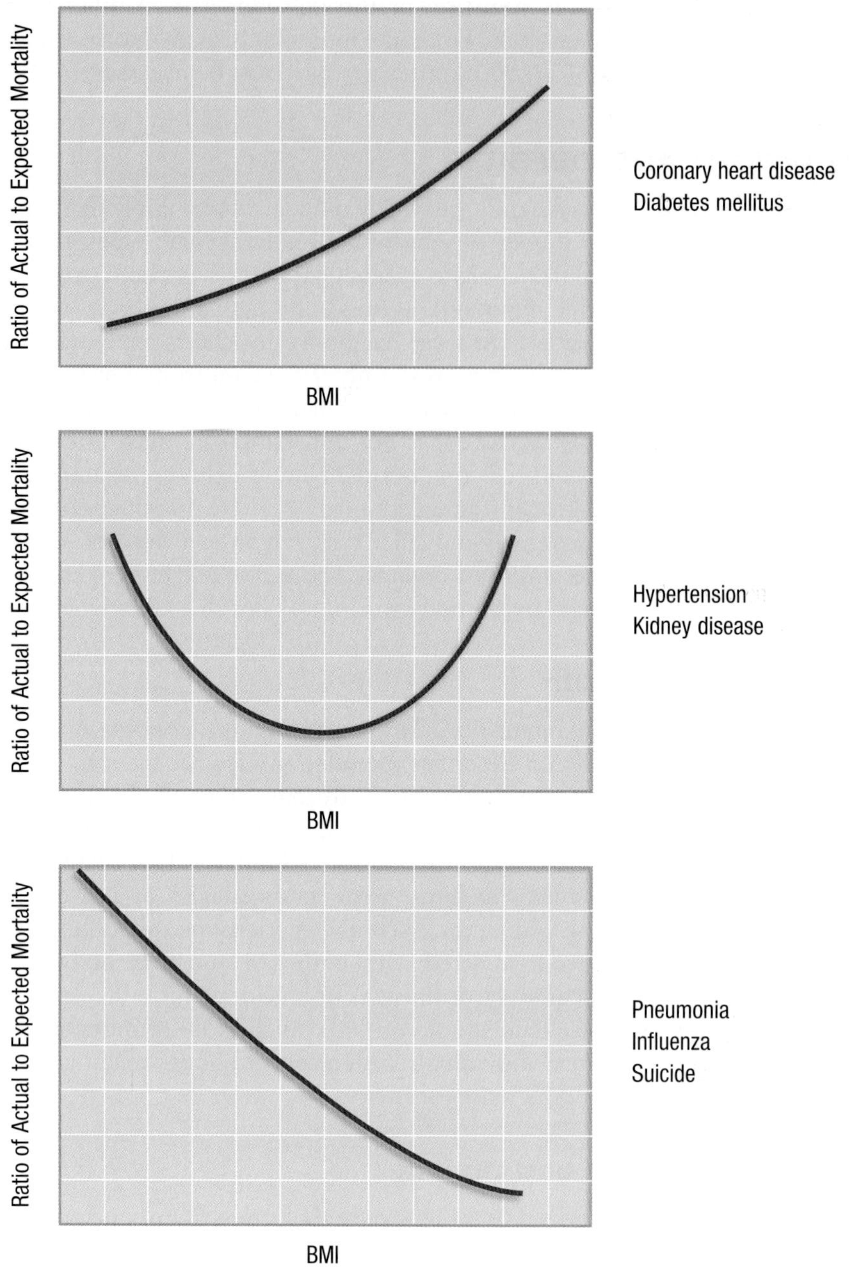

hyperplastic obesity

a non-obese person. In **hyperplastic obesity,** there is a higher number (75 to 100 billion) of enlarged fat cells. It is generally accepted that:

1. The number of fat cells in the human body is established primarily during three critical periods of rapid growth: (a) the latter part of gestation, (b) the first year of infancy, and (c) the adolescent growth spurt. There is also a gradual and less pronounced increase in the number of fat cells between 1 and 10 years of age.[20]
2. Once established, the number of fat cells normally remains constant in spite of weight gain or loss. The exception to this rule is in the case of severe hypertrophic obesity, when new fat cells may develop.[19] Reducing body fatness is

especially difficult (but not impossible) for those with a high number of fat cells (hyperplastic obesity).

3. The size of fat cells can change with weight gain or loss.

Americans today are much more sedentary than ever before and are taking in far more calories than they expend. This imbalance has led to an obesity epidemic, which in turn is the cause of many of the disease conditions facing the American population.

Caloric Balance

Weight gain and loss conform to the physical laws that govern energy exchange. The **law of energy balance** or law of thermodynamics describes the relationship between the number of calories we take in from food versus the number we expend, primarily from basal metabolism and physical activity. If the number of calories taken in exceeds those expended, we gain body weight from a **positive caloric balance.** On the other hand, when the number of calories expended exceeds those taken in, we lose body weight from a **negative caloric balance.** When the number of calories taken in is equal to the number expended, body weight remains fairly constant and we have an **isocaloric state.** Table 9.3 provides the approximate caloric expenditure rates for some common physical activities and sports.

- law of energy balance
- positive caloric balance
- negative caloric balance
- isocaloric state

Physical Activity and Weight Loss

In a safe and effective weight loss program, physical activity and caloric restriction work together. Physical activity contributes to caloric expenditure in a number of ways:[3,17]

1. Calories are expended during physical activity. Jogging one mile, independent of pace, expends approximately 100 kilocalories. While this may not seem like many in the short term, over the course of a year the calories add up. For example, jogging two miles, three times per week for 52 weeks expends 31,200 kilocalories. Given

table 9.3 Approximate caloric expenditure rates for some common physical activities and sports.*

SPORT/ACTIVITY	KILOCALORIES PER HOUR
1. Baseball	198–330
2. Basketball	450–750
3. Circuit resistance training	276–462
4. Bicycling (9.4 miles per hour)	324–540
5. Football	432–714
6. Golf	276–462
7. Racquetball	582–966
8. Running (7.5 miles per hour)	696–1,116
9. Soccer	450–744
10. Swimming (crawl stroke – slow)	420–696
11. Tennis	354–588
12. Walking (3.5 miles per hour)	282–468

*Ranges based on 120–200 pound individual (male or female). Adapted from Katch, F. I., and McArdle, W. D. *Introduction to Nutrition, Exercise, and Health,* 4th Edition. Philadelphia: Lea and Febiger, 1993, 390–401.

that a pound of fat equals 3,500 kilocalories, this modest exercise program accounts for approximately 8.9 pounds of fat (31,200 / 3,500) over the course of a year that otherwise would not be expended.

2. Additional calories are expended after exercise. Metabolic rate can remain elevated above resting levels for a period of time after the bout of physical activity has ended. Over the course of a year, these metabolic aftereffects of exercise could account for additional weight loss over and above the energy cost of the exercise itself. The calories expended during exercise, however, are greater than those expended by the elevated metabolic rate after exercise.

basal metabolic rate

3. A program of physical activity helps to maintain **basal metabolic rate** (BMR), while caloric restriction alone, typically, results in a decrease in BMR. BMR is the energy expended to maintain normal body functions and is measured at rest. Most of the energy we expend is due to BMR, and a reduction in BMR would therefore negatively affect weight loss. The major determinant of BMR is fat-free weight, which includes muscle, bone, connective tissue, organs, and so forth. A regular program of physical activity tends to maintain or even increase fat-free weight, particularly muscle. Weight loss from caloric restriction alone includes fat-free weight as well as fat. The combination of physical activity with caloric restriction usually results in a greater loss of fat and little, if any, reduction in fat-free weight.

4. A common misconception regarding physical activity and weight loss is that appetite increases in direct proportion to increased activity. Generally, moderate amounts of physical activity, perhaps up to about one hour per day, do not increase and may actually decrease appetite. Very strenuous and long-duration physical activity, however, does increase appetite.

spot reducing

5. **Spot reducing** does not work.[19] It is commonly believed that exercising a specific area of the body preferentially decreases fat stores at that location. This is not the case: exercise-induced fat mobilization occurs throughout the body, particularly the areas of greatest fat accumulation. Thus, sit-ups will not specifically reduce abdominal fat stores, although they will strengthen the underlying muscles.

General Recommendations for Combining Caloric Restriction and Physical Activity for Weight Management[3]

1. Prolonged fasting and diet programs that severely restrict caloric intake are scientifically undesirable and can be medically dangerous.

2. Fasting and diet programs that severely restrict caloric intake result in the loss of large amounts of water, electrolytes, minerals, glycogen stores, and other fat-free tissue (including proteins within fat-free tissues), with minimal amounts of fat loss.

3. Mild caloric restriction (500 to 1,000 kilocalories less than the usual daily intake) results in a smaller loss of water, electrolytes, minerals, and other fat-free tissue and is less likely to cause malnutrition.

4. Dynamic exercise of large muscles helps to maintain fat-free tissue, including muscle mass and bone density, and it results in losses of body weight. Weight loss resulting from an increase in energy expenditure is primarily in the form of fat weight.

5. A nutritionally sound diet resulting in mild caloric restriction, coupled with an exercise program and behavioral modification of existing eating habits, is recommended for weight reduction.

6. To maintain proper weight control and optimal body fat levels, a lifetime commitment to proper eating habits and regular physical activity is required.

Therefore, a desirable weight management program is one that:[2–4]

1. Provides a caloric intake not lower than approximately 1,200 kilocalories per day for typical adults, including a proper blend of foods to meet nutritional requirements. (Note: this requirement may be different for children, older individuals, athletes, etc.)

2. Includes foods acceptable to the dieter from viewpoints of sociocultural background, usual habits, taste, cost, and ease in acquisition and preparation.

3. Provides a negative caloric balance (not to exceed 500 to 1,000 kilocalories per day lower than recommended), resulting in gradual weight loss without metabolic derangements. In most cases, weight loss should not exceed approximately 1 kg per week. Reduce dietary fat intake to less than 30 percent of total energy intake.

4. Includes guidelines for individuals who are overweight and obese, targeting a minimum reduction in body weight of at least 5 to 10 percent of initial body weight over a three- to six-month period.

5. Includes the use of behavior modification techniques to identify and eliminate dieting habits that contribute to improper nutrition.

6. Combines caloric restriction and physical activity.

The ACSM's[2] recommended exercise prescription for individuals who are overweight or obese includes:

Frequency: Greater than or equal to five days per week.

Intensity: Moderate- to vigorous-intensity aerobic activity should be encouraged. Initial exercise training intensity should be moderate (i.e., 40% to less than 60% $\dot{V}O_2$ reserve or heart rate reserve). Eventual progression to more vigorous exercise intensity (i.e., greater than or equal to 60% $\dot{V}O_2$ reserve or heart rate reserve) may result in further health and fitness benefits.

Time: A minimum of 30 minutes per day (i.e., 150 minutes per week) progressing to 60 minutes per day (i.e., 300 minutes per week) of moderate-intensity aerobic activity. Incorporating more vigorous-intensity exercise should be encouraged in individuals who are both capable and willing to exercise at a higher than moderate-intensity level of physical exertion with recognition that vigorous-intensity exercise is associated with the potential for greater injuries. Accumulation of intermittent exercise in bouts of at least 10 minutes is an effective alternative to continuous exercise and may be a particularly useful way to initiate exercise.

Type: The primary mode of exercise should be aerobic physical activities that involve the large muscle groups. As part of a balanced exercise program, resistance training and flexibility exercise should be incorporated (see Chapters 11 and 12).

PHYSICAL ACTIVITY AND CANCER

Epidemiological studies have provided equivocal findings regarding the relationship between physical activity and cancer.[23] When all forms of cancer are considered together, there is no consensus that physical activity or fitness reduces the risk of developing the disease. In addition, there is little evidence to suggest associations between physical activity and rectal, prostate, or testicular cancers.[23]

On the other hand, there is compelling evidence to suggest that the level of physical activity is inversely related to colon cancer (Figure 9.6). It is possible that the favorable effect of physical activity on colon cancer is related to increased peristalsis of the digestive tract and reduced transit time. Furthermore, Frisch et al.[15] found that women who had competed in athletics in college exhibited lower incidences of cancers of the uterus, ovaries, cervix, vagina, and breasts than non-athletes. These findings are particularly interesting because they describe a relationship between physical activity and cancers that, usually, are not diagnosed for 20 years or more. Although far from conclusive, these results suggest that activity patterns during adolescence and early adulthood influence the risk of developing cancer later in life.

It must be emphasized that none of these studies provides evidence of a direct cause-and-effect relationship between physical activity and prevention of cancer. Exercise is not being advanced as a panacea for cancer prevention. However, if a life of regular physical activity can make a contribution, no matter how small in a statistical sense, to the prevention of this disease, this information (even though causal relationships are not scientifically validated) may be extremely important.

Exercise can also help cancer patients combat ailments associated with prolonged bed rest, reduce stress, relieve fatigue, and reduce the side effects of cancer therapies such as chemotherapy. The ACSM's[2] recommended exercise prescription for individuals with cancer includes:

Frequency: For those who have completed treatment, the goal for aerobic exercise should be to increase gradually from the current physical activity level to three to five days per week with resistance training two to three days per week. Flexibility activities can occur daily, even during treatment. Evidence indicates that even individuals currently undergoing systemic cancer treatments can increase their daily physical activity sessions over the course of one month.

Intensity: Exercise tolerance may be highly variable during active treatment. Patients who have completed treatment may increase intensity slowly for all physical activities. Heart rate may be less reliable for monitoring intensity for those patients currently undergoing treatment. Therefore, educating these individuals to use perceived exertion to monitor intensity may be advisable. If exercise is tolerated without adverse effects on symptoms or side effects, exercise intensity need not differ from that of healthy populations.

figure 9.6 The relationship between physical activity and the risk of developing colon cancer is inverse.

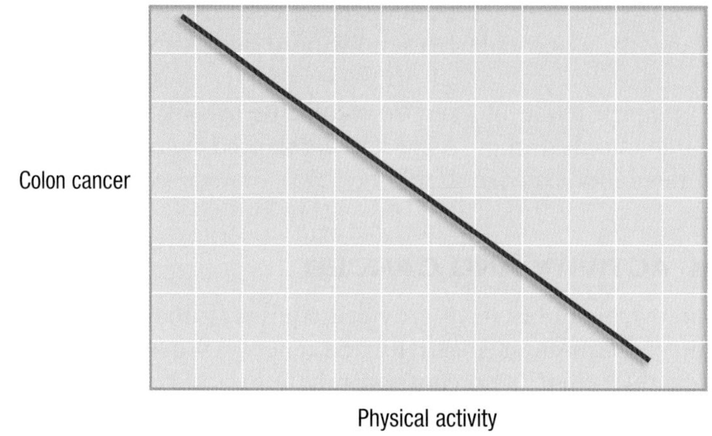

Aerobic exercise should be moderate (i.e., 40% to less than 60% $\dot{V}O_2$ reserve or heart rate reserve or RPE of 12 to 13 on a scale of 6 to 20) to vigorous (60 to 85% $\dot{V}O_2$ reserve or heart rate reserve or RPE of 12 to 16 on a scale of 6 to 20) intensity. Moderate-intensity resistance exercise should be 60 to 70% of one-repetition maximum (1-RM; see Chapter 11). Range of motion restrictions resultant to surgery and/or radiation therapy may affect flexibility intensity (see Chapter 12).

Time: Several short bouts per day rather than a single bout may be useful, particularly during active treatment. Patients who have completed treatment can increase duration as tolerated for all activities. When tolerated without exacerbation of symptoms or side effects, exercise session duration should be no different from that prescribed for healthy populations. Aerobic exercise should consist of 75 minutes per week of vigorous-intensity activity or 150 minutes per week of moderate-intensity activity or an equivalent combination of the two. Resistance training should consist of at least one set of 8 to 12 repetitions.

Type: Aerobic exercise should consist of prolonged rhythmic activities using large muscle groups (e.g., walking, cycling, swimming). Resistance exercise should consist of work with weights or resistance machines or weight-bearing functional tasks (e.g., sit-to-stand) targeting all major muscle groups. Flexibility exercise should consist of stretching or range of motion exercises of all major muscle groups also addressing specific areas of joint or muscle restriction that may have resulted from treatment with steroids, radiation, or surgery.

Progression: Slower progression may be needed among individuals with cancer compared to healthy adults. Awareness of the highly variable impact of exercise on symptoms for individuals undergoing treatment is needed. If exercise progression leads to an increase in fatigue or other common adverse symptoms, the amount of exercise should be reduced to a level that is better tolerated.

Exercise and breast cancer

It is clear that genetic factors play a role in determining who is at risk for developing breast cancer; however, body fatness and estradiol (a form of estrogen) levels appear to be contributing factors, as well. It has been estimated that each 5 kg/m^2 increase in BMI increases a woman's postmenopausal breast cancer risk by approximately 12 percent. It has also been estimated that survival rates of women with breast cancer decrease by as much as 30 percent in those with higher BMIs. The type of exercise that appears to lower estradiol levels, thereby reducing the risk of developing post-menopausal breast cancer, is moderate- to vigorous-intensity aerobic exercise lasting 150 to 225 minutes per week, continued for 12 months. This type of exercise program leads to reductions in body fat and in estradiol level and can have a significant impact not only on a woman's risk for developing breast cancer but also on her prognosis for survival following diagnosis.[21]

PHYSICAL ACTIVITY AND DIABETES MELLITUS

Diabetes mellitus is a metabolic disorder characterized by elevated blood glucose levels.[23] It has been estimated that more than 20 million Americans are diabetic. Diabetes mellitus is a risk factor for coronary heart disease and is closely associated with obesity. There are two primary classifications of diabetes mellitus: type 1 (formerly called insulin-dependent) and type 2 (formerly called non–insulin-dependent). **Type 1 diabetes mellitus** is caused by destruction of the beta cells of the pancreas and, therefore, is characterized by a deficiency of the hormone insulin in circulation. Most diabetics (over 90%) have **type 2 diabetes mellitus,** in which case insulin may be elevated but is not effective at normalizing blood glucose levels, or insulin secretion from the pancreas may be impaired.

- diabetes mellitus
- type 1 diabetes mellitus
- type 2 diabetes mellitus

Physical activity may improve the control of blood glucose levels in type 1 diabetics by increasing insulin sensitivity.[2] Much care is needed, however, to coordinate the timing and dosages of insulin supplementation with bouts of physical activity. This coordination can be very complex and requires much experience,

hypoglycemia
hyperglycemia

as well as supervision by a physician to avoid **hypoglycemia** (low blood glucose levels) or **hyperglycemia** (high blood glucose levels).

For type 2 diabetics, evidence shows that regular physical activity improves insulin sensitivity and glucose tolerance.[2]

The ACSM's[2] recommended exercise prescription for individuals with diabetes mellitus includes:

Frequency: Three to seven days per week.

Intensity: 40% to less than 60% $\dot{V}O_2$ reserve, corresponding to an RPE of 11 to 13 on a scale of 6 to 20. Better blood glucose control may be achieved at higher exercise intensities (greater than or equal to 60% $\dot{V}O_2$ reserve), so individuals who have been participating in regular exercise may consider raising the exercise intensity to this level of physical exertion.

Time: Individuals with type 2 diabetes mellitus should engage in a minimum of 150 minutes per week of exercise undertaken at moderate intensity or greater. Aerobic activity should be performed in bouts of at least 10 minutes and should be spread throughout the week. Moderate-intensity exercise totaling 150 minutes per week is associated with reduced mortality in observational studies in all populations. Additional benefits are accrued by increasing to greater than or equal to 300 minutes per week of moderate- to vigorous-intensity physical activity.

Type: Emphasize activities that use large muscle groups in a rhythmic and continuous fashion. Personal interest and desired goals of the exercise program should be considered.

Progression: Because maximizing caloric expenditure will always be a high priority, progressively increase exercise duration (either continuous or accumulated). As individuals improve physical fitness, adding higher-intensity physical activity to promote beneficial adaptations and combat boredom may be warranted.

Resistance training should be encouraged for individuals with diabetes mellitus or prediabetes in the absence of contraindications. The recommendations for healthy individuals generally apply to individuals with diabetes mellitus. Given that many patients may present with comorbidities, it may be necessary to tailor the resistance training prescription accordingly (see Chapter 11).

There is some evidence that a combination of aerobic and resistance training improves blood glucose control more than either modality alone.[10,22] Whether the added benefits are caused by greater overall caloric expenditure or are specific to the combination of aerobic and resistance training has not yet been resolved.

No more than two consecutive days of physical inactivity per week should be allowed. A greater emphasis should eventually be placed on vigorous-intensity exercise if cardiorespiratory fitness is a primary goal. On the other hand, greater amounts of moderate-intensity exercise that result in a caloric energy expenditure of greater than or equal to 2,000 kilocalories per week (greater than seven hours per week), including daily exercise, may be required if weight loss maintenance is the goal, as is the case for most individuals with type 2 diabetes mellitus.

PHYSICAL ACTIVITY AND OSTEOPOROSIS

osteoporosis

Osteoporosis is a disease characterized by low bone mass and microarchitectural deterioration of bone tissue, leading to enhanced bone fragility and a consequent increase in fracture risk.[2] Osteoporosis, which affects approximately 20 million women and 5 million men in the United States, is most common in older individuals, but bone density begins to decline between 25 and 35 years of age.[11] Thus, osteoporosis should not be viewed as only a geriatric disease. Furthermore, osteoporosis is most common in post-menopausal women.[11] Women tend to be more susceptible than men to osteoporosis because they[23] (1) have lower peak bone mass, (2) lose bone mass at an accelerated rate after menopause due to decreased estrogen levels, and (3) have a longer life span.

Fractures, particularly of the spine, femoral neck, and wrist, are the primary health consequence of osteoporosis. Fractures of the femoral neck, often called hip fractures, account for over 15 percent of all fractures attributed to osteoporosis. In older individuals, hip fractures can be devastating and frequently result in long-term disability.[23]

Physical activity may reduce the risk of osteoporosis by aiding in the development of bone mass and density during adolescence and young adulthood, helping to maintain bone mass and density through middle age, and supplementing the effect of prescribed estrogen therapy on the retention and development of bone density in post-menopausal women.[23] Physical activity, however, is not a replacement for estrogen therapy when prescribed.

The beneficial effect of physical activity on bone health is primarily due to its load-bearing characteristics.[11,23] In general, the higher the load on a bone, the greater the bone mass. Thus, weight-bearing activities such as fast walking, running, and stair climbing are prescribed to increase bone mass of the femur in an attempt to reduce hip fractures and falls.

The ACSM's[2] recommended exercise prescriptions for individuals at risk for osteoporosis (at least one risk factor including current low bone mass, age, and being female) or individuals with diagnosed osteoporosis include:

Exercise and bone density

Osteoporosis affects more than 20 million people in the United States. As bone density declines with age, particularly in post-menopausal women, the risk of fractures of the vertebrae and hip rises. Exercise is commonly recommended as a way to combat bone loss. The authors of a review article[8] present four considerations to take into account when developing an exercise program for post-menopausal women:

1. The wrong type of exercise can do more harm than good, e.g., jogging could cause a fracture in individuals with low bone mass.
2. Weight training can improve bone density while at the same time increasing muscular strength and balance, which may result in fewer falls and subsequent fractures.
3. Adequate calcium intake is essential for exercise to improve bone density.
4. Exercise is not a substitute for estrogen replacement therapy (ERT) when prescribed.

WWW

National Osteoporosis Foundation
www.nof.org

Exercise prescription for individuals at risk for osteoporosis to help preserve bone health

Frequency: Weight-bearing aerobic activities three to five days per week and resistance exercise two to three days per week.

Intensity of aerobic exercise: Moderate (e.g., 40 to 60% $\dot{V}O_2$ reserve or heart rate reserve) to vigorous (e.g., greater than or equal to 60% $\dot{V}O_2$ reserve or heart rate reserve) intensity.

Intensity of resistance exercise: Moderate (e.g., 60 to 80% 1-RM, 8 to 12 repetitions with exercises involving each major muscle group) to vigorous (e.g., 80 to 90% 1-RM, 5 to 6 repetitions with exercises involving each major muscle group) intensity in terms of bone-loading forces.

Time: 30 to 60 minutes per day of a combination of weight-bearing aerobic and resistance activities.

Type: Weight-bearing aerobic activities (e.g., tennis, stair climbing/descending, and walking with intermittent jogging), activities that involve jumping (e.g., volleyball and basketball), and resistance exercise (e.g., weight lifting).

Exercise prescription for individuals with osteoporosis to help prevent disease progression

Frequency: Weight-bearing aerobic activities three to five days per week and resistance exercise two to three days per week.

Intensity: Moderate intensity (i.e., 40% to less than 60% $\dot{V}O_2$ reserve or heart rate reserve) for weight-bearing aerobic activities and moderate intensity (e.g., 60 to 80% 1-RM, 8 to 12 repetitions of exercises involving each major muscle group) in terms of bone-loading forces, although some individuals may be able to tolerate more intense exercise.

Time: 30 to 60 minutes per day of a combination of weight-bearing aerobic and resistance activities.

Type: Weight-bearing aerobic activities (e.g., stair climbing/descending, walking, and other activities as tolerated) and resistance exercise (e.g., weight lifting).

PHYSICAL ACTIVITY AND ASTHMA

asthma

Asthma involves chronic inflammation of the airways of the lungs and is characterized by obstruction of the flow of air due to bronchoconstriction, wheezing, coughing, shortness of breath, and tightness of the chest.[2] Sometimes the symptoms of asthma occur during exercise or can be made worse by exercise and, therefore, may lead to reduced participation in exercise and sports. The reduced participation in physical activity can result in reduced levels of fitness and tolerance for exercise.

The ACSM's[2] recommended aerobic exercise prescription for individuals with asthma includes:

Frequency: At least two to three days per week.

Intensity: Approximately at the ventilatory anaerobic threshold or at least 60% $\dot{V}O_{2Peak}$ determined from progressive exercise testing with measurement of expired gases or 80% of maximal walking speed determined from the 6-minute walk test.

Time: At least 20 to 30 minutes per day.

Type: Aerobic activities using large muscle groups such as walking, running, or cycling. Swimming (preferably in a nonchlorinated pool) is less asthmogenic and, therefore, a better tolerated form of exercise.

Progression: After the first month, if the exercise prescription is well tolerated, greater health/fitness benefits may be gained by increasing the intensity to approximately 70% $\dot{V}O_{2Peak}$, the time of each exercise session to 40 minutes per day, and frequency to five days per week.

The exercise prescription for resistance training and flexibility should be the same as for healthy adults (see Chapters 11 and 12).

PHYSICAL ACTIVITY AND CHRONIC OBSTRUCTIVE PULMONARY DISEASE

chronic obstructive pulmonary disease

Chronic obstructive pulmonary disease (COPD) consists of bronchitis and/or emphysema and is characterized by limited airflow to the lungs that is not fully reversible.[2] Often COPD results in shortness of breath during exercise, which limits participation in physical activity. The lack of regular physical activity can result in severe deconditioning. Chronic exercise, however, can reduce the functional impairment associated with COPD by promoting cardiovascular and musculoskeletal adaptations and thereby reducing the demands on the pulmonary system.

The ACSM's[2] recommended exercise prescription for individuals with chronic obstructive pulmonary disease includes:

Frequency: At least three to five days per week.

Intensity: For patients with COPD, light (30 to 40% of peak work rates) and vigorous (60 to 80% of peak work rates) intensities have been recommended. Light-intensity training results in improvements in symptoms, health-related quality of life, and performance of activities of daily living, whereas vigorous-intensity training has been shown to result in greater physiologic improvements (e.g., reduced minute ventilation and heart rate at a given workload). Because of these greater physiologic improvements, high-intensity training can be encouraged if tolerated. However, it should be recognized that some patients may not be able to exercise at these intensities, and light-intensity exercise is recommended for such patients.

Time: Individuals with moderate or severe COPD may be able to exercise only at a specified intensity for a few minutes at the start of the training program. Intermittent exercise may also be used for the initial training sessions until the individual tolerates exercise at sustained higher intensities and durations of activity. Shorter periods of vigorous-intensity exercise separated by periods of rest (i.e., interval training) have been used with those with COPD and shown to result in lower symptom scores despite high training work rates.

Type: Walking and/or cycling.

Resistance and flexibility training should be encouraged for individuals with COPD. The exercise prescription for resistance and flexibility training for these individuals should be the same as for healthy adults and/or older adults (see Chapters 11 and 12).

PHYSICAL ACTIVITY AND MENTAL HEALTH

The most frequently reported mental disorders are mood disturbances, such as depression, and anxiety disorders.[23] It is commonly believed that physically active and fit individuals are less likely to suffer from these disorders (Figure 9.7) and have a more positive outlook, greater self-esteem, and an enhanced ability to respond to stressors. In general, this conventional wisdom is supported by epidemiological, laboratory, and clinical research.[23] Most epidemiological studies have reported that physical activity is associated with reduced symptoms of depression. Regular physical activity also has positive effects on **trait** (how a person feels right now) and **state** (how a person generally feels) **anxiety.** Furthermore, single bouts of physical activity can reduce anxiety and muscle tension.[23] The physiological mechanism underlying the benefits of physical activity to mental health are unknown but may involve endorphins and enkephalins, brain neuroreceptors for monoamines, hormonal factors, and changes in core body temperature.[23]

- trait anxiety
- state anxiety

There is no definitive information regarding the optimal characteristics of a physical activity program for improving mental health. It appears, however, that daily physical activity is necessary to reduce anxiety on a long-term basis.

figure 9.7 High fit individuals are less likely than low fit individuals to suffer from anxiety or depression.

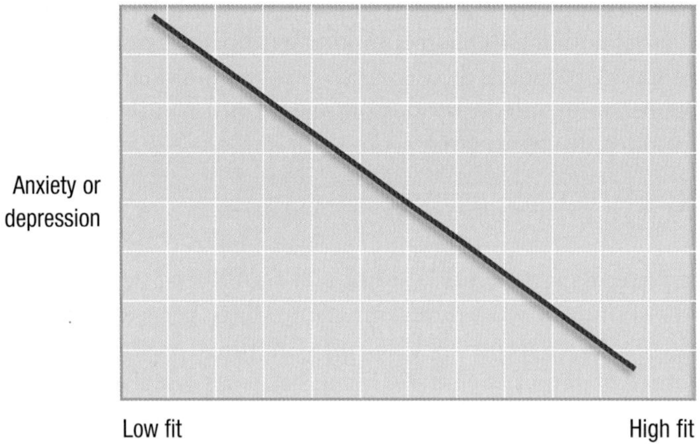

PHYSICAL ACTIVITY AND PREGNANCY AND CHILDBIRTH

Some women may be concerned that regular physical activity during pregnancy may cause miscarriage, premature delivery, or maternal injury. For normal pregnancies, these concerns have not been supported. For example, according to the ACSM,[5] "participation in regular weight-bearing exercise has been shown to improve maternal fitness, restrict weight gain without compromising fetal growth, and hasten postpartum recovery."

The ACSM[2] has provided a list of relative and absolute contraindications for exercising during pregnancy (Table 9.4). The ACSM's[2] recommended aerobic exercise prescription for pregnant women who are not limited by these contraindications includes:

Frequency: Three to four days of the week.

Intensity: Moderate intensity based on BMI and HR.

BMI < 25 kg • m²			BMI ≥ 25 kg • m²	
AGE	FITNESS LEVEL	HR RANGE (bpm)	AGE	HR RANGE (bpm)
<20		140–155	20–29	102–124
20–29	Low	129–144	30–39	101–120
	Active	135–150		
	Fit	145–160		
30–39	Low	128–144		
	Active	130–145		
	Fit	140–156		

Time: At least 15 minutes per day gradually increasing to at least 30 minutes per day of accumulated moderate-intensity physical activity to total 120 minutes per week.

Type: Dynamic, rhythmic physical activities that use the large muscle groups, such as walking and cycling.

Normal pregnancy and childbirth have no effects on subsequent exercise and athletic performance. For athletes in various sports who have more than one child, it is not uncommon for them to compete successfully even at international levels.

www

Exercise During Pregnancy
www.aafp.org/afp/
https://www.acsm.org/docs/current-comments/exerciseduringpregnancy.pdf

table 9.4 Relative and absolute contraindications for exercising during pregnancy.[2]

RELATIVE CONTRAINDICATIONS
1. Severe anemia
2. Unevaluated maternal cardiac dysrhythmia
3. Chronic bronchitis
4. Poorly controlled type 1 diabetes mellitus
5. Extreme morbid obesity
6. Extreme underweight
7. History of extremely sedentary lifestyle
8. Intrauterine growth restriction in current pregnancy
9. Poorly controlled hypertension
10. Orthopedic limitations
11. Poorly controlled seizure disorder
12. Poorly controlled hyperthyroidism
13. Heavy smoker
ABSOLUTE CONTRAINDICATIONS
1. Hemodynamically significant heart disease
2. Restrictive lung disease
3. Incomplete cervix/cerclage
4. Multiple gestation at risk for premature labor
5. Persistent second- or third-trimester bleeding
6. Placenta previa after 26 weeks of gestation
7. Premature labor during the current pregnancy
8. Ruptured membranes
9. Preeclampsia/pregnancy-induced hypertension

summary

During the twentieth century, the illnesses that affect American society changed from predominantly infectious diseases such as tuberculosis, diphtheria, and poliomyelitis to degenerative diseases such as cardiovascular diseases, hypertension, and cancer. Physical activity can have positive effects on many degenerative diseases. For example, epidemiological and clinical evidence suggests that there are inverse relationships between physical activity and all-cause mortality, coronary heart disease, atherosclerosis, stroke, hypertension, peripheral artery disease, obesity, colon cancer, diabetes mellitus, osteoporosis, asthma, COPD, and certain mental disorders. In some cases, there are dose–response relationships between physical activity and the risk of disease, such that higher levels of activity and/or improved fitness reduce the risk of developing the disease. Physical activity also has a positive effect on other health conditions such as asthma and pregnancy. The ACSM has provided recommended exercise prescriptions for individuals with many health conditions.

questions for review

1. What is the relationship among physical activity, fitness, and all-cause mortality?
2. How does physical activity reduce the risk of CHD? Of stroke?
3. What is the relationship of physical activity to blood pressure? To peripheral artery disease?
4. Can you generalize about the risk of death with a low or high body weight? Why or why not?
5. In what ways does physical activity contribute to weight loss?
6. What are some common misconceptions regarding physical activity and weight loss?
7. As an exercise professional, a coach, or a physical educator, what advice might you give regarding a weight loss program?
8. What do current studies conclude about the relationship of physical activity to cancer?
9. What health benefits of physical activity would you stress if you were giving a presentation to a group of parents? To a group of older adults? To a group of women?
10. As an exercise professional, what are some factors you would consider when designing an exercise program for a post-menopausal woman?
11. What precautions would you suggest to an individual starting an aerobic training program who is pregnant?

student companion website

For further review of this book's chapters and for test preparation, visit the book's website, **www.hhpcommunities.com/exercisephysiology**, to take practice quizzes, review the vocabulary terms, use the study guide, and view the digital image bank.

references

1. American College of Sports Medicine. *ACSM's Resource Manual for Guidelines for Exercise Testing and Prescription*, 7th edition. Baltimore: Wolters Kluwer/Lippincott Williams & Wilkins, 2014.
2. American College of Sports Medicine. *ACSM's Guidelines for Exercise Testing and Prescription*, 9th edition. Baltimore: Wolters Kluwer/Lippincott Williams & Wilkins, 2014.
3. American College of Sports Medicine. Position Stand. Proper and improper weight loss programs. *Med. Sci. Sports Exerc.* 15: ix–xi, 1983.
4. American College of Sports Medicine. Position Stand. Appropriate physical activity intervention strategies for weight loss and prevention of weight regain in adults. *Med. Sci. Sports Exerc.* 41: 459–471, 2009.
5. American College of Sports Medicine. Current Comment Fact Sheet. Exercise during pregnancy. 2015. Retrieved from https://www.acsm.org/docs/current-comments/exerciseduringpregnancy.pdf?sfvrsn=4.
6. Andres, R. Discussion: Assessment of health status. In *Exercise, Fitness, and Health, A Consensus of Current Knowledge*, eds. C. Bouchard, R. J. Shephard, T. Stephens, J. R. Sutton, and B. D. McPherson, 133–136. Champaign, IL: Human Kinetics, 1990.
7. Barnard, R. J. Physical activity, fitness, and claudication. In *Physical Activity, Fitness, and Health, International Proceedings and Consensus Statement*, eds. C. Bouchard, R. J. Shephard, and T. Stephens. Champaign, IL: Human Kinetics, 1994, pp. 622–632.

8. Bemben, D. A., and Fetters, N. L. The independent and additive effects of exercise training and estrogen on bone metabolism. *J. Str. Cond. Res.* 14: 114–120, 2000.

9. Blair, S. N., Kohl, H. W., Barlow, C. E., Paffenbarger, R. S., Gibbons, L. W., and Macera, C. A. Changes in physical fitness and all-cause mortality: A prospective study of health and unhealthy men. *JAMA* 273: 1093–1098, 1995.

10. Cuff, D. J., Meneilly, G. S., Martin, A., Ignaszewski, A., Tildesley, H. D., and Frohlich, J. J. Effective exercise modality to reduce insulin resistance in women with type 2 diabetes. *Diabetes Care*. 26: 2977–82, 2003.

11. Dembo, L., and McCormick, K. M. Exercise prescription to prevent osteoporosis. *ACSM's Health and Fitness Journal* 4: 32–38, 2000.

12. Durstine, J. L., and Thompson, R. W. Exercise modulates blood lipids and lipoproteins, a great explanation and exercise plan. *ACSM's Health and Fitness Journal* 4: 7–12, 2000.

13. Flegal, K. M., Carroll, M. D., Ogden, C. L., and Johnson, C. L. Prevalence and trends in obesity among U.S. adults. *JAMA* 288: 1723–1727, 2002.

14. Freedman, D. S., Khan, L. K., Serdula, M. K., Galuska, D. A., and Dietz, W. H. Trends and correlates of class 3 obesity in the United States from 1990 through 2000. *JAMA* 288: 1758–1761, 2002.

15. Frisch, R. E., Wyshak, G., Albright, N. L., Albright, T. E., Schiff, I., Koff, E., and Marguglio, M. Lower prevalence of breast cancer and cancers of the reproductive system among former college athletes compared to nonathletes. *Br. J. Cancer* 52: 885–891, 1985.

16. Fryar, C. D., Carroll, M. D., and Ogden, C. L. Prevalence of overweight, obesity, and extreme obesity among adults: United States, trends 1960–1962 through 2009–2010. National Center for Health Statistics, 2012. Available at http://www.cdc.gov/nchs/data/hestat/obesity_adult_09_10/obesity_adult_09_10.htm.

17. Hill, J. O., Drougas, H. J., and Peters, J. C. Physical activity, fitness, and moderate obesity. In *Physical Activity, Fitness, and Health, International Proceedings and Consensus Statement,* eds. C. Bouchard, R. J. Shephard, and T. Stephens. Champaign, IL: Human Kinetics, 1994, pp. 684–695.

18. Hubert, H. B., Feinleib, M., McNamara, P. M., and Castelli, W. P. Obesity as an independent risk factor for cardiovascular disease: a 26-year follow-up of participants in the Framingham Heart Study. *Circulation* 67: 968–977, 1983.

19. Katch, F. I., and McArdle, W. D. *Introduction to Nutrition, Exercise, and Health,* 4th edition. Philadelphia: Lea and Febiger, 1993.

20. McArdle, W. D., Katch, F. I., and Katch, V. L. *Exercise Physiology, Energy, Nutrition, and Human Performance,* 8th edition. Baltimore: Wolters Kluwer/Lippincott, Williams & Wilkins, 2014.

21. Neilson, H. K., Conroy, S. M., and Friedenreich, C. M. The influence of energetic factors on biomarkers of postmenopausal breast cancer risk. *Curr. Nutr. Rep.* 3: 22–34, 2014.

22. Sigal, R. J., Kenny, G. P., Boulé, N. G., Sigal, R. J., Kenny, G. P., et al. Effects of aerobic training, resistance training, or both on glycemic control in type 2 diabetes: a randomized trial. *Ann. Intern. Med.* 147: 357–69, 2007.

23. U. S. Department of Health and Human Services. *Physical Activity and Health: A Report of the Surgeon General.* Atlanta: U.S. Department of Health and Human Services, Centers for Disease Control and Prevention, National Center for Chronic Disease Prevention and Health Promotion, 1996.

24. U. S. Department of Health and Human Services. *2008 Physical Activity Guidelines for Americans.* Atlanta: U. S. Department of Health and Human Services, 2008. Available at www.health.gov/paguidelines.

CHAPTER 9

lab Anthropometric Measures of Health Risk

BACKGROUND

Three primary anthropometric-based parameters that can provide information regarding the risk of developing cardiovascular disease, type 2 diabetes, dyslipidemia, obesity, and/or hypertension are: body mass index (BMI), waist-to-hip ratio, and waist circumference.[1,3,4,5,8] Each of these parameters can be used to classify individuals with regard to their health risk. In addition, they are commonly used in epidemiological studies because they are associated with various diseases and risk factors, require few measurements, and are simple to calculate.

In this laboratory, the techniques and landmarks for measuring height and body weight, as well as waist 1, waist 2, and hips circumferences, will be described, and you will use them to determine the BMI, waist-to-hip ratio, and waist 2 circumference. You will also learn to classify an individual's health risk based on these parameters.

TERMS & ABBREVIATIONS

- ☐ anthropometric = relating to the measurement of the size and proportions of the human body
- ☐ BMI = body mass index: body weight in kg/height in meters squared ($kg \cdot m^2$)
- ☐ epidemiological studies = studies performed on human populations that attempt to link health effects to a cause; e.g., waist circumference and type 2 diabetes

PROCEDURES[1,5,6]

1. Measure the subject's height in meters (cm/100) and body weight in kg with the shoes removed (see photos 9.1 and 9.2). Record the values on Worksheet 9.1.
2. Identify the landmarks for the waist 1, waist 2, and hips circumferences (see photos 9.3, 9.4, and 9.5).
3. Place the tape parallel to the floor (horizontal).
4. Hold the tape firmly around the circumference site, but do not compress the underlying tissue.
5. Take three measurements per site and use the mean of repeated recordings that agree within 0.5 cm. Record measurements on Worksheet 9.1.

photo 9.1

Measurement of height.

Circumference Sites in cm[1,2,6,8]

Waist 1 (see photo 9.3): at the level of the "natural waist," midway between the xyphoid process and umbilicus

Waist 2 (see photo 9.4): at the level of the umbilicus and iliac crests

Hips (see photo 9.5): at the level of the pubis symphysis and the maximal protrusion of the gluteal muscles

SAMPLE CALCULATIONS

Gender: Male

Body weight: 80 kg

Height: 1.85 m

Waist 1 circumference: 84.0 cm

Waist 2 circumference: 87.0 cm

Hips circumference: 96 cm

body mass index (BMI) = body weight in kg / height in meters squared ($kg \cdot m^2$)

BMI = 80 / 1.85^2 = 80 / 3.42 = 23.4

waist-to-hip ratio = waist 1 circumference in cm / hips circumference in cm

waist-to-hip ratio = 84.0/96.0 = 0.875

waist 2 circumference = 87.0 cm

Tables L9.1, L9.2, and L9.3 provide mean height, body weight, and BMI values by age categories.[8]

Tables L9.4, L9.5, and L9.6 provide health risk classifications for BMI, waist-to-hip ratio, and waist 2 circumference.[3,4,5,6,7]

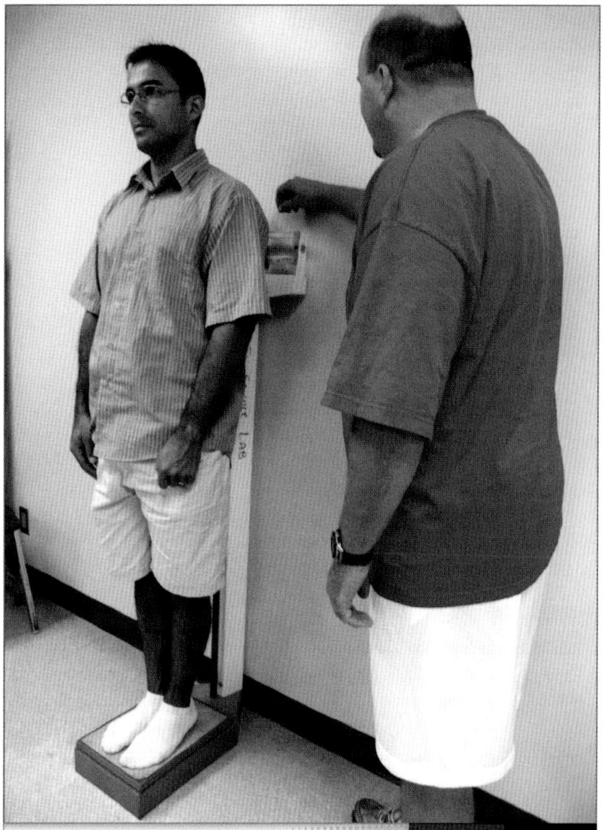

photo 9.2

Measurement of weight.

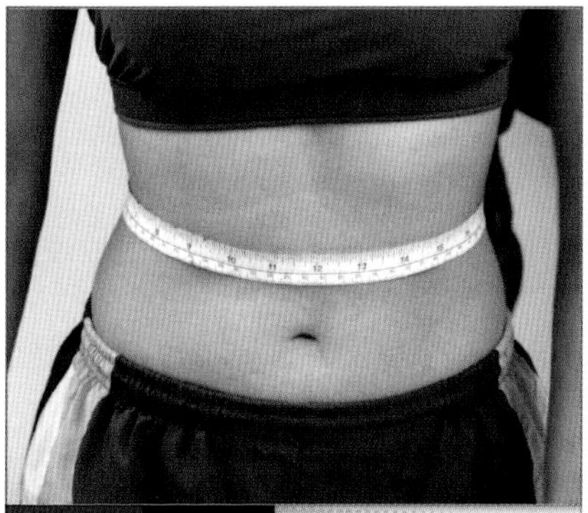

photo 9.3

Measurement of waist 1 circumference, at the natural waist.

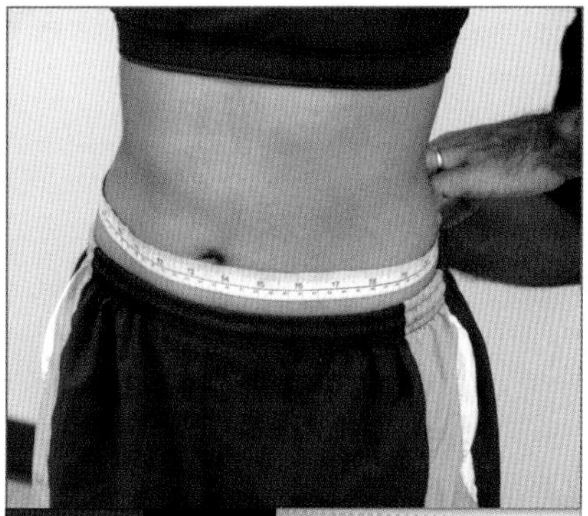

photo 9.4

Measurement of waist 2 circumference, at the level of the umbilicus and iliac crests.

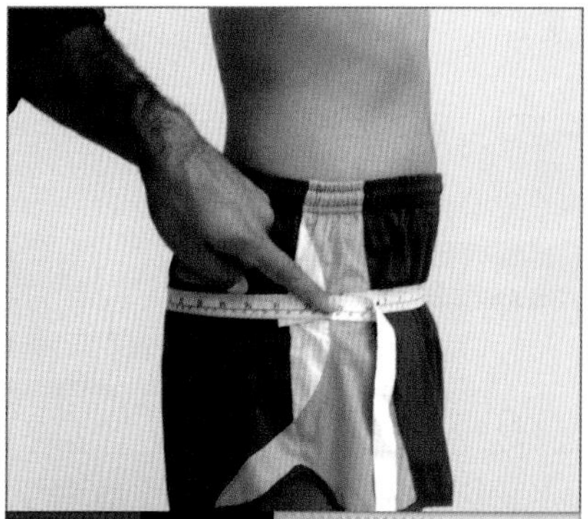

photo 9.5

Measurement of hips circumference, at the level of the symphysis pubis and maximal gluteal protrusion.

table L9.1 Mean (± SEM) height (cm) values by age categories.[8]

AGE (YEARS)	MALES	FEMALES
17	175.3 ± 0.57	163.1 ± 0.56
18	176.4 ± 0.65	163.1 ± 0.44
19	176.7 ± 0.64	162.9 ± 0.64
20–29	176.7 ± 0.29	162.8 ± 0.31
30–39	176.4 ± 0.26	163.1 ± 0.28
40–49	177.2 ± 0.33	163.4 ± 0.24
50–59	175.8 ± 0.32	162.3 ± 0.35
60–69	174.8 ± 0.33	160.6 ± 0.27
70–79	172.7 ± 0.44	159.0 ± 0.31
80 and over	170.7 ± 0.44	155.8 ± 0.34

table L9.2 Mean (± SEM) body weight (kg) values by age categories.[8]

AGE (YEARS)	MALES	FEMALES
17	75.6 ± 1.38	61.7 ± 1.21
18	75.6 ± 1.12	65.2 ± 1.52
19	78.2 ± 1.29	67.9 ± 1.21
20–29	83.4 ± 0.70	71.1 ± 0.90
30–39	86.0 ± 0.90	74.1 ± 0.91
40–49	89.1 ± 0.73	76.5 ± 1.09
50–59	88.8 ± 0.94	76.9 ± 1.15
60–69	88.2 ± 0.73	76.3 ± 0.76
70–79	82.7 ± 0.71	71.0 ± 0.76
80 and over	76.0 ± 0.66	63.7 ± 1.31

table L9.3 Mean (± SEM) BMI values by age categories.[8]

AGE (YEARS)	MALES	FEMALES
17	24.5 ± 0.41	23.1 ± 0.41
18	24.2 ± 0.34	24.4 ± 0.48
19	24.9 ± 0.36	25.5 ± 0.43
20–29	26.6 ± 0.19	26.8 ± 0.29
30–39	27.5 ± 0.26	27.9 ± 0.33
40–49	28.4 ± 0.25	28.6 ± 0.40
50–59	28.7 ± 0.31	29.2 ± 0.40
60–69	28.9 ± 0.20	29.6 ± 0.30
70–79	27.7 ± 0.18	28.0 ± 0.29
80 and over	26.1 ± 0.23	26.1 ± 0.48

table L9.4 Health risk classifications for BMI.[5]

BMI (kg • m^{-2})	WEIGHT CLASSIFICATION	HEALTH RISK
<18.5	Underweight	Increased
18.5–24.9	Normal weight	Average
25.0–29.9	Overweight	Increased
⩾30	Obese	High

Note: Underweight, overweight, and obese classifications are associated with various diseases such as hypertension, dyslipidemia, and cardiovascular disease.[1]

table L9.5 Health risk classifications for cardiovascular disease associated with waist-to-hip ratio by age categories.[4,6,7]

MALES				
Age (years)	Low	Moderate	High	Very High
20–29	<0.83	0.83–0.88	0.89–0.94	>0.94
30–39	<0.84	0.84–0.91	0.92–0.96	>0.96
40–49	<0.88	0.88–0.95	0.96–1.00	>1.00
50–59	<0.90	0.90–0.96	0.97–1.02	>1.02
60–69	<0.91	0.91–0.98	0.99–1.03	>1.03
FEMALES				
Age (years)	Low	Moderate	High	Very High
20–29	<0.71	0.71–0.77	0.78–0.82	>0.82
30–39	<0.72	0.72–0.78	0.79–0.84	>0.84
40–49	<0.73	0.73–0.79	0.80–0.87	>0.87
50–59	<0.74	0.74–0.81	0.82–0.88	>0.88
60–69	<0.76	0.76–0.83	0.84–0.90	>0.90

Note: Waist-to-hip ratio uses waist 1 circumference.

table L9.6 Chronic disease classifications for waist 2 circumference.[3]

CHRONIC DISEASE RISK	FEMALES	MALES
Very low	<70	<80
Low	70–89	80–99
High	90–109	100–120
Very high	>110	>120

Note: Chronic diseases include type 2 diabetes, hypertension, and cardiovascular disease.[1]

worksheet 9.1 ANTHROPOMETRIC MEASURES OF HEALTH RISK FORM

NAME ______________________________ DATE ______________

Gender: ______________

Age: ______________ years

Body weight: ______________ kg

Height: ______________ cm / 100 = ______________ meters

	TRIAL 1	TRIAL 2	TRIAL 3	MEAN
Waist 1 circumference (cm)				
Waist 2 circumference (cm)				
Hips circumference (cm)				

BMI = body weight in kg / height in m^2 = ______________ kg / ______________ m^2 = ______________

Classification = ______________ (Table L9.4)

Waist-to-hip ratio = waist 1 circumference in cm / hips circumference in cm =

______________ cm / ______________ cm = ______________

Classification = ______________ (Table L9.5)

Waist 2 circumference = ______________ cm

Classification = ______________ (Table L9.6)

EXTENSION ACTIVITIES

worksheet 9.2

NAME ______________________ DATE ______________________

Use the following data and Tables L9.4, L9.5, and L9.6 to answer the questions below.

Gender: Female

Age: 20 years

Body weight: 78 kg

Height: 1.75 m

Waist 1 circumference = 82.0 cm

Waist 2 circumference = 89.0 cm

Hips circumference = 98.0 cm

1. Calculate the subject's BMI and classify her health risk (see Table L9.4).

   BMI = ______________________

   Classification = ______________________

2. Calculate the subject's waist-to-hip ratio and classify her health risk for cardiovascular disease (see Table L9.5).

   Waist-to-hip ratio = ______________________

   Classification = ______________________

3. Based on the subject's waist 2 circumference, classify her health risk for chronic diseases (see Table L9.6).

   Classification = ______________________

EXTENSION QUESTIONS

1. What are some common mistakes that may occur in administering this lab?

2. Identify possible sources of error in this lab.

3. Assess the practicality of using this lab in the field.

4. Research the reliability and/or validity of this lab using online resources, journal articles, and other credible sources.

REFERENCES

1. American College of Sports Medicine. *ACSM's Guidelines for Exercise Testing and Prescription,* 9th edition. Baltimore: Wolters Kluwer/Lippincott Williams & Wilkins, 2014.
2. Behnke, A. R., and Wilmore, J. H. *Evaluation and Regulation of Body Build and Composition.* Englewood Cliffs, NJ: Prentice-Hall, 1974.
3. Bray, G. A. Don't throw the baby out with the bath water. *Am. J. Clin. Nutr.* 79: 347–349, 2004.
4. Bray, G. A., and Gray, D. S. Obesity Part 1—Pathogenesis. *West. J. Med.* 149: 429–441, 1988.
5. Expert Panel on the Identification, Evaluation, and Treatment of Overweight in Adults. Clinical guidelines on the identification, evaluation, and treatment of overweight and obesity in adults: Executive summary. *Am. J. Clin. Nutr.* 68: 899–917, 1998.
6. Heyward, V. H., and Stolarczyk, L. M. *Applied Body Composition Assessment.* Champaign, IL: Human Kinetics, 1996, pp. 81–82.
7. Hoffman, J. *Norms for Fitness, Performance, and Health.* Champaign, IL: Human Kinetics, 2006, p. 87.
8. McDowell, M. A., Fryar, C. D., Hirsch, R., and Ogden, C. L. *Anthropometric Reference Data for Children and Adults: U.S. Population, 1999–2002.* Hyattsville, MD: Centers for Disease Control and Prevention, 2005.

10 Aerobic Exercise Prescriptions for Public Health, Cardiorespiratory Fitness, and Athletics

As a result of reading this chapter you will:

Know the characteristics of an aerobic exercise prescription for public health.

Understand the differences between aerobic exercise prescriptions for public health and the improvement of cardiorespiratory fitness.

Understand the frequency, intensity, time, type, volume, and progression or pattern of training necessary to improve cardiorespiratory fitness.

Know the effects of detraining on cardiorespiratory fitness.

Recognize the primary physiological factors that determine endurance performance in athletes.

Know basic considerations related to warming up and cooling down.

Understand the characteristics of an endurance training program for athletes.

key concepts

anaerobic threshold
controlled frequency breathing (CFB)
cooling down
cruise intervals
detraining
drafting
duration
economy of movement
Fartlek training
FITT-VP
frequency
heart rate reserve
high risk
hypercapnic training
hypoxic training
intensity
interval training
lactate threshold
long slow distance (LSD) training
low risk
metabolic equivalent (MET)
mode
moderate risk
rating of perceived exertion (RPE)
repetition (REP) training
target heart rate
tempo-pace training
ventilatory threshold
$\dot{V}O_2$ reserve
volume of exercise
warming up

Exercise professionals, physical educators, and often coaches are called upon to advise school children, as well as young, middle-aged, and older adults, about exercise training programs. The general public and allied health professionals now recognize the importance of physical activity for health.[2,3,18]

No single prescription for aerobic exercise will meet the needs and goals of all individuals. Therefore, this chapter presents prescriptions for aerobic exercise for the following categories of individuals:

1. The general public interested in the health-related benefits of exercise.
2. Healthy individuals interested in developing cardiorespiratory fitness and increasing maximal oxygen consumption rate ($\dot{V}O_2$ max).
3. Endurance athletes.

PRESCRIPTIONS FOR ALL TYPES OF AEROBIC TRAINING PROGRAMS

Medical Evaluations

In some cases, an individual should receive a medical examination prior to beginning an exercise program. According to the American College of Sports Medicine's *Guidelines for Exercise Testing and Prescription,*[2] the need for a medical examination is dependent on the level of risk posed by the exercise program. Individuals are categorized as low, moderate, or high risk.

Low risk: Asymptomatic and fewer than two of the following risk factors: (1) Men greater than or equal to 45 years of age and women greater than or equal to 55, (2) family history of coronary artery disease, (3) current cigarette smoking, (4) hypertension, (5) dyslipidemia, or abnormalities in blood lipid and lipoprotein concentrations, (6) impaired fasting glucose (pre-diabetes), (7) obesity, and (8) sedentary lifestyle. A high-density lipoprotein (HDL) cholesterol level of ≥ 60 mg • dL^{-1} in the serum decreases cardiovascular disease risk, and one risk factor can, therefore, be subtracted from an individual's total. Individuals in the low-risk category do not need a medical exam or graded exercise text supervised by a physician prior to participation in a moderate-intensity (40 to 59% $\dot{V}O_2$ reserve) or vigorous-intensity ($\geq$60% $\dot{V}O_2$ reserve) exercise program.[2]

Moderate risk: Asymptomatic and greater than or equal to two of the risk factors listed above. For individuals at moderate risk, a medical exam is recommended prior to beginning a vigorous-intensity exercise program but not a moderate-intensity exercise program. An exercise test, however, is not necessary prior to beginning a moderate- or vigorous-intensity exercise program.[2]

High risk: Individuals who are symptomatic or with known cardiac, pulmonary, or metabolic disease, or any person who has unstable or new or possible symptoms of cardiovascular disease or one or more of the following conditions:

1. Diabetes mellitus and at least one of the following:
   - Age greater than 35 years or
   - Type 2 diabetes mellitus greater than 10-year duration or
   - Type 1 diabetes mellitus greater than 15-year duration or
   - Hypercholesterolemia or
   - Hypertension or
   - Smoking or

low risk
moderate risk
high risk

Warming up

Exercise scientists, physical educators, athletic trainers, and coaches should be aware that warming up reduces the risk of musculoskeletal injuries. Warming up prior to exercise increases blood flow to muscles and the temperature of tendons and ligaments. Thus, warming up decreases the risk of muscle pulls and tears, as well as damage to the connective tissues that may occur if exercise is performed when these tissues are at comparatively low temperatures.[15]

- Family history of coronary artery disease in first-degree relative less than 60 years of age or
- Microvascular disease or
- Peripheral artery disease or
- Autonomic neuropathy

2. End-stage renal disease
3. Symptomatic or diagnosed pulmonary disease including chronic obstructive pulmonary disease (COPD), asthma, interstitial lung disease, or cystic fibrosis.

WWW

Physical Activity and Health Executive Summary

www.cdc.gov/nccdphp/sgr/sgr.htm

It is recommended that high-risk individuals have a medical examination and physician-supervised maximal or submaximal graded exercise test prior to beginning a moderate-intensity or vigorous-intensity exercise program.[2]

Warming Up and Cooling Down

The warm-up prior to a training session and the cool-down following it are very important for everyone who exercises and particularly for athletes who engage in very demanding training and competition. The principles of good warm-up and cool-down procedures apply to all individuals who perform physical activity for health, fitness, or athletic competition.

Warming up

warming up

Warming up prior to vigorous physical activity provides a number of important health and performance-related benefits. The increased muscle temperature from warming up can improve muscle strength and anaerobic muscle power and improve performance in running, cycling, and swimming. These improvements in performance may result from interactions among the following mechanisms:

1. Muscles relax and contract faster at higher temperatures.
2. Increased temperature decreases viscous resistance in the muscles and improves efficiency.
3. Hemoglobin and myoglobin give up more oxygen and dissociate more rapidly at higher temperatures.
4. The rates of metabolic processes increase with temperature.
5. Warm-up provides more time for aerobic metabolism to supply the energy needs of the activity and, thereby, may reduce lactate accumulation during the subsequent exercise bout.
6. Vascular resistance decreases with increasing temperature.
7. Total pulmonary resistance to blood flow decreases with increasing temperature.

Perhaps the most important health-related benefit of warming up is the gradual increase in blood flow to the heart. Vigorous physical activity without a warm-up period can lead to electrical abnormalities within the heart (electrocardiogram [ECG or EKG] abnormalities) that result from inadequate blood flow (ischemia). Proper warm-up can dramatically reduce or eliminate these symptoms.[15]

Typically, warming up involves physical activity that increases general body temperature (i.e., increasing rectal temperature 1–2°C), as well as the temperature of the muscles involved in the sport or physical activity. Most athletes and recreational exercisers use low- to moderate-intensity physical activity for warming up. Furthermore, stretching to improve flexibility should not be used as a substitute for warming up and should follow the warm-up period (see Chapter 12 on flexibility).

The most effective warm-up involves low- to moderate-intensity exercise that is related to the sporting event or physical activity to follow. For example, runners normally warm up by jogging, while weight lifters generally perform a number of repetitions and sets prior to a competitive maximal lift. A warm-up that mimics the upcoming sporting event may also be beneficial as a rehearsal prior to competition.[15,16]

What is the most effective combination of exercise intensity and duration for warming up? The answer depends on the individual. For some, 10 to 15 minutes of light exercise may be sufficient, while others may need higher-intensity physical activity for a longer period of time (e.g., 30 minutes). As a rule of thumb, the onset of sweating occurs when the internal (rectal) body temperature increases sufficiently to indicate an adequate warm-up. Of course, too much activity, resulting in excessive sweating and fatigue, is not appropriate for warming up and should be avoided because of the negative effects on subsequent performance. Furthermore, body temperature can return to normal within approximately 45 minutes of the end of exercise; therefore, athletes who compete in intermittent competitive events (such as running various heats for track events) may need to warm up prior to each race or activity.[16]

Cooling down

cooling down

As with warming up prior to physical activity, an active **cooling down** period usually involves low- to moderate-intensity activity. Cool-down following exercise is important for a number of reasons. For example, an active cooling down helps to clear lactate from the blood far more rapidly than a passive (inactive) cool-down. The increased rate of lactate removal during active recovery is probably due to greater blood flow and increased utilization of lactate as a fuel source by skeletal muscles.

Probably the most important reason for a gradual cool-down is to prevent blood pooling, particularly in the lower extremities. During exercise the vessels of the legs dilate to supply more blood to the working muscles. If the exercise bout is stopped abruptly (as in passive recovery), blood tends to pool in the legs, which decreases venous return to the heart and can cause dizziness due to reduced blood flow to the brain. An active cool-down, however, takes advantage of the muscles' pumping action, which facilitates venous blood return to the heart from the lower extremities. An active cool-down also helps to maintain increased muscle and connective tissue temperature. This adds to the beneficial effects of stretching for increasing flexibility.

WWW

Physical Activity and Fitness: Healthy People 2020
http://health.gov/our-work/healthy-people

AEROBIC EXERCISE PRESCRIPTION FOR IMPROVING PUBLIC HEALTH

For many years, recommendations for aerobic training programs focused on the mode, frequency, intensity, and duration of exercise required to increase $\dot{V}O_2$ max. Increased $\dot{V}O_2$ max was taken as a sign of improved fitness, which theoreti-

table 10.1 Health-related physical activity guidelines for children and adolescents, ages 6 to 17.[17]

1. Children and adolescents should do 60 minutes (one hour) or more of physical activity daily.		
Aerobic: Most of the 60 or more minutes a day should be either moderate- (noticeably increases breathing, sweating, and heart rate) or vigorous-intensity (substantially increases breathing, sweating, and heart rate) aerobic physical activity and should include vigorous-intensity physical activity at least three days a week. Examples of aerobic activities include running, hopping, skipping, jumping rope, swimming, dancing, and bicycling.	**Muscle strengthening:** As part of their 60 or more minutes of daily physical activity, children and adolescents should include muscle-strengthening physical activity on at least three days of the week. Muscle-strengthening activities can include resistance training or less structured activities such as playing on playground equipment, climbing trees, and playing tug-of-war.	**Bone strengthening:** As part of their 60 or more minutes of daily physical activity, children and adolescents should include bone-strengthening physical activity on at least three days of the week. Examples of bone-strengthening activities include running, jumping rope, basketball, tennis, and hopscotch.
2. It is important to encourage young people to participate in physical activities that are appropriate for their age, that are enjoyable, and that offer variety.		

cally reduced the risk of cardiovascular and other diseases. It was widely accepted that to gain health-related benefits, it was necessary to engage in an exercise training program that increased $\dot{V}O_2$ max. It is now clear, however, that substantial health benefits can be gained from less structured training programs that do not necessarily meet the previously recommended minimum standards, especially for exercise intensity. In fact, from a public health perspective, probably the greatest benefit to society is to encourage sedentary individuals simply to become more active. Increases in cardiorespiratory fitness, however, provide additional benefits.

The U.S. Department of Health and Human Services[17] health-related physical activity guidelines for children and adolescents (6–17 years of age), based on moderate-intensity and vigorous-intensity physical activities, are presented in Table 10.1.

It is possible to integrate these guidelines into physical education curricula in elementary, middle, and high schools and to use them to support a daily physical education requirement.[6,7,14] Such a requirement would be consistent with the Centers for Disease Control and Prevention's *Guidelines for School and Community Programs to Promote Lifelong Physical Activity Among Young People.*[6] These guidelines[6] have been successfully integrated into physical education curricula through the teaching of lifetime sports such as racquet sports, bowling, and Frisbee golf; fitness activities such as resistance training, walking, running, and aerobic dance; outdoor activities such as bicycling, orienteering, downhill skiing, and white-water rafting; and adventure education activities such as in-line skating, indoor climbing, and canoeing.[15]

In addition to those for children, the U.S. Department of Health and Human Services[17] has provided the health-related physical activity guidelines for adults 18–64 years of age presented in Table 10.2. Table 10.3 provides examples of moderate-intensity and vigorous-intensity physical activities.

The U.S. Department of Health and Human Services[17] has provided examples of ways that moderate-intensity exercise, vigorous-intensity exercise, and muscle strengthening can be combined to accomplish the 150 minutes per week of physical activity guidelines and provide substantial health benefits:

1. Thirty minutes of brisk walking (moderate-intensity) on five days, exercising with resistance bands (muscle strengthening) on two days.
2. Twenty-five minutes of running (vigorous-intensity) on three days, lifting weights on two days (muscle strengthening).

table 10.2 Health-related physical activity guidelines for adults ages 18 to 64.[17]

All adults should avoid inactivity. Some physical activity is better than none, and adults who participate in any amount of physical activity gain some health benefits.	For substantial health benefits, adults should do at least 150 minutes (2.5 hours) a week of moderate-intensity, or 75 minutes (1 hour and 15 minutes) a week of vigorous-intensity, aerobic physical activity or an equivalent combination of moderate-intensity and vigorous-intensity activity. Aerobic activity should be performed in episodes of at least 10 minutes, and preferably it should be spread throughout the week.	For additional and more extensive health benefits, adults should increase their aerobic physical activity to 300 minutes (5 hours) a week of moderate-intensity, or 150 minutes (2.5 hours) of vigorous-intensity, aerobic physical activity or an equivalent combination of moderate-intensity and vigorous-intensity activity. Additional health benefits are gained by engaging in physical activity beyond this amount.	Adults should also do muscle-strengthening activities that are moderate or high intensity and involve all major muscle groups on two or more days a week, as these activities provide additional health benefits.

3. Thirty minutes of brisk walking on two days, 60 minutes (one hour) of social dancing (moderate intensity) on one evening, 30 minutes of mowing the lawn (moderate intensity) on one afternoon, heavy gardening (muscle strengthening) on two days.
4. Thirty minutes of biking to and from work on three days (moderate intensity), playing softball for 60 minutes on one day (moderate intensity), using weight machines on two days (muscle strengthening).

table 10.3 Examples of moderate-intensity (40 to 59% $\dot{V}O_2$ reserve and heart rate reserve; 46 to 63% $\dot{V}O_2$ max; 64 to 76% maximum heart rate; rating of perceived exertion [RPE] from 12 to 13) and vigorous-intensity (60 to 89% $\dot{V}O_2$ reserve and heart rate reserve; 64 to 90% $\dot{V}O_2$ max; 77 to 95% maximum heart rate; RPE from 14 to 17) physical activities.[2,3]

MODERATE INTENSITY (3–6 metabolic equivalents [METs])	**VIGOROUS INTENSITY** (>6 METs)
1. Walking at 3–4 mph (3–5 METs)	1. Walking at 4.5 mph (6.3 METs)
2. Cleaning, heavy—washing windows, car, clean garage (3.0)	2. Walking/hiking at moderate pace and grade with no or light pack (7.0)
3. Sweeping floors or carpet, vacuuming, mopping (3–3.5)	3. Hiking at steep grades and pack 10–42 pounds (7.5–9.0)
4. Carpentry—general (3.6)	4. Jogging/running at 5–7 mph (8–11.5)
5. Carrying and stacking wood (5.5)	5. Shoveling sand, coal, etc. (7.0)
6. Mowing lawn—walking power mower (5.5)	6. Carrying heavy loads such as bricks (7.5)
7. Badminton—recreational (4.5)	7. Heavy farming such as baling hay (8.0)
8. Basketball—shooting around (4.5)	8. Shoveling, digging ditch (8.5)
9. Bicycling on flat—light effort at 10–12 mph (6.0)	9. Basketball game (8.0)
10. Dancing—ballroom, slow or fast (3–4.5)	10. Bicycling on flat at 12–16 mph (8–10)
11. Fishing from riverbank and walking (4.0)	11. Cross-country skiing at 2.5–7.9 mph (7–9)
12. Golf—walking, pulling clubs (4.3)	12. Soccer, casual to competitive (7–10)
13. Sailing boat, wind surfing (3.0)	13. Swimming, moderate to hard (8–11)
14. Swimming leisurely (6.0)	14. Tennis singles (8.0)
15. Table tennis (4.0)	15. Volleyball—competitive at gym or beach (8.0)
16. Tennis doubles (5.0)	
17. Volleyball—noncompetitive (3–4)	

5. Forty-five minutes of doubles tennis on two days (moderate intensity), lifting weights after work on one day (muscle strengthening), hiking for 30 minutes and rock climbing (muscle strengthening) on one day.

For adults who are already doing at least 150 minutes of moderate-intensity physical activity, the following are a few ways to do even more. Physical activity at this level has even greater health benefits.[17]

1. Forty-five minutes of brisk walking every day, exercising with resistance bands on two or three days.
2. Forty-five minutes of running on three or four days, circuit weight training in a gym on two or three days.
3. Thirty minutes of running on two days, 45 minutes of brisk walking on one day, 45 minutes of an aerobics and weights class on one day, 90 minutes (1 hour and 30 minutes) of social dancing on one evening, 30 minutes of mowing the lawn plus some heavy garden work on one day.
4. Ninety minutes of playing soccer on one day, brisk walking for 15 minutes on three days, lifting weights on two days.
5. Forty-five minutes of stationary bicycling on two days, 60 minutes of basketball on two days, calisthenics on three days.

For older adults (≥65 years), the U.S. Department of Health and Human Services makes the recommendations shown in Table 10.4.[17]

table 10.4 Health-related physical activity guidelines for older adults, ≥65 years of age.[17]

All older adults should avoid inactivity. Some physical activity is better than none, and older adults who participate in any amount of physical activity gain some health benefits.
For substantial health benefits, older adults should do at least 150 minutes (2.5 hours) a week of moderate-intensity, or 75 minutes (1 hour and 15 minutes) a week of vigorous-intensity, aerobic physical activity or an equivalent combination of moderate-intensity and vigorous-intensity activity. Moderate-intensity activities are equal to 5 or 6 on a 10-point scale, where 0 is sitting and 10 is the greatest possible effort. Vigorous intensity is a 7 or 8 on a 10-point scale. Aerobic activity should be performed in episodes of at least 10 minutes, and preferably it should be spread throughout the week. Examples of recommended aerobic activities for older adults include walking, dancing, swimming, water aerobics, jogging, aerobic exercise classes, bicycle riding (stationary or on a path), gardening, raking leaves, mowing the lawn, tennis, and golf (without a cart).
For additional and more extensive health benefits, older adults should increase their aerobic physical activity to 300 minutes (5 hours) a week of moderate-intensity, or 150 minutes (2.5 hours) of vigorous-intensity, aerobic physical activity or an equivalent combination of moderate-intensity and vigorous-intensity activity. Additional health benefits are gained by engaging in physical activity beyond this amount.
Older adults should also do muscle-strengthening activities that are moderate or high intensity and involve all major muscle groups on two or more days a week, as these activities provide additional heath benefits. Examples of recommended muscle-strengthening activities for older adults include exercises using exercise bands, weight machines, or hand-held weights; calisthenics exercises using body weight as the resistance; digging, lifting, and carrying as part of gardening; carrying groceries; some yoga exercises; and some tai chi exercises.
THE FOLLOWING GUIDELINES ARE JUST FOR OLDER ADULTS:
When older adults cannot do 150 minutes of moderate-intensity aerobic activity a week because of chronic conditions, they should be as physically active as their abilities and conditions allow. Older adults should do exercises that maintain or improve balance if they are at risk of falling. Older adults should determine their level of effort for physical activity relative to their level of fitness. Older adults with chronic conditions should understand whether and how their conditions affect their ability to do regular physical activity safely.

AEROBIC EXERCISE PRESCRIPTION FOR DEVELOPING CARDIORESPIRATORY FITNESS AND IMPROVING $\dot{V}O_2$ max

Individuals who already meet the U.S. Department of Health and Human Services[17] physical activity guidelines can derive additional health- and fitness-related benefits from becoming even more active. Increased physical activity and improved cardiorespiratory fitness are associated with reduced risk of developing a number of degenerative diseases. The ACSM[2,3] has provided recommendations for designing aerobic exercise programs for developing and maintaining cardiorespiratory capacity and endurance in healthy adults (Table 10.5). These recommendations consider six components: frequency of exercise, intensity of exercise, time (duration) of exercise, type (mode) of exercise, volume (amount) of exercise, and progression (advancement) or pattern of exercise. The ACSM[2,3] refers to this as the **FITT-VP** (frequency, intensity, time, type, volume, and progression or pattern) principle of aerobic exercise prescription.

FITT-VP

Frequency of Exercise

frequency

The **frequency** of exercise is how many times per week exercise is performed. Depending on the intensity (moderate intensity or vigorous intensity), three to five days per week is recommended.[2,3] One workout per week gives little training effect, but improvements in cardiorespiratory fitness accelerate rapidly when workout frequency is increased to three to five days per week. Bear in mind that for the low to moderately fit, the payoff for six or seven vigorous exercise sessions per week may not outweigh the potential increase in musculoskeletal injuries, decrease in adherence, and risk of overtraining.

Intensity of Exercise

intensity

A number of methods are available to determine the **intensity** (the degree of physiological strain or challenge) of exercise. These include monitoring heart rate (HR), oxygen consumption rate ($\dot{V}O_2$), metabolic equivalents (METs), and ratings of perceived exertion (RPEs). Generally, an aerobic training program prescribes a target range of values that includes the recommended minimum and maximum intensities necessary for improving cardiorespiratory fitness.

Target heart rate range

target heart rate

There are two common methods for estimating a **target heart rate** range: (1) as a percentage of maximum HR, and (2) as a percentage of HR reserve.

Percentage of maximum heart rate. The recommended target HR range for moderate-intensity exercise is 64 to 76 percent of maximum HR and for vigorous-intensity exercise is 77 to 95 percent of maximum HR. The following is an example of the calculation of a target HR range for moderate-intensity exercise (64–76% of maximum HR) for a 20-year-old individual. Maximum HR (the highest HR attainable during exercise) can be estimated with reasonable accuracy from the formula: maximum HR = 220 – age in years.[2]

$$220 - 20 = 200 \text{ beats per minute (bpm) maximum HR}$$

$$0.64 \times 200 = 128 \text{ bpm}$$

$$0.76 \times 200 = 152 \text{ bpm}$$

$$\text{Target HR range} = 128 \text{ to } 152 \text{ bpm}$$

ACSM recommendations for developing cardiorespiratory capacity and endurance.[2,3] **table 10.5**

FREQUENCY OF EXERCISE	
Three to five days per week is the recommended overall frequency.	
Moderate-intensity aerobic exercise should be performed at least five days per week.	
Vigorous-intensity aerobic exercise should be performed at least three days per week.	
A combination of moderate-intensity and vigorous-intensity aerobic exercise performed three to five days per week is recommended for most adults.	
INTENSITY OF EXERCISE	
1. Moderate Intensity	2. Vigorous Intensity
40–59% $\dot{V}O_2$ reserve	60–89% $\dot{V}O_2$ reserve
40–59% heart rate reserve	60–89% heart rate reserve
46–63% $\dot{V}O_2$ max	64–90% $\dot{V}O_2$ max
64–76% maximum heart rate	77–95% maximum heart rate
3–5.9 METs	6–8.7 METs
12–13 RPE	14–17 RPE
TIME (DURATION) OF EXERCISE	
1. Moderate-intensity exercise should be performed for 30 to 60 minutes per day for a total of at least 150 minutes per week.	
2. Vigorous-intensity exercise should be performed for at least 20 to 60 minutes per day for a total of at least 75 minutes per week.	
3. For most adults, a combination of moderate-intensity and vigorous-intensity exercise can be performed daily.	
TYPE (MODE) OF EXERCISE	
1. Uses large muscle groups	3. Must be rhythmical
2. Can be maintained continuously	4. Must be aerobic in nature
VOLUME OF EXERCISE	
1. Greater than or equal to 500–1000 MET-min • wk^{-1}. Calculated as METs associated with one or more activities times number of minutes that activities were performed (METs x minutes) per week.	
2. Caloric expenditure of 1000 kcal • wk^{-1} through moderate-intensity exercise.	
3. Pedometer counts of greater than or equal to 7000 steps • d^{-1}.	
Exercising below these volumes may still be beneficial for individuals unable or unwilling to reach this amount of exercise.	
PROGRESSION OF EXERCISE	**PATTERN OF EXERCISE**
1. A gradual progression of exercise volume achieved by adjusting exercise duration, frequency, and/or intensity is reasonable until the desired exercise goal (maintenance) is attained.	1. Exercise may be performed in one (continuous) session per day or in multiple sessions of greater than or equal to 10 minutes to accumulate the desired duration and volume of exercise per day.
2. This approach may enhance adherence and reduce risks of musculoskeletal injury and adverse cardiac events.	2. Exercise bouts of less than 10 minutes may yield favorable adaptations in very deconditioned individuals.

Heart rate response during an sECG

It is common practice to recommend that individuals be screened for potential cardiac abnormalities prior to beginning an exercise program. The assumption is that the results of the stress electrocardiogram (sECG) can be applied to sport activities. However, St. Clair Gibson et al.* have shown that heart rate (HR) responses elicited during an sECG are not the same as HR responses in social or competitive sporting activities. The subjects in the study were either social or competitive runners and squash players between the ages of 45 and 60 years. The subjects performed a laboratory sECG test to exhaustion using a stationary bike and two field tests (either running or squash).

The most interesting finding in this study was that while maximum HR during the sECG ranged from 148 to 156 beats per minute (bpm), the peak HRs during the sporting activities ranged from 167 to 177 bpm, with the mean HR ranging from 155 to 159 bpm. This suggests that care needs to be taken in prescribing exercise based on the results of sECG tests, since the sECG HR may not be indicative of the maximal HR achieved while exercising. This is particularly true of individuals who already exercise on a regular basis, where their normal training HRs are higher than those achieved during an sECG test. The authors suggest that "routine sECG using a cycle ergometer is a submaximal test of exercise performance, and should be interpreted as such."

* St. Clair Gibson, A., Perold, J., Watermeyer, G. A., Latouf, S. E., Hawley, J. A., Lambert, M. I., and Noakes, T. D. Veteran athletes exercise at higher maximum heart rates than are achieved during standard exercise (stress) testing. *S. Afr. Med. J.* 90: 141–146, 2000.

An unfit 20-year-old may want to begin the exercise program at an intensity near the lower end of this range, while a moderately fit 20-year-old may want to exercise near the upper end of this range.

heart rate reserve

Percentage of heart rate reserve. The recommended target HR range is 40 to 59 percent of **heart rate reserve** for moderate-intensity exercise and 60 to 89 percent of HR reserve for vigorous-intensity exercise. The HR reserve is defined as the difference between maximum HR and resting HR. The resting HR should be taken after a period of relaxation so that it is truly a "resting" HR (see **Chapter 10 Lab A**). If we assume, for the sake of this example, that the 20-year-old has a resting HR of 70 bpm, we can calculate the target HR range for moderate-intensity exercise using the HR reserve method.

220 – 20 = 200 bpm maximum HR

200 – 70 (resting HR) = 130 bpm HR reserve

$0.40 \times 130 = 52$

$0.59 \times 130 = 76.7$ (round to 77)

52 + 70 (resting HR) = 122 bpm

77 + 70 (resting HR) = 147 bpm

Target HR range = 122 to 147 bpm

Unfit individuals are likely to see a training effect at intensities as low as 40 to 49 percent of HR reserve, while moderately fit individuals should use 50 percent of HR reserve as the minimum training HR. For the 20-year-old in the present example, 40 to 49 percent of HR reserve is equal to 122 to 134 bpm, and 50 percent equals 135 bpm.

In practical terms, you may choose either method (percentage of maximum HR or HR reserve) for determining a target HR range. There are, however, theoretical and physiological differences between the methods. For example, the percentage of HR reserve method more closely tracks the relationship between $\dot{V}O_2$ reserve ($\dot{V}O_2$ max minus resting $\dot{V}O_2$) and exercise intensity than does the percentage of maximum

HR method. That is to say, 50 percent of HR reserve is about the same as 50 percent of $\dot{V}O_2$ reserve. It would, however, require about 60 to 70 percent of maximum HR to equal 50 percent of $\dot{V}O_2$ reserve. In addition, aerobic training causes a decrease in resting HR and, therefore, the calculation of a target HR range from the percentage of HR reserve method accounts for training-induced changes in the physiological parameter, resting HR. The target HR range from the percentage of maximum HR method is affected only by age (and the accuracy of the estimated maximum HR). Even with these differences, either method can be used with confidence to prescribe a target HR range for improving cardiorespiratory fitness. It is important, however, that exercise professionals recognize those individuals whose maximum HR is not accurately predicted from the 220 – age formula and adjust the target HR range accordingly. For those whose maximum HR is substantially lower or higher than predicted, the target HR range may have to be reduced or increased, respectively. In these situations, the science and art of exercise prescription meet.

Target oxygen consumption rate range

Percentage of $\dot{V}O_2$ max. Exercise intensity can be calculated as a percentage of maximal oxygen consumption rate ($\dot{V}O_2$ max). The use of this method, however, requires the measurement or estimation of $\dot{V}O_2$ max (see laboratories for Chapters 3, 6, and 19). The target range for moderate-intensity exercise is 46 to 63 percent of $\dot{V}O_2$ max, and vigorous-intensity exercise is defined as 64 to 90 percent of $\dot{V}O_2$ max. The percentage of $\dot{V}O_2$ max associated with moderate-intensity exercise, however, is dependent on the individual's fitness level. For example, the recommended moderate-intensity target range is 52 to 67 percent $\dot{V}O_2$ max for low-fit individuals, 46 to 63 percent $\dot{V}O_2$ max for moderately fit individuals, and 43 to 61 percent $\dot{V}O_2$ max for highly fit individuals.[3] Greater than or equal to 68 percent $\dot{V}O_2$ max is considered vigorous-intensity exercise for all individuals. The following is an example of the calculation of the target range as a percent of $\dot{V}O_2$ max (expressed relative to body weight in mL • kg^{-1} • min^{-1}) for moderate-intensity exercise (46–63% $\dot{V}O_2$ max) for a moderately fit individual:

$$\dot{V}O_2 \text{ max} = 35 \text{ mL} \bullet \text{kg}^{-1} \bullet \text{min}^{-1}$$
$$0.46 \times 35 = 16.1 \text{ mL} \bullet \text{kg}^{-1} \bullet \text{min}^{-1}$$
$$0.63 \times 35 = 22.1 \text{ mL} \bullet \text{kg}^{-1} \bullet \text{min}^{-1}$$
$$\text{Target range} = 16.1 \text{ to } 22.1 \text{ mL} \bullet \text{kg}^{-1} \bullet \text{min}^{-1}$$

Hence, in this example, moderate-intensity exercise involves activities that require an oxygen consumption rate ($\dot{V}O_2$) of 16.1 to 22.1 mL • kg^{-1} • min^{-1}.

Table 10.6 provides examples of various types of physical activity and their metabolic equivalents. One MET is equal to 3.5 mL • kg^{-1} • min^{-1}. Thus, the $\dot{V}O_2$ associated with each activity in Table 10.6 can be calculated by multiplying the MET value by 3.5. For example, the $\dot{V}O_2$ for a doubles tennis match from Table 10.6 can be calculated as:

$$3.5 \text{ mL} \bullet \text{kg}^{-1} \bullet \text{min}^{-1} \times 5 \text{ METs} = 17.5 \text{ mL} \bullet \text{kg}^{-1} \bullet \text{min}^{-1}$$

Thus, in the current example, a doubles tennis match would be an example of moderate-intensity exercise within the target range as a percentage of $\dot{V}O_2$ max for this individual.

Percentage of $\dot{V}O_2$ reserve. According to the percentage of $\dot{V}O_2$ reserve method, the $\dot{V}O_2$ range for moderate-intensity exercise is 40 to 59 percent of $\dot{V}O_2$ reserve and for vigorous-intensity exercise is 60 to 89 percent of $\dot{V}O_2$ reserve. These are the same percentages used for the percentage of HR reserve method. The **$\dot{V}O_2$ reserve** is defined

$\dot{V}O_2$ reserve

table 10.6 Leisure activities in METs: sports, exercise classes, games, dancing (moderate intensity = 3–5.9 METs and vigorous intensity = 6–8.7 METs).[1,2,3]

ACTIVITY	AVERAGE MET
Archery	3.5
Badminton (recreational)	4.5
Basketball	
Game playing	8.0
Shooting around	4.5
Bicycling (10–12 mph)	6.0
Billiards	2.5
Bowling	3.0
Boxing	
In-ring	12.0
Sparring	9.0
Calisthenics	8.0
Circuit weight training	8.0
Cricket	5.0
Croquet	2.5
Dancing (aerobic)	6.5
Dancing (ballroom)	3.0–4.5
Fencing	6.0
Field hockey	8.0
Fishing	
From bank	4.0
Wading in stream	6.0
Football (touch)	8.0
Golf	
Power cart	3.5
Walking (carrying bag or pulling cart)	4.3
Handball	12.0
Hiking	7.0–9.0
Horseback riding	
Trotting	6.5
Walking	2.5
Horseshoe pitching	3.0
Hunting (bow or gun)	
Small game (walking, carrying light load)	5.0
Big game (dragging carcass, walking)	6.0
Jazzercise	6.0
Judo	10.0
Mountain climbing	8.0
Music playing	2.5
Paddleball, racquetball	9.0
Rock climbing	11.0
Rope jumping	
Slow	8.0
Moderate	10.0
Fast	12.0
Running	
5 mph	8.0
6 mph	10.0
7 mph	11.5
8 mph	13.5
9 mph	15.0
10 mph	16.0
Sailing	3.0
Scuba diving	7.0
Shuffleboard	3.0
Skating, ice and roller	7.0
Skiing, snow	
Downhill (moderate effort)	6.0
Cross-country (moderate effort)	7.0–9.0
Skiing, water	7.0
Sledding, tobogganing	7.0
Snowshoeing	8.0
Soccer	7.0–10.0
Squash	12.0
Stair climbing	8.0
Swimming (leisurely to hard)	6.0–11.0
Table tennis	4.0
Tennis (doubles to singles)	5.0–8.0
Volleyball (noncompetitive to competitive)	3.0–8.0
Walking	
2 mph	2.5
3 mph	3.0
4 mph	6.0
Water aerobics	4.0
Weight lifting	3.0

as the difference between $\dot{V}O_2$ max and resting $\dot{V}O_2$. Thus, to use the percentage of $\dot{V}O_2$ reserve method for aerobic exercise prescription, you must know the individual's $\dot{V}O_2$ max, resting $\dot{V}O_2$ (usually about 0.25 to 0.30 L • min^{-1}), and the oxygen cost of various activities (Table 10.6). The following is an example of the calculation of a target range for moderate-intensity exercise as a percentage of $\dot{V}O_2$ reserve.

$\dot{V}O_2$ max = 3.3 L • min^{-1}
$\dot{V}O_2$ resting = 0.3 L • min^{-1}
3.3 – 0.3 = 3.0 $\dot{V}O_2$ reserve
0.40 × 3.0 = 1.2 L • min^{-1}
1.2 + 0.3 L • min^{-1} ($\dot{V}O_2$ resting) = 1.5 L • min^{-1}
0.59 × 3.0 = 1.77 L • min^{-1}
1.77 + 0.3 L • min^{-1} = 2.07 L • min^{-1}
Target range = 1.5 to 2.07 L • min^{-1}

According to the percentage of $\dot{V}O_2$ reserve method, the range of $\dot{V}O_2$ values associated with moderate-intensity exercise for the individual in this example is 1.5 to 2.07 L • min^{-1}.

Metabolic equivalents

Metabolic equivalents (METs) are multiples of the resting $\dot{V}O_2$ level. A value of 3.5 mL • kg^{-1} • min^{-1} is considered the average resting $\dot{V}O_2$ and is defined as 1 MET. The intensity of exercise can be described as a multiple of the resting $\dot{V}O_2$, such as 1 MET, 2 METs, and so on. The target range for moderate-intensity exercise is 3 to 5.9 METs and for vigorous-intensity exercise is 6 to 8.7 METs. Tables 10.3 and 10.6 provide the average MET values for various activities.

metabolic equivalent

Borg Rating of Perceived Exertion

The **Rating of Perceived Exertion** (RPE) Scale, developed by Gunnar Borg, is used to quantify an individual's subjective experience of exercise intensity (Figure

rating of perceived exertion

Borg Rating of Perceived Exertion (RPE). **figure 10.1**

THE SCALE

6	No exertion at all
7	
	Extremely light
8	
9	Very light
10	
11	Light
12	
13	Somewhat hard
14	
15	Hard (heavy)
16	
17	Very hard
18	
19	Extremely hard
20	Maximal exertion

Borg RPE Scale® © Gunnar Borg, 1970, 1985, 1998, 2004.

INSTRUCTIONS to the Borg-RPE Scale®

During the work, we want you to rate your perception of exertion (i.e., how heavy and strenuous the exercise feels to you and how tired you are). The perception of exertion is mainly felt as strain and fatigue in your muscles and as breathlessness or aches in the chest. All work requires some effort, even if this is only minimal. This is true also if you only move a little (e.g., walking slowly).

Use this scale from 6 to 20, with 6 meaning "no exertion at all" and 20 meaning "maximal exertion."

6 "No exertion at all" means that you don't feel any exertion whatsoever (e.g., no muscle fatigue, no breathlessness or difficulties breathing).

9 "Very light" exertion, as taking a shorter walk at your own pace.

13 A "somewhat hard" work, but it still feels OK to continue.

15 It is "hard" and tiring, but continuing isn't terribly difficult.

17 "Very hard." This is very strenuous work. You can still go on, but you really have to push yourself and you are very tired.

19 An "extremely" strenuous level. For most people this is the most strenuous work they have ever experienced.

Try to appraise your feeling of exertion and fatigue as spontaneously and as honestly as possible, without thinking about what the actual physical load is. Try not to underestimate and not to overestimate your exertion. It's your own feeling of effort and exertion that is important, not how this compares with other people's. Look at the scale and the expressions and then give a number. Use any number you like on the scale, not just one of those with an explanation behind it. Any questions?

Note: For correct usage of the scale, the exact design and instructions given in Borg's folders must be followed.

10.1). The advantages of this scale include simplicity and the lack of need to measure a physiological variable such as heart rate or $\dot{V}O_2$. The primary disadvantage is its subjective nature. An RPE of 12 to 13 is moderate-intensity exercise and 14 to 17 is vigorous-intensity exercise.[3]

Time (Duration) of Exercise

duration

The time or **duration** describes how long exercise is performed each day. Depending on intensity, the total daily duration of exercise necessary to improve cardiorespiratory fitness in healthy adults ranges from 20 to 60 minutes. To promote or maintain weight loss, however, 50 to 60 minutes per day is recommended.[2] Within this range, the daily duration can be accomplished from a single continuous bout of exercise or multiple bouts of at least 10 minutes each. Improved cardiorespiratory fitness is associated with the total volume of energy expended each day, and as long as the minimum intensity threshold is met, it doesn't matter if the exercise is continuous or intermittent. Sometimes due to time conflicts or motivation, it is more convenient to exercise more frequently but for shorter periods of time. For some individuals, being able to use intermittent bouts of activity may result in better adherence to an exercise training program.

Type (Mode) of Exercise

mode

You may choose any type (or **mode**) of physical activity as long as it (1) uses large muscle groups, (2) can be maintained continuously, (3) is rhythmical, and (4) is aerobic in nature. The most common types of exercise for improving cardiorespiratory fitness are jogging, walking, cycling, swimming, cross-country skiing, rope skipping, stair climbing, and skating. Thus, you have many options to choose from when selecting or prescribing an aerobic activity, and you may therefore also want to consider such factors as equipment availability and the preferred type of exercise.

Volume of Exercise

volume of exercise

The **volume of exercise** reflects the total amount of physical activity performed and is the product of the frequency, intensity, and time of exercise.[2] For example, if an individual jogged three days per week at an intensity of 7 METs for 30 minutes per session, the volume of exercise would be calculated as follows:

$$3 \times 7 \times 30 = 630 \text{ MET-min} \bullet \text{wk}^{-1}$$

According to the ACSM,[2] compelling evidence supports the importance of the volume of exercise for realizing the health and fitness outcomes of an exercise program. The volume of exercise performed may be of particular importance for body composition and weight management outcomes.

Progression of Exercise

The progression of exercise describes the need to increase the volume of exercise as fitness improves. That is, at the beginning of an exercise program for an unconditioned individual, it may be necessary to perform a limited volume of exercise at the low end of the frequency, intensity, and time recommendations. As the exercise program is continued and the individual's fitness level improves, progressively increasing the volume of exercise is necessary to manifest even greater improvements in fitness. During the initial phase of an exercise program, it is recommended that the volume of exercise be increased by increasing the duration of each exercise session by 5 to 10 minutes every one to two weeks for the first four to six weeks.[2]

Detraining and Maintenance of Cardiorespiratory Fitness

detraining

Detraining refers to the cessation of a training program. That is, you stop exercising. Decreases in cardiorespiratory fitness may occur in as little as two weeks after detraining.[4] In some cases, detraining can result in the loss of almost all of the improvement in cardiorespiratory fitness in only about 10 weeks, depending on how long an individual had been training.[4] Those who have trained for many years tend to retain more of the improvement in cardiorespiratory fitness for a longer period of time than do individuals with a shorter training history.

If training intensity is unchanged, a person can maintain cardiorespiratory fitness with substantial reductions in training frequency and duration.[4] Training one to two days per week is probably enough to maintain cardiorespiratory fitness. A reduction in training intensity, however, typically results in a decrease in $\dot{V}O_2$ max in several weeks. Thus, training intensity is an important factor in maintaining cardiorespiratory fitness.

AEROBIC TRAINING FOR ENDURANCE ATHLETES

The characteristics of aerobic training programs for endurance athletes differ substantially from the exercise prescriptions typically recommended for improving public health or developing cardiorespiratory fitness. Generally, to compete successfully, athletes must train at higher intensities, for longer durations, and more frequently than do individuals whose goal is to improve health. These differences result in athletes performing a much greater volume of training than non-athletes. Furthermore, it is important for athletes to use a mode of training that mimics the sport in which they compete, while the health-related benefits of aerobic physical activity are largely independent of the mode of exercise. The aerobic training programs for endurance athletes tend to be far more specialized and complex than those appropriate for the general public interested in health-related fitness.

Factors Affecting Aerobic Aspects of Endurance Performance of Athletes

In developing training programs for athletes, a coach or trainer needs to take into account several aerobic aspects of endurance performance. Endurance events that last longer than approximately three to four minutes (e.g., running more than approximately 1,500 meters or swimming more than 400 to 800 meters) rely predominantly on aerobic energy production (see Chapter 3). Running greater distances, such as the marathon or triathlon, is almost totally aerobic in nature. Three primary physiological factors interact to determine performance in endurance events for both recreational and elite athletes: maximal oxygen consumption rate ($\dot{V}O_2$ max), the fraction of $\dot{V}O_2$ max that can be maintained (which is related to the so-called *anaerobic threshold*), and the economy (or efficiency) of movement. These factors are modifiable with aerobic training, and the relative improvements (percent change) are generally comparable for females and males.

$\dot{V}O_2$ max and endurance performance

Maximal oxygen consumption rate ($\dot{V}O_2$ max) describes the maximum amount of oxygen that can be utilized (as the final electron acceptor) in the electron transport system (ETS) to produce adenosine triphosphate (ATP) (see Chapter 3). The greater the amount of oxygen that can be utilized, the more ATP that can be produced to supply energy during endurance (aerobic) activities. A number of factors contribute to the ability to produce ATP aerobically, including lung ventilation, pulmonary diffusion, oxygen and carbon dioxide transportation in the blood,

WWW

Sports Coach—$\dot{V}O_2$ max
www.brianmac.co.uk/vo2max.htm

cardiac function, vascular adaptation (vasodilation of active tissues and vasoconstriction of inactive tissues), and the physical condition of the muscles involved.

Typically, successful endurance athletes are characterized by high $\dot{V}O_2$ max values. It is not unusual for elite competitors to have $\dot{V}O_2$ max values >70 mL • kg^{-1} • min^{-1}, while young adult non-athletes average about 35 to 45 mL • kg^{-1} • min^{-1}. Although $\dot{V}O_2$ max is not the only factor that determines endurance performance, it is correct to say that a high $\dot{V}O_2$ max is a prerequisite for elite performance.

Anaerobic threshold and endurance performance

anaerobic threshold

Conceptually, the anaerobic threshold describes the fraction of $\dot{V}O_2$ max that can be maintained during an endurance event. Specifically, the **anaerobic threshold** can be defined as the intensity of exercise just below that at which lactate builds up in the blood (metabolic acidosis) and the associated changes in gas exchange occur. In theory, the anaerobic threshold is the exercise intensity above which the oxygen demand exceeds the oxygen supply. Aerobic energy supply must then be supplemented by anaerobic metabolism, which results in a substantial increase in the production of metabolic byproducts (see Chapter 14). Traditionally, identification of the anaerobic threshold has been accomplished by measuring the ventilatory responses from expired gas samples (usually called the **ventilatory threshold** [see **Chapter 10 Lab B**] or gas exchange threshold) or blood lactate levels (the **lactate threshold**) (see Figure 10.2).

ventilatory threshold

lactate threshold

An endurance athlete with a high anaerobic threshold can, theoretically, maintain a high percentage (fraction) of $\dot{V}O_2$ max for a long period of time without fatigue. For example, an athlete with a $\dot{V}O_2$ max of 65 mL • kg^{-1} • min^{-1} and an anaerobic threshold that corresponds to 90 percent of $\dot{V}O_2$ max could maintain an exercise intensity equivalent to 58.5 mL • kg^{-1} • min^{-1} for the duration of an endurance event. On the other hand, an athlete with a higher $\dot{V}O_2$ max of 72 mL • kg^{-1} • min^{-1} but a lower anaerobic threshold of 75 percent of $\dot{V}O_2$ max could maintain an exercise intensity of only 54 mL • kg^{-1} • min^{-1}. This example demonstrates the interaction between $\dot{V}O_2$ max and anaerobic threshold as it relates to endurance performance.

WWW

Anaerobic Threshold
www.rice.edu/~jenky/sports/anaerobic.threshold.html

Economy of movement and endurance performance

economy of movement

Economy of movement, or the efficiency with which a movement (such as running, bicycling, swimming, etc.) is performed, is often determined by measuring the oxygen cost of the activity. For example, running economy has been defined as "the aerobic demand ($\dot{V}O_2$) of submaximal running."[13] Individuals can differ substantially in the $\dot{V}O_2$ associated with running at the same submaximal velocity. In this case, the person with the lowest $\dot{V}O_2$ is more efficient and the more economical (in terms of energy expenditure) of two runners. The high degree of running economy that characterizes elite athletes can be observed during a race in the "smooth" appearance of the strides of some runners. Observers often comment that these athletes "make running look easy." We can quantify the level of efficiency by assessing the $\dot{V}O_2$ cost of submaximal running or running economy. The same concept of efficiency or economy applies to other endurance sports (such as swimming, bicycling, and cross-country skiing); we compare differences among athletes in the $\dot{V}O_2$ cost of the activity at the same intensity.

Many factors can influence the efficiency with which we perform endurance activities. These factors include:

1. Age. Children are less economical runners than adults, but they improve steadily throughout childhood and adolescence.[12] Children and adults differ in running economy for three primary reasons:[12] (1) Children have higher resting metabolic rates,

(2) children have greater ventilatory equivalents for oxygen, and (3) children have disadvantageous stride rates and stride lengths.

2. Fiber type. At the same running velocity, athletes with a high percentage of fast-twitch fibers require more oxygen than those with a high percentage of slow-twitch fibers.[5]

3. Gender. At the same submaximal velocity, elite male runners tend to be more economical than elite female runners.

4. Fatigue. During a submaximal, constant power output, fatiguing task on a cycle ergometer, the electrical activity within the working muscle increases (see Chapter 14 on neuromuscular fatigue). As fatigue occurs, more and more motor units are activated to replace those that fatigue and can no longer contribute to force production. To recruit additional motor units requires greater energy usage. Since the power output remains constant, the increased energy use indicates reduced efficiency.

5. Altitude. The oxygen cost of submaximal running tends to be lower at altitude than at sea level, possibly due to lowered work of breathing and/or less air resistance because of less dense air.[13]

6. Environmental temperature. Exercising at a higher temperature results in greater energy expenditure than exercising at a lower temperature. The decreased efficiency is probably due to an increased load on the circulatory system (increased heart rate, etc.) for meeting the demand for increased peripheral circulation to transport heat from the core of the body to the skin.

figure 10.2

Theoretical representation of the anaerobic threshold from respiratory (ventilatory threshold or gas exchange threshold) and lactate (lactate threshold) responses to incremental exercise.

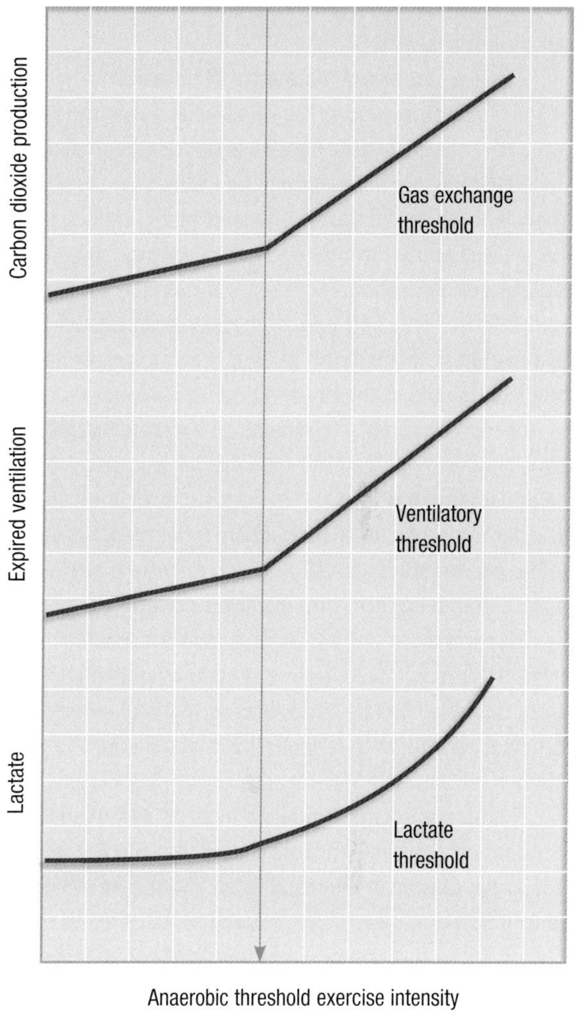

7. Wind. Overcoming air resistance, even on a calm day, requires additional energy of approximately 7.8 percent for sprinting, 4 percent for middle distances, and 2 percent for marathons.[9] One might think that the wind would help as much when running with the wind as it hurts when running against it, but this is not the case. The help received is not nearly so great as the losses. It has been estimated that for a wind velocity equal to running velocity, the overall cost is a loss of about four seconds per 400 meters.[9]

Of potential interest to runners is the concept of drafting. **Drafting** involves running directly behind another runner (usually one to two meters) so that the wind and air resistance is reduced and energy expenditure is conserved. Drafting may reduce the energy cost of running by 3 to 6 percent. This level of energy savings may be beneficial, particularly at the end of a distance event. Drafting is even more important where velocity is greater, as in ice skating and bicycling competition.

drafting

8. Acceleration–deceleration versus smooth movement. In some activities (such as swimming) the smoothness of movement is important to efficiency.

The anaerobic threshold controversy

Although it is a potentially valuable tool for assessing endurance capabilities, as well as the effectiveness of training programs, the anaerobic threshold concept has been the center of considerable controversy for a number of reasons.

First, using blood lactate as the criterion against which respiratory and other noninvasive methods are evaluated has problems. Lactate is not only produced by the active muscle but also may be consumed simultaneously by both the active muscle and other inactive muscle, as well as by the liver and kidneys. Thus, the blood lactate concentration represents a balance between lactate entry into and exit from the plasma. Besides this problem, it has been shown that the relationship between lactate in the plasma and its concentration in muscle, which is really the matter of interest, is at best a poor one. Another factor to be considered in interpreting blood lactate concentration is the time delay for lactate transfer from the site of production in the muscle tissue to the site of blood sampling, which may be a matter of several minutes. Furthermore, for a number of years it was accepted that the reduced lactate accumulation in trained persons results from a greater oxidative capacity and decreased lactate production in skeletal muscle. It is now clear that endurance training affects not the production of lactate but its clearance from the blood.

Perhaps the most serious criticisms of the classical concept of anaerobic threshold are these: (1) Since lactate in the plasma is the result of an equilibrium between production and clearance from the blood, it cannot be considered a true measure of the magnitude of anaerobic metabolism per se; and (2) the relationship of lactate versus exercise intensity during an incremental test may be a smooth curvilinear rise rather than a breakpoint or threshold, as depicted in Figure 10.2. In light of these considerations, it is not surprising that the exercise intensities at the ventilatory threshold, gas exchange threshold, and lactate threshold do not always correspond.

In swimming the butterfly stroke, for example, if constant velocity could be maintained throughout the various events of the single-stroke cycle (the pull, the arm recovery, and the leg drive), maximal efficiency would be achieved. This is so because at a constant velocity, a constant amount of energy is required to overcome the resistance of the body's movement through the water. This resistance is called *drag*. If the stroke is coordinated so that the leg drive sustains the velocity achieved by the arm pull during the recovery phase of the arms, only the force of drag must be overcome. If the coordination is such that the swimmer comes to a virtual standstill during arm recovery, then, in addition, the body must be accelerated by each arm pull. The energy required for acceleration is very costly because it varies as the square of the velocity. To double the velocity, then, requires four times the energy output.

9. Pace and efficiency. The question of how best to pace an endurance event cannot be answered simply. First, we have seen that efficiency for most activities (but not running) falls off beyond some optimum velocity. Second, the level of fatigue must be considered, inasmuch as efficiency falls off rapidly as fatigue brings about greater recruitment of muscle fibers to do the same job and possibly interferes with neuromuscular coordination.

In events that are largely aerobic, a constant pace is probably the most efficient. This is true even in running, in which efficiency does not vary with velocity under aerobic conditions (see below). Even though the varying paces may be equally efficient, the changes in pace cost additional energy.

Constant pace does not necessarily mean running or swimming equal split times. For example, it is typical in distance swimming that the number of strokes per minute remains constant throughout the 1,500-meter swim, but each successive 100 meters shows a small decrement in velocity of two or three seconds, or more, depending on the swimmer. This is the result of fatigue. Even though cadence remains the same, the force developed and consequently the distance per stroke decrease.

A steady pace may also be preferred for distance running. Starting out too fast can result in an earlier accumulation of metabolic byproducts (see Chapter 14) and the onset of fatigue, which can cause the race to be run less efficiently. On the other hand, starting out slowly and then increasing the pace during the race may delay the negative effects of fatigue. Whether the slow–fast pace is better than the steady pace for distance running performance requires further research.

10. Velocity of running, walking, and cycling. In running, efficiency tends to remain stable in spite of changes in velocity. Interindividual differences in running efficiency appear to be primarily influenced by stride length and the amount of vertical movement. In general, better runners tend to use longer and faster strides and have greater forward lean. Interestingly, well-trained runners tend to choose voluntarily a combination of stride length and frequency that is very close to their optimal condition. Therefore, in most cases, coaches would be wise not to dictate a particular stride profile for an athlete.

The most economical rate of walking is typically about 4 km • hr^{-1} (2.4 mph), at which the energy consumption is about one-half kilocalorie per kilometer walked per kilogram of body weight. The energy consumption of aerobic running is about twice that value, regardless of speed.

In walking more slowly than 4 km • hr^{-1}, energy is apparently wasted in static components of muscle activity because weight is supported too long with respect to the amount of useful work done. In walking faster, energy consumption increases faster than the useful work done and efficiency again falls off, presumably because of a disproportionate increase of energy wasted in accelerating and decelerating body parts. As a result of the increasing inefficiency at increasing rates, energy consumption of walking at about 8 km • hr^{-1} (4.8 mph) becomes greater than that required for running, so that running is more efficient than walking above 8 km • hr^{-1}.

On a stationary cycle ergometer, pedaling rate efficiency tends to increase with increases in power output. Hagberg and co-workers,[11] however, found the average preferred pedaling rate for experienced racing bicyclists to be 91 rpm. This discrepancy is probably due to differences between the stationary ergometer and the bicyclists' own racing equipment.

Training Methods for Distance Events

As we have seen, the three primary physiological factors that determine endurance performance are $\dot{V}O_2$ max, the anaerobic (or lactate) threshold, and the economy or efficiency of movement. Thus, endurance training programs for athletes should be designed with improving these factors in mind. Table 10.7 provides informa-

table 10.7 Characteristics of training methods listed from easiest to hardest (slowest to fastest).

	EASY (E)	LONG (L)	TEMPO (T)	CRUISE (C)	INTERVAL (I)	REP (R)
Purpose	Warm up Recovery Cool down Early season buildup	Skeletal and cardiac muscle adaptation	Improve endurance by raising lactate threshold		Improve $\dot{V}O_2$ max	Improve speed and running economy
Intensity	Conversational 70% of $\dot{V}O_2$ max		Comfortably hard 85% of $\dot{V}O_2$ max 15 seconds *per mile* slower than 10-K race pace		5-K race pace or slightly slower 95–100% of $\dot{V}O_2$ max	5 seconds *per 400 m* faster than interval pace or race pace, whichever is faster
Duration of each work bout	20–60 minutes	60–120 minutes	20 minutes	3–10 minutes	1/2–5 minutes	30–90 seconds
Recovery time between work bouts	Not applicable	Not applicable	Not applicable	1 minute	1:1 work to rest ratio	1:5 work to rest ratio
Number of work bouts in one session	Not applicable	Not applicable	Not applicable	Repeat work bouts until quality work totals 8% of weekly mileage; not over 6 miles/session		5% of weekly mileage; not over 5 miles/session

From Daniels, J. Training Distance Runners—A Primer. *Gatorade Sports Science Exchange:* 1(11), 1989.

Gatorade Sports Science Institute
www.gssiweb.com

tion for several methods of training for distance running. Although the table was designed for distance running, the basic design and strategies can be applied to any endurance activity. It is important to recognize that during a year of training, an endurance athlete will probably utilize many, if not all, of the methodologies listed in Table 10.7. The relative emphasis on one type of training versus another depends on the goals of the athlete and the timing of major competitions.

Daniels[8] has identified three key points regarding the training of endurance athletes:

1. There are many types of training for endurance events, each one varying in intensity and duration. The coach and athlete first must set goals and then determine the best training regimen to reach those goals.
2. Each athlete's strengths and weaknesses must be considered in the development of a training program. Place early season emphasis on weaknesses and late season emphasis on strengths.
3. An effective training program results from efficient long-range planning, the judicious use of rest and recovery days, and gradual increases in training intensity and duration.

Long slow distance training

long slow distance (LSD) training

The purpose of **long slow distance (LSD) training** is to develop the cardiorespiratory system and circulatory blood supply to the active muscles and to enhance the muscles' metabolic characteristics. These adaptations tend to increase $\dot{V}O_2$ max. Normally, LSD training is performed for one or two hours at an intensity equal to approximately 65 to 70 percent of $\dot{V}O_2$ max.[8] In terms of running velocity, this intensity usually corresponds to one or two minutes slower than the athlete's 10-kilometer race pace.[8]

Tempo-pace training

tempo-pace training

cruise intervals

Training at the lactate threshold is called tempo-pace (or cruise interval) training.[8] **Tempo-pace training** refers to continuous work bouts of approximately 20 minutes duration, while **cruise intervals** are discontinuous and usually last 3 to 10 minutes with 1-minute rest periods (total distance for a cruise interval for running session should not exceed 6 miles; see Table 10.7). The typical intensity for endurance athletes at the lactate threshold (used for both tempo-pace and cruise intervals) is approximately 85 percent of $\dot{V}O_2$ max or a running velocity of 15 to 20 seconds per mile slower than the 10-kilometer race pace.[8]

Interval training

interval training

Interval training consists of short periods of work alternating with short rest intervals, as distinct from work bouts that are continuous (Table 10.7). Thus an individual training for a 1,500-meter swim, instead of swimming long distances continuously (as in LSD training), might be trained largely on 100-meter swims at a faster pace. The endurance (or training) factor would be gained through manipulation of (1) the speed at which the 100s are swum, (2) the total number of 100s accomplished, and (3) the duration of the rest intervals.

One of the primary goals of a training program is to perform the greatest total amount of work with the smallest physiological strain (fatigue). This can best be achieved through the method of interval training. At the same intensity, far more total work can be accomplished intermittently (with rest intervals) than continuously. Furthermore, rest intervals of 30 to 45 seconds train both the cardiorespiratory and muscle glycolytic systems. Thus, one of the advantages of interval training lies in the simultaneous development of aerobic and anaerobic capabilities, both of which are essential to many sports.

Interval training for events that are largely aerobic can be developed around work intervals ranging from 30 seconds to 5 minutes, with alternating rest intervals of approximately the same duration. The shorter the rest interval, the greater the training effect on anaerobic capacity, while longer rest intervals are more effective for improving $\dot{V}O_2$ max. Thus, the selection of work and rest intervals depends largely on the nature of the endurance event.

Repetition training

Repetition training is intended to improve speed and running economy.[8] Generally, **repetition (REP) training** involves an intensity that is greater than that used for interval training, with individual work bouts lasting 30 to 90 seconds. For runners, Daniels[8] has recommended that REP training be performed at an intensity equal to three to five seconds per 400 meters faster than interval training pace, particularly when training for races longer than 5,000 meters, or up to five seconds per 400 meters faster than current race pace (using the race of primary importance as the standard). The ratio of work to recovery intervals should be 1:5. As indicated in Table 10.7, the total distance performed during a REP training session should not exceed five miles.

repetition (REP) training

Fartlek training

Fartlek training has also been called "speed play" because the athlete varies the speed of running frequently during a session.[8] The foundation of Fartlek training is an easy continuous running pace with short, high-intensity bursts interspersed. Frequently, this form of training is performed over a varied terrain where the pace is, in part, determined by running up or down hills.[8] Fartlek training is, generally, not highly structured, with the athlete deciding when, how much, and for how long to alter the running speed.

Fartlek training

"Hypoxic training" for swimmers

For many years swimming coaches have used changes in the frequency of breathing as a training mechanism. Breathing once every stroke cycle in the crawl stroke means breathing every second arm stroke and consequently breathing on the same side. Most coaches realized long ago that turning the head from the midline to breathe resulted in slower times. Therefore they experimented with **controlled frequency breathing (CFB)**, in which the swimmer breathed every fourth or sixth stroke and even less frequently in short sprints. Others also used breathing every third stroke to combine CFB with achieving a more symmetrical swim style. However, it was proposed that this less-frequent breathing constituted what was called **"hypoxic training"** in the belief that the reduction in inspired air resulted in a decreased oxygen delivery to the musculature.

controlled frequency breathing (CFB)

hypoxic training

Controlled experiments, however, have shown that as ventilatory volume decreases in CFB, oxygen extraction and tidal volume increase to maintain a constant oxygen consumption rate for a given velocity of swimming. Estimated alveolar partial pressure of oxygen decreased while carbon dioxide increased. Thus, the training could be called **"hypercapnic training"** but not "hypoxic training."[10] If there are any performance advantages to such training they would be associated with improved tolerance to high alveolar levels of carbon dioxide rather than to hypoxia.

hypercapnic training

Analysis of pace as an indicator of training needs

In middle-distance and distance athletic events, where pace is established on a voluntary basis, considerable insight can be gained into training needs by comparing split times with those of championship performances in the same event. If an athlete's split times, for example, are in the same proportion as those of championship performances but slower for each split, further improvement probably depends on increased power or better technique. In this case, resistance training and interval training, with rate as the variable for progression, should be utilized.

On the other hand, if an athlete meets the championship pace on the first splits but fades badly late in the race, the fault probably stems from cardiorespiratory factors, and endurance work is needed (such as increasing the number of repeats of an interval training workout).

summary

Physical activity, health, and cardiorespiratory fitness are closely related. It is clear that health-related benefits can be gained from moderate-intensity continuous or intermittent physical activity, and it is not necessary to follow a rigidly structured exercise training program. Many of the activities that we participate in during the normal course of our daily lives, such as gardening and walking, as well as occupational and recreational activities, contribute to the recommended 150 minutes per week of moderate-intensity physical activity. Additional health benefits, however, result from greater activity. To improve cardiorespiratory fitness, aerobic exercise should be performed at approximately 64 to 76 percent of maximum heart rate, for at least 30 minutes (continuously or in minimum 10-minute work bouts), on at least five days per week.

Three primary physiological factors interact to determine endurance performance in athletes: $\dot{V}O_2$ max, anaerobic threshold, and the economy or efficiency of movement. Typically, the aerobic training programs for endurance athletes involve a much greater volume of training and are more specialized and complex than those designed for improving public health or developing cardiorespiratory fitness.

questions for review

1. Identify the characteristics of low-risk, moderate-risk, and high-risk individuals according to ACSM's *Guidelines for Exercise Testing and Prescription.*[2] Describe the appropriate training program for each group.
2. What are the health and performance benefits of warming up before and cooling down after vigorous physical activity?
3. What are the two common methods for estimating target heart rate range? How is each computed? What are the physiological differences between the two measures?
4. How is the target oxygen consumption rate range calculated?
5. What are the advantages and disadvantages of using the RPE scale to quantify exercise intensity?
6. What is detraining?
7. What is the most important factor in maintaining cardiorespiratory fitness?
8. What are the criticisms of using the anaerobic threshold to assess endurance capabilities?
9. What factors influence economy of movement?

10. As a physical educator, how might you integrate the physical activity guidelines from the U.S. Department of Health and Human Services[17] into your school curriculum?
11. Prescribe an exercise training program for an adult, 60 years of age, whose primary goal is to obtain health benefits from physical activity.
12. Prescribe an exercise training program for an adult, 30 years of age, whose primary objective is to improve cardiorespiratory fitness. Include exercise frequency, intensity, time, type, volume, and progression or pattern. For exercise intensity, use the heart rate reserve method to determine the appropriate target heart rate range. Assume a resting heart rate of 75 bpm.
13. In prescribing an aerobic training program for endurance athletes, what key points must a coach or trainer consider?
14. What specialized training methods might be used in training athletes? What are the characteristics of each?

student companion website

For further review of this book's chapters and for test preparation, visit the book's website, **www.hhpcommunities.com/exercisephysiology**, to take practice quizzes, review the vocabulary terms, use the study guide, and view the digital image bank.

references

1. Ainsworth, B. E., Haskell, W. L., Whitt, M. C., et al. Compendium of physical activities: An update of activity codes and MET intensities. *Med. Sci. Sports Exerc.* 32, Suppl. S498–S516, 2000.
2. American College of Sports Medicine. *ACSM's Guidelines for Exercise Testing and Prescription,* 9th edition. Baltimore: Wolters Kluwer/Lippincott Williams & Wilkins, 2014.
3. American College of Sports Medicine. *ACSM's Resource Manual for Guidelines for Exercise Testing and Prescription,* 7th edition. Baltimore: Wolters Kluwer/Lippincott Williams & Wilkins, 2014.
4. American College of Sports Medicine. Position Stand. Quantity and quality of exercise for developing and maintaining cardiorespiratory, musculoskeletal, and neuromotor fitness in apparently healthy adults: Guidance for prescribing exercise. *Med. Sci. Sports Exerc.* 43: 1334–1359, 2011.
5. Bosco, C., Montanari, G., and Ribacchi, R. Relationship between the efficiency of muscular work during jumping and the energetics of running. *Eur. J. Appl. Physiol.* 56: 138–143, 1987.
6. Centers for Disease Control and Prevention. Guidelines for school and community programs to promote lifelong physical activity among young people. *MMWR* 46 (No. RR-6): 1–24, 1997.
7. Corbin, C. B., and Pangrazi, R. P. What you need to know about the Surgeon General's Report on Physical Activity and Health. In *Physical Activity and Fitness Research Digest,* eds. C. Corbin and R. P. Pangrazi. Washington, DC: President's Council on Physical Fitness and Sports, series 2, number 6, 1996.
8. Daniels, J. Training distance runners—A primer. *Gatorade Sports Sci. Exch.* 1(11), 1989.
9. Davies, C. T. M. Effects of wind assistance and resistance on the forward motion of a runner. *J. Appl. Physiol.* 48: 702–709, 1980.
10. Dickers, S. G., Lofthus, G. K., Thornton, N. W., and Brooks, G. A. Respiratory and heart rate responses to tethered controlled frequency breathing swimming. *Med. Sci. Sports Exerc.* 12: 20–23, 1980.
11. Hagberg, J. M., Mullin, J. P., Grese, M. D., and Spitznagel, E. Effect of pedaling rate on submaximal exercise responses of competitive cyclists. *J. Appl. Physiol.* 51: 447–451, 1981.
12. Krahenbuhl, G. S., and Williams, T. J. Running economy: Changes with age during childhood and adolescence. *Med. Sci. Sports Exerc.* 24: 462–466, 1992.
13. Morgan, D. W., and Craib, M. Physiological aspects of running economy. *Med. Sci. Sports Exerc.* 24: 456–461, 1992.
14. Sammann, P. *Active Youth: Ideas for Implementing CDC Physical Activity Promotion Guidelines.* Champaign, IL: Human Kinetics, 1998.
15. Shellock, F. G. Physiological benefits of warm-up. *Phys. Sportsmed.* 11: 134–139, 1983.

16. Shellock, F. G., and Prentice, W. E. Warming-up and stretching for improved physical performance and prevention of sports-related injuries. *Sports Med.* 2: 267–278, 1985.

17. U.S. Department of Health and Human Services. *2008 Physical Activity Guidelines for Americans.* Atlanta: U.S. Department of Health and Human Services. www.health.gov/paguidelines, 2008.

18. U.S. Department of Health and Human Services. *Physical Activity and Health: A Report of the Surgeon General.* Atlanta: U.S. Department of Health and Human Services, Centers for Disease Control and Prevention, National Center for Chronic Disease Prevention and Health Promotion, 1996.

Measuring Heart Rate

BACKGROUND

Several different physical fitness assessments may involve the measurement of a basic vital sign: heart rate (HR). Sometimes the measurement is performed at rest, which can help determine the pre-exercise health status of the individual or the return to resting conditions after exercise. During exercise, monitoring of HR can be an effective method to estimate the intensity of exercise, especially during aerobic exercise. HR is directly related to exercise intensity, and this relationship is most predictable between 50 and 90 percent of the maximum HR.[1] In addition, for exercise at the same absolute work rate, the HR of an aerobically trained individual will be lower than that of an untrained or unfit person. Thus, for someone who is less physically fit, the HR will generally be higher after completing a fitness test. For example, the Astrand-Rhyming submaximal cycle ergometer test to estimate $\dot{V}O_2$ max (Chapter 19 Lab) is based on the assumption that less fit individuals will have a higher HR at a given power output than subjects who are more physically fit. Therefore, measuring HR before, during, and after exercise is an important aspect of physical fitness testing.

On average, most people have resting HR values between 60 and 80 beats per minute (bpm).[3] However, the average resting HR for women tends to be 7 to 10 bpm higher than for men.[3] Table L10.1 provides specific normative values for resting HR. There are three common clinical classifications of resting HR:

1. Bradycardia, defined as a slow HR of less than 60 bpm
2. Tachycardia, a fast HR of greater than 100 bpm
3. Normal rhythm, a resting HR of 60 to 100 bpm

Two primary methods are used for assessing resting HR: (1) palpation and (2) HR monitor. The most common and cost-effective method for measuring HR is palpation. A more expensive but convenient method that has become increasingly popular is a digital-display HR monitor. Procedures for both methods are described below.

table L10.1 Norms for resting heart rate in men and women (age = 18–65+ years).

CLASSIFICATION	RESTING HEART RATE (BPM)	
	MEN	WOMEN
Low	35–56	39–58
Moderately low	57–61	59–63
< Average	62–65	64–67
Average	66–71	68–72
> Average	72–75	73–77
Moderately high	76–81	78–83
High	82–103	84–104

Data from Golding, L. A. (2000). *YMCA fitness testing and assessment manual,* 4th ed. Champaign, IL: Human Kinetics.

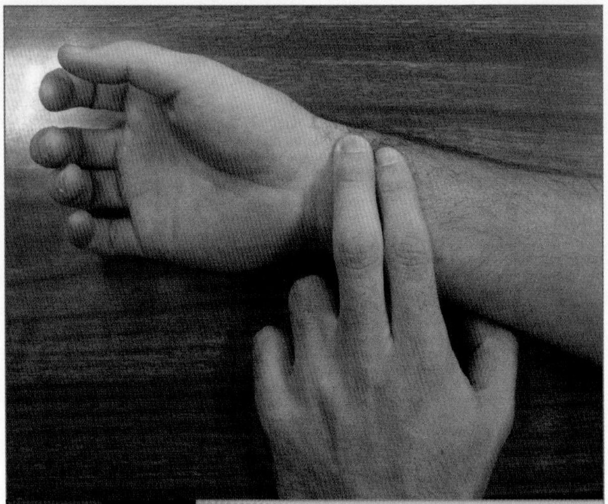

photo 10.1

Palpation of the radial artery pulse.

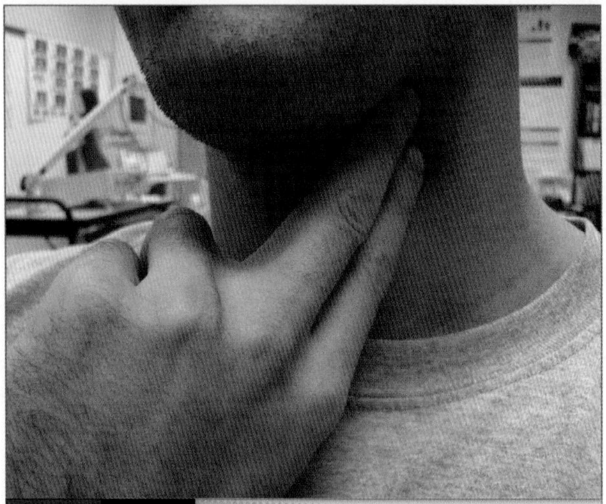

photo 10.2

Palpation of the carotid artery pulse.

photo 10.3

A stopwatch.

TERMS & ABBREVIATIONS

- HR = heart rate, measured in beats per minute (bpm)
- HR monitor = equipment used to measure and monitor HR; includes a chest strap (identifies the heartbeats and transmits the signal telemetrically) and a digital display (displays the signal as a real-time HR value)
- palpation = the act of examining by touch

PROCEDURES

Palpation[6]

1. To palpate the HR (or pulse), use the tips of the index and middle fingers. Avoid using the thumb, since small arteries running through the thumb can be confused with the actual palpable HR.
2. Palpate one of the following anatomical landmarks to find the pulse:
   a. The radial artery, which is located on the anterior-lateral surface of the wrist, in line with the base of the thumb.[3] The best location is usually just medial to the styloid process of the radius. The tips of the index and middle fingers should be placed gently on the skin over this area (photo 10.1).
   b. The carotid artery can be found on the anterior surface of the neck, just lateral to the larynx (photo 10.2).[3] Care should be taken when palpating the pulse of the carotid artery, because applying too much pressure may artificially lower the resultant HR value.[4,8] This may be due to negative feedback from the baroreceptors, which sense pressure, in the aortic arch. There is some debate in the literature whether carotid artery palpation elicits enough pressure to trigger the baroreceptors.[2,5,7]
3. Once the pulse is located, use a stopwatch (photo 10.3) to keep the time while counting the beats. If the stopwatch is started at the moment the counting begins, count the first beat as "0." If the stopwatch has been running, count the first beat as "1."
4. The HR should be counted for a set period of time, such as 10, 15, 30, or 60 seconds. Use one of the following calculations to determine the HR in beats per minute (bpm):
   a. Counting for 10 seconds: Take the number of beats counted and multiply by 6.

b. Counting for 15 seconds: Take the number of beats counted and multiply by 4.
c. Counting for 30 seconds: Take the number of beats counted and multiply by 2.

5. Generally, the shorter-duration HR counts (10 and 15 seconds) are used during and after exercise, when it is important to attain a momentary HR. Since HR can increase with exercise intensity and decrease during recovery, it is sometimes necessary to count the beats during short time periods to obtain an accurate representation of HR at a specific moment during exercise or recovery. By contrast, resting HR measurements are often counted for 30 or 60 seconds to reduce the risk of miscounts and error.

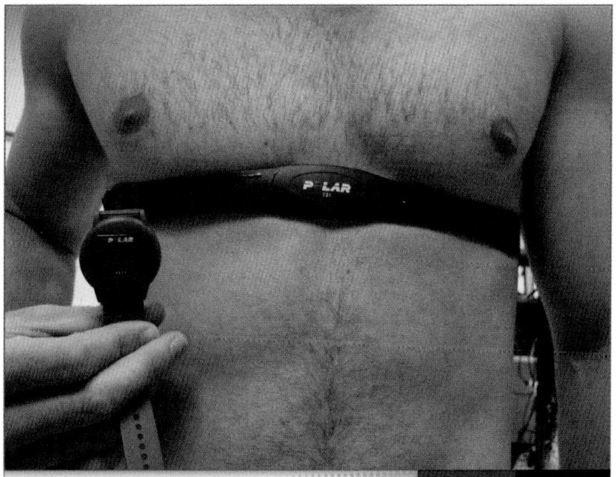

photo 10.4

Placement of the heart rate monitor strap and the digital display of resting heart rate.

Heart Rate Monitor

Generally, an HR monitor consists of a chest strap and a digital display (photo 10.4). The chest strap contains sensors that identify the heartbeats, and the resultant signal is transmitted telemetrically to the digital display as a real-time HR value in bpm. As with all equipment, different HR monitors may function slightly differently, and the manufacturer's directions should be read and followed. However, most HR monitors work in a similar fashion, and the procedure is as follows:

1. Most chest straps require a little moisture (water) applied with a damp cloth over the sensor areas to improve their ability to sense heartbeats.
2. Once the chest strap has been wetted, place the strap just distal to the pectoralis major muscles by adjusting the elastic band (see photo 10.5). The strap should be firm, but not tight enough to indent the skin. For both men and women, the chest strap should be placed in direct contact with the skin.
3. When properly placed, the digital display should provide HR values that update regularly (within seconds).

SAMPLE CALCULATIONS

Gender: Female Age: 24 years

Resting HR count (radial pulse) for 30 seconds: 38 beats

Step 1: Calculate the resting HR in beats per minute (bpm).

38 beats x 2 = 76 bpm

Step 2: Compare the resting HR (bpm) to the norms in Table L10.1.

A score of 76 bpm would be classified as "> Average" for a woman, according to Table L10.1.

worksheet 10.1 RESTING HEART RATE FORM

NAME ______________________ DATE ______________

Gender: ______________

Age: ______________

30-second radial pulse count: ______________

1. Resting HR (bpm) = ______________
2. Resting HR classification = ______________ (see Table L10.1)

worksheet 10.2 EXTENSION ACTIVITIES

NAME ______________________ DATE ______________

Use the following data with Table L10.1 to answer the questions below.

Gender: Female

Age: 32 years

30-second radial pulse count: 41 beats

1. Calculate the subject's resting HR.

   Resting HR (bpm) = ______________

2. Classify the subject's resting HR based on Table L10.1.

   Resting HR classification = ______________

REFERENCES

1. Beam, W. C., and Adams, G. M. *Exercise Physiology Laboratory Manual,* 7th edition. New York: McGraw-Hill, 2014.
2. Couldry, W. C., Corbin, C. B., and Wilcox, A. Carotid vs. radial pulse counts. *Phys. Sportsmed.* 10(12): 67–72, 1982.
3. Heyward, V. H. *Advanced Fitness Assessment and Exercise Prescription,* 7th edition. Champaign, IL: Human Kinetics, 2014.
4. McArdle, W. D., Katch, F. I., and Katch, V. L. *Exercise Physiology: Energy, Nutrition, and Human Performance,* 6th edition. Philadelphia: Lippincott Williams & Wilkins, 2007.
5. Oldridge, N. B., Haskell, W. L., and Single, P. Carotid palpation, coronary heart disease and exercise rehabilitation. *Med. Sci. Sports Exerc.* 13(1): 6–8, 1981.
6. Ryan, E. D., and Cramer, J. T. Fitness testing protocols and norms. In *NSCA's Essentials of Personal Training,* eds. R. W. Earle and T. R. Baechle, 2nd edition. Champaign, IL: Human Kinetics, 2012, pp. 201–250.
7. Sedlock, D. A., Knowlton, R. G., Fitzgerald, P. I., Tahamont, M. V., and Schneider, D. A. Accuracy of subject-palpated carotid pulse after exercise. *Phys. Sportsmed.* 11(4): 106–116, 1983.
8. White, J. R. EKG changes using carotid artery for heart rate monitoring. *Med. Sci. Sports Exerc.* 9: 88, 1977.

CHAPTER 10

lab B Non-Exercise-Based Estimation of the Ventilatory Threshold

BACKGROUND

Theoretically, the ventilatory threshold (VT) is an estimation of the exercise intensity above which anaerobic adenosine triphosphate (ATP) production must supplement aerobic metabolism. Thus, in theory, exercise intensities below the VT are non-fatiguing and are maintained from aerobic ATP production only, while those above the VT are fatiguing and utilize anaerobic plus aerobic ATP production. Typically, the VT occurs at approximately 50 to 60% of maximal oxygen consumption rate ($\dot{V}O_2$ max) in untrained to moderately trained individuals, but 80% of $\dot{V}O_2$ max or above in highly trained endurance athletes.[4]

The VT has been used as a measure of aerobic fitness in clinical populations including patients with HIV[6] and cystic fibrosis,[7] as well as endurance athletes such as marathon runners.[3,5] The VT has also been used to assess the effectiveness of endurance training programs.[1]

Endurance athletes with a high VT can maintain a high percentage (fraction) of their $\dot{V}O_2$ max for a long time without fatigue. Thus, an athlete with a high VT can maintain a faster race pace than a competitor with a lower VT and, therefore, perform better in endurance events. In fact, some elite distance runners with very high VT values can maintain a race pace that corresponds to approximately 90% of their $\dot{V}O_2$ max for the entire duration of a marathon.

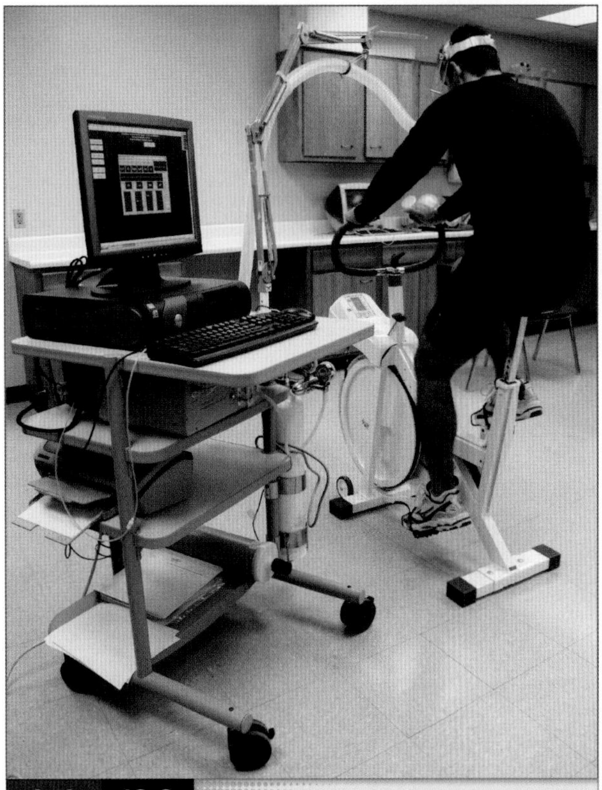

photo 10.6

Estimation of VT using a metabolic cart.

The VT is estimated from expired gas samples collected during an incremental test to exhaustion. During the test, the subject breathes through a two-way valve to collect expired gas samples, which are then analyzed by a metabolic cart (see photo 10.6) to determine the volume of oxygen consumed ($\dot{V}O_2$ in L • min^{-1}) and the volume of gas expired (called minute ventilation, $\dot{V}_E$). As the exercise intensity increases, more oxygen is consumed per minute ($\dot{V}O_2$ increases) for ATP production, and a greater volume of gas is expired. The $\dot{V}_E$ increases linearly with exercise intensity ($\dot{V}O_2$) until the VT is reached. Above the VT, there is a disproportionate increase in $\dot{V}_E$ (relative to $\dot{V}O_2$) as a result of the accelerated contribution of anaerobic energy to the metabolism. The VT is defined as the $\dot{V}O_2$ value (L • min^{-1}) that corresponds to the "breakpoint" (nonlinear increase) in the $\dot{V}_E$ versus $\dot{V}O_2$ relationship (see Figure L10.1).

Direct determination of the VT in a laboratory setting requires a metabolic cart to analyze expired gas samples collected during the incremental test to exhaustion. In this laboratory, however, the VT for adult males and females can be estimated using a multiple regression equation that utilizes only age and height as predictor variables.[2]

Method for determining the ventilatory threshold (VT). **figure L10.1**

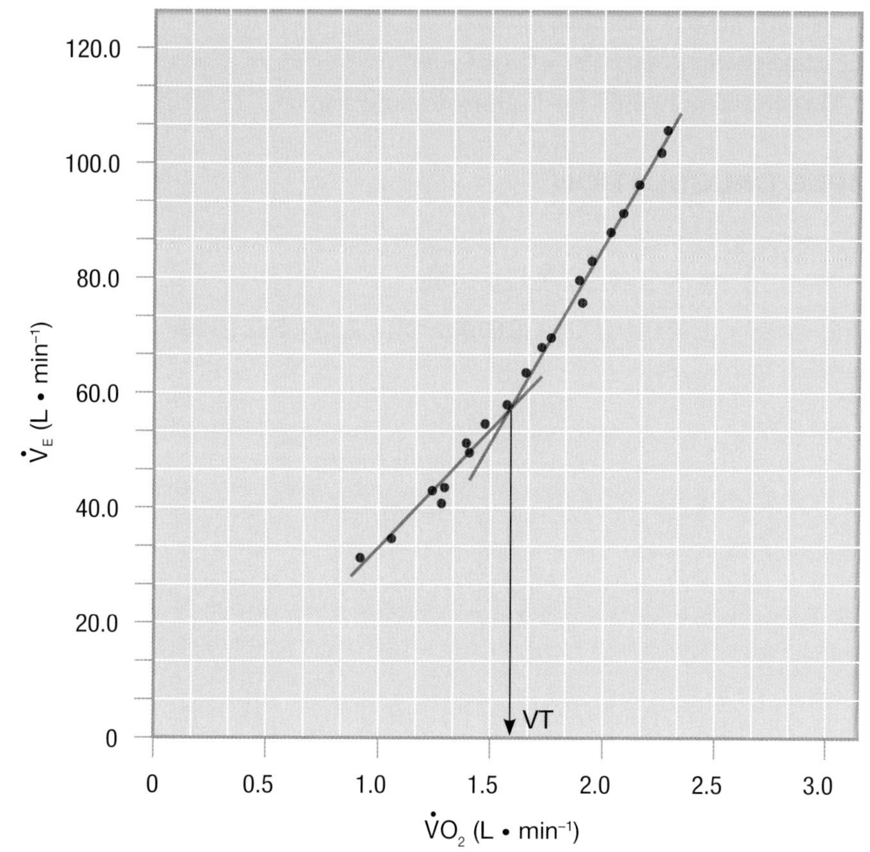

TERMS & ABBREVIATIONS

- ☐ ATP = adenosine triphosphate
- ☐ $\dot{V}_E$ = volume of gas expired, or minute ventilation
- ☐ $\dot{V}O_2$ = oxygen consumption rate, an indirect measure of aerobic energy production
- ☐ $\dot{V}O_2$ max = maximal oxygen consumption rate
- ☐ VT = ventilatory threshold, an estimation of the exercise intensity above which anaerobic ATP production must supplement aerobic metabolism

PROCEDURES

1. Record the subject's age in years and height in cm (inches × 2.54) on Worksheet 10.3.
2. Use the equation on the following page to calculate the VT.

Equation[2]

VT ($L \cdot min^{-1}$) = (0.024 × height in cm) – (0.0074 × age in years) – 2.43

R (multiple correlation coefficient) = 0.651

SEE (standard error of estimate) = 0.316 $L \cdot min^{-1}$

Note: This equation is used for both males and females.

SAMPLE CALCULATION

Age: 21 years

Height: 70 inches (or 177.8 cm)

VT ($L \cdot min^{-1}$) = (0.024 × 177.8) – (0.0074 × 21) – 2.43 = 1.68 $L \cdot min^{-1}$

NON–EXERCISE-BASED ESTIMATION OF VENTILATORY THRESHOLD FORM — worksheet 10.3

NAME ______________________ DATE ______________

Age: ______________ yrs

Height: ______________ cm

VT ($L \cdot min^{-1}$) = (0.024 × height in cm) – (0.0074 × age in years) – 2.43 = ________

EXTENSION ACTIVITIES — worksheet 10.4

NAME ______________________ DATE ______________

Use the following data to answer the questions below.

Age: 23 years

Height: 182 cm

$\dot{V}O_2$ max: 3.3 $L \cdot min^{-1}$

1. Calculate the VT.

   VT = ______________ $L \cdot min^{-1}$

2. What percentage of $\dot{V}O_2$ max is this VT value?

   VT = ______________ % $\dot{V}O_2$ max

EXTENSION QUESTIONS

1. What are some common mistakes that may occur in administering this lab?

2. Identify possible sources of error in this lab.

3. Assess the practicality of using this lab in the field.

4. Research the reliability and/or validity of this lab using online resources, journal articles, and other credible sources.

REFERENCES

1. Jones, A. M., and Carter, H. The effects of endurance training on parameters of aerobic fitness. *Sports Med.* 29: 373–386, 2000.
2. Jones, N. L., Makrides, L., Hitchcock, C., Chypchar, T., and McCartney, N. Normal standards for an incremental progressive cycle ergometer test. *Am. Rev. Respir. Dis.* 131: 700–708, 1985.
3. Maffulli, N., Testa, V., and Gapasso, G. Anaerobic threshold determination in master endurance runners. *J. Sports Med. Phys. Fitness* 34: 242–249, 1994.
4. Malek, M. H., Housh, T. J., Coburn, J. W., Schmidt, R. J., and Beck, T. W. Cross-validation of ventilatory threshold prediction equations on aerobically trained men and women. *J. Strength Cond. Res.* 21: 29–33, 2007.
5. Tanaka, K., and Matsuura, Y. Marathon performance, anaerobic threshold, and onset of blood lactate accumulation. *J. Appl. Physiol.* 57: 640–643, 1984.
6. Tesiorowski, A. M., Harris, M., Chan, K. J., Thompson, C. R., and Montaner, J. S. Anaerobic threshold and random venous lactate levels among HIV-positive patients on antiretroviral therapy. *J. Acquir. Immune Defic. Syndr.* 31: 250–251, 2002.
7. Thin, A. G., Linnane, S. J., McKone, E. F., Freaney R., Fitzgerald, M. X., Gallagher, C. G., and McLoughlin, P. Use of the gas exchange threshold to noninvasively determine the lactate threshold in patients with cystic fibrosis. *Chest* 121: 1761–1770, 2002.

11

Muscle Strength and Resistance Training for Health and Athletics

As a result of reading this chapter you will:

Understand the twitch response of a muscle contraction.

Understand how muscle length and joint angle affect force production.

Be able to compare and contrast isometric, dynamic constant external resistance, isokinetic, concentric, and eccentric muscle actions.

Be able to describe the potential health-related benefits of resistance training.

Know the basic characteristics of a resistance training program for athletes.

Know the basic adaptations to resistance training in females as they relate to athletic performance.

key concepts

agonist
all-or-none law
antagonist
bilateral deficit
concentric
conductivity
contractility
contraction phase
cross-education effect
delayed onset muscle soreness (DOMS)
dynamic constant external resistance (DCER) muscle action
eccentric
hyperplasia
hypertrophy
irritability
isokinetic
isometric
isotonic

Muscle strength is important for both health and athletic performance. A minimum level of muscle strength is necessary to perform activities of daily living. On the other hand, athletic participation usually requires a high level of strength, and in the case of the sports of power lifting and Olympic lifting, maximal expression of muscle strength defines success.

The popularity of resistance training has grown dramatically. This is true for males and females, athletes and non-athletes. In Chapters 18 and 19 we discuss various aspects of muscle strength and resistance training in children, adolescents, and the elderly. In this chapter we will discuss muscle strength and resistance training for health and athletic competition in adults.

Resistance training increases muscle strength and size and improves athletic performance and functional capabilities. Resistance training is not only a requirement for success in athletics, but it is now also routinely recommended as a part of a total health-related fitness program for non-athletes.[3] Exercise science professionals, physical educators, athletic trainers, and coaches are often looked to as experts in physical conditioning for health and athletics. Thus, it is important that we understand and be able to apply the scientific aspects of muscle strength and resistance training.

FACTORS ASSOCIATED WITH MUSCLE STRENGTH

To develop an effective resistance training program, you need to understand the factors associated with muscle strength. Muscle tissue is specifically differentiated for the purpose of contraction; thus its most important physiological property is **contractility,** or the ability to contract. However, it possesses other properties as well, including irritability and conductivity. **Irritability** is muscle tissue's responsiveness to adequate stimuli with its typical response, contraction. **Conductivity** means that an adequate stimulus will be propagated throughout any one muscle fiber in skeletal muscle and from fiber to fiber in smooth and cardiac muscles (see Chapter 2).

contractility
irritability
conductivity
latent period

Muscle Twitch

When a muscle is removed from a laboratory animal (called an *excised muscle*) and electrically stimulated, it responds with a muscle twitch (Figure 11.1). After the stimulus is applied, a short delay before contraction occurs, called the **latent period.**

figure 11.1 The muscle twitch consists of a latent period, a shortening period, and a relaxation period.

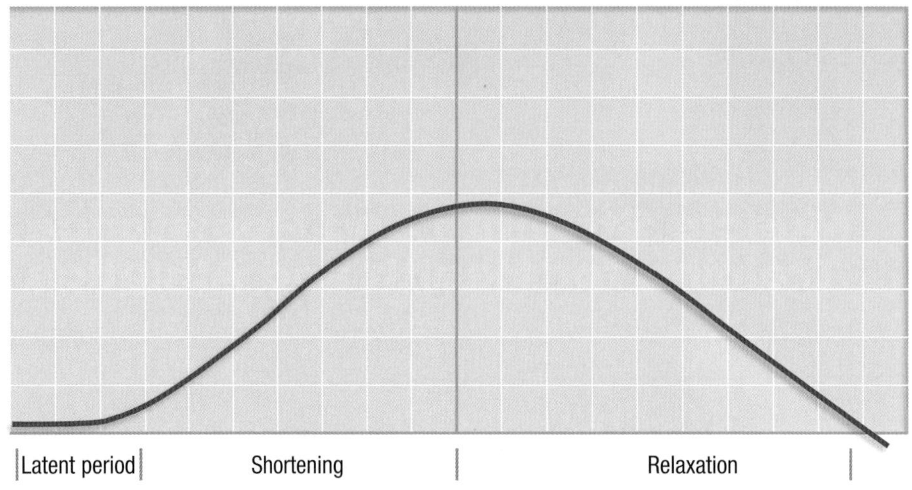

The period of shortening of the muscle is called the **shortening period** (or **contraction phase**), and the subsequent lengthening is called the **relaxation period.**

To better conceptualize how muscles produce tension, it is important to understand that the stimulation of excised muscle and the normal stimulation and contraction processes in intact muscle differ in two basic ways:

1. In the laboratory preparation (excised muscle), nearly all of the nerve fibers for the whole muscle are stimulated simultaneously because all the fibers of the nerve are shocked at the same time. The stimulation of normal human muscle, however, is asynchronous, motor unit by motor unit. We might say that each nerve fiber is stimulated individually at varying points in time.

2. In the laboratory preparation, the muscle twitch is in response to a single stimulation (shock). This probably never occurs in intact muscle, for we know that stimulation of human muscle is accomplished by volleys of nerve impulses, ranging from 5 or 6 per second to as many as 80 or 90.

Summation of twitches and tetanus

If we electrically stimulate an excised muscle a second time, before it has relaxed from an initial stimulation, tension can be increased considerably (Figure 11.2). The second twitch adds tension to that of the first twitch. This additive tension is called the **summation of twitches.** If, however, we stimulate the excised muscle too frequently, the muscle twitch becomes prolonged, and **tetanus,** fusion of the individual muscle responses, occurs (Figure 11.3). If a partial relaxation phase occurs, as shown in curves A, B, C, and D of Figure 11.3, the tetanus is called *partial* or *incomplete.* If the relaxation phases are completely eliminated, as in curve E, it is called *complete tetanus.* In complete tetanus, the tension that develops may be three to four times that of a single muscle twitch.

Temperature and muscle contraction

Heating a muscle causes it to contract and relax more rapidly, while cooling causes it to contract and relax more slowly. When a muscle is cooled, the relaxation phase slows two to three times as much as the contraction phase. In practical terms, this difference may contribute to muscle injury after improper or insufficient warm-up. Under conditions where deep-muscle temperature is low, the muscle causing the movement (**agonist**) may contract while the opposing muscle (**antagonist**) is relax-

key concepts

- latent period
- muscle atrophy
- oligomenorrhea
- overload
- overtraining
- periodization
- plyometrics
- progression
- rate coding
- recruitment
- relaxation period
- relaxin
- repetition maximum (RM) load
- shortening period
- size principle
- specificity
- summation of twitches
- tetanus
- torque
- unilateral imagined training

- shortening period
- relaxation period
- summation of twitches
- tetanus
- agonist
- antagonist

figure 11.2 The summation of twitches can increase force production.

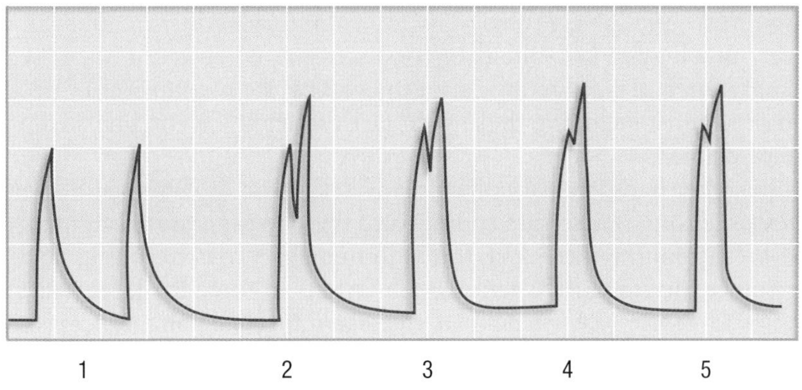

figure 11.3 Muscle twitch responses showing incomplete (A, B, C, and D) and complete (E) tetanus.

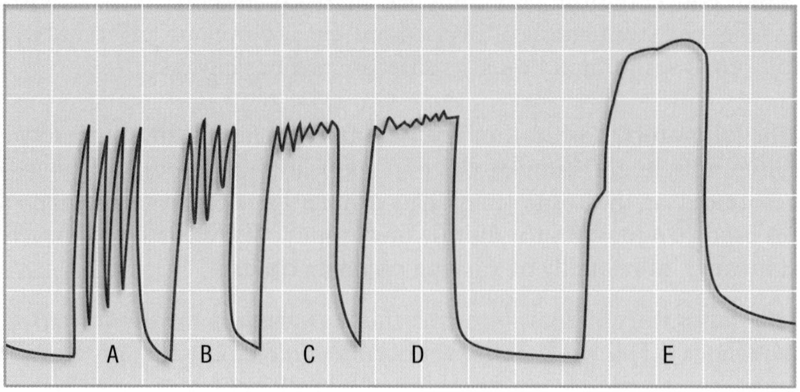

ing but is still partially contracted. This could cause the slowly relaxing antagonist muscle to be injured (a pulled muscle).

The all-or-none law

If a muscle fiber (or motor unit) is stimulated by a single impulse at or above threshold value, it responds by contracting. Stimulation by impulses much larger than threshold value, however, will change neither the amount of shortening nor the force of contraction. This is referred to as the **all-or-none law** of muscle contraction.

all-or-none law

The all-or-none law, however, has been widely misinterpreted to mean that a muscle fiber or motor unit is capable of producing no more force than that exhibited following stimulation by a single impulse at or above the threshold for contraction. This interpretation is clearly in error given that successive stimuli can result in increased force production by a muscle fiber or motor unit due to summation of twitches.

Gradation of response

The all-or-none law applies to the contraction of motor units and muscle fibers, but not whole muscles. Whole muscles are capable of very small gradations in the force of contraction. The nervous system achieves these gradations by two methods: (1) **recruitment,** which means varying the number of motor units activated, and (2) **rate coding,** which means increasing or decreasing the rate of firing for the motor units involved.

recruitment

rate coding

Smaller motor units, and those composed of slow-twitch oxidative fibers in particular, have the lowest thresholds for voluntary activation and are therefore selectively involved in low-intensity contractions. When recruitment is involved, increasingly forceful contractions are achieved by the recruitment of progressively larger motor units, including those with fast-twitch glycolytic fibers. This is called the **size principle.**[24]

size principle

On the other hand, motor units already active can discharge at higher frequencies (they are responsive to rate coding) and thereby generate greater tensions. The method for generating increasing forces in humans varies from muscle to muscle.

During isometric muscle actions, gradations in force for large muscles of the extremity such as the biceps brachii are mediated by concomitant increases in motor unit recruitment and firing rates up to approximately 80 to 90 percent of maximal voluntary contraction (MVC).[37,38] At about 80 to 90 percent MVC, new motor

WWW

Physical Factors Behind the Action Potential
http://psych.hanover.edu/Krantz/neural/actionpotential.html

unit recruitment ends, and increases in motor unit firing rates alone account for the remaining increases in force production to MVC.[37,38] For smaller muscles such as those of the hand and fingers (e.g., adductor pollicis), however, recruitment ends at approximately 50 percent MVC, and rate coding accounts for increases in force from about 50 to 100 percent MVC.[37,38]

During dynamic muscle actions, the motor control strategies (contributions of motor unit recruitment and firing rates) that modulate force production are muscle-specific as well as specific to the type of muscle action (concentric or eccentric) involved. For example, unlike isometric muscle actions, torque production during concentric muscle actions of the biceps brachii is modulated primarily by motor unit recruitment with little or no changes in firing rates.[5a,5b,32] Torque production during concentric muscle actions of the vastus medialis muscle of the thigh, however, may be controlled by motor unit recruitment alone[12] or by concurrent changes in recruitment and firing rates.[13] During eccentric muscle actions of the vastus medialis, torque is modulated by concurrent increases in motor unit recruitment and firing rates to 100 percent of peak torque.[14] For the biceps brachii, however, eccentric torque may be controlled by motor unit recruitment alone[32] or by concurrent increases in recruitment to approximately 60 percent of peak torque and then increases in firing rates alone to between 60 and 100 percent of peak torque.

Mechanical Factors in Force Production

Two important factors contribute to the external force that a muscle can produce: (1) the angle of pull of the muscle and (2) the length of the muscle.

Angle of pull

The angle of pull for a muscle on a bone influences the ability to overcome an external resistance. When the muscle pulls at right angles (90°) to the bone, all of the muscle's internal force becomes available to do external work such as lift a weight. At angles other than 90°, less of the muscle's internal force is available for external work, and therefore, less weight can be lifted.

For example, the most difficult points in a chin-up seem to be at the very bottom and top of the exercise. Subjects who are able to start chinning themselves can probably get past the midpoint, where the angle of pull is favorable, but may have difficulty stretching their necks over the bar at the top. Figure 11.4 provides a simplified example of the relationship between strength and joint angle for the forearm flexion movement. Note that the ability to produce tension to overcome external resistance depends on the joint angle and is a function of the angle of pull of the muscles involved.

Length of muscle

The length of the muscle determines how much internal force or tension it can generate. Figure 11.5 describes the basic pattern for the tension versus muscle length relationship for isolated muscle fibers

figure 11.4

Force production depends on the angle of pull of the muscle and the joint angle at which the muscle action occurs.

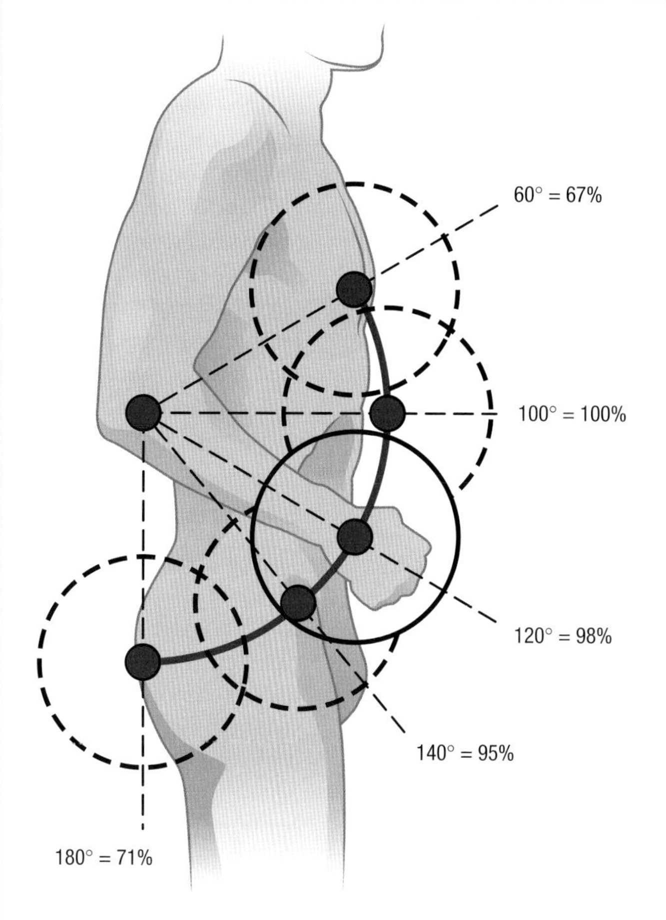

figure 11.5 The relationship between tension and muscle length. Maximum tension is produced at the resting muscle length.

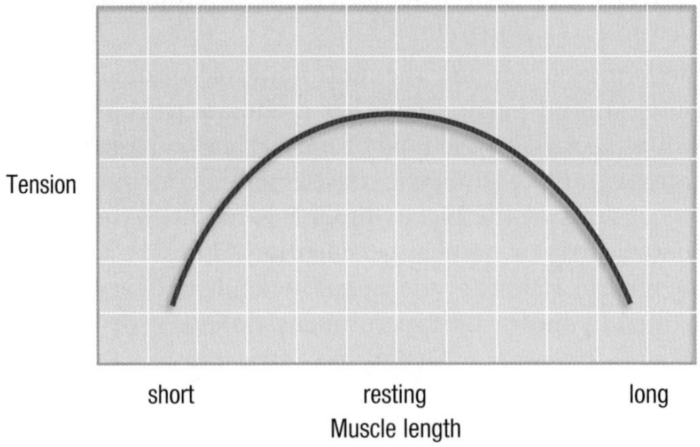

as well as intact skeletal muscle. Maximum tension occurs at about resting length and then decreases with greater or lesser lengths.

The tension versus muscle length relationship can be explained, in large part, by the degree of overlap of actin and myosin filaments within the sarcomeres of muscle fibers (see Chapter 2 for information about the contractile proteins actin and myosin). When a muscle is stretched too far, there is little overlap between the actin and myosin filaments, and little tension can be produced. At approximately resting length, the overlap of actin and myosin is optimal, and maximum tension can be produced. When a muscle is shortened substantially, tension is reduced because the extensive overlap of the actin and myosin filaments interferes with the formation of cross-bridges and the rigidity of the thick myosin filaments probably absorbs some of the tension that is generated.

Under normal conditions it is difficult to stretch a muscle to the point where tension is dramatically reduced, because our range of motion is limited by the anatomical structure of our skeleton. Thus, in most cases, if we put the muscle on stretch, we can obtain the greatest force of which the muscle is capable. The stretch factor, however, that provides the greatest internal forces may work at odds with the angle of pull of the muscle, which determines how much of the internal force can be used for external work. Thus, both factors—angle of pull of the muscle and length of the muscle—interact to influence our force production capabilities.

Bilateral Deficit in Strength

bilateral deficit

The **bilateral deficit** refers to a decrease in the strength of a muscle group when the contralateral limb (same muscle group on the opposite side of the body) is concurrently performing a maximal contraction.[19,29] To demonstrate this, we can determine the maximal strength for a specific movement in each limb (e.g., leg extension) unilaterally (one limb at a time) and then measure the maximal strength in both limbs concurrently (bilaterally). The additive strength for the limbs measured individually is usually 5 to 25 percent greater than the strength when both limbs are measured concurrently.[19] The bilateral deficit is more apparent in muscle groups that normally function in a reciprocal manner (they contract in an alternating fashion, such as the quadriceps during walking) than in those that function concurrently (they contract at the same time, such as with many functions of the arms).[19]

RESEARCH

Resting metabolic rate

It is generally thought that as fat-free weight (FFW) increases following a strength training program, resting metabolic rate (RMR) also goes up. However, a study by Lemmer et al.* suggested that when gender is included in the analysis, only men showed a significant increase in RMR (9%), even though both male and female subjects experienced similar gains in FFW (~2 kg). These results must be interpreted with caution because the sample sizes in this study were small. However, if true, this information has implications for the benefits of strength training with respect to weight control in women.

* Lemmer, J. T., Ivey, F. M., Ryan, A. S., Martel, G. F., Hurlbut, D. E., Metter, J. E., Fozard, J. L., Fleg, J. L., and Hurley, B. F. Effect of strength training on resting metabolic rate and physical activity: age and gender comparisons. *Med. Sci. Sports Exerc.* 33: 532–541, 2001.

The bilateral deficit may have a neural basis. When muscle groups on opposite sides of the body work concurrently to produce maximal force, the electrical activation as measured by electromyography (EMG) (see Chapter 4) from one of the muscle groups is less than if it were contracting maximally alone.[29] The decrease in EMG is proportional to the bilateral deficit in force production. These findings suggest a neural inhibitory mechanism during maximal bilateral contractions.

It also appears that the bilateral deficit is modifiable with training, if the training exercises utilize concurrent contractions of the same muscle groups on both sides of the body.[19] Thus, familiarity with concurrent bilateral contractions affects the magnitude of the bilateral deficit. For example, Howard and Enoka[29] found a bilateral deficit in elite bicyclists (who normally train using reciprocal movements) and control subjects, but bilateral facilitation (increased bilateral strength compared to the sum of unilateral measurements) in weight lifters (who train using concurrent contractions).

Gender Differences in Strength

Females tend to be about 40 to 80 percent as strong as males, depending on the muscle groups involved.[21] In terms of the absolute weight that can be lifted, adult females are typically 40 to 50 percent as strong as adult males for upper body movements such as forearm flexion and extension (at the elbow), but 50 to 80 percent as strong for lower body movements such as leg flexion and extension (at the knee). These differences can be explained, in part, by gender differences in body weight, fat-free weight, and muscle mass. Males tend to be stronger because they are bigger and have more muscle. If strength is expressed relative to muscle cross-sectional area, however, the gender differences in strength disappear. Thus, there is no qualitative difference in strength per unit of muscle between the genders. An equal quantity of muscle from a typical male and female will produce the same amount of force.

TYPES OF MUSCLE ACTIONS

The phrase "muscle contraction" implies shortening of the activated muscle fibers. We know, however, that force can be produced while the muscle is shortening, lengthening, or maintaining a constant length. Therefore, a more accurate descriptive phrase is "muscle action." Types of muscle actions include isometric, dynamic constant external resistance (DCER), isokinetic, concentric, and eccentric.

Isometric Muscle Actions

An **isometric** muscle action (also called *static* muscle action) involves producing tension without movement at the joint or shortening of the muscle fibers. Examples of

isometric

isometric muscle actions are squeezing a hand grip dynamometer or pushing against an immovable object. Squeezing a hand grip dynamometer also provides a measure of hand grip strength—a simple measure for checking overall body strength (see **Chapter 11 Lab A**).

Most of the sports we participate in are dynamic (involve movement) and not static. There are, however, aspects of certain sports that involve isometric muscle actions, such as arm wrestling or the iron-cross maneuver on the gymnastics rings. Amateur wrestlers also perform isometric muscle actions when holding an opponent down. For the most part, however, sports are characterized by movement, and therefore, isometric strength does not predict success in sporting activities very well.

Isometric strength is joint angle specific, as illustrated in Figure 11.4. As discussed above, joint angle differences in isometric strength result from the effects of muscle length on the overlap of actin and myosin, as well as biomechanical considerations associated with the angle of pull of the muscle. Thus, to quantify isometric strength and compare it between individuals, it is necessary to define the characteristics of the task precisely, including the joint angle. To develop a composite of an individual's strength we must measure isometric strength at many points throughout the range of motion.

Dynamic Constant External Resistance Muscle Actions

dynamic constant external resistance (DCER) muscle actions

isotonic

Dynamic constant external resistance (DCER) **muscle actions** used to be commonly known as **isotonic** muscle actions. The term *isotonic,* however, suggests a dynamic activity in which the muscle generates the same amount of force throughout the range of motion. Typically, as depicted in Figure 11.4, different amounts of force are generated at the various joint angles. Thus, for example, when describing the muscle actions associated with lifting free weights, it is more accurate to say DCER instead of isotonic, because the amount of weight lifted (external resistance) remains constant throughout the movement while the internal tension produced by the muscle changes with the joint angle.

DCER muscle actions are commonly used for resistance training by recreational lifters as well as athletes. Furthermore, the sports of power lifting and Olympic lifting involve DCER muscle actions. In addition to free weights, a number of commercial resistance training machines, such as those found in health clubs and schools, utilize DCER muscle actions; however, some use variable resistance that allows the resistance to change during the movement to accommodate joint angle differences in strength. Because DCER muscle actions are dynamic, they are more closely related to the movements involved in most sports than are isometric muscle actions.

repetition maximum (RM) load

DCER strength is often expressed in terms of a **repetition maximum (RM) load,** the maximum amount of weight you can lift for a specific number of repetitions. One repetition involves moving the weight through the full range of motion. For the bench press, one repetition would include lowering the barbell to your chest and pushing it back up completely. A 1-RM load is the maximum weight that you can lift only one time; you cannot lift it twice. A 10-RM load is the weight you can lift 10 times, but not 11. There is an inverse relationship between the weight lifted and the number of repetitions you can complete (Figure 11.6). Thus, a 1-RM load is heavier than a 10-RM load.

Testing DCER strength often involves a trial-and-error procedure. That is, a certain amount of weight is attempted, and a successful trial involves moving the weight through the complete range of motion. This procedure continues until the 1-RM load is determined. Because strength is joint angle specific, the weight that can be lifted is limited by the weakest point in that range of motion. Therefore, a 1-RM load describes the maximum weight that can be lifted at the weakest point in the range of motion.

figure 11.6

There is an inverse relationship between the weight lifted and the number of repetitions that can be performed.

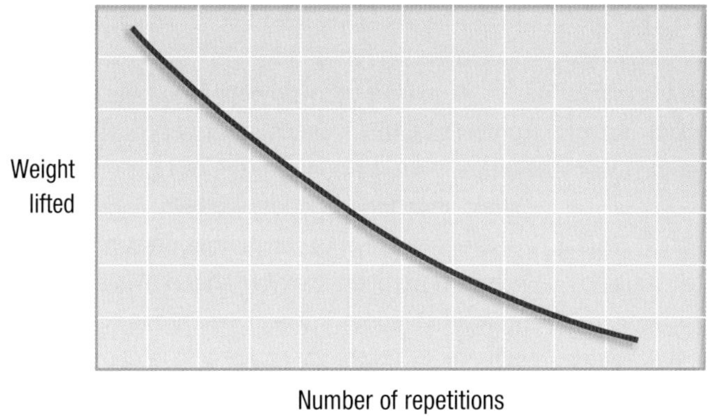

Isokinetic Muscle Actions

Isokinetic muscle actions have a constant velocity of movement.[8] To limit the velocity of the movement, the athlete can use a dynamometer, which allows for the selection of a predetermined muscle action velocity. The dynamometer is set to the desired velocity prior to the muscle action, and the lever arm attached to your limb will move no faster than the predetermined velocity—no matter how hard you try. Any force (or **torque,** which is rotary force production, such as rotating around a joint) that is greater than that necessary to move the dynamometer lever arm at the predetermined velocity is recorded as your strength. The resistance to the movement provided by the dynamometer accommodates the amount of torque exerted by your limb against the lever arm. The harder you push, the more resistance.

isokinetic

torque

Physical therapists and athletic trainers commonly use isokinetic testing and training procedures in rehabilitative settings. Unlike DCER, isokinetic testing allows for the measurement of maximum torque production at all points in the range of motion. Figure 11.7 illustrates a typical recording of a torque curve from an isokinetic dynamometer for a movement such as leg extension (kicking motion). From this curve, the maximum torque production at each point in the range of motion can be determined. The highest level of torque production is called the *peak torque.*

figure 11.7

The relationship between torque production and the range of motion.

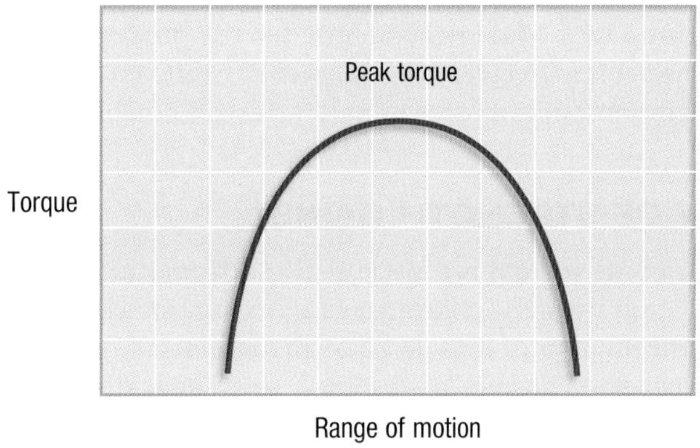

Eccentric muscle actions and delayed onset muscle soreness

Delayed onset muscle soreness (DOMS) is the pain that you feel 24 to 48 hours after an exercise bout. Everyone who exercises has, at one time or another, overexerted with unaccustomed activity and become sore. Eccentric muscle actions are primarily responsible for DOMS,[11] while concentric muscle actions rarely result in DOMS.

It is commonly believed that lactate accumulation causes muscle soreness. This is not the case. Eccentric muscle actions cause tiny tears in the microscopic structure of sarcomeres, which cause fibers to degenerate and a substantial loss in strength for up to a week or more in some cases.[11] Soreness probably originates from this muscle tissue damage, the resulting swelling, and an inflammatory response by white blood cells, which release chemicals that activate pain receptors.

A number of treatments have been proposed to reduce or prevent DOMS, including topical analgesics, anti-inflammatory drugs, heat, cold, massage, electrical stimulation, warm-up, static stretching, and low-intensity exercise. The effectiveness of these treatments varies from person to person, but no treatments have been identified that prevent or permanently reduce muscle soreness.[11] It is interesting to note, however, that we apparently adjust very quickly to eccentric muscle actions. A single bout of eccentric activity seems to make the muscle less susceptible to tissue damage and reduces DOMS following a subsequent exercise session.[11]

Concentric Muscle Actions

concentric

A **concentric** muscle action involves the production of force while the muscle is shortening. An example of a concentric muscle action is the biceps curl movement (forearm flexion). If you hold a barbell with your arms fully extended and then curl it up to your chest (full flexion), the forearm flexor muscles (including the biceps) shorten. This is a concentric muscle action of the forearm flexors. Dynamic activities including isokinetic and DCER muscle actions can be performed concentrically.

Concentric strength decreases as the velocity of movement increases (Figure 11.8). During maximal concentric muscle actions at slow velocities, both slow- and fast-twitch muscle fibers contribute to force production. At fast velocities, however, slow-twitch fibers, although activated, cannot contract rapidly enough to contribute to the force production. Therefore, at fast velocities, fewer muscle fibers (only fast-twitch) result in less force production.

Eccentric Muscle Actions

eccentric

An **eccentric** muscle action involves force production while the muscle is lengthening. Letting the body down slowly from a chin-up is an example of an eccentric muscle action of the forearm flexors. Everyday activities such as walking, running, or squatting to tie your shoes include eccentric muscle actions of the quadriceps muscles.

Unlike concentric muscle actions (Figure 11.8), eccentric strength changes little with velocity (Figure 11.9). Maximal eccentric force is produced when myosin heads pull apart from the actin molecules (see Chapter 2) as the muscle lengthens.[52] In theory, it takes the same amount of force to pull the myofilaments apart at all velocities.

PHYSIOLOGY OF STRENGTH GAINS

hypertrophy
hyperplasia

Resistance training increases muscle size and strength. The increase in muscle size could result from the enlargement of existing muscle fibers (**hypertrophy**) or an increase in the number of muscle fibers (**hyperplasia**). Although some evidence indicates that hyperplasia occurs in response to resistance training in laboratory animals,[23] there is little compelling evidence that hyperplasia contributes to training-induced increases in muscle size in humans. Thus, it is generally accepted that,

The relationship between concentric strength and velocity of muscle action. Concentric strength decreases as the velocity of muscle action increases.

figure 11.8

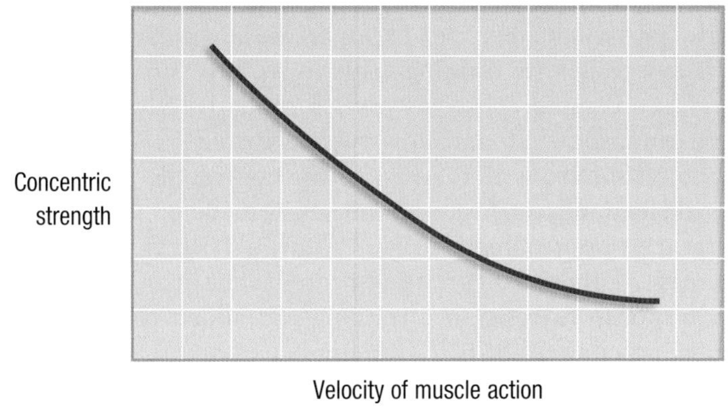

The relationship between eccentric strength and the velocity of muscle action. There is no change with velocity for eccentric strength.

figure 11.9

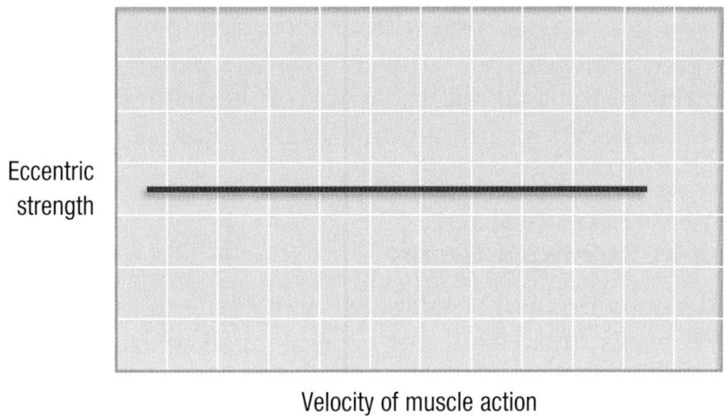

in humans, muscles increase in size in response to resistance training due to hypertrophy and not hyperplasia.[39,40]

It has been suggested[15] that eccentric muscle actions are necessary to stimulate hypertrophy, and therefore, concentric training by itself does not result in an increase in the size of the trained muscle. Studies,[27,43] however, have used magnetic resonance imaging to show increases in the cross-sectional area of the leg extensor muscles (quadriceps) following concentric-only, isokinetic training. It is also interesting to note that each of the quadriceps muscles (vastus lateralis, vastus medialis, vastus intermedius, and rectus femoris) hypertrophied to a different degree. It is clear from these findings that hypertrophy does not require eccentric muscle actions.

WWW
Strength Training
www.sport-fitness-advisor.com/strengthtraining.html

The increase in muscle strength that accompanies resistance training may result from hypertrophy or neural adaptations.[41] In some cases, hypertrophy alone can account for strength increases, while under different conditions, neural adaptations cause strength to increase to a much greater degree than muscle size.

Hypertrophy

The amount of muscle mass that we have (usually about 40–45% of total body weight) is determined by the relationship between protein synthesis and degradation.[28] We are constantly breaking down and rebuilding the proteins within our muscles. Resistance training not only increases protein synthesis but may also decrease the breakdown of existing proteins, causing a net gain in muscle mass.

Resistance training results in hypertrophy of both fast- and slow-twitch muscle fibers, although fast-twitch fibers tend to increase in size to a greater degree.[21,39] Furthermore, heavy resistance training leads to a conversion of fast-twitch glycolytic (FG) fibers (see Chapter 2) to fast-twitch oxidative glycolytic (FOG) but no conversion between fast-twitch and slow-twitch fibers.[21,51]

Hypertrophy results from an increase in the contractile protein content (actin and myosin) of skeletal muscle.[28] Skeletal muscle is made up primarily of water and proteins in a ratio of approximately 4:1.[28] Thus, a 1-kg increase in muscle mass requires an increase of about 200 grams of protein. The actin and myosin filaments synthesized in response to resistance training are added to existing sarcomeres, which leads to enlarged myofibrils.[39] The number of myofibrils also increases due to longitudinal splitting. Therefore, resistance training increases actin and myosin content as well as myofibril size and number within skeletal muscle.

The protein synthesis associated with hypertrophy is mediated by complex interactions among various hormones. The anabolic (growth-promoting) hormones testosterone, growth hormone, insulin, and insulin-like growth factor 1 contribute to increased muscle mass through increased protein synthesis and/or decreased degradation.[28] Cortisol, however, also increases in the blood with resistance exercise and is associated with an increased rate of protein degradation (protein catabolic). Thus, cortisol works to decrease muscle mass.[28] The interplay between the effects of the anabolic and catabolic hormones influences the degree of hypertrophy that occurs as a result of resistance training.

Hypertrophy Versus Neural Adaptations in Strength Gains

If an untrained person begins a resistance training program, strength will increase in the first few weeks, but it will not be accompanied by hypertrophy.[41] This initial increase in strength is generally attributed to neural adaptations. In some cases, untrained individuals may not be able to activate fully all of their motor units during a maximal effort, particularly those with high-threshold, fast-twitch muscle fibers.[48] During the first few weeks of a resistance training program, the individual "learns" to recruit these fibers; therefore, total muscle activation increases, and more force can be produced even though hypertrophy has not occurred. After the first three to four weeks, additional strength increases result mostly from hypertrophy.

There may also be a neural component to strength gains in advanced resistance trained athletes.[21] After many years of resistance training, an athlete may approach the genetic limit to muscle size, and it becomes more and more difficult to increase muscle mass further. Performance in strength and power events, however, may continue to improve without substantial hypertrophy, possibly due to increased muscle activation.[21]

Maximal force output can also be affected by antagonist co-activation. For example, during a leg extension movement the agonist muscles (prime movers for the task) are the quadriceps, and the antagonists (muscles opposing the task) are the hamstrings. Activation of the quadriceps causes the leg extension movement, but it also activates, to some degree, the hamstrings (called *co-activation*). Resistance training can result in a decrease in the level of antagonist co-activation and, therefore, reduce the opposing force to the task, which leads to greater maximal voluntary force production.[48]

RESEARCH

Number of sets for health and strength gains

How many sets should a person do for strength gains? Surprisingly, the answer to this question is not yet clear, and it probably depends on the interaction of a number of factors. Hass et al.* have tried to clarify the matter by examining the effectiveness of single versus multiple sets. The subjects were recreational weight lifters who had been lifting for at least a year using one set for each exercise on a nine-exercise circuit. The training program consisted of a nine-exercise circuit performed once (Group 1) or three times (Group 2), three times per week for 13 weeks. The groups did not differ in 1-RM strength levels prior to the training program. The results showed no statistically significant difference in strength gains between the two groups following training. Overall strength increased 8 to 14 percent depending on the exercise. It seems that if health and fitness are the goals of an exercise program, then one set is just as effective as three and is sufficient to stimulate strength gains even in individuals who are already lifting. Certainly most of the health benefits of resistance training can be realized with the shorter program. The additional strength gains one might expect to see from doing more sets should be balanced with the time cost of the program and a concern for high dropout rates as demands on an individual increase.

* Hass, C. J., Garzarella, L., De Hoyos, D., and Pollock, M. L. Single versus multiple sets in long-term recreational weightlifters. *Med. Sci. Sports Exerc.* 32: 235–242, 2000.

Cross-education

If you resistance train one limb (unilateral training), you will see strength increases not only in that limb but also in the corresponding untrained limb on the other side of the body (contralateral limb). This is called the **cross-education** (or *cross-training*) **effect,** and it has been demonstrated for unilateral isometric, DCER, and isokinetic training of both the arms and legs.[58]

cross-education effect

The cross-education effect has important health-related implications for maintaining muscle tone and preventing atrophy in immobilized muscles. In situations where one limb cannot be exercised due to injury, disease, or surgery, it may be possible, through cross-education, to maintain muscle integrity by resistance training the contralateral limb. Maintenance of strength through cross-education may also reduce the amount of time necessary for rehabilitation when the affected limb can once again be trained.

The increase in strength in the contralateral limb following unilateral resistance training is not as great as that of the trained limb. Normally the strength increase in the untrained limb is less than or equal to about 60 percent of that of the trained limb.[58] Furthermore, the cross-education effect is specific, in several ways, to the type of training. For example, unilateral training of the right leg may increase strength of the left leg but not the left arm. Furthermore, the cross-education effect is greatest for the type of muscle action used in the training. That is, if you train concentrically, the increase in strength in the untrained limb will be greater when tested concentrically than eccentrically. In addition, training with eccentric muscle actions seems to be most effective for inducing cross-education.[58]

Although it is generally accepted that increases in strength from cross-education are not a result of changes in muscle morphology, such as hypertrophy, the mechanism that is responsible for this phenomenon is unclear. Three potential mechanisms, however, have been suggested: (1) central neural mechanisms, (2) postural mechanisms, and (3) humoral mechanisms.

Central neural mechanisms. Three distinct central neural mechanisms have been suggested to explain the cross-education effect. The first involves nerve fibers of the pyramidal tract (see Chapter 4). About 85 percent or more of these pyramidal nerve fibers cross over (decussate) in the spinal cord to activate muscles on the opposite side of the body. The remaining 10 to 15 percent of the pyramidal nerve fibers do not decussate; they activate muscles on the same side of the body (ipsilaterally). Thus, when we voluntarily activate the muscles in one limb, the corresponding muscles in the contralateral limb are also activated, but to a smaller degree. The cross-education effect may result from the small percentage of pyramidal nerve fibers that fail to cross over in the spinal cord and activate muscles ipsilaterally.

The second neural mechanism that may explain the cross-education effect involves the activation of the contralateral (on the opposite side) cortex during unilateral voluntary movements.[36] It may be difficult or even impossible to isolate one-half of the motor cortex and not call into action the contralateral cortex. This potential mechanism is supported by the observation that **unilateral imagined training** (thinking about but not actually performing resistance training with only one limb) increases contralateral strength.[57]

unilateral imagined training

The third potential central neural mechanism that may account for the cross-education effect occurs at the level of the spinal cord. Involuntary muscle training using electrical stimulation has resulted in contralateral effects, suggesting the involvement of a spinal mechanism.

Postural mechanisms. Contracting the muscles in one limb may lead to the contraction of the corresponding muscles of the contralateral limb in order to maintain postural stability and aid in force production.[58] During high-intensity, unilateral muscle actions there is a noticeable tensing on the contralateral side of the body to maintain the proper position for optimal force production. It is debatable, however, if the degree of activation of the muscles of the contralateral limb is sufficient to stimulate the amount of strength gains normally associated with cross-education.[26]

Humoral mechanisms. It was initially suggested[57] that the involvement of some blood-borne factor may potentially provide a mechanism for increases in contralateral strength as a result of unilateral training. The absence of a generalized training effect throughout all muscle groups, however, has discredited this theory as a potential cross-education mechanism.[42]

Disuse and atrophy

muscle atrophy

Anyone who has had a limb in a cast can attest to the results of **muscle atrophy** (shrinking of a muscle). Immobilization of a limb results in decreased muscle fiber size, but no loss in the number of fibers. Thus, to maintain muscle size and strength, resistance training must be performed regularly.

Placing a muscle on stretch (in a lengthened position) may retard atrophy. Because of this, physicians try to cast limbs in positions that allow the greatest resting muscle length.

RESISTANCE TRAINING FOR HEALTH-RELATED OUTCOMES

Resistance training is now widely accepted as an integral part of a total health and fitness program.[3,20,46] According to the American College of Sports Medicine,[3] the goals of a health-related resistance training program should be to:

1. Make activities of daily living such as climbing stairs and carrying groceries less physiologically demanding and stressful.
2. Effectively manage, attenuate, and prevent chronic diseases such as osteoporosis, type 2 diabetes mellitus, and obesity.

The many health-related outcomes of resistance training include increased bone mineral density, favorable changes in body composition, increased functional strength for daily living, improved insulin sensitivity, increased basal metabolic rate, decreased diastolic blood pressure, reduced risk of low back pain, decreased risk of injury during physical activity and sports, and improved blood lipid profiles.[45,55]

Resistance Training Prescription for Health-Related Outcomes

The ACSM[3] recommends that resistance training programs, like aerobic exercise, follow the FITT-VP principles (frequency, intensity, time, type, volume, and progression or pattern) of exercise prescription. Resistance training prescriptions consider a number of factors, including the number of repetitions (individual muscle actions), the number of sets (a group of muscle actions), the resistance used (i.e., weight), the frequency of training (how often you train), the mode of training (type of muscle action, such as isometric or DCER, etc.), the rest periods between sets, the muscle groups involved, and the volume of training (sets × repetitions × resistance).

The ACSM's[3] recommended resistance exercise prescription for health-related purposes for adults includes:

Frequency: Each major muscle group should be trained on two or three days per week.

Intensity: 60 to 70% 1-RM (moderate to vigorous intensity) for novice to intermediate exercisers to improve strength. Greater than or equal to 80% 1-RM (vigorous to very vigorous intensity) for experienced strength trainers to improve strength. An intensity of 40 to 50% RM (very light to light intensity) for older individuals beginning exercise to improve strength. Intensities of 40 to 50% 1-RM (very light to light intensity) may be beneficial for improving strength in sedentary individuals beginning a resistance training program. Less than 50% 1-RM (light to moderate intensity) is recommended to improve muscular endurance, while 20 to 50% 1-RM is recommended in older adults to improve power.

Time: No specific duration of training has been identified for effectiveness.

Type: Resistance exercises involving each major muscle group are recommended. Multi-joint exercises affecting more than one muscle group and targeting agonist and antagonist muscle groups are recommended for all adults. In addition, single joint exercises targeting major muscle groups may also be included in a resistance training program, typically after performing multi-joint exercise(s) for that particular muscle group. A variety of exercise equipment and/or body weight can be used to perform these exercises.

Repetitions: To improve strength and power in most adults, 8 to 12 repetitions are recommended. For improving strength in middle-aged and older individuals starting exercise, 10 to 15 repetitions are effective. To improve muscular endurance, 15 to 20 repetitions are recommended.

Sets: Two to four sets are recommended for most adults to improve strength and power. A single set of resistance exercise can be effective, especially among older and novice exercisers. One or two sets are effective in improving muscular endurance.

Progression: A gradual progression of greater resistance and/or more repetitions per set and/or increasing frequency is recommended.

Pattern: Rest intervals of two to three minutes between each set of repetitions are effective. A rest of greater than or equal to 48 hours between sessions for any single muscle group is recommended.

Effects from Very-Short-Term Training

Exercise Prescription
www.exrx.net

As discussed earlier in this chapter, the increase in muscle strength that accompanies resistance training may be a result of neural adaptations, muscle hypertrophy, or both. We have discussed the work of Moritani and deVries,[41] who found that during a resistance training program the initial gains in strength are due to neural adaptations, whereas the gains achieved later are due to muscle hypertrophy. Evidence suggests that short-term training, lasting as few as two sessions, can result in strength gains that are proportional to those achieved after several weeks of training.[1,47,51] This evidence has practical implications for allied health professionals, who, because of managed care, may see a patient only a few times. For example, a physician may opt to try a short-term physical therapy resistance training treatment, rather than jump into surgery if improvements in strength and function can be attained quickly. Also, patients would more likely adhere to a rehabilitation program lasting only two or three sessions than one lasting several weeks.

RESISTANCE TRAINING FOR STRENGTH AND HYPERTROPHY IN HEALTHY ADULTS

In addition to the health-related benefits, two of the primary reasons to engage in a resistance training program are to increase muscular strength and/or increase muscle size (hypertrophy). The ACSM[2] has provided recommendations regarding the design of novice, intermediate, and advanced resistance training programs for increasing muscular strength and hypertrophy. These programs include recommendations related to type of muscle action, loading, volume, exercise selection, use of free weights and machines, exercise order, rest periods, velocity of muscle action, and frequency of training. Table 11.1 provides a summary of the ACSM's[2] recommendations for increasing muscular strength in healthy adults. Table 11.2 provides a summary of the ACSM's[2] recommendations for increasing muscle size through hypertrophy in healthy adults.

RESISTANCE TRAINING FOR ATHLETES

It is widely accepted that to compete successfully, an athlete must include resistance training as a part of a total conditioning program. In fact, it is quite common to find strength and conditioning coaches in high schools as well as colleges.

USA Weightlifting
www.teamusa.org/USA-Weightlifting

There are many reasons to include resistance training in a conditioning program for athletes. Not only does resistance training increase muscle strength and modify body composition, but it also contributes to improving sports performance by increasing muscle power, muscle endurance, and the rate of force production; improving flexibility; and reducing the risk of injury. From a rehabilitative standpoint, resistance training is commonly used to strengthen muscles following injury or surgery and aids the athlete's return to practice and competition.[45]

Body Composition and Body Build

One of the primary reasons that athletes (and non-athletes) resistance train is to modify their body composition. Resistance training has been shown to decrease

ACSM's recommendations for increasing muscular strength in healthy adults.[2] **table 11.1**

VARIABLE	NOVICE	INTERMEDIATE	ADVANCED
Type of muscle action	concentric, eccentric, and isometric	concentric, eccentric, and isometric	concentric, eccentric, and isometric
Loading	60–70% of 1-RM for 8–12 repetitions	60–70% of 1-RM for 8–12 repetitions	80–100% of 1-RM
Volume	1–3 sets per exercise	multiple sets	multiple sets
Exercise selection	unilateral and bilateral single- and multi-joint exercises	unilateral and bilateral single- and multi-joint exercises	unilateral and bilateral single- and multi-joint exercises
Free weights and/or machines	free weights and machines	free weights and machines	emphasis on free weights, with machine exercises as a complement
Exercise order	large-muscle groups before small-muscle group exercise; multi-joint before single-joint exercise; high intensity before lower intensity; rotate upper and lower body exercises; rotate agonist and antagonist exercises	large-muscle groups before small-muscle group exercise; multi-joint before single-joint exercise; high intensity before lower intensity; rotate upper and lower body exercises; rotate agonist and antagonist exercises	large-muscle groups before small-muscle group exercise; multi-joint before single-joint exercise; high intensity before lower intensity; rotate upper and lower body exercises; rotate agonist and antagonist exercises
Rest periods	2–3 minutes	2–3 minutes	2–3 minutes
Velocity of muscle actions	slow and moderate	moderate	slow, moderate, and fast
Frequency of training	2–3 days per week	3–4 days per week	4–6 days per week

ACSM's recommendations for increasing muscle size through hypertrophy in healthy adults.[2] **table 11.2**

VARIABLE	NOVICE	INTERMEDIATE	ADVANCED
Type of muscle action	concentric, eccentric, and isometric	concentric, eccentric, and isometric	concentric, eccentric, and isometric
Loading and volume	70–85% of 1-RM for 8–12 repetitions for 1–3 sets per exercise	70–85% of 1-RM for 8–12 repetitions for 1–3 sets per exercise	70–100% of 1-RM for 1–12 repetitions for 3–6 sets per exercise
Exercise selection	single- and multi-joint exercises	single- and multi-joint exercises	single- and multi-joint exercises
Free weights and/or machines	free weights and machines	free weights and machines	free weights and machines
Exercise order	performed in the same order as for increasing muscular strength from Table 11.1	performed in the same order as for increasing muscular strength from Table 11.1	performed in the same order as for increasing muscular strength from Table 11.1
Rest periods	1–2 minutes	1–2 minutes	2–3 minutes for heavy loading; 1–2 minutes for moderate loading
Velocity of muscle actions	slow and moderate	slow and moderate	slow, moderate, and fast
Frequency of training	2–3 days per week	2–4 days per week	4–6 days per week

RESEARCH

Effects of resistance training programs on men and women

As more women enter physically demanding fields such as the military and firefighting, they must be able to meet the physical requirements of the job, including high levels of strength. Since females typically have about half the upper body strength of males, proper exercise programs are important. Ribeiro et al.* have investigated the effects of a progressive resistance training program on men and women. They found that during the first eight weeks of the training program, which included both upper and lower body exercises, the women in the study improved in overall strength more than the men. During the second eight weeks of strength training, the women and men had similar increases in strength. When only the upper body exercises were analyzed, however, the women improved in strength more than the men in both the first and the second eight weeks of training. The results indicate that 16 weeks of strength training has a significant impact on the strength of both men and women and that upper body strength in women continues to improve well into the strength training program. Therefore, a longer program may be more beneficial to women, who tend to have a greater need for upper body strength increases than men.

*Ribeiro, A. S., Avelar, A., Schoenfeld, B. J., Fleck, S. J., Souza, M. F., Padilha, C. S., and Cyrino, E. S. Analysis of the training load during a hypertrophy-type resistance training programme in men and women. *Eur. J. Sport Sci.* 15: 256–264, 2015.

percent body fat and increase fat-free weight (FFW). For example, short-term DCER and isokinetic resistance training programs of 6 to 20 weeks in duration have been shown to decrease percent body fat by 0.2 to 4.0 percent and increase FFW by 0.3 to 6.0 kg.[21] Furthermore, experienced bodybuilders, power lifters, and Olympic lifters tend to possess less percent body fat (Table 11.3) and more FFW than non-athletes. The absolute amount (in kg) of FFW, of course, depends on an individual's competitive weight class.

Competitive weight lifters and bodybuilders are also characterized by unique physiques that differ from those of non-athletes as well as athletes in other sports. Male and female weight lifters and bodybuilders tend to exhibit great muscularity, broad shoulders, and large muscle circumferences. These traits probably result from a combination of many years of resistance training and genetically determined body build characteristics (e.g., height and limb length). See **Chapter 11 Lab B** for performing somatotyping to determine body build characteristics.

Basic Principles of Resistance Training for Athletes

Four basic principles are associated with resistance training for athletes: specificity, overload, progression, and periodization. To integrate these principles into a resistance training program to enhance an athlete's performance, one must have a thorough understanding of the athlete's sport.

table 11.3 Percent body fat of bodybuilders, power lifters, Olympic lifters, and non-athletes.[21,22,30,50]

	MALES	FEMALES
Bodybuilders	6.6–9.3% fat	13.2–18.7% fat
Power lifters	9.7–15.6% fat	21.5% fat
Olympic lifters	8.9–12.2% fat	20.4% fat
College-age non-athletes	14.0–16.0% fat	20.0–24.0% fat

Specificity

The **specificity** principle suggests that adaptations to a resistance training program be specific to the characteristics of the program. Application of the specificity principle helps to ensure that the adaptations will transfer to the sport in which the athlete competes. The primary types of specificity are metabolic, movement pattern, and velocity.

specificity

Metabolic specificity, as it relates to resistance training, indicates that the primary adaptations will occur in the ATP–PC system and anaerobic glycolysis (see Chapter 3). Because resistance training involves predominantly anaerobic energy production, there are, typically, few adaptations to the aerobic systems.

Movement pattern specificity means that the resistance training exercises should mimic, as closely as possible, the athlete's sport. For example, because of the trajectory used by a shot putter when putting the shot, the incline bench press exercise is a logical choice to include (along with other exercises) in a resistance training program. Another example is internal and external rotation exercises for a baseball pitcher.

Velocity specificity indicates that the resistance training exercises should be performed at velocities that are similar to the demands of the sport in which the athlete participates. Although it is very difficult during resistance training to mimic the velocity of the leg during sprinting, rapid, explosive movements are more likely to transfer to improved sprinting performance than are slow or isometric muscle actions.

Overload

According to the **overload** principle, to promote strength gains and hypertrophy, a resistance training program must demand more of a muscle or muscle group than it normally performs. Unless a muscle or muscle group is taxed, it will not adapt with increases in strength or size. This does not mean, however, that each workout must result in complete exhaustion. Furthermore, the volume of training that an athlete can endure is related to the level of conditioning at a particular point in time. Thus, a resistance training program that results in an overload during the off season may not be sufficient to overload muscles during a period of heavy training.

overload

Progression

The principle of **progression** indicates that to maintain an overload and continue to see adaptations from a resistance training program, it is necessary periodically to increase the volume of training. This can be accomplished by increasing the resistance, number of repetitions, and/or number of sets and by altering the repetition speed and rest periods according to the goals of the program.[34] Typically, as an athlete becomes stronger, resistance is increased first.

progression

Periodization

Periodization involves systematic changes in the resistance, number of repetitions, and/or number of sets of a resistance training program. Because many athletes resistance train year round and need to peak for athletic competitions, it is necessary periodically to change the characteristics of the resistance training program to minimize boredom and facilitate adherence.[33,53] Furthermore, periodized programs tend to result in greater and more consistent strength gains than traditional nonperiodized programs. There are three primary periodization models: linear, reverse linear, and nonlinear. The linear (also called *classic*) periodization model, illustrated in Figure 11.10, is composed of a macrocycle, mesocycles, and microcycles.[21,53]

periodization

For athletes, a *macrocycle* is usually about one year in length, corresponding to the time from one competitive season to the next. The macrocycle is divided into several *mesocycles* (usually two to three months in length) depending on the sport, and each is designed to produce specific adaptations.

For developing strength and power, the mesocycles may include a hypertrophy phase, a strength phase, a power phase, a peaking phase, and an active rest phase. As the athlete moves through the phases (from hypertrophy phase to active rest phase) the total volume of training decreases and the resistance increases. For example:[21,53]

Hypertrophy phase: 3–5 sets of various movements at an 8–20 RM load

Strength phase: 3–5 sets at a 2- to 6-RM load

Power phase: 3–5 sets at a 2- to 3-RM load

Peaking phase: 1–3 sets at a 1- to 3-RM load

Active rest phase: light physical activity

The mesocycles are composed of *microcycles*, which involve variations in training intensity from one training session to the next throughout the week. For example, the first training session of the week usually involves the highest resistance, with decreasing resistance during the second and third sessions. The microcycle then starts over at the beginning of the next week.

figure 11.10 Linear periodization model.

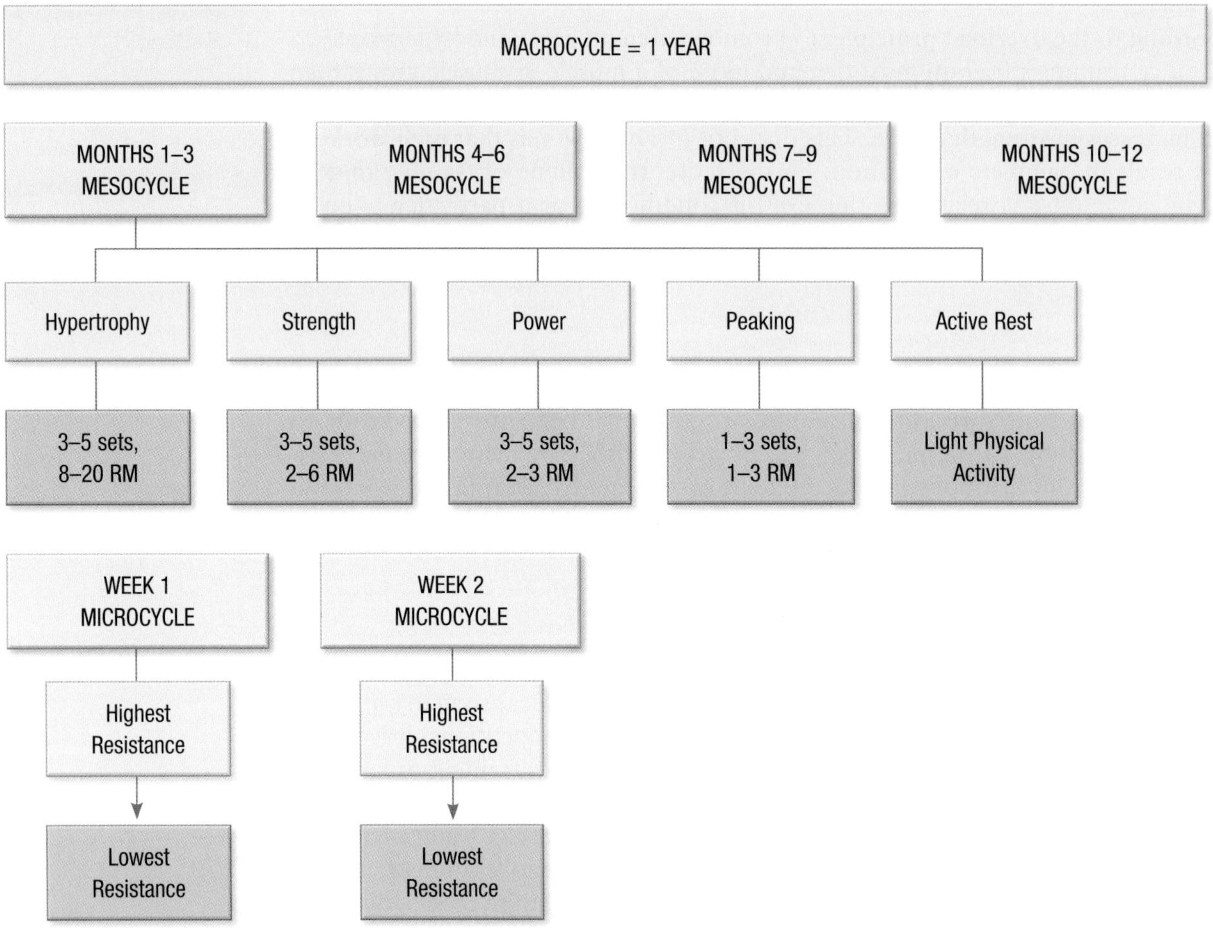

In addition to the linear periodization model, a reverse linear model has been studied.[2] In this model, the loading is initially the highest and volume of training the lowest. Over time, the intensity decreases and volume increases. This is the inverse of the classic, linear periodization model. The reverse linear model has been shown to improve local muscular endurance, but it is not as effective as the linear model for increasing strength.[2]

The nonlinear (sometimes called the undulating) periodization model involves rotating heavy (3–5 RM), moderate (8–10 RM), and light (12–15 RM) loads either systematically or randomly. The nonlinear periodization model compares favorably with other models for increasing strength.[2]

Periodization models for resistance training programs can be developed for any sport. The specific designs of the macrocycle, mesocycles, and microcycles depend on the demands of the sport. Properly applying the science of resistance training to individual athletes is one example of the art of coaching.

Resistance Training Prescription for Athletes

The National Strength and Conditioning Association (NSCA) has provided basic guidelines for the resistance training of athletes.[45] These guidelines can be used as the basis for coaches to design specific individualized resistance training programs for athletes in various sports. There is, however, no single resistance training program that meets the needs of all athletes in all sports. Therefore, the coach and the athlete must design an individualized resistance training prescription using a combination of the scientific bases of resistance training and their own practical experiences.

The NSCA has provided the following basic recommendations for designing a resistance training prescription for athletes.[45]

1. Schedule training at least three days a week, with a minimum of 24 hours' rest between training sessions.
2. Design programs so that all of the major muscle groups are targeted during training sessions.
3. Take into account appropriate muscle balance across joints as well as both the upper and lower body muscle groups.
4. Periodize training to vary volume and intensity.
5. Plan recovery periods to help avoid any overtraining symptoms.
6. Generally, require no more than two exercises per body part; however, different exercises per body part may be used throughout the week.
7. Limit specific large-muscle group exercises to two times per week (e.g., parallel squat performed on Mondays and Fridays).
8. Use warm-up sets that involve a very light resistance.
9. Allow adequate recovery for muscle groups during a training week (e.g., use split programs or split body part programs depending on the program goals).
10. Perform large-muscle group exercises first in a workout.
11. Allow rest between sets depending on the goals of the training program. If maximal strength is the goal, then a longer rest period is desirable (e.g., two to three minutes). If skeletal muscle hypertrophy is the primary goal, then short rest periods may be desirable (less than one minute).
12. Using a four-day-per-week training protocol, one can divide the selected lifts into two groups: (a) chest and shoulders and (b) back and legs. This arrangement is most often used by experienced lifters and is the basis for many collegiate programs.

13. A well-balanced program will make use of multi-joint and Olympic-style lifts with free weights as well as isolated movements on resistance machines to promote targeted muscle hypertrophy.

Resistance Training for Female Athletes

Female athletes respond favorably to resistance training, and in general the rates of training-induced increases in strength (as a percentage of initial levels) are similar in females and males. Typically, however, males exhibit greater absolute gains.

The recommendations for designing resistance training programs for athletes presented above apply to both genders.[45] In addition, the NSCA has prepared a position paper, *Strength Training for Female Athletes,*[44] that is based on a thorough review of the literature. The NSCA has endorsed the following statements:[56]

> It appears that proper strength and conditioning exercise programs may increase athletic performance, improve physiological function, and reduce the risk of injuries. These effects are as beneficial to female athletes as they are to males. The question that has to be addressed is whether female athletes require different training modalities, programs, or personnel than those required by male athletes.
>
> Due to similar physiological responses, it appears that males and females should train for strength in the same basic way, employing similar methodologies, programs, and types of exercises. Coaches should assess the needs of each athlete, male or female, individually, and train that athlete accordingly. Coaches should keep in mind that there may be more differences between individuals of the same gender than between males and females. Still, there may be psychological and/or physiological considerations that should be taken into account in training female athletes.

WWW

The Physician and Sports Medicine: Strength Training for Females

www.stumptuous.com/ebben.html

The NSCA position paper discusses the following important physiological aspects of strength training in female athletes:[44]

Total body strength. Data at this time suggest that in untrained individuals, the absolute total body strength of females is approximately two-thirds that of males, although this difference is not consistent for all muscle groups. Absolute lower body strength ranges from 60 to 80 percent that of males, and absolute upper body strength from 35 to 79 percent that of males. It should be noted that these differences are based on studies involving non-athletic subjects; the studies primarily involved tests of static strength. Studies assessing the relative and absolute strength of highly trained female athletes are needed. Strength differences in the studies to date are largely attributable to the greater body size of males and their higher lean body mass to fat ratio.

When the gender differences in body size and lean body mass are taken into consideration, relative strength differences are considerably less appreciable. In the lower body, in fact, the relative strength (strength to lean body mass) of untrained women appears to be approximately equal to that of males. Researchers who have examined the ability to generate force per unit of cross-sectional muscle have found no significant gender differences.

Testosterone. The role of the hormone testosterone in strength expression is not clearly understood at this time. Although it is known that the rate of secretion is 5 to 10 milligrams per day for males and less than 0.1 milligram per day for females, studies have yet to demonstrate that higher testosterone levels alone (in either males or females) correlate with greater strength values. Both empirical and some objective evidence suggests, however, that the exogenous administration of testosterone does positively affect strength expression in both males and females who practice weight training.

Steroid use. Little statistical evidence is available to document the existence of anabolic steroid use by female athletes. (Anabolic steroids are synthetic derivatives of the male hormone testosterone.) Because success in many competitive sports results in part from greater physical size and strength, however, the temptation for females to use anabolic steroids appears to be as great as for males. Furthermore, a growing body of anecdotal evidence suggests that a large number of women athletes have experimented with these drugs. Strength and conditioning coaches should help athletes pursue excellence through improved training methods and nutritional counseling. This approach should help coaching staffs avoid endangering the health of female athletes or compromising the ethics of sport.

Effects of resistance exercise. Short-term studies and empirical evidence have shown female hypertrophy as a consequence of resistance exercise. The relative degree of hypertrophy as a result of resistance training is equal to that of males, although the absolute degree is smaller. The genetic predisposition to hypertrophy and any exogenous androgen use most likely play significant roles in determining the degree of hypertrophy achieved.

Female athletes appear to have fiber-type distributions similar to those of their male counterparts, although the fibers of females appear to be smaller in cross-sectional area. Whether this is genetically determined or training-induced is not clear at this time. Heavy resistance training has been demonstrated to increase fiber cross-sectional area, with corresponding increases in strength and power.

Some have raised the question of whether the relatively narrow shoulder width of most females may pose problems in certain overhead lifts. Thus far no data have been found to substantiate this concern. Coaches should pay close attention to hand spacing and to the carrying angle at the elbow. In the lower body, the typical greater pelvic width and the Q-angle (quadriceps angle) of the knee may pose problems for female weight trainers. The Q-angle is the angle formed between the longitudinal axis of the femur that represents the pull of the quadriceps muscles and a line that represents the patellar ligament. Again, although this has been raised as a point of concern, no data at this time support it. Coaches who are concerned about this condition may wish to caution female weight trainers with large Q-angles to squat with a toe-forward stance. Development of quadriceps strength can act as a strong deterrent of injuries in female athletes.

Menstrual cycle. There is little research evidence that suggests the onset of a normal menstrual period affects athletic performance. There is tremendous variability, however, in the physical and psychological ways in which women respond to their menses. If circumstances permit individualized strength programs, the monthly onset of menstruation should be considered during program design. Discussions of the menstrual cycle should be handled with tact and sensitivity by strength and conditioning personnel. Athletes who experience extreme difficulty before or during menstruation should seek advice from their gynecologists regarding proper medical intervention. Irregular menstrual cycles (**oligomenorrhea**) and/or the cessation of the menses (amenorrhea) may pose health risks to female athletes. Amenorrheic athletes have an increased likelihood of developing musculoskeletal injuries (especially stress fractures and osteoporotic fractures) due to the weakening of the bones from reduced estrogen levels. It is strongly urged that all athletes experiencing amenorrhea or other menstrual irregularities consult a gynecologist. Proper nutritional intakes (e.g., calcium, iron) also must be evaluated. Finally, resistance training utilizing multi-joint and structural exercises is recommended to induce sufficient stresses on the skeletal system and to enhance calcium storage in the bone.

oligomenorrhea

Pregnancy. Few data exist at this time regarding weight training and pregnancy. Anecdotal evidence suggests, however, that women may safely weight train during pregnancy. Of course, common sense should be employed when selecting training intensities, exercises, and loads during critical stages of pregnancy. Due to the influx of the hormone **relaxin,** which softens the tendons and ligaments in preparation for delivery, caution is warranted in performing heavy multi-joint free weight exercises (squats, dead lifts, snatches, and cleans) after the first trimester. Also, the potential for hyperthermia (increase in body temperature) in pregnant women warrants precautions in dress and environmental conditions during all types of exercise. Following childbirth, many women have returned to successful athletic careers.

relaxin

Body fat. Athletes of different sports show considerable variation in percent body fat. It is important to understand that the performance and health of the individual must be carefully considered before any attempt to alter body composition. Furthermore, athletes and coaches need to be aware of societal norms regarding body image and the implications for the development of eating disorders. Proper nutrition is an important consideration in strength training for female athletes. Finally, resistance training has demonstrated favorable changes in body composition with minimal change in body weight.

Resistance Training for Muscular Power

Muscular power is defined as the amount of work performed per unit of time and is essential for successful athletic performance in almost all sports. For example, an explosive, powerful vertical jump is important in many sports such as basketball, volleyball, football, track and field events, baseball, softball, and many others. Because work is calculated as the product of force times distance, the ability to produce force is an important aspect of muscular power. Thus, resistance training programs not only increase strength but also contribute to the ability to perform powerful movements related to athletic performance. Table 11.4 provides a summary of the ACSM's recommendations for increasing muscular power through resistance training.[2]

table 11.4 ACSM's recommendations for increasing muscular power through resistance training.[2]

VARIABLE	NOVICE	INTERMEDIATE	ADVANCED
Type of muscle action	multi-joint	multi-joint	multi-joint
Loading and volume	30–60% of 1-RM for upper body exercises and 0–60% of 1-RM for lower body exercises	30–60% of 1-RM for upper body exercises and 0–60% of 1-RM for lower body exercises	85–100% of 1-RM for increasing force and 30–60% of 1-RM for upper body exercises and 0–60% of 1-RM for lower body exercises for increasing fast force production
Repetitions	3–6 repetitions per set	3–6 repetitions per set	1–6 repetitions per set
Sets	1–3 sets per exercise	1–3 sets per exercise	3–6 sets per exercise
Rest periods	2–3 minutes for core exercises and 1–3 minutes for assistance exercises	2–3 minutes for core exercises and 1–3 minutes for assistance exercises	2–3 minutes for core exercises and 1–3 minutes for assistance exercises
Frequency	2–3 days per week	3–4 days per week	4–5 days per week

Note: The power training component should be included concurrently with the athlete's normal resistance training program.

Plyometric Training

Athletes use plyometric training to increase explosive muscular power. The origin of the term *plyometric* is unknown; it may come from the Greek words *pleythein,* "to increase," or *plio,* meaning "more," and *metric,* meaning "to measure."[17] **Plyometrics** (also called the *stretch–shortening cycle*) includes both upper and lower body exercises and involves stretching a muscle through an eccentric (lengthening) phase followed by a forceful concentric (shortening) muscle action. This can be accomplished through lower body exercises such as depth jumps from an elevated stand, bounding with loping strides, leaping over objects, and hopping on one or both feet.[17] Upper body plyometric exercises include such activities as the scoop toss, overhead throw, lateral toss, two-handed put throw, wood chop throw, and chest throw using a medicine ball.[10] The eccentric phase of the exercise is a preparatory movement to increase the elastic energy stored in muscle and connective tissue.[31] That is, when the athlete jumps from an elevated stand and lands on the floor, the quadriceps muscles must absorb the weight of the body through an eccentric muscle action that stretches the muscle. The subsequent concentric muscle action of the quadriceps is then more forceful than it would be if it were not preceded by the eccentric phase of the movement.

plyometrics

Plyometric training improves performance in anaerobic activities such as jumping (high jump, long jump, triple jump, and vertical jump) and maximizes squat strength. Therefore, plyometric training is particularly beneficial for athletes who compete in sports that require a high level of explosive power, such as track and field, football, volleyball, basketball, and Olympic-style weight lifting.

It is normally recommended that plyometrics be used as a supplement to other forms of training such as resistance training and sprinting to enhance the functional capabilities of athletes.[17] As a supplement for advanced athletes, plyometric training should be utilized no more than two times per week.[17] Excessive use of plyometric training can result in overuse injuries such as tendonitis, particularly of the knee joint. Of the various plyometric techniques, the depth jump from an elevated stand, apparently, is most likely to cause injury.[17]

WWW

Plyometrics

www.brianmac.co.uk/plymo.htm

Concurrent Strength and Endurance Training

Many athletes as well as non-athletes interested in health-related fitness perform both strength and endurance training. In an attempt to enhance both cardiorespiratory fitness and muscular strength, it is common for individuals to engage in aerobic activity several days per week and strength training on the same or alternate days. The ACSM[3] recommends a moderate-intensity resistance training program.

Studies of the effects of concurrent strength and endurance training have indicated that:[6,25,49]

1. Concurrent strength and endurance training results in improvements in both muscular strength and aerobic capabilities.
2. The increases in muscular strength as a result of concurrent strength and endurance training tend to be less than those that result from strength training alone.
3. There is no difference in the increase in aerobic power that results from concurrent strength and endurance training versus endurance training alone.

WWW

Concurrent Resistance and Endurance Training

http://jap.physiology.org/content/abstract/85/2/695

http://collegesportsscholarships.com/home-gym-aerobic-resistance.htm

Concurrent strength and endurance training is clearly beneficial for individuals interested in health-related fitness. This may not be true, however, for strength and power athletes such as weight lifters, power lifters, and football players. Dudley and Fleck[18] have stated, "It may be advised that athletes involved in pure strength/power type activities should not perform large volumes of endurance type training."

Vibration Training and Strength

Vibration, a mechanical stimulus that alters the gravitational field, has been shown to serve as an effective method for improving strength and power production. Vibration treatments may be applied via specialized vibrating weights or cable systems or via whole-body vibration using vibrating plates. Both acute and chronic vibration treatments have been shown to result in improvements in muscular strength, vertical jump height, and mechanical power.[7,9,16,54] Even though these improvements appear to be short-lived, disappearing 60 minutes after the treatment,[54] vibration treatment could provide a critical edge if utilized immediately prior to performance in athletic events of relatively short duration.

The mechanism responsible for these improvements is not well understood, but it most likely involves the hypergravity imposed by the high accelerations that occur during the vibrations. This results in fast and short changes in the length of the muscle–tendon complex and subsequent activation of muscle spindles, the gamma system, and the stretch–reflex loop. Vibration may also enhance muscular performance by inhibiting the activation of antagonist muscle via Ia-inhibitory neurons. In addition, vibration, which activates the supplementary motor area of the brain, may increase the excitatory state of the peripheral and central nervous systems, which in turn may facilitate subsequent voluntary activity. Hormonal factors may also play a role in the neuromuscular adaptations that occur with vibration training. Hypergravity, which accompanies both strength training and vibration training, has been shown to increase blood levels of both testosterone and growth hormone. These hormones, which serve as facilitators of many intracellular physiological mechanisms, may alter calcium movement within the muscle cell and other critical aspects of muscle function.

Overtraining

overtraining

Overtraining, sometimes called *staleness* or *burnout,* is of concern to both coaches and athletes because of the potential negative effects on health and performance.[35] Overtraining is often the result of increasing the total volume of a resistance training program too quickly. It can affect an individual muscle or muscle group or the athlete's entire body.[45] Factors that may contribute to developing overtraining include:

1. Overly frequent competitions
2. Pre-existing illnesses such as colds, influenza, or allergies
3. Dietary inadequacies
4. Psychological stress related or unrelated to training and competition
5. Excessively heavy time demands, including travel and media commitments
6. Inadequate sleep

According to the NSCA,[45] general symptoms of overtraining include:

1. A plateau followed by decrease of strength gains
2. Increased resting diastolic blood pressure
3. Increased resting heart rate by 5 to 10 beats per minute
4. Sleep disturbances
5. Decreased lean body weight (when not dieting)
6. Decreased appetite
7. A cold that just won't go away
8. Persistent flu-like symptoms

9. Loss of interest in the training program
10. Feelings of fatigue upon rising in the morning
11. Excessive muscle soreness

The most effective way to cure overtraining is rest.[45] It is not uncommon for it to take several weeks or months to overcome the effects of overtraining and restore peak sports performance.[35] Probably the best way to reduce the risk of overtraining is to periodize the athlete's resistance training program.

Detraining

Detraining results from the cessation of resistance training.[21] Normally, detraining is characterized by decreases in strength that level off after a few weeks. Typically, athletes retain a level of strength that is greater than prior to the resistance training program. It may be possible, however, to maintain training-induced strength gains with only one resistance training session per week.[21]

summary

Resistance training is important to both health and athletic performance. The potential health-related benefits of resistance training include increased bone mineral density, favorable changes in body composition, increased functional strength for daily living, improved insulin sensitivity, increased basal metabolic rate, possibly decreased diastolic blood pressure, reduced risk of low back pain, decreased risk of injury during physical activity and sports, and improved blood lipid profiles. It is recommended that healthy adults perform two to four sets of multi-joint exercises (at least one exercise for each major muscle group), using 40 to ≥80% 1-RM loads, 8–12 repetitions, two to three days per week.

It is widely accepted that for an athlete to compete successfully, resistance training must be a part of a total conditioning program. Four basic principles are associated with resistance training for athletes: specificity, overload, progression, and periodization. The NSCA has provided basic recommendations for designing a resistance training program for athletes, but no single program will meet the needs of all athletes in all sports. Athletic and non-athletic males and females can benefit from properly designed aerobic and resistance training programs.

questions for review

1. What happens when a muscle is heated? Cooled? What are the implications for exercise?
2. What factors contribute to the external force a muscle can produce? How?
3. How can the bilateral deficit be modified with training?
4. List the advantages and disadvantages of isometric, DCER, and isokinetic training methods.
5. What causes delayed onset muscle soreness? Can it be treated or prevented? If so, how?
6. Discuss the health implications of the cross-education effect.
7. You are preparing an orientation session for a group of new healthy, middle-aged members who joined your fitness club primarily to use your aerobics equipment.

You would like to encourage them to incorporate resistance training into their workout routine. What potential health-related benefits of resistance training could you stress to encourage them to begin such a program? Prescribe an appropriate program for a member of this group.

8. Answer both parts of question 7 for a group of older adults.
9. Discuss the four principles associated with resistance training for athletes. How can they be incorporated in a resistance training program for enhancing performance?
10. What precautions would you suggest to an individual starting a resistance training program who is pregnant?
11. Prescribe a resistance training program for a competitive weight lifter who would like to maintain a minimal level of cardiovascular fitness while not compromising strength gains.
12. What are the advantages and disadvantages of using plyometric training?
13. What causes overtraining and how can it be prevented?
14. How many sets should you recommend to a person who is interested in beginning a resistance training program for health benefits?

student companion website

For further review of this book's chapters and for test preparation, visit the book's website, **www.hhpcommunities.com/exercisephysiology**, to take practice quizzes, review the vocabulary terms, use the study guide, and view the digital image bank.

references

1. Akima, H., Takahashi, H., Kuno, S. Y., Masuda, K., Masuda, T., Shimojo, H., Anno, I., Itai, Y., and Katsuta, S. Early phase adaptations of muscle use and strength to isokinetic training. *Med. Sci. Sports Exerc.* 31: 588–594, 1999.
2. American College of Sports Medicine. Position Stand. Progression Models in Resistance Training for Healthy Adults. *Med. Sci. Sports Exerc.* 41: 687–708, 2009.
3. American College of Sports Medicine. *ACSM's Guidelines for Exercise Testing and Prescription,* 9th edition. Baltimore: Wolters Kluwer/Lippincott Williams & Wilkins, 2014.
4. Beck, T. W., Housh, T. J., Johnson, G. O., Weir, J. P., Cramer, J. T., Coburn, J. W., and Malek, M. H. Mechanomyographic and electromyographic responses during submaximal to maximal eccentric isokinetic muscle actions of the biceps brachii. *J. Strength Cond. Res.* 20: 184–191, 2006.

5a. Beck, T. W., Housh, T. J., Johnson, G. O., Weir, J. P., Cramer, J. T., Coburn, J. W., and Malek, M. H. Mechanomyographic amplitude and mean power frequency versus torque relationships during isokinetic and isometric muscle actions of the biceps brachii. *J. Electromyogr. Kinesiol.* 14: 555–564, 2004.

5b. Beck, T. W., Housh, T. J., Johnson, G. O., Weir, J. P., Cramer, J. T., Coburn, J. W., and Malek, M. H. Mechanomyographic and electromyographic time and frequency domain responses during submaximal to maximal isokinetic muscle actions of the biceps brachii. *Eur. J. Appl. Physiol.* 92: 352–359, 2004.

6. Bell, G. J., Petersen, S. R., Wessel, J., Bagnall, K., and Quinney, H. A. Physiological adaptations to concurrent endurance training and low velocity resistance training. *Int. J. Sports Med.* 12: 384–390, 1991.
7. Bosco, C., Cardinale, M., Colli, R., Tihanyi, J., von Duvillard, S. P., and Viru, A. The influence of whole body vibration on jumping ability. *Biol. Sport.* 15: 157–164, 1998.
8. Brown, L. E. *Isokinetics in Human Performance.* Champaign, IL: Human Kinetics, 2000.
9. Cardinale, M., and Bosco, C. The use of vibration as an exercise intervention. *Exerc. Sport Sci. Rev.* 31: 3–7, 2003.
10. Chandler, T. J., and Brown, L. E. *Conditioning for Strength and Human Performance,* 2nd edition. Baltimore: Wolters Kluwer/Lippincott Williams & Wilkins, 2013.

11. Clarkson, P. M. Oh, those aching muscles: Causes and consequences of delayed onset muscle soreness. *ACSM's Health and Fitness Journal* 1: 12–17, 1997.

12. Coburn, J. W., Housh, T. J., Cramer, J. T., Weir, J. P., Miller, J. M., Beck, T. W., Malek, M. H., and Johnson, G. O. Mechanomyographic and electromyographic responses of the vastus medialis muscle during isometric and concentric muscle actions. *J. Strength Cond. Res.* 19: 412–420, 2005.

13. Coburn, J. W., Housh, T. J., Cramer, J. T., Weir, J. P., Miller, J. M., Beck, T. W., Malek, M. H., and Johnson, G. O. Mechanomyographic time and frequency domain responses of the vastus medialis muscle during submaximal to maximal isometric and isokinetic muscle actions. *Electromyogr. Clin. Neurophysiol.* 44: 247–255, 2004.

14. Coburn, J. W., Housh, T. J., Weir, J. P., Malek, M. H., Cramer, J. T., Beck, T. W., and Johnson, G. O. Mechanomyographic responses of the vastus medialis to isometric and eccentric muscle actions. *Med. Sci. Sports Exerc.* 36: 1916–1922, 2004.

15. Cote, C., Simoneau, J., Lagasse, P., Boulay, M., Thibault, M., Marcotte, M., and Bouchard, C. Isokinetic strength training protocols: Do they induce skeletal muscle fiber hypertrophy? *Arch. Phys. Med. Rehabil.* 69: 281–285, 1988.

16. Cunnington, R., Windischberger, C., Deecke, L., and Moser, E. The preparation and execution of self-initiated and externally triggered movement: A study of event-related fMRI. *Neuroimage* 15: 373–385, 2002.

17. Duda, M. Plyometrics: A legitimate form of power training? *Phys. Sportsmed.* 16: 213–218, 1988.

18. Dudley, G. A., and Fleck, S. J. Strength and endurance training: Are they mutually exclusive? *Sports Med.* 4: 79–85, 1987.

19. Enoka, R. M. Muscle strength and its development: New perspectives. *Sports Med.* 6: 146–168, 1988.

20. Feigenbaum, M. S., and Pollock, M. L. Prescription of resistance training for health and disease. *Med. Sci. Sports Exerc.* 31: 38–45, 1999.

21. Fleck, S. J., and Kraemer, W. J. *Designing Resistance Training Programs,* 4th edition. Champaign, IL: Human Kinetics, 2014.

22. Fry, A. C., Cisar, C. T., and Housh, T. J. A comparison of anthropometric equations for estimating body density in male competitive body builders. *J. Appl. Sport Sci. Res.* 1: 61–65, 1987.

23. Gonyea, W. J. Role of exercise in inducing increases in skeletal muscle fiber number. *J. Appl. Physiol.* 48: 421–426, 1980.

24. Henneman, E., Somjen, G., and Carpenter, D. O. Functional significance of cell size in spinal motorneurons. *J. Neurophysiol.* 28: 560–580, 1965.

25. Hortobagyi, T., Katch, F. I., and LaChance, P. F. Effects of simultaneous training for strength and endurance on upper and lower body strength and running performance. *J. Sports Med.* 31: 20–30, 1991.

26. Hortobagyi, T., Scott, K., Lambert, J., Hamilton, G., and Tracy, J. Cross-education of muscle strength is greater with stimulated than voluntary contractions. *Motor Control* 3: 205–219, 1999.

27. Housh, D. J., Housh. T. J., Johnson, G. O., and Chu, W. Hypertrophic response to unilateral concentric isokinetic resistance training. *J. Appl. Physiol.* 73: 65–70, 1992.

28. Houston, M. E. Gaining weight: The scientific basis of increasing skeletal muscle mass. *Can. J. Appl. Physiol.* 24: 305–316, 1999.

29. Howard, J. D., and Enoka, R. M. Maximum bilateral contractions are modified by neurally mediated interlimb effects. *J. Appl. Physiol.* 70: 306–319, 1991.

30. Johnson, G. O., Housh, T. J., Powell, D. R., and Ansorge, C. J. A physiological comparison of female body builders and power lifters. *J. Sports Med.* 30: 361–364, 1990.

31. Komi, P. V., and Bosco, C. Utilization of stored elastic energy in leg extensor muscles by men and women. *Med. Sci. Sports* 10: 261–265, 1978.

32. Kossev, A., and Christova, P. Discharge pattern of human motor units during dynamic concentric and eccentric contractions. *Electroencephalogr. Clin. Neurophysiol.* 109: 245–255, 1998.

33. Kraemer, W. J., and Fleck, S. J. Resistance training: Exercise prescription (part 4 of 4). *Phys. Sportsmed.* 16: 69–81, 1988.

34. Kraemer, W. J., and Ratamess, N. A. Fundamentals of resistance training: Progression and exercise prescription. *Med. Sci. Sports Exerc.* 36: 674–688, 2004.

35. Kreider, R. B., Fry, A. C., and O'Toole, M. L. (eds.). *Overtraining in Sport.* Champaign, IL: Human Kinetics, 1998.

36. Kristeva, R., Cheyne, D., and Deecke, L. Neuromagnetic fields accompanying unilateral and bilateral voluntary movements: Topography and analysis of cortical sources. *Electroencephalogr. Clin. Neurophysiol.* 81: 284–298, 1991.

37. Kukulka, C. G., and Clamann, H. P. Comparison of the recruitment and discharge properties of motor units in human brachial biceps and adductor pollicis during isometric contractions. *Brain Res.* 219: 45–55, 1981.

38. Lawrence, J. H., and De Luca, C. J. Myoelectric signal versus force relationship in different human muscles. *J. Appl. Physiol.* 54: 1653–1659, 1983.

39. MacDougall, J. D. Hypertrophy or hyperplasia. In *Strength and Power in Sport,* ed. P. V. Komi. Oxford: Blackwell Scientific Publications, 1992, pp. 230–238.

40. MacDougall, J. D. Morphological changes in human skeletal muscle following strength training and immobilization. In *Human Muscle Power,* eds. N. L. Jones, N. McCartney, and A. J. McComas. Champaign, IL: Human Kinetics, 1986, pp. 269–285.

41. Moritani, T., and deVries, H. A. Neural factors vs. hypertrophy in the time course of muscle strength gain. *Am. J. Phys. Med.* 58: 115–130, 1979.

42. Munn, J., Herbert, R. D., and Gandevia, S. C. Contralateral effects of unilateral resistance training: A meta-analysis. *J. Appl. Physiol.* 96: 1861–1866, 2004.

43. Narici, M. V., Roi, G. S., Landoni, L., Minetti, A. E., and Cerretelli, P. Changes in force, cross-sectional area and neural activation during strength training and detraining of the human quadriceps. *Eur. J. Appl. Physiol.* 59: 310–319, 1989.

44. National Strength and Conditioning Association. *Position Paper on Strength Training for Female Athletes.* Lincoln, NE: NSCA, 1990.

45. Pearson, D., Faigenbaum, A., Conley, M., and Kraemer, W. J. The National Strength and Conditioning Association's Basic Guidelines for the Resistance Training of Athletes. *Strength Cond. J.* 22: 14–27, 2000.

46. Pollock, M. L., and Evans, W. J. Resistance training for health and disease: Introduction. *Med. Sci. Sports Exerc.* 31: 10–11, 1999.

47. Prevost, M. E., Nelson, A. G., and Maraj, B. K. V. The effect of two days of velocity-specific isokinetic training on torque production. *J. Strength Cond. Res.* 13: 35–39, 1999.

48. Sale, D. G. Neural adaptation to strength training. In *Strength and Power in Sport,* ed. P. V. Komi. Oxford: Blackwell Scientific Publications, 1992, pp. 249–265.

49. Sale, D. G., Jacobs, I., MacDougall, J. D., and Garner, S. Comparison of two regimens of concurrent strength and endurance training. *Med. Sci. Sports Exerc.* 22: 348–356, 1990.

50. Sinning, W. E. Body composition in athletes. In *Human Body Composition,* eds. A. F. Roche, S. B. Heymsfield, and T. G. Lohman. Champaign, IL: Human Kinetics, 1996, pp. 257–273.

51. Staron, R. S., Karapondo, D. L., Kraemer, W. J., Fry, A. C., Gordon, S. E., Falkel, J. E., Hagerman, F. C., and Hikida, R. S. Skeletal muscle adaptations during the early phase of heavy-resistance training in men and women. *J. Appl. Physiol.* 76: 1247–1255, 1994.

52. Stauber, W. T. Eccentric action of muscles: Physiology, injury, and adaptations. *Exerc. Sport Sci. Rev.* 17: 157–185, 1989.

53. Stone, M. H., O'Bryant, H., and Garhammer, J. A hypothetical model for strength training. *J. Sports Med.* 21: 342–351, 1981.

54. Torvinen, S., Kannus, P., Sievanen, H., Jarvinen, T. A. H., Pasanen, M., Kontulainen, S., Jarvinen, T. L. N., Jarvinen, M., Oja, P., and Vuori, I. Effect of a vibration exposure on muscular performance and body balance. *Clin. Physiol. Funct. Imaging* 22: 145–152, 2002.

55. U. S. Department of Health and Human Services. *Physical Activity and Health: A Report of the Surgeon General.* Atlanta: U. S. Department of Health and Human Services, Centers for Disease Control and Prevention, National Center for Chronic Disease Prevention and Health Promotion, 1996.

56. U. S. Department of Health and Human Services. *2008 Physical Activity Guidelines for Americans.* Atlanta: U.S. Dept. Of Health and Human Services. www.health.gov/paguidelines, 2008.

57. Yue, G., and Cole, K. J. Strength increases from the motor program: Comparison of training with maximal voluntary and imagined muscle contractions. *J. Neurophysiol.* 67: 1114–1123, 1992.

58. Zhou, S. Chronic neural adaptations to unilateral exercise: Mechanisms of cross education. *Exerc. Sport Sci. Rev.* 28: 177–184, 2000

CHAPTER 11 lab A

Assessment of Isometric Hand Grip Strength

BACKGROUND

Isometric hand grip strength is an important component of physical fitness and provides a simple method for characterizing overall body strength.[1,2] The performance of many manual labor activities, such as yard and garden work and lifting and carrying large objects, depends on a certain degree of hand grip strength. Thus, the purpose of this lab is to describe the procedures for measuring isometric hand grip strength with a hand grip dynamometer.

TERMS & ABBREVIATIONS

- ☐ hand grip dynamometer = an instrument that measures isometric hand grip strength, which provides a simple method for characterizing overall body strength
- ☐ isometric strength = tension production by a muscle without movement at the joint or shortening of the muscle fibers
- ☐ percentile rank = in this lab, a score between 10 and 90% that shows how the subject performed relative to others in the age group. A percentile ranking of 70, for example, indicates that the subject's grip strength is higher than 70% of the others in the age group and lower than 30% of the others in the age group.

PROCEDURES

The isometric hand grip strength test can be performed with a variety of dynamometers (photo 11.1).

1. Prior to beginning the test, adjust the length of the handle on the hand grip dynamometer so that it feels comfortable in the hand. For individuals with very small hands, the handle of the dynamometer should be shortened, while for those with very large hands, the handle should be lengthened.[1]
2. Have the subject hold the hand grip dynamometer in the right hand with the palm facing up and the elbow at approximately 90° (photo 11.2). When

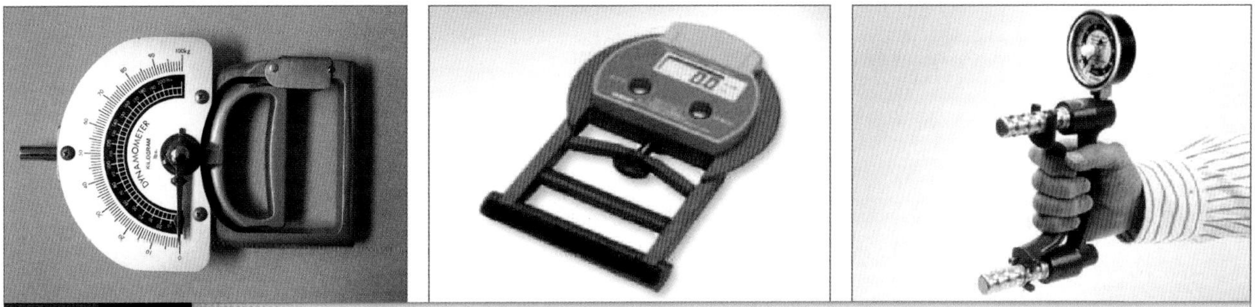

photo 11.1

Three different hand grip dynamometers.

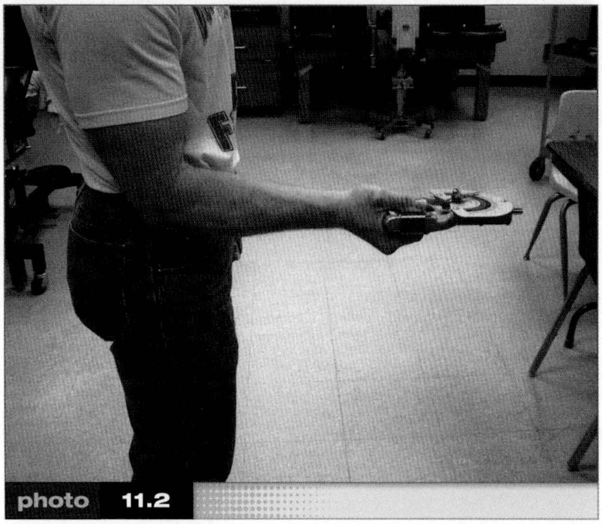

photo 11.2

The correct elbow position for performing the hand grip dynamometer strength test.

ready, the subject should squeeze the dynamometer maximally for three seconds. Read the force value (kg) from the dynamometer and record it on Worksheet 11.1. Perform the strength test two more times with the right hand, separating the trials by two minutes of rest.

3. Repeat the procedures described in step 2 for the left hand.
4. Add the highest strength value (kg) for the right hand to that from the left hand and record the value on Worksheet 11.1. Divide the sum by body weight in kg and record this value on Worksheet 11.1.
5. Percentile rank norms by age and gender are provided in Tables L11.1 through L11.4. Compare the sum of right and left hand grip strength to the values in Tables L11.1 and L11.2 based on age and gender. Compare the sum of right and left hand grip strength divided by body weight to the values in Tables L11.3 and L11.4 based on age and gender.

table L11.1 Percentile ranks for sum of grip strengths (kg, right plus left) for males.

PERCENTILE RANK	AGE (yrs)															
	10	11	12	13	14	15	16	17	18	19	20-24	25-29	30-34	35-39	40-44	45-49	50-59
90	34	42	52	69	89	96	106	111	117	118	122	123	124	123	123	116	110
80	30	37	47	60	80	90	99	105	106	113	115	115	115	115	115	108	102
70	26	34	41	53	72	84	95	99	101	109	110	110	110	109	108	104	96
60	24	32	38	48	66	80	91	93	98	104	105	107	106	106	103	99	93
50	22	29	34	44	61	76	87	89	96	101	102	103	102	102	100	95	89
40	20	26	31	42	58	73	84	85	93	98	99	100	98	98	97	91	85
30	18	23	30	39	54	69	78	81	90	94	94	95	95	93	93	82	81
20	15	21	27	34	49	64	74	76	86	90	89	90	90	88	87	81	75
10	11	16	23	28	39	55	68	70	81	84	80	81	82	79	81	75	66

Adapted from Montoye, H. J., and Lamphiear, D. E. Grip and arm strength in males and females, age 10 to 69. *Research Quarterly for Exercise and Sport,* Vol. 48, pp. 109–120, 1977. Reprinted with permission of the publisher, Taylor & Francis Ltd., tandfonline.com.

Percentile ranks for sum of grip strengths (kg, right plus left) for females. **table L11.2**

PERCENTILE RANK	AGE (yrs)															
	10	11	12	13	14	15	16	17	18	19	20-24	25-29	30-34	35-39	40-44	45-49	50-59
90	30	37	44	49	65	60	58	61	59	63	61	67	65	66	64	64	57
80	25	33	40	44	50	54	53	54	55	59	57	62	60	59	58	57	52
70	22	30	36	41	48	49	49	50	52	54	53	57	57	55	54	53	48
60	20	27	33	38	44	45	48	47	49	50	50	53	53	53	51	52	45
50	18	25	31	36	41	43	43	44	46	48	48	49	49	51	49	49	43
40	17	23	28	34	39	41	41	42	43	46	45	48	47	49	47	47	40
30	15	20	26	32	36	38	39	39	39	42	42	46	44	46	43	44	38
20	14	17	22	30	32	36	36	36	36	39	38	43	41	43	40	40	34
10	10	12	18	26	27	31	33	31	31	36	34	37	36	36	36	34	30

Adapted from Montoye, H. J., and Lamphiear, D. E. Grip and arm strength in males and females, age 10 to 69. *Research Quarterly for Exercise and Sport,* Vol. 48, pp. 109–120, 1977. Reprinted with permission of the publisher, Taylor & Francis Ltd., tandfonline.com.

Percentile ranks for ratio of sum of grip strengths to body weight (kg/kg body weight) for males. **table L11.3**

PERCENTILE RANK	AGE (yrs)														
	10	11	12	13	14	15	16	17	18	19	20-24	25-29	30-34	35-39	40-49	50-59
90	0.89	1.04	1.10	1.20	1.40	1.45	1.56	1.62	1.62	1.75	1.73	1.72	1.64	1.62	1.54	1.39
80	0.83	0.94	0.97	1.13	1.28	1.36	1.49	1.48	1.50	1.54	1.59	1.54	1.52	1.51	1.41	1.30
70	0.76	0.85	0.93	1.03	1.23	1.29	1.43	1.44	1.47	1.44	1.53	1.47	1.45	1.42	1.34	1.22
60	0.69	0.80	0.86	0.98	1.15	1.25	1.39	1.39	1.44	1.36	1.45	1.40	1.39	1.35	1.28	1.19
50	0.65	0.77	0.80	0.93	1.09	1.22	1.30	1.35	1.37	1.33	1.39	1.35	1.33	1.28	1.24	1.14
40	0.62	0.71	0.74	0.86	1.02	1.17	1.19	1.28	1.33	1.29	1.32	1.28	1.29	1.23	1.19	1.10
30	0.52	0.66	0.70	0.80	0.96	1.14	1.14	1.21	1.31	1.24	1.26	1.20	1.24	1.17	1.14	1.03
20	0.45	0.58	0.66	0.77	0.90	1.06	1.09	1.16	1.22	1.17	1.18	1.12	1.18	1.11	1.07	0.98
10	0.38	0.48	0.61	0.65	0.81	0.95	0.98	1.01	1.16	1.12	1.08	1.01	1.10	1.02	0.99	0.89

Adapted from Montoye, H. J., and Lamphiear, D. E. Grip and arm strength in males and females, age 10 to 69. *Research Quarterly for Exercise and Sport,* Vol. 48, pp. 109–120, 1977. Reprinted with permission of the publisher, Taylor & Francis Ltd., tandfonline.com.

table L11.4 Percentile ranks for ratio of sum of grip strengths to body weight (kg/kg body weight) for females.

PERCENTILE RANK	AGE (yrs)															
	10	11	12	13	14	15	16	17	18	19	20-24	25-29	30-34	35-39	40-49	50-59
90	0.71	0.91	0.92	0.96	1.08	1.04	0.98	1.12	1.02	1.10	1.04	1.12	1.05	1.07	1.02	0.90
80	0.65	0.80	0.80	0.86	0.96	0.92	0.94	1.02	0.95	1.04	0.97	1.02	1.00	1.00	0.93	0.83
70	0.62	0.72	0.75	0.81	0.86	0.89	0.84	0.96	0.90	0.94	0.91	0.97	0.94	0.93	0.87	0.78
60	0.57	0.68	0.72	0.79	0.81	0.84	0.79	0.89	0.82	0.85	0.86	0.91	0.89	0.87	0.81	0.71
50	0.54	0.64	0.66	0.73	0.76	0.79	0.76	0.83	0.78	0.80	0.81	0.86	0.83	0.84	0.77	0.68
40	0.50	0.57	0.61	0.68	0.71	0.76	0.73	0.78	0.72	0.77	0.77	0.82	0.78	0.80	0.73	0.63
30	0.46	0.53	0.57	0.65	0.67	0.69	0.71	0.71	0.69	0.74	0.72	0.75	0.72	0.75	0.69	0.59
20	0.42	0.45	0.54	0.63	0.65	0.65	0.65	0.66	0.65	0.69	0.68	0.68	0.66	0.69	0.63	0.52
10	0.32	0.33	0.47	0.52	0.58	0.57	0.57	0.52	0.58	0.64	0.61	0.61	0.60	0.60	0.54	0.48

Adapted from Montoye, H. J., and Lamphiear, D. E. Grip and arm strength in males and females, age 10 to 69. *Research Quarterly for Exercise and Sport,* Vol. 48, pp. 109–120, 1977. Reprinted with permission of the publisher, Taylor & Francis Ltd., tandfonline.com.

SAMPLE CALCULATIONS

Gender: Male

Age: 21 years

Body weight: 75 kg

	Trial 1 (kg)	Trial 2 (kg)	Trial 3 (kg)	Max of three trials (kg)
Right hand	50	52	53	53
Left hand	51	50	52	52

Sum of right and left = 105 kg

Approximate percentile rank = 60 (Table L11.1)

Sum of right and left (kg)		Body weight (kg)		Grip strength ratio (kg/kg body weight)
105	/	75	=	1.40

Approximate percentile rank = 51 (Table L11.3)

ISOMETRIC HAND GRIP STRENGTH FORM worksheet 11.1

NAME ______________________________ DATE ______________________________

AGE ______________ BODY WEIGHT ______________ GENDER ______________

	Trial 1 (kg)	Trial 2 (kg)	Trial 3 (kg)	Max of three trials (kg)
Right hand	________	________	________	________
Left hand	________	________	________	________
			Sum of right plus left	________

Percentile rank (see Tables L11.1 and L11.2) = ______________

Sum of right and left (kg)		Body weight (kg)		Grip strength ratio (kg/kg body weight)
______________	/	______________	=	______________

Percentile rank (see Tables L11.3 and L11.4) = ______________

worksheet 11.2 EXTENSION ACTIVITIES

NAME ______________________________ DATE ______________

1. Using your own data, report the sum of your right and left hand grip strength scores (kg) and percentile ranking.

2. Using your own data, report the ratio of the sum of your grip strengths to body weight (kg/kg body weight) and percentile ranking.

3. Describe three activities that you regularly perform that depend on possessing a high degree of hand grip strength.

4. Describe three sporting activities that, in part, require a high degree of hand grip strength.

5. Report the approximate percentile rankings for a 26-year-old, 70-kg (body weight) male with a sum of grip strengths (kg, right plus left) of 103 kg.

   a. percentile ranking for sum of right and left hand grip strength scores (kg) = ______________

   b. percentile ranking for the ratio of the sum of grip strengths to body weight (kg/kg body weight) = ______________

6. Report the approximate percentile rankings for a 21-year-old, 60-kg (body weight) female with a sum of grip strengths (kg, right plus left) of 50 kg.

   a. percentile ranking for sum of right and left hand grip strength scores (kg) = ______________

   b. percentile ranking for the ratio of the sum of grip strengths to body weight (kg/kg body weight) = ______________

EXTENSION QUESTIONS

1. What are some common mistakes that may occur in administering this lab?
2. Identify possible sources of error in this lab.
3. Assess the practicality of using this lab in the field.
4. Research the reliability and/or validity of this lab using online resources, journal articles, and other credible sources.

REFERENCES

1. Montoye, H. J., and Faulkner, J. A. Determination of the optimum setting of an adjustable grip dynamometer. *Res. Q. Exerc. Sport* 35: 29–36, 1964.
2. Montoye, H. J., and Lamphiear, D. E. Grip and arm strength in males and females, age 10 to 69. *Res. Q. Exerc. Sport* 48: 109–120, 1977.

lab B Anthropometric Somatotyping Determinations of Body Build Characteristics

BACKGROUND

Body build characteristics describe an individual's physique.[1,4,5,6] Unlike body composition measurements that determine the relative proportions of fat and fat-free tissue (see the lab for Chapter 15, covering skinfold estimates), body build assessments describe the distribution of body weight on the skeleton.

Athletes in various sports, as well as non-athletes, tend to have certain unique body build characteristics. For example, basketball players tend to be tall and thin, while football linemen are usually much heavier with a lower center of gravity. Wrestlers and gymnasts, however, tend to be lean and muscular.

In addition to contributing to successful sports performance, body build characteristics can have health-related implications.[6] For example, the endomorphic rating from the somatotyping procedures in this laboratory has been associated with the risk of developing a number of diseases including coronary heart disease, obesity, and diabetes.[6] Thus, there are both performance and health-related reasons for assessing body build characteristics.

Somatotyping

Somatotyping characterizes body build in terms of the predominance of each of three components: endomorphy, mesomorphy, and ectomorphy. There are a number of ways to perform somatotyping, including the use of photographs (photoscopic method), anthropometry (using height, weight, skinfolds, circumferences, and diameters), or a combination of the two. In this laboratory, the anthropometric method is used to determine the "decimalized anthropometric somatotype."[5,6]

Endomorphy. *Endomorphy,* the first component of the somatotyping classification, rates the individual in terms of fatness or roundness characteristics.

Mesomorphy. *Mesomorphy,* the second somatotype component, describes the individual's muscularity or musculoskeletal development.

Ectomorphy. The third component of the somatotyping classification, *ectomorphy,* rates the individual in terms of linearity of body build based on the relationship between height and weight.

After the separate endomorphy, mesomorphy, and ectomorphy components are calculated, the individual's somatotype characteristics are defined by a three-number combination of the components. That is, an individual who has an endomorphic rating of 2, mesomorphic rating of 3.5, and ectomorphic rating of 5.5 has a somatotype rating of 2-3.5-5.5 (read as 2, 3.5, 5.5). The first (endomorphy), second (mesomorphy), and third (ectomorphy) components are always listed in the same order. There is no upper limit to the rating scale for each component, but values of 2–2.5 are considered low, 3–5 moderate, 5.5–7 high, and 7.5 or greater very high.[5] Thus, an individual with a somatotype rating of 2-3.5-5.5 has a body build characterized by a low level of fatness (endomorphic rating of 2), moderate muscularity (mesomorphic rating of 3.5), and a high degree of linearity (ectomorphic rating of 5.5). This somatotype rating is typical of a basketball player at the center or forward position.[6] On the other hand, a male body builder may have a somatotype rating of 2-8-1, which reflects a low level of fatness (endomorphic rating of 2), extreme muscularity (mesomorphic rating of 8), and a very low linearity of build (ectomorphic rating of 1).[6] Table L11.5 lists examples of somatotype ratings for non-athletes and athletes in various sports.

table L11.5 Examples of somatotype ratings for non-athletes and athletes in various sports.

FEMALES	ENDOMORPHY	MESOMORPHY	ECTOMORPHY
1. College students[6]	4.2	3.7	2.6
2. Non-athletes[3]	3.57	3.35	2.90
3. Junior Olympic swimmers[14]	3.6	3.4	3.3
4. Professional soccer players[4]	3.07	3.55	2.43
5. Olympic canoers[9]	2.8	4.0	2.9
6. Olympic gymnasts[9]	2.2	3.9	3.4
7. Olympic rowers[9]	3.0	3.9	2.8
8. Olympic swimmers[9]	3.2	3.8	3.1
9. Olympic track & field athletes[9]	2.3	3.4	3.5
10. College basketball players[6]	3.3	3.5	2.8
11. College volleyball players[6]	3.1	3.4	3.2
12. South Australian athletes[17]	3.8	4.2	2.6
13. Body builders[6]	2.5	5.1	2.5
MALES	**ENDOMORPHY**	**MESOMORPHY**	**ECTOMORPHY**
1. College students[6]	3.1	5.1	2.7
2. Physical Education majors[7]	2.9	5.4	2.4
3. Young adults 18–29 years[6]	4.1	4.4	2.7
4. Junior Olympic swimmers[14]	2.8	4.5	3.3
5. High school wrestlers[8]	2.77	4.49	3.15
6. South Australian track & field athletes[16]	2.0	4.7	3.4
7. International soccer players[6]	2.5	5.0	2.5
8. Olympic canoers[6]	1.8	5.4	2.6
9. Olympic gymnasts[6]	1.4	5.8	2.5
10. Olympic rowers[6]	2.3	5.0	2.7
11. Olympic swimmers[6]	2.1	5.1	2.8
12. Olympic marathoners[6]	1.4	4.4	3.4
13. Olympic sprinters[6]	1.7	5.2	2.8
14. Olympic basketball players[6]	2.0	4.2	3.5
15. Olympic volleyball players[6]	2.3	4.4	3.4
16. Body builders[6]	1.6	8.7	1.2
17. College football players[6]	4.6	6.3	1.4

TERMS & ABBREVIATIONS

- ectomorphy = the third component of the somatotyping classification, a rating of the individual in terms of linearity of body build based on the relationship between height and weight
- endomorphy = the first component of the somatotyping classification, a rating of the individual in terms of fatness or roundness characteristics
- mesomorphy = the second somatotype component, a rating of the individual in terms of the individual's muscularity or musculoskeletal development
- ponderal index = height in cm / cube root of body weight in kg – height/weight ratio, estimated either from a nomogram or by use of a calculator
- somatochart = a two-dimensional graph on which the X and Y coordinates are calculated from the three somatotype components (endomorphy, mesomorphy, and ectomorphy)

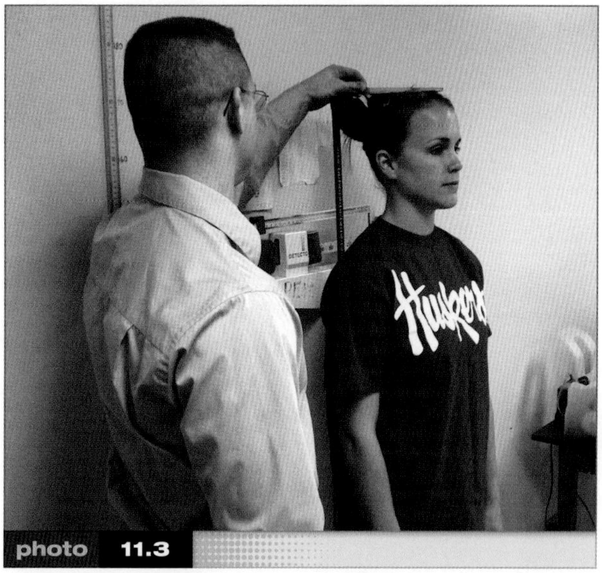

photo 11.3

Height measurement.

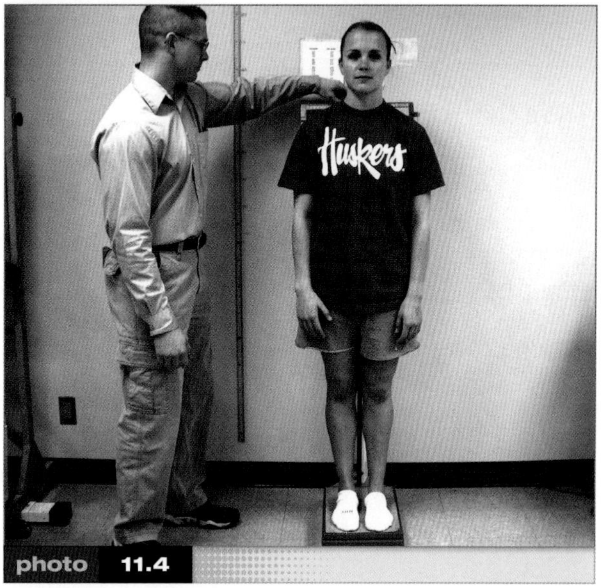

photo 11.4

Body weight measurement.

PROCEDURES

To calculate the three components of the somatotype rating, 10 anthropometric measurements need to be taken: height, body weight, four skinfolds, two diameters, and two circumferences. The following list includes all of the measurements needed to determine an individual's somatotype rating.

1. Height in centimeters without shoes (inches × 2.54 = cm; see photo 11.3)
2. Body weight in kilograms without shoes (pounds / 2.2046 = kg; see photo 11.4)
3. Skinfolds in millimeters (inches × 25.4 = mm)

Procedures to measure skinfolds:

a. Measure and mark the anatomical site with a marker (see sites below).
b. Take all measurements on the right side of the body.
c. Grasp the skinfold firmly with the thumb and finger and pull away from the body.
d. Hold the caliper perpendicular to the skinfold. The caliper should be approximately 1 cm away from the thumb and forefinger so that the pressure of the caliper will not be affected.
e. Read the skinfold size approximately one to two seconds after the caliper thumb grip has been released.
f. Take three measurements per site at least 15 seconds apart to allow the skinfold site to return to normal. Record the skinfold values on Worksheet 11.3. If the repeated measurements vary by more than 1 mm, more measurements should be taken. Use the mean of the recorded measurements that agree within 1 mm.

Skinfold Sites[6,10,12]

Triceps: a vertical fold on the posterior midline of the upper arm, halfway between the acromion and olecranon processes; the elbow should be extended and relaxed (see photo 11.5).

Suprailium: a diagonal fold above the crest of the ilium at the spot where an imaginary line would come down from the anterior axillary line (see photo 11.6).

Subscapular: a diagonal fold adjacent to the inferior angle of the scapula (see photo 11.7).

Medial calf: a vertical fold on the medial side of the leg, at the level of maximum circumference of the calf (see photo 11.8).

4. Procedures to measure diameters:
   a. Palpate for bony landmarks of the right limbs (see sites below).
   b. Hold anthropometer so that the tips of the index fingers are adjacent to the tips of the blades of the anthropometer.
   c. Position the blades of the anthropometer with sufficient pressure to ensure they are measuring bony landmarks.
   d. Take three measurements per site and use the mean of repeated recordings that agree within 0.5 cm. Record the diameter values on Worksheet 11.3.

Diameter Sites[6,15]

Elbow: the distance between the medial and lateral epicondyles of the humerus (see photo 11.9).

Knee: the distance between the medial and lateral epicondyles of the femur (see photo 11.10).

5. Procedures to measure circumferences:
   a. Identify the landmarks of the right limbs (see sites below).
   b. Place the tape perpendicular to the long axis of the limb.
   c. Hold the tape tightly around the limb, but do not compress the underlying tissue.
   d. Take three measurements per site and use the mean of repeated recordings that agree within 0.5 cm. Record the circumference values on Worksheet 11.3.

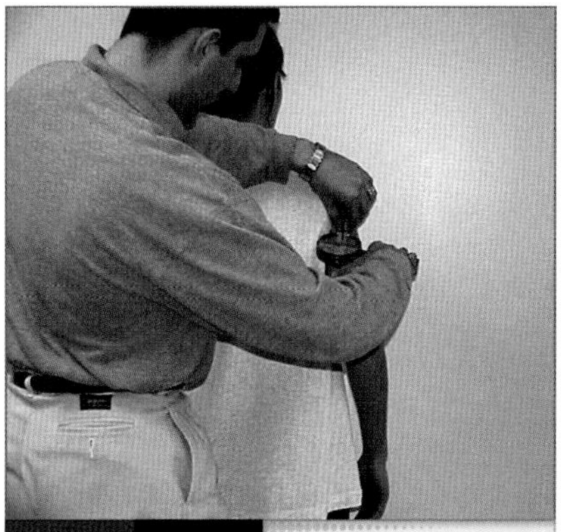

photo 11.5

Triceps skinfold measurement.

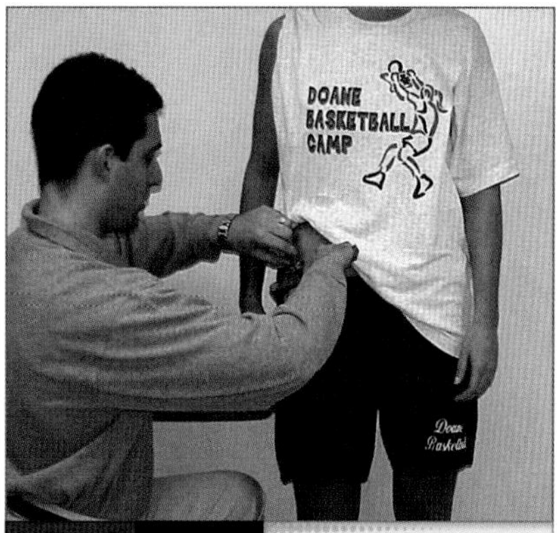

photo 11.6

Suprailium skinfold measurement.

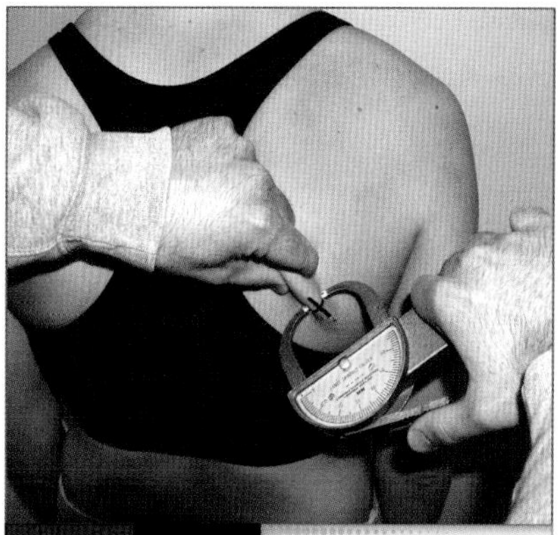

photo 11.7

Subscapular skinfold measurement.

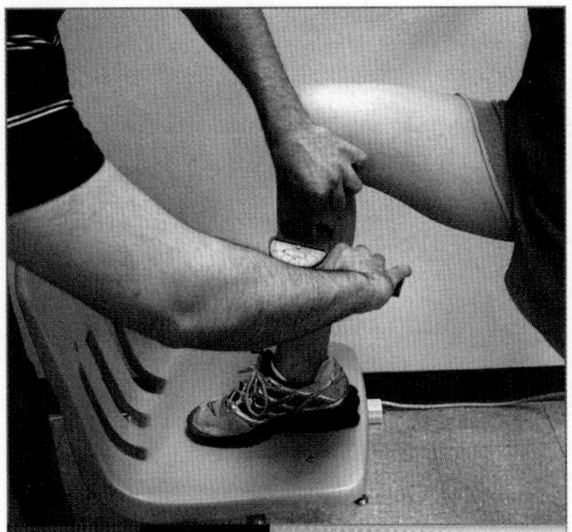

photo 11.8

Medial calf skinfold measurement.

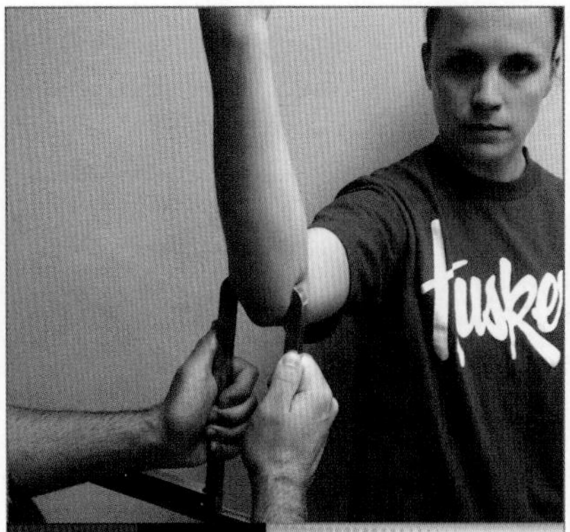

photo 11.9

Elbow diameter measurement.

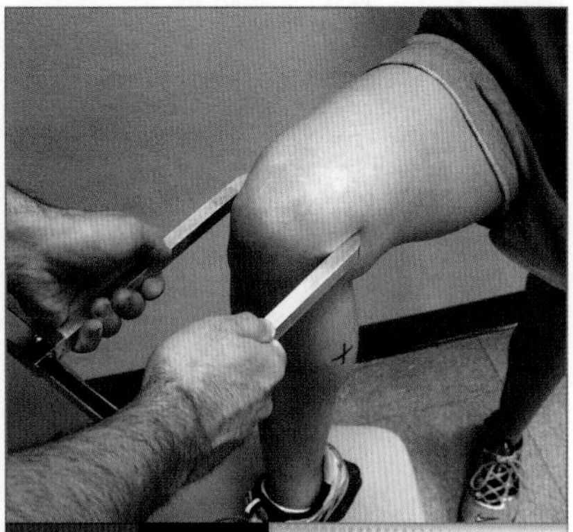

photo 11.10

Knee diameter measurement.

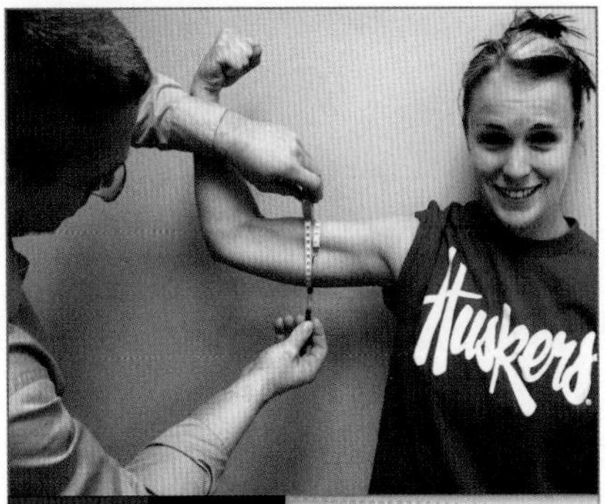

photo 11.11

Flexed arm circumference measurement.

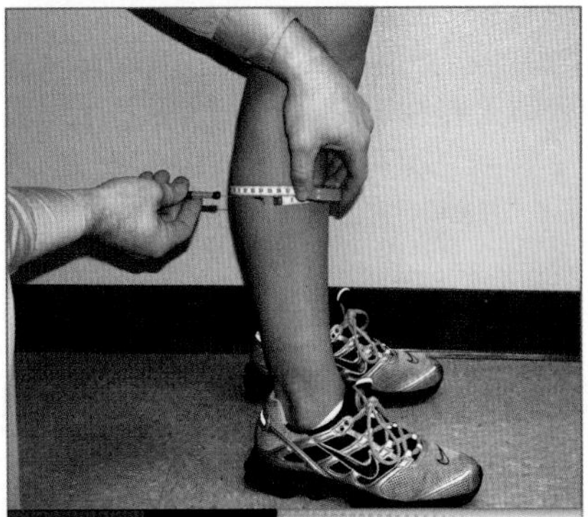

photo 11.12

Calf circumference measurement.

Circumference Sites[2,6]

Flexed arm: the maximal distance around the flexed biceps and triceps (see photo 11.11).

Calf: the maximal distance around the calf with the subject standing and feet slightly apart (see photo 11.12).

Equations

The following equations are used to calculate the endomorphic, mesomorphic, and ectomorphic ratings.[5,6]

Endomorphy

Height-corrected endomorphic rating

$$= -0.7182 + 0.1451\,((\text{sum of triceps, suprailium, and subscapular skinfolds}) \times (170.18 / \text{height in cm}))$$
$$- 0.00068\,(\text{sum of 3 skinfolds} \times (170.18 / \text{height in cm}))^2$$
$$+ 0.0000014\,(\text{sum of 3 skinfolds} \times (170.18 / \text{height in cm}))^3$$

Mesomorphy

Mesomorphic rating

$$= [(0.858 \times \text{elbow diameter}) \times (0.601 \times \text{knee diameter})$$
$$+ (0.188 \times (\text{flexed arm circumference} - \text{triceps skinfold} / 10))$$
$$+ (0.161 \times (\text{calf circumference} - \text{medial calf skinfold} / 10))]$$
$$- (0.131 \times \text{height}) + 4.50$$

Ectomorphy

The ectomorphic rating is based on the height–body weight ratio or ponderal index.[3,11]

ponderal index = height in cm/cube root of body weight in kg

The ponderal index can be estimated from the nomogram in Figure L11.1. The cube root of body weight can be determined by use of a calculator with a y^x key. To get the cube root, enter body weight, press y^x, enter 0.333, and press "equals."[5]

Based on the ponderal index, the ectomorphic rating is determined as follows:

If the ponderal index is greater than or equal to 40.75, then the ectomorphic rating = (0.732 × ponderal index) – 28.58.

Nomogram for determining the ponderal index (height in cm/cube root of weight in kg). figure L11.1

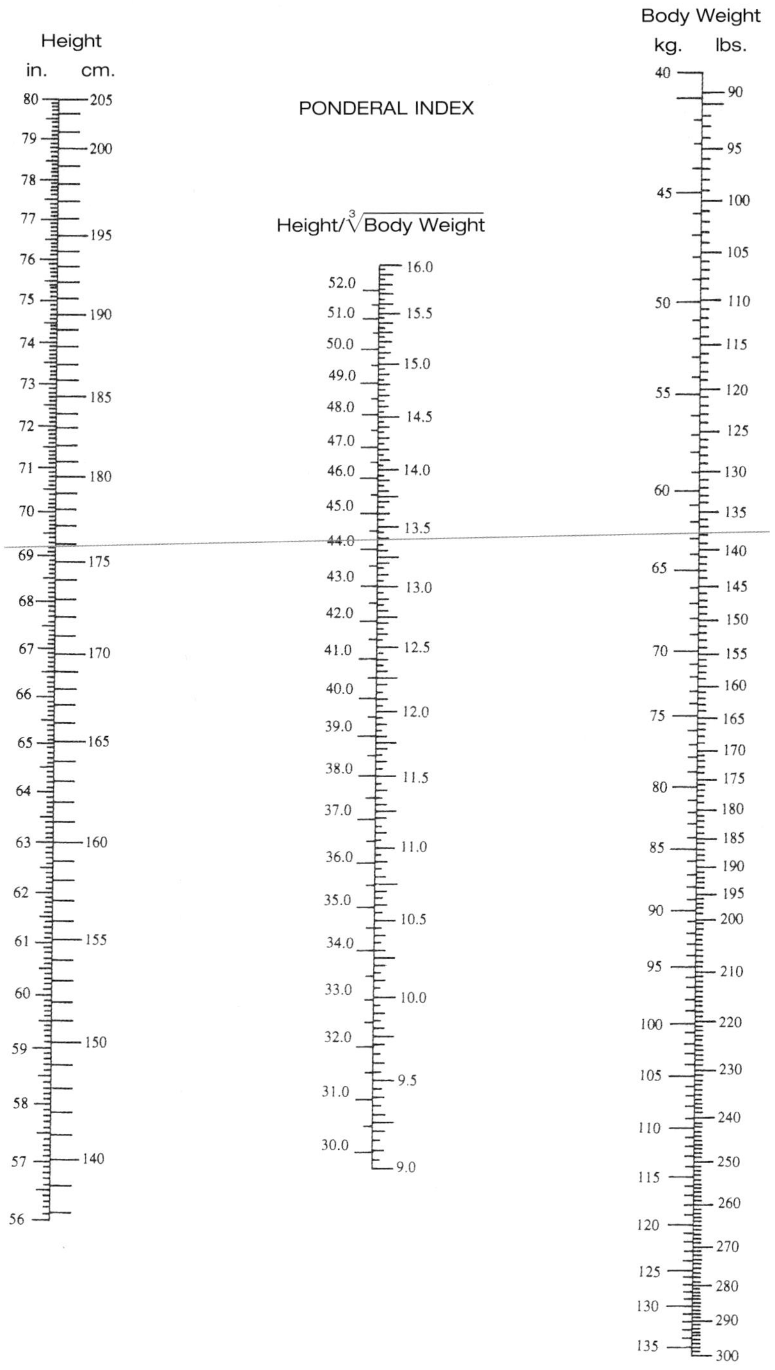

To estimate the ponderal index, lay a ruler between the height on the left column and body weight on the right column. Read the ponderal index value where the ruler crosses the center column. For example, the subject in the sample calculation had a height of 176.0 cm, body weight of 62.8 kg, and a ponderal index of 44.33.

If the ponderal index is less than 40.75 and greater than 38.25, then the ectomorphic rating = (0.463 × ponderal index) – 17.63.

If the ponderal index is equal to or less than 38.25, then the ectomorphic rating = 0.1.

SAMPLE CALCULATIONS

Height: 176.0 cm

Body weight: 62.8 kg

Triceps skinfold: 11.0 mm

Suprailium skinfold: 14.0 mm

Subscapular skinfold: 9.0 mm

Medial calf skinfold: 15.0 mm

Elbow diameter: 6.5 cm

Knee diameter: 9.0 cm

Flexed arm circumference: 27.85 cm

Calf circumference: 35.75 cm

Height-corrected endomorphic rating = – 0.7182 + 0.1451 ((11 + 14 + 9) × (170.18 / 176)) – 0.00068 $(32.9)^2$ + 0.0000014 $(32.9)^3$ = 3.36

Mesomorphic rating = [(0.858 × 6.5) + (0.601 × 9.0) + (0.188 × (27.85 – 1.1)) + (0.161 × (35.75 – 1.5))] – (0.131 × 176) + 4.50 = 3.03

Ectomorphic rating

ponderal index = $176.0/\sqrt[3]{62.8}$ = 176.0 / 3.97 = 44.33

Thus, ectomorphic rating = 0.732 × 44.33 – 28.58 = 3.87

Somatotyping rating = 3.36 – 3.03 – 3.87

Somatochart

Somatotype ratings can be visualized and compared with characteristics of various populations by plotting them on a somatochart (Figures L11.2–L11.4). While the somatotype includes three components (endomorphy, mesomorphy, and ectomorphy), the somatochart plots the somatotype on a two-dimensional graph. To do so, X and Y coordinates are calculated from the three components as follows:[5,13]

X = ectomorphic rating – endomorphic rating

Y = 2 × mesomorphic rating – (endomorphic + ectomorphic ratings)

The X and Y coordinates can then be plotted on the somatochart. For example, Figure L11.2 is the somatochart for the individual with a somatotype of 3.36 (endomorphy)-3.03 (mesomorphy)-3.87 (ectomorphy).

X = 3.87 – 3.36 = 0.51

Y = 2 × 3.03 – (3.36 + 3.87) = –1.17

Figures L11.3 and L11.4 include the somatotypes of various male and female athletes as well as the non-athletes in Table L11.5. Figures L11.5 and L11.6 are blank somatocharts.

figure L11.2 Somatochart for somatotype ratings of 3.36-3.03-3.87 (X coordinate = 0.51 and Y coordinate = −1.17).

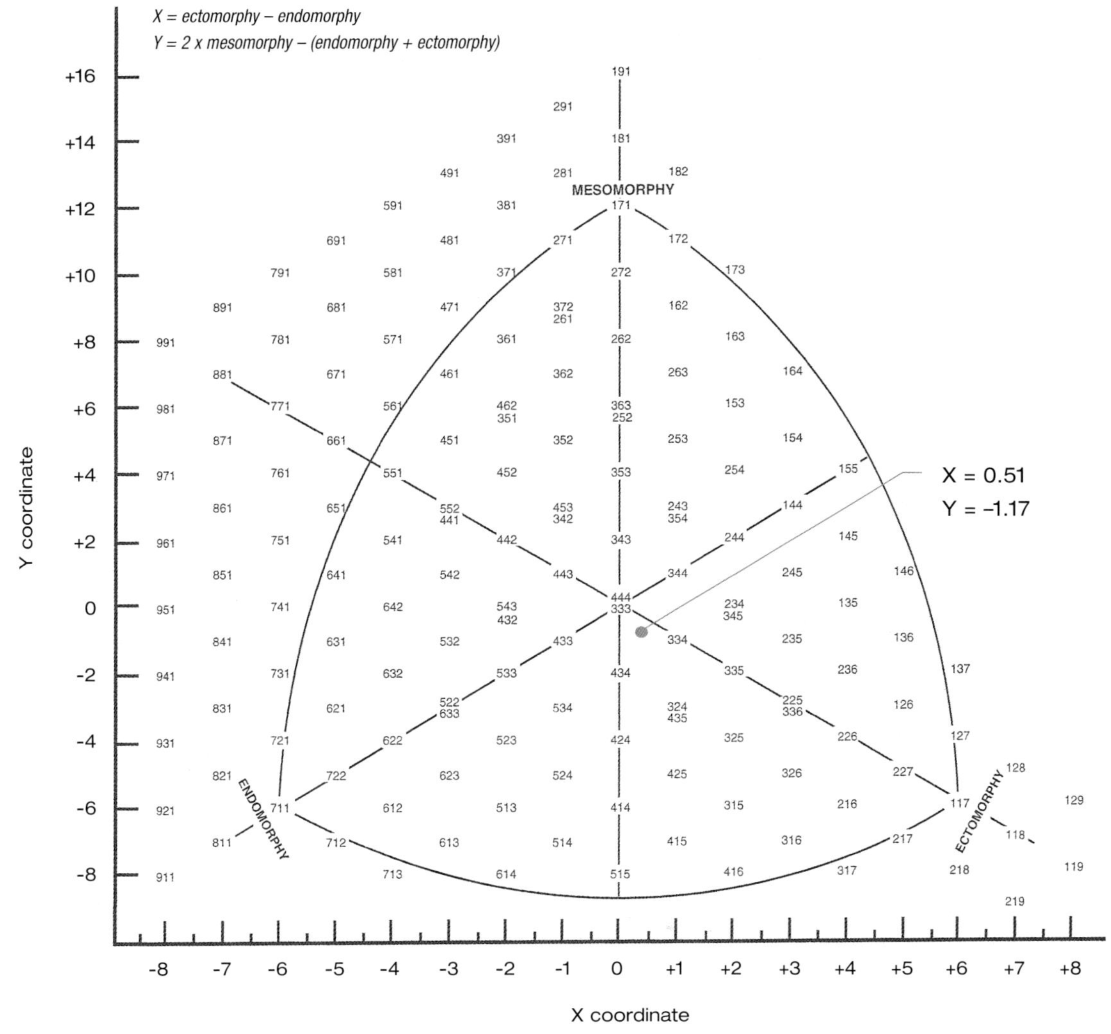

figure L11.3 Somatochart examples of male athletes and non-athletes (see Table L11.5).

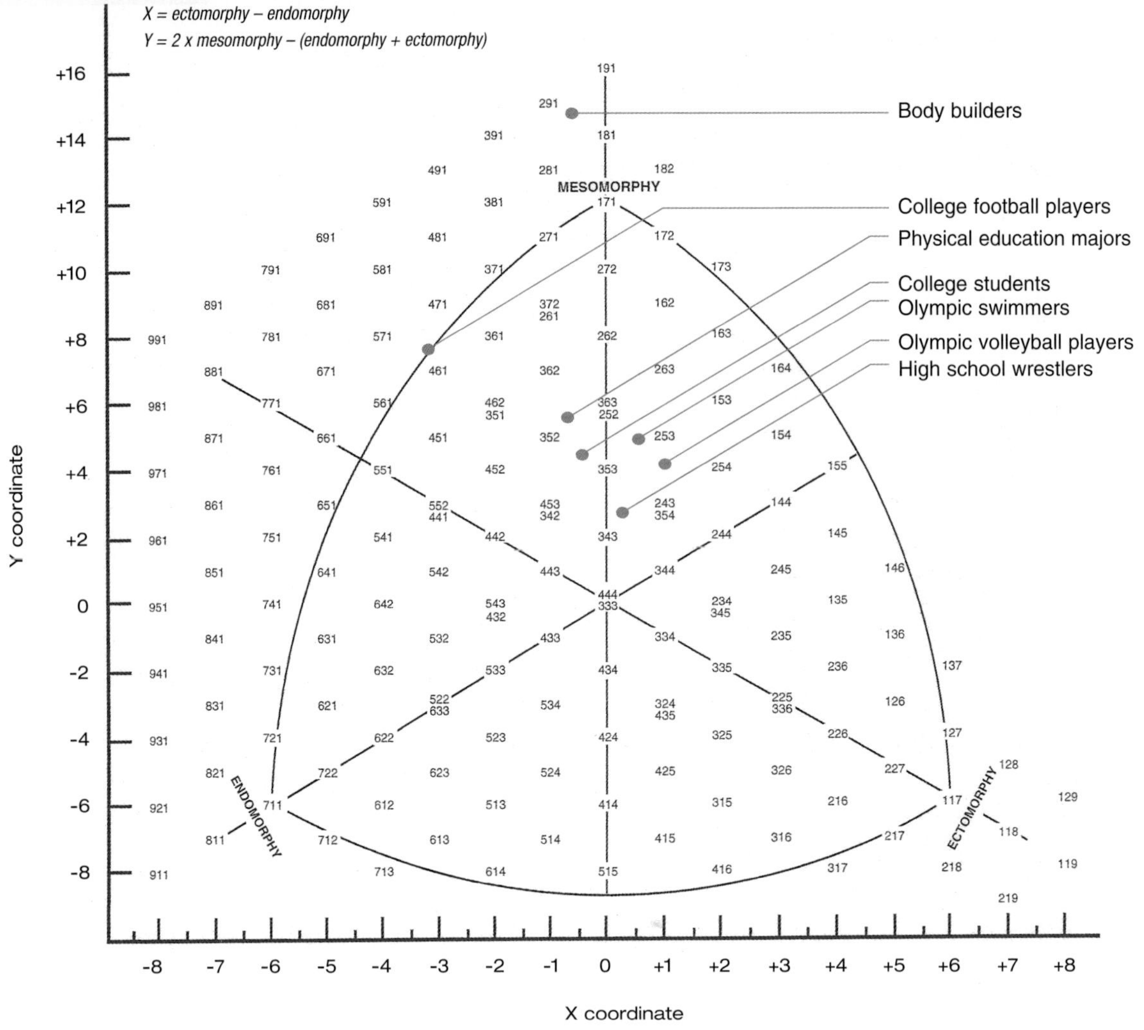

Somatochart examples of female athletes and non-athletes (see Table L11.5). **figure L11.4**

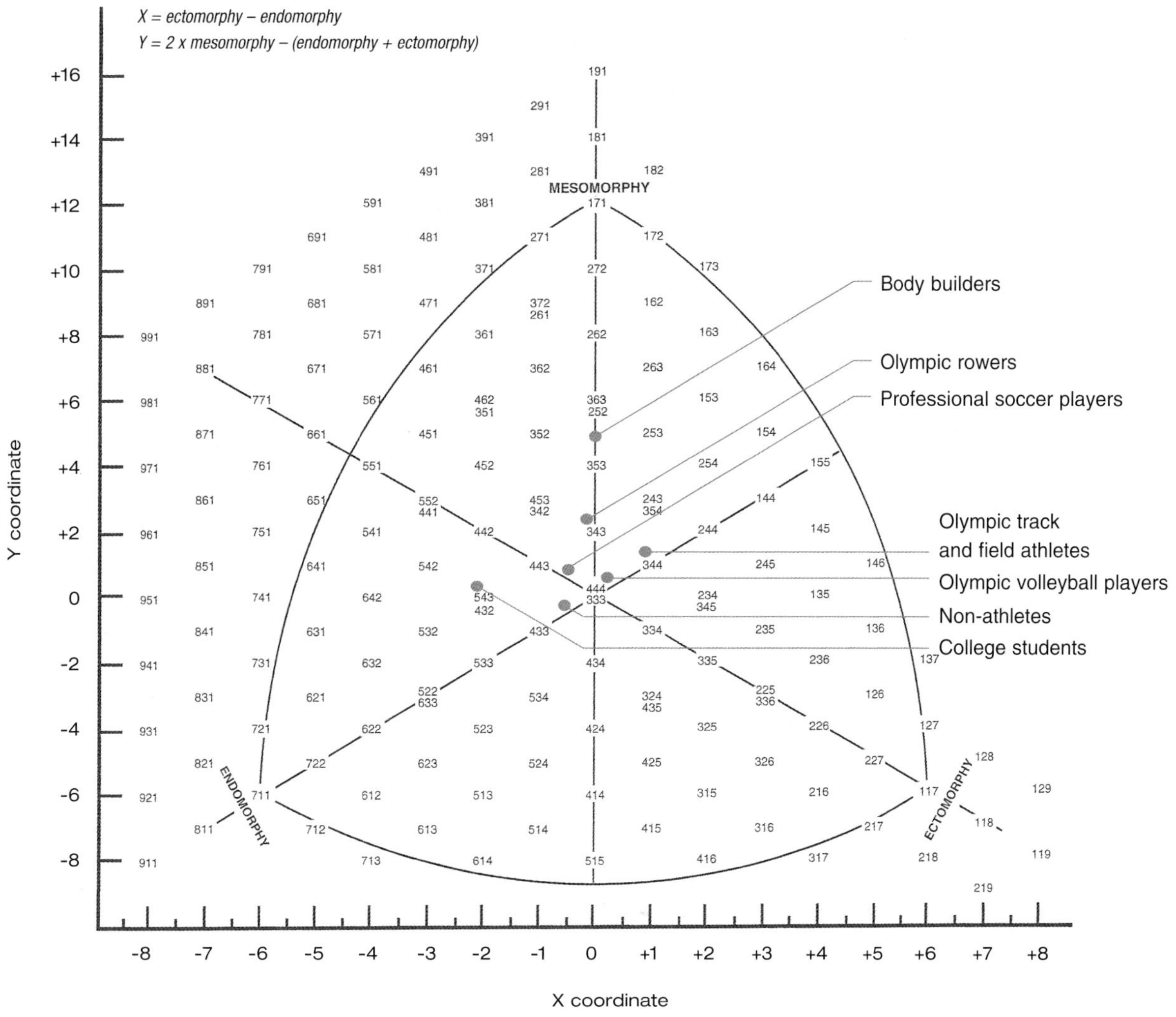

worksheet 11.3 SOMATOTYPING

NAME ______________________________ DATE ______________

Height: ________________ cm

Height-correction = 170.18 / height in cm: ________________

Body weight: ________________ kg

Trial	1	2	3	Mean
Triceps skinfold (mm)	______	______	______	______
Suprailium skinfold (mm)	______	______	______	______
Subscapular skinfold (mm)	______	______	______	______
Sum of triceps, suprailium, and subscapular skinfolds (mm) =				______
Medial calf skinfold (mm)	______	______	______	______
Elbow diameter (cm)	______	______	______	______
Knee diameter (cm)	______	______	______	______
Flexed arm circumference (cm)	______	______	______	______
Flexed arm circumference (cm) minus triceps skinfold (mm) / 10 =				______
Calf circumference	______	______	______	______
Calf circumference (cm) minus medial calf skinfold (mm) / 10 =				______

Endomorphic rating: ________________

Mesomorphic rating: ________________

Ectomorphic rating: ________________

Somatotype rating: ________________ – ________________ – ________________

X coordinate: ________________

Y coordinate: ________________

Somatochart: Use Figure L11.5.

Blank somatochart. **figure L11.5**

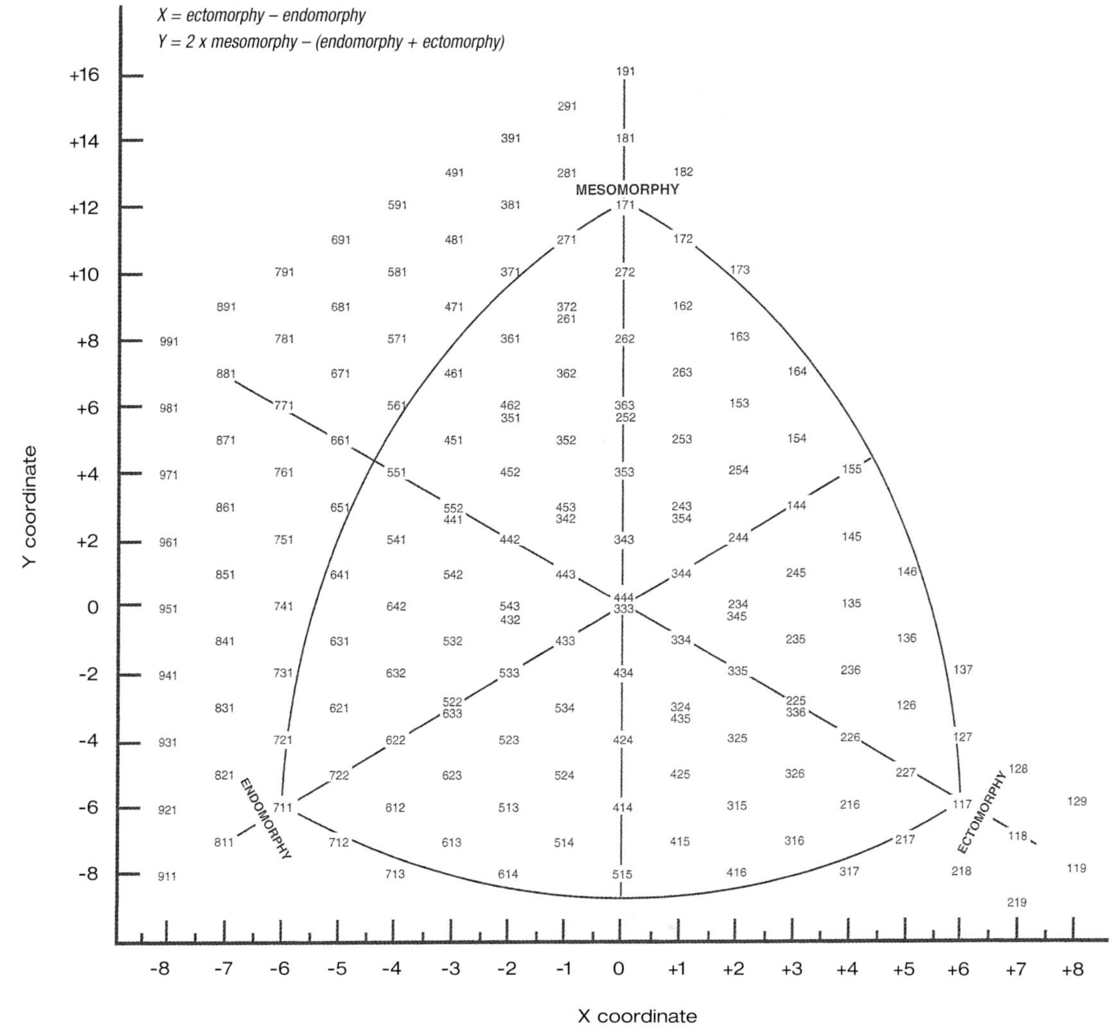

worksheet 11.4 EXTENSION ACTIVITIES

NAME ____________________ DATE ____________________

1. Given the following data, calculate (a) endomorphic rating, (b) mesomorphic rating, (c) ectomorphic rating, (d) X coordinate, and (e) Y coordinate.

Data:

Height: 172.0 cm

Body weight: 68.5 kg

Triceps skinfold: 17.0 mm

Suprailium skinfold: 16.0 mm

Subscapular skinfold: 13.0 mm

Medial calf skinfold: 14.0 mm

Elbow diameter: 7.5 cm

Knee diameter: 9.0 cm

Flexed arm circumference: 29.6 cm

Calf circumference: 37.9 cm

a. Endomorphic rating: ____________

b. Mesomorphic rating: ____________

c. Ectomorphic rating: ____________

d. X coordinate: ____________

e. Y coordinate: ____________

2. Using the somatotype ratings in Table L11.5 (a) calculate the X and Y coordinates for female Junior Olympic swimmers, female Olympic canoers, and male Olympic marathoners; and (b) plot these three sets of X and Y coordinates on the blank somatochart in Figure L11.6.

	X	Y
Female Junior Olympic swimmers	____________	____________
Female Olympic canoers	____________	____________
Male Olympic marathoners	____________	____________

Blank somatochart. **figure L11.6**

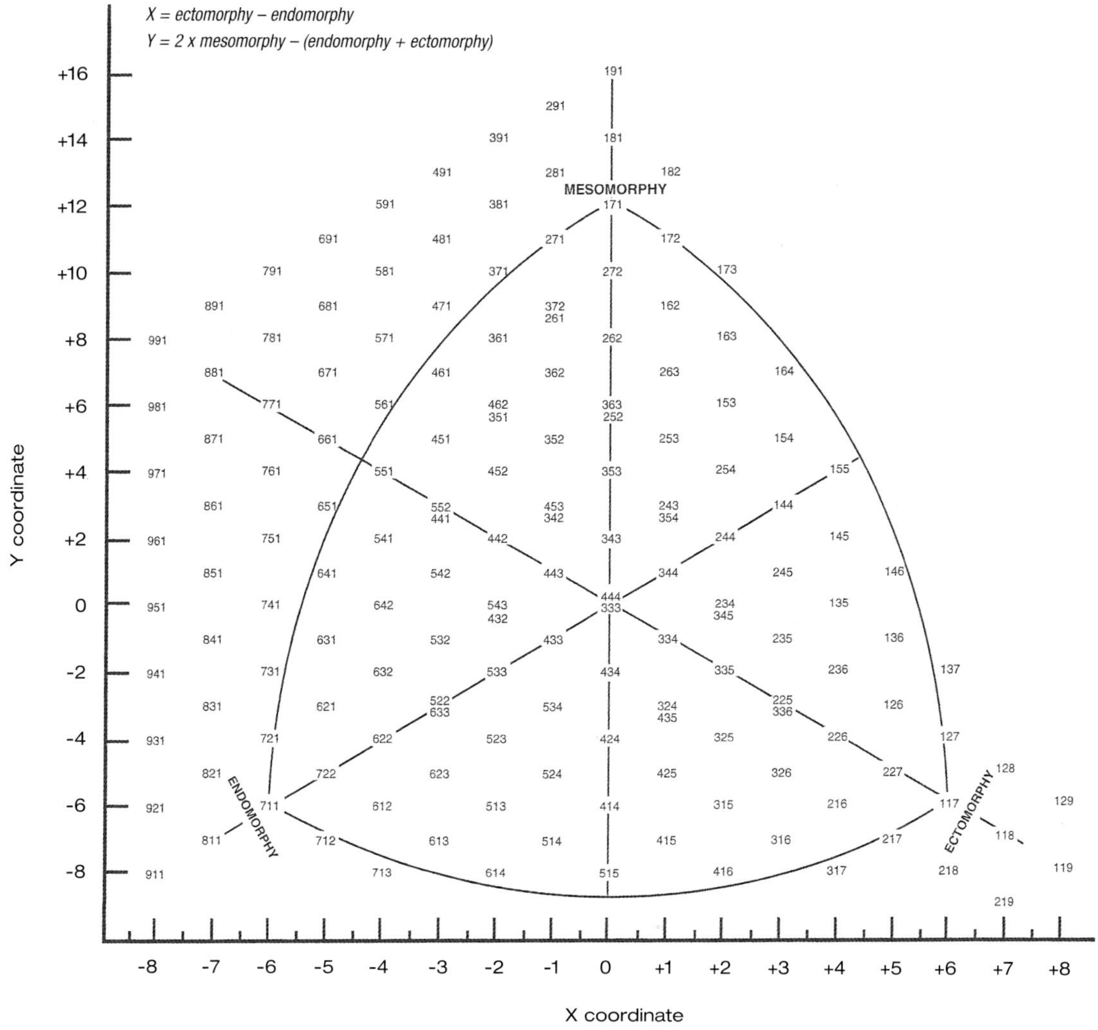

EXTENSION QUESTIONS

1. What are some common mistakes that may occur in administering this lab?

2. Identify possible sources of error in this lab.

3. Assess the practicality of using this lab in the field.

4. Research the reliability and/or validity of this lab using online resources, journal articles, and other credible sources.

REFERENCES

1. Behnke, A. R., and Wilmore, J. H. *Evaluation and Regulation of Body Build and Composition.* Englewood Cliffs, NJ: Prentice Hall, 1974.
2. Callaway, C. W., Chumlea, W. C., Bouchard, C., Himes, J. H., Lohman, T. G., Martin, A. D., Mitchell, C. D., Mueller, W. H., Roche, A. F., and Seefeldt, V. D. Circumferences. In *Anthropometric Standardization Reference Manual,* eds. T. G. Lohman, A. F. Roche, and R. Martorell. Champaign, IL: Human Kinetics, 1988, pp. 39–54.
3. Can, F., Yilmaz, I., and Erden, Z. Morphological characteristics and performance variables of women soccer players. *J. Strength Cond. Res.* 18: 480–485, 2004.
4. Carter, J. E. L. *The Heath–Carter Somatotype Method.* San Diego, CA: San Diego University Press, 1980.
5. Carter, J. E. L. Somatotyping. In *Anthropometrica,* eds. K. Norton and T. Olds. Sidney, Australia: University of New South Wales Press, 1996, pp. 147–170.
6. Carter, J. E. L., and Heath, B. H. *Somatotyping—Development and Applications.* Cambridge, MA: Cambridge University Press, 1990.
7. Carter, J. E. L., Stepnicka, J., and Clarys, J. P. Somatotypes of male physical education majors in four countries. *Res. Q.* 44: 361–371, 1973.
8. Cisar, C. J., Johnson, G. O., Fry, A. C., Housh, T. J., Hughes, R. A., Ryan, A. J., and Thorland, W. G. Preseason body composition, build, and strength as predictors of high school wrestling success. *J. Appl. Sport Sci. Res.* 1: 66–70, 1987.
9. Cressie, N. A. C., Withers, R. T., and Craig, N. P. The statistical analysis of somatotype data. *Year. of Phys. Anthropol.* 29: 197–208, 1986.
10. Harrison, G. G., Buskirk, E. R., Carter, J. E. L., Johnston, F. E., Lohman, T. G., Pollock, M. L., Roche, A. F., and Wilmore, J. Skinfold thicknesses and measurement techniques. In *Anthropometric Standardization Reference Manual,* eds. T. G. Lohman, A. F. Roche, and R. Martorell. Champaign, IL: Human Kinetics, 1988, pp. 55–70.
11. Housh, T. J., Thorland, W. G., Johnson, G. O., Tharp, G. D., and Cisar, C. J. Anthropometric and body build variables as discriminators of event participation in elite adolescent male track and field athletes. *J. Sports Sci.* 2: 3–11, 1984.
12. Jackson, A. S., and Pollock, M. L. Practical assessment of body composition. *Phys. Sportsmed.* 13: 76–90, 1985.
13. Ross, W. D., and Wilson, B. D. A somatotype dispersion index. *Res. Q.* 44: 372–374, 1973.
14. Thorland, W. G., Johnson, G. O., Housh, T. J., and Refsell, M. J. Anthropometric characteristics of elite adolescent competitive swimmers. *Hum. Biol.* 55: 735–748, 1983.
15. Wilmore, J. H., Frisancho, R. A., Gordon, C. G., Himes, J. H., Martin, A. D., Martorell, R., and Seefeldt, V. D. Body breadth equipment and measurement techniques. In *Anthropometric Standardization Reference Manual,* eds. T. G. Lohman, A. F. Roche, and R. Martorell. Champaign, IL: Human Kinetics, 1988, pp. 27–38.
16. Withers, R. T., Craig, N. P., and Norton, K. I. Somatotypes of South Australian male athletes. *Hum. Biol.* 58: 337–356, 1986.
17. Withers, R. T., Whittingham, N. O., Norton, K. I., and Dutton, M. Somatotypes of South Australian female games players. *Hum. Biol.* 59: 575–584, 1987.

12 Flexibility

As a result of reading this chapter you will:

Be able to define flexibility.

Know the factors that can limit the range of motion at a joint.

Know the differences between static and dynamic flexibility.

Understand the theory and implications of static, ballistic, and proprioceptive neuromuscular facilitation stretching methods.

key concepts

ballistic stretching
contract–relax (CR)
contract–relax with agonist-contraction (CRAC)
dynamic flexibility
flexibility
proprioceptive neuromuscular facilitation (PNF)
static flexibility
static stretching
stretch reflex

Flexibility, put simply, is the range of motion at a joint (as in the hip joint) or series of joints (as when the spinal column is involved). Flexibility is specific to a given joint or combination of joints. An individual can have some joints that are unusually flexible, some that are inflexible, and some of average flexibility. Therefore, no single test can adequately represent overall body flexibility; tests are specific to the joint (see **Chapter 12 Labs A and B** for the sit-and-reach test to measure the flexibility in the lower back and hamstring muscles and the shoulder elevation and trunk extension flexibility tests of the shoulder joints and lower back).

The need for flexibility in specific joints varies with the athletic endeavor. For example, a hurdler must have exceptional hip flexion and extension flexibility. In competitive swimming, shoulder and ankle flexibility can be decisive factors, and a diver who cannot execute a deep pike position will never achieve outstanding success.

For non-athletes, flexibility contributes to efficient movement in walking and running. The maintenance of good joint mobility also prevents, or to a large extent relieves, the aches and pains that grow more common with increasing age.

PHYSIOLOGY OF FLEXIBILITY

What Sets the Limits of Flexibility

flexibility

For some joints the bony structure sets a very definite limit on range of motion. For example, extension at the elbow and knee joints is limited in this fashion. These mechanical factors cannot be greatly modified.

In other joints such as the ankle or hip, the limitation of range of motion is imposed by soft tissues, including (1) muscle; (2) connective tissue including the fascial sheaths, tendons, ligaments, and joint capsules; and (3) the skin.

If you stretch a resting muscle passively (no contraction), the greater the length, the greater the force you need to hold the stretch. This resistance to stretch does not lie in the contractile elements of the muscle, but is due to the connective tissue sheaths associated with the muscle as well as the sarcolemma of the muscle fiber. Thus, as we pursue flexibility, we are concerned primarily with the connective tissue components of muscle tissue.

Physical Properties Important to Stretching Theory

static stretching
ballistic stretching

The time required to stretch connective tissue a given amount varies inversely with the force applied. That is, a low-force stretching method requires more time to produce a given elongation than does a higher-force method. The proportion of elongation that remains after stretching, however, is greater for the low-force, long-duration stretch. Low-force, long-duration stretching is consistent with **static stretching** methods. On the other hand, **ballistic stretching** represents a relatively high-force method. The high-force stretching methods tend to produce more structural weakening than the slow, low-force methods.

www

Types of Stretching
www.bath.ac.uk/masrjb/Stretch/stretching_4.html

Furthermore, the amount of structural weakening produced by a given amount of tissue elongation varies inversely with the temperature. This emphasizes the importance of using warm-up procedures before stretching. Unfortunately, many coaches and athletes have been misled into using static stretching as a warm-up. Athletes and others should be advised to "break a sweat" by slow jogging, brisk walking, or other mild exercise before attempting any stretching procedures. Otherwise, the very procedure designed to prevent muscular problems may itself become a source of problems. The ACSM[1] has recommended that for individuals engaged in a general fitness program, flexibility exercises can be performed after cardiorespiratory or resistance exercise.

Static Versus Dynamic Flexibility

The fact that an individual can flex and extend at a joint through a wide range of motion does not mean the person necessarily can use that same joint to move the limb quickly with little resistance to the movement. Range of motion is only one factor. How easily the limb can be moved in the middle of the range of motion, where the speed is necessarily greatest, is quite another factor.

We should therefore consider two separate components of flexibility: (1) **static flexibility,** which is what we ordinarily measure as range of motion, and (2) **dynamic flexibility,** which reflects joint stiffness and resistance to limb movement. Dynamic flexibility may be of greater importance in physical performance than is the ability to achieve an extreme degree of flexion or extension at a joint.[14,16]

- static flexibility
- dynamic flexibility

The primary physical factor that contributes to joint stiffness, and therefore limits dynamic flexibility, is lack of elasticity and plasticity of the joint and associated muscles.

Stretch Reflexes and Flexibility

A muscle that is stretched with a jerky motion responds with a contraction (**stretch reflex**) whose amount and rate vary directly with the amount and rate of the movement that causes the stretch. This is the result of the myotatic reflex that originates in the muscle spindle (Chapter 4). On the other hand, a firm, steady, static stretch invokes the inverse myotatic reflex, which brings about inhibition not only of the muscle whose tendon organ was stretched but also of the entire functional group of muscles involved.

- stretch reflex

Some therapists have suggested the use of tension in the agonist—either before or when stretching the antagonist—to take advantage of the inhibition brought about by reciprocal inhibition, the neuromuscular function that serves to turn off one of a pair of muscles when its opponent is activated in reciprocating type movements. However, for most subjects the lowest levels of innervation during passive stretching were attained by the static stretching technique.[20] Attempts at implementing the reciprocal inhibition principle are not as effective in reducing activation as the static method.

METHODS FOR IMPROVING RANGE OF MOTION

Static Versus Ballistic Stretching

Typically, ballistic stretching used to improve flexibility involves bobbing, bouncing, or jerky movements in which one body segment is put in movement by active contraction of a muscle group and the momentum is then arrested by the antagonists at the end of the range of motion. Thus, the antagonists are stretched by the dynamic movements of the agonists (Figure 12.1).

WWW

Stretching and Flexibility

www.exrx.net/ExInfo/Stretching.html

Static stretching, by contrast, consists of held stretches. Static stretching methods are in many cases derived from Hatha Yoga, and both depend on the same physiological principles. The differences, however, are significant, so the term "static stretching" was coined to distinguish the methods. The most important differences are:

1. Static stretching refers to stretches performed for physical and physiological purposes, whereas Yoga is a system of meditation and mental concentration often pursued for both physical and spiritual purposes.

figure 12.1 Examples of ballistic stretching methods.

1. **Trunk lifter.**
   a. Hands behind neck.
   b. Raise head and chest vigorously.
   c. Partner holds feet.

2. **Leg lifter.**
   a. Arms down at side.
   b. Raise both legs off floor and return vigorously.

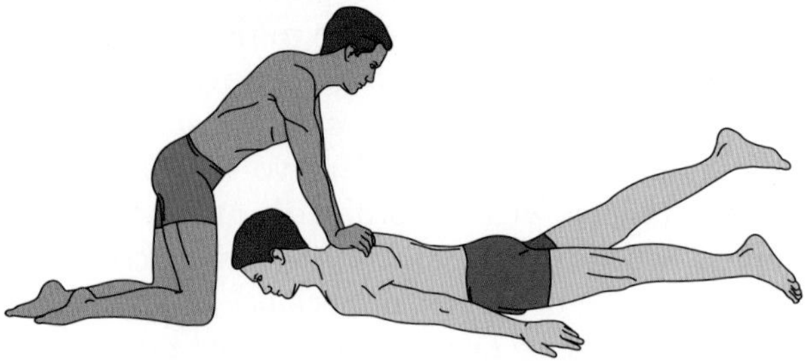

3. **Trunk bender.**
   a. Legs apart and straight.
   b. Hands behind neck.
   c. Bend trunk forward and downward in a bouncing fashion.
   d. Keep back straight.

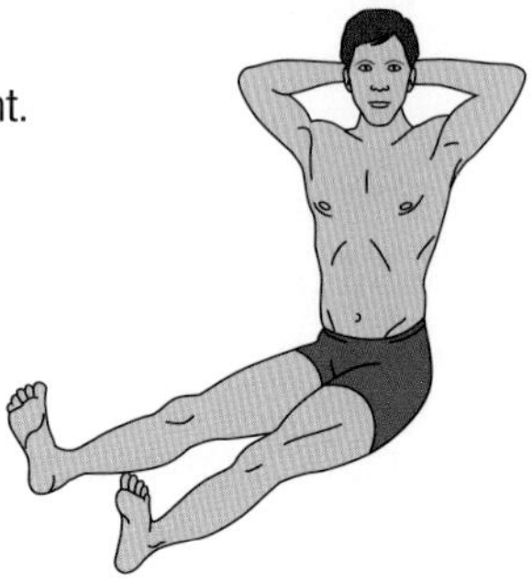

4. **Upper back stretcher.**
   a. Legs crossed, sitting position.
   b. Try to touch head to floor.
   c. Use vigorous bouncing motion.

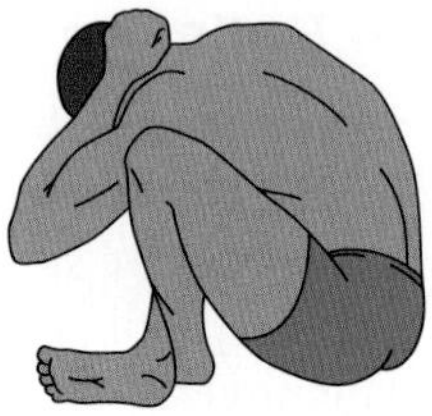

5. **Trunk rotator.**
   a. Arms extended laterally.
   b. Twist to left and then to right.

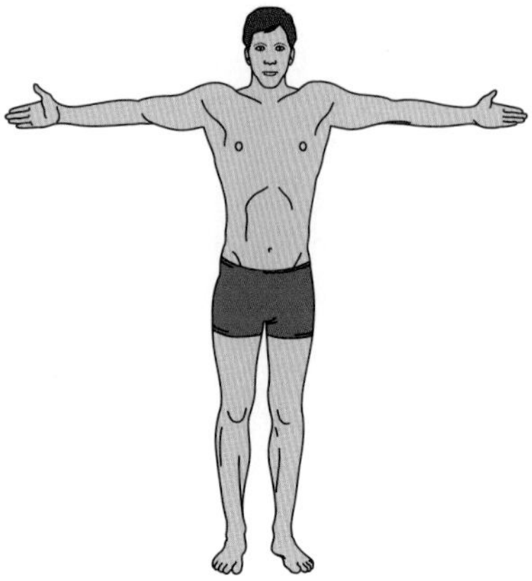

6. **Gastrocnemius stretcher.**
   a. Stand on raised surface on balls of feet.
   b. Lower weight and return rapidly.
   c. Use partner to balance if necessary.

7. **Single leg raiser.**
   a. Front leaning rest position.
   b. Keep feet in extended position.
   c. Raise one leg at time, alternately.

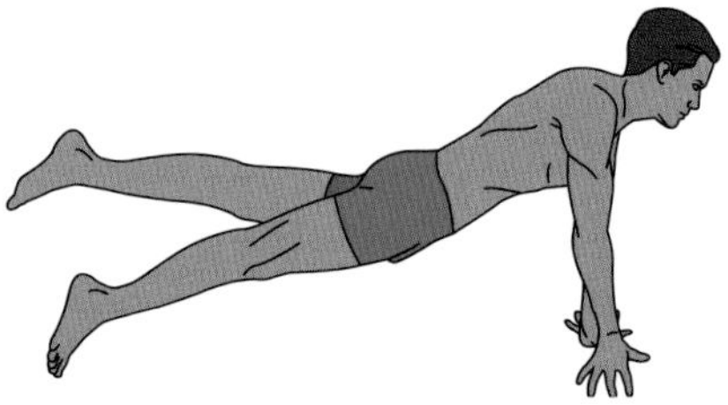

8. **Arm and leg lifter.**
   a. Supine position, arms and legs extended.
   b. Whip arms and legs up and down alternately.
   c. Right arm and left leg come up simultaneously and vice versa.

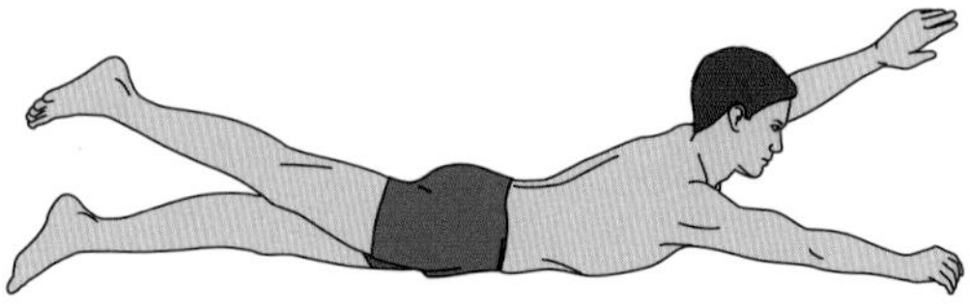

2. Static stretching is based on neurophysiological principles with better health and performance as the goals, whereas Yoga is based primarily on both physical and spiritual principles.

3. Yogic stretching is directed largely to the joints and musculature of the trunk, whereas static stretching is equally concerned with the limb muscles.

The static stretching method involves holding a static position (very little or no movement) for 10 to 60 seconds, during which the muscles and connective tissues are stretched to the point of feeling tightness or slight discomfort (Figure 12.2).[1]

Both static and ballistic stretching methods can increase static flexibility. It is important to note, however, that static stretching before exercise does not prevent muscular soreness.[17] Furthermore, increases in flexibility gained by stretching exercises can persist for eight weeks or more after stretching is discontinued.

Proprioceptive Neuromuscular Facilitation (PNF)

Proprioceptive neuromuscular facilitation (PNF) provides a basis for techniques aimed at improving muscle compliance during stretching exercises by stretching a muscle immediately after a contraction.[1,3] Several variations of PNF techniques are used by athletes and non-athletes for maintaining or increasing flexibility as well as in clinical settings for restoring the range of motion following injury. Probably the most common PNF procedures involve contract–relax and contract–relax with agonist-contraction stretching techniques.[7,8] The **contract–relax** (CR) technique involves isometrically contracting the lengthened muscle, then relaxing and further passively lengthening the muscle (Figure 12.3). The **contract–relax with agonist-contraction** (CRAC) technique is identical to CR except that during the final stretching phase the muscle opposite the one stretched is concentrically contracted.[7,8]

- proprioceptive neuromuscular facilitation (PNF)
- contract–relax
- contract–relax with agonist-contraction

Theoretically, contracting the stretched (antagonist) or opposite (agonist) muscles should facilitate autogenic and reciprocal inhibition, respectively.[7] Thus, it should be possible to increase the length of the stretched muscle because of the inhibition to contraction, and the inhibitory influences may add up, as utilized in the CRAC technique.[7]

There is conflicting evidence regarding the effectiveness of PNF techniques compared to static or ballistic stretching. Some studies have found PNF methods to be more effective than static or ballistic stretching, while others have not.[7,8,14,15] In a review, however, Etnyre and Lee[7] stated, "Based upon applications and experimental procedures among the various comparative investigations, PNF methods are more efficient than static or ballistic stretching techniques." This conclusion was based largely on their findings that "of the 10 comparative studies which equated the amount of time stretching, nine found the PNF methods produced a greater range of motion than static or ballistic stretching methods, which suggests that the PNF methods should be considered generally more effective and more efficient." It should also be noted, however, that Etnyre and Lee[7] went on to say, "the problem of which stretching method is most effective is still not clearly resolved. Also, the effectiveness of each method on muscle groups other than the hamstring and lower back muscles has not been adequately addressed."

WWW

PNF Stretching

www.sport-fitness-advisor.com/pnfstretching.html

Although evidence supports the effectiveness of PNF techniques, further research is necessary before a definitive recommendation can be made regarding the use of static stretching or PNF.

figure 12.2 Examples of static stretching methods.

1. **Upper trunk stretcher.**
   a. Keep pelvis on floor.
   b. Extend arms.

2. **Lower trunk stretcher.**
   a. Grasp ankles from behind and pull.
   b. Hold head up.

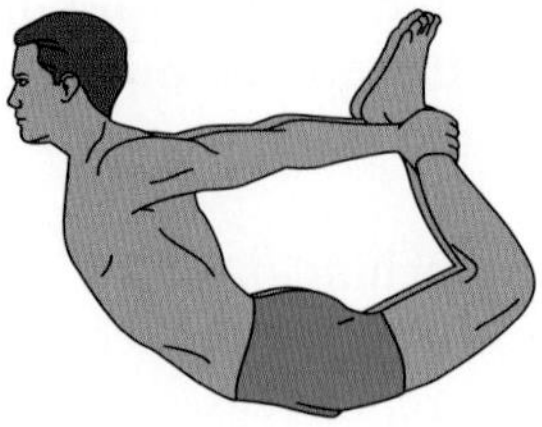

3. **Lower back stretcher.**
   a. Legs extended, toes pointed.
   b. Grasp outer borders of feet and pull head downward.

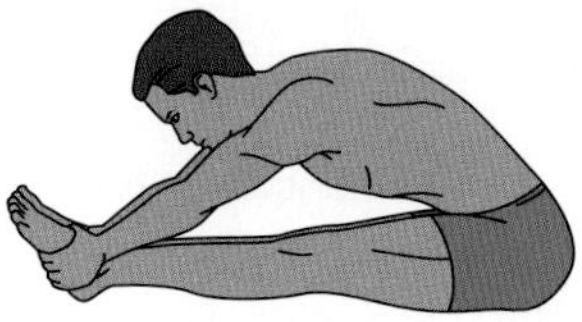

4. **Upper back stretcher.**
   a. Raise legs up and over head.
   b. Rest extended toes on floor.
   c. Leave hands and arms flat on floor.

5. **Gastrocnemius stretcher.**
   a. Place feet 3 to 4 feet from wall.
   b. Keep body straight.
   c. Lean on wall.
   d. Keep feet parallel and heels on floor.

6. **Toe pointer.**
   a. Sit on feet, toes and ankles stretched backward.
   b. Raise knees from floor slightly.
   c. Balance weight with both hands on floor just behind hips.

7. **Shoulder stretcher.**
   a. Bring right hand to upper back from above.
   b. Bring left hand to upper back from below and hook fingers of the two hands.
   c. Repeat on other side.

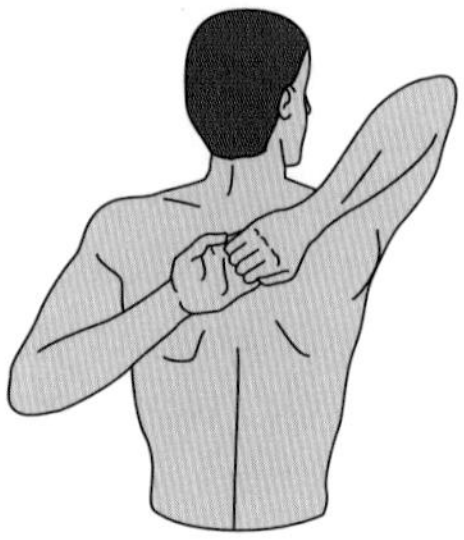

Example of contract-relax (CR) proprioceptive neuromuscular facilitation (PNF) stretching method. **figure 12.3**

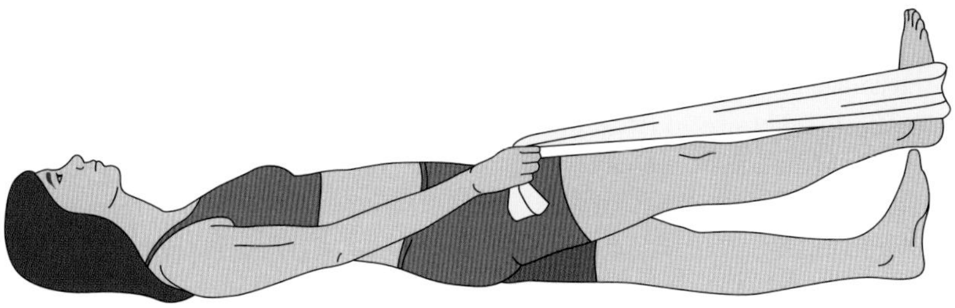

1. Lie on your back and place a towel around the bottom of one foot.
2. Fully straighten leg and lift until you feel moderate resistance.
3. Contract hamstring muscle for 6 seconds.
4. Pull on the towel to stretch the hamstring muscle further.

STRETCHING, INJURY, PERFORMANCE, AND THE STRETCHING-INDUCED FORCE DEFICIT

Stretching prior to exercise and athletic events is often performed to increase flexibility, enhance performance, and reduce the risk of injury.[1] There is little compelling evidence, however, that stretching prior to physical activity reduces the risk of injury.[1] Furthermore, it has been suggested that pre-exercise stretching may temporarily decrease a muscle's ability to produce maximal force during isometric,[19] concentric isokinetic,[5,6,9] and dynamic constant external resistance (DCER) muscle actions,[4] but not eccentric muscle actions.[4] In addition, stretching may compromise vertical jumping performance[21,22] and balance.[2] The negative effects of stretching on strength and performance have been called the "stretching-induced force deficit" and apply to athletes and non-athletes as well as adults and adolescents of both genders.[2,5,6,9,11,19,21,22] Furthermore, the deficit in exercise performance may, in some cases, last up to an hour after stretching.[5] Thus, stretching prior to competition may adversely affect performance, particularly in athletes involved in strength and power events.

Two primary hypotheses have been proposed to explain the stretching-induced force deficit:[8,10,19]

1. mechanical factors, such as decreases in musculotendonous stiffness and changes in the muscle's length–tension relationship
2. neural factors, such as decreases in muscle activation

Although it is likely that the precise mechanism(s) underlying the stretching-induced force deficit depends on the type of activity that is being performed, it is generally accepted that both mechanical and neural factors contribute to the compromised performance.

Guidelines for Stretching to Increase Flexibility

The ACSM's[1] recommended flexibility exercise prescription includes:

Frequency: Stretch each major muscle group greater than or equal to two or three days per week, with a daily regimen being most effective.

Intensity: Stretch to the point of feeling tightness or slight discomfort.

Time: Holding a static stretch for 10 to 30 seconds is recommended for most adults. In older individuals, holding a stretch for 30 to 60 seconds may confer greater benefit. For PNF stretching, a 3- to 6-second light to moderate contraction

RESEARCH

Stretching prior to practice and competition

It is common practice for athletes to perform stretching exercises prior to practice and competition. However, stretching prior to activity has been reported to inhibit maximal strength. This is a concern for any athlete involved in sports where maximal efforts are required. Nelson et al.* were interested in whether this is a general effect or whether it occurs at specific velocities of movement. They tested 15 subjects for maximal concentric, isokinetic torque production of the knee extensors at five different movement velocities. This was done prior to and 10 minutes after stretching. The subjects performed three different stretching exercises, with each stretch repeated four times. The results showed that maximal torque production declined following stretching for only the two slowest velocities (1.05 and 1.57 rad • sec^{-1}). The authors suggest that the inhibitory effect of stretching on maximal force output is velocity-specific. For a sport such as power lifting, where success depends on maximal force production, it may be advisable to avoid stretching immediately prior to competition.

* Nelson, A. G., Guillory, I. K., Cornwell, A., and Kokkonen, J. Inhibition of maximal voluntary isokinetic torque production following stretching is velocity-specific. *J. Str. Cond. Res.* 15: 241–246, 2001.

(e.g., 20–75% of maximum voluntary contraction) followed by a 10- to 30-second assisted stretch is desirable.

Type: A series of flexibility exercises for each of the major muscle–tendon units is recommended. Static flexibility (i.e., active or passive), dynamic flexibility, ballistic flexibility, and PNF exercises are effective.

Volume: A reasonable target is to perform 60 seconds of total stretching time for each flexibility exercise.

Pattern: Repetition of each flexibility exercise two to four times is recommended. Flexibility exercise is most effective when the muscle is warmed through light to moderate aerobic activity or passively through external methods such as moist heat packs or hot baths.

FACTORS AFFECTING FLEXIBILITY

WWW
Flexibility Basics
http://sportsmedicine.about.com/cs/flexibility/a/aa040703a.htm

Activity. Active and physically fit individuals tend to be more flexible than inactive individuals.[13]

Weight training. Although there is conflicting evidence, it is generally believed that resistance training has no negative effects on flexibility (or may increase flexibility) as long as[12] (1) exercises are performed through the full range of motion, (2) both agonist and antagonist muscle groups are trained, and (3) stretching exercises are included with the resistance training program.

Gender. Females tend to be more flexible than males.[13] This difference exists at all ages and throughout the lifespan.

Age. Elementary school–age children become less flexible as they grow older, reaching a low point in flexibility between 10 and 12 years of age. From this age upward, flexibility seems to improve toward young adulthood, but it never again achieves the levels of early childhood. Dynamic flexibility grows steadily poorer, from childhood on, with increasing age. Age-related decreases also occur in static flexibility of the head, shoulder, ankle, and hip joints in males and females across adulthood.[20] (See Figure 12.4.)

figure 12.4

Sit-and-reach flexibility declines throughout adulthood for both males and females.

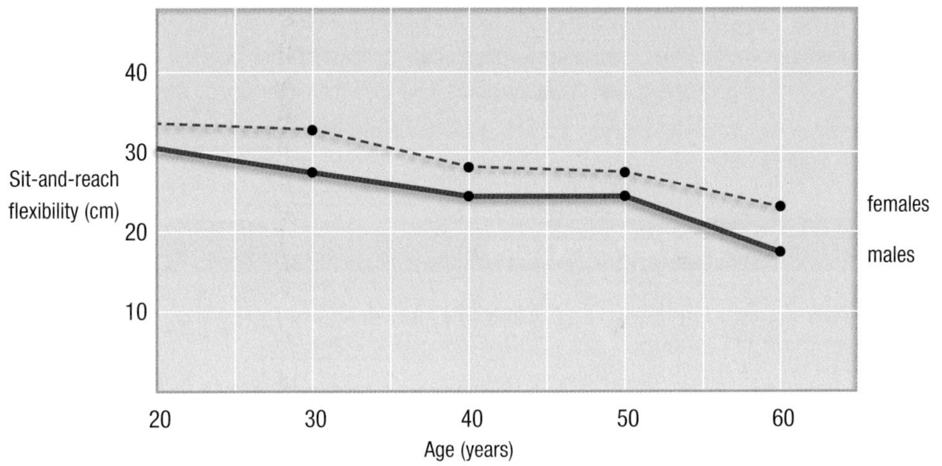

Temperature. Flexibility tends to increase with local warming and to decrease with cooling.[1,18] This supports the need for warm-up prior to stretching.

summary

Flexibility is the range of motion at a joint or series of joints. Flexibility is joint specific, and an individual can therefore have outstanding range of motion at one joint but limited flexibility at another. The range of motion at a joint can be limited by bone structures, muscle, connective tissue, and the skin. In general, females are more flexible than males, and flexibility decreases throughout adulthood in both genders.

The most common stretching methods of increasing flexibility are static, ballistic, and proprioceptive neuromuscular facilitation. Static stretching involves holding a position with very little or no movement for 10 to 60 seconds, while ballistic stretching involves bouncing or jerky movements. PNF methods include stretching a muscle immediately following a contraction of agonist or antagonist muscles. All three types of stretching—static, ballistic, and PNF—have been shown to increase flexibility.

questions for review

1. How are the limits of flexibility set in the human body?
2. Describe the difference between static and dynamic flexibility. Which is of greater concern to a coach?
3. Discuss the advantages and disadvantages of static versus ballistic stretching.
4. Describe the evidence about the effectiveness of PNF stretching techniques compared with static or ballistic stretching.
5. Prescribe a stretching program for a healthy adult who is seeking greater flexibility.
6. What factors influence flexibility?
7. What is the recommended interval for holding a static stretch? Why?

student companion website

For further review of this book's chapters and for test preparation, visit the book's website, **www.hhpcommunities.com/exercisephysiology**, to take practice quizzes, review the vocabulary terms, use the study guide, and view the digital image bank.

references

1. American College of Sports Medicine. *ACSM's Guidelines for Exercise Testing and Prescription,* 9th edition. Baltimore: Walters Kluwer/Lippincott Williams & Wilkins, 2014.
2. Behm, D. G., Bambury, A., Cahill, F., and Power, K. Effect of acute static stretching on force, balance, reaction time, and movement time. *Med. Sports Exerc.* 36: 1397–1402, 2004.
3. Burke, D. G., Culligan, C. J., and Holt, L. E. The theoretical basis of proprioceptive neuromuscular facilitation. *J. Strength Cond. Res.* 14: 496–500, 2000.
4. Cramer, J. T., Housh, T. J., Coburn, J. W., Beck, T. W., and Johnson, G. O. Acute effects of static stretching on maximal eccentric torque production in women. *J. Strength Cond. Res.* 20: 354–358, 2006.
5. Cramer, J. T., Housh, T. J., Johnson, G. O., Miller, J. M., Coburn, J. W., and Beck, T. W. The acute effects of static stretching on peak torque in women. *J. Strength Cond. Res.* 18: 176–182, 2004.
6. Cramer, J. T., Housh, T. J., Weir, J. P., Johnson, G. O., Coburn, J. W., and Beck, T. W. The acute effects of static stretching on peak torque, mean power output, electromyography, and mechanomyography. *Eur. J. Appl. Physiol.* 93: 530–539, 2005.
7. Etnyre, B. R., and Lee, E. J. Comments on proprioceptive neuromuscular facilitation stretching techniques. *Res. Q. Exerc. Sport* 58: 184–188, 1987.
8. Etnyre, B. R., and Lee, E. J. Chronic and acute flexibility of men and women using three different stretching techniques. *Res. Q. Exerc. Sport* 59: 222–228, 1988.
9. Evetovich, T. K., Nauman, N. J., Conley, D. S., and Todd, J. B. Effect of static stretching of the biceps brachii on torque, electromyography, and mechanomyography during concentric isokinetic muscle actions. *J. Strength Cond. Res.* 17: 484–488, 2003.
10. Fowles, J. R., Sale, D. G., and MacDougall, J. D. Reduced strength after passive stretch of the human plantarflexors. *J. Appl. Physiol.* 89: 1179–1188, 2000.
11. Fry, A. C., McLellan, E., Weiss, L. W., and Rosato, F. D. The effects of static stretching on power and velocity during the bench press exercise. *Med. Sci. Sports Exerc.* 35: S264, 2003.
12. Girouard, C. K., and Hurley, B. F. Does strength training inhibit gains in range of motion from flexibility training in older adults? *Med. Sci. Sports Exerc.* 27: 1444–1449, 1995.
13. Golding, L. A. Flexibility, stretching, and flexibility testing. Recommendations for testing and standards. *ACSM's Health and Fitness Journal* 1: 17–38, 1997.
14. Hardy, L., and Jones, D. Dynamic flexibility and proprioceptive neuromuscular facilitation. *Res. Q. Exerc. Sport* 57: 150–153, 1986.
15. Hartley-O'Brien, S. J. Six mobilization exercises for active range of hip flexion. *Res. Q.* 51: 625–635, 1980.
16. Hedrick, A. Dynamic flexibility training. *Strength Cond. J.* 22: 33–38, 2000.
17. High, D. M., Howley, E. T., and Franks, B. D. The effects of static stretching and warm-up on prevention of delayed-onset muscle soreness. *Res. Exerc. Sport* 60: 357–361, 1989.
18. Moore, M. A., and Hutton, R. S. Electromyo-graphic evaluation of muscle stretching techniques. *Med. Sci. Sports* 12: 322–329, 1980.
19. Nelson, A. G., Allen, J. D., Cornwell, A., and Kokkonen, J. Inhibition of maximal voluntary isometric torque production by acute stretching is joint-angle specific. *Res. Q. Exerc. Sport* 72: 68–70, 2001.
20. Shephard, R. J., and Berridge, M. On the generality of the "sit and reach" test: An analysis of flexibility data for an aging population. *Res. Q. Exerc. Sport* 61: 326–330, 1990.
21. Wallmann, H. W., Mercer, J. A., and McWhorter, J. W. Surface electromyographic assessment of the effect of static stretching of the gastrocnemius on vertical jump performance. *J. Strength Cond. Res.* 19: 684–688, 2005.
22. Young, W. B., and Behm, D. G. Effects of running, static stretching, and practice jumps on explosive force production and jumping performance. *J. Sports Med. Phys. Fitness* 43: 21–27, 2003.

Sit-and-Reach Flexibility

BACKGROUND

Flexibility is a measure of the range of motion at a specific joint. Just because an individual has a large range of motion at the shoulder joint does not mean the person is also "flexible" at the hip joint. Therefore, no single test can adequately represent overall body flexibility. However, many people experience low back pain, which is often related to poor flexibility in the low back and hamstring muscles. Therefore, the sit-and-reach test is the most commonly used measure of flexibility. The sit-and-reach test requires the subject to reach forward, stretching the muscles of the low back and hamstrings. In this laboratory experience, you will learn how to use the sit-and-reach test to evaluate an individual's flexibility, and you will compare the results with norms for individuals of the same age and gender (see Tables L12.1 and L12.2).

table L12.1 Percentile norms for the sit-and-reach (in), females.[1]

	AGE						
PERCENTILE	<20	20–29	30–39	40–49	50–59	60+	CLASSIFICATION
99	>24.3	>24.5	>24.0	>22.8	>23.0	>23.0	
95	24.3	24.5	24.0	22.8	23.0	23.0	Superior
90	24.3	23.8	22.5	21.5	21.5	21.8	
85	22.5	23.0	22.0	21.3	21.0	19.5	
80	22.5	22.5	21.5	20.5	20.3	19.0	Excellent
75	22.3	22.0	21.0	20.0	20.0	18.0	
70	22.0	21.5	20.5	19.8	19.3	17.5	
65	21.8	21.0	20.3	19.1	19.0	17.5	
60	21.5	20.5	20.0	19.0	18.5	17.0	Good
55	21.3	20.3	19.5	18.5	18.0	17.0	
50	21.0	20.0	19.0	18.0	17.9	16.4	
45	20.5	19.5	18.5	18.0	17.0	16.1	
40	20.5	19.3	18.3	17.3	16.8	15.5	Fair
35	20.0	19.0	17.8	17.0	16.0	15.2	
30	19.5	18.3	17.3	16.5	15.5	14.4	
25	19.0	17.8	16.8	16.0	15.3	13.6	
20	18.5	17.0	16.5	15.0	14.8	13.0	Poor
15	17.8	16.4	15.5	14.0	14.0	11.5	
10	14.5	15.4	14.4	13.0	13.0	11.5	
5	14.5	14.1	12.0	10.5	12.3	9.2	
1	<14.5	<14.1	<12.0	<10.5	<12.3	<9.2	Very poor

table L12.2 Percentile norms for the sit-and-reach (in), males.[1]

	AGE						
PERCENTILE	<20	20-29	30-39	40-49	50-59	60+	CLASSIFICATION
99	>23.4	>23.0	>22.0	>21.3	>20.5	>20.0	
95	23.4	23.0	22.0	21.3	20.5	20.0	Superior
90	22.6	21.8	21.0	20.0	19.0	19.0	
85	22.4	21.0	20.0	19.3	18.3	18.0	
80	21.7	20.5	19.5	18.5	17.5	17.3	Excellent
75	21.4	20.0	19.0	18.0	17.0	16.5	
70	20.7	19.5	18.5	17.5	16.5	15.5	
65	19.8	19.0	18.0	17.0	16.0	15.0	
60	19.0	18.5	17.5	16.3	15.5	14.5	Good
55	18.7	18.0	17.0	16.0	15.0	14.0	
50	18.0	17.5	16.5	15.3	14.5	13.5	
45	17.3	17.0	16.0	15.0	14.0	13.0	
40	16.5	16.5	15.5	14.3	13.3	12.5	Fair
35	16.0	16.0	15.0	14.0	12.5	12.0	
30	15.5	15.5	14.5	13.3	12.0	11.3	
25	14.1	15.0	13.8	12.5	11.2	10.5	
20	13.2	14.4	13.0	12.0	10.5	10.0	Poor
15	11.9	13.5	12.0	11.0	9.7	9.0	
10	10.5	12.3	11.0	10.0	8.5	8.0	
5	9.4	10.5	9.3	8.3	7.0	5.8	
1	<9.4	<10.5	<9.3	<8.3	<7.0	<5.8	Very poor

TERMS & ABBREVIATIONS

- ☐ flexibility = a measure of the range of motion at a specific joint
- ☐ percentile rank = in this lab, a score between 1 and 99% that shows how the subject performed relative to others in the age and gender group. A percentile ranking of 70, for example, indicates that the subject's low back and hamstring muscles are equal to or more flexible than 70% of the others in the age and gender group and less flexible than 30% of the others in the age and gender group.

PROCEDURES

1. Have the subject warm up by walking or riding a stationary cycle ergometer and by doing static stretching exercises.
2. Leg position: Have the subject sit down with shoes off with full extension at the knees and feet no more than 8 inches apart. The heels should be at the 15-inch mark on the measuring scale (see note below).
3. Arm position: The arms should be extended straight forward with one hand over the top of the other, fingertips even, and palms down (see photo 12.1).
4. For the test, have the subject reach forward along the measuring scale and hold the position for one or two seconds. Record the point reached on Worksheet 12.1, and repeat for a total of three trials.

5. Record on Worksheet 12.1 the most distant point reached to the nearest .25 inch. If the fingertips are uneven or if flexion at the knee occurs, the test should be repeated (see photo 12.2).

Note: A sit-and-reach box can easily be constructed. The box should be 12 inches high with an overlap toward the subject so that readings can be obtained if the subject is unable to reach the feet. The foot line is set at 15 inches. A bench (or a floor) with a ruler taped onto it can also be used (see photo 12.3).

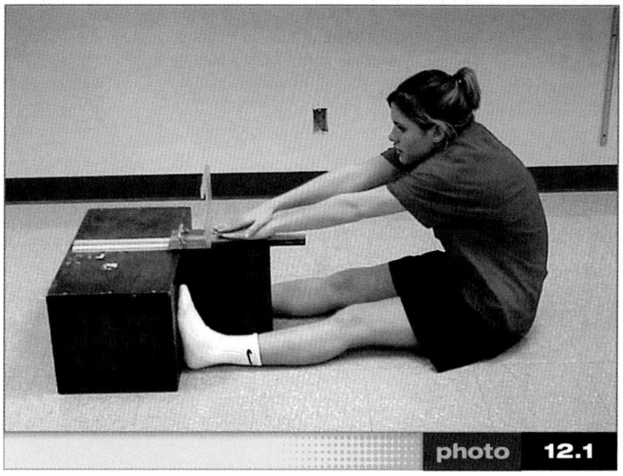

photo 12.1

Position using a sit-and-reach box.

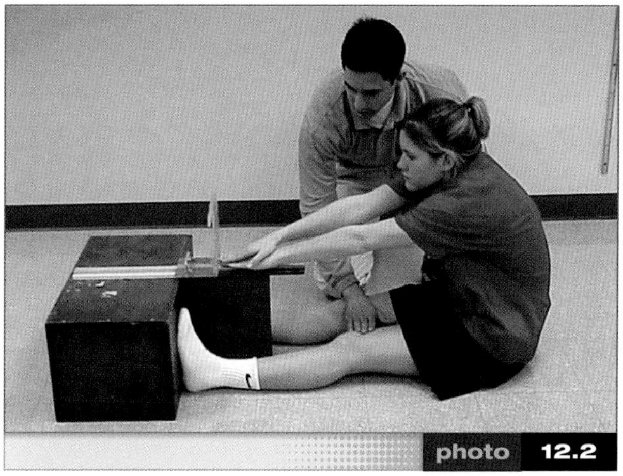

photo 12.2

A partner can make sure that the knees do not flex.

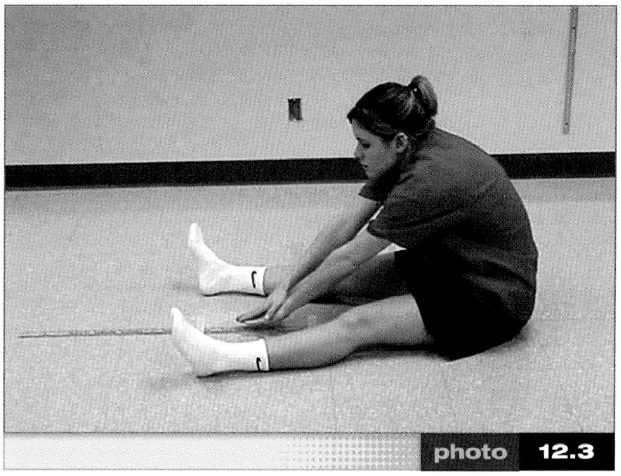

photo 12.3

Position using a ruler taped to the floor.

SAMPLE CALCULATIONS

Gender: Female

Age: 20 years

Trial	1	2	3
	20	22	21

High score = 22 inches

Approximate percentile rank = 75
(Table L12.1)

Classification = good (Table L12.1)

worksheet 12.1 SIT-AND-REACH TEST FORM

NAME ______________________________ DATE ______________

GENDER ______________________________ AGE ______________

	Trial 1	Trial 2	Trial 3
Score (in)	________	________	________

High score (in) ________________

Percentile rank ________________

Classification ________________

worksheet 12.2 EXTENSION ACTIVITIES

NAME ______________________________ DATE ______________

1. Briefly describe the limitation of using a single test of range of motion, such as the sit-and-reach test, as it relates to overall flexibility.

2. Use your own data from the sit-and-reach test to determine your percentile rank and classification (see Tables L12.1 and L12.2). What does your percentile rank mean?

3. Use the following data from the sit-and-reach test to determine the subjects' percentile rank and classification.
   a. 28-year-old male with a sit-and-reach of 19.0 inches
      percentile rank = ________________
      classification = ________________
   b. 32-year-old female with a sit-and-reach of 22.0 inches
      percentile rank = ________________
      classification = ________________

EXTENSION QUESTIONS

1. What are some common mistakes that may occur in administering this lab?

2. Identify possible sources of error in this lab.

3. Assess the practicality of using this lab in the field.

4. Research the reliability and/or validity of this lab using online resources, journal articles, and other credible sources.

REFERENCES

1. *Physical Fitness Assessments and Norms for Adults and Law Enforcement*, 2007. Cooper Institute, Dallas. Available online at www.cooperinstitute.org.

lab B Shoulder Elevation and Trunk Extension Flexibility

BACKGROUND

Flexibility is a measure of the range of motion at a specific joint. Just because an individual has a large range of motion at the hip joint does not mean the person is also "flexible" at the shoulder joint. Furthermore, the need for flexibility at a specific joint depends on the sports or activities in which the individual participates. For example, baseball pitchers, gymnasts, swimmers, and wrestlers require great flexibility at the shoulder joint, while swimmers, dancers, divers, and jumpers (long jump, high jump, triple jump, etc.) need substantial ankle flexibility. Therefore, flexibility assessments should be selected based on the demands of the sport or activity.

In this laboratory, you will learn to use the shoulder elevation and trunk extension tests to evaluate an individual's flexibility, and you will compare the results to gender-specific norms for young adults.

TERMS & ABBREVIATIONS

- flexibility = a measure of the range of motion at a specific joint
- percentile rank = in this lab, a score between 10 and 90% that shows how the subject performed relative to others in the gender group. A percentile ranking of 70, for example, indicates that the subject's flexibility rating and scores are higher than 70% of the others in the gender group and lower than 30% of the others in the gender group.
- static stretching = a stretching method where specified joints are locked into a position that places the muscles and connective tissues passively at their greatest possible length, and held for 10 to 60 seconds

PROCEDURES

Shoulder Elevation Test[1,2]

1. The shoulder elevation test requires measuring the subject's arm length, which is defined as the distance between the acromion process (top of the shoulder) and the palm of the hand. To do so, have the subject stand and grasp a yardstick with the arms fully extended and hands pronated (see photo 12.4). Measure the distance (in inches) between the acromion process and the top of the yardstick. Record the arm length on Worksheet 12.3.
2. Have the subject warm up by walking or riding a stationary cycle ergometer and doing static stretching exercises of the trunk, shoulders, and arms.
3. Have the subject lie face-down on the floor with the arms fully extended above the head and grasp a yardstick (see photo 12.5). The chin should be touching the floor. Have the subject slowly raise the yardstick from the floor as high as possible. It

photo 12.4

Measurement of arm length.

is important that the subject keep the chin on the floor and arms fully extended while raising the yardstick. Record the distance (in inches) between the yardstick and floor on Worksheet 12.3. Repeat for a total of four trials. Use the greatest distance from the four trials in all calculations.

4. Calculate the shoulder elevation score as:

   greatest shoulder elevation distance in inches
   × 100 / arm length in inches

5. Determine the subject's approximate percentile rank and flexibility rating from Table L12.3.

photo 12.5

Measurement of shoulder elevation distance.

SAMPLE CALCULATIONS

Gender: Male

Arm length: 29 inches

Greatest shoulder elevation distance: 20 inches

shoulder elevation score = 20 inches × 100 / 29

= 2000 / 29 = 69 inches

approximate percentile rank: 49 (see Table L12.3)

flexibility rating: below average (see Table L12.3)

Trunk Extension Test[1,2]

1. The trunk extension test requires measuring the subject's trunk length, which is defined as the distance between the tip of the nose and the seat of the chair in which the subject is sitting (see photo 12.6). To do so, have the subject sit in a chair, with the back straight and chin level. Place the zero end of a yardstick on the seat of the chair between the subject's legs, and measure the distance between the seat of the chair and the tip of the subject's nose. Record the trunk length on Worksheet 12.4.
2. Have the subject warm up by walking or riding a stationary cycle ergometer and doing upper-body static stretching exercises.
3. Have the subject lie face-down on the floor and place the hands on the lower back (see photo 12.7). Have a second person hold down the legs to stabilize

table L12.3 Percentile ranks, flexibility ratings, and shoulder elevation scores.[1]

		SHOULDER ELEVATION SCORE (IN)	
PERCENTILE RANK	RATING	MALES	FEMALES
90	Well above average	106–123	105–123
70	Above average	88–105	86–104
50	Average	70–87	68–85
30	Below average	53–69	50–67
10	Well below average	35–52	31–49

photo 12.6

Measurement of trunk length.

photo 12.7

Measurement of trunk extension distance.

the subject. The subject then slowly raises the trunk (hyperextending the back) from the floor as high and as far back as possible. Record the distance (in inches) between the floor and the tip of the subject's nose on Worksheet 12.4. Repeat for a total of four trials. Use the greatest distance from the four trials in all calculations.

4. Calculate the trunk extension score as:

   greatest trunk extension distance in inches × 100 / trunk length in inches

5. Determine the subject's approximate percentile rank and flexibility rating from Table L12.4.

SAMPLE CALCULATIONS

Gender: Female

Trunk length: 34 inches

Greatest trunk extension distance: 13 inches

trunk extension score = 13 inches × 100 / 34

= 1300 / 34 = 38 inches

approximate percentile rank: 60 (see Table L12.4)

flexibility rating: average (see Table L12.4)

table L12.4 Percentile ranks, flexibility ratings, and trunk extension scores.[1]

		SHOULDER ELEVATION SCORE (IN)	
PERCENTILE RANK	RATING	MALES	FEMALES
90	Well above average	50–64	48–63
70	Above average	43–49	42–47
50	Average	37–42	35–41
30	Below average	31–36	29–34
10	Well below average	28–30	23–28

SHOULDER ELEVATION TEST FORM

worksheet **12.3**

NAME ______________________________ DATE ______________________________

Gender: ______________________

Arm length: ______________________ inches

Shoulder elevation distance (inches)

1	2	3	4
________	________	________	________

Shoulder elevation score = ______________________

Greatest shoulder elevation distance in inches × 100 / arm length in inches

__________ inches × 100 / __________ inches = __________ inches

Approximate percentile rank: ______________________ (see Table L12.3)

Flexibility rating: ______________________ (see Table L12.3)

worksheet 12.4 TRUNK EXTENSION TEST FORM

NAME ____________________ DATE ____________________

Gender: ____________________

Trunk length: ____________________ inches

Trunk extension distance (inches)

1	2	3	4
________	________	________	________

Trunk extension score = ____________________

Greatest trunk extension distance in inches × 100 / trunk length in inches

________ inches × 100 / ________ inches = ________ inches

Approximate percentile rank: ____________________ (see Table L12.4)

Flexibility rating: ____________________ (see Table L12.4)

EXTENSION ACTIVITIES

worksheet 12.5

NAME ______________________ DATE ______________________

1. Use your own data from the shoulder elevation test to determine your approximate percentile rank and flexibility rating (see Table L12.3).

   Approximate percentile rank: ______________________

   Flexibility rating: ______________________

2. Use your own data from the trunk extension test to determine your approximate percentile rank and flexibility rating (see Table L12.4).

   Approximate percentile rank: ______________________

   Flexibility rating: ______________________

3. Briefly interpret the meaning of a percentile rank of 50.

4. Identify athletes who might benefit from above average shoulder extension and/or trunk extension flexibility.

EXTENSION QUESTIONS

1. What are some common mistakes that may occur in administering this lab?

2. Identify possible sources of error in this lab.

3. Assess the practicality of using this lab in the field.

4. Research the reliability and/or validity of this lab using online resources, journal articles, and other credible sources.

REFERENCES

1. Acevedo, E. O., and Starks, M. A. *Exercise Testing and Prescription Lab Manual.* Champaign, IL: Human Kinetics, 2003, pp. 76–79.
2. Johnson, B. L., and Nelson, J. K. *Practical Measurements for Evaluation in Physical Education.* Edina, MN: Burgess Publishing, 1986, pp. 91–95.

As a result of reading this chapter you will:

Know the primary factors that contribute to the intrinsic speed of a muscle contraction.

Know the relationships among strength, flexibility, and speed of movement.

Understand the differences between the start, acceleration phase, and high-velocity phase of a sprinting event.

Be knowledgeable about sprint-resisted and sprint-assisted training methods.

Know the relative contributions of various factors to sprint running, swimming, bicycling, and speed skating performance.

13 Sprinting and Speed Training

key concepts

acceleration phase
high-velocity phase
specificity of speed
speed
sprint-assisted training
sprint-resisted training
start

Speed of movement is very important in athletics. By carefully analyzing the factors affecting speed, we can better understand this aspect of human performance and thus be in a better position to improve this function in athletics.

Speed, the result of applying force to a mass, implies movement at a constant rate. The movement of a human body at a constant rate requires sufficient driving force to overcome the forces that resist movement.

We can think of a balance of positive and negative forces with respect to propulsion of the body or any of its parts. The positive force that propels the body is provided by muscular contractions, aided in some cases by elastic energy associated with the recoil of stretched soft tissue such as muscle. The negative forces depend on the nature of the activity.

In running, for example, the positive force developed by the muscles is counterbalanced by negative forces including gravity, velocity changes, acceleration of limbs, deceleration of limbs, and air resistance. Thus, speed can be improved either by increasing the positive force or by decreasing the negative factors. For example, improving strength may be an important positive factor in increasing the forces of muscular contractions. Negative factors might be reduced through improved neuromuscular coordination (skill) and increased flexibility.

INTRINSIC SPEED OF MUSCLE CONTRACTION

www

Speed Training
www.brianmac.co.uk/speed.htm

Muscles differ in their ability to produce fast movement. This, of course, reflects the differences in their proportions of fast-twitch (FT) and slow-twitch (ST) fibers (see Chapter 2). For example, there are considerable intrinsic differences between the postural muscles, which tend to be predominately ST, and other muscles composed of more FT fibers. There are also interindividual differences in speed of movement for the same muscle group or type of movement. The speed of a muscle action also varies greatly from one animal species to another, approximately in inverse ratio to size.

Several factors influence a muscle fiber's contraction speed. Of these, the primary factors believed to differentiate FT from ST fibers in terms of speed of contraction include:[9]

1. The level of myosin ATPase activity (see Chapter 3). Inherently, FT fibers have greater activity of this enzyme and therefore liberate the stored energy from ATP more effectively.
2. ST fibers have poorly developed sarcoplasmic reticulum, which may interfere with the rate of calcium release and muscle contraction.
3. There are slight differences between the myosin molecules (myosin isoforms) found in FT and ST fibers.
4. There may be differences between FT and ST fibers in the ability of calcium to bind with troponin.

It is likely that ultimate maximal speed capacity is limited by the intrinsic speed of an individual's muscle tissue, the efficacy of that person's neuromuscular coordination patterns, and the metabolic considerations discussed in Chapter 3.

SPECIFICITY OF SPEED

www

USA Track and Field
www.usatf.org

It is commonplace to speak of an individual as fast or slow, but speed is not a general characteristic. Indeed, an individual with a fast arm movement may well have slow leg movements. In fact, there is practically no association between the speeds with which one can perform an arm movement and a leg movement and only a small relationship between speed of movement in a forward arm swing and a backward arm swing. This might lead us to describe an individual as fast in a backward swing of the right leg! Obviously this makes no sense, but neither does it make sense to speak of a fast or slow individual. We can speak of a fast runner, but this does not mean that the same individual can effectively throw a fastball in baseball. This phenomenon is referred to as **specificity of speed.**

specificity of speed

STRENGTH AND SPEED

Differences in strength among individuals or between groups of individuals do not accurately predict sprinting performance. That is, the strongest person is not always the fastest. On the other hand, strength gains within an individual, such as from a resistance training program, often translate into improved sprinting performance, particularly for the acceleration phase of a race. Based on the specificity principle discussed in Chapter 11, a training program to improve sprint times should consist of dynamic resistance training such as dynamic constant external resistance (DCER) or isokinetic training, and the movements should be performed at velocities that mimic the sprinting activity as closely as possible.

FLEXIBILITY AND SPEED

Theoretically, improving flexibility should decrease the negative forces (resistance) involved in sprinting and thus improve speed. For example, during sprint running, flexion and extension at the hip joint may influence speed, while sprint swimming requires exceptional range of motion at the shoulder. Thus, lack of flexibility at specific joints may limit sprinting performance, while increased flexibility may improve performance. The combination of flexibility and resistance training may be especially beneficial to sprinting performance.

FACTORS AFFECTING SPRINT PERFORMANCE

The duration of a sprint activity is normally no longer than two to three minutes (i.e., less than or equal to a 200-meter swim, 800-meter run, one-kilometer bicycling time trial, or 1500-meter speed skating trial), and sprinting relies heavily on energy produced from the ATP–PC system and anaerobic glycolysis (see Chapter 3). Strategically, sprints require maximal or near maximal efforts from start to finish, even though there may be some reduction in velocity at the end of the race.

The relative contributions of various factors to sprinting performance differ depending on the sport (running, swimming, bicycling, skating, etc.) as well as the duration of the event. That is, strength, flexibility, and skill may have a different order of relative importance in sprint running versus speed skating. In addition, these (and other factors) may be more important at the beginning of a sprinting event than at the end. Generally, sprint events can be divided into three phases: (1) the **start,** (2) the **acceleration phase,** which involves increasing the movement velocity after the start, and (3) the **high-velocity phase,** which involves maintaining the highest possible velocity after the acceleration phase. It is important that coaches and athletes understand these issues in order to design training programs that emphasize the factors most likely to contribute to successful performance.

start
acceleration phase
high-velocity phase

Sprint Running

In sprint running, the start and acceleration phases are critical in optimizing performance.[7] This is especially true for short sprints such as the 60- and 100-meter dashes and, to a lesser degree, longer sprints (e.g., 400 meters). The start of a sprint race (pushing out of the blocks) and the acceleration phase require very powerful movements that may exceed four horsepower.[5,7] A good start and rapid accel-

RESEARCH

Sprinting and sloped surface training

Sprinters use both downhill and uphill sprint training to improve their horizontal sprint performance. The athletes hope that these methods of training will result in greater strength and power and improved maximal running time. Paradisis and Cooke* have looked at the effect of using a sloped surface on kinematic and postural characteristics during sprinting. Eight subjects were filmed while running uphill, horizontally, and downhill. The slope of the platform was 3 percent. The results showed that maximum running speed was 3.0 percent slower for uphill and 9.2 percent faster for downhill sprinting compared with horizontal sprinting. These changes were due to changes in step length of +7.1 percent and −5.2 percent for downhill and uphill sprinting, respectively. Step rate did not change significantly. These changes were accompanied by postural changes, the discovery of which led the authors to question how effective training on uphill or downhill slopes is in increasing horizontal maximal running speed. Further research will be needed to understand the implications regular training on sloping surfaces will have on maximal horizontal running speed.

* Paradisis, G. P., and Cooke, C. B. Kinematic and postural characteristics of sprint running on sloping surfaces. *J. Sports Sci.* 19: 149–159, 2001.

WWW

Sprint Training for Developing Athletes
www.oztrack.com/devsp.html

eration require very strong flexor and extensor muscles of the lower extremities, which can be developed through resistance training.[3,10] Maintenance of the high-velocity phase, however, requires substantially less average power output and is influenced by many factors including technique, training, equipment, posture, and body composition.[7,10] Interestingly, large extensor muscles are beneficial to a powerful start and rapid acceleration, but they may hinder the high-velocity phase by increasing the moment of inertia associated with acceleration and deceleration of the legs. In general, improvements in performance during the high-velocity phase are brought about by increasing the length of the stride and shortening ground contact time[6] rather than by increasing the rate of the movements. Efficient sprint running technique is characterized by a high knee lift, a long running stride, and placement of the feet beneath the runner's center of gravity.

sprint-resisted training

sprint-assisted training

The most commonly used test of running speed is the 40-yard dash (see **Chapter 13 Lab**). Two of the most commonly used methods for improving sprint running performance are (1) sprint-resisted training and (2) sprint-assisted training. **Sprint-resisted training** includes such techniques as weighted-vest running, sand running, and resisted-towing activities.[4] **Sprint-assisted training** (sometimes called *overspeed, supramaximal,* or *assisted speed training*) often involves activities such as assisted-towing, downhill running, and high-speed treadmill running.[4] Sprint-resisted training is appropriate for any sport or distance that requires rapid acceleration, repetitive bouts of acceleration, or changes of direction, while sprint-assisted training may be most appropriate for distances greater than 40 meters, where the maintenance of maximal velocity is required.[4] Table 13.1 describes various aspects of sprint-resisted and sprint-assisted training.

Sprint Swimming

The start of a sprint swimming event and the pushoff from the pool wall during turns require powerful movements of the legs. The start is characterized by strong contractions of the hip and leg extensors and plantar flexors. After the start, swimmers remain underwater for a period of time to gain full advantage of the initial acceleration.

Typically, increased speed of swimming is achieved through a combination of increasing stroke rate and decreasing distance per stroke.[2] Simply stroking faster and disregarding efficiency of stroking, however, is not effective. The decreasing distance per stroke is not a cause of increased speed but is rather a result of faster stroking.

table 13.1 Sprint-resisted and sprint-assisted training.

METHOD	SPORT REQUIREMENTS	FACTORS AFFECTED	PRESCRIPTION	PRECAUTIONS
Sprint-Resisted Training				
1. Weighted-vest running	Most appropriate for sports that require vertical movements as opposed to horizontal movements	Improved force production	Add 3–8% of body weight with vest	Athletes should have resistance training experience and advanced vertical power capabilities
2. Sand running	Best applied to sports that demand rapid bouts of acceleration and multi-directional movements May be useful for rehabilitation of lower-limb injuries	Improved strength Improved stabilization Improved acceleration	Can be used during any phase of training	Should be alternated with normal running conditions
3. Resisted-towing (parachute or rubber cord, etc.)	Appropriate for sports that involve change of direction and forceful acceleration	Increased force throughout acceleration	Used in conjunction with resistance and technique training	Athletes should have proper technique and experience in resistance training
Sprint-Assisted Training				
1. Assisted-towing (motorized towing device, rubber cord, or rocket rope, etc.)	Useful for activities that require the maintenance of maximal velocity for over 40 meters	Reduced ground contact time May increase stride length Possibly improved running technique and efficiency Improved stretch-shortening cycle	Running at 101–103% of maximal unassisted velocity Often used in season	Athletes must have expert technique, high-speed running experience, and a resistance training background
2. Downhill running	Most appropriate for events that involve downhill running Used for high-velocity activities	Improved running velocity Improved running form	Declines not to exceed a 3% grade	Athletes should have expert technique and resistance training experience Should be used only short term to reduce potential of decreasing rear leg thrust
3. High-speed treadmill running	Most useful for linear activities May be useful for rehabilitating hamstring injuries	Improved running technique at high velocities Increased hamstring conditioning	Used in conjunction with resistance training	Requires substantial eccentric strength Athletes must be experienced with high-velocity running and resistance training Should be used only short term

Adapted from Morgan, T. Picking up speed: A no-nonsense look at overspeed and resistance training. *Training and Conditioning,* August: 45–51, 1998.

Swim coaches have long known that improved performance involves considerable practice swimming with slow stroke rates to develop greater distance per stroke. In support of this concept, Toussaint[8] concluded that "on average the better swimmer distinguishes himself from the poorer one by a greater distance per stroke rather than a higher stroke frequency." Improving the distance per stroke should probably be accomplished early in the season, while establishing power and efficiency at race speeds should be emphasized in the late season.

Are you a sprinter or a runner?

Why are some people good sprinters and others better suited to distance running? It appears that muscle fiber shortening velocity (MFSV) is an important factor. MFSV is determined both by biochemical factors (e.g., fiber type/enzyme activity) and by the architecture of the muscle. Sprinters have been found to have thicker muscles, longer muscle fascicle lengths, and an altered muscle shape (i.e., greater muscle thickness in the upper part of the anterior thigh, but not in the lower part) compared to long-distance runners. These factors all would contribute to an increase in MFSV and improved sprint performance. It is still unclear whether these differences are due to training specificity or are genetic.[1]

Sprint Bicycling

Sprint bicycle racing at distances of 500 and 1,000 meters is affected by the characteristics of both the rider and the equipment. For example, the force produced by the rider must be transferred through the pedal to produce horizontal movement of the bicycle. This transfer results in a substantial reduction in the force produced at the pedal and at the rear wheel.[7] Thus, improved sprint bicycling performance can result from conditioning of the rider (i.e., resistance training to improve power production) and from changes in equipment (i.e., streamlining, or changing gear ratios). Traditionally, gear ratios are selected to optimize the high-velocity phase of the race at the expense of the start.[7] Thus, the initial velocity during sprint bicycling is far less (approximately 65–75% less) than that for sprint running, but the maximal velocity attained during the race is much greater.

Sprint Speed Skating

The start and initial acceleration phases of sprint speed skating are similar to those in sprint running, but without the advantage of starting blocks. At the start of a race, speed skaters use a running technique by pushing off against the ice.[7] The initial acceleration velocity for sprint skating tends to be greater than in sprint cycling, but only about one-half that of sprint running. After the start and initial acceleration phase (usually about five seconds into the race), skaters use a gliding motion for most of the race that is characterized by:[7] (1) a horizontal trunk position and a small knee joint angle to reduce air friction, (2) a short push-off phase, and (3) a long gliding phase without powerful plantar flexion.

WWW

The President's Council on Fitness, Sports, and Nutrition
www.fitness.gov

Improvements in sprint speed skating performance may be possible through:[7] (1) increasing strength of the lower-body extensor muscles and plantar flexors to aid in the start and the maintenance of speed during the gliding phase, (2) reducing the moment of inertia caused by the weight of the skates, (3) improving technique to reduce air and ice friction, and (4) perfecting new starting techniques such as beginning with hands on the ice.

summary

Sprinting involves short-duration (no longer than two to three minutes), high-intensity (all-out effort) activities at distances of no more than 200 meters for swimming, 800 meters for running, one kilometer for bicycling, and 1,500 meters for speed skating. Sprinting and speed training activities rely heavily on energy produced from the ATP–PC system and anaerobic glycolysis.

Sprinting performance is determined by the balance between muscular contractions that propel the body and the forces that resist movement. Exercise training for improved strength and flexibility can increase the propelling force of the muscles and reduce the forces that resist acceleration and deceleration of the limbs.

Generally, sprinting events can be divided into three phases: (1) the start, (2) the acceleration phase, and (3) the high-velocity phase. The relative importance of the phases of a sprinting event depend on the activity involved. For example, the start and acceleration phases are more important in sprint running than in bicycling, but the speed obtained during the high-velocity phase of bicycling is far greater than that of running.

questions for review

1. What factors contribute to the intrinsic speed of a muscle contraction?
2. What are the implications of specificity of speed for coaches?
3. How can flexibility and strength training improve sprinting performance?
4. Using Table 13.1, select several sprint-assisted and sprint-resisted training activities to recommend to the following athletes and explain why the activities will improve their performance:
   - Sprint runner
   - Long jumper
   - Football running back
5. How can speed be increased in running? In swimming? In sprint bicycling? In sprint speed skating?
6. What are the physiological reasons some people are good sprinters while others are better suited to distance running?

student companion website

For further review of this book's chapters and for test preparation, visit the book's website, **www.hhpcommunities.com/exercisephysiology**, to take practice quizzes, review the vocabulary terms, use the study guide, and view the digital image bank.

references

1. Abe, T., Kumagai, K., and Brechue, W. F. Fascicle length of leg muscles is greater in sprinters than distance runners. *Med. Sci. Sports Exerc.* 32: 1125–1129, 2001.
2. Craig, A. B., and Pendergast, D. R. Relationship of stroke rate, distance per stroke, and velocity in competitive swimming. *Med. Sci. Sports* 11: 278–283, 1979.
3. Kirksey, B., and Stone, M. Periodizing a college sprint program: Theory and practice. *Strength Cond. J.* 20: 42–47, 1998.
4. Morgan, T. Picking up speed: A no-nonsense look at overspeed and resistance training. *Train. Cond.* August: 45–51, 1998.
5. Nesser, T. W., Latin, R. W., Berg, K., and Prentice, E. Physiological determinants of 40-meter sprint performance in young male athletes. *J. Strength Cond. Res.* 10: 263–267, 1996.
6. Rimmer, E., and Sleivert, G. Effects of a plyometrics intervention program on sprint performance. *J. Strength Cond. Res.* 14: 295–301, 2000.
7. Schenau, G. J. V. I., deKoning, J. J., and deGrout, G. Optimization of sprinting performance in running, cycling, and skating. *Sports Med.* 17: 259–275, 1994.
8. Toussaint, H. M. Differences in propelling efficiency between competitive and triathlon swimmers. *Med. Sci. Sports Exerc.* 22: 409–415, 1990.
9. Vrbova, G. Influence of activity on some characteristic properties of slow and fast mammalian muscles. *Exerc. Sport Sci. Rev.* 7: 181–213, 1979.
10. Young, W., and Pryor, J. Resistance training for short sprints and maximum-speed sprints. *Strength Cond. J.* 23: 7–13, 2001.

lab 40-Yard Dash Test of Speed

BACKGROUND

Speed describes the ability to cover a specific distance as fast as possible. One of the most commonly used tests of speed is the 40-yard dash, and it is often included in a battery of tests for male and female athletes who compete in sports such as football, basketball, volleyball, and baseball.[1,2,3,4] Although it is likely that the original selection of 40 yards for this test was somewhat arbitrary, this distance has now become standard, and many coaches and athletes are familiar with the sprint times associated with this distance.[4]

In this laboratory, you will learn to perform and record the time for the 40-yard dash. You will also learn to estimate the approximate percentile rank associated with 40-yard dash times by gender and age and to compare 40-yard dash times with those of athletes in various sports.

TERMS & ABBREVIATIONS

- speed = the ability to cover a specific distance as fast as possible
- percentile rank = in this lab, a score between 10 and 90% that shows how the subject performed relative to others in the age group. A percentile ranking of 70, for example, indicates that the subject can run the 40-yard dash faster than 70% of the others in the age group and slower than 30% of the others in the age group.

PROCEDURES[4]

(see photos 13.1 and 13.2)

1. Typically, the 40-yard dash is performed on a track or football field, but any open area of sufficient size will work.
2. Mark off a distance of 40 yards using cones (on a field) or tape (on a track).
3. Have the subject warm up by jogging (and stretching if desired). After the initial warm-up, the subject should complete four to six intermittent sprints of approximately 10 to 20 yards of 80 to 100% of maximal speed.
4. Have the subject place one or two hands on the starting line of the 40-yard dash (for an example of a four-point stance, see photo 13.1). When ready, the subject starts running as fast as possible. The timer is located at the end line of the 40 yards and begins timing with a stopwatch when the subject's hands leave the starting line. The subject must run as fast as possible for the full 40 yards. The timer stops the stopwatch precisely when the subject crosses the end line (see photo 13.2).

photo 13.1

Four-point stance at the starting line of the 40-yard dash.

5. The timer records the 40-yard dash time to the nearest 0.01 second on Worksheet 13.1.
6. Repeat for a total of three trials and select the fastest time. The subject should rest for approximately three minutes (or more) between trials.
7. Table L13.1 provides the percentile ranks for 40-yard dash times in seconds for young males and females (12–18 years of age). For college-age subjects, use the percentile ranks in Table L13.1 for 16- to 18-year-olds (even though the subject may be older than 18) for the appropriate gender. Table L13.2 provides mean 40-yard dash times in seconds for male and female athletes in selected sports.

photo 13.2

Subject being timed as he crosses the finish line.

SAMPLE CALCULATION

Gender: Male

Age: 15 years

40-yard dash time (to the nearest 0.01 second):

Trial 1	Trial 2	Trial 3
5.31	5.30	5.24

Fastest trial = 5.24 seconds

Approximate percentile rank = 70 (see Table L13.1)

table L13.1 Percentile ranks for 40-yard dash times in seconds for young (age 12–18) males and females.[4]

	12–13 YEARS		14–15 YEARS		16–18 YEARS	
PERCENTILE RANK	MALES	FEMALES	MALES	FEMALES	MALES	FEMALES
90	5.41	5.79	5.02	5.36	4.76	4.93
80	5.63	6.14	5.15	5.68	4.85	5.22
70	5.77	6.49	5.24	6.01	4.90	5.52
60	5.84	6.84	5.32	6.33	4.98	5.82
50	5.97	7.19	5.46	6.65	5.10	6.11
40	6.08	7.54	5.54	6.97	5.13	6.41
30	6.25	7.89	5.78	7.30	5.21	6.71
20	6.32	8.24	6.02	7.62	5.30	7.00
10	6.64	8.59	6.08	7.95	5.46	7.31

table L13.2 Mean (±SD) 40-yard dash times in seconds for male and female athletes in selected sports.[1,2,3,4]

SPORT	GENDER	AGE	$\bar{X} \pm SD$
American football	M	14–15 years	5.40 ± 0.53
American football	M	16–18 years	5.15 ± 0.45
American football	M	College (NCAA Division III)	4.99 ± 0.35
American football	M	College (NCAA Division II)	4.88 ± 0.30
American football	M	College (NCAA Division I)	4.74 ± 0.30
Basketball	M	College (NCAA Division I)	4.81 ± 0.26
Soccer	M	College (NCAA Division III)	4.73 ± 0.18
Ice hockey	F	8–16 years ($\bar{X} \pm SD$ = 12.2 ± 2.1 years)	7.19 ± 0.70
Soccer	F	College (NCAA Division III)	5.34 ± 0.17
Volleyball	F	College (NCAA Division I)	5.62 ± 0.24

40-YARD DASH FORM

worksheet **13.1**

NAME ____________________ DATE ____________________

Gender: ____________________

Age: ____________________

40-yard dash time (to the nearest 0.01 second):

Trial	**1**	**2**	**3**
	________	________	________

Fastest trial = ____________________ seconds

Percentile rank = ____________________ (see Table L13.1)

EXTENSION ACTIVITIES

worksheet **13.2**

NAME ____________________ DATE ____________________

1. Use your own data from the 40-yard dash to determine the approximate percentile rank based on the column in Table L13.1 for 16- to 18-year-olds (even though you may be older than 18 years) of your gender.

   40-yard dash time = ____________________ seconds

   Approximate percentile rank = ____________________ (see Table L13.1)

2. For your gender, which sport and age category in Table L13.2 is your 40-yard dash time closest to?

   Sport: ____________________

   Age category: ____________________

3. What is the approximate percentile rank for a 17-year-old female who runs the 40-yard dash in 5.50 seconds?

   Approximate percentile rank = ____________________

EXTENSION QUESTIONS

1. What are some common mistakes that may occur in administering this lab?

2. Identify possible sources of error in this lab.

3. Assess the practicality of using this lab in the field.

4. Research the reliability and/or validity of this lab using online resources, journal articles, and other credible sources.

REFERENCES

1. Bracko, M. R., and George, J. D. Prediction of ice skating performance with off-ice testing in women's ice hockey players. *J. Strength Cond. Res.* 15: 116–122, 2001.
2. Fry, A. C., Kramer, W. J., Weseman, C. A., Conroy, B. P., Gordon, S. E., Hoffman, J. R., and Maresh, C. M. The effects of an off-season strength and conditioning program on starters and non-starters in women's intercollegiate volleyball. *J. Appl. Sports Sci. Res.* 5: 174–181, 1991.
3. Garstecki, M. A., Latin, R. W., and Cuppett, M. M. Comparison of selected physical fitness and performance variables between NCAA Division I and II football players. *J. Strength Cond. Res.* 18: 292–297, 2004.
4. Hoffman, J. *Norms for Fitness, Performance, and Health.* Champaign, IL: Human Kinetics, 2006, pp. 107–112.

14 Neuromuscular Fatigue

As a result of reading this chapter you will:

Be able to define neuromuscular fatigue.

Understand basic concepts regarding the central and peripheral causes of fatigue.

Be able to describe and discuss the task-dependency model, the central governor model, the accumulation hypothesis, and the depletion hypothesis of fatigue.

Understand the basic concepts of electromyography and the electromyographic observations of fatigue.

key concepts

accumulation hypothesis
central fatigue
central governor model
depletion hypothesis
fatigue
glycogen depletion
neuromuscular fatigue
peripheral fatigue
phosphagen depletion
runner's wall
Setchenov phenomenon
task-dependency model

During physical activity, and especially in athletics, we are constantly involved directly or indirectly with the concept of fatigue. In all events in which time or distance is a criterion of success we are of necessity concerned with an endpoint largely determined by fatigue. See the **Chapter 14 Lab**, which measures critical velocity, or the maximal running velocity that can be maintained without fatigue, and the time limit or time to exhaustion.

But what is **fatigue?** The general term has been defined as "that state, following a period of mental or bodily activity, characterized by a lessened capacity for work and reduced efficiency of accomplishment, usually accompanied by a feeling of weariness, sleepiness or irritability; may also supervene when, from any cause, energy expenditure outstrips restorative processes."[11] Thus, fatigue is not a single entity but, rather, includes many different aspects.

This chapter deals with neuromuscular fatigue, but it should be recognized that other systems, including the cardiovascular, pulmonary, and endocrine systems, also contribute to some aspects of fatigue. **Neuromuscular fatigue** can be defined as a transient decrease in muscular performance, usually seen as a failure to maintain or develop a certain expected force or power output.

EFFECTS OF FATIGUE ON STRENGTH, REFLEXES, AND COORDINATION

fatigue
neuromuscular fatigue

Fatigue causes a loss of muscle strength. Figure 14.1 describes the basic relationships between the force that a muscle produces and the duration that the muscle action can be maintained. For any given duration of work, a continuous isometric muscle action is far more fatiguing than intermittent isometric (alternating periods of work and rest) or dynamic muscle actions. The differences result from the fact that continuous isometric muscle actions occlude circulation (above about 15–20 percent of maximum), whereas intermittent isometric and dynamic muscle actions allow blood flow to the muscle.

The effect of fatigue on reflex activity has been well known but somewhat neglected since the turn of the twentieth century. The classic work of Sherrington[26] demonstrated clearly the fading of a reflex with repeated stimulation. The phenomenon of reflex fatigue hinges on Sherrington's basic observation that conduction in the reflex arc is much more "fatiguable" than is conduction in the nerve fiber itself.

figure 14.1 The relationships between force production and time to exhaustion for continuous isometric, intermittent isometric, and dynamic muscle actions.

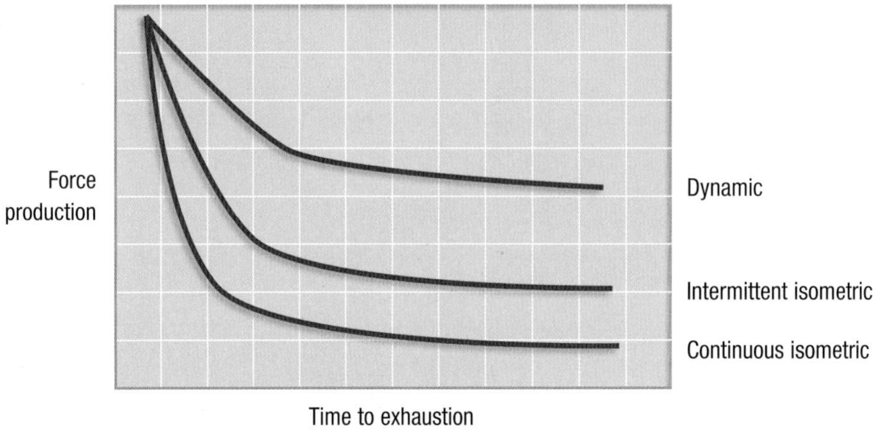

Where a nerve fiber may fail to respond to an artificial stimulus after, say, 100 trials, a reflex becomes inelicitable after far fewer trials, and the more interneurons or synapses are involved in the reflex arc, the more quickly it becomes fatigued.

Since fatigue has rather dramatic effects on both strength and reflexes, it is not surprising that fatigue also affects coordination of the complex movements involved in athletics. Anyone who has ever watched the degraded performance of marathon runners at the finish line needs no further evidence. In addition, fatigue also affects the physical work rate that industrial workers can sustain throughout a work day. Clearly, undue fatigue affects not only productivity but also worker safety. Frequent rest periods can reduce fatigue in industrial settings.

WWW

Fatigue in Exercise

http://coachsci.sdsu.edu/csa/vol65/table.htm

CAUSES OF FATIGUE

Depending on the characteristics of the physical activity or work, the deterioration of motor performance with fatigue may result from central or peripheral mechanisms.[17] The mechanisms underlying **central fatigue** occur proximal to the motor neurons (i.e., mainly in the brain), while those associated with **peripheral fatigue** reside within the motor units (i.e., the motor neurons, the peripheral nerves, the motor endplates, and the muscle fibers themselves). The following are several proposed explanations for causes of fatigue.

- central fatigue
- peripheral fatigue

The Task-Dependency Model: Central and Peripheral Causes of Fatigue

The most widely accepted model for explaining the causes of neuromuscular fatigue involves the concept of task dependency. In general, the **task-dependency model** suggests that the cause of fatigue is dependent on the characteristics of the exercise task that is being performed:[3,6,18]

- task-dependency model

- type and intensity of exercise
- load of the muscle action
- muscle(s) involved
- environment in which the task is performed

For example, fatigue during a high-intensity task such as the final repetition of a maximal set of three bench press exercises is due to different factors than fatigue manifested by a runner near the end of a marathon race. Based on the extreme differences that exist in the characteristics of different types of exercise, it is likely that both central and peripheral mechanisms contribute to fatigue during various tasks.[3]

The site of the physiological changes in the neuromuscular system that lead to fatigue also depends on the task involved (Figure 14.2). For example, during low-intensity, long-duration (several hours) exercise, fatigue is probably due to a central mechanism and a failure of nervous system drive (central fatigue). High-intensity exercise, however, is probably limited by factors within the muscle (peripheral fatigue) and not the central nervous system. Under various exercise conditions, fatigue can also occur from changes at the spinal or motor neuron levels. Thus, as described by Enoka[12] the task-dependency model indicates that "fatigue is not caused by the impairment of a single process, but rather by several mechanisms, both motor and sensory, and that these vary from one condition to another" (p. 374).

Central Mechanism of Fatigue

The physiological mechanisms that underlie central fatigue result in a decrease in neural drive from the brain. Although the precise causes are unknown, central

figure 14.2 Sites of fatigue in the neuromuscular system.

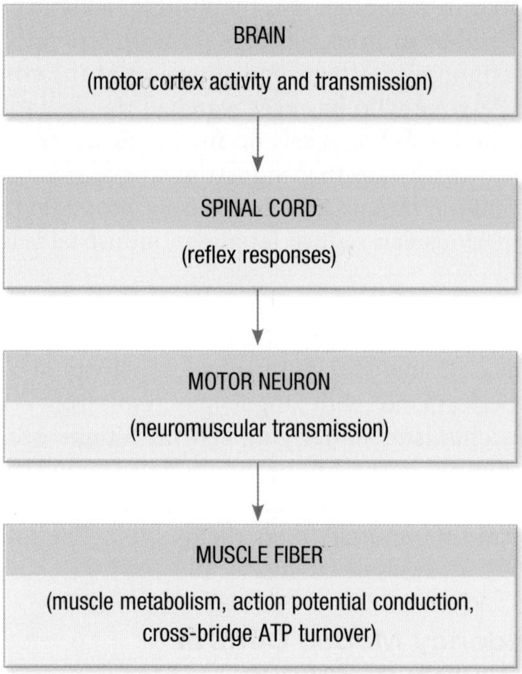

fatigue may arise from the inhibition of neural drive as a result of sensory feedback from working muscles or the effects of either exercise-induced accumulation of the metabolite ammonia or an increase in the neurotransmitter serotonin in the brain (or some combination of these).

Setchenov phenomenon

The **"Setchenov phenomenon"** refers to the fact that more work can be produced after a pause with diverting activity than after a passive rest pause.[1] During a fatiguing task, such as continuous or intermittent isometric muscle actions, sensory feedback of nerve impulses from the fatigued muscles impinges on a part of the reticular formation in the brain and causes an inhibition of the voluntary effort. Diverting activities such as exercise with some non-fatigued muscle group or counting backward (either during the exercise or during the rest pause), on the other hand, produce an increased inflow of impulses from non-fatigued parts of the body to the facilitatory part of the reticular formation, thus shifting the balance between inhibition and facilitation toward facilitation.[17]

www

Neuromuscular Research Center
http://nmrc.bu.edu

It is also possible that ammonia accumulation contributes to the decrease in neural drive from the brain that is associated with central fatigue. Exercise increases ammonia production.[7,17] In the brain, ammonia can alter the levels of neurotransmitters and ATP as well as contribute to the perception of fatigue by causing *hyperpnea* (deep and labored breathing).

The level of the neurotransmitter serotonin in the brain may be associated with central fatigue during long-duration activities.[5,7,14] With prolonged exercise, serotonin builds up in the brain and can impair central nervous system function and endurance performance.[7] The build-up of serotonin results from increased transport of the amino acid tryptophan (along with the branched-chain amino acids leucine, isoleucine, and valine) across the blood–brain barrier during exercise. Tryptophan is a precursor to serotonin. Supplementation with branched-chain amino acids may reduce tryptophan uptake from the blood into the brain and thereby decrease the effects of central fatigue. This hypothesis, however, has not been confirmed.

Historical perspectives

Early studies on muscle fatigue were carried out on animal preparations both on isolated muscle and "in situ." In the late 1800s Angelo Mosso, an Italian physiologist, studied muscle fatigue. It was Mosso's opinion that muscle fatigue probably originated in the nervous system, based on the fact that mental (emotional) excitement reduced the decrease in strength caused by fatigue.[1]

In the early years of the twentieth century, many investigators examined the question of central versus peripheral location of fatigue. For many years, a common technique for examining neuromuscular fatigue utilized voluntary muscle actions (differing rates of both static and dynamic muscle actions) to fatigue a muscle thoroughly. The fatigued muscle was then stimulated by electric shock to the motor nerve. The shock to the motor nerve produced sizable contractions.[27] These findings constituted strong evidence that the central nervous system is a primary site of fatigue but, of course, did not rule out peripheral sites such as the neuromuscular junction and the muscle fiber itself.

In the mid-1950s, however, Merton[19,20] found that when fatigue had progressed to the point where even maximal electrical stimulation of the motor nerve could no longer produce evidence of a muscle twitch, the muscle action potentials were relatively unaffected. He concluded that "fatigue is peripheral and is due to failure of muscle to contract when motor impulses reach it." Because there was no significant falling off in the voltage of the muscle action potentials, he also concluded that the muscle's failure to respond was not because impulses were blocked at the neuromuscular junction. To further confuse matters, in 1967 Ikai et al.[16] demonstrated, in the same muscle preparation used by Merton,[19,20] that electrical stimulation could enhance contractile force after voluntary muscle action had produced fatigue.

Bigland-Ritchie et al.[2] attempted to resolve the question: "Does fatigue arise because the muscle machinery is failing or because the subject is not willing to go on driving it with the same motivation as at the start?" Or more succinctly: Is fatigue caused by central versus peripheral mechanisms? They found that in sustained maximum voluntary contractions of the quadriceps, central fatigue may account for an appreciable proportion of the force loss, and they found no evidence that failure at the neuromuscular junction was a limiting factor. Five of their nine subjects consistently showed central fatigue while the rest did not. From this, we may conclude that both central and peripheral fatigue can be important factors, and many individual differences are involved.

Central Governor Model of Fatigue

More recently, a model has been proposed to explain the mechanism underlying fatigue; it is called the central governor model.[23,28] The **central governor model** postulates that the central nervous system regulates exercise performance to "ensure that catastrophic physiological failure does not occur during normal exercise in humans" (p. 511).[23] This is accomplished by the subconscious brain, which regulates the number of active motor units in the working muscles and provides a "pacing strategy that will allow completion of the task in the most efficient way while maintaining internal homeostasis and a metabolic and physiological reserve capacity" (p. 801).[28] According to the central governor model, the regulation of motor unit recruitment and power output by the subconscious brain occurs in "all forms of exercise" (p. 801).[28] Furthermore, the central governor model redefines fatigue by stating that "fatigue should no longer be considered a physical event but rather a sensation or emotion, separate from an overt physical manifestation—for example, the reduction in force output by the active muscles" (p. 121).[23]

central governor model

Thus, unlike the task-dependency model, the central governor model places the mechanism of fatigue under all exercise conditions in the brain (central fatigue) and indicates that exercise-induced physiological changes in the spinal cord as well as motor neuron and muscle fiber (peripheral fatigue) do not cause fatigue.

Accumulation and Depletion Hypotheses of Peripheral Fatigue

For many years it was commonly accepted that oxygen delivery alone limited exercise performance. Thus, performance limits, particularly during maximal but also during submaximal exercise, were explained largely in terms of oxygen transport to the muscle, oxygen utilization by the muscle, and availability of fuel to the muscle. To some degree, this "tunnel vision" limited the exploration of other factors determining muscle contractile function, while we concentrated on cardiovascular and respiratory limits to exercise performance.

Subsequent evidence suggested that we should question whether oxygen limitation develops during exercise.[22] It is now widely accepted that the factors limiting exercise performance might be better explained in terms of an interaction between oxygen limitations and a failure of muscle contractility.

With respect to the mechanisms underlying peripheral fatigue, two hypotheses have remained tenable over the years: (1) the accumulation of metabolites and (2) the depletion of energy substrates (fuels). Under various conditions (intensity and duration of physical activity), fatigue can be explained by either the accumulation hypothesis or the depletion hypothesis.[17]

Accumulation hypothesis

accumulation hypothesis

The **accumulation hypothesis** describes the fatigue-causing effects of the build-up of metabolic byproducts (metabolites) within muscle fibers. The metabolic byproducts that have received the most attention in this regard are lactate, inorganic phosphate, and ammonia.[17] High-intensity physical activities (about 85–95% of maximum) that can be maintained for approximately 20 to 30 seconds to 2 or 3 minutes, such as (but not limited to) 400- to 800-meter runs, 100- to 200-meter swims, gymnastics, field hockey, and speed skating, rely primarily on anaerobic glycolysis for adenosine triphosphate (ATP) production to sustain muscular activity (see Chapter 3). A naturally occurring metabolic byproduct of anaerobic glycolysis is lactate. Thus, fatigue occurs due to a build-up of lactate (with a concomitant increase in hydrogen ions and acidity, and decrease in pH) within the activated muscle fibers. The build-up of lactate interferes with muscle contraction in a number of ways. The processes affected by lactate include:

1. Calcium release from the sarcoplasmic reticulum
2. Actin–myosin binding
3. ATP breakdown (through reduced activity of the enzyme myosin ATPase)
4. ATP production (through decreased effectiveness of the various enzymes in the metabolic pathways)

However, the conventional wisdom that lactate build-up and the concomitant increase in acidity of the muscle cellular environment (decreased pH) cause fatigue has been challenged.[15,25] For example, it has been suggested that there is no biochemical support for lactate accumulation causing cellular acidosis[25] and that increased lactate production as a result of insufficient oxygen in the cellular environment is the exception and not the rule.[15] Furthermore, Gladden[15] has stated, "Lactate can no longer be considered the usual suspect for metabolic 'crimes,' but is instead a central player in cellular, regional and whole body metabolism" (p. 5). The primary theme of this hypothesis is that lactate can be shuttled from muscle fiber to muscle fiber and used for various metabolic processes including aerobic metabolism.[15] Thus, instead of lactate production causing fatigue and having a negative effect on exercise performance, it is hypothesized that it contributes positively to energy metabolism and may enhance exercise performance.[15,25]

Westerblad et al.[31] have suggested that the primary cause of fatigue during high-intensity exercise may be the build-up of inorganic phosphate in the muscle fiber instead of lactate. Inorganic phosphate accumulation may lead to fatigue by affecting a number of cellular processes including:[31]

1. Actin–myosin binding
2. Myofibrillar calcium sensitivity for binding with troponin
3. Calcium release from the sarcoplasmic reticulum
4. Calcium uptake by the sarcoplasmic reticulum

Muscle fibers

Less than 20 percent of available muscle fibers are used at any one time during variable-intensity 100-km cycling time trials. That is, muscle fibers seem to take turns working, and fatiguing fibers are continually replaced with "fresh" ones. To control this process the nervous system must keep track of the pattern of motor unit recruitment that has occurred. This phenomenon may be important as we learn how to avoid muscular fatigue and optimize performance.[29]

Depletion hypothesis

The **depletion hypothesis** describes fatigue in terms of the depletion of the fuels used to produce ATP. The depletion hypothesis has two basic aspects: (1) phosphagen depletion and (2) glycogen depletion. Which of these is responsible for fatigue depends on the intensity of the physical activity. **Phosphagen depletion** occurs during very-high-intensity activity, whereas **glycogen depletion** causes fatigue over a long period of time during moderate-intensity exercise.

- depletion hypothesis
- phosphagen depletion
- glycogen depletion

1. *Phosphagen depletion.* The phosphagens ATP and phosphocreatine are stored in small amounts within the muscle fibers and serve to supply energy for muscular contraction during maximal- or near-maximal-intensity physical activity (see Chapter 3). The phosphagens are the fuels for the ATP–PC energy production system, which functions during activities that last up to approximately 15 to 20 seconds, such as 100- to 200-meter runs, power lifting, Olympic lifting, and high jumping. If very-high-intensity physical activity is continued, fatigue occurs when phosphocreatine stores within the muscle fibers are depleted (and ATP levels may be reduced).

2. *Glycogen depletion.* During moderate-intensity and long-duration physical activities such as the marathon or triathlon, ATP is produced primarily through aerobic metabolism of carbohydrates and fats. While we have a huge amount of energy stored in the form of fat, we have limited stores of glycogen within skeletal muscle. Over the course of long-duration activities such as distance running or cycling, the glycogen stores are gradually depleted. For example, it has been suggested that the **"runner's wall"** that marathon runners experience at around 18 to 20 miles is probably caused by glycogen depletion in the most active fibers of the quadriceps muscles. When fatigue occurs due to glycogen depletion, the runner must slow down and may continue the marathon (at a slower pace) using only the aerobic metabolism of fats.

- runner's wall

MUSCLE TEMPERATURE AND FATIGUE

Deep muscle temperature affects fatigue. Figure 14.3 illustrates the inverted U-shaped relationship between time to exhaustion and muscle temperature during submaximal isometric muscle actions. At high muscle temperatures, the reduction in endurance may be due to a rapid accumulation of metabolites within the activated muscle fibers. Low muscle temperature may lead to fatigue by affecting neuromuscular electrical transmission or the contractile properties of the muscle.

figure 14.3 The relationship between time to exhaustion and muscle temperature during submaximal isometric muscle actions.

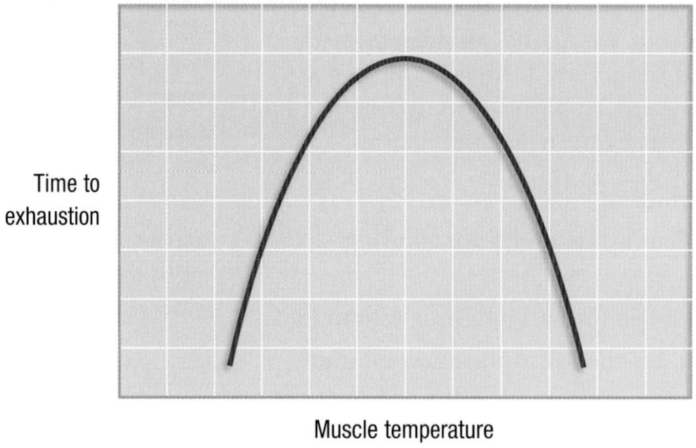

MYOELECTRIC MANIFESTATIONS OF FATIGUE

Time Domain

Chapter 4 provides a description of electromyography (EMG) and its uses in examining muscle function including neuromuscular fatigue. The electrical activity (EMG amplitude) in muscle tissue increases over time during submaximal fatiguing tasks.[13,21] Under most conditions, the fatigue curves that come from measuring EMG responses from a working muscle over time during a fatiguing task are linear, and the EMG voltage–time relationship is inversely related to the endurance time (see Figure 14.4). Similar fatigue curves are found for isometric and dynamic muscle actions as well as for cycle ergometry.[9,10,21,24,30] Figure 14.5 shows EMG fatigue curves during non-fatiguing and fatiguing cycle ergometer work bouts.[10] Riding at the lowest power output for two minutes resulted in no fatigue and, therefore, no increase in EMG voltage. At the two higher power outputs, however, fatigue was demonstrated by increases in EMG voltage throughout the two-minute

figure 14.4 The relationship between EMG voltage and time to exhaustion during fatiguing tasks with increasing force outputs. As the slope of the EMG voltage–time relationship increases, time to exhaustion decreases.

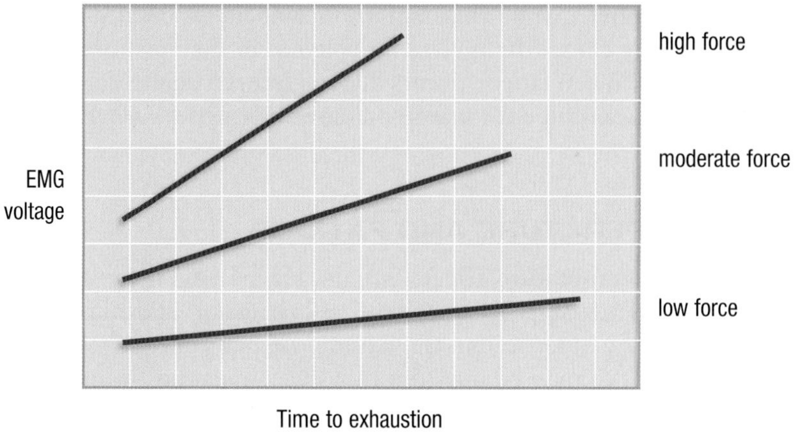

figure 14.5

The relationship between EMG voltage and time at non-fatiguing and fatiguing power outputs during cycle ergometry. During non-fatiguing work bouts, there is no increase in EMG voltage over time. With fatigue, however, EMG voltage increases over time.

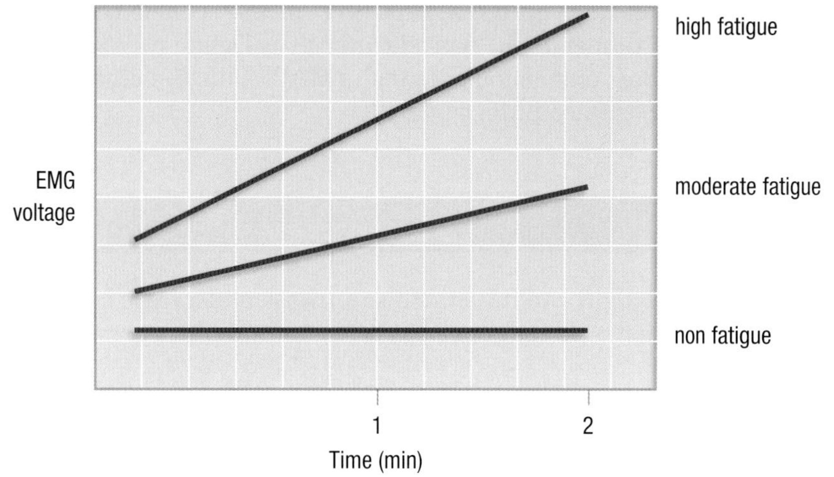

work bouts. The increase in electrical activity during a fatiguing task results from both the recruitment of additional motor units and increases in the firing rate of already activated motor units to make up for the force that is lost as motor units fatigue and can no longer contribute to the activity.

Frequency Domain

Neuromuscular fatigue results in a shift in the power density spectrum (PDS; see Chapter 4 under "Frequency Domain") of the surface EMG signal to lower frequencies. As shown in Figure 14.6, with fatigue the PDS shifts to the left, and more of the power of the EMG signal is located in the lower frequency range. As discussed in Chapter 4, the most common variables used to describe the characteristics of the PDS of the surface EMG signal are the mean power frequency (MPF)

figure 14.6

Effect of fatigue on the power density spectrum (PDS) of the surface EMG signal.

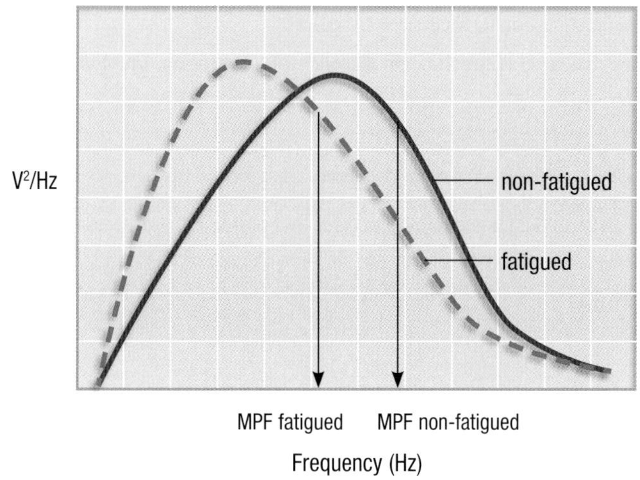

and median power frequency (MDPF) (see Chapter 4, Figure 4.11). Both the MPF and MDPF of the EMG signal decrease with fatigue (Figure 14.6). The exact physiological mechanism(s) that causes the fatigue-induced decrease in MPF and MDPF is unknown.[4] It has been suggested, however, that under some conditions, exercise-induced changes in the acidity (pH) of the cellular environment due to the accumulation of metabolic byproducts such as lactate decrease the conduction velocity of the motor unit action potentials (MAPs) and, therefore, reduce the MPF and MDPF of the surface EMG signal.[4,8]

summary

Neuromuscular fatigue can be defined as a transient decrease in muscular performance usually seen as a failure to maintain or develop a certain expected force or power output.

The mechanisms underlying neuromuscular fatigue can be of central or peripheral origin. Central fatigue involves mechanisms that are located proximal to the motor neurons, while peripheral fatigue involves motor neurons and muscle fibers. Central fatigue is normally associated with a reduction in the level of excitation from the brain. Peripheral fatigue is caused by the accumulation of metabolic byproducts in the muscle fiber (the accumulation hypothesis) or the depletion of energy substrates (phosphagens or glycogen) within the muscle fiber (the depletion hypothesis). The causes of fatigue vary under varying exercise conditions (intensity and duration).

The amplitude of the electromyographic (EMG) signal quantifies the electrical activity within skeletal muscle, which increases over time during submaximal fatiguing tasks. This increase results from the recruitment of additional motor units and increases in motor unit firing rates.

questions for review

1. Discuss the evidence for central versus peripheral mechanisms of fatigue.
2. What are the implications of the Setchenov phenomenon for coaches and exercise professionals?
3. How does exercise cause central fatigue?
4. How does exercise cause peripheral fatigue?
5. What can coaches and exercise professionals learn by studying EMG curves?

student companion website

For further review of this book's chapters and for test preparation, visit the book's website, **www.hhpcommunities.com/exercisephysiology**, to take practice quizzes, review the vocabulary terms, use the study guide, and view the digital image bank.

references

1. Asmussen, E. Muscle fatigue. *Med. Sci. Sport.* 11: 313–321, 1979.
2. Bigland-Ritchie, B., Jones, D. A., Hosking, G. P., and Edwards, R. H. T. Central and peripheral fatigue in sustained maximum contractions of human quadriceps muscle. *Clin. Mol. Med.* 54: 609–614, 1978.
3. Bigland-Ritchie, B., Rice, C. L., Garland, S. J., and Walsh, M. L. Task-dependent factors in fatigue of human voluntary contractions. *Adv. Exp. Med. Biol.* 384: 361–380, 1995.
4. Brody, L. R., Pollock, M. T., Roy, S. H., De Luca, C. J., and Celli, B. pH-induced effects on median frequency and conduction velocity of the myoelectric signal. *J. Appl. Physiol.* 71: 1878–1885, 1991.
5. Burke, E. R. Nutritional ergogenic aids. In *Nutrition for Sport and Exercise,* 2nd edition. J. R. Berning and S. N. Steen (eds.). Gaithersburg, MD: Aspen Publishers, 1998, pp. 119–142.
6. Cairns, S. P., Knicker, A. J., Thompson, M. W., and Sjogaard, G. Evaluation of models used to study neuromuscular fatigue. *Exerc. Sport Sci. Rev.* 33: 9–16, 2005.
7. Davis, J. M., and Bailey, S. P. Possible mechanisms of central nervous system fatigue during exercise. *Med. Sci. Sports Exerc.* 29: 45–57, 1997.
8. De Luca, C. J. The use of surface electromyography in biomechanics. *J. Appl. Biomech.* 13: 135–163, 1997.
9. deVries, H. A. Method for evaluation of muscle fatigue and endurance from electromyographic fatigue curves. *Am. J. Phys. Med.* 47: 125–135, 1968.
10. deVries, H. A., Tichy, M. W., Housh, T. J., Smyth, K. D., Tichy, A. M., and Housh, D. J. A method for estimating physical working capacity at the fatigue threshold (PWCFT). *Ergonomics* 30: 1195–1204, 1987.
11. Dirckx, J. H. *Stedman's Concise Medical Dictionary for the Health Professions,* 4th edition. Baltimore: Lippincott Williams & Wilkins, 2001.
12. Enoka, R. M. *Neuromechanics of Human Movement,* 3rd edition. Champaign, IL: Human Kinetics, 2002.
13. Enoka, R. M., and Stuart, D. G. Neurobiology of muscle fatigue. *J. Appl. Physiol.* 72: 1631–1648, 1992.
14. Gibala, M. J., Hargreaves, M., and Tipton, K. Amino acids, proteins, and exercise performance. *Gatorade Sports Sci. Exch.* 11: 1–4, 2000.
15. Gladden, L. B. Lactate metabolism: A new paradigm for the third millennium. *J. Physiol.* 558: 5–30, 2004.
16. Ikai, M., Yabe, K., and Ishii, K. Muskelkraft und muskulare ermudung bei willkurlicher anspannung und elektrisher reizung des muskels. *Sportartz. un sportmedizin.* 5: 197–211, 1967.
17. MacLaren, D. P. M., Gibson, H., Parry-Billings, M., and Edwards, R. H. T. A review of metabolic and physiological factors in fatigue. *Exerc. Sport Sci. Rev.* 17: 29–68, 1989.
18. Maluf, K. S., and Enoka, R. M. Task failure during fatiguing contractions performed by humans. *J. Appl. Physiol.* 99: 389–396, 2005.
19. Merton, P. A. Voluntary strength and fatigue. *J. Physiol.* 123: 553–564, 1954.
20. Merton, P. A. Problems of muscular fatigue. *Brit. Med. Bull.* 12: 219–221, 1956.
21. Moritani, T., and Yoshitake, Y. The use of electromyography in applied physiology. *J. Electromyogr. Kinesiol.* 8: 363–381, 1998.
22. Noakes, T. D. Implications of exercise testing for prediction of athletic performance: A contemporary perspective. *Med. Sci. Sports Exerc.* 20: 319–330, 1988.
23. Noakes, T. D., St. Clair Gibson, A., and Lambert, E. V. From catastrophe to complexity: A novel model of integrative central neural regulation of effort and fatigue during exercise in humans: Summary and conclusions. *Br. J. Sports Med.* 38: 511–514, 2004.
24. Petrofsky, J. S. Frequency and amplitude analysis of the EMG during exercise on the bicycle ergometer. *Eur. J. Appl. Physiol.* 41: 1–15, 1979.
25. Robergs, R. A., Ghiasvand, F., and Parker, D. Biochemistry of exercise-induced metabolic acidosis. *Am. J. Physiol. Regul. Integr. Comp. Physiol.* 287: R502–R516, 2004.
26. Sherrington, C. S. *The Integrated Action of the Nervous System.* New Haven, CT: Yale University Press, 1947.
27. Simonson, E. *Physiology of Work Capacity and Fatigue.* Springfield, IL: Charles C. Thomas Publisher, 1971.
28. St. Clair Gibson, A., and Noakes, T. D. Evidence for complex system integration and dynamic neural regulation of skeletal muscle recruitment during exercise in humans. *Br. J. Sports Med.* 38: 797–806, 2004.
29. St. Clair Gibson, A., Schabort, E. J., and Noakes, T. D. Reduced neuromuscular activity and force generation during prolonged cycling. *Am. J. Physiol. Regul. Integr. Comp. Physiol.* 281: R187–R196, 2001.
30. Stegman, D. F., Blok, J. H., Hermens, H. J., and Roeleveld, K. Surface EMG models: Properties and applications. *J. Electromyogr. Kinesiol.* 10: 313–326, 2000.
31. Westerblad, H., Allen, D. G., and Lannergren, J. Muscle fatigue: Lactic acid or inorganic phosphate the major cause? *News Physiol. Sci.* 17: 17–21, 2002.

Critical Velocity for Track Running Test

BACKGROUND

The purpose of this lab is to describe the procedures for performing the critical velocity (CV) test on a running track. The CV test estimates three parameters of physical working capacity:[1,2,3,4,5] (1) the maximal running velocity that can be maintained for an extended period of time without fatigue, called the CV; (2) the total distance that can be run using only stored energy sources within the activated muscles, such as creatine phosphate, glycogen, and oxygen bound to myoglobin, called the anaerobic running capacity (ARC); and (3) the time to exhaustion or time limit (TL) during continuous running at any velocity (V) greater than the CV. The CV test uses linear mathematical modeling of the relationship between the total distance (TD) at different velocities and the corresponding TL values to simultaneously estimate the CV, ARC, and TL at any V greater than the CV (Figure L14.1).

Critical velocity (CV). The CV is an estimate of the maximal running velocity that can be maintained for an extended period of time without fatigue and is conceptually analogous to the anaerobic threshold.[2,4] The anaerobic threshold is

figure L14.1 Curvilinear velocity (V) versus time limit (TL) relationship.

Figure L14.1a represents the negative, curvilinear velocity (V) versus time limit (TL) relationship and provides the equation that can be used to estimate the TL for any V greater than the CV. Please note that, theoretically, any V less than the CV can be maintained indefinitely without exhaustion. In reality, however, the CV can often be maintained for an extended period of time (usually > 30 minutes), but not indefinitely. Figure L14.1b represents the linear relationship between total distance (TD) and TL, and provides the equation that can be used to estimate the CV and anaerobic running capacity (ARC).

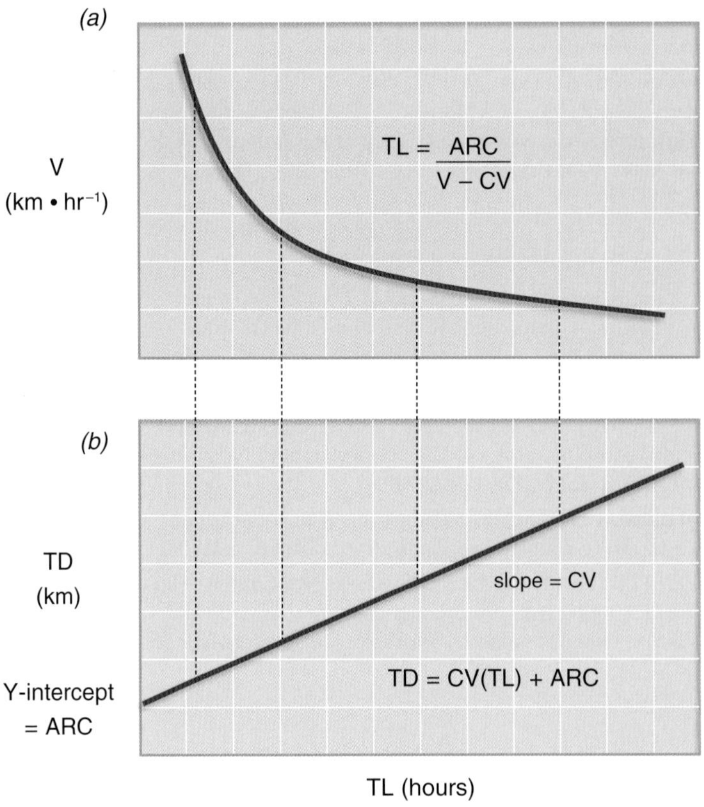

one of three primary physiological factors (along with $\dot{V}O_2$ max and economy of movement) that contribute to performance in endurance events. The anaerobic threshold is typically determined from the measurement of blood lactate levels (the lactate threshold) or expired gas samples (the gas exchange threshold or ventilatory threshold). A salient feature of the critical velocity for track running test, however, is that it requires only a running track, markers (e.g., orange cones, reflective tape) placed at 100-meter intervals around the track, and a stopwatch.

Anaerobic running capacity (ARC). The ARC is an estimate of the total distance that can be run using only stored energy sources within the activated muscles, such as creatine phosphate, glycogen, and oxygen bound to myoglobin.[3] Theoretically, the ARC represents the capacity to produce ATP from anaerobic metabolic pathways. Thus, the CV test provides estimates of physical working capacity associated with both aerobic (the CV) and anaerobic (ARC) ATP production.

Time to exhaustion or time limit (TL). There is a negative, curvilinear (asymptotic) relationship between V and TL that is called the V versus TL curve (Figure L14.1a). Based on fitness level, each individual has a unique V versus TL curve. The linear mathematical model used to estimate CV and ARC (Figure L14.1b) can also be used to derive an individual's V versus TL curve and, therefore, an equation to predict the person's TL for any V greater than the CV. Theoretically, the CV is the asymptote of the V versus TL curve (Figure L14.1a) and, thus, any V $\leq$ CV should be able to be continued indefinitely. In reality, however, the CV can often be maintained for an extended period of time (usually > 30 minutes), but not indefinitely.[2,4,5]

TERMS & ABBREVIATIONS

- ☐ ARC = anaerobic running capacity (km), defined as the y-intercept of the total distance (TD) versus TL relationship (Figure L14.1b)
- ☐ CV = critical velocity ($km \cdot hr^{-1}$), defined as the slope coefficient of the total distance (TD) versus TL relationship (Figure L14.1b).
- ☐ TL = time to exhaustion or time limit (TL) (hours)
- ☐ V = velocity ($km \cdot hr^{-1}$)

PROCEDURES

(see photo 14.1)

The CV test can be performed on either a 400-meter or a 200-meter track (or other length tracks with appropriate modifications for time splits). The equipment required for the test includes stopwatches and two or four markers that will be placed at 100-meter increments around the track. Four markers are used for a 400-meter track, and two markers are used for a 200-meter track. The three parameters of physical working capacity that will be determined are the CV, ARC, and TL for any running V greater than the CV.

photo 14.1

Subject completing the critical velocity test.

1. As stated previously, an important feature of the CV test is that it uses very little equipment. The test does, however, require two (or more) exhaustive runs, each of which is performed at a different constant velocity. To achieve constant velocities during the runs, the subject will be required to reach 100-meter intervals on the track at designated time points, or splits. For example, with a 400-meter track, four markers are placed at 100-meter intervals around the track. If a subject is required to run at a velocity of 18 km • hr^{-1} (11.18 mph), he or she should reach the first marker (i.e., 100 meters away from the starting line) in 20 seconds, the second marker in 40 seconds, the third marker in 60 seconds, and the starting line in 80 seconds (Figure L14.2). Figure L14.2 shows the 100-meter time splits required for four different velocities. It is important to note that the same time splits can be used for a 200-meter track. With a 200-meter track, however, only two markers (one at the starting line and another one 100 meters away from the starting line) are used. For untrained subjects, the recommended 100-meter time splits when using only two runs for the CV test are 30 seconds (12 km • hr^{-1} or 7.45 mph) and 20 seconds (18 km • hr^{-1} or 11.18 mph). For trained subjects or experienced runners, the recommended 100-meter time splits are 25 seconds (14.4 km • hr^{-1} or 8.94 mph) and 15 seconds (24 km • hr^{-1} or 14.91 mph).
2. Warm-up. Prior to the warm-up, record a pre-exercise heart rate. The CV test should be preceded by a warm-up that includes three minutes of walking and then three minutes of jogging at a comfortable pace around the track.
3. Following the warm-up and a two-minute rest period, instruct the subject that during the test, he or she should run at the designated time splits for as long as possible. The run ends when the subject cannot maintain the designated split time.

figure L14.2 Example of the marker locations for the critical velocity (CV) test with a 400-meter track.

The 100-meter time splits are shown. Note that the CV test can also be performed with a 200-meter track, in which case only two markers would be used (one at the starting line, and another one that is 100 meters away from the starting line).

100-meter time splits for four running velocities:

15-second time splits = 24 km • hr^{-1} or 14.91 mph

20-second time splits = 18 km • hr^{-1} or 11.18 mph

25-second time splits = 14.4 km • hr^{-1} or 8.94 mph

30-second time splits = 12 km • hr^{-1} or 7.45 mph

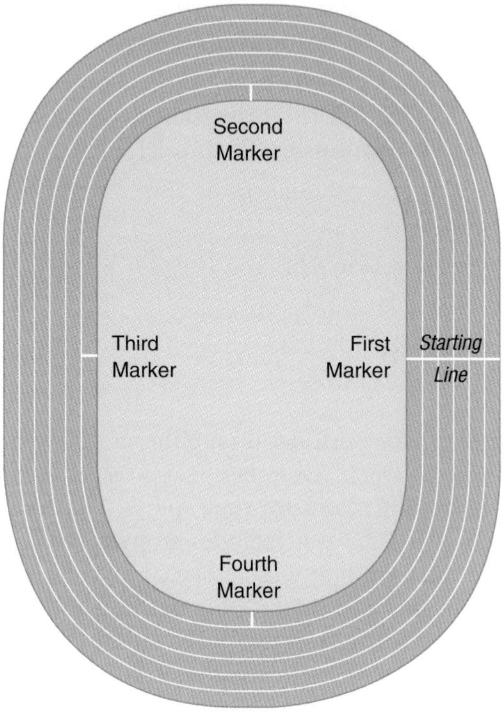

4. When the subject is ready to begin the test, have him or her start a stopwatch and run toward the first marker to complete the first time split. If the subject is unable to accomplish any of the first four time splits, he or she should stop the test and rest until his or her heart rate is within 10 beats per minute of the resting heart rate. The test should then be restarted at a lower velocity.
5. For each run, the TL is recorded on Worksheet 14.1 when the subject can no longer complete the designated time splits. The TL is then calculated with the following equation:

   TL = number of time splits (each 100 meters) successfully completed
   × duration (in seconds) of each split

   For example, if the subject ran 20-second time splits and was able to complete eight splits, then the TL was 160 seconds (8 time splits × 20 seconds per split), or 0.044 hours. The corresponding TD can then be calculated with the following equation:

   TD = number of time splits successfully completed × distance (in meters) of each split

   Thus, the TD for this example would be 800 meters (8 time splits × 100 meters per split), or 0.8 km.
6. Cool-down. After each exhaustive run, have the subject walk around the track at a comfortable pace for as long as desired.
7. No more than two exhaustive runs at different velocities (time splits) should be performed on a single day. If a second run is to be performed on the same day, have the subject rest (following the cool-down) until his or her heart rate returns to within 10 beats per minute of the pre-exercise level to ensure that the individual is fully recovered before performing the second run. This usually takes at least 30 minutes.

SAMPLE CALCULATIONS

Calculations of CV and ARC, as well as the derivation of the equation used to estimate the TL for any V greater than the CV, follow.

1. Calculate the TL and TD for each of the two or more track runs at different velocities.

   FIRST RUN

   100 meter time split = 20 seconds (18 km • hr^{-1})

   Number of time splits successfully completed = 8

   TL = 8 time splits × 20 seconds per split = 160 seconds = 0.044 hours

   TD = 8 time splits × 100 meters per split = 800 meters = 0.8 km

   SECOND RUN

   100 meter time split = 30 seconds (12 km • hr^{-1})

   Number of time splits successfully completed = 14

   TL = 14 time splits × 30 seconds per split = 420 seconds = 0.117 hours

   TD = 14 time splits × 100 meters per split = 1400 meters = 1.4 km

2. Use a simple linear regression analysis (y = b(x) + a) to characterize the relationship for the TD (km) values for the two track runs versus the corresponding TL (hours) values (Figure L14.3b). Simple linear regression can be performed using

many handheld calculators or software (such as Microsoft Excel and others). The slope coefficient and y-intercept values for the linear TD versus TL relationship are the CV and ARC, respectively (Figure L14.3b).

	TD (km)	TL (hours)
First run (20-second time splits)	0.8	0.044
Second run (30-second time splits)	1.4	0.117

Simple linear regression equation: TD = 8.22 (TL) + 0.44

Thus,

$$CV = 8.22\ km \bullet hr^{-1} \text{ and } ARC = 0.44\ km$$

3. The linear regression analysis used to determine the CV and ARC for each subject is also used to derive the equation to estimate the TL for any V greater than the CV (Figure L14.3a). The equation is derived by equalizing the two mathematical expressions for determining the TD. That is,

$$TD = V(TL) = CV(TL) + ARC$$

Thus,

$$CV(TL) + ARC = V(TL)$$

$$ARC = V(TL) - CV(TL)$$

$$ARC = TL(V - CV)$$

$$\frac{ARC}{(V - CV)} = \frac{TL(V - CV)}{(V - CV)}$$

$$TL = \frac{ARC}{V - CV}$$

If a subject's CV = 8.22 km • hr^{-1} and ARC = 0.44 km, what is his or her TL at a V of 16 km • hr^{-1}?

$$TL = \frac{0.44}{16 - 8.22} = 0.057 \text{ hours (3.42 minutes)}$$

Graphic representation of sample calculations for critical velocity (CV = 8.22 km • hr^{-1}), anaerobic running capacity (ARC = 0.44 km), and the estimated time limit (TL = 0.057 hours) at 16 km • hr^{-1}.

figure L14.3

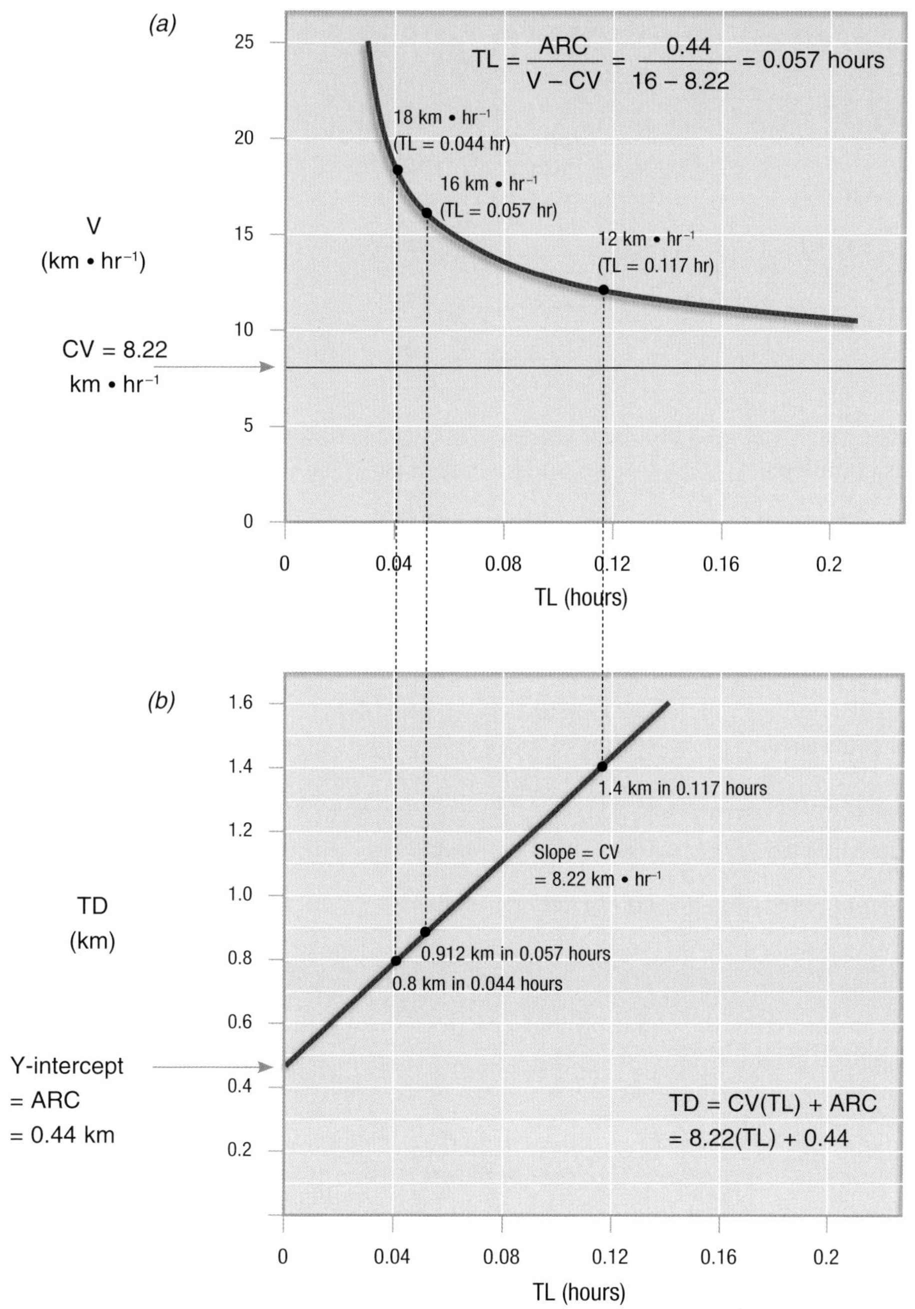

worksheet 14.1 CRITICAL VELOCITY FOR TRACK RUNNING TEST FORM

NAME ______________________________ DATE ______________

Pre-exercise Heart Rate ______________

Velocity (V) *Time splits*

Velocity 1: ____________ $km \bullet hr^{-1}$ ____________ sec

Velocity 2: ____________ $km \bullet hr^{-1}$ ____________ sec

Velocity 3 (if used): ____________ $km \bullet hr^{-1}$ ____________ sec

Velocity 4 (if used): ____________ $km \bullet hr^{-1}$ ____________ sec

Time Limit (TL)

Velocity 1: Number of splits completed ___ × ___ seconds per split = ___ seconds ÷ 3600 = ___ hours

Velocity 2: Number of splits completed ___ × ___ seconds per split = ___ seconds ÷ 3600 = ___ hours

Velocity 3: Number of splits completed ___ × ___ seconds per split = ___ seconds ÷ 3600 = ___ hours

Velocity 4: Number of splits completed ___ × ___ seconds per split = ___ seconds ÷ 3600 = ___ hours

Total Distance (TD)

Velocity 1: Number of splits completed ____ × 100 meters per split = ____ m ÷ 1000 = ____ km

Velocity 2: Number of splits completed ____ × 100 meters per split = ____ m ÷ 1000 = ____ km

Velocity 3: Number of splits completed ____ × 100 meters per split = ____ m ÷ 1000 = ____ km

Velocity 4: Number of splits completed ____ × 100 meters per split = ____ m ÷ 1000 = ____ km

TD vs. TL Relationship

Use linear regression analysis to determine the equation that describes the TD versus TL relationship:
TD = CV(TL) + ARC (see Figure L14.3b)

CV = ______________ $km \bullet hr^{-1}$

ARC = ______________ km

Equation for estimating the TL at any V greater than the CV (see Figure L14.3a)

$$TL = \frac{ARC}{V - CV} = \_\_\_\_\_\_\_\_\_\_\_\_\_\_ \text{ hours}$$

EXTENSION ACTIVITIES

worksheet 14.2

NAME ______________________________ DATE ______________________________

1. A critical velocity for track running test resulted in the following data:

TD (km)	V ($km \bullet hr^{-1}$)	TL (hours)
2.64	______	______
2.32	______	______
1.20	______	______
1.12	______	______

Given the expected relationships among TD, V, and TL, fill in the blanks with the V and TL values from the randomly ordered choices below.

V ($km \bullet hr^{-1}$) = 18.5, 16.9, 19.3, 17.7

TL (hours) = 0.065, 0.058, 0.131, 0.156

2. Given a CV of 15.94 $km \bullet hr^{-1}$ and an ARC of 0.19 km, what is the estimated TL for a V of 18.0 $km \bullet hr^{-1}$?

3. Use your own data to calculate the following:

   a. CV = ______________ $km \bullet hr^{-1}$

   b. ARC = ______________ km

   c. TL at a V of CV + 2.0 $km \bullet hr^{-1}$ = ______________ hours

EXTENSION QUESTIONS

1. What are some common mistakes that may occur in administering this lab?

2. Identify possible sources of error in this lab.

3. Assess the practicality of using this lab in the field.

4. Research the reliability and/or validity of this lab using online resources, journal articles, and other credible sources.

REFERENCES

1. Housh, T. J., Cramer, J. T., Bull, A. J., Johnson, G. O., and Housh, D. J. The effect of mathematical modeling on critical velocity. *Eur. J. Appl. Physiol.* 84: 469–475, 2001.
2. Housh, T. J., Johnson, G. O., McDowell, S. L., Housh, D. J., and Pepper, M. Physiological responses at the fatigue threshold. *Int. J. Sports Med.* 12: 305–308, 1991.
3. Housh, T. J., Johnson, G. O., McDowell, S. L., Housh, D. J., and Pepper, M. The relationship between anaerobic running capacity and peak plasma lactate. *J. Sports Med. Phys. Fitness* 32: 117–122, 1992.
4. Hughson, R. L., Orok, C. J., and Staudt, L. E. A high velocity treadmill running test to assess endurance running potential. *Int. J. Sports Med.* 5: 23–25, 1984.
5. Pepper, M. L., Housh, T. J., and Johnson, G. O. The accuracy of the critical velocity test for predicting time to exhaustion during treadmill running. *Int. J. Sports Med.* 13: 121–124, 1992.

15 Nutrition for Fitness and Athletics

As a result of reading this chapter you will:

Understand the importance of diet for fitness and athletics.

Know the approximate daily caloric intake recommendations for adult athletes and non-athletes.

Know the American College of Sports Medicine recommendations for the percentages of carbohydrates, proteins, and fats in the diet for athletes and non-athletes.

Understand the importance of carbohydrate intake prior to, during, and after exercise.

Know the basic vitamin and mineral needs of athletes and non-athletes.

Understand the importance of fluid ingestion prior to, during, and after exercise.

Be familiar with general recommendations for pre-exercise meals and snacks.

key concepts

complete protein
complex carbohydrate
disaccharide
essential amino acid
frank anemia
hemochromatosis
hypoglycemia
latent iron deficiency
monosaccharide
prelatent iron deficiency
recommended daily caloric intake
simple carbohydrate
sports anemia

A proper diet can contribute to the health and well-being of all individuals. In addition, with ever-increasing levels of competition, athletes and coaches have developed considerable interest in nutrition. Unfortunately, sports nutrition is an area in which misinformation from faddists and self-proclaimed experts often obscures scientifically valid information.

Furthermore, exercise professionals and coaches are sometimes influenced by the success of athletes whose training regimens include such dietary fads as royal jelly, kelp, blackstrap molasses, or other substances thought to have miraculous properties for improving athletic performance. More often than not, when these substances are tested by scientific methods in controlled experiments, it turns out that an athlete's success was achieved in spite of, not because of, the unusual dietary modifications.

Along with training, skill, genetics, and motivation, a sound diet is essential for long-term successful athletic and exercise performance, and performance can deteriorate rapidly if the diet is less than optimal. According to the American College of Sports Medicine, American Dietetic Association, and Dietitians of Canada,[2] "physical activity, athletic performance, and recovery from exercise are enhanced by optimal nutrition." Furthermore, a nutritious diet can be obtained in many different ways, and the best diet for one athlete may not be the best diet for another athlete. Individual differences exist in our sense of taste as well as in our systems of enzymes, which are necessary for digestion and absorption.

LONG-TERM DIETARY CONSIDERATIONS AND REQUIREMENTS

Caloric Intake

recommended daily caloric intake

Table 15.1 provides the **recommended daily caloric intake** for males and females of various ages and levels of physical activity.[35] These recommendations were designed for the maintenance of good health for healthy persons in the United States. For moderately active adult males and females, daily caloric intakes of 2200 to 2800 and 1800 to 2200 kilocalories per day, respectively, are recommended.[35] It should be recognized, however, that these caloric intake values would not be sufficient for athletes involved in heavy training, who often consume 4000 to 7000 kilocalories per day.

Athletes must consume enough food daily to meet the energy demands of their training programs. If they eat less than this, they will burn body tissues to make up the deficit. If they consume more food than they need, the result will be increases in body weight and body fatness with the accompanying disadvantages in performance.

Proportion of Macronutrients (Carbohydrate, Protein, and Fat) in the Diet

www

Nutrition Information
www.choosemyplate.gov

Thirty years ago, a typical American diet contained approximately 46 percent carbohydrate, 12 percent protein, and 42 percent fat.[17] Today, however, it is slightly higher in carbohydrate (48–50%) and protein (16%) intake and lower in fat (34%) content.[34] It is recommended that a healthful diet include approximately 45 to 65 percent carbohydrate, 10 to 35 percent protein, and 20 to 35 percent fat.[15] An athlete's diet, however, should be composed of approximately 55 to 65 percent carbohydrate, 12 to 15 percent protein, and 20 to 35 percent fat.[3] Furthermore, it is recommended that saturated fat make up no more than 10 percent of total calories (10–25% of total calories from mono- and polyunsaturated fats),[3] and the carbohydrate component of the diet should consist of approximately 45 to 55 percent starches and 10 percent simple sugars.[3] See Figure 15.1.

table 15.1 Estimated caloric needs per day by age, gender, and physical activity level.

Estimated amounts of kilocalories[a] needed to maintain calorie balance for various gender and age groups at three different levels of physical activity. The estimates are rounded to the nearest 200 kilocalories. An individual's caloric needs may be higher or lower than these average estimates.

AGE	MALE			FEMALE[b]		
	SEDENTARY	MODERATELY ACTIVE	ACTIVE	SEDENTARY	MODERATELY ACTIVE	ACTIVE
2 to 3	1,000	1,000–1,400	1,000–1,400	1,000	1,000–1,200	1,000–1,400
4 to 8	1,200–1,400	1,400–1,600	1,600–2,000	1,200–1,400	1,400–1,600	1,400–1,800
9 to 13	1,600–2,000	1,800–2,200	2,000–2,600	1,400–1,600	1,600–2,000	1,800–2,200
14 to 18	2,000–2,400	2,400–2,800	2,800–3,200	1,800	2,000	2,400
19 to 30	2,600–2,400	2,800–2,600	3,000	2,000–1,800	2,200–2000	2,400
31 to 50	2,400–2,200	2,600–2,400	3,000–2,800	1,800	2,000	2,200
51 to 75	2,200–2,000	2,400–2,200	2,800–2,600	1,600	1,800	2,200–2,000
75+	2000	2,200	2,400	1,600	1,800	2,000

Note: *Sedentary* means a lifestyle that includes only the light physical activity associated with typical day-to-day life. *Moderately active* means a lifestyle that includes physical activity equivalent to walking about 1.5 to 3 miles per day at 3 to 4 miles per hour, in addition to the light physical activity associated with typical day-to-day life. *Active* means a lifestyle that includes physical activity equivalent to walking more than 3 miles per day at 3 to 4 miles per hour, in addition to the light physical activity associated with typical day-to-day life.

a. Based on Estimated Energy Requirements (EER) equations, using reference heights (average) and reference weights (healthy) for each age–gender group. For children and adolescents, reference height and weight vary. For adults, the reference man is 5 feet 10 inches tall and weighs 154 pounds. The reference woman is 5 feet 4 inches tall and weighs 126 pounds. EER equations are from the Institute of Medicine. *Dietary Reference Intakes for Energy, Carbohydrate, Fiber, Fat, Fatty Acids, Cholesterol, Protein, and Amino Acids.* Washington, D.C.: The National Academies Press, 2002.

b. Estimates for females do not include women who are pregnant or breastfeeding.

Source: U.S. Department of Agriculture and U.S. Department of Health and Human Services. *Dietary Guidelines for Americans, 2015,* 8th edition, Washington, DC: U.S. Government Printing Office, 2015. Available at http://health.gov/dietaryguidelines/2015/guidelines/appendix-2/ footnote-1

figure 15.1 Comparison of typical to recommended adult American diet.

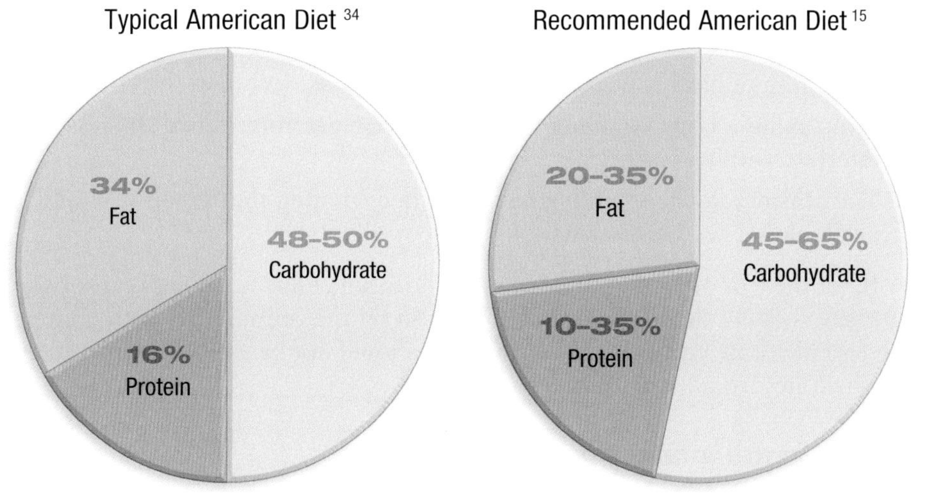

Dietary Carbohydrate Intake for Fitness and Athletics

Recommendation: 55 to 65 percent of total calories from carbohydrates with approximately 10 percent in the form of simple sugars: 6–10 grams per kilogram of body weight per day.[2,3]

Carbohydrates have been called the "master fuel" because of their importance in energy metabolism and their potential in preventing diseases.[12,37] Dietary carbohydrates contribute to energy production during exercise in the form of blood glucose and stored muscle glycogen. Manipulation of carbohydrate intake and exercise can result in larger than normal stores of muscle glycogen and increased endurance time for moderate-intensity, long-duration activities such as the marathon and triathlon (see Chapter 16 on ergogenic aids).

Although fat produces more than twice as much energy per gram as carbohydrate (4 kcal per gram of carbohydrate and 9 kcal per gram of fat),[37] fat requires more oxygen for each calorie (213 mL per kcal of fat compared with 198 mL per kcal of carbohydrate). In athletic events where energy production per unit of oxygen consumed is an important factor, carbohydrates offer an advantage of some 7.5 percent.

Simple and complex carbohydrates

complex carbohydrates

simple carbohydrates

monosaccharides

disaccharides

Complex carbohydrates (such as starches) are a combination of three or more glucose molecules, while simple carbohydrates (sugars) contain only one or two sugar molecules joined together. **Simple carbohydrates** can be further subdivided into **monosaccharides** (such as glucose, fructose, and galactose) and **disaccharides** (such as sucrose, lactose, and maltose). Disaccharides are two simple sugar molecules in combination (e.g., glucose plus fructose to form sucrose).

It is generally recommended that only approximately 10 percent of total caloric intake be in the form of simple sugars found in such foods as fruit and honey. Complex carbohydrates, commonly found in such foods as vegetables, pasta, and grains, are nutrient dense and provide more B vitamins, fiber, and iron than do simple sugars.[12]

High-carbohydrate supplements

Some athletes have difficulty eating enough food to account for the energy demands of very high volumes of training. Inadequate total caloric intake often results in less than optimal carbohydrate consumption. Coleman[12] has identified three reasons athletes sometimes have difficulty consuming enough carbohydrates:

1. The stress of hard training can decrease appetite.
2. Consuming a large volume of food can cause gastrointestinal distress and interfere with training.
3. The athlete may be spending so much time training that few rest hours are available for replenishment.

If, for these or other reasons, an athlete does not consume enough carbohydrates, he or she is likely to benefit from supplementing the normal diet with commercial high-carbohydrate products. These products should not be used as a replacement for carbohydrates from a nutritionally sound diet.

Carbohydrate intake prior to exercise

Athletes should avoid eating large amounts (200–300 kcal) of sugar 30 to 45 minutes prior to exercise.[13,18] Consuming sugar causes increases in blood glucose, which stimulates the release of insulin into circulation from the pancreas. Over a period of time, the combination of elevated insulin and exercise facilitates glucose removal from the blood and can result in **hypoglycemia** (depressed blood glucose), which may hinder performance.

hypoglycemia

Eating a meal that contains 200 to 300 grams of carbohydrates, three to four hours before exercise, has been shown to enhance performance.[2] It is important to emphasize, however, that individual athletes differ substantially in their responses to pre-exercise ingestion of sugar.[22] That is, consuming sugar shortly before an endurance event may hinder performance in some athletes but not affect the performance of others. In this regard, Sherman[32] has recommended, "Every athlete should initially test the effectiveness of pre-exercise meals on exercise capacity during training and not during an important competition." Coaches' recommendations regarding sugar intake prior to exercise should be based on personalized data regarding the response of each individual athlete.

WWW

Food and Nutrition Information Center
http://ndb.nal.usda.gov

Carbohydrate intake during exercise

Ingestion of high-carbohydrate food or drink increases endurance time during long-duration exercise. Carbohydrates ingested during exercise help to maintain blood glucose levels and provide a source of glucose for energy metabolism when muscle glycogen stores are reduced or depleted. Carbohydrate ingestion is particularly useful when athletes have not carbohydrate loaded, have not consumed pre-exercise meals, or have restricted food intake for weight loss.[2] The maintenance of blood glucose by carbohydrate feeding may help to reduce the perception of fatigue during prolonged exercise.[5] For events of one hour or less, sports drinks that contain 6 to 8 percent carbohydrates have been shown to improve endurance performance. For longer events (>1 hour), endurance performance is enhanced by consuming 30 to 60 grams of carbohydrates per hour, divided into 15- to 20-minute intervals.[2]

Carbohydrate intake after exercise

Consuming carbohydrates after strenuous exercise helps to replenish muscle glycogen stores.[2] Restoration of glycogen stores is very important for athletes involved in heavy training or competition on a daily basis. Failure to replenish muscle glycogen stores can result in premature fatigue and diminished performance.

The rate of glycogen synthesis following exercise is, in part, dependent on when the carbohydrates are consumed. Muscle glycogen synthesis is greatest when carbohydrate intake occurs immediately after exercise.[24] The greater the delay between the end of exercise and carbohydrate feeding, the slower the rate of muscle glycogen synthesis. Three potential explanations for the greater rate of glycogen synthesis immediately following exercise have been proposed:[12]

1. There is greater blood flow to the muscle.
2. The muscle fiber is more likely to take up glucose.
3. The muscle fiber is more sensitive to the effects of insulin.

Within 30 minutes after exercise, athletes should consume 1.0 to 1.5 grams of carbohydrate per kilogram of body weight at two-hour intervals for up to six hours.[2]

Low-carbohydrate diets and exercise performance

It is well accepted that a person's energy intake must include a large carbohydrate component to maintain optimum physical performance. However, low-carbohydrate diets, such as the Atkins, South Beach, and Zone diets, are popular as a method of weight loss. The relationship between diet and nutrient metabolism during exercise leads one to wonder how these popular diets, containing less than 10 percent carbohydrates and composed primarily of protein and fat, may alter this relationship and, in turn, alter performance.

As discussed in Chapter 3, most of the energy that is available during exercise is in the form of intramuscular glycogen and triglycerides as well as plasma glucose and free fatty acids. During low-intensity exercise, the primary fuel source is fat. As the exercise intensity increases, however, carbohydrate use becomes more prevalent. The energy sources used during the exercise are replenished through the dietary intake of nutrients. Low-carbohydrate diets have been shown to lead to several metabolic and hormonal changes that tend to promote glycogen sparing and increase the use of triglycerides and fatty acids for energy.[22,30] Because of these and other metabolic adaptations that occur during exercise, it has been suggested that low-carbohydrate diets may allow for maintaining, but not improving, endurance performance,[22] but that performance during anaerobic activities, such as weight lifting and sprinting, may be diminished as a result of the low muscle glycogen levels and decreased glycogen use that occur with a diet low in carbohydrates. Therefore, the metabolic limitations imposed by a low-carbohydrate diet may not pose a problem during low-intensity, everyday activities, but they do not allow for optimum performance during high-intensity exercise or competitive athletic events.[31]

Dietary Protein Intake for Fitness and Athletics

Recommendation: 12 to 15 percent of total calories from proteins: for endurance athletes, 1.2 to 1.4 grams per kilogram of body weight per day; for strength athletes, 1.4 to 1.7 grams per kilogram of body weight per day.[3]

Under normal dietary conditions, approximately 5 to 18 percent of energy production during exercise comes from protein sources (see Chapter 3). Under conditions of reduced muscle glycogen stores, protein catabolism may be even greater.

Factors that affect protein catabolism during exercise include the mode, frequency, intensity, and duration of exercise; the training status of the individual; and the quality of the proteins.

WWW
Academy of Nutrition and Dietetics
www.eatright.org

Effect of mode of exercise on protein metabolism. In general, it appears that high-intensity, anaerobic activities derive less energy production from protein sources than does continuous aerobic exercise. For example, strenuous weight training derives less than 5 percent of the energy needs from protein, whereas 15 percent of the energy needed for prolonged endurance exercise comes from protein catabolism.[18]

Effect of frequency of exercise on protein metabolism. It is commonly believed that the frequency of training affects protein degradation and synthesis.[23] Training that is too frequent may result in reduced gains in strength and muscle mass, possibly due to increased protein catabolism.[27] Unfortunately, it is not possible to recommend an optimal frequency of exercise based on the available evidence regarding protein metabolism.

Effect of intensity of exercise on protein metabolism. Typically, very-low-intensity exercise (<50% of $\dot{V}O_2$ max) is not characterized by substantial energy production from protein sources.[26] However, measurable protein catabolism is evident during continuous exercise with an intensity as low as 55 percent of $\dot{V}O_2$ max.

RESEARCH

Antioxidant supplements and muscle damage

Strenuous exercise is associated with an elevation in free radicals and other reactive oxygen and nitrogen species, all of which have been implicated as contributors to muscle damage. Previous research in the area has indicated that antioxidant supplements do not improve performance, but they may decrease the amount of exercise-induced muscle injury and may help athletes recover from the oxidative damage caused by free radicals. One source of natural antioxidants is the fruit of the Amazonian palm tree *Euterpe oleracea Mart,* commonly called açai. Açai is typically mixed with other fruit juices to produce a number of commercial beverages.

Sadowska-Krepa et al.* utilized an açai berry–based juice to determine the effects of this supplement on sprint performance, blood antioxidant status, and lipid profile in young athletes. The subjects for this study were seven junior hurdlers (17.5 ± 1.2 years) who were participating in a pre-season conditioning camp. Each subject consumed 100 ml of the açai juice blend once a day for six weeks. At the beginning and the end of the camp, the athletes ran a 300-meter sprint test on a track, and blood was sampled before, immediately after, and one hour after the tests. The blood was analyzed for antioxidant status based on the activities of several antioxidant enzymes and was also analyzed for creatine kinase and lactate dehydrogenase levels, as markers for muscle damage. Triglyceride and cholesterol levels were also measured in order to evaluate the potential health benefits of the açai berry supplement. The results showed that six weeks of açai berry–based juice blend had no effect on sprint performance. There was, however, a significant increase in the total antioxidant capacity of plasma, a significant improvement in the blood lipid profile, and a moderate attenuation of the exercise-induced muscle damage. These findings strongly support the utilization of an açai berry–based juice blend for its health benefits, which include higher in vivo antioxidants, higher hypocholesterolemic activity levels, and markedly decreased indicators of muscle damage.

*Sadowska-Krepa, E., Klapcinska, B., Podqorski, T., Szade, B., Tyl, K., and Hadzik, A. Effects of supplementation with acai (Euterpe oleracea Mart.) berry-based juice blend on the blood antioxidant defence capacity and lipid profile in junior hurdlers. A pilot study. *Biol. Sport* 32: 161–168, 2015.

Effect of duration of exercise on protein metabolism. Protein degradation tends to increase substantially after approximately one hour of continuous exercise.[20] This increase in amino acid oxidation may be related to a decrease in carbohydrate availability.[23,29]

Effect of training status on protein metabolism. A transient increase in protein degradation takes place at the beginning of an exercise program in previously untrained subjects,[6,8] and trained subjects have greater protein requirements than do untrained subjects. The additional dietary protein may contribute to energy production and repair of muscle tissue in trained individuals, while in untrained subjects it may reduce the loss of blood proteins.[28]

Quality of protein. During digestion, all proteins break down to amino acids, so these may be considered the units or building blocks for the synthesis of the proteins found in the human body. Of the 23 amino acids normally present in animal protein, only 13 can be synthesized in the cells. The other 10 must be supplied in the diet and are therefore called **essential amino acids.**

essential amino acids

Supplying the essential amino acids is no problem for those who eat meat and animal products. The fact that **complete proteins** (those that include all the essential amino acids) can be obtained from milk, eggs, and meat solves the problem quite easily. Thus, for most athletes, protein or amino acid supplementation is unnecessary. This is true for strength and power athletes as well as endurance athletes.[2] For vegetarians, however, the problem is more complicated. Vegetarians can include all the essential amino acids in their diet by eating a diversity of vegetable products such as leaves, seeds, roots, and fruits.[2] Again, in most cases, protein supplementation is not necessary, but it is recommended that vegetarian athletes consult a

complete proteins

Predicting body fat

Skinfold assessment equations and other indirect measures are commonly used to predict body fat (see **Chapter 15 Lab**). These prediction formulae are generally validated against underwater weighing. What is not well known is that our direct knowledge of the density values of body tissues (e.g., fat, bone, muscle) rests on a very limited number of cadaver dissections. Prior to 1984, only 15 human cadaver dissections had been reported in the nineteenth and twentieth centuries for the purpose of body composition analysis; complete information regarding skin, adipose tissue, muscle, and bone was reported for only nine subjects. A study in 1984 extended this number to 34 subjects and was the first to take extensive anthropometric measurements. Even with the data now available, it is important to realize that the data may not be generalizable to young, non-White individuals, and further research still needs to be done.[10]

sports dietician to avoid potential nutrition-related problems.[2] To account for the incomplete digestion of plant proteins, it is recommended that vegetarian athletes consume 1.3 to 1.8 grams of protein per kilogram of body weight per day.[2]

Dietary Fat Intake for Fitness and Athletics

Recommendation: 20 to 35 percent of total calories from fat, with no more than 10 percent of total calories in the form of saturated fat.[3]

Fatty acids are energy rich (9 kcal per gram) and are the primary energy source during low-intensity activity. As the intensity of exercise increases, the contribution of carbohydrates to energy production also increases.

At the initiation of exercise, the circulating level of free fatty acids decreases.[7] After a few minutes of continuous exercise, fatty acids stored in adipose tissue mobilize, which results in an increase in circulating free fatty acids.[7] Thus, the fatty acids used for energy metabolism initially (at the beginning of an exercise bout) come from existing circulatory sources, while those that contribute to energy production during prolonged exercise are derived from stored sources.

A high-fat diet (>70% of total caloric intake) does not improve endurance performance.[2] Therefore, a high-fat diet is not recommended for athletes.

Endurance training improves the ability to metabolize both fats and carbohydrates.[7] Furthermore, training results in an increase in the utilization of fatty acids at a given absolute submaximal exercise intensity—but not when the workload is expressed as a percentage of maximal aerobic power.[20,31] The enhanced ability to metabolize fats during submaximal exercise may result in a sparing of carbohydrate stores and thereby increase the duration of moderate- to high-intensity activity.

Vitamins

WWW

Vitamins and Nutrition Center
www.vitamins-nutrition.org
www.nlm.nih.gov/medlineplus/vitamins.html

Table 15.2 lists the recommended daily dietary reference intakes (a system of nutrition recommendations that broadens the older recommended daily allowances, or RDAs), dietary sources, major body functions, and possible roles important during exercise for common vitamins and minerals.[14] The need for vitamins in the human diet is well established, but a question of recurring interest is whether people need vitamins to supplement their normal diets. It was at one time thought that vitamin requirements increased much more rapidly than the increase in metabolism that is attributable to exercise. This is not the case, and ingestion of larger amounts of food as daily workout levels increase usually provides the needed increase in vitamins (if the diet is sound to begin with). Athletes (as well as non-athletes) who do not have optimal nutritional habits may wish to take a multiple vitamin.

Some investigators have claimed that vitamin supplementation has improved athletic performance in their subjects. However, when the proper controls are instituted, ensuring that subjects are on an adequate diet before starting the experiment, these improvements in performance can no longer be demonstrated. Thus, in all likelihood the reported improvements in performance with vitamin supplementation were the result of having improved previously inadequate diets.[4,25,36]

Vitamins and minerals. **table 15.2**

VITAMIN OR MINERAL	DAILY DIETARY REFERENCE INTAKES (mg) FOR HEALTHY ADULTS		DIETARY SOURCES	MAJOR BODY FUNCTIONS	POSSIBLE ROLES IMPORTANT DURING EXERCISE
	MEN	WOMEN			
Minerals					
Calcium	1000–1200	1000–1200	Dairy products, dark green leafy vegetables, dried legumes	Bone and tooth formation; blood clotting; nerve transmission	Muscle contraction; glycogen breakdown
Phosphorus	700	700	Milk, cheese, meat, poultry, grains	Bone and tooth formation; acid–base balance	Formation of ATP and creatine phosphokinase; release of oxygen from red blood cells
Potassium	4700	4700	Meats, milk, many fruits	Acid–base balance; body water balance; nerve function	Nerve impulse transmission; muscle contraction; glycogen storage
Sodium	1200–1500	1200–1500	Common salt	Acid–base balance; body water balance; nerve function	Nerve impulse transmission; muscle contraction; water balance
Magnesium	400–420	310–320	Whole grains, green leafy vegetables	Activates enzymes; involved in protein synthesis	Muscle contraction; glucose metabolism in muscle cells
Iron	8	8–18	Eggs, lean meats, legumes, whole grains, green leafy vegetables	Constituent of hemoglobin and enzymes involved in energy metabolism	Oxygen transport by red blood cells; oxygen utilization in muscle cells
Zinc	11	8	Widely distributed in foods	Constituent of enzymes involved in digestion	Energy production in muscle cells
Chromium	0.30–0.35	0.20–0.25	Fats, vegetables, oils, meats	Involved in glucose and energy metabolism	Glucose and energy metabolism; normal blood sugar metabolism
Copper	0.9	0.9	Meats, drinking water	Constituents of enzymes associated with iron metabolism	Oxygen transport and utilization; close work with iron
Selenium	0.055	0.055	Seafood, meat, grains	Functions in close association with Vitamin E	Antioxidant
Fat-soluble vitamins					
A (retinol)	0.9	0.7	Provitamin A (β-carotene) widely distributed in green vegetables; retinol present in milk, butter, cheese, fortified margarine	Constituent of rhodopsin (visual pigment); maintenance of epithelial tissues; role in mucopolysaccharide synthesis	Antioxidant; prevention of red blood cell damage
D	0.005–0.015	0.005–0.015	Cod-liver oil, eggs, dairy products, fortified milk, margarine	Promotes growth and mineralization of bones; increases absorption of calcium	Calcium transport in muscle
E (tocopherol)	15	15	Seeds, green leafy vegetables, margarines, shortenings	Functions as antioxidant to prevent cell membrane damage	Antioxidant; prevention of red blood cell damage; promotion of aerobic energy production
K (phylloquinone)	0.12	0.11	Green leafy vegetables; small amounts in cereals, fruits, and meats	Important in blood clotting (involved in formation of active prothrombin)	None determined

(continued)

table 15.2 Continued.

VITAMIN OR MINERAL	DAILY DIETARY REFERENCE INTAKES (mg) FOR HEALTHY ADULTS		DIETARY SOURCES	MAJOR BODY FUNCTIONS	POSSIBLE ROLES IMPORTANT DURING EXERCISE
	MEN	WOMEN			
Water-soluble vitamins					
B_1 (thiamin)	1.2	1.1	Pork, organ meats, whole grains, legumes	Coenzyme (thiamin pyrophosphate) in reactions involving removal of carbon dioxide	Energy release from carbohydrate; formation of hemoglobin; proper nervous system functioning
B_2 (riboflavin)	1.3	1.1	Widely distributed in foods	Constituent of two flavin nucleotide coenzymes involved in energy metabolism (FAD and FMN)	Energy release from carbohydrate and fat
Niacin	16	14	Liver, lean meats, grains, legumes (can be formed from tryptophan)	Constituent of two coenzymes involved in oxidation-reduction reactions (NAD and NADP)	Energy release from carbohydrate, both aerobic and anaerobic; inhibition of FFA release from adipose tissue
B_6 (pyridoxine)	1.3–1.7	1.3–1.5	Meats, vegetables, whole-grain cereals	Coenzyme (PLP) involved in amino acid metabolism	Energy release from carbohydrate; formation of hemoglobin and oxidative enzymes; proper nervous system functioning
Pantothenic acid	5	5	Widely distributed in foods	Constituent of CoA, which plays a central role in energy metabolism	Energy production from carbohydrate and fat
Folacin	0.4	0.4	Legumes, green vegetables, whole-wheat products	Coenzyme (reduced form) involved in transfer of single-carbon units in nucleic acid and amino acid metabolism	Red blood cell production
B_{12}	0.0024	0.0026	Muscle meats, eggs, dairy products (not present in plant foods)	Coenzyme involved in transfer of single-carbon units in nucleic acid metabolism	Red blood cell production
Biotin	0.3	0.3	Legumes, vegetables, meats	Coenzyme required for fat synthesis, amino acid metabolism, glycogen (animal starch) formation	Carbohydrate and fat synthesis
C (ascorbic acid)	90	75	Citrus fruits, tomatoes, green peppers, salad greens	Maintains intercellular matrix of cartilage, bone, dentine; important in collagen synthesis	Antioxidant; increased absorption of iron; formation of epinephrine; promotion of aerobic energy production; formation of connective tissue

Sources: National Academy of Sciences, 2004: www.nasonline.org and J. R. Berning and S. N. Steen, *Sports Nutrition for the 90s,* pp. 136–139, © 1991 by Aspen Publishers.

FLUID INGESTION

Proper hydration during exercise promotes health and optimal athletic performance.[1] Table 15.3 provides recommendations regarding fluid ingestion prior to, during, and after exercise.

Fluid ingestion prior to, during, and after exercise.[1] **table 15.3**

PRIOR TO EXERCISE
1. Prehydrating with beverages, if needed, should be initiated at least several hours before the exercise task to enable fluid absorption and allow urine output to return toward normal levels.
2. When hydrating prior to exercise, slowly drink 5 to 7 mL per kg of body weight at least four hours before the exercise task.
3. Pre-exercise beverages should contain sodium (20–50 mEq • L^{-1}). Eating salted snacks or foods will help stimulate thirst and retain the fluids consumed.
DURING EXERCISE
1. Individuals should develop customized fluid replacement programs to prevent excessive (>2% body weight loss from water deficit) dehydration.
2. The measurement of pre- and post-exercise body weights is useful for determining the characteristics of the customized fluid replacement program.
3. Endurance athletes such as marathon runners should consume 0.4 to 0.8 L per hour of a sports drink that contains approximately 20 to 30 mEq • L^{-1} of sodium, 2 to 5 mEq • L^{-1} of potassium, and 5 to 10% carbohydrate.
AFTER EXERCISE
1. Normal meals and beverages can restore hydration.
2. For rapid return to normal hydration, drink approximately 1.5 L of fluid for each kilogram of body weight lost during exercise.
3. Consuming beverages and snacks with sodium will expedite rehydration by stimulating thirst and fluid retention.
4. Intravenous fluid replacement is generally not advantageous unless medically merited due to severe dehydration (>7% of body weight loss).

SPECIAL DIETARY CONSIDERATIONS FOR ATHLETES

The following section discusses several special dietary issues that pertain to athletes.

Iron Deficiency and Sports Anemia

As with vitamins, there is very little evidence that exercise (in comfortable climates) increases the need for minerals beyond the requirement of increased daily food consumption for metabolic demands. The one exception to this is for iron.

While a normal diet usually provides sufficient mineral constituents, some groups of athletes may require iron supplementation (under medical guidance). These groups include male and female endurance athletes, adolescent athletes, athletes who lose weight for competition, and vegetarian athletes.[16,19,21,33] It has been known for many years that highly trained distance runners are likely to have low hemoglobin and hematocrit values. The term **sports anemia** was coined to describe anemia that occurs in response to heavy endurance training in the absence of any recognizable disease process.

sports anemia

Iron deficiency is commonly divided into three stages: prelatent iron deficiency, latent iron deficiency, and frank anemia. The earliest stage, **prelatent iron deficiency,** is characterized by a decrease or absence of storage iron (iron is stored as ferritin and hemosiderin in the liver, bone marrow, and spleen). Following exhaustion of the body's iron stores, the iron supply to developing red cells is diminished, and iron-

prelatent iron deficiency

latent iron deficiency

frank anemia

WWW

Sports Nutrition
http://sportsmedicine.about.com/od/sportsnutrition

deficient erythropoiesis (formation of red blood cells) occurs. This second stage of iron deficiency, **latent iron deficiency,** is characterized by an increased total iron binding capacity and reduced serum iron.

In the first and second stages of iron deficiency, the hemoglobin level remains essentially in the normal range. Only in the third stage of iron deficiency, **frank anemia,** does the hemoglobin level drop significantly below normal values. Thus the detection of anemia represents an advanced stage of iron deficiency. Even the early stages of iron deficiency without anemia can substantially reduce an athlete's ability to maximize performance and constitute a clearly undesirable condition.[11] In frank anemia, the evidence is clear that optimal energy release is impossible because of the combined effects of inefficient cell metabolism and decreased oxygen transport.

Pre-Exercise Meals

Generally, eating three to four hours prior to exercise or athletic competition improves performance (compared with fasting). The consumption of food should leave the athlete neither hungry nor with undigested food in the stomach. Generally, pre-exercise meals or snacks should:[2]

1. Have sufficient fluid to maintain hydration.
2. Be low in fat and fiber to facilitate gastric emptying and minimize gastrointestinal distress.
3. Be high in carbohydrate to maintain blood glucose and maximize glycogen stores.
4. Be moderate in protein.
5. Be composed of food familiar to the athlete.

Eating to Increase Body Weight and Muscle Mass

Although athletes such as wrestlers, gymnasts, ballet dancers, and jockeys must often reduce body weight for their sports, others, including football, basketball, volleyball, and baseball players, frequently try to gain body weight to improve performance and potentially reduce the risk of injury.[9] This is true for adolescent and adult athletes of both genders. For some individuals, it can be difficult to gain body weight (particularly muscle) because of their genetic makeup as well as the volume of exercise training they perform. Gaining body weight and muscle mass requires not only taking in more calories than are expended (a positive caloric balance) but also ensuring that the extra calories are from both carbohydrate and protein sources. As indicated earlier in the chapter, strength athletes should ingest approximately 1.4 to 1.7 grams of protein and 6 to 10 grams of carbohydrates per kilogram of body weight per day.[2,3] Many athletes, however, have accepted the myth that to build muscle requires protein supplementation in the form of powders or drinks. This is not the case, and filling up on protein-rich foods or supplements may negatively affect resistance training due to inadequate carbohydrate intake.[9] Clark[9] has provided six key concepts for weight gain.

1. Consistently eat three meals per day. It is not unusual for athletes to skip meals because of practice or other commitments. Furthermore, some athletes eat one large meal instead of three normal-sized meals. The caloric intake from one large meal may not equal that of three meals. Three meals each day can also reduce the possibility of decreased caloric intake following a day of large caloric intake.

CLINICAL APPLICATIONS

Preventing iron deficiency in athletes

Coaches, athletic trainers, and allied health professionals should be aware that typically a diet high in iron sources such as meat, poultry, and fish (heme-iron) and non-heme-iron foods such as dried peas and beans, nuts, whole-grain breads and cereals, leafy vegetables, eggs, and dried fruits can prevent iron deficiency problems. But it is very difficult to correct an iron deficiency by diet alone once it has been established. On the other hand, iron supplements should not be given routinely to athletes without medical supervision, because of the possibility of inducing deficiencies of other trace minerals such as copper and zinc. Also, a high iron intake can produce an iron overload **(hemochromatosis)** in some people, which can negatively affect health and performance.

2. Eat larger than normal portions. For example, instead of eating one sandwich at a meal, eat two.
3. Eat extra (healthy) snacks at mid-morning, at mid-afternoon, and before bedtime.
4. Eat higher-calorie foods. For example, cranberry juice has more calories per glass than orange juice.
5. Drink lots of beverages such as juice and milk. These drinks provide extra calories that water does not.
6. Resistance train for strength and hypertrophy (see Chapter 11).

summary

A healthful diet is important for successful exercise and athletic performance. Too often, however, athletes and coaches are influenced by misinformation. Moderately active adult males and females should consume approximately 2,200 to 2,800 and 1,800 to 2,200 kilocalories per day, respectively, whereas athletes involved in heavy training sometimes consume 4,000 to 7,000 kilocalories per day. It is generally recommended that the diet of athletes consist of 55 to 65 percent carbohydrate, 12 to 15 percent protein, and 20 to 35 percent fat.

Typically, the increased daily caloric intake associated with heavy training provides the vitamin needs of athletes. In some cases, however, when the athlete's diet is not optimal, supplementation with a multiple vitamin can be beneficial.

As with vitamins, a nutritionally balanced diet usually meets an athlete's mineral needs. This may not be true, however, for iron. An iron deficiency can lead to anemia and impaired exercise performance.

Proper hydration promotes health and optimal athletic performance. It is important that athletes consider hydration status prior to, during, and after exercise training and competition.

questions for review

1. What are the recommended daily caloric intakes for moderately active adults? For athletes?
2. What are the ACSM guidelines for the percentages of carbohydrate, protein, and fat in the diet for athletes and non-athletes?

3. What recommendations should coaches give regarding carbohydrate intake before exercise? During exercise? After exercise? Why?
4. Should coaches recommend iron supplements? Why or why not?
5. What recommendations would you give an athlete about fluid ingestion prior to, during, and after exercise?
6. What guidelines would you give athletes regarding pre-exercise meals?
7. Does antioxidant supplementation decrease muscle damage resulting from strenuous exercise?

student companion website

For further review of this book's chapters and for test preparation, visit the book's website, **www.hhpcommunities.com/exercisephysiology**, to take practice quizzes, review the vocabulary terms, use the study guide, and view the digital image bank.

references

1. American College of Sports Medicine. Position Stand. Exercise and fluid replacement. *Med. Sci. Sports Exerc.* 39: 377–390, 2007.
2. American College of Sports Medicine, American Dietetic Association, and Dietitians of Canada. Joint Position Statement. Nutrition and athletic performance. *Med. Sci. Sports Exerc.* 41: 709–731, 2009.
3. American College of Sports Medicine. *ACSM's Resource Manual for Guidelines for Exercise Testing and Prescription,* 7th edition. Baltimore: Wolters Kluwer/Lippincott Williams & Wilkins, 2014.
4. Belko, A. Z. Vitamins and exercise: An update. *Med. Sci. Sports Exerc.* 19 (Supplement): S191–S196, 1987.
5. Burgess, M. L., Robertson, R. J., Davis, J. M., and Norris, J. M. RPE, blood glucose, and carbohydrate oxidation during exercise: Effects of glucose feeding. *Med. Sci. Sports Exerc.* 23: 353–359, 1991.
6. Butterfield, G. E. Whole-body protein utilization in humans. *Med. Sci. Sports Exerc.* 19 (Supplement): S157–S165, 1987.
7. Butterfield, G. Fat as a fuel for exercise. In *Sports Nutrition for the 90s,* eds. J. R. Berning and S. N. Steen. Gaithersburg, MD: Aspen Publishers, Inc., 1991.
8. Butterfield, G. E., and Calloway, D. H. Physical activity improves protein utilization in young men. *Br. J. Nutr.* 51: 171–184, 1984.
9. Clark, N. Bulking up: Helping clients gain weight healthfully. *ACSM's Health & Fitness Journal* 9: 15–19, 2005.
10. Clarys, J. P., Martin, A. D., and Drinkwater, D. T. Gross tissue weights in the human body by cadaver dissection. *Hum. Biol.* 56: 459–473, 1984.
11. Clement, D. B., and Sawchuk, L. L. Iron status and sports performance. *Sports Med.* 1: 65–74, 1984.
12. Coleman, E. Carbohydrates: The master fuel. In *Sports Nutrition for the 90s,* eds. J. R. Berning and S. N. Steen. Gaithersburg, MD: Aspen Publishers, Inc., 1991.
13. Costill, D. L., Coyle, E., Dalsky, G., Evans, W., Fink, W., and Hoopes, D. Effects of elevated plasma FFA and insulin on muscle glycogen usage during exercise. *J. Appl. Physiol.* 43: 695–699, 1977.
14. Dietary Reference Intakes for Calcium, Phosphorus, Magnesium, Vitamin D, and Fluoride (1997); DRI for Thiamin, Riboflavin, Niacin, Vitamin B6, Folate, Vitamin B12, Pantothenic Acid, Biotin, and Choline (1998); DRI for Vitamin C, Vitamin E, Selenium, and Carotenoids (2000); DRI for Vitamin A, Vitamin K, Arsenic, Boron, Chromium, Copper, Iodine, Iron, Manganese, Molybdenum, Nickel, Silicon, Vanadium, and Zinc (2001); DRI for Water, Potassium, Sodium, Chloride, and Sulfate (2004). National Academy of Sciences, 2004. Available: www.nap.edu.
15. Dietary Reference Intakes for Energy, Carbohydrates, Fiber, Fat, Fatty Acids, Cholesterol, Protein, and Amino Acids (2002/2005). National Academy of Sciences, 2005. Available: www.nap.edu.
16. Eichner, E. Sports anemia: Poor terminology of a real phenomenon. *Gatorade Sports Sci. Exch.* 1(6), 1988.
17. Falls, H. B., Baylor, A. M., and Dishman, R. K. *Essentials of Fitness.* Philadelphia: Saunders College/Holt, Rinehart and Winston, 1980.
18. Foster, C., Costill, D. L., and Fink, W. J. Effects of pre-exercise feedings on endurance performance. *Med. Sci. Sports* 11: 1–5, 1979.
19. Grandjean, A. C. The vegetarian athlete. *Phys. Sportsmed.* 15: 191–194, 1987.
20. Haralambie, G., and Berg, A. Serum urea and amino nitrogen changes with exercise duration. *Eur. J. Appl. Physiol.* 36: 39–48, 1976.

21. Haymes, E. M. Nutritional concerns: Need for iron. *Med. Sci. Sports Exerc.* 19 (Supplement): S197–S200, 1987.
22. Helge, J. W. Long-term fat diet adaptation effects on performance, training capacity, and fat utilization. *Med. Sci. Sports Exerc.* 34: 1499–1502, 2002.
23. Houck, J., and Slavin, J. Protein nutrition for the athlete. In *Sports Nutrition for the 90s,* eds. J. R. Berning and S. N. Steen. Gaithersburg, MD: Aspen Publishers, Inc., 1991.
24. Ivy, J. L., Katz, A. L., Cutler, C. L., Sherman, W. M., and Coyle, E. F. Muscle glycogen synthesis after exercise: Effect of time of carbohydrate ingestion. *J. Appl. Physiol.* 64: 1480–1485, 1988.
25. Kris-Etherton, P. M. The facts and fallacies of nutritional supplements for athletes. *Gatorade Sports Sci. Exch.* 2(18), 1989.
26. Lemon, P. W. R. Effect of intensity on protein utilization during prolonged exercise. *Med. Sci. Sports Exerc.* 16: 151 (Abstract), 1984.
27. Lemon, P. W. R. Protein and exercise: Update 1987. *Med. Sci. Sports Exerc.* 19 (Supplement): S179–S190, 1987.
28. Lemon, P. W. R. Influence of dietary protein and total energy intake on strength improvement. *Gatorade Sports Sci. Exch.* 2, 1989.
29. Lemon, P. W. R., and Mullin, J. P. Effect of initial muscle glycogen levels on protein catabolism during exercise. *J. Appl. Physiol.* 48: 624–629, 1980.
30. Peters, S. J., and LeBlanc, P. J. Metabolic aspects of low carbohydrate diets and exercise. *Nutr. Metab.* 1: 7–14, 2004.
31. Phinney, S. D. Ketogenic diets and physical performance. *Nutr. Metab.* 1: 2–8, 2004.
32. Sherman, W. M. Pre-event nutrition. *Gatorade Sports Sci. Exch.* 1(12), 1989.
33. Steen, S. N. Nutritional concerns of athletes who must reduce body weight. *Gatorade Sports Sci. Exch.* 2(20), 1989.
34. U.S. Department of Agriculture. Agricultural Research Service. *Energy Intakes: Percentages of Energy from Protein, Carbohydrate, Fat, and Alcohol, by Gender and Age, What We Eat in America,* NHANES 2007–2008. Available: ars.usda.gov/ba/bhnrc/fsrg.
35. U.S. Department of Health and Human Services and U.S. Department of Agriculture. *Dietary Guidelines for Americans,* 2015–2020, 8th edition. Washington, DC: U.S. Government Printing Office, 2015. Available: http://health.gov/dietaryguidelines/2015/guidelines.
36. Whitmire, D. Vitamins and minerals: A perspective in physical performance. In *Sports Nutrition for the 90s,* eds. J. R. Berning and S. N. Steen. Gaithersburg, MD: Aspen Publishers, Inc., 1991.
37. Williams, M. H., Anderson, D. E., and Rawson, E. S. *Nutrition for Health, Fitness & Sport,* 10th edition. New York: McGraw-Hill Education, 2013.

lab

Skinfold Estimations of Body Composition

BACKGROUND

Laboratory methods for body composition assessment represent the most accurate means available for determining the amount of fat and fat-free tissue in live subjects. Generally, underwater weighing is considered the "gold standard" for determining body composition characteristics. Often, however, underwater weighing is not practical for assessing large groups of subjects in field situations.

Assessment of body composition by skinfold measurements is a simple and relatively accurate method that requires minimal equipment and can be used with large numbers of subjects in a field setting. Skinfold measurements can be used in multiple regression "prediction" equations to estimate body composition (body density [DB], percent fat [% FAT], fat-free weight [FFW], fat weight [FW]). The results of skinfold methods of determining body composition are usually within 3 to 5% of underwater weighing.

The ability to predict body composition from skinfolds is based on the fact that fat or fat-free tissues accumulate in relatively predictable patterns in similarly aged individuals of the same gender. Therefore, if specific sites are measured, the measurements will be influenced by the amount of the individual's adipose or fat-free tissue.

In this laboratory the technique for skinfold measurement will be outlined, and you will use the measurements for predicting various aspects of body composition.

TERMS & ABBREVIATIONS

- DB = body density
- FFW = fat-free weight
- FW = fat weight
- % FAT = percent fat

PROCEDURES[2]

1. Measure and mark the anatomical sites with a marker (see sites below in photos 15.1–15.15). Three sites are to be measured for each gender. Both males and females are measured at the thigh site. Males are also measured at the chest and abdomen, females at the triceps and suprailium.
2. Take all measurements on the right side of the body.
3. Grasp the skinfold of the subject firmly with the thumb and forefinger and pull away from the body.
4. Hold the skinfold caliper perpendicular to the skinfold. The caliper should be approximately 1 cm away from the thumb and forefinger so that the pressure of the caliper will not be affected.
5. Read the skinfold size approximately one to two seconds after the caliper thumb grip has been released.

Skinfold Sites[3]

CHEST (see photos 15.1–15.3): a diagonal fold taken one half of the distance between the anterior axillary line and the nipple (males).

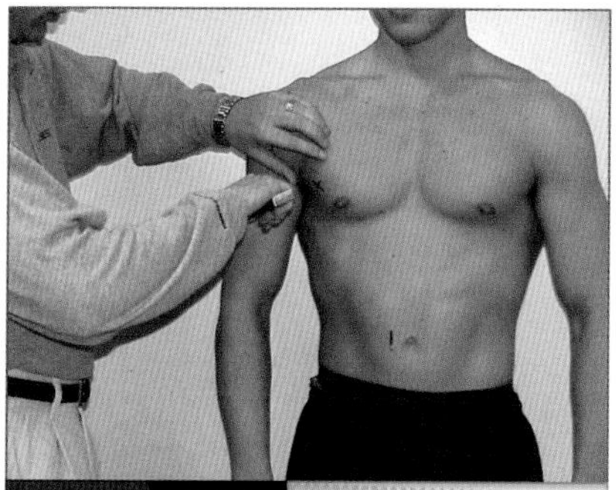
photo 15.1

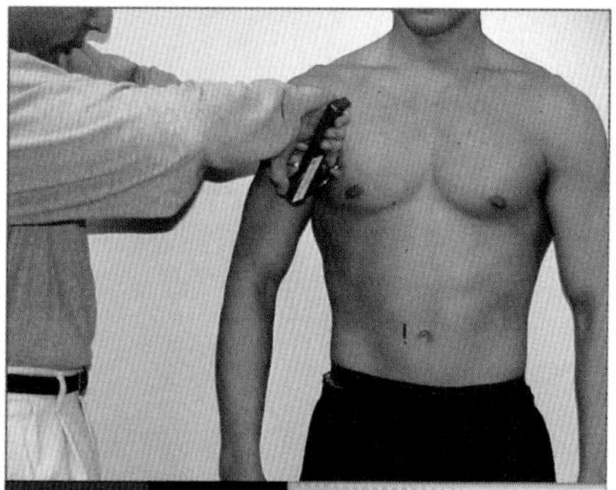
photo 15.2

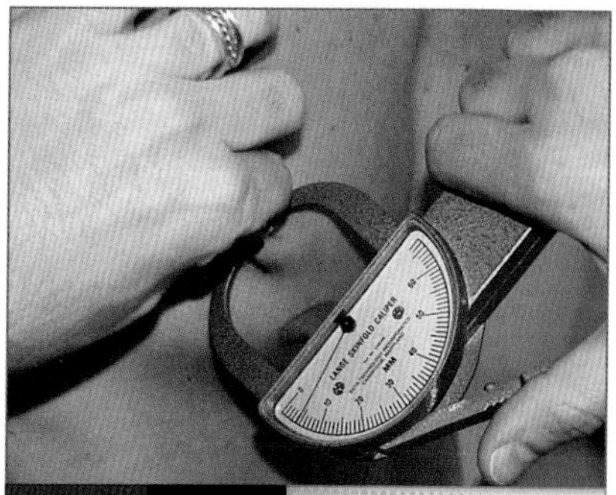
photo 15.3

Chest skinfold measurement.

ABDOMEN (see photos 15.4–15.6): a vertical fold taken at a lateral distance of approximately 2 cm from the umbilicus (males).

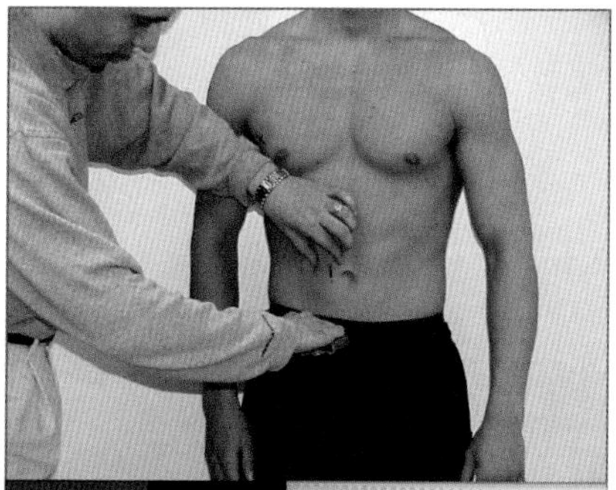
photo 15.4

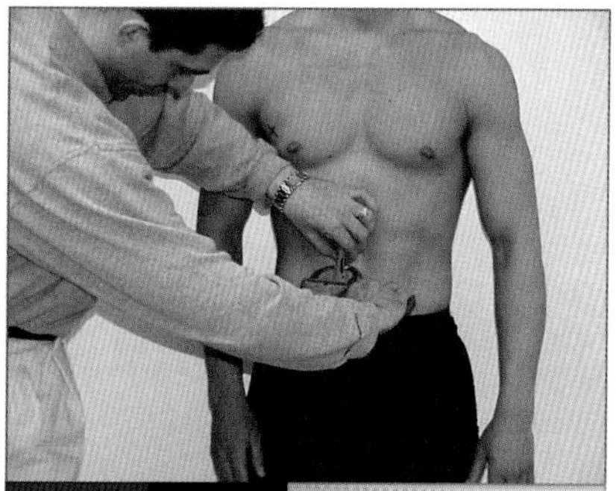
photo 15.5

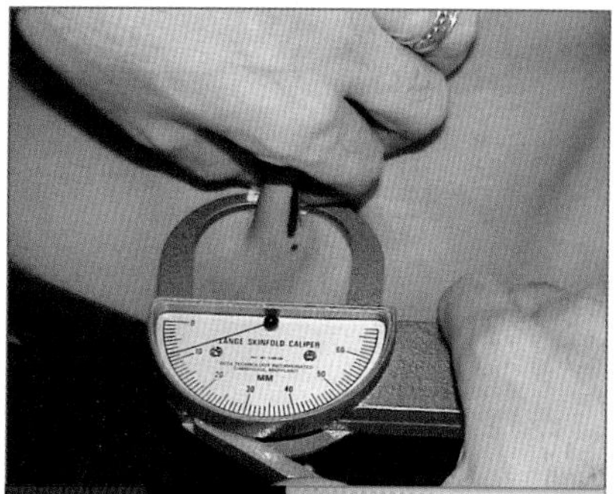
photo 15.6

Abdomen skinfold measurement.

THIGH (see photos 15.7–15.9): a vertical fold on the anterior aspect of the thigh, midway between hip and knee joints (males and females).

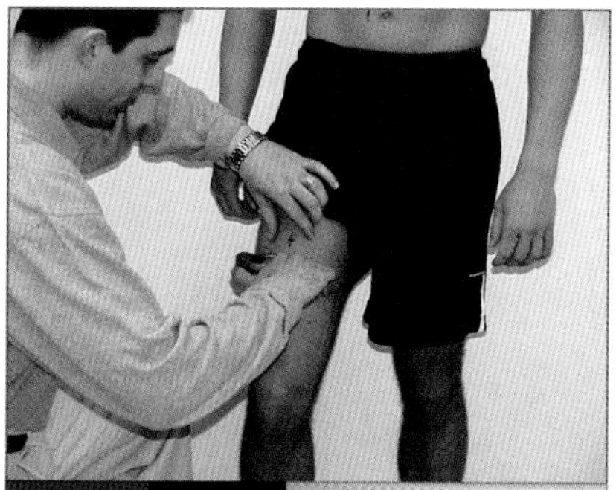
photo 15.7

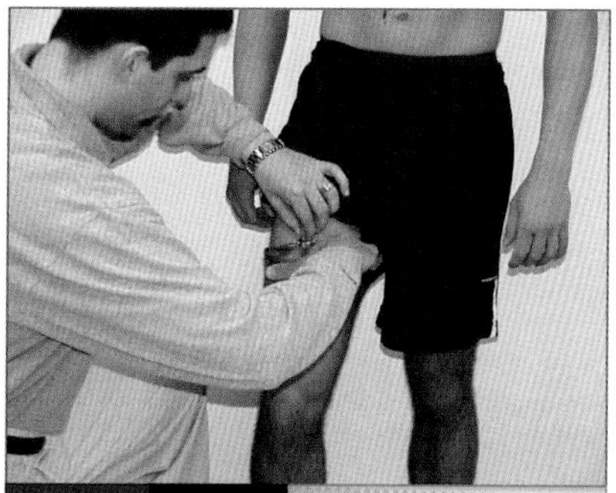
photo 15.8

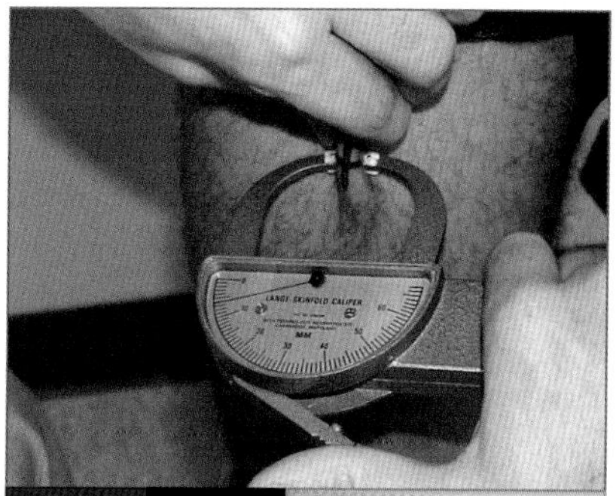
photo 15.9

Thigh skinfold measurement.

TRICEPS (see photos 15.10–15.12): a vertical fold on the posterior midline of the upper arm, halfway between the acromion and olecranon processes; the elbow should be extended and relaxed (females).

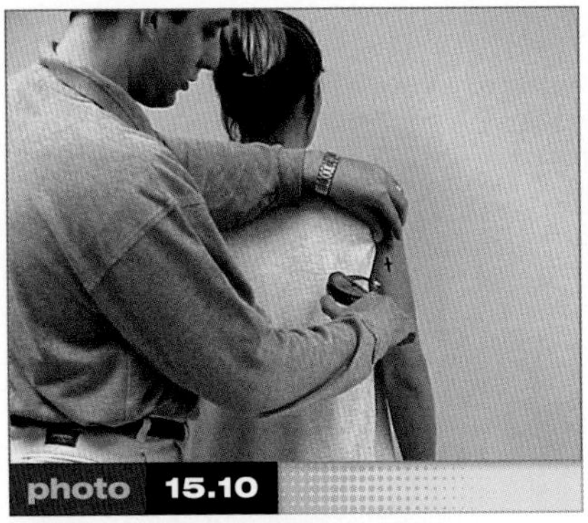

photo 15.10

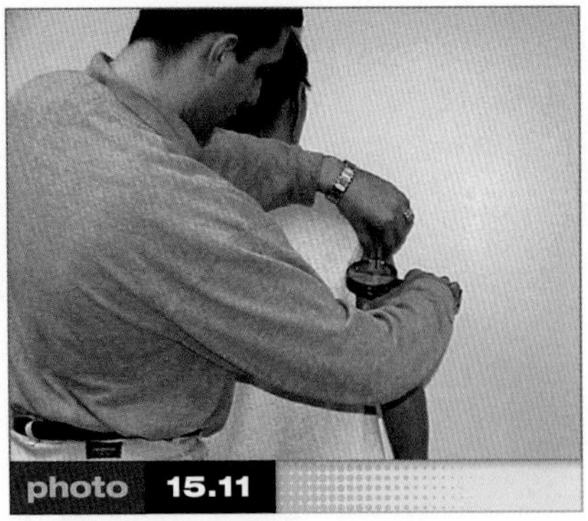

photo 15.11

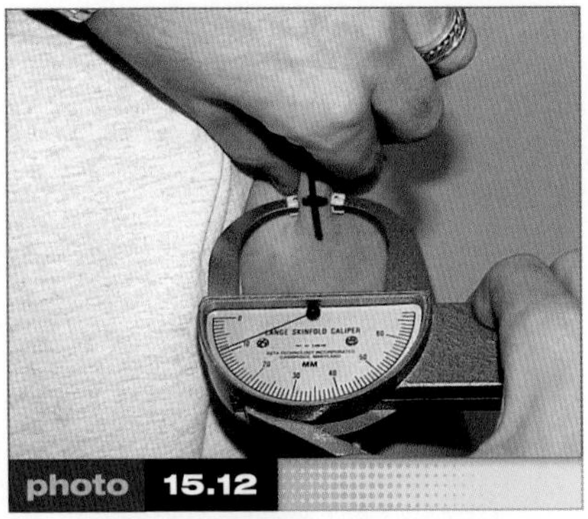

photo 15.12

Triceps skinfold measurement.

SUPRAILIUM (see photos 15.13–15.15): a diagonal fold above the crest of the ilium at the spot where an imaginary line would come down from the anterior axillary line (females).

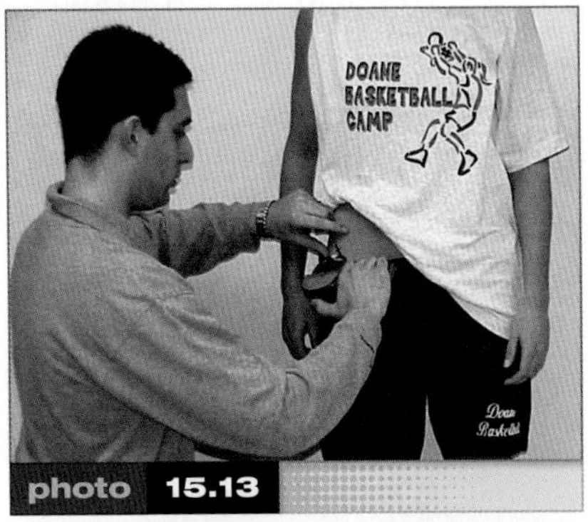

photo 15.13

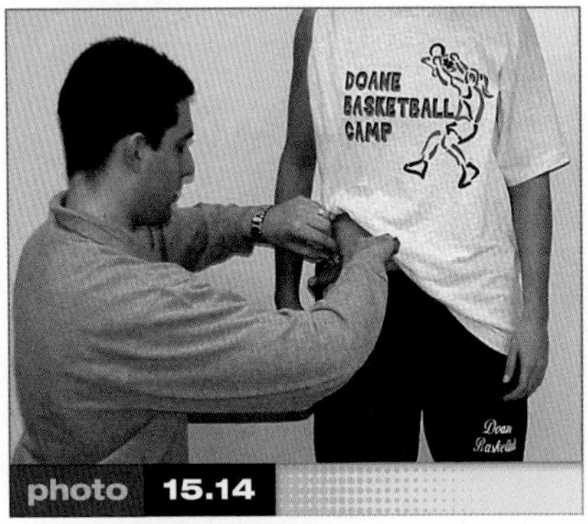

photo 15.14

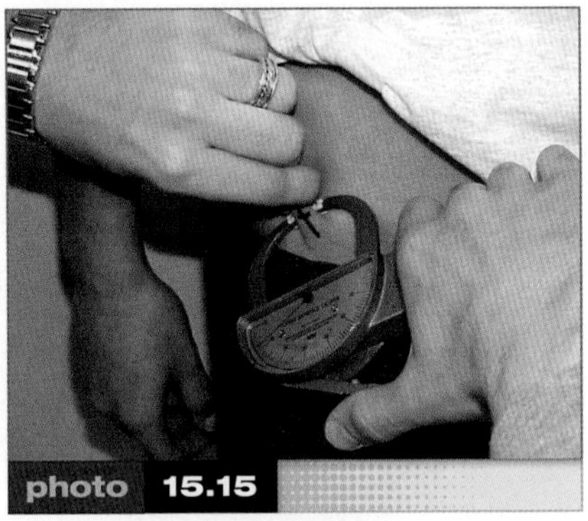

photo 15.15

Suprailium skinfold measurement.

Note: For accurate measures, do not take measurements when the skin is wet, immediately after exercise, or when the subject is overheated.

6. Take three measurements per site at least 15 seconds apart to allow the skinfold site to return to normal. If the repeated measurements vary by more than 1 mm, more measurements should be taken. Use the mean of the recorded measurements that are within 1 mm as the representative skinfold value in the equation.
7. Calculate body composition characteristics using Worksheet 15.1.

Equations

Males (ages 18–61 years)[3]

$$DB = 1.1093800 - [0.0008267 (X_2)] + [0.0000016 (X_2)^2] - [0.0002574 (X_4)]$$

$R = 0.91$

$SEE = 0.008\ kg \bullet L^{-1}$

X_2 = sum of chest, abdomen, and thigh skinfolds in mm

X_4 = age in years

Females (ages 18–55 years)[3]

$$DB = 1.099421 - [0.0009929 (X_3)] + [0.0000023 (X_3)^2] - [0.0001392 (X_4)]$$

$R = 0.84$

$SEE = 0.009\ kg \bullet L^{-1}$

X_3 = sum of triceps, thigh, and suprailium skinfolds in mm

X_4 = age in years

SEE = standard error of estimate, R = multiple correlation coefficient

% FAT = {[(4.57 / DB) – 4.142] × 100} (Reference[1])

FW = body weight × (% FAT / 100)

FFW = body weight – FW

body weight goal = FFW / [1 – (Target % FAT / 100)]

SAMPLE CALCULATIONS

Gender: Male

Body weight: 80.0 kg

Age: 25

Sum of chest, abdomen, and thigh skinfolds: 40 mm

$$DB = 1.1093800 - [0.0008267 (40)] + [0.0000016 (40)^2] - [0.0002574 (25)]$$

$$DB = 1.1093800 - 0.03307 + 0.00256 - 0.006435 = 1.0724\ kg \bullet L^{-1}$$

% FAT = [(4.57 / 1.0724) – 4.142] × 100 = 11.9 % FAT

FW = 80.0 × (11.9 / 100) = 9.5 kg

FFW = 80.0 – 9.5 = 70.5 kg

body weight goal of 8.0 % FAT = 70.5 / [1 – (8.0 / 100)] = 76.6 kg

Gender: Female

Body weight: 65 kg

Age: 30

Sum of triceps, thigh, and suprailium skinfolds: 55 mm

$$DB = 1.099421 - [0.0009929 (55)] + [0.0000023 (55)^2] - [0.0001392 (30)]$$

$$DB = 1.099421 - 0.05461 + 0.00696 - 0.004176 = 1.0476$$

% FAT = [(4.57 / 1.0476) – 4.142] × 100 = 22.0 % FAT

FW = 65 × (22.0 / 100) = 14.3 kg

FFW = 65 – 14.3 = 50.7 kg

body weight goal of 15.0 % FAT = 50.7 / [1 – (15.0 / 100)] = 59.6 kg

worksheet 15.1 SKINFOLD ESTIMATIONS OF BODY COMPOSITION

NAME ______________________________ DATE ______________

Gender: ______________________

Age: ______________________ years

Body weight: ______________________ kg

Skinfold Measurements (mm)

	TRIAL 1	TRIAL 2	TRIAL 3	MEAN
Triceps				
Suprailium				
Abdomen				
Thigh				
Chest				

Sum of chest, abdomen, and thigh skinfolds = ______________________

Sum of triceps, thigh, and suprailium skinfolds = ______________________

Use the gender-specific equations on pp. 350–351 to calculate DB.

DB = ______________________ $kg \cdot L^{-1}$

Use the equations on p. 351 to calculate % FAT, FW, and FFW.

% FAT = ______________ % FW = ______________ kg FFW = ______________ kg

EXTENSION ACTIVITIES

worksheet **15.2**

NAME DATE

1. A subject's % FAT, determined by skinfolds, was estimated to be 16.9% (DB = 1.0600 kg • L^{-1}). If the SEE of the predicted body density value is equal to 0.0050 kg • L^{-1}, then this subject's % FAT is likely to fall between what two values?

2. List potential sources of error when estimating body composition from skinfold equations.

3. Using the skinfold prediction equations on pages 350–351, calculate your body density and convert this value to % FAT.

4. Using the following data and the skinfold prediction equations on pages 350–351, calculate each subject's body density and convert this value to % FAT.

   a. gender = male

      age = 25 years

      chest skinfold = 12 mm

      abdomen skinfold = 18 mm

      thigh skinfold = 15 mm

      body density = ______ kg • L^{-1}

      % FAT = ______ %

   b. gender = female

      age = 30 years

      triceps skinfold = 16 mm

      thigh skinfold = 14 mm

      suprailium skinfold = 19 mm

      body density = ______ kg • L^{-1}

      % FAT = ______ %

EXTENSION QUESTIONS

1. What are some common mistakes that may occur in administering this lab?

2. Assess the practicality of using this lab in the field.

3. Research the reliability and/or validity of this lab using online resources, journal articles, and other credible sources.

REFERENCES

1. Brozek, J., Grande, F., Anderson, J. T., and Keys, A. Densitometric analysis of body composition: Revision of some quantitative assumptions. *Ann. N.Y. Acad. Sci.* 110: 113–140, 1963.
2. Harrison, G. G., Buskirk, E. R., Carter, J. E. L., Johnston, F. E., Lohman, T. G., Pollock, M. L., Roche, A. F., and Wilmore, J. Skinfold thicknesses and measurement techniques. In *Anthropometric Standardization Reference Manual,* eds. T. G. Lohman, A. F. Roche, and R. Martorell. Champaign, IL: Human Kinetics, 1988, pp. 55–70.
3. Jackson, A. S., and Pollock, M. L. Practical assessment of body composition. *Phys. Sportsmed.* 13: 76–90, 1985.

As a result of reading this chapter you will:

Know the definition of ergogenic aids.

Know the conditions under which the use of ergogenic aids is considered acceptable or unacceptable.

Have a basic understanding of how ergogenic aids can improve sports and exercise performance.

Be able to describe the potential ergogenic and health-related effects of selected ergogenic aids.

16 Ergogenic Aids for Fitness and Athletics

key concepts

amphetamine
anabolic steroid
androstenedione
arginine
beta-alanine
beta-hydroxy-beta-methylbutyrate (HMB)
blood doping
caffeine
creatine
creatine loading
dehydroepiandrosterone (DHEA)
ergogenic aid
erythrocythemia
erythropoietin
glycogen supercompensation
growth hormone
phosphate loading
prohormone
pyruvate
sodium bicarbonate
sodium phosphate

Ergogenic aids (*ergo* = work; *genic* = producing) are often used by athletes to enhance exercise and sports performance and less frequently by non-athletes to increase muscle mass and improve physique. Most ergogenic aids are nutritional (such as protein drinks) or pharmacologic (such as drugs) agents. The popularity of ergogenic aids is growing in adults of both genders as well as younger populations such as junior and senior high school athletes. It has been estimated that almost half of all Americans regularly use some kind of supplement. The most common reasons for supplement use are:

1. to increase energy level
2. to increase muscle mass
3. to decrease body fat

The incidence of supplement use appears to vary according to (1) sport (runners, cyclists, and weight lifters use supplements more than gymnasts, wrestlers, and basketball players), (2) gender (females tend to use supplements more than males), and (3) level of competition (elite athletes use supplements more than high school or college athletes).[28] Thus, it is important for exercise professionals, physical educators, and coaches to know the potential benefits and hazards associated with the use of ergogenic aids.

The most common use of ergogenic aids is to improve athletic performance. Very small improvements in athletic performance of 1 to 2 percent can make the difference between average and championship achievement. For example, an improvement of only 2 percent in a 4-minute mile brings the time down to 3:55.2.

Small improvements in performance are very difficult to obtain by normal training methods when performance approaches record times or championship levels. Thus, coaches and athletes have tried to improve performance through the use of ergogenic aids. The use of ergogenic aids is generally acceptable as long as they are used to supplement, not to supplant, dedication to training and conditioning, constitute no hazard to the athletes, and are not illegal or banned by sanctioning bodies.

ergogenic aids

Ergogenic aids usually function by (1) improving the capacity of the muscles and/or the oxygen transport and utilization systems to do work or (2) removing or reducing inhibitory mechanisms to allow use of previously untapped reserves. In general, the use of drugs to improve athletic performance falls into the second category and is cause for disqualification by the United States Olympic Committee (USOC), the International Olympic Committee (IOC), the Amateur Athletic Union (AAU), and the National Collegiate Athletic Association (NCAA). Even more important, some drugs used by athletes as well as non-athletes (such as the amphetamines and anabolic steroids) can be habit forming and have many other harmful effects.

AMPHETAMINES

amphetamine

An **amphetamine,** in all its various forms (primarily d-amphetamine sulfate and its European relative, Pervitin), mimics the activity of the sympathetic nervous system (see Chapter 4 for information on the nervous system), and it is used in medicine as a central nervous system stimulant. Many dangerous side-effects are associated with the use of amphetamines, including restlessness, tremor, irritability, confusion, psychotic behavior, vomiting, diarrhea, abdominal cramps, headaches, elevated heart rate, hypertension, severe weight loss, hallucinations, and paranoia.[15]

Research regarding the ergogenic effects of amphetamines gives conflicting results. Under some conditions amphetamines may improve swimming, running, weight-throwing performance, reaction time, and balance, but these drugs have no consistent effect in all individuals nor a reproducible effect on any one individual.[15] Amphetamines are banned by sports sanctioning bodies including the IOC and NCAA.

CAFFEINE

caffeine

Caffeine, a central nervous system stimulant, increases arousal from the sympathetic nervous system (see Chapter 4). It is also a diuretic. Medicinal dosage ranges from 100 to 500 milligrams. A cup of coffee usually contains 100 to 150 milligrams of caffeine, and tea contains slightly less.

Caffeine is a mental stimulant, but it may impair motor performance in activities that require great manual dexterity and calmness such as target shooting, archery, golf, and billiards. In general, caffeine ingested at doses ranging from 3 to 13 milligrams per kilogram of body weight about one hour prior to exercise increases endurance performance (activities lasting longer than approximately five minutes) in cycling, running, and swimming.[27] Research on the ergogenic effects of caffeine on performance in sprint-type activities (less than 90 seconds) and muscle strength is inconclusive.[9] The mechanisms underlying the ergogenic effects of caffeine may include (depending on the activity) an increase in plasma fatty acid concentrations, a carbohydrate sparing effect for muscle glycogen, an increase in the release of epinephrine (adrenaline) from the adrenal gland, and an effect on the release of calcium from the sarcoplasmic reticulum.[7,15,27,47,50] Habitual caffeine use may dampen these responses.[27]

Caffeine ingestion may have side-effects including irritability, restlessness, diarrhea, insomnia, anxiety, diuresis, heart arrhythmias, dehydration, and stomach distress.[7,9,27,47] Clearly, these potentialities should be considered by coaches and athletes prior to the use of caffeine as an ergogenic aid. Caffeine, however, is not banned by the World Anti-Doping Agency (www.wada-ama.org).

ANABOLIC STEROIDS

anabolic steroids

Anabolic steroids are synthetically developed cholesterol-based drugs that resemble naturally occurring hormones such as testosterone and have anabolic (growth-promoting) and androgenic (masculinizing) effects.[1] Anabolic steroids are particularly popular with strength and power athletes as well as body builders because, if taken in high enough doses, they can substantially increase strength, muscle mass, and body weight. Some endurance athletes, however, also use anabolic steroids in an attempt to improve performance by increasing red blood cells.

WWW

NIDA Research Report—
Steroid Abuse and Addiction

www.drugabuse.gov/publications/research-reports/anabolic-steroid-abuse/letter-director

In many cases, laboratory studies of anabolic steroid administration in conjunction with resistance training have demonstrated only modest effects (or no effect) on strength and body weight.[36] Athletic testimonials, however, suggest that the use of anabolic steroids results in very large increases in strength and muscle mass.[7] Coaches should be on the lookout for large, rapid increases in body weight and muscle mass in their athletes as a possible indicator of anabolic steroid use. This is true not only for adult athletes but also for those in junior and senior high school.

The differences between laboratory studies and athletic testimonials are probably due primarily to the dosages of anabolic steroids used. Athletes have reported taking dosages that are 10 to 100 times those used therapeutically.[47] It is clear that when administered under the conditions typically used by athletes, anabolic steroids are effective at increasing strength, body weight, and muscle mass. There are, however, many negative health-related side-effects associated with anabolic steroid use, and the risk of developing the side-effects is dose- and duration-dependent. That is, the longer steroids are administered and the higher the dosages used, the more likely an individual is to manifest health-related difficulties. Anabolic steroids are banned by all major athletic sanctioning bodies and are classified as a controlled substance. Some of the most serious health-related side-effects of anabolic steroid use are:

- Liver dysfunction
- Liver cancer
- Peliosis hepatis (blood-filled cysts)
- Cholestasis (arrest of bile flow)
- Hypertension
- Elevated blood lipids (total cholesterol and triglycerides)
- Reduced high-density lipoprotein cholesterol
- Oligospermia (reduced sperm count)
- Azoospermia (lack of sperm)
- Gynecomastia (mammary development in males)
- Testicular atrophy
- Amenorrhea (absence of menstruation)
- Prostatic cancer
- Depressed immune function
- Premature closure of epiphyseal plates in children

GROWTH HORMONE

growth hormone

Growth hormone is a naturally occurring polypeptide secreted by the anterior pituitary gland (see Chapter 7). The use of growth hormone by athletes and non-athletes has increased because it can now be synthesized.[7,36,45] Strength and power athletes self-administer growth hormone to increase muscle size and strength and to improve performance. Clinically, growth hormone is supplemented in deficient children to facilitate normal growth and development. Growth hormone has been marketed as an anti-aging agent.[36,45] Growth hormone promotes increases in muscle mass directly by increasing amino acid transport and protein synthesis in skeletal muscle and indirectly by stimulating the production of insulin-like growth factor (see Chapter 11).

Little scientific data is available regarding the effectiveness of growth hormone administration for increasing strength, muscle mass, and athletic performance. Athletic testimonials, however, indicate that growth hormone use results in dramatic increases in strength and body weight in as little as 10 weeks.[7] Some athletes are now combining the use of anabolic steroids and growth hormone.

Growth hormone use by adults can have severe adverse health-related consequences, including cardiomegaly (enlarged heart), heart disease, acromegaly (enlarged bones in the head, face, and hands), diabetes, osteoporosis, and arthritis. Growth hormone use is banned by the IOC and other sanctioning bodies.

SODIUM BICARBONATE

sodium bicarbonate

Sodium bicarbonate (sold commercially as baking soda) is a naturally occurring buffer of acids in the blood. Sodium bicarbonate supplementation, also called *bicarbonate loading,* is used by athletes to reduce the fatigue-causing effects of lactate buildup during moderate- to high-intensity physical activity (see Chapter 14). As discussed in Chapter 3, lactate is the end product of the anaerobic glycolysis that is primarily responsible for ATP production during activities that can be maintained for approximately 20 to 30 seconds to 2 to 3 minutes, such as 400- to 800-meter runs and 100- to 200-meter swims. Theoretically, ingestion of sodium bicarbonate at a typical dosage of 0.3 grams per kilogram of body weight (usually taken up to one hour before an athletic event or exercise

CLINICAL APPLICATIONS

Natural steroid hormones as ergogenic aids

There has been great interest in the use of **androstenedione** and **dehydroepiandrosterone (DHEA)** as ergogenic aids for increasing strength and muscle mass. Both are steroid hormones produced naturally in the body by the adrenal gland and testes and are sometimes marketed as **"prohormones"** because they are precursors to testosterone and estrogen.[29,35] The effectiveness of these steroids is questionable, and further research is needed in this area.[5,35] It is likely that many of the side-effects associated with anabolic steroids are also of concern for androstenedione and DHEA administration. Both are banned by the IOC and other athletic governing bodies.

bout) increases blood alkaline reserves and blood pH, which facilitates the movement of lactate out of the muscle. During high-intensity exercise, the removal of lactate from the muscle fiber creates a more favorable cellular environment for ATP production.

In general, bicarbonate loading does not affect performance in short-term, very-high-intensity activities that last no more than 20 to 30 seconds, probably because of the contribution of the ATP–PC system to the ATP demands.[54] On the other hand, sodium bicarbonate supplementation has been shown to increase performance in activities that rely heavily on anaerobic glycolysis for ATP production, such as supramaximal (greater than $\dot{V}O_2$ max) and repeated laboratory tests that last up to approximately two minutes, as well as sprint running, swimming, and rowing.[30,55] Bicarbonate loading may also enhance performance in activities that utilize a substantial proportion of aerobic ATP production and last up to about seven to eight minutes.[30]

Generally, bicarbonate loading at typical dosages does not result in substantial health risk, although gastrointestinal distress and diarrhea are not uncommon. Excessive sodium bicarbonate supplementation at doses much higher than the 0.3 grams per kilogram of body weight normally used, however, can cause heart arrhythmias and cardiac arrest. Currently bicarbonate loading is not banned by sanctioning athletic organizations.

ARGININE

arginine

Arginine is a semi-essential amino acid that is involved in a number of metabolic pathways and the production of biologically active compounds. For example, arginine contributes to the removal of excess ammonia from the body and may attenuate the production of lactate and other metabolic byproducts of exercise.[12,13] In addition, arginine is involved in the synthesis of creatine and glutamate. Potentially the most important role of arginine with regard to exercise is as the precursor of nitric oxide. Nitric oxide is a powerful vasodilator that affects blood flow to the heart and skeletal muscle. Arginine is found in a variety of foods including dairy products, beef, pork, seafood, wheat germ, flour, oatmeal, and soybeans. A typical diet results in the uptake of approximately 4 to 6 grams of arginine per day.

In clinical populations such as patients with pulmonary and cardiovascular diseases, arginine supplementation has been shown to increase exercise tolerance, isometric hand-grip strength, and muscle blood flow. In healthy subjects, arginine supplementation has been shown to increase upper body strength, the anaerobic threshold, physical working capacity at the fatigue threshold, and peak and mean power from the Wingate test.[12,13]

The dosing protocols used for arginine supplementation in previous studies have typically ranged from approximately 5.2 to 12.6 grams per day for one to six weeks.[12,13] More recent studies, however, have examined the effects of polyethylene glycosylated (PEG) arginine supplementation on exercise performance. PEG is a nontoxic, water-soluble polymer that is frequently used to enhance the absorption and delivery of medications, vitamins, electrolytes, and other nutritional supplements. Supplementing with 1.5 to 3.0 grams per day of PEG-arginine for four weeks increased the gas exchange threshold and physical working capacity at the fatigue threshold, but it had no effect on $\dot{V}O_2$ max.[12,13] The improved exercise performance associated with arginine supplementation is probably attributable to reduced concentrations of metabolic byproducts such as lactate and ammonia or to improved blood flow from increased nitric oxide synthesis. Supplementation with arginine is not associated with any harmful side-effects and is not banned by athletic sanctioning bodies.

BETA-ALANINE

beta-alanine

Beta-alanine is a nonproteogenic (not involved in protein synthesis) amino acid produced in the liver. The role of beta-alanine in exercise performance is related to its involvement in the synthesis of carnosine in skeletal muscle. Carnosine is synthesized from beta-alanine and L-histidine via the enzyme carnosine synthetase. The rate-limiting point in the synthesis of carnosine in skeletal muscle is the availability of beta-alanine.[4]

Carnosine acts as an intramuscular buffer for the hydrogen ions (H^+) that accumulate during high-intensity exercise as a result of ATP production via anaerobic glycolysis (see Chapter 3). The buffering process helps to maintain a favorable cellular environment for ATP production. It has been estimated that under normal conditions, carnosine contributes approximately 10 percent of the total buffering capacity in skeletal muscle. Beta-alanine supplementation, however, can increase muscle carnosine concentration by up to approximately 65 percent and, therefore, increase the carnosine contribution to total muscle buffering capacity to about 15 percent.[4]

An effective dose of beta-alanine supplementation for increasing muscle carnosine is 6.4 grams per day. The highest tolerated single dose of beta-alanine, however, is approximately 800 mg. Thus, 6.4 grams per day requires eight daily doses (separated by three hours) of 800 mg each. Single doses higher than 800 mg often result in unpleasant symptoms of numbness, tingling, or a "pins and needles" feeling called paresthesia. Beta-alanine can also be supplemented using controlled release capsules and four 1600-mg doses per day. The controlled release capsules eliminate the symptoms of paresthesia and can increase muscle carnosine by approximately 40 percent after four weeks of beta-alanine supplementation. Other than paresthesia associated with high single doses (>800 mg), there do not appear to be any side-effects associated with beta-alanine supplementation.[4]

Beta-alanine supplementation has been shown to increase the ventilatory threshold, lactate threshold, physical working capacity at the fatigue threshold (PWC_{FT}), and time to exhaustion during a graded exercise test, but it does not increase the maximal oxygen consumption rate ($\dot{V}O_2$ max). In addition, supplementation with beta-alanine has been shown to increase the total work accomplished during a resistance training session, but not maximal strength. Thus, beta-alanine supplementation has been shown to delay the onset of metabolic and neuromuscular fatigue and to increase high-intensity work output but not to affect $\dot{V}O_2$ max or muscular strength.[4] Beta-alanine supplementation is not banned by athletic sanctioning bodies.

Effects of creatine supplementation supported by research

Creatine (Cr) supplementation is, as one manufacturer states, "at the pinnacle of sports supplementation" due to its "ability to dramatically increase strength and hypertrophy of muscle tissue." While this may be something of an overstatement, creatine supplementation does appear to increase Cr and phosphocreatine (PCr) concentrations in the muscle, thereby making PCr more available to replenish ATP for muscle contraction. Effects of Cr supplementation that are substantiated by research include an increase in strength and a delay of fatigue, and Preen et al.* found that it improved performance during an 80-minute repeated sprint exercise. An improvement in performance in high-intensity exercise is important in sports such as football and soccer, where athletes have to be able to perform multiple sprints intermittently throughout the game.

* Preen, D., Dawson, B., Goodman, C., Lawrence, S., Beilby, J., and Ching, S. Effect of creatine loading on long-term sprint exercise performance and metabolism. *Med. Sci. Sports Exerc.* 33: 814–821, 2001.

CREATINE

Creatine is synthesized primarily in the liver (but also the pancreas and kidneys) from the amino acids arginine, glycine, and methionine.[3] As a dietary element, creatine is found in abundance in meat and fish.[3] Skeletal muscle takes up creatine from circulation and stores it predominately (approximately 50–70%) as phosphocreatine.[3] As discussed in Chapter 3, phosphocreatine is used as a fuel source for very-high-intensity exercise through the ATP–PC energy production system. Fatigue during maximal- or near-maximal-intensity physical activity lasting up to 15 to 20 seconds results from phosphocreatine depletion (see Chapter 14). Theoretically, increasing phosphocreatine stores within skeletal muscle could delay the onset of fatigue during very-high-intensity, short-term activities.

- creatine

Creatine loading using creatine monohydrate at a dosage of 20 grams per day (usually 5 grams four times per day) for four to seven days increases muscle phosphocreatine stores by an average of approximately 20 percent.[3] Over a longer period of time (approximately 30 days) as little as 3 grams per day will increase muscle phosphocreatine to the same level. Phosphocreatine accumulation in muscle may be further enhanced by combining creatine supplementation with ingestion of simple carbohydrates.[3] To do so requires approximately 100 grams of carbohydrates per 5 grams of creatine. Individuals show substantial differences in the effectiveness of creatine supplementation; some individuals show no increase in muscle phosphocreatine stores at all. Furthermore, creatine supplementation tends to have a greater effect on phosphocreatine storage in fast-twitch fibers (particularly FG fibers; see Chapter 2) than in slow-twitch fibers.

- creatine loading

Creatine supplementation has been shown to improve anaerobic capabilities, body composition characteristics, and muscular strength but has not been shown to improve aerobic performance.[3] With regard to short-term, high-intensity anaerobic activities such as all-out cycling, sprinting, repeated jumping, swimming, and rowing, creatine supplementation is especially beneficial for repeated exercise bouts.[3] Performance in the latter bouts of a series of three to five repetitions of an activity may be improved by 5 to 20 percent.[3]

WWW
Creatine Supplementation
www.rice.edu/~jenky/sports/creatine.html

Creatine supplementation, particularly in conjunction with resistance training, increases body weight, fat-free weight, and muscle mass.[39] The increased rate of hypertrophy with creatine supplementation may be due to greater protein synthesis and/or reduced protein breakdown.[39] Furthermore, the increase in muscle mass associated with the combination of resistance training and creatine supplementation can result in greater maximum isometric and dynamic strength.[39] (See **Chapter 16 Lab,** Anthropometric Estimation of Thigh Muscle Cross-Sectional Area.)

WWW
Sports Science Creatine Review
http://sportsci.org/traintech/creatine/rbk.html

There is no compelling evidence to indicate that there are health risks associated with short- or long-term creatine supplementation.[39] Although anecdotal reports have described increased cramping, muscle injury, gastrointestinal difficulties, renal problems, liver dysfunction, and hypertension due to creatine supplementation, these are not supported by research. Research is continuing, however, to assess the long-term effects of creatine supplementation on various health parameters. Creatine supplementation is not currently banned by major athletic sanctioning bodies.

PYRUVATE

pyruvate

Pyruvate is a 3-carbon metabolite of carbohydrate metabolism and an intermediate in the glycolytic energy production pathway (see Chapter 3).[31] Theoretically, pyruvate supplementation may provide additional substrate for the Krebs cycle, increase aerobic production of ATP, and improve performance in endurance activities.[46] Pyruvate has also been marketed as a weight-loss agent, an antioxidant, and a cholesterol-reducing agent.[46]

There is some evidence that high dosages (25 grams per day for seven days) of pyruvate supplementation (along with 75 grams of dihydroxyacetone) improve submaximal endurance performance.[42,43] This dosage, however, is substantially higher than the less than 1 gram typically found in commercial products.[46] Currently there is no compelling evidence that these lower dosages of pyruvate supplementation enhance endurance performance. In fact, a single administration of pyruvate may reduce endurance performance.[31]

As a weight-loss agent, pyruvate has the potential to accelerate the loss of fat weight by increasing energy expenditure.[30,46] It appears again, however, that doses of pyruvate of greater than 28 grams, substantially higher than marketed commercially, may be necessary to elicit accelerated fat loss.[46] Furthermore, no conclusive evidence supports the claim that pyruvate supplementation results in a more favorable cholesterol profile or acts as an effective antioxidant.

The low doses of pyruvate in commercially marketed products are probably not associated with substantive health risk. Higher doses, however, consistent with those that have shown ergogenic effects on endurance performance or accelerated fat loss, may result in gastrointestinal dysfunction such as diarrhea.[46] Pyruvate supplementation is not banned by athletic sanctioning bodies.

BETA-HYDROXY-BETA-METHYLBUTYRATE (HMB)

beta-hydroxy-beta-methylbutyrate

Beta-hydroxy-beta-methylbutyrate (HMB) is a metabolite produced from the breakdown of the essential, branched-chain amino acid leucine. HMB is used primarily in conjunction with resistance training to increase muscle mass and strength and decrease fat weight. The effect of HMB supplementation on muscle damage from long-distance running has also been examined.[33] Theoretically, HMB supplementation may increase muscle mass by decreasing protein breakdown during vigorous physical activity. Typical dosages for HMB supplementation range from approximately 1.5 to 6.0 grams per day.[23,24]

HMB supplementation during resistance training has been shown to increase maximal isometric strength, concentric and eccentric isokinetic peak torque, and fat-free weight.[23] These beneficial effects of HMB may have been due to reduced muscle breakdown.[23]

It does not appear that HMB supplementation with dosages less than approximately 6 grams per day results in negative effects on health. Gallagher et al.[24] reported that short-term (eight weeks) HMB supplementation of 6 grams per day had no effects on liver, kidney, or immune function. Additional research is needed to determine the potential health-related effects of longer-term supplementation with higher dosages of HMB. The use of HMB is not banned by athletic sanctioning bodies.

PHOSPHATE LOADING

Oral administration of **sodium phosphate** has been used as an ergogenic aid. **Phosphate loading** normally involves ingesting approximately 600 to 1,000 mg of sodium phosphate, four to six times per day for three to six days prior to exercise.[11,18,22,34,44,49] Kreider et al.[34] have identified six potential mechanisms through which phosphate supplementation may affect human performance: (1) elevations in serum and intracellular phosphate promoting phosphate-stimulated glycolysis, (2) increased availability of phosphate for oxidative phosphorylation and creatine phosphate synthesis, (3) increased red cell anaerobic glycolysis and efficiency, (4) an elevation in red cell 2,3-diphosphoglycerate (2,3-DPG) promoting a reduced oxyhemoglobin affinity at a given oxygen tension, (5) enhanced myocardial and cardiovascular efficiency, and (6) a possible increase in anaerobic threshold.

- sodium phosphate
- phosphate loading

There is conflicting evidence concerning the ergogenic effects of phosphate loading. While some investigations have reported increases in $\dot{V}O_2$ max[11,34,44] and anaerobic threshold,[34] in general, phosphate loading has not been shown to improve endurance performance significantly during running,[18,34] bicycling,[34,49] or isokinetic leg extension activities.[18] Stewart et al.,[44] however, reported 10 to 25 percent increases in the time to exhaustion during an incremental cycle ergometer test as a result of phosphate loading, compared with placebo or control situations. Because of the lack of consistent findings among investigations, Williams[53] has stated, "Whether or not phosphate salt supplementation confers an ergogenic effect is still questionable." Considerable additional research is necessary before phosphate loading should be considered an effective ergogenic aid to performance. Phosphate loading is not banned by athletic sanctioning bodies.

BLOOD DOPING (ERYTHROCYTHEMIA)

Blood doping (more properly called **erythrocythemia**) usually involves removing approximately two pints of blood, 8 to 12 weeks prior to an endurance competition.[2,16] The red blood cells (RBCs) are then separated and frozen. The athlete continues to train as usual, and the body restores the RBC count to normal levels through a process called *hemopoiesis*. During the week prior to competition, the RBCs are reinfused.[16] This process results in an increase in RBC concentration and, thus, improved oxygen transport capability.[2,25,51,52]

- blood doping
- erythrocythemia

Blood doping can significantly improve maximal oxygen consumption rate ($\dot{V}O_2$ max) as well as submaximal and maximal endurance performance because of the increase in hemoglobin level and enhanced oxygen transport.[2,8,20,21,25,26,52] Previous work[17,48,51] that failed to find significant improvements in exercise performance may have been confounded by: (1) inadequate reinfusion volumes, (2) premature reinfusion before subjects had recovered from the anemia following blood withdrawal, or (3) improper storage of blood.

WWW
U.S. Anti-Doping Agency
www.usada.org

Ethical questions surround blood doping. For example, the Medical Commission of the International Olympic Committee defines doping as "the administration of, or the use by a competing athlete of, any substance foreign to the body or of any physiological substance taken in abnormal quantity or taken by an abnormal route of entry into the body with the sole intention of increasing in an artificial and unfair manner his or her performance in competition." On the other hand, it might be argued that blood doping offers only the same advantage in enhancing hemoglobin concentration that some athletes enjoy by training at high elevation to compete at sea level. Blood doping appears to be an effective method of improving distance running performance, but it has been banned by the IOC and the NCAA.[16]

ERYTHROPOIETIN

erythropoietin

The drug **erythropoietin** has been approved by the Food and Drug Administration for use primarily in patients with various forms of anemia or kidney disease. The function of erythropoietin is to stimulate bone marrow to produce red blood cells. Erythropoietin is also a naturally occurring hormone produced by the kidneys that responds to low blood hemoglobin levels.[2,16]

Exogenous administration of erythropoietin can theoretically improve endurance exercise performance in the same way as conventional blood doping procedures.[2] In essence, erythropoietin mimics the results of blood doping by increasing hematocrit (percentage of RBCs) and thereby enhancing oxygen transport to the working muscles.[2,16]

Like traditional blood doping, the use of erythropoietin can improve endurance performance,[2] and anecdotal evidence has suggested that endurance performance may be improved by as much as 19 percent.[10] Ekblom[19] has reported that seven weeks of erythropoietin injections increased endurance performance by a minimum of 10 percent. A study by Schena et al.[38] found that blood levels of endogenous erythropoietin were increased by 15 to 24 percent following endurance running and bicycle races. These changes were transient, however, with no change reported in basal erythropoietin levels.

WWW

NCAA Drug Testing
www.ncaa.org/health-and-safety/policy/drug-testing

A number of side-effects are associated with the drug erythropoietin including elevated blood pressure and flu-like symptoms.[2] Furthermore, elevation of hematocrit above 55 percent is generally considered risky.[16] Theoretically, excessive doses of erythropoietin could elevate hematocrit to 80 percent.[16] In addition, hematocrit is generally increased due to fluid loss as a result of long-duration endurance activity such as the marathon. The thickened blood clots more quickly and can increase the risk of heart attack, stroke, and pulmonary edema.[16] It has been suggested that some competitive athletes may have died as a result of erythropoietin abuse.[10] Because of the potential health hazards, the IOC has banned the use of artificial erythropoietin.[41]

GLYCOGEN SUPERCOMPENSATION (CARBOHYDRATE LOADING)

As described in Chapter 14, moderate-intensity, long-duration activities such as the marathon, triathlon, and endurance bicycling utilize aerobic metabolism of carbohydrates (and fats) to supply ATP. Over the course of one to two hours or longer of this kind of activity, glycogen stores within the activated muscle fibers can be depleted. To continue the activity, the athlete must decrease exercise intensity. Thus, the duration that these activities can be maintained before glycogen depletion causes fatigue is determined largely by the size of the glycogen stores within the muscle. **Glycogen supercompensation** procedures (sometimes called *carbohydrate loading*) are designed to increase the amount of glycogen stored within muscle and thereby delay the onset of fatigue during endurance activities.[14]

glycogen supercompensation

Karlsson and Saltin[32] demonstrated the effect of glycogen stores on endurance performance when they had 10 subjects run the same 30-km race twice, three weeks apart, once after a carbohydrate-enriched diet and once after a mixed diet. They found the muscle glycogen level in the quadriceps for the high-carbohydrate diet to be double that for the mixed diet, and every subject turned in the better performance after the high-carbohydrate diet. Interestingly, identical pace was maintained after both diets in the early part of the race when glycogen content was high, but pace fell off earlier after the mixed diet as glycogen stores were emptied.

The classic work of the original investigators in this area, Bergstrom and colleagues,[6] provided suggestions for depleting muscle glycogen stores and then modifying the diet to best prepare for prolonged endurance-type events through glycogen supercompensation. To achieve the highest possible level of muscle glycogen for such events, the athlete was to work the same muscles to exhaustion about one week prior to the event. For the next three days, the diet was to be made up almost exclusively of fat and protein, since it was shown that a low-carbohydrate diet followed by a high-carbohydrate diet results in the greatest possible glycogen storage. About three days were to be left for a carbohydrate-rich diet with only very light workouts to produce the maximum possible glycogen storage in the muscles. The low-carbohydrate diet consisted of 1,500 kcal of protein and 1,300 kcal of fat for a total daily energy expenditure estimated at 2,800 kcal. The high-carbohydrate diet made up the same total with 2,300 kcal of carbohydrate and 500 kcal of protein.[6]

Work by Sherman and his co-workers[40] modified the classic method, which was both physically and psychologically taxing for the athlete. Their group of runners consumed three different trial diets in preparation for three separate 13-mile performance runs. In preparation for each performance run, the runners all ran on a treadmill at 73 percent $\dot{V}O_2$ max for 90, 40, 40, 20, and 20 minutes and then rested one day of the six days before each of the 13-mile performance runs. The diet for the first trial was from the classic regimen: 15 percent carbohydrate for the first three days and 70 percent for the last three. The second trial diet was 50 percent carbohydrate for the first three days and 70 percent for the last three. The third trial diet was an average diet (50% carbohydrate for all six days). Muscle biopsies showed that the low–high carbohydrate regimen (15–70%) elevated muscle glycogen to 207 millimoles per kilogram; the second regimen of average–high carbohydrate (50–70%) yielded 203 millimoles per kilogram; and the normal regimen (50% on all six days) produced only 160 millimoles per kilogram. Thus, it appears that this much more moderate regimen can accomplish the same supercompensation as the difficult classic approach. It should be noted that this procedure, which relies heavily on the declining level of training in the six days before competition for its glycogen storage effect, is not greatly different from what knowledgeable coaches have recommended for many decades past.

Acupuncture

Is acupuncture an ergogenic aid? While many theoretical reasons as to why acupuncture should improve strength, aerobic conditioning, and flexibility have been proposed, there has been very little research that supports these claims. Probably the most promising use for acupuncture in athletics is in the area of pain management. By controlling pain the athlete may be able to perform at a higher level. Further research needs to be done to establish the usefulness of acupuncture in exercise and sport and to determine the potential side-effects and ethical considerations that need to be addressed.[37]

summary

Ergogenic (*ergo* = work; *genic* = producing) aids are special aids to performance used to enhance the results of training. Generally, the use of supplements or ergogenic procedures is acceptable as long as they do not supplant training and conditioning, are not hazardous to the athlete's health, and are not banned by sanctioning bodies. Ergogenic aids usually function by improving the capacity of muscles and/or the oxygen transport systems, or by removing or reducing inhibitory mechanisms. Typically, the use of drugs falls into the second category and can lead to disqualification by various sport sanctioning bodies.

Marketers of ergogenic supplements sometimes make unsubstantiated claims for their products. Although some supplements improve athletic performance under specific conditions, many do not. In some cases, the use of supplements not only is useless in terms of athletic performance but also can be harmful to an athlete's health.

questions for review

1. Define ergogenic aids. Why do exercise professionals, physical educators, and coaches need to be aware of the properties of ergogenic aids?
2. How do ergogenic aids work to improve performance?
3. What are the benefits and hazards of steroid use?
4. What are the signs of steroid use for which coaches should be on the lookout?
5. Discuss the pros and cons of creatine loading.
6. What is the ethical dilemma associated with blood doping?
7. Describe the protocols used for carbohydrate loading and the advantages and disadvantages of each.
8. As a coach, what recommendations regarding ergogenic aids would you give to an adult professional athlete who wants to improve sprinting performance? Endurance? Strength?
9. As a coach, what recommendations regarding ergogenic aids would you give to a high school athlete who wants to improve sprinting performance? Endurance? Strength?
10. As an exercise professional, what recommendations regarding ergogenic aids would you give to a client who wants to increase muscle size and definition?

student companion website

For further review of this book's chapters and for test preparation, visit the book's website, **www.hhpcommunities.com/exercisephysiology**, to take practice quizzes, review the vocabulary terms, use the study guide, and view the digital image bank.

references

1. American College of Sports Medicine. Position Stand. The use of anabolic-androgenic steroids in sports. *Me. Sci. Sports Exerc.* 19: 534–539, 1987.
2. American College of Sports Medicine Position Stand. The use of blood doping as an ergogenic aid. *Med. Sci. Sports Exerc.* 28: i–viii, 1996.
3. American College of Sports Medicine. Roundtable. The physiological and health effects of oral creatine supplementation. *Med. Sci. Sports Exerc.* 32: 706–717, 2000.
4. Artioli, G. G., Gualano, B., Smith, A., Stout, J., and Lancha Jr., A. H. Role of beta-alanine supplementation on muscle carnosine and exercise performance. *Med. Sci. Sports Exerc.* 42: 1162–1173, 2010.
5. Ballantyne, C. S., Phillips, S. M., MacDonald, J. R., Tarnopolsky, M. A., and MacDougall, J. D. The acute effects of androstenedione supplementation in healthy young males. *Can. J. Appl. Physiol.* 25: 68–78, 2000.
6. Bergstrom, J., Hermansen, L., Hultman, E., and Saltin, B. Diet, muscle glycogen, and physical performance. *Acta Physiol. Scand.* 71: 140–150, 1967.
7. Brooks, G. A., Fahey, T. D., White, T. P., and Baldwin, K. M. *Exercise Physiology: Human Bioenergetics*

and Its Applications, 3rd edition. Mountain View, CA: Mayfield Publishing Co., 2000, pp. 711, 722–723.

8. Buick, F. J., Gledhill, N., Froese, A. B., Spriet, L., and Meyers, E. C. Effect of induced erythrocythemia on aerobic work capacity. *J. Appl. Physiol.* 48: 636–642, 1980.
9. Burke, E. R. Nutritional ergogenic aids. In *Nutrition for Sport and Exercise,* 2nd edition, eds. J. R. Berning and S. N. Steen. Gaithersburg, MD: Aspen Publishers Inc., 1998, pp. 119–142.
10. Burke, E., Coyle, E. F., Eichner, E. R., Nadel, E. R., and Williams, M. H. Blood doping and plasma volume expansion: Benefits and dangers. *Gatorade Sports Sci. Exch.* (Roundtable) Spring, 1991.
11. Cade, R., Conte, M., Zauner, C., Mars, D., Peterson, J., Lunne, D., Hommen, N., and Packer, D. Effects of phosphate loading on 2,3-diphosphoglycerate and maximal oxygen uptake. *Med. Sci. Sports Exerc.* 16: 263–268, 1984.
12. Camic, C. L., Housh, T. J., Mielke, M., Zuniga, J. M., Hendrix, C. R., Johnson, G. O., Schmidt, R. J., and Housh, D. J. The effects of 4 weeks of an arginine-based supplement on the gas exchange threshold and peak oxygen uptake. *Appl. Physiol. Nutr. Metab.* 35: 286–293, 2010.
13. Camic, C. L., Housh, T. J., Zuniga, J. M., Hendrix, C. R., Mielke, M., Johnson, G. O., Schmidt, R. J. Effects of arginine-based supplements on the physical working capacity at the fatigue threshold. *J. Strength Cond. Res.* 24: 1306–1312, 2010.
14. Coleman, E. J. Carbohydrate—The master fuel. In *Nutrition for Sport and Exercise,* 2nd edition, eds. J. R. Berning and S. N. Steen. Gaithersburg, MD: Aspen Publishers Inc., 1998, pp. 21–44.
15. Conlee, R. K. Amphetamine, caffeine, and cocaine. In *Ergogenics: Enhancement of Performance in Exercise and Sport,* eds. D. R. Lamb and M. H. Williams. Dubuque, IA: Brown and Benchmark, 1991, pp. 285–330.
16. Cowart, V. S. Erythropoietin: A dangerous new form of blood doping? *Phys. Sportsmed.* 17: 115–118, 1989.
17. Cunningham, K. G. The effect of transfusional polycythemia on aerobic work capacity. *J. Sports Med. Phys. Fitness* 18: 353–358, 1978.
18. Duffy, D. J., and Conlee, R. K. Effects of phosphate loading on leg power and high intensity treadmill exercise. *Med. Sci. Sports Exerc.* 18: 674–677, 1986.
19. Ekblom, B. Effects of iron deficiency, variations in hemoglobin concentration and erythropoietin injections on physical performance and relevant physiological parameters. *Proceedings of First I.O.C. World Congress on Sports Sciences,* pp. 9–11, 1989.
20. Ekblom, B., Goldbarg, A. N., and Gullbring, B. Response to exercise after blood loss and reinfusion. *J. Appl. Physiol.* 33: 175–180, 1972.
21. Ekblom, B., Wilson, G., and Astrand, P. O. Central circulation during exercise after venesection and reinfusion of red blood cells. *J. Appl. Physiol.* 40: 379–383, 1976.
22. Fukuda, D. H., Smith, A. E., Kendall, K. L., and Stout, J. R. Phosphate supplementation: An update. *Strength Cond. J.* 32: 53–56, 2010.
23. Gallagher, P. M., Carrithers, J. A., Godard, M. P., Schulze, K. E., and Trappe, S. W. β-hydroxy-β-methylbutyrate ingestion, Part I: Effects on strength and fat free mass. *Med. Sci. Sports Exerc.* 32: 2109–2115, 2000.
24. Gallagher, P. M., Carrithers, J. A., Godard, M. P., Schulze, K. E., and Trappe, S. W. β-hydroxy-β-methylbutyrate ingestion, Part II: Effects on hematology, hepatic and renal function. *Med. Sci. Sports Exerc.* 32: 2116–2119, 2000.
25. Gledhill, N. Blood doping and related issues: A brief review. *Med. Sci. Sports Exerc.* 14: 183–189, 1982.
26. Gledhill, N. The ergogenic effect of blood doping. *Phys. Sportsmed.* 11: 87–90, 1983.
27. Graham, T. E., and Spriet, L. L. Caffeine and exercise performance. *Gatorade Sports Sci. Exch.* 9(1), 1996.
28. Grandjean, A. C., and Ruud, J. Dietary supplement use by athletes. *Strength Cond. J.* 25: 72–73, 2003.
29. Gwartney, D. L., and Stout, J. R. Androstenedione: Physical and ethical considerations relative to its use as an ergogenic aid. *Strength Cond. J.* 21: 65–66, 1999.
30. Heigenhauser, G. J. F., and Jones, N. L. Bicarbonate loading. In *Ergogenics: Enhancement of Performance in Exercise and Sport,* eds. D. R. Lamb and M. H. Williams. Dubuque, IA: Brown and Benchmark, 1991, pp. 183–212.
31. Ivy, J. L. Effect of pyruvate and dihydroxyacetone on metabolism and aerobic endurance capacity. *Med. Sci. Sports Exerc.* 30: 837–843, 1998.
32. Karlsson, J., and Saltin, B. Diet, muscle glycogen, and endurance performance. *J. Appl. Physiol.* 31: 203–206, 1971.
33. Knitter, A. E., Patton, L., Rathmacher, J. A., Petersen, A., and Sharp, R. Effects of beta-hydroxy-beta-methylbutyrate on muscle damage after a prolonged run. *J. Appl. Physiol.* 89: 1340–1344, 2000.
34. Kreider, R. B., Miller, G. W., Williams, M. H., Somma, C. T., and Nasser, T. A. Effects of phosphate loading on oxygen uptake, ventilatory anaerobic threshold, and run performance. *Med. Sci. Sports Exerc.* 22: 250–256, 1990.
35. Leutholtz, B. C. Update on DHEA. *Strength Cond. J.* 20: 74–75, 1998.
36. Lombardo, J. A., Hickson, R. C., and Lamb, D. R. Anabolic/androgenic steroids and growth hormone. In *Ergogenics: Enhancement of Performance in Exercise and Sport,* eds. D. R. Lamb and M. H. Williams. Dubuque, IA: Brown and Benchmark, 1991, pp. 249–284.
37. Pelham, T. W., Holt, L. E., and Stalker, R. Acupunture in human performance. *J. Strength Cond. Res.* 15: 266–271, 2001.
38. Schena, F., Cevese, A., Guidi, G. G., Mosconi, C., and Pattini, A. Serum erythropoietin changes in runners and

mountain-bikers after a 42 km race. *Med. Sci. Sports Exerc.* 22 (supplement): S135, 1990.

39. Schilling, B. K., Stone, M. H., Utter, A., Kearney, J. T., Johnson, M., Coglianese, R., Smith, L., O'Bryant, H. S., Fry, A. C., Starks, M., Keith, R., and Stone, M. E. Creatine supplementation and health variables: A retrospective study. *Med. Sci. Sports Exerc.* 33: 183–188, 2001.
40. Sherman, W. M., Costill, D. L., and Fink, W. J. Effect of exercise–diet manipulation on muscle glycogen and its subsequent utilization during performance. *Int. J. Sports Med.* 2: 114–117, 1981.
41. Spriet, L. L. Blood doping and oxygen transport. In *Ergogenics: Enhancement of Performance in Exercise and Sports,* eds. D. R. Lamb and M. H. Williams. Dubuque, IA: Brown and Benchmark, 1991, pp. 213–248.
42. Stanko, R. T., Robertson, R. J., Galbreath, R. W., Reilly, Jr., J. J., Greenawalt, K. D., and Goss, F. L. Enhanced leg exercise endurance with a high-carbohydrate diet and dihydroxyacetone and pyruvate. *J. Appl. Physiol.* 69: 1651–1656, 1990.
43. Stanko, R. T., Robertson, R. J., Spina, R. J., Reilly Jr., J. J., Greenawalt, K. D., and Goss, F. L. Enhancement of arm exercise endurance capacity with dihydroxyacetone and pyruvate. *J. Appl. Physiol.* 68: 119–124, 1990.
44. Stewart, I., McNaughton, L., Davies, P., and Tristram, S. Phosphate loading and the effects on $\dot{V}O_2$ max in trained cyclists. *Res. Q. Exerc. Sport* 61: 80–84, 1990.
45. Stone, M. H. Human growth hormone: Physiological functions and ergogenic efficacy. *Strength Cond. J.* 17: 72–74, 1995.
46. Sukala, W. R. Pyruvate: Beyond the marketing hype. *Int. J. Sport Nutr.* 8: 241–249, 1998.
47. Thein, L. A., Thein, J. M., and Landry, G. L. Ergogenic aids. *Phys. Ther.* 75: 426–439, 1995.
48. Videman, T., and Rytomaa, T. Effect of blood removal and autotransfusion on heart rate response to a submaximal workload. *J. Sports Med. Phys. Fitness* 17: 387–390, 1977.
49. Weathermax, R. S., Ahlberg, A., Deady, M., Otto, R. M., Perez, H. R., Cooperstein, D., and Wygand, J. Effects of phosphate loading on bicycle time trial performance. *Med. Sci. Sports Exerc.* 18 (supplement): S11–S12, 1986.
50. Wilcox, A. R. Caffeine and endurance performance. *Gatorade Sports Sci. Exch.* 3(26), 1990.
51. Williams, M. A., Goodwin, A. R., Perkins, R., and Bocrie, J. Effect of blood reinjection upon endurance capacity and heart rate. *Med. Sci. Sports* 5: 181–186, 1973.
52. Williams, M. H. Blood doping: An update. *Phys. Sportsmed.* 9: 59–64, 1981.
53. Williams, M. H. Ergogenic aids. In *Sports Nutrition for the 90s,* eds. J. R. Berning and S. N. Steen. Gaithersburg, MD: Aspen Publishers, Inc., 1991.
54. Williams, M. H. Bicarbonate loading. *Gatorade Sports Sci. Exch.* 4(36), 1992.
55. Williams, M. H. *The Ergogenic Edge.* Champaign, IL: Human Kinetics, 1998.

Anthropometric Estimation of Thigh Muscle Cross-Sectional Area

BACKGROUND

The quantification of muscle cross-sectional area (CSA) has been used clinically to evaluate the nutritional status of children, the elderly, and individuals with muscle-wasting diseases or injuries.[3] In nonclinical settings, the quantification of muscle CSA has been used to describe and compare athletic and non-athletic populations, predict muscular strength and strength per unit of muscle CSA, and examine the effects of various interventions on hypertrophy and atrophy.[3]

The most common laboratory techniques used to determine muscle CSA are computed tomography (CT scan) and magnetic resonance imaging (MRI), which are valid and reliable but also expensive (see photos 16.1 and 16.2). Many laboratories do not have access to this technology and, therefore, must rely on more practical methods, such as anthropometry, for assessing muscle CSA. Multiple regression equations for estimating thigh muscle CSA have been developed based on the measurement of the anterior thigh skinfold and mid-thigh circumference.[3] The accuracy (validated against MRI) of these equations is comparable to that of skinfold estimates of percent body fat (see Chapter 15 lab) as well as field tests such as the Astrand–Rhyming test (see Chapter 19 Lab) for estimating maximal oxygen consumption rate ($\dot{V}O_2max$).[3] The equations are applicable to both males and females. The mid-thigh circumference reflects all tissues of the thigh, including muscle, skin, subcutaneous fat, bone, connective tissue, and vessels. Theoretically, the skinfold accounts for the amount of subcutaneous fat (and skin) that covers the muscle.

In this laboratory, the mid-thigh circumference and anterior thigh skinfold will be measured and used in multiple regression equations to estimate the quadriceps CSA, hamstrings CSA, and total thigh muscle CSA. The quadriceps CSA includes the vastus intermedius, vastus lateralis, vastus medialis, and rectus femoris muscles. The hamstrings CSA includes the semimembranosus, semitendinosus, and biceps femoris muscles. The total thigh muscle CSA includes the quadriceps, hamstrings, adductor longus, adductor magnus, gracilis, and sartorius muscles.

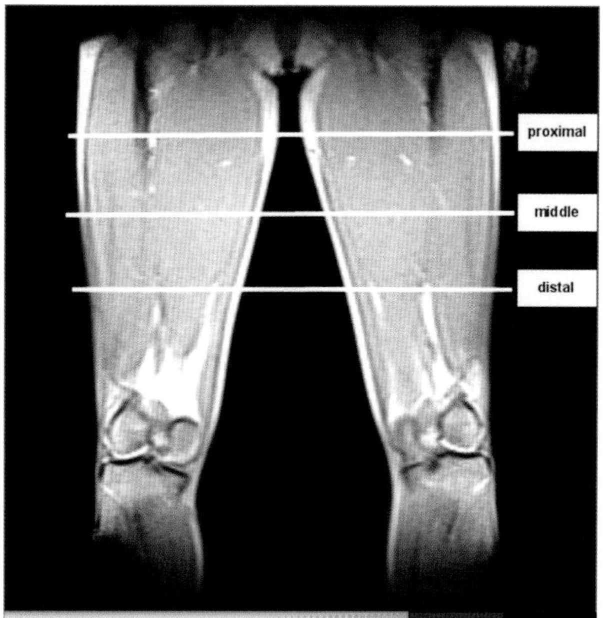

photo 16.1

Coronal MRI scan of the thighs.

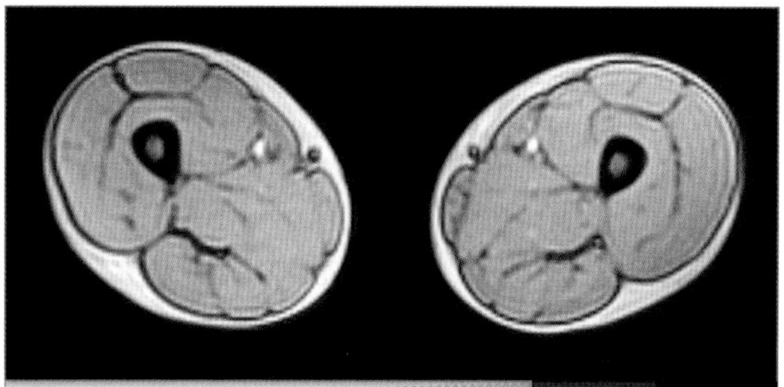

photo 16.2

Cross-sectional MRI images of the thighs.

TERMS & ABBREVIATIONS

- ☐ anthropometry = the measurement of the size and proportions of the human body
- ☐ CSA = cross-sectional area. Muscle CSA in this lab is determined using circumferences, skinfolds, and multiple regression equations.
- ☐ CT scan = computed tomography scan

- MRI = magnetic resonance imaging
- multiple regression equation = a combination of a number of measurements (independent variables) that best predict a common variable (the dependent variable, in this case muscle CSA)
- R = multiple correlation coefficient, a numerical measure of how well a dependent variable can be predicted from a combination of independent variables (a number between −1 and 1)
- SEE = standard error of estimate, a measure of the accuracy of predictions made using a regression equation

PROCEDURES

1. Measure and mark the anatomical sites with a marker (see sites below). The mid-thigh circumference and anterior thigh skinfold measurements are taken on the dominant limb. To determine the dominant limb, ask the subject, "Which leg do you prefer to kick with?"
2. Calculate quadriceps CSA, hamstrings CSA, and total thigh muscle CSA using Worksheet 16.1. The CSA values from the equations are expressed in cm^2.

Skinfold Site[2]

Anterior thigh (see photos 16.3–16.5): a vertical fold (measured in mm) on the anterior aspect of the thigh, midway between the hip (inguinal fold) and knee joints (photo 16.3; superior border of the patella).

a. Grasp the skinfold firmly with the thumb and forefinger and pull away from the body (photo 16.3).
b. Hold the skinfold caliper perpendicular to the skinfold (photo 16.4). The caliper should be approximately 1 cm away from the thumb and forefinger so that the pressure of the caliper will not be affected.
c. Read the skinfold size approximately one to two seconds after the caliper thumb grip has been released.
d. Take three measurements (record the measurements on Worksheet 16.1) at least 15 seconds apart to allow the skinfold site to return to normal. If the repeated measurements vary by more than 1 mm, more measurements should be taken. Use the mean of the recorded measurements that are within 1 mm as the representative skinfold value in the equations.

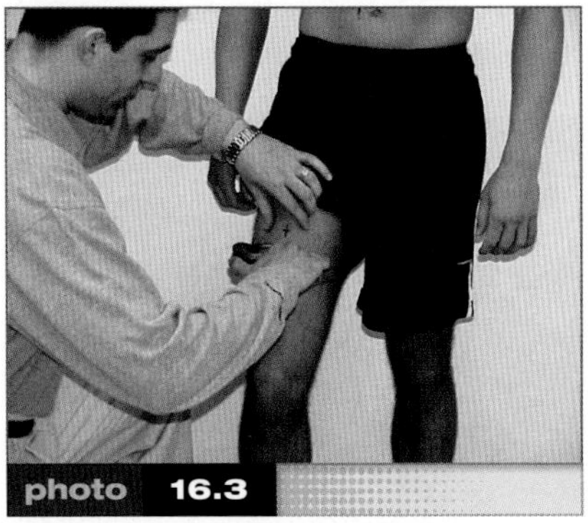
photo 16.3

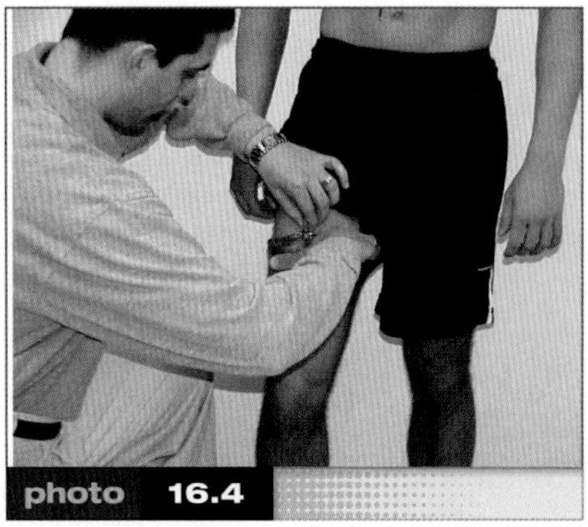
photo 16.4

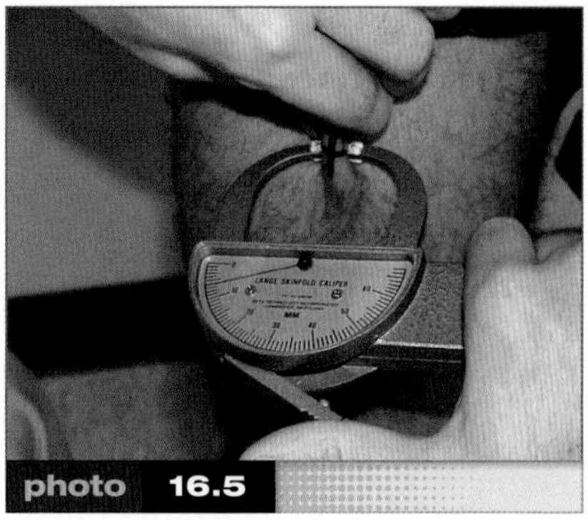
photo 16.5

Anterior thigh skinfold measurement.

Circumference Site[1]

Mid-thigh (see photo 16.6): the distance (expressed in cm) around the thigh, midway between the hip (inguinal fold) and knee joints (superior border of the patella), with the subject standing and feet slightly apart.

a. Place the tape perpendicular to the long axis of the limb.
b. Hold the tape tightly around the limb, but do not compress the underlying tissue.
c. Take three measurements (record the measurements on Worksheet 16.1) and use the mean of repeated recordings that agree within 0.5 cm.

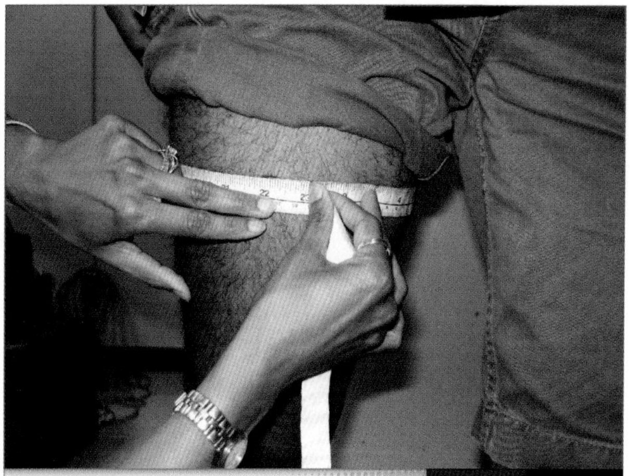
photo 16.6

Mid-thigh circumference measurement.

Equations[3]

Quadriceps CSA (cm^2) = (2.52 × mid-thigh circumference in cm) – (1.25 × anterior thigh skinfold in mm) – 45.13

R = 0.86

SEE = 5.2 cm^2

Hamstrings CSA (cm^2) = (1.08 × mid-thigh circumference in cm) – (0.64 × anterior thigh skinfold in mm) – 22.69

R = 0.75

SEE = 3.5 cm^2

Total thigh muscle CSA (cm^2) = (4.68 × mid-thigh circumference in cm) – (2.09 × anterior thigh skinfold in mm) – 80.99

R = 0.86

SEE = 9.5 cm^2

SAMPLE CALCULATIONS

TRIAL	1	2	3	MEAN
Anterior thigh skinfold (mm)	19.5	20.5	20.0	20
Mid-thigh circumference (cm)	55.0	54.8	55.2	55

Quadriceps CSA (cm^2) = (2.52 × 55) – (1.25 × 20) – 45.13 = 68.5 cm^2

Hamstrings CSA (cm^2) = (1.08 × 55) – (0.64 × 20) – 22.69 = 23.9 cm^2

Total thigh muscle CSA (cm^2) = (4.68 × 55) – (2.09 × 20) – 80.99 = 134.6 cm^2

Table L16.1 includes typical quadriceps, hamstrings, and total thigh muscle CSA values.

table L16.1 Typical mean (± SD) values for quadriceps, hamstrings, and total thigh muscle cross-sectional area.[3]

MUSCLE GROUP	MEAN ± SD
Quadriceps CSA	75.5 ± 9.9 cm^2
Hamstrings CSA	27.5 ± 5.1 cm^2
Total thigh muscle CSA	145.9 ± 18.3 cm^2

Note: The values listed in this table are for untrained adults (age range = 19–36 years). Training status and age will likely affect the subject's estimated CSA values.

ANTHROPOMETRIC ESTIMATION OF THIGH MUSCLE CROSS-SECTIONAL AREA — worksheet 16.1

NAME ______________________ DATE ______________

Measurements

Trial	1	2	3	Mean
Anterior thigh skinfold (mm)	________	________	________	________
Mid-thigh circumference (cm)	________	________	________	________

Use the equations on page 371 to calculate:

Quadriceps CSA = ______________________ cm^2

Hamstrings CSA = ______________________ cm^2

Total thigh muscle CSA = ______________________ cm^2

EXTENSION ACTIVITIES — worksheet 16.2

NAME ______________________ DATE ______________

1. A subject's quadriceps CSA estimated from the anthropometric equation in the present laboratory is 70.5 cm^2. Given that the SEE for this equation is 5.2 cm^2, the subject's true quadriceps CSA is likely to fall between what two values?

2. Have your anterior thigh skinfold and mid-thigh circumference measured, and use the anthropometric equations on page 371 to calculate your:

   Quadriceps CSA = ______________________ cm^2

   Hamstrings CSA = ______________________ cm^2

   Total thigh muscle CSA = ______________________ cm^2

EXTENSION QUESTIONS

1. What are some common mistakes that may occur in administering this lab?

2. Identify possible sources of error in this lab.

3. Assess the practicality of using this lab in the field.

4. Research the reliability and/or validity of this lab using online resources, journal articles, and other credible sources.

REFERENCES

1. Callaway, C. W., Chumlea, W. C., Bouchard, C., Himes, J. H., Lohman, T. G., Martin, A. D., Mitchell, C. D., Mueller, W. H., Roche, A. F., and Seefeldt, V. D. Circumferences. In *Anthropometric Standardization Reference Manual,* eds. T. G. Lohman, A. F. Roche, and R. Martorell. Champaign, IL: Human Kinetics, 1988, pp. 39–54.
2. Harrison, G. G., Buskirk, E. R., Carter, J. E. L., Johnston, F. E., Lohman, T. G., Pollock, M. L., Roche, A. F., and Wilmore, J. Skinfold thicknesses and measurement technique. In *Anthropometric Standardization Reference Manual,* eds. T. G. Lohman, A. F. Roche, and R. Martorell. Champaign, IL: Human Kinetics, 1988, pp. 55–70.
3. Housh, D. J., Housh, T. J., Weir, J. P., Weir, L. L., Johnson, G. O., and Stout, J. R. Anthropometric estimation of thigh muscle cross-sectional area. *Med. Sci. Sports Exerc.* 27: 784–791, 1995.

17 Environment and Exercise

As a result of reading this chapter you will:

Know the basic physiological responses to exercise in cold and hot environments.

Understand specific elements of acclimatization to cold and hot climates.

Know the primary health-related risks of exercising in the cold and heat.

Be aware of the potential effects of exercising at high altitudes on health and performance.

key concepts

altitude acclimatization
chilblain
chilling
cold acclimatization
conduction
convection
core temperature
evaporation
exertional heat exhaustion
exertional heat stroke
exertional hyperthermia
frostbite
heat acclimatization
heat strain
heat stress
heat syncope
hypothermia
jet lag
muscle (heat) cramps
orthostatic dizziness
radiation
temperature regulatory center
trenchfoot
wind chill factor

www

Environmental Physiology Lab
www.mayo.edu/research/labs/human-integrative-environmental-physiology

The efficiency with which humans perform work or exercise can vary between 15 and 40 percent. This means that, of the energy consumed, only 15 to 40 percent is converted into useful work, while the remaining energy (60–85%) is wasted as heat energy. This wasted heat energy must be dissipated, or body temperature will increase. Furthermore, in a hot climate the body also absorbs heat from the environment. These two factors tend to increase the body's heat stores and thus increase body temperature.

Cold environments also pose challenges. In some cases, the heat produced by increased metabolic activity may not be sufficient to maintain body temperature, and performance therefore decreases.

PHYSIOLOGY OF ADAPTATION TO HEAT AND COLD

The body can maintain thermal balance by losing heat to the environment in four ways:

1. Conduction. Heat exchange by conduction is accomplished through physical contact between one substance and another substance. The rate of exchange is determined by the temperature difference between the two substances and by their thermal conductivities. For example, the body loses heat through conduction when submerged in cold water.

2. Convection. In convection, heat is transferred by a moving fluid (liquid or gas). Thus, in the example of a man submerged in cold water, the heat that is transferred from the body to the water by conduction is carried away from the body by convection (the water that has been warmed rises, making way for new molecules to be heated by conduction, etc.).

3. Radiation. The process of heat transfer by means of electromagnetic waves is radiation. At rest, we are constantly giving off heat through radiation. These waves can pass through air without imparting much heat to it; however, when they strike a body, their energy is largely transformed into heat. This is the means by which the sun heats the earth, which also explains why one can be perfectly comfortable in air that is below the freezing point if one receives enough solar radiation. (Skiing in high mountains in subtropical latitudes is an example. The air may be cold due to the altitude, yet the sun's declination is such that it transfers considerable radiant heat.)

4. Evaporation. Changing a liquid into a gas is called *evaporation,* or *vaporization,* and requires large amounts of heat energy. Thus, while one kilocalorie can raise the temperature of one liter of water one degree centigrade, it takes 580 kilocalories to evaporate one liter of water at body temperature. These 580 kilocalories are taken from the water's surroundings. This of course is the principle that underlies the operation of a kitchen refrigerator. Human beings function much as refrigerators when they leave a swimming pool and the atmosphere absorbs the water on their skin.

Thus, the body encounters two problems in adjusting to thermal environments: (1) heat dissipation in hot climates and (2) heat conservation in cold climates. We can gain heat from two sources: environment and metabolism. We can lose heat from one, two, or more of the following factors: conduction, convection, radiation, and evaporation.

Under normal indoor atmospheric conditions, resting individuals maintain body temperature equilibrium within narrow limits. In this situation heat gain is entirely due to metabolism, and heat loss is estimated to occur approximately 40 percent by convection, 40 percent by radiation, and 20 percent by evaporation (insensible perspiration). Conduction is usually negligible. Input is balanced by output, and body temperature remains constant at, or close to, 98.6° F. In fact, within the range of about 30°F to 170°F environmental temperature, the body temperature of a nude human is maintained at a constant temperature within about 1°F of normal resting temperature. This very precise regulatory function is brought about by nervous feedback mechanisms operating through the **temperature regulatory center** in the hypothalamus. The receptors that feed into this temperature regulatory center sense the body temperature at the preoptic area of the anterior hypothalamus, in the skin, and probably in some of the internal organs.

temperature regulatory center

When the body temperature is too high, the temperature regulatory center in the hypothalamus increases the rate of heat loss from the body in two principal ways: (1) by stimulating the sweat glands to secrete, which results in evaporative heat losses from the body, and (2) by inhibiting the sympathetic centers in the posterior hypothalamus, thus reducing the vasoconstrictor tone of the arterioles and microcirculation in the skin. This allows vasodilation of the skin vessels and thus better transport of metabolic heat to the periphery for cooling.

When the body temperature is too low, three mechanisms are brought into play to produce more metabolic heat and conserve the heat produced within the body. Heat production is increased by hypothalamic stimulation of (1) shivering, which can increase metabolic rate two- to fourfold; (2) catecholamine release, which increases the rate of cellular oxidation; and (3) the thyroid gland, which increases metabolic rates considerably. Heat conservation is brought about by vasoconstriction of the skin vessels and abolition of the sweating response.

EXERCISE IN THE COLD

Exercising in the cold can have adverse effects on both health and performance.[1] Three potentially dangerous outcomes of exposure to the cold are hypothermia, frostbite, and nonfreezing cold injuries.[1] **Hypothermia** is severely reduced **core temperature** (rectal temperature, which reflects the temperature of the central nervous system and internal organs) and occurs when the loss of body heat is greater than that produced from the increased metabolic rate. **Frostbite** results from the crystallization of fluids in the skin or subcutaneous tissues due to exposure to cold temperatures.

hypothermia

core temperature

frostbite

The most common nonfreezing cold injuries are **trenchfoot** and **chilblain.**[1] Chilblain is typically less severe than trenchfoot and can occur with only one to five hours of exposure of bare skin to cold (<60°F) and wet conditions. The symptoms of chilblain include swollen, tender, itchy, and painful lesions on the fingers, ears, face, and other exposed skin areas. After rewarming, there are no long-lasting effects of chilblain.[1] Trenchfoot, however, often develops after many hours (usually >12 hours) of exposure to cold, wet conditions when socks and shoes are worn continuously. Thus, trenchfoot is not typically associated with most sports but can occur during winter hiking, camping, and expeditions. The symptoms include swelling and numbness of the feet.[1]

trenchfoot

chilblain

Cold environmental temperatures can also affect exercise performance, particularly when core temperature is reduced.[1] Under cold conditions, performance in maximal and submaximal aerobic exercise, anaerobic activities, and muscle strength can be adversely affected.

Some sports and athletic activities are of necessity carried on in cold environments. Skiing and ice skating depend on snow and ice, and many other sports, such as football and soccer, are occasionally played in very cold weather. A cold

Cold and cardiovascular events

People exercising or working in a cold environment are more prone to adverse cardiovascular events, as indicated by the increased incidence of these events during the winter months. Koutnik et al.* examined several cardiovascular indices, during isometric exercise, in an effort to understand this phenomenon better. Several hemodynamic markers were measured in 20 healthy, normotensive males who were evaluated on two separate occasions, separated by at least 48 hours. During the evaluation sessions, the subjects entered an environmental chamber and were exposed to either a cold (4°C) or temperate (24°C) environmental condition. During each session, the subjects were instructed to enter the environmental chamber and rest in a supine position on an air mattress, wearing only shorts and a T-hirt, for 30 minutes in order for temperature equilibration to occur. Cardiovascular measures were performed in the last 90 seconds of the rest period, the last 90 seconds of a 3-minute isometric handgrip exercise, and the last 90 seconds of a 3-minute post-exercise time period.

The results of this study indicated that cold exposure increases both peripheral and central blood pressure and that isometric exercise in the cold significantly increases indices of pulse wave analysis that are superior indicators of cardiovascular events and disease. Analysis of these indices suggests that the cold-induced pressor response is more dependent upon peripheral arteriolar vasoconstriction than on central arteriolar stiffening. Although the precise mechanisms underlying the differences observed in the hemodynamic variables studied remain unclear, the data suggest that increased aortic pressure and an impaired cardiovagal response appear to be important contributing factors. The authors concluded that cold exposure during isometric exercise significantly increases cardiovascular stress and may lead to adverse cardiovascular events.

*Koutnik, A. P., Figueroa, A., Wong, A., Ramirez, K. J., Ormsbee, M. J., and Sanchez-Gonzalez, M. A. Impact of acute whole-body cold exposure with concurrent isometric handgrip exercise on aortic pressure waveform characteristics. *Eur. J. Appl. Physiol.* 114: 1779–1787, 2014.

environment ordinarily poses few problems for athletes, because increased metabolic heat produced by the activity soon warms them to a normal temperature. Heat dissipation to the atmosphere occurs easily by radiation, convection, and when sweating starts, by evaporation.

chilling

The main problem in this situation is to prevent sudden changes in temperature (**chilling**). Athletic dress is extremely important, especially when there are intermittent periods of activity and rest (as in football). Athletes must be dressed in attire that (1) keeps them comfortably warm while they are waiting to perform and warming up and (2) can be removed (in part) after warm-up has been accomplished.

Metabolic rates can increase by as much as 25 to 30 times basal values in very vigorous activity. This means that even in the coldest weather (but no wind) an athlete has large heat loads to dissipate if a sport is extremely vigorous. Many athletes sweat profusely even in cold environments, so the clothing worn (after warm-up) should be as light as possible in weight and provide as little barrier to passage of water vapor (sweat) as possible. Otherwise, sweat will accumulate on the skin or in soaked jerseys, thus leading to chilling in the time between the end of exercise and showering.

In winter sports that are less physically active, such as hiking, snowmobiling, ice fishing, and so on, metabolic heat contributes less to the body heat, and clothing becomes even more important. For short exposure it has been shown that heavily insulating the hands and feet prevents cold discomfort, while overinsulating the hands and feet in comparison with the torso for longer exposures may result in decreasing core temperature and shivering.[8] More thermal insulation over the torso than the hands and feet complements the normal physiological heat conservation mechanisms and maintains core temperature. The popular down-filled vest is excellent for this purpose. It has also been found that superficial warming of the hand will stimulate blood flow to it, but blood flow will not return to the foot unless the whole body is sufficiently warm. Therefore, we see again how important torso protection is even for protection of the feet from cold damage.

Cold Acclimatization

Continued exposure to cold environments results in greater ability to withstand cold. The most important factor is the maintenance of core temperature. Core temperature is maintained at a fairly constant 98.6°F even though skin temperature may fall from its normal average temperature of 92°F to as low as 60°F.

The body can react to cold by reduction of heat loss and by increased metabolism. When a resting human is cooled from a comfortable environment of 85°F to approximately 72°F, no increase in metabolism occurs, and heat is conserved by vasoconstriction of blood vessels in the skin that prevents loss of the heat carried by the blood from the core. Below 72°F, increased metabolism results from shivering. The involuntary contraction of the muscles in shivering may raise the metabolic rate to two to four times the resting rate.

Long-term **cold acclimatization** likely involves increased basal metabolic rate, decreased peripheral circulation, and increased body fatness. The relative contribution of these factors to cold acclimatization as well as the importance of psychological influences may vary considerably from individual to individual. Table 17.1 provides a summary of exercising in cold environments.

cold acclimatization

Wind Chill and Exercise

Table 17.2 shows the combined effect of wind and temperature, the **wind chill factor,** as it is usually called. A temperature of –20°F with no wind is not likely to cause tissue damage (frostbite) for a properly clothed individual. But there is danger of freezing exposed flesh at the same temperature if the wind is blowing 5 to 20 mph, and the danger increases with higher winds. Vigorous exercise moderates the wind chill factor by virtue of the metabolic heat produced.

wind chill factor

EXERCISE IN THE HEAT

Exercise in hot environmental conditions can be a more serious problem than exercise in the cold. In a cold climate the increased metabolic heat production combats the increased heat loss to the environment, but in a hot climate metabolism and environment combine to increase heat gain in body tissues. The problem is further

Exercising in cold environments. **table 17.1**

Effects	Loss of body heat countered by increased metabolic heat produced by activity Heat dissipation occurs by radiation, convection, and evaporation (through sweating)
Risks	Hypothermia Frostbite Nonfreezing cold injuries
Precautions	Dress in warm clothes and layers Wear dry socks and shoes
Acclimatization effects	Increased basal metabolic rate Decreased peripheral circulation Increased body fatness

table 17.2 The combined effect of wind and temperature (wind chill factor).[1]

WIND SPEED (mph)	When the thermometer reads (°F)								
	40	30	20	10	0	−10	−20	−30	−40
	the temperature equals this in its effect on exposed flesh								
Calm	40	30	20	10	0	−10	−20	−30	−40
5	36	25	13	1	−11	−22	−31	−46	−57
10	34	21	9	−4	−16	−28	−41	−53	−66
15	32	19	6	−7	−19	−32	−45	−58	−71
20	30	17	4	−9	−22	−35	−48	−61	−74
30	29	15	1	−12	−26	−39	−53	−67	−80
40	27	13	−1	−15	−29	−43	−57	−71	−84
Little danger if properly clothed			Danger of freezing exposed flesh				Great danger of freezing exposed flesh		

complicated by the fact that when environmental temperature approaches skin temperature (approximately 92°F), heat loss through convection and radiation gradually comes to an end, so that at temperatures above skin temperature the only means for heat loss is evaporation of sweat. Radiation and convection reverse their direction and add heat to the body.

Sweating, then, is the only avenue for heat loss at temperatures above skin temperature, and it is the most important avenue at temperatures that approach skin temperature. Of course sweating is not in itself effective in dissipating heat; liquid sweat must be converted to a gas by evaporation before any heat loss occurs. Sweat that merely rolls off is virtually ineffective, but large heat losses can result when the weather is so dry that the liquid evaporates from the skin rapidly. Under such conditions sweating is sometimes imperceptible.

Hot, Dry Environment

When a person works or plays in a hot and dry environment, cooling of the skin is brought about by evaporation of sweat. There is no problem because dry air can absorb considerable moisture before becoming saturated. Cooling the skin is not the desired end result, however; it is the internal environment that must be cooled. Greater volume of slow-moving blood in and close to the skin better transfers heat to the evaporative surfaces and thus enhances cooling.

Along with the improved cooling, however, the volume of the blood in and near the skin increases by a considerable amount due to vasodilation. Under these conditions, venous return to the heart is somewhat impaired, which results in a decreased stroke volume. To maintain a constant cardiac output for the demands of both exercising muscles and skin circulation, the heart rate must increase. Because increases in heart rate depress cardiac efficiency, exercise at temperatures close to or above skin temperature can impose very severe loads on the cardiovascular system even when the air is relatively dry.

Since the process of heat dissipation in hot, dry environments depends on elimination of water in perspiration, it is obvious that dehydration is a distinct possibility. A man walking in the desert can lose up to one quart of water per hour. Furthermore, while voluntary thirst results in adequate water replacement during rest, it does not during work or exercise.

CLINICAL APPLICATIONS

National Athletic Trainers' Association: Signs and symptoms for heat-related illnesses[4]

Muscle (heat) cramps

- Dehydration
- Thirst
- Sweating
- Transient muscle cramps
- Fatigue

Heat syncope

- Dehydration
- Fatigue
- Tunnel vision
- Pale or sweaty skin
- Decreased pulse rate
- Dizziness
- Lightheadedness
- Fainting

Heat exhaustion

- Normal or elevated body core temperature
- Dehydration
- Dizziness
- Lightheadedness
- Syncope
- Headache
- Nausea
- Anorexia
- Diarrhea
- Decreased urine output
- Persistent muscle cramps
- Pallor
- Profuse sweating
- Chills
- Cool, clammy skin
- Intestinal cramps
- Urge to defecate
- Weakness
- Hyperventilation

Heat stroke

- High body core temperature *(>40°C [104°F])*
- Central nervous system changes
  - *Dizziness*
  - *Drowsiness*
  - *Irrational behavior*
  - *Confusion*
  - *Irritability*
  - *Emotional instability*
  - *Hysteria*
  - *Apathy*
  - *Aggressiveness*
  - *Delirium*
  - *Disorientation*
  - *Staggering*
  - *Seizures*
  - *Loss of consciousness*
  - *Coma*
- Dehydration
- Weakness
- Hot and wet or dry skin
- Tachycardia *(100 to 120 beats per minute)*
- Hypotension
- Hyperventilation
- Vomiting
- Diarrhea

Hot, Humid Environment

When the air surrounding an individual is not only hot but is also loaded with moisture, evaporative cooling is impaired because evaporation cannot take place unless volumes of air are available to take up the water vapor given off. To illustrate this, let us take the extreme example where the air is completely saturated (100% relative humidity) and the air temperature is higher than the skin temperature. Under these conditions no heat dissipation can occur. Consequently, the metabolic heat accumulates and raises body temperature, which can cause death (body temperatures of 108°F to 110°F can be fatal).

The problems during exercise in a hot, dry environment are related to increased cardiovascular loads and dehydration if water intake is insufficient. In a hot, humid environment the same problems exist and are aggravated by a decreased ability to unload water vapor into an already loaded ambient atmosphere.

Fluid Replacement for Exercise in the Heat

The following guidelines can help athletes maintain proper hydration during practice and competition in hot weather.[5,12]

1. Weigh in without clothes before and after exercise, especially during hot weather. For each pound of body weight lost during exercise, drink two cups of fluid.
2. Drink a rehydration beverage containing sodium to replenish lost body fluids quickly. The beverage should also contain 6 to 8 percent glucose or sucrose.

Athletes and Fluid Replacement
http://sportsmedicine.about.com/od/hydrationandfluid/

3. Drink 17 to 20 fluid ounces of water or sports drink, two to three hours before practice or competition.
4. Drink 7 to 10 fluid ounces of water or sports drink, 10 to 20 minutes before the event.
5. Drink 7 to 10 fluid ounces of water or sports drink every 10 to 20 minutes during training and competition.
6. Do not restrict fluids before or during an event.
7. Avoid beverages containing caffeine or alcohol, because they increase urine production and add to dehydration.

Human Limitations in the Heat

Coaches, athletic trainers, exercise professionals, and athletes should be familiar with the following definitions associated with exercise in the heat.[2,4,13]

heat stress

Heat stress. The sum of the metabolic and environmental heat loads. The total thermal load is related to the exercise intensity (metabolic load), the environmental temperature, and the evaporative potential of the environment (itself related to the ambient water vapor pressure, or humidity).

heat strain

Heat strain. The bodily effect of heat stress, i.e., the relative elevation of body core temperature, average skin temperature, and heart rate over that occurring in a cool environment.

muscle (heat) cramps

Muscle (heat) cramps. Acute, painful, and involuntary muscle contractions due to dehydration, electrolyte imbalances, and/or neuromuscular fatigue.

heat syncope
orthostatic dizziness

Heat syncope. Also called **orthostatic dizziness.** Dizziness associated with high environmental temperatures due to peripheral vasodilation, postural pooling of blood, diminished venous return, dehydration, reduced cardiac output, and/or cerebral ischemia.

exertional hyperthermia

Exertional hyperthermia. An elevated core body temperature greater than 104°F that occurs during athletic or recreational activities. It is influenced by exercise intensity, environmental conditions, clothing, and equipment.

exertional heat exhaustion

Exertional heat exhaustion. The fatigue that develops during exercise in the heat. This fatigue may be caused by excess body heat, which occurs when the rate of heat loss from the body is not sufficient to balance the body's rate of heat production and/or gain from the environment. Heat exhaustion may also be caused by dehydration, which can lead to an inability to maintain adequate blood flow to the contracting skeletal muscles.

exertional heat stroke

Exertional heat stroke. A potentially fatal disorder that occasionally follows heat exhaustion. It is characterized by an elevated core body temperature greater than 104°F; loss of consciousness (coma) following exertion; and clinical symptoms of damage to the central nervous system, liver, and kidneys.

Effects of Age, Gender, and Obesity on Exercise in the Heat

Age. Prepubertal girls and boys have less tolerance for exercise in the heat than do adults, possibly due to a lower sweating rate and/or the instability of an immature cardiovascular system.[3,7] In addition, older individuals do not respond as well to

CLINICAL APPLICATIONS

Reducing the likelihood of heat-related illnesses

Listed below are some practical considerations that coaches and athletic trainers can use to reduce the likelihood of heat-related illnesses.[13]

Education. It is important to understand that the heat produced during exercise cannot be readily dissipated from the body in a hot and/or humid environment. Exercise intensity should be moderated in the heat.

Clothing. Clothing adds insulation to the body and reduces the effective surface area for heat transfer. It is important to minimize clothing to provide an optimal skin surface area from which evaporation can occur. Moisture-wicking fabric can also aid evaporation and ventilation, helping to keep the body cool during exercise in the heat.[6]

Hydration. Progressive dehydration reduces sweating and blood flow to the skin and leads to excessive body heating. It is essential to keep well hydrated before, during, and following exercise in the heat.

Fitness. Physical training and heat acclimatization can expand blood volume and provide a more sensitive heat dissipation response to an increase in body core temperature. The majority of heat illness victims are novice runners, older adults, and those with circulatory or respiratory disorders. These are people who have become unfit by choice or due to an inability to remain active. People at risk should avoid extremes of heat or activity.

heat exposure as do young people, possibly because of their lower aerobic capacity and/or age-related changes in blood flow to the skin.[7,9]

Gender. Females tend to tolerate hot and wet climates better than males, while males tolerate hot and dry conditions better than females.[16] This finding is largely explained by the fact that, on the average, females have a higher ratio of body surface area to weight, an advantage in hot and wet climates but a disadvantage under hot and dry conditions. This is so because heat production is mainly weight dependent, whereas heat dissipation is related to the skin surface area. Since evaporation is not a factor in hot and wet environments, the more surface area available for radiation and convection losses in relation to heat production, the better the adjustment. In hot and dry conditions, a high ratio of surface area to weight is disadvantageous because it allows more heat gain by convection and radiation.

Obesity. Exercise in the heat is more stressful for the obese than the lean individual. Heat production is related to the volume of metabolizing tissue, while the ability to dispose of the heat is related to the skin surface area. Therefore, obese individuals tend to have a poorer capacity for heat dissipation.

Acclimatization to Hot Environments

In these days of rapid transportation, individual athletes and whole teams frequently travel far enough for their competitions to encounter a severe climatic change. Going from a cold to a hot climate will bring about a considerable decrement in performance if the event involves heavy demands on the cardiovascular system.

For this reason, coaches and exercise physiologists have explored the possibility of improving heat tolerance through physical conditioning in a normally cool environment. Considerable controversy has arisen concerning the possible magnitude of such an acclimatization procedure, but there is little doubt that heat tolerance can be improved to some extent by conditioning alone. For example, conditioning can improve the function of the sweating mechanism, expand the plasma volume, and increase the sensitivity of the sweating response so the sweating occurs at lower skin and core temperatures. Thus, trained individuals store less

Jet lag and athletic performance

Jet lag is defined as a group of symptoms resulting from the physiologic adaptations that occur when one travels to a new time zone. High-performance athletes often travel great distances to compete, and the jet lag they experience can have very negative effects on an athlete's performance. The fatigue associated with jet lag is caused by a number of interacting factors, including loss of sleep, change in diet, dehydration, and circadian rhythm changes. Samuels recommends a comprehensive approach to the management of jet lag.[15] This approach includes three primary components, related to the timing of the intervention: (1) preflight component, (2) in-flight component, and (3) post-flight component.

The preflight component is accomplished within seven days of travel and includes reducing the training volume and intensity, adjusting the training time to the destination time zone, choosing an evening flight for eastbound travel, and getting plenty of sleep in the days prior to travel. The in-flight component includes adjusting watches immediately upon boarding the plane, creating a comfortable environment for resting (pillows, eyeshades, earplugs, and minimum use of electronic devices), eating in-flight meals on the destination schedule, drinking plenty of water, and sleeping according to the destination schedule. He also recommends the use of sleep aids such as sedatives or melatonin to aid in the adjustment to the sleep schedule of the destination time zone. The post-flight component occurs during the two to four days after arrival. The eating, sleeping, training, recovery, and rest schedules of the athlete should be altered as quickly as possible to the new time zone to accomplish rapid circadian rhythm changes. Interventions such as light therapy, light avoidance, caffeine, and melatonin can be effective during this adjustment period.

This comprehensive program may be challenging to incorporate into the athlete's travel plans at times. However, by following the recommendations listed above, an athlete can reduce jet lag and travel fatigue dramatically. With a reduction in jet lag and travel fatigue, the athlete will be better adjusted to the new time zone, and this should translate into a better athletic performance.

heat in the transient phase of starting to exercise in the heat, arrive at a thermal steady state sooner, and maintain a lower internal temperature at equilibrium.[11] In the long term, then, the results of physical conditioning for **heat acclimatization** per se are cooler skin and core temperatures, which in turn reduce the level of skin blood flow needed for regulation of body temperature.[14] This results in a greater portion of the cardiac output being available to muscle blood flow, which is what improves performance in the heat. The major physiological adjustments associated with acclimatization to hot environments usually take 7 to 14 days to occur.[10] Table 17.3 provides a summary of exercising in hot environments.

heat acclimatization

table 17.3 Exercising in hot environments.

Effects	Sweating the only means for heat loss Radiation and convection add heat to the body		
Risks	Dehydration Heat strain Heat stroke	Muscle (heat) cramps Heat stress Heat exhaustion	Heat syncope
Precautions	Maintain proper hydration Moderate exercise intensity Minimize clothing		
Acclimatization effects	Cooler skin and core temperatures Greater portion of cardiac output available to muscle blood flow Reduction of the level of skin blood flow needed for temperature regulation		

EXERCISE AT HIGH ALTITUDES

Travel to athletic competition often involves not only changes in temperature and humidity but large changes in altitude as well. It has been known since the turn of the twentieth century and the advent of aviation that whenever humans ascend to higher altitudes they encounter lower atmospheric pressures. Because oxygen maintains a constant 20.93 percent of decreasing total pressure regardless of altitude, a gradually decreasing partial pressure drives less oxygen into the blood. This decreasing availability of oxygen to the tissues hampers physical performance.

The oxygen saturation of arterial blood at sea level approaches 100 percent, even under conditions of exercise. But at 19,000 feet, saturation is only 67 percent at rest, and exercise at this altitude causes the value to drop below 50 percent. We do not have to go to this extreme altitude, however, to find changes that may be of great importance in athletic competition. At 3,000 feet even acclimatized subjects have lost 5 percent of their aerobic power, and at 6,500 feet 15 percent.

This decreased aerobic power ($\dot{V}O_2$ max) results from a combination of factors, probably the most important of which are reduction in oxygen saturation of arterial blood and the higher cost of increased lung ventilation. Impaired lung diffusion results from the lowered oxygen pressure gradient, which leads to increased lung ventilation at higher altitudes in an attempt to get the same number of molecules of oxygen by breathing more air. The increased effort of the respiratory muscles increases their oxygen consumption and lowers their efficiency.

WWW

The High Altitude Medicine Guide

www.high-altitude-medicine.com

Limitations in Performance at High Altitudes

Not all athletic performances suffer because of the hypoxia at higher altitudes. Obviously, athletes participating in one-maximal-effort activities, such as the shot put, long jump, and high jump, do not suffer because they do not depend on oxygen transport. Furthermore, events lasting less than one minute, such as the 100- and 200-meter sprints, are also performed very largely anaerobically. Consequently performances are unimpaired at high altitude, but recovery times are longer.

In events that last two minutes or more, aerobic power is important, and this importance increases as duration increases. Considerable losses in performance of 20 to 30 percent may be expected in such events unless athletes have had adequate time for acclimatization.

Acclimatization to High Altitudes

The process of **altitude acclimatization** can be accomplished by various systems of physical conditioning taking place, if possible, at progressively higher altitudes. If altitude cannot be increased systematically, a progressive conditioning program at the same altitude is undertaken in which progressively increasing demands gradually improve cardiorespiratory endurance.

altitude acclimatization

Altitudes below 3,000 feet probably require no acclimatization, the problem is slight up to about 5,000 feet, and few athletic competitions occur above 10,000 feet. Thus, the primary area of concern is for altitudes between 5,000 and 10,000 feet.

Acclimatization to the decrease in aerobic performance at high altitude can take weeks or months.[17] Thus, the coach whose athletes will compete at a site such as Mexico City at an altitude of 7,350 feet must time the trip to arrive several weeks early to allow time for acclimatization. This, of course, is usually not possible. Perhaps

WWW

OA Guide to High Altitude: Acclimatization and Illness

www.princeton.edu/~oa/safety/altitude.html

RESEARCH

Altitude and exercise performance

The mechanisms responsible for diminished exercise performance at high altitudes are quite complex. Both peripheral (associated with changes in the peripheral nerves and the muscles) and central (associated with changes in the brain or spinal cord) fatigue have been implicated and found to be associated with this diminished performance; however, in conditions of hypoxia, central fatigue appears to become the primary limitation to exercise. Goodall et al.* wanted to know if this type of fatigue could be reduced with acclimatization to the hypoxic environment. He studied seven recreational cyclists and found that 14 days of chronic hypoxia served to acclimatize the subjects to the hypoxic conditions of high altitude. The authors concluded that a reduction in the development of central fatigue during the acclimatization process may be attributable to an increase in cerebral oxygen delivery and consequent increase in corticospinal excitability. It appears, therefore, that a period of two weeks of exercise under hypoxic conditions can reduce central fatigue, is beneficial for acclimatizing athletes to the hypoxia experienced at high altitudes, and can serve to improve their performance in acute hypoxic conditions.

*Goodall, S., Twomey, R., Amann, M., Ross, E. A., Lovering, A. T., Romer, L. M., Subudhi, A. W., and Roach, R. C. AltitudeOmics: exercise-induced supraspinal fatigue is attenuated in healthy humans after acclimatization to high altitude. *Acta Physiol.* 210: 875–888, 2014.

the only real solutions for flatlanders are to limit competitions at high altitude or to accept the alternative of a predictable loss of performance in aerobic events.

The primary physiological mechanisms that bring about altitude acclimatization include increases in red blood cell count, hemoglobin content in the blood, plasma volume, lung ventilation, aerobic enzyme activity, capillary density, and mitochondrial density in skeletal muscle.[17] Table 17.4 provides a summary of exercising at high altitudes.

Administration of Oxygen to Improve Performance

There is no evidence that breathing enriched mixtures of oxygen before an athletic event has a significant effect on the subsequent performance. Use of oxygen during work at high altitudes, however, is not only advantageous but absolutely necessary for activities such as mountain climbing at 18,000 to 20,000 feet or more for most people without a long acclimatization period.

One use of oxygen for athletes that rests on sound theoretical and experimental bases is for shortening recovery times at high altitude. In sports that involve rest periods between heavy endurance workouts, such as basketball and soccer, recovery can be hastened in unacclimatized athletes who are competing at an altitude substantially higher than the altitude they are used to.

table 17.4 Exercising in high altitudes.

Effects	Reduction in oxygen saturation of arterial blood Higher cost of increased lung ventilation
Risks	Decreased performance in aerobic activities at altitudes greater than about 3,000 feet
Precautions	Use oxygen to shorten recovery times
Acclimatization effects	Increase in red blood cell count, hemoglobin content in the blood, plasma volume, lung ventilation, aerobic enzyme activity, capillary density, and mitochondrial density in skeletal muscle

summary

There are potential risks to health and performance from exercising in the cold or heat as well as at high altitude. Exercising in cold environments can lead to hypothermia (severely reduced core temperature), frostbite (crystallization of fluids in the skin or subcutaneous tissues), or other nonfreezing injuries including trenchfoot and chilblain. Normally, however, individuals can maintain core temperature while exercising in the cold through increased metabolic rate and proper clothing.

During exercise in hot environments, metabolic heat can be dissipated by conduction, convection, radiation, and evaporation. In a hot, dry environment, evaporation of sweat from the skin contributes to cooling. In a hot, humid environment, however, less water vapor can be taken up by the air, and evaporation is therefore not as effective at cooling. Some of the more common problems associated with exercise in the heat include heat stress, heat strain, heat exhaustion, and heat stroke.

Exercising at altitudes above approximately 5,000 feet above sea level can adversely affect performance. This is particularly true for aerobic activities, because of the reduced oxygen saturation of arterial blood. Maximal strength and anaerobic activities, however, are normally not affected by altitude, although it takes longer to recover between work bouts. Acclimatization to altitude can take weeks or months. Therefore, it is typically not possible for athletes to acclimatize prior to competition unless they can arrive at the site several weeks prior to the event.

questions for review

1. Describe the four means by which the body can maintain thermal balance by losing heat to the environment.
2. What mechanisms are used by the body to raise and lower body temperature?
3. What steps can an individual take to avoid problems when exercising in extreme temperatures (hot or cold)?
4. What physiological changes are involved in long-term cold acclimatization?
5. Why is exercising in the heat a more serious problem than exercising in the cold?
6. Contrast the effects on the body of exercising in a hot, dry environment with those of exercising in a hot, humid environment.
7. What are the guidelines for hydration during exercise?
8. What are the possible heat-related illnesses of which coaches and physical educators need to be aware and what are their symptoms?
9. What physiological changes are involved in long-term heat acclimatization?
10. What is the effect of altitude on health and exercise performance?
11. How can acclimatization to higher altitudes be accomplished?

student companion website

For further review of this book's chapters and for test preparation, visit the book's website, **www.hhpcommunities.com/exercisephysiology**, to take practice quizzes, review the vocabulary terms, use the study guide, and view the digital image bank.

references

1. American College of Sports Medicine Position Stand. Prevention of cold injuries during exercise. *Med. Sci. Sports Exerc.* 38: 2012–2029, 2006.
2. American College of Sports Medicine Position Stand. Exertional heat illness during training and competition. *Med. Sci. Sports Exerc.* 39: 556–572, 2007.
3. Bar-Or, O. Children's responses to exercise in hot climates: Implications for performance and health. *Gatorade Sports Sci. Exch.* 7(2), 1994.
4. Binkley, H. M., Beckett, J., Casa, D. J., Kleiner, D. M., and Plummer, P. E. National Athletic Trainers' Association Position Statement: Exertional heat illness. *J. Athl. Train.* 37: 329–343, 2002.
5. Casa, D. J., Armstrong, L. E., Hillman, S. K., Montain, S. J., Reiff, R. V., Rich, B. S. E., Roberts, W. O., and Stone, J. A. National Athletic Trainers' Association Position Statement: Fluid replacement for athletes. *J. Athl. Train.* 35: 212–224, 2000.
6. De Sousa, J., Cheatham, C., and Wittbrodt, M. The effects of a moisture-wicking fabric shirt on the physiological and perceptual responses during acute exercise in the heat. *Appl. Ergonomics* 45: 1447–1453, 2014.
7. Drinkwater, B. L., Kupprat, I. C., Denton, J. E., Crist, J. L., and Horvath, S. M. Response of prepubertal girls and college women to work in the heat. *J. Appl. Physiol.* 43: 1046–1053, 1977.
8. Kaufman, W. C. Cold-weather clothing for comfort or heat conservation. *Phys. Sportsmed.* 10: 71–75, 1982.
9. Kenney, W. L. The older athlete: Exercise in hot environments. *Gatorade Sports Sci. Exch.* 6(3), 1993.
10. Maughan, R. J., and Shirreffs, S. M. Preparing athletes for competition in the heat: Developing an effective acclimatization strategy. *Gatorade Sports Sci. Exch.* 10(2), 1997.
11. Nadel, E. R. Control of sweating rate while exercising in the heat. *Med. Sci. Sports* 11: 31–35, 1979.
12. Nadel, E. R. New ideas for rehydration during and after exercise in hot weather. *Gatorade Sports Sci. Exch.* 1(3), 1988.
13. Nadel, E. R. Limits imposed on exercise in a hot environment. *Gatorade Sports Sci. Exch.* 3(27), 1990.
14. Roberts, M. F., and Wenger, C. B. Control of skin circulation during exercise and heat stress. *Med. Sci. Sports* 11: 36–41, 1979.
15. Samuels, C. H. Jet lag and travel fatigue: a comprehensive management plan for sport medicine physicians and high-performance support teams. *Clin. J. Sports Med.* 22: 268–273, 2012.
16. Shapiro, Y., Pandolf, K. B., Avellini, B. A., Pimental, N. A., and Goldman, R. F. Physiological responses of men and women to humid and dry heat. *J. Appl. Physiol.* 49: 1–8, 1980.
17. Sutton, J. R. Exercise training at high altitude: Does it improve endurance performance at sea level? *Gatorade Sports Sci. Exch.* 6(4), 1993.

18 Growth, Development, and Exercise in Children and Adolescents

As a result of reading this chapter you will:

Be able to compare and contrast growth, development, and maturation.

Be able to define infancy, childhood, and adolescence.

Be able to discuss the basic changes that occur at puberty in males and females for height, weight, aerobic capacity, anaerobic fitness, and muscle strength.

Be able to describe the age-related changes during childhood and adolescence for absolute and relative maximal oxygen consumption, anaerobic capabilities, and muscle strength.

Know the effects of training on maximal oxygen consumption, anaerobic capabilities, and muscle strength in children and adolescents.

Understand the effects of exercise and athletic participation on the menstrual cycle, including factors related to the age of menarche, athletic menstrual cycle irregularities (AMIs), performance, and the female athlete triad.

key concepts

acute musculoskeletal injury
adolescence
amenorrhea
athletic menstrual cycle irregularities (AMIs)
body building
childhood
chronic musculoskeletal injury
core strengthening
development
disordered eating
dysmenorrhea
epiphyseal growth plate
female athlete triad
growth
infancy
making weight
maturation
mean power
peak height velocity
peak power
peak weight velocity
power lifting
puberty
strength training
Tanner scale
weight lifting

Many exercise professionals, physical educators, and coaches work with individuals between the ages of 5 and 18 years. This is especially true for teachers and coaches in public and private schools. In addition, the interest and participation of children in competitive sports has increased dramatically, and therefore, professionals must be knowledgeable in the areas of normal growth and development as well as the effects of exercise on young competitors. Frequently, athletes, parents, and the community at large count on personal trainers, physical educators, and coaches to advise them on the potential benefits and hazards of certain types of exercise for young populations. Responding to questions with scientifically based information affords an opportunity to dispel popular but inaccurate myths and improve the health and performance of children and adolescents.

GROWTH, DEVELOPMENT, AND MATURATION

Growth, development, and maturation can be defined as follows:[31]

1. **Growth** is an increase in the size of the body as a whole or the size attained by specific parts of the body.
2. The term **development** is often used in two distinct contexts. In a biological context, development is the differentiation of cells along specialized lines of function. In the behavioral context, the term relates to the development of competence in a variety of interrelated domains as the child adjusts to his or her cultural milieu—the amalgam of symbols, values, and behaviors that characterize a population.
3. **Maturation** refers to the tempo and timing of progress toward the mature biological state.

growth
development
maturation

Clearly, growth, development, and maturation are related concepts, and the terms are commonly (but incorrectly) used interchangeably. Growth is often expressed in absolute terms such as the change in height in centimeters (cm) or body weight in kilograms (kg) or as a rate such as change in height or body weight per year (cm per year or kg per year), while maturation reflects the percentage of height or body weight attained compared to adult expectations. For example, increases in height from 138 to 142 cm between 10 and 11 years of age for a male and female would reflect a similar growth rate (4 cm per year), but it is likely that the male would be less mature since adult males on the average tend to be approximately 12 cm taller than adult females. Thus, in this example, at 11 years of age, the female would have attained 87 percent of her expected adult stature (approximately 163 cm) while the male would have attained only 81 percent of his expected adult stature (approximately 175 cm). The term *development* is often used in a broad sense to include both growth and maturation as they relate to the functions of the systems of the body or to the behavior of the child.

Infancy, Childhood, and Adolescence

www

Physical Fitness and Activity in Schools
http://pediatrics.aappublications.org/content/pediatrics;105/5/1156.full.pdf

Infancy, childhood, and adolescence can be defined as follows:[14,31]

infancy
childhood

1. **Infancy** is defined as the first year of life and is a time of rapid growth in almost all bodily functions and physical characteristics.

2. **Childhood,** defined as the time between the first birthday and puberty, is characterized by steady growth and maturation with particularly rapid progress in motor development. The relatively stable rate of growth makes childhood a good time for the introduction and development of motor skills.

3. The beginning of **adolescence** is usually defined by the adolescent growth spurt and the onset of puberty. For females and males, the adolescent growth spurt normally occurs from 10.5 to 13 and 12.5 to 15 years of age, respectively. The age of adolescence, however, ranges from 8 to 19 and 10 to 22 years for females and males, respectively. The difference in these age ranges reflects the high degree of variability in the maturational status among individuals of this age group. Clearly some children mature late and others mature much earlier. Differences in maturity are manifested in dramatic differences in strength, sports skill, and performance.

adolescence

WWW

American Academy of Pediatrics
www.aap.org

Puberty

The term **puberty** is derived from the Latin word "pubertas," which means the period of life at which the ability to reproduce—or the time of sexual maturation—begins. It is important to be able to identify the onset of puberty because normal growth patterns as well as the responses to exercise training are substantially different in children than in adolescents. Coaches, athletes, and physical educators should have very different expectations for a training program, depending on the participants' levels of maturation.

puberty

In females, the beginning of puberty is marked by the development of breasts and appearance of pubic hair. This is followed by the first menstruation (*menarche*).[14] The onset of menarche provides a definitive landmark for the assessment of maturation in females; a similar landmark is not available for males.[14,42] In males, the circulating level of testosterone is an indicator of puberty. During adolescence the testosterone concentration increases ten- to thirtyfold from the childhood value of 20 to 60 ng • dL^{-1} to the adult value of approximately 600 ng • dL^{-1}.[14] In contrast, females exhibit low (prepubescent) testosterone levels throughout life. The measurement of blood testosterone as an indicator of maturational development in males requires invasive procedures, however, which limits its common usage.

Tanner scale
peak height velocity
peak weight velocity

Puberty in both genders can also be assessed indirectly based on the level of development of secondary sex traits such as the breasts and genitals. A commonly used technique, the **Tanner scale,** utilizes a 1 to 5 scale based on direct visual observation or nude photographs.[31] Stage 1 is characterized by an absence of development of the secondary sex traits and is clearly prepubertal; Stage 5 indicates adult standards of maturity. Stages 2, 3, and 4 represent varying levels of development with defined characteristics. Although the stages overlap to some degree, making the judgment somewhat arbitrary, the determination of Tanner stages can be very useful for identifying an individual's approximate level of maturity.

Additional procedures for assessing the timing of the adolescent growth spurt are called **peak height velocity** and **peak weight velocity** (Figures 18.1 and 18.2). If longitudinal height and body weight data are available for an individual, it is possible to identify the adolescent growth spurt by examining the yearly change in height or body weight as a function of age. The dramatic increases in height and body weight coincide with the onset of puberty and are reflected in increases in the rate of height and body weight changes from approximately 5 cm per year to 10 cm per year and 3 kg per year to 10 kg per year, respectively.[31]

Steroids and growth hormones

Adolescent athletes want to get bigger and stronger and, like adult athletes, some are willing to try almost anything that claims to have an anabolic effect. Aside from the ethical and health implications of taking some of the substances, young athletes need to take care to scrutinize the "science" behind some manufacturers' claims. As one example, while testosterone has proven to be an effective anabolic agent, the possible anabolic effects of androstenedione (popularized by reports in the late 1990s of its use by MLB star Mark McGwire) seem to be offset by the fact that once in the body most of the androstenedione is converted to estrogen, not testosterone! During the critical years of growth and development, adolescents need to be encouraged to make good decisions concerning their own bodies and also their responsibility to play fair in their chosen sport.[40]

figure 18.1 Peak height velocity occurs at approximately 13 years of age for females and 14 years of age for males.

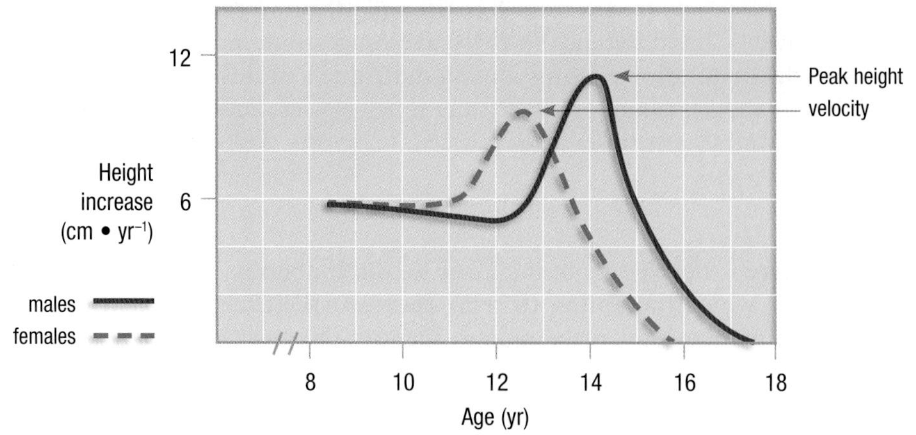

figure 18.2 Peak weight velocity occurs at approximately 12 to 13 years of age for females and 14 years of age for males.

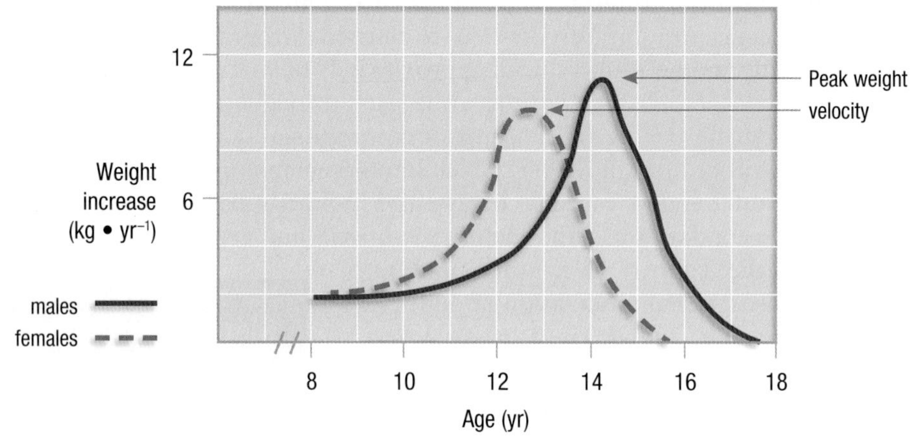

Normal Growth Patterns

Height and body weight

Normal growth in height and body weight develops along an S-shaped curve from birth through adolescence (Figure 18.3).[14] During infancy, rapid increases in both parameters are greater than those during childhood. At the time of the adolescent growth spurt, males exhibit a dramatic increase in height and body weight while the growth curves for females begin to level off as they approach adult standards of maturity.

Of interest to coaches, parents, and athletes is the effect of exercise and competitive sports on normal growth and development patterns. That is, does athletic participation have a beneficial, detrimental, or no effect on body size? It is generally accepted that participation in athletics does not accelerate or decelerate the growth and maturation of young athletes. Furthermore, exercise training has no effect on height, body build, or biological maturation.

(a) Height and (b) body weight develop along an S-shaped curve throughout childhood and adolescence. **figure 18.3**

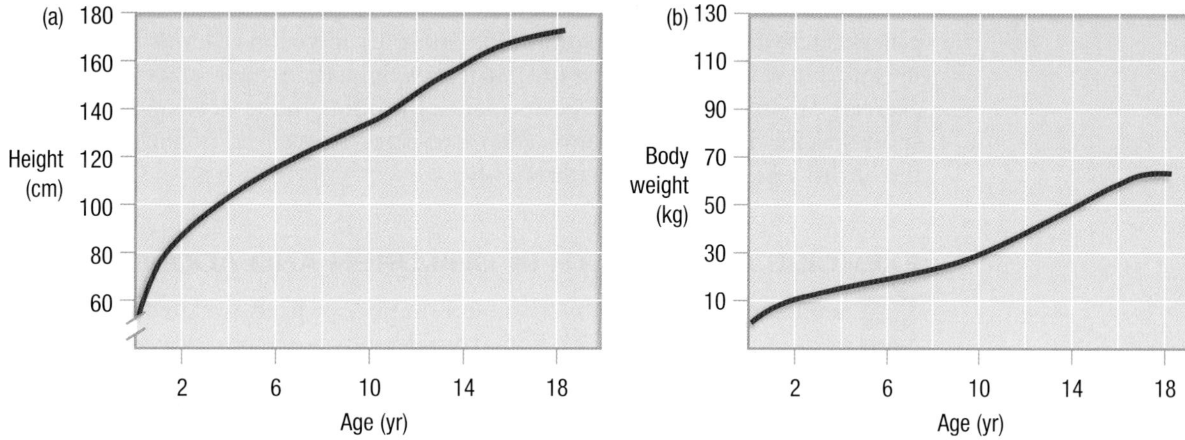

Body composition

Figure 18.4 describes the normal growth patterns for percent body fat, fat weight, and fat-free weight from birth to 20 years of age. Fat weight and fat-free weight increase gradually throughout childhood in both males and females. At the adolescent growth spurt, males exhibit an increased rate of development in fat-free weight while females tend to maintain a constant level from approximately 14 to 20 years of age.

Changes in (a) fat-free weight, (b) fat weight, and (c) percent body fat during childhood and adolescence in males and females. **figure 18.4**

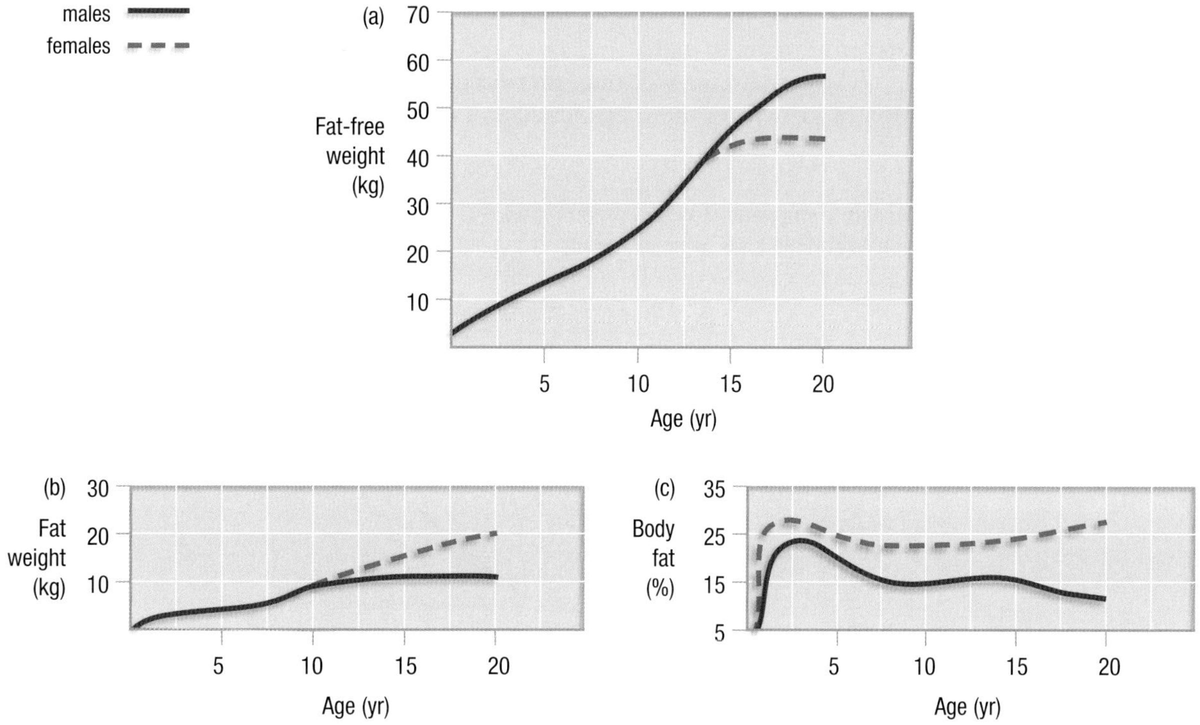

Percent body fat increases dramatically during infancy for both genders. Throughout childhood and adolescence, however, females remain stable or increase slightly in percent body fat, while males decrease gradually.

Physical activity has beneficial effects on body composition characteristics. In general, active children and adolescents not only have lower levels of percent body fat and fat weight but also more fat-free weight than their inactive peers. Thus, exercise can improve athletic performance by aiding in the development of optimal sport-specific body composition characteristics as well as potentially decreasing the health risks associated with obesity.

EXERCISE AND HEALTH IN CHILDREN AND ADOLESCENTS

Exercise and physical activity have a number of health-related benefits in children and adolescents.[7,50] For example, physical activity can have positive effects on cardiovascular disease risk factors and obesity, which when present in youth, tend to track into adulthood. In addition, physically active youth have higher levels of cardiorespiratory fitness, stronger muscles and bones, and reduced levels of anxiety and depression. Furthermore, physical activity can positively affect academic performance and self-esteem. Refer back to Table 10.1 (p. 197) for health-related physical activity recommendations for children and adolescents.[7,50]

EXERCISE AND AEROBIC FITNESS IN CHILDREN AND ADOLESCENTS

Maximal oxygen consumption ($\dot{V}O_2$ max) is often used as an indicator of aerobic fitness because it reflects the efficiency of the cardiorespiratory system as well as the effectiveness with which the active muscles are able to utilize oxygen. Figure 18.5 describes the typical developmental patterns of absolute (L • min^{-1}) $\dot{V}O_2$ max during childhood and adolescence for both genders. In general, males and females increase in absolute $\dot{V}O_2$ max throughout childhood. During adolescence, however, males tend to continue to increase while females level off at about 14 years of age.[9,42]

The increase in $\dot{V}O_2$ max that occurs throughout childhood is, in part, a function of growth in the lungs, circulatory system, and musculature.[9,45] Therefore, to

figure 18.5 Absolute maximal oxygen consumption ($\dot{V}O_2$ max), expressed in L • min^{-1}, increases in males and plateaus at approximately 14 years of age in females.

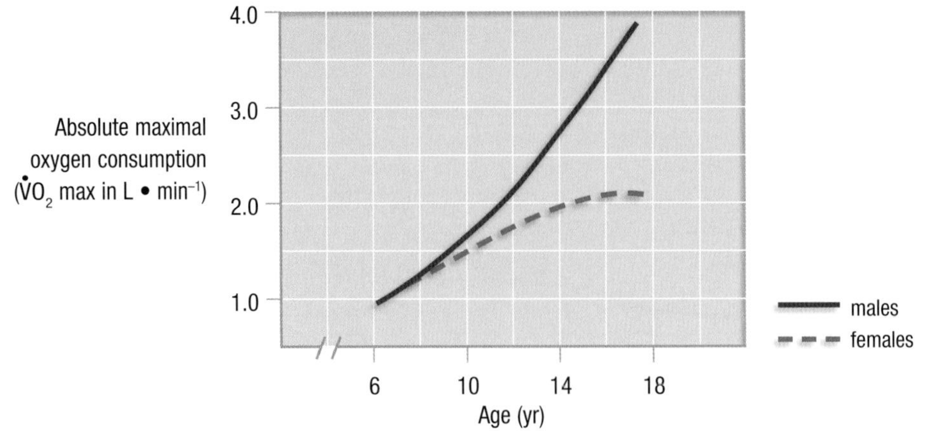

compare children of different ages and body sizes validly or to examine the effect of growth on $\dot{V}O_2$ max, it is necessary to normalize the values based on a parameter that will account for maturational differences.[42] The most common way to normalize $\dot{V}O_2$ max values is to express them relative to body weight (mL • kg^{-1} • min^{-1}). Figure 18.6 describes the changes in $\dot{V}O_2$ max expressed in mL • kg^{-1} • min^{-1} for both genders between approximately 6 and 18 years of age. The trends indicate that the relative $\dot{V}O_2$ max of males remains stable throughout these ages while that of females tends to decrease gradually.[42] In females, this pattern may reflect the increase in fat weight that normally occurs throughout childhood and adolescence.[11,42]

It should be noted at this point that controversy surrounds the appropriateness of normalizing $\dot{V}O_2$ max by expressing it relative to body weight.[42,43,45,52] Other potential normalizing parameters have been suggested, such as body surface area, fat-free weight, skeletal age, and height.[42,45] Rowland[45] has stated, "It appears prudent to investigate means of normalizing $\dot{V}O_2$ max independently of body dimension." No consensus regarding the most valid method for normalizing maximal oxygen uptake values in children and adolescents currently exists.

Aerobic Fitness and Endurance Performance

In adults, $\dot{V}O_2$ max is a valuable determinant of endurance performance. In children, however, the relationship between $\dot{V}O_2$ max and age-related changes in endurance performance is less clear because of the confounding influences of normal growth and development. The multifactorial nature of endurance performance requires an examination of the interactions among many contributing parameters, such as $\dot{V}O_2$ max, submaximal exercise economy, qualitative changes in oxygen delivery not indicated by $\dot{V}O_2$ max, biomechanical factors, speed, and strength.[43] The interrelationships are clearly evidenced by the fact that while relative $\dot{V}O_2$ max (mL • kg^{-1} • min^{-1}) remains stable or declines during childhood and adolescence, endurance performance on tests such as timed runs steadily improves.[43] Thus, factors other than $\dot{V}O_2$ max must influence endurance performance in children. Rowland[43] has suggested that "maximal oxygen uptake [$\dot{V}O_2$ max] in children may therefore be a less valid indicator of cardiopulmonary function, endurance capacity, and response to training than in adult subjects."

Relative (to body weight) maximal oxygen consumption ($\dot{V}O_2$ max), expressed in mL • kg^{-1} • min^{-1}, remains stable during childhood and adolescence in males and decreases across age in females.

figure 18.6

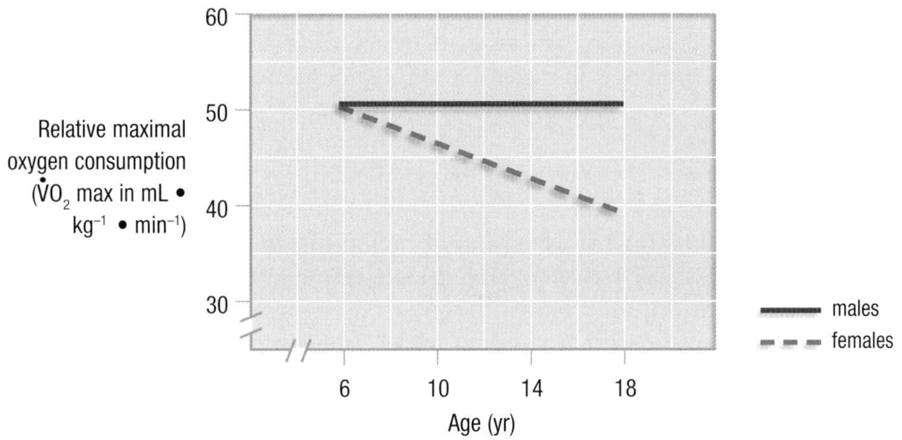

R E S E A R C H

Relationship of age, body weight, and strength

Everyone knows that as children get older they get bigger and stronger. However, the relationship between age, body weight, and strength is not as straightforward as it first appears. Weir et al.* investigated this issue in young wrestlers. The study divided 258 wrestlers into two age groups: high school wrestlers (age 14.3 to 18.6 years) and young wrestling club members (age 8.1 to 13.9 years). Both groups underwent identical testing procedures to measure concentric, isokinetic peak torque of the leg extensors and flexors. Body composition was also assessed to determine fat-free weight (FFW). The results of this study showed that the relationship between FFW and isokinetic peak torque varied with age. In other words, pound for pound the older wrestlers were stronger than the younger ones. In the younger wrestlers, as age increased, peak torque increased even after the age-associated increase in FFW was removed. This effect was not as pronounced for the older wrestlers, although it was present. Possible reasons for this "age effect" include maturation of the neuromuscular system, changes in skeletal muscle such that it makes up a greater proportion of FFW or that the proportion of muscle mass in the lower extremities increases with age, and perhaps changes in the muscle tissue itself. The authors suggest that in the interest of fair competition, young wrestlers should be matched for age as well as body weight.

* Weir, J. P., Housh, T. J., Johnson, G. O., Housh, D. J., and Ebersole, K. T. Allometric scaling of isokinetic peak torque: the Nebraska wrestling study. *Eur. J. Appl. Physiol.* 80: 240–248, 1999.

Endurance Training and Aerobic Fitness

There is some controversy regarding the trainability of children with respect to aerobic fitness. Rowland[44] reviewed the results of longitudinal studies of endurance training in children and concluded that when the exercise protocol was consistent with that which has been shown to improve aerobic fitness in adults,[7] most of the studies with children demonstrated increases of 7 to 26 percent in $\dot{V}O_2$ max. Thus, it appears that adult standards such as those recommended by the American College of Sports Medicine[7] can be utilized for improving $\dot{V}O_2$ max in children.

Long-Distance Running for Children

WWW

ACSM Current Comment—Preseason Conditioning for Young Athletes
www.acsm.org/docs/current-comments/preseasonconditioning.pdf

The popularity of running for adults has led to an increase in the participation of children in long-distance running. The American Academy of Pediatrics[3] has identified many potential hazards associated with long-distance running in children, including heel cord injuries, epiphyseal growth plate injuries, chronic joint trauma, thermal intolerance, and psychological problems as a result of unrealistic goals. In addition, Rowland and Walsh[47] reported that shin splints was the most common injury reported among runners 8 to 15 years of age. Do these potential hazards preclude children from running? The answer to this question is clearly no. Thousands of children, some as young as four years of age, run safely in recreational as well as competitive situations.[46,47]

Several authorities[3,32,46] have made recommendations regarding the distances children should run. The American Academy of Pediatrics[3] has not made specific recommendations regarding maximal racing distances for children but has suggested that the total distance covered during training, rather than the distance run during competition, may entail the greatest risk to the health of children. Micheli[32] has recommended that children under 14 years of age not train or compete at distances greater than 10 km. Furthermore, Rowland and Hoontis[46] have suggested that a two-mile race over a flat course is appropriate for children aged 12 and younger.

Making weight in athletics

Although physical activity and sports participation, per se, do not adversely affect normal growth and development patterns, it is possible that **making weight,** the excessive weight loss associated with such sports as wrestling, boxing, and gymnastics, may have detrimental effects. In many sports, competition is organized into divisions by body weight. Also, some states set up high school and junior high school athletics on the basis of a classification system that depends, at least in part, on the weight of the athletes. It is generally accepted by coaches and athletes that there are advantages to competing in the lowest possible weight class.

For mature athletes, making weight is not a large health problem because experience has taught them what their normal weight should be. However, extreme cases of weight loss by high school athletes sometimes arise, such as the loss of 15 or more pounds in an athlete whose normal weight is 150 to 160 pounds. This practice should be condemned in the strongest terms, for these short-term weight losses are often obtained through drastic changes in caloric intake and water metabolism (sweating, water restriction, starvation, and purging), causing attendant changes in kidney and cardiovascular function (whose consequences are difficult to evaluate). In high school athletes, a 5 percent weight loss should certainly be the outside limit of prudence, and it is quite likely that even this amount (without medical supervision) is too great for some of the leaner athletes.

The American College of Sports Medicine[5] has made the following recommendations with respect to weight loss in wrestlers.

1. Educate coaches and wrestlers about the adverse consequences of prolonged fasting and dehydration on physical performance and physical health.
2. Discourage the use of rubber suits, steam rooms, hot boxes, saunas, laxatives, and diuretics for "making weight."
3. Adopt new state or national governing body legislation that schedules weigh-ins immediately prior to competition.
4. Schedule daily weigh-ins before and after practice to monitor weight loss and dehydration. Weight lost during practice should be regained through adequate food and fluid intake.
5. Assess the body composition for each wrestler prior to the season using valid methods for this population. Males 16 years and younger with a body fat below 7 percent or those over 16 years with a body fat below 5 percent need medical clearance before being allowed to compete. Female wrestlers need a minimum body fat of 12 to 14 percent.
6. Emphasize the need for daily caloric intake obtained from a balanced diet high in carbohydrates (more than 55% of calories), low in fat (less than 30% of calories), with adequate protein (15 to 20% of calories, 1.0 to 1.5 g • kg^{-1} body weight) determined on the basis of nutrition guidelines and physical activity levels. The minimal caloric intake for wrestlers of high school and college age should range from 1,700 to 2,500 kcal • d^{-1}, and rigorous training may increase the requirement up to an additional 1,000 kilocalories per day. Wrestlers should be discouraged by coaches, parents, school officials, and physicians from consuming less than their minimal daily needs. Combined with exercise, this minimal caloric intake will allow for gradual weight loss. After the minimal weight has been attained, caloric intake should be increased sufficiently to support the normal developmental needs of the young wrestler.
7. Permit more participants per team to compete by adding weight classes between 119 lb and 151 lb or by allowing more than one representative at a given weight class, just as swimming and track teams do in competition.
8. Standardize regulations concerning the eligibility rules at championship tournaments so that severe and rapid weight loss is discouraged at the end of the season (e.g., a wrestler dropping one or more weight classes).
9. Encourage cooperative efforts between coaches, exercise scientists, physicians, dietitians, and wrestlers to collect data systematically on the body composition, hydration state, energy and nutritional demands, growth, maturation, and psychological development of wrestlers.

There is a substantial difference between high-pressure competitive racing and recreational or health-related training. It is important that children participate without excessive parental and peer pressure to succeed. Children should engage in regular physical activity because it is enjoyable and encourages a lifelong commitment to a healthy lifestyle.

EXERCISE AND ANAEROBIC FITNESS IN CHILDREN AND ADOLESCENTS

mean power

peak power

Children have a substantially lower capacity for performing anaerobic exercise than do adolescents and adults.[10,11,25,51,56] This is clear when we examine the age-related changes in **mean power** (total work performed during a maximal 30-second cycle ergometer test) and **peak power** (greatest amount of work performed during a 5-second period) from the Wingate Anaerobic Test. It is generally assumed that mean power represents principally the capacity of the glycolytic energy production pathway, whereas peak power reflects the efficiency of the phosphagen system (ATP and CP breakdown). The vertical jump test is also commonly used to assess anaerobic muscular power of the legs in young males and females as well as adults (see **Chapter 18 Lab**). Figures 18.7 and 18.8 describe the positive relationships (in males and females) for absolute mean and peak power (expressed in watts, W) versus age. As illustrated in Figures 18.9 and 18.10, the same general trends, although less pronounced, are true when mean and peak power are expressed relative to body weight ($W \cdot kg^{-1}$). Thus, as children develop throughout childhood, their performance capacity in anaerobic sports and activities increases.

figure 18.7 Absolute mean power expressed in W from the Wingate Anaerobic Test increases throughout childhood in males and females.

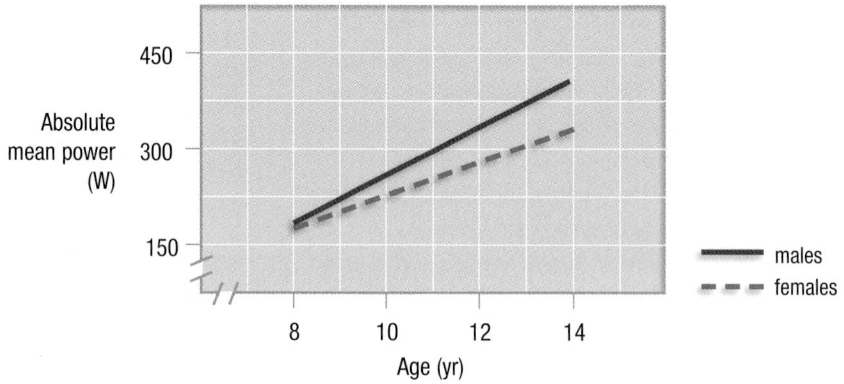

figure 18.8 Absolute peak power expressed in W from the Wingate Anaerobic Test increases throughout childhood in males and females.

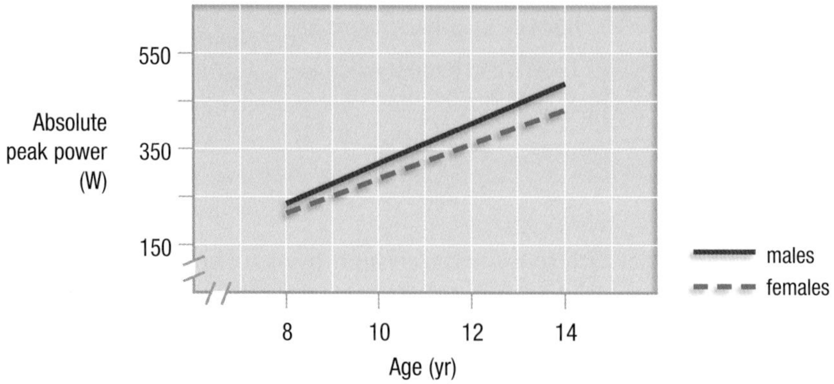

Relative (to body weight) mean power expressed in W • kg^{-1} from the Wingate Anaerobic Test increases throughout childhood in males and females.

figure 18.9

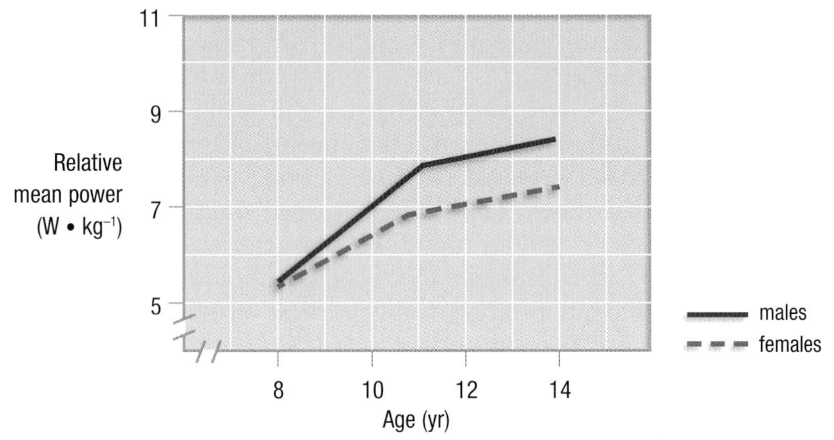

Relative (to body weight) peak power expressed in W • kg^{-1} from the Wingate Anaerobic Test increases throughout childhood in males and females.

figure 18.10

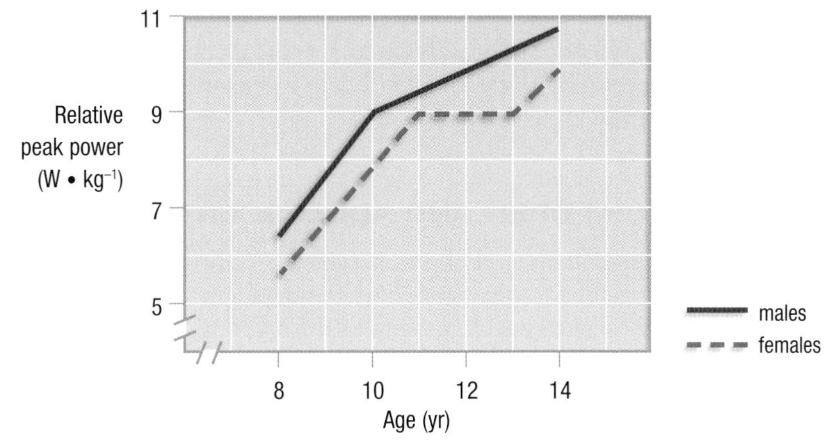

The ability to perform anaerobic activities is limited by the availability of stored energy sources (ATP, CP, and glycogen) and the enzyme activity of the anaerobic energy systems. Although there is conflicting research,[51] it is possible that children have a diminished capacity for anaerobic activity, in part, because they have smaller creatine phosphate stores and lower concentrations of the glycolytic enzyme phosphofructokinase than adults.[10,18] Thus, compared with adults, the anaerobic metabolic systems of children are less effective at ATP production, which translates into poorer performance in high-intensity, short-duration activities.

www

Weight Training for Children and Adolescents

http://weighttraining.about.com/od/weighttrainingforgroups/a/0408weightskids.htm

The Effect of Anaerobic Training in Children and Adolescents

Children and adolescents respond favorably to anaerobic training.[11,42] The metabolic adaptations associated with anaerobic training include increased phosphofructokinase, myosin ATPase, creatine phosphokinase, and adenylate kinase activity as well as increased stores and rate of utilization of ATP, CP, and glycogen.[10,17,20,42] These metabolic changes are manifested as improvements in the performance of anaerobic activities.

Unlike for aerobic exercise, research designed to identify the optimal protocol for improving anaerobic capabilities has been limited. In general, the studies that have reported improved anaerobic capacity following training in children and adolescents have utilized sprint running[20,24,41] or stationary cycling,[17,18,24] submaximal[2] to supramaximal exercise intensities,[24] and three[41] to six[23] exercise sessions per week for six[24] to 16 weeks.[18]

Previous authors[21,55] have recommended sprint training protocols for adults, but it is not clear that these standards are appropriate for children. For example, Wilt[55] has recommended repeated maximal sprints of 60 to 70 yards with full recovery between repetitions. Fox[21] has suggested multiple sprints of approximately 100 to 220 yards with a ratio of work to rest (walking) of 1:3. That is, if the 100-yard sprint is performed in 15 seconds, it should be followed by 45 seconds of walking. Although the applicability of these recommended adult protocols to children is uncertain, it is appropriate to utilize a training program that closely mimics the intended sporting activity with respect to the mode (type) of exercise as well as the metabolic demands. That is, if the training is designed to improve 100-meter sprint running performance, the exercise should consist of running as opposed to stationary cycling or other modes of activity. Furthermore, it is important to identify which anaerobic metabolic system (phosphagen or glycolysis) is more responsible for the energy production for the intended sporting activity. To use the example of the 100-meter sprint, which utilizes primarily the phosphagen system, the training protocol should include repetitions that tax the phosphagen system to a high degree, such as 100-meter sprints, as opposed to longer sprints (200 to 400 meters), which rely heavily on anaerobic glycolysis for energy production. This level of specificity of training will help to ensure favorable physiological adaptations and improved performance.

STRENGTH IN CHILDREN AND ADOLESCENTS

Figure 18.11 illustrates the changes in strength during childhood and adolescence for both genders. In general, both genders increase in strength with age, with males only slightly stronger than females throughout childhood.[31] At approximately 13 to 14 years of age (corresponding to the adolescent growth spurt), males begin to increase in strength at a greater rate than females. The changes in strength during childhood and adolescence coincide with increases in body weight (Figure

figure 18.11 Prior to puberty, males and females increase in strength at approximately the same rate. During adolescence, however, males increase in strength at a greater rate than do females.

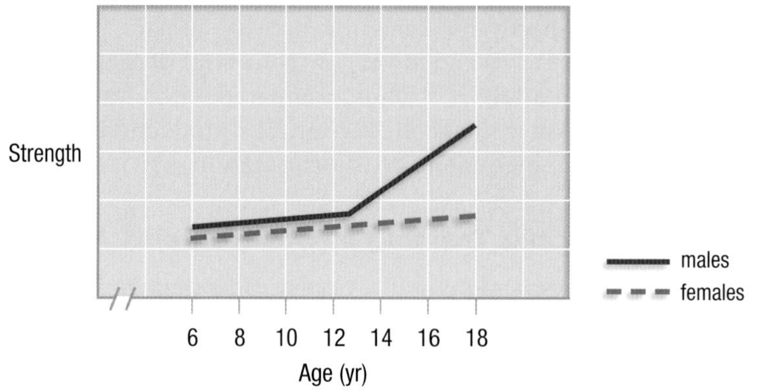

Muscle mass increases throughout childhood and adolescence in males and females. **figure 18.12**

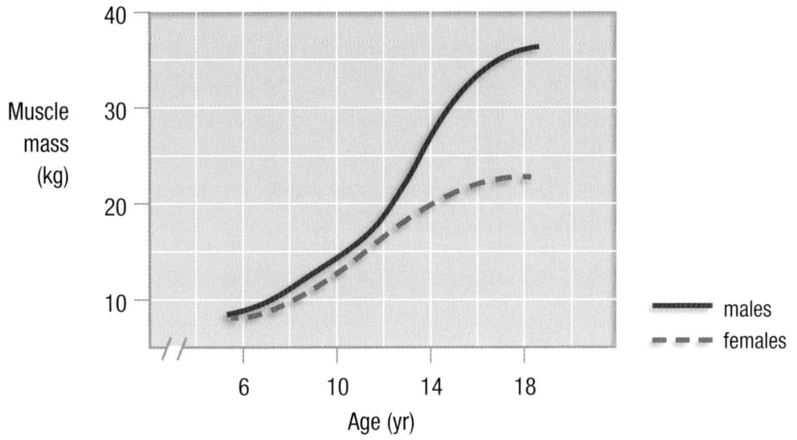

18.3) and muscle mass (Figure 18.12). It is likely that the accelerated increase in strength during puberty in males reflects the anabolic effect of circulating testosterone as well as neural maturation.[1,14,31]

Resistance Training During Prepubescence and Postpubescence

It has long been known that after puberty, resistance training results in increased strength. For many years, however, a controversy existed regarding the effectiveness of resistance training in prepubescent children.[16,26,29] Conventional wisdom held that prepubescent children should not perform resistance training for three primary reasons: (1) low levels of circulating androgens make significant increases in strength impossible; (2) strength gains do not improve motor performance or reduce the risk of sports-related injuries in children; and (3) the potential hazards associated with weight training in children outweigh the benefits.[16,29] Research studies, however, have shown these ideas to be in error.

www

Strength Training for Children
www.issaonline.edu/blog/index.cfm/2011/6/1/Strength-Training-for-Children-a-review-of-research-literature

A number of studies have shown that resistance training results in increased strength in prepubescent children.[19,33,36,37,38,48,49,53] These increases normally range from approximately 5 to 40 percent depending on the characteristics of the training program and are substantially larger than the small increases exhibited in short-term studies (5 to 20 weeks) by age-matched control groups.[28] Thus, the increases in strength as a result of resistance training are greater than those attributable to normal growth and development. Strength increases in prepubertal children have been shown to result from resistance training that involved hydraulic resistance,[52] dynamic constant external resistance exercise,[37,38] weight-bearing activities,[49] and variable resistance (Nautilus and CAM II) training.[48] These investigations indicate that prepubescent children respond favorably to a variety of resistance training modalities. In addition to the increases in strength associated with resistance training, other potential benefits for prepubescent children include:

- improved flexibility[53]
- favorable changes in blood lipid profiles[54]
- enhanced bone and connective tissue development[28]
- favorable changes in body composition[49]
- reduced musculoskeletal injuries during sports participation[28]

Resistance training for young populations

It has been estimated that between 1978 and 1998 more than 188,000 resistance training injuries occurred in individuals between 5 and 14 years of age.[27] In addition, it is likely that each year many unreported and less serious injuries result from resistance training. Therefore it should be recognized that risks are associated with resistance training as well as maximal competitive weight lifting in young populations.[4,33] The degree of risk, however, for supervised submaximal resistance training programs is low, and therefore it is generally accepted that the benefits outweigh the potential hazards.[8,28,33,39]

- improved motor skills[8,53]
- increased muscular endurance[8]
- positive psychological effects[8]

Mechanisms of Strength Increases in Prepubescent Children

It is likely that the strength increases in response to resistance training in prepubescent children are, primarily, a result of neural adaptations,[28,38] although hypertrophy may also occur.[22] The neural factors that contribute to strength gains are primarily associated with increased neural drive and synchronization of motor unit firing.[44] Furthermore, part of the strength increase is probably a function of improved lifting technique.[38]

Potential Hazards Associated with Resistance Training in Children and Adolescents

An issue of importance to parents, athletes, and coaches is the safety of resistance training for young populations. The potential hazards associated with resistance training in children and adolescents fall into two primary categories:[33] acute musculoskeletal injuries and chronic musculoskeletal injuries.

Acute musculoskeletal injuries

acute musculoskeletal injuries

epiphyseal growth plate

Acute musculoskeletal injuries result from trauma experienced during a single episode of resistance training.[33] Examples of this type of injury include epiphyseal fractures, ruptured intervertebral disks, and low-backbone disruption. Of these, damage to the **epiphyseal growth plate** at the end of long bones has received the most attention. The epiphyseal growth plate contributes to the normal development of long bones, and premature closure due to trauma may result in long-term deformity of the limb.

Lifting excessive amounts of weight or using improper technique can result in epiphyseal fractures in children and adolescents.[12] The number of epiphyseal fractures as a result of resistance training, however, is small compared with the number that result from contact sports such as football, hockey, and basketball.[12] In addition, it has been estimated that 5 percent or fewer of all epiphyseal injuries result in a measurable variation in growth.[34] Therefore, although the risk of epiphyseal damage as a result of resistance training in children and adolescents is small, and long-term deformity unlikely, it is important that those individuals responsible for supervision of the training sessions teach proper lifting techniques and take steps to prevent such injuries.[4,8,33]

Strength training, core strengthening, weight lifting, power lifting, and body building

The American Academy of Pediatrics[4] has recommended the following definitions to differentiate among strength training, core strengthening, weight lifting, power lifting, and body building.

1. **Strength training** is the use of resistance methods to increase one's ability to exert or resist force. The training may include use of free weights, the individual's own body weight, machines, and/or other resistance devices to attain this goal.
2. **Core strengthening** is focusing a strengthening program on the muscles that stabilize the trunk of the body. The training emphasizes strengthening of the abdominal, low back, and gluteal muscles as well as flexibility of muscular attachments to the pelvis, such as the quadriceps and hamstring muscles.
3. **Weight lifting** is a competitive sport that involves maximum lifting ability. Weight lifting (which is sometimes called Olympic lifting) includes the snatch and the clean and jerk.
4. **Power lifting** is a competitive sport that also involves maximum lifting ability. Power lifting includes the dead lift, the squat, and the bench press.
5. **Body building** is a competitive sport in which muscle size, symmetry, and definition are judged.

Chronic musculoskeletal injuries

chronic musculoskeletal injuries

Chronic musculoskeletal injuries are generally a result of repeated micro-trauma due to overuse.[33] Examples of these injuries include stress fractures, musculotendinous strains, and osteochondrites dissecans of the knee and elbow.[33] With respect to resistance training, the risk of these injuries can be reduced through a properly supervised program that avoids an excessive frequency and number of repetitions. If resistance training is conducted properly by children and adolescents, the risk of developing severe chronic musculoskeletal injuries is considered small.[8,33]

Characteristics of a Resistance Training Program for Children and Adolescents

The American Academy of Pediatrics[4] has made the following recommendations:

1. Proper resistance techniques and safety precautions should be followed so that strength-training programs for preadolescents and adolescents are safe and effective. Whether it is necessary or appropriate to start such a program and which level of proficiency the youngster already has attained in his or her sport activity should be determined before a strength-training program is started.
2. Preadolescents and adolescents should avoid power lifting, body building, and maximal lifts until they reach physical and skeletal maturity.
3. Athletes should not use performance-enhancing substances or anabolic steroids. Athletes who participate in strength-training programs should be educated about the risks associated with the use of such substances.
4. When pediatricians are asked to recommend or evaluate strength-training programs for children and adolescents, the following issues should be considered:
   a. Before beginning a formal strength-training program, a medical evaluation should be performed by a pediatrician or family physician. Youths with uncontrolled hypertension, seizure disorders, or a history of childhood cancer and chemotherapy should be withheld from participation

until they receive additional treatment or evaluation. When indicated, a referral may be made to a pediatric or family physician sports medicine specialist who is familiar with various strength-training methods as well as risks and benefits for preadolescents and adolescents.

b. Children with complex congenital cardiac disease (cardiomyopathy, pulmonary artery hypertension, or Marfan syndrome) should have a consultation with a pediatric cardiologist before beginning a strength-training program.
c. Aerobic conditioning should be coupled with resistance training if general health benefits are the goal.
d. Strength-training programs should include periods of 10 to 15 minutes for warm-up and cool-down.
e. Athletes should have adequate intake of fluids and proper nutrition, because both are vital in maintaining muscle energy stores, in recovery, and in performance.
f. Specific strength-training exercises should be learned initially with no load (no resistance). Once the exercise technique has been mastered, incremental loads can be added using either body weight or other forms of resistance. Strength training should involve two to three sets of higher repetitions (8 to 15) two to three times per week and be at least eight weeks in duration.
g. A general strengthening program should address all major muscle groups, including the core, and exercise through the complete range of motion. More sports-specific areas may be addressed subsequently.
h. Any sign of illness or injury from strength training should be evaluated fully before allowing resumption of the exercise program.
i. Instructors or personal trainers should have certification reflecting specific qualifications in pediatric strength training.
j. Proper technique and strict supervision by a qualified instructor are critical safety components in any strength-training program involving preadolescents and adolescents.

Several authorities have recommended resistance training programs for children.[8,28,33] While all are similar in philosophy, the recommendations in Table 18.1 provide specifics for a progression from a novice program to an advanced program for the goal of increasing strength.[33] The National Strength and Conditioning Association has also provided recommendations for a resistance training progression program in children for increasing power (Table 18.2).[33] Typically, the order of the exercises involves large muscle group exercises performed before smaller muscle group exercises and multi-joint exercises performed before single-joint exercises.[33]

THE MENSTRUAL CYCLE, EXERCISE, AND ATHLETICS

Menarche. Loucks[30] has addressed the issue of whether athletic participation during childhood delays menarche. Compelling evidence shows that biased sampling procedures have led to the spurious conclusion that the exercise training associated with athletic participation causes a delay in menarche. After a thorough review of the available evidence, Loucks[30] concluded that "at present, it is correct to say that the average age of menarche is later in athletes than non-athletes, but there is no experimental evidence that athletic training delays menarche in anyone."

Resistance training progression for children for strength.[33] table 18.1

	NOVICE PROGRAM	INTERMEDIATE PROGRAM	ADVANCED PROGRAM
1. Muscle action	Eccentric and concentric	Eccentric and concentric	Eccentric and concentric
2. Exercise choice	Single joint and multi-joint	Single joint and multi-joint	Single joint and multi-joint
3. Intensity	50–70% 1-RM*	60–80% 1-RM	70–85% 1-RM
4. Volume	1–2 sets x 10–15 reps	2–3 sets x 8–12 reps	≥3 sets x 6–10 reps
5. Rest periods between sets	1 minute	1–2 minutes	2–3 minutes
6. Frequency	2–3 times per week	2–3 times per week	3–4 times per week

*RM (repetition maximum) = the maximal amount of weight that can be lifted for a specific number of repetitions. For example, a 1-RM load is the maximal amount of weight that can be lifted only one time. A 10-RM load is the maximal amount of weight that can be lifted 10 times but not 11.

Resistance training progression for children for power.[33] table 18.2

	NOVICE PROGRAM	INTERMEDIATE PROGRAM	ADVANCED PROGRAM
1. Muscle action	Eccentric and concentric	Eccentric and concentric	Eccentric and concentric
2. Exercise choice	Multi-joint	Multi-joint	Multi-joint
3. Intensity	30–60% 1-RM* velocity	30–60% 1-RM velocity 60–70% 1-RM strength	30–60% 1-RM velocity 70–≥80% 1-RM strength
4. Volume	1–2 sets x 3–6 reps	2–3 sets x 3–6 reps	≥3 sets x 1–6 reps
5. Rest periods between sets	1 minute	1–2 minutes	2–3 minutes
6. Velocity	Moderate/fast	Fast	Fast
7. Frequency	2 times per week	2–3 times per week	2–3 times per week

*RM (repetition maximum) = the maximum amount of weight that can be lifted for a specific number of repetitions. For example, a 1-RM load is the maximal amount of weight that can be lifted only one time. A 10-RM load is the maximal amount of weight that can be lifted 10 times but not 11.

Participation in sports and exercise during menstruation. At present there is no conclusive evidence that participation in exercise or sporting events during menstruation is harmful. In addition, it is unclear whether menstruation per se or the discomfort associated with primary **dysmenorrhea** (pain from uterine contractions or ischemia during menstruation) affects performance.[15]

- dysmenorrhea

Athletic menstrual cycle irregularity (AMI). Regular, asymptomatic menstruation is usually considered a measure of general good health in females after a regular rhythm has been established. **Athletic menstrual cycle irregularities** (AMIs) such as **amenorrhea** (cessation of the menstrual cycle) are reported with greater frequency as adolescent and adult women become more involved in high-intensity, year-round training programs,[13,15] but it is not known whether AMI constitutes a threat to health or future reproductive function or is simply a normal variation in function that is reversible. AMI could be caused by physical or psychological stress, changes in hormonal function or body composition, or a combination of these factors.

- athletic menstrual cycle irregularities
- amenorrhea

The female athlete triad

The **female athlete triad** refers to the interrelationships among energy availability, menstrual function, and bone density, which may have clinical manifestations, including disordered eating, amenorrhea, and osteoporosis.[35] This syndrome affects physically active females of various ages and is most commonly associated with sports that emphasize low body weight and thin appearance such as gymnastics, figure skating, diving, and cheerleading. The female athlete triad is also common to sports that use weight categories, including horse racing, martial arts, wrestling, and rowing. The necessity to maintain a low body weight for competition can lead to **disordered eating,** including potentially pathogenic behaviors such as anorexia nervosa and bulimia nervosa. These behaviors not only affect performance but also can lead to amenorrhea. Amenorrhea is associated with decreased bone mineral density, which can result in osteoporosis, a condition characterized by low bone mass and microarchitectural deterioration of bone tissue.[6] Osteoporosis can lead to bone weakness and an increased risk of fractures (see Chapter 9).

The prevalence of the female athlete triad is unknown, but it is likely to increase as sports participation increases. Coaches, athletic trainers, physical educators, and exercise professionals need to recognize the early signs of disordered eating, such as excessive weight loss and avoidance of food, as well as the use of laxatives, diuretics, and vomiting, and work to prevent the development of the female athlete triad.[35]

www

Female Athlete Triad: eMedicine Sports Medicine *http://emedicine.medscape.com/article/89260-overview*

Effect of the menstrual cycle on performance. There is no definitive information to support the widespread impression that performance is impaired during certain periods of the menstrual cycle. For some athletes, the menstrual cycle has no effect on performance, while for others, performance tends to be best in the postmenstrual or intermenstrual phases. Generally, for athletes affected by the menstrual cycle, performance is worst in the two to three days preceding menstruation or during menstruation.[15]

summary

Many exercise professionals, physical educators, and coaches work with children and adolescents and it is important to understand normal growth and development patterns and how they affect the responses to physical activity and training.

Growth refers to an increase in the size of the body, while development describes the differentiation of cells along specialized lines of function. Maturation is the timing of progress toward the mature state.

Maximal oxygen consumption ($\dot{V}O_2$ max), expressed in absolute ($L \cdot min^{-1}$) terms, increases throughout childhood in both males and females. During adolescence absolute $\dot{V}O_2$ max continues to increase in males, but plateaus in females at about 14 years of age. Relative $\dot{V}O_2$ max ($mL \cdot kg^{-1} \cdot min^{-1}$), however, remains stable during childhood and adolescence in males, but decreases with age in females. Endurance training increases $\dot{V}O_2$ max during childhood and adolescence.

Children have a lower capacity for anaerobic activities than do adolescents and adults. Thus, they tend not to perform as well during high-intensity, explosive activities that utilize the ATP–PC or anaerobic glycolytic energy production systems. The diminished capacity for anaerobic activity in children, compared with adults, may be due to smaller creatine phosphate stores and lower levels of the glycolytic enzyme phosphofructokinase. Anaerobic training in children increases phosphagen and glycogen stores as well as the activity of the anaerobic enzymes phosphofructokinase, myosin ATPase, creatine phosphokinase, and adenylate kinase.

Muscle strength increases throughout childhood at approximately the same rate in males and females. After the onset of puberty, however, the rate of strength increase is greater in males than females, probably due to the anabolic effects of increased circulating levels of the hormone testosterone. Resistance training results in increased strength in both children and adolescents.

There is little compelling evidence that athletic participation affects the age of menarche or that competitive athletic participation during menstruation is harmful. Athletic menstrual cycle irregularities such as amenorrhea are reported more frequently as women become involved in high-intensity, year-round training and competition. It is unclear if AMI has any long-term reproductive implications.

questions for review

1. Compare and contrast the terms *growth, development,* and *maturation.*
2. Define the stages of infancy, childhood, and adolescence.
3. How can you determine if a child has reached puberty?
4. Why should making weight be of special concern to coaches of children and adolescents?
5. Why do children have a lower capacity for anaerobic activities than adults?
6. What factors should an exercise professional, a coach, or a physical educator consider before planning a running program for children? An anaerobic training program?
7. What are the mechanisms of strength increases in prepubescent children?
8. What potential hazards are associated with a resistance training program for children and adolescents?
9. Design a weight training program for a 10-year-old boy who has not engaged in regular physical activity or athletic competition. Include exercises to work each major muscle group and increase intensity, duration, frequency, and rest interval length.
10. Discuss the relationships among age, body weight, and strength in children.
11. What are the effects of the menstrual cycle on performance?
12. What are the effects of exercise and athletic participation on the menstrual cycle?
13. Explain the female athlete triad. What signs should coaches and physical educators look for to identify this syndrome?
14. How is the demand for leanness in certain sports detrimental to female athletes?

student companion website

For further review of this book's chapters and for test preparation, visit the book's website, **www.hhpcommunities.com/exercisephysiology**, to take practice quizzes, review the vocabulary terms, use the study guide, and view the digital image bank.

references

1. Adams, R. D., and Victor, M. *Principles of Neurology.* St. Louis: McGraw-Hill Book Co., 1985.
2. Adeniran, S. A., and Toriola, M. A. Effects of continuous and interval running programmes on aerobic and anaerobic capacities in schoolgirls aged 13 to 17 years. *J. Sports Med. Phys. Fitness* 28: 260–266, 1988.
3. American Academy of Pediatrics. Risks in distance running for children. *Pediatrics* 86: 799–800, 1990.

4. American Academy of Pediatrics. Strength training by children and adolescents. *Pediatrics* 121: 835–840, 2008.
5. American College of Sports Medicine. Position Stand. Weight loss in wrestlers. *Med. Sci. Sports Exerc.* 28: ix–xii, 1996.
6. American College of Sports Medicine. Position Stand. The female athlete triad. *Med. Sci. Sports Exerc.* 39: 1867–1882, 2007.
7. American College of Sports Medicine. *Guidelines for Exercise Testing and Prescription,* 9th edition. Baltimore: Wolters Kluwer/Lippincott Williams & Wilkins, 2014.
8. American Orthopaedic Society for Sports Medicine. *Proceedings of the Conference on Strength Training and the Prepubescent,* ed. B. R. Cahill. Chicago: AOSSM, 1988.
9. Armstrong, N., and Welsman, J. R. Development of aerobic fitness during childhood and adolescence. *Ped. Exer. Sci.* 12: 128–149, 2000.
10. Bar-Or, O. Pediatric sports medicine for the practitioner. In *Physiologic Principles of Clinical Applications.* New York: Springer-Verlag, 1983.
11. Bar-Or, O. Trainability of the prepubescent child. *Phys. Sportsmed.* 17: 65–82, 1989.
12. Benton, J. W. Epiphyseal fracture in sports. *Phys. Sportsmed.* 10: 63–71, 1982.
13. Bonen, A., and Keizer, H. A. Athletic menstrual cycle irregularity: Endocrine response to exercise and training. *Phys. Sportsmed.* 12: 78–94, 1984.
14. Brooks, G. A., Fahey, T. D., and Baldwin, K. M. *Exercise Physiology: Human Bioenergetics and Its Applications,* 4th edition. Boston: McGraw-Hill Higher Education, 2004.
15. Carlberg, K., Peake, G. T., and Buckman, M. T. Exercise and the menstrual cycle. In *Sports Medicine,* 3rd edition, ed. O. Appenzeller. Baltimore: Urban and Schwarzenberg, 1988, pp. 161–180.
16. Duda, M. Prepubescent strength training gains support. *Phys. Sportsmed.* 14: 157–161, 1986.
17. Eriksson, B. O. Physical training, oxygen supply and muscle metabolism in 11–13 year old boys. *Acta Physiol. Scand.* (Suppl.) 384: 1–48, 1972.
18. Eriksson, B. O., Gollnick, P. D., and Saltin, B. Muscle metabolism and enzyme activities after training in boys 11–13 years old. *Acta Physiol. Scand.* 87: 485–497, 1973.
19. Faigenbaum, A. D., Wescott, W. L., Loud, R. L., and Long, C. The effects of different resistance training protocols on muscular strength and endurance development in children. *Pediatrics* 104: E5, 1999.
20. Fournier, M., Ricci, J., Taylor, A. W., Ferguson, R. J., Montpetit, R. R., and Chaitman, B. R. Skeletal muscle adaptation in adolescent boys: Sprint and endurance training and detraining. *Med. Sci. Sports Exerc.* 14: 453–456, 1982.
21. Fox, E. L. Physical training: Methods and effects. *Ortho. Clin. North Amer.* 8: 533–548, 1977.
22. Funkunaga, T., Funato, K., and Ikegawa, S. The effects of resistance training on muscle area and strength in prepubescent age. *Ann. Physiol. Anthrop.* 11: 357–364, 1992.
23. Grodjinovsky, A., and Bar-Or, O. Influence of added physical education hours upon anaerobic capacity, adiposity, and grip strength in 12–13 year-old children enrolled in a sports class. In *Children and Sport,* eds. J. Ilmarinen and I. Valimaki. Berlin: Springer-Verlag, 1984.
24. Grodjinovsky, A., Bar-Or, O., Dotan, R., and Inbar, O. Training effect on the anaerobic performance of children as measured by the Wingate anaerobic test. In *Children and Exercise,* eds. K. Berg and B. O. Eriksson. Baltimore: University Park Press, 1980.
25. Inbar, O., and Bar-Or, O. Anaerobic characteristics in male children and adolescents. *Med. Sci. Sports Exerc.* 18: 264–269, 1986.
26. Jacobson, B. H., and Kulling, F. A. Effect of resistive weight training in prepubescents. *J. Orthop. Sports Phys. Ther.* 11: 96–99, 1989.
27. Jones, C. A., Christensen, C., and Young, M. Weight training injury trends: A 20-year survey. *Phys. Sportsmed.* 28: 61–72, 2000.
28. Kraemer, W. J., Fry, A. C., Frykman, P. N., Conroy, B., and Hoffman, J. Resistance training and youth. *Ped. Exer. Sci.* 1: 336–350, 1989.
29. Legwold, G. Does lifting weights harm a prepubescent athlete? *Phys. Sportsmed.* 10: 141–144, 1982.
30. Loucks, A. B. Effects of exercise training on the menstrual cycle: Existence and mechanisms. *Med. Sci. Sports Exerc.* 22: 275–280, 1990.
31. Malina, R. M., Bouchard, C., and Bar-Or, O. *Growth, Maturation, and Physical Activity,* 2nd edition. Champaign, IL: Human Kinetics, 2004.
32. Micheli, L. J. Complications of recreational running. *Ped. Alert* 6: 1–2, 1981.
33. National Strength and Conditioning Association. Position Statement. Youth resistance training: Updated position statement paper from the National Strength and Conditioning Association. *J. Strength Cond. Res.* 23: 560–579, 2009.
34. Pappas, A. M. Epiphyseal injuries in sports. *Phys. Sportsmed.* 11: 140–148, 1983.
35. Payne, J. M., and Kirchner, J. T. Should you suspect the female athlete triad? *J. Fam. Prac.* 63: 187–192, 2014.
36. Payne, V. G., Morrow, J. R., Johnson, L., and Dalton, S. N. Resistance training in children and youth: A meta-analysis. *Res. Q. Exerc. Sport* 68: 80–88, 1997.
37. Pfeiffer, R. D., and Francis, R. S. Effects of strength training on muscle development in prepubescent, pubescent and postpubescent males. *Phys. Sportsmed.* 14: 134–143, 1986.
38. Ramsay, J. A., Blimkie, C. J. R., Smith, K., Garner, S., MacDougall, J. D., and Sale, D. G. Strength training effects in prepubescent boys. *Med. Sci. Sports Exerc.* 22: 605–614, 1990.
39. Rians, C. B., Weltman, A., Cahill, B. R., Janney, C. A., Tippett, S. R., and Katch, F. I. Strength training for

prepubescent males: Is it safe? *Am. J. Sports Med.* 15: 483–489, 1987.

40. Rogol, A. D. Sex steroid and growth hormone supplementation to enhance performance in adolescent athletes. *Curr. Opin. Pediatr.* 12: 382–387, 2000.
41. Rotstein, A., Dotan, R., Bar-Or, O., and Tenenbaum, G. Effect of training on anaerobic threshold, maximal aerobic power and anaerobic performance of preadolescent boys. *Int. J. Sports Med.* 7: 281–286, 1986.
42. Rowland, T. W. *Children's Exercise Physiology,* 2nd edition. Champaign, IL: Human Kinetics, 2004.
43. Rowland, T. W. Oxygen uptake and endurance fitness in children: A developmental perspective. *Ped. Exer. Sci.* 1: 313–328, 1989.
44. Rowland, T. W. *Exercise and Children's Health.* Champaign, IL: Human Kinetics, 1994.
45. Rowland, T. W. "Normalizing" maximal oxygen uptake, or the search for the holy grail (per kg). *Ped. Exer. Sci.* 3: 95–102, 1991.
46. Rowland, T. W., and Hoontis, P. P. Organizing road races for children: Special concerns. *Phys. Sportsmed.* 13: 126–132, 1985.
47. Rowland, T. W., and Walsh, C. A. Characteristics of child distance runners. *Phys. Sportsmed.* 13: 45–53, 1985.
48. Sewall, L., and Micheli, L. J. Strength training for children. *J. Ped. Ortho.* 6: 143–146, 1986.
49. Siegel, J. A., Camaione, D. N., and Manfredi, T. G. The effects of upper body resistance training on prepubescent children. *Ped. Exer. Sci.* 1: 145–154, 1989.
50. U.S. Department of Health and Human Services. *2008 Physical Activity Guidelines for Americans.* Atlanta: U.S. Department of Health and Human Services. www.health.gov/paguidelines, 2008.
51. Van Praagh, E. Development of anaerobic function during childhood and adolescence. *Ped. Exer. Sci.* 12: 150–173, 2000.
52. Welsman, J. R., and Armstrong, N. Statistical techniques for interpreting body size-related exercise performance during growth. *Ped. Exer. Sci.* 12: 112–127, 2000.
53. Weltman, A., Janney, C., Rians, C. B., Strand, K., Berg, B., Tippitt, S., Wise, J., Cahill, B. R., and Katch, F. I. The effects of hydraulic resistance strength training in pre-pubertal males. *Med. Sci. Sports Exerc.* 18: 629–638, 1986.
54. Weltman, A., Janney, C., Rians, C. B., Strand, K., and Katch, F. I. The effects of hydraulic-resistance strength training on serum lipid levels in prepubertal boys. *Am. J. Dis. Child.* 141: 777–780, 1987.
55. Wilt, F. Training for competitive running. In *Exercise Physiology,* ed. H. Falls. New York: Academic Press, 1968.
56. Zwiren, L. D. Anaerobic and aerobic capacities of children. *Ped. Exer. Sci.* 1: 31–44, 1989.

lab Vertical Jump Test for Measuring Muscular Power of the Legs

BACKGROUND

The vertical jump is a commonly used test to assess muscular power of the legs.[1,2,3,4,5,6] Power is defined as (*force* × *distance*) / *time*. Thus, performing the vertical jump and producing great muscular power depend on the ability to produce a high level of force very rapidly. There are two primary ways to test the vertical jump: the squat jump and the countermovement jump. During the squat jump, the subject lowers into the squat position, pauses for a moment, and then jumps vertically as high as possible. During the countermovement jump, the subject starts from a standing position, descends rapidly into a squat position, and then, without stopping at the bottom of the squat, performs a maximal vertical jump. The countermovement jump results in jump heights that are approximately 2 to 4 cm higher than the squat jump.[1] This occurs because there is a rapid transition from the descent (eccentric phase) to the ascent (concentric phase) of the movement. The squat jump, however, tends to result in more reliable scores, presumably due to the variability associated with the countermovement. In addition, muscular power of the legs is more accurately estimated using the squat jump than the countermovement jump.[5]

It is not necessary to use advanced equipment such as a force plate or Vertec device to determine vertical jump height. Vertical jump height can be measured simply by placing chalk on the fingertips of the subject, then having the subject jump next to a wall and touch the wall at the top of the jump. Vertical jump height is measured as the difference between the height of the chalk mark at the level of the highest jump and the height of a chalk mark made while standing with the arm fully extended overhead.

Power output cannot be measured directly from jump height alone, but for the squat jump technique, it can be estimated for both males and females from vertical jump height and body weight using the following regression equation of Sayers et al.:[5]

$$\text{Muscular power (watts)} = [60.7 \times \text{vertical jump height (cm)}] + [45.3 \times \text{body weight (kg)}] - 2055.$$

Multiple correlation coefficient (R) = 0.94

Standard error of estimate (SEE) = 372.9 watts

In addition, a nomogram has been developed[3] from the equation of Sayers et al.[5] to simplify the estimation of muscular power.

In this laboratory, you will learn to administer the vertical jump test using the squat jump technique and calculate muscular power of the legs from vertical jump height and body weight using the equation of Sayers et al.[5] You will also learn to use the nomogram of Keir et al.[3] to estimate muscular power. You will then compare the subject's vertical jump height in cm and muscular power in watts to percentile rank norms based on age and gender (Tables L18.1–L18.4).

Percentile ranks for vertical jump muscular power (watts) for males by age.[4] **table L18.1**

PERCENTILE RANK	15-19	20-29	30-39	40-49	50-59	60-69
90	≥4978	≥5676	≥5602	≥5271	≥4841	≥4106
80	4643	5093	4859	4319	4018	3766
70	4506	4882	4685	3992	3703	3466
60	4184	4639	4388	3699	3566	3290
50	4049	4411	4222	3550	3342	3248
40	3857	4296	3966	3241	2937	2842
30	3678	4018	3750	3040	2747	2512
20	3322	3774	3484	2707	2511	2382
10	2908	3456	2764	2511	2080	1636
<10	<2908	<3456	<2764	<2511	<2080	<1636

Note: The percentile ranks in this table are for the squat jump technique.

Percentile ranks for vertical jump muscular power (watts) for females by age.[4] **table L18.2**

PERCENTILE RANK	15-19	20-29	30-39	40-49	50-59	60-69
90	≥3514	≥3667	≥3581	≥2989	≥2742	≥2604
80	3166	3249	3192	2674	2558	2474
70	2945	3007	2844	2503	2470	1779
60	2794	2803	2549	2287	2160	1717
50	2590	2628	2388	2157	1956	1465
40	2398	2477	2334	2100	1700	1316
30	2280	2374	2258	1824	1497	1262
20	2155	2270	2146	1687	1385	1197
10	1878	1971	1692	1330	1006	570
<10	<1878	<1971	<1692	<1330	<1006	<570

Note: The percentile ranks in this table are for the squat jump technique.

table L18.3 Percentile ranks for vertical jump height (cm) for males by age.[4]

PERCENTILE RANK	15–19	20–29	30–39	40–49	50–59	60–69
90	≥57	≥60	≥54	≥51	≥47	≥34
80	55	57	51	42	40	32
70	53	55	48	38	36	30
60	50	53	45	35	34	28
50	47	50	42	33	30	26
40	45	47	39	31	27	24
30	43	44	36	29	24	22
20	41	41	30	25	17	17
10	38	38	23	21	10	12
<10	<38	<38	<23	<21	<10	<12

Note: The percentile ranks in this table are for the squat jump technique.

table L18.4 Percentile ranks for vertical jump height (cm) for females by age.[4]

PERCENTILE RANK	15–19	20–29	30–39	40–49	50–59	60–69
90	≥41	≥40	≥37	≥32	≥26	≥20
80	39	37	35	30	24	18
70	37	35	33	28	22	16
60	35	33	31	26	20	14
50	33	30	29	24	18	12
40	31	28	27	22	15	10
30	29	26	25	20	12	8
20	27	24	23	17	9	6
10	25	19	19	14	5	3
<10	<25	<19	<19	<14	<5	<3

Note: The percentile ranks in this table are for the squat jump technique.

TERMS & ABBREVIATIONS

- maximal effort vertical jump = total jump height
- nomogram = a graph that shows the relationship between variables. In this case, the nomogram shows the relationship between vertical jump height, body weight, and muscular power in watts.
- power = (force × distance) / time
- R = multiple correlation coefficient, a numerical measure of how well a dependent variable can be predicted from a combination of independent variables (a number between –1 and 1)
- SEE = standard error of estimate, a measure of the accuracy of predictions made using a regression equation

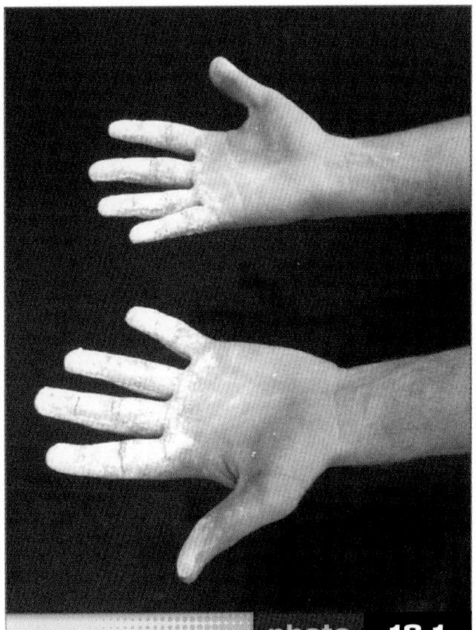

photo 18.1

Chalk on fingers.

PROCEDURES (see photos 18.1 to 18.4)

1. Measure the subject's body weight (kg) and record it on Worksheet 18.1.
2. Measure the subject's standing reach height by putting chalk on the person's fingertips (photo 18.1) and having him or her stand next to a wall, reach as high as possible, and touch the wall (photo 18.2). The distance between the floor and the chalk mark on the wall is the standing reach height. Record the standing reach height on Worksheet 18.1.
3. Have the subject perform a general warm-up of jogging or cycle ergometry for five minutes and three to five practice jumps at approximately 50% of maximal capability.
4. Place chalk on the fingertips prior to each maximal effort vertical jump.
5. Have the subject assume a squat position with the knees at approximately 90 degrees[5] and then pause for one to two seconds prior to initiating a maximal vertical jump (photo 18.3). The feet should be approximately shoulder-width apart and the dominant arm should be toward the wall. The arms should be positioned posterior to the torso so that they can be thrust upward during the jump. Have the subject touch his chalked fingers to the wall at the highest point of the jump. The subject should perform at least three maximal effort vertical jumps or continue until a plateau in performance is achieved. Provide at least one minute of rest between attempts.[6] Record the height (from the floor to the chalk mark) of each maximal effort vertical jump (photo 18.4; called the total jump height) on Worksheet 18.1.
6. Calculate the vertical jump height, defined as the difference in cm between the total jump height and the standing reach height (vertical jump height = total jump height – standing reach height; see Worksheet 18.1).
7. Calculate muscular power using the equation of Sayers et al.[5] based on the subject's best vertical jump height and body weight (see sample calculation below). Alternatively, muscular power can be estimated using the nomogram of Keir et al.,[3] which is derived from the equation of Sayers et al.[5] (see sample estimation given in Figure L18.1).

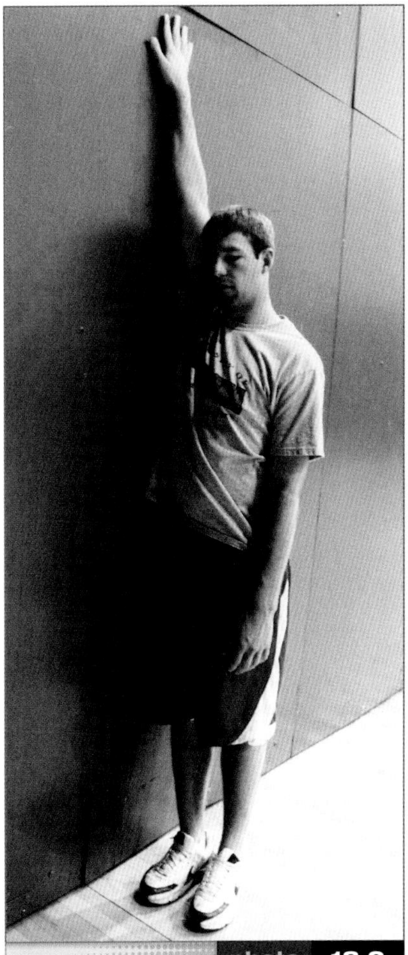

photo 18.2

Standing reach height.

photo 18.3

Squat position prior to initiating a maximal vertical jump.

photo 18.4

Touch the chalked fingers to the wall at the highest point of the maximal vertical jump.

8. Compare the subject's vertical jump height in cm and muscular power in watts to the percentile rank norms in Tables L18.1 through L18.4.[4] These percentile rank norms are for the squat jump technique only and cannot be used for the countermovement jump technique.

SAMPLE CALCULATIONS

Gender: Male

Body weight: 81.6 kg

Height: 153 cm

Age: 21 years

standing reach height 205 cm

total jump height # 1 243 cm

total jump height – standing reach height = vertical jump height

243 cm – 205 cm = 38 cm

total jump height # 2 245 cm

total jump height – standing reach height = vertical jump height

245 cm – 205 cm = (40) cm

total jump height # 3 244 cm

total jump height – standing reach height = vertical jump height

244 cm – 205 cm = 39 cm

muscular ~~power~~ = (60.7 × 40 cm) + (45.3 × 81.6 kg) – 2055
= (4069) watts

estimated muscular power from the nomogram (see Figure 18.1)
= 4050 watts

percentile rank based on muscular power (watts) 32nd percentile
(see Table L18.1)

percentile rank based on vertical jump height (cm) 18th percentile
(see Table L18.3)

Nomogram example for estimating muscular power in watts from vertical jump height and body weight.[3,5]

figure L18.1

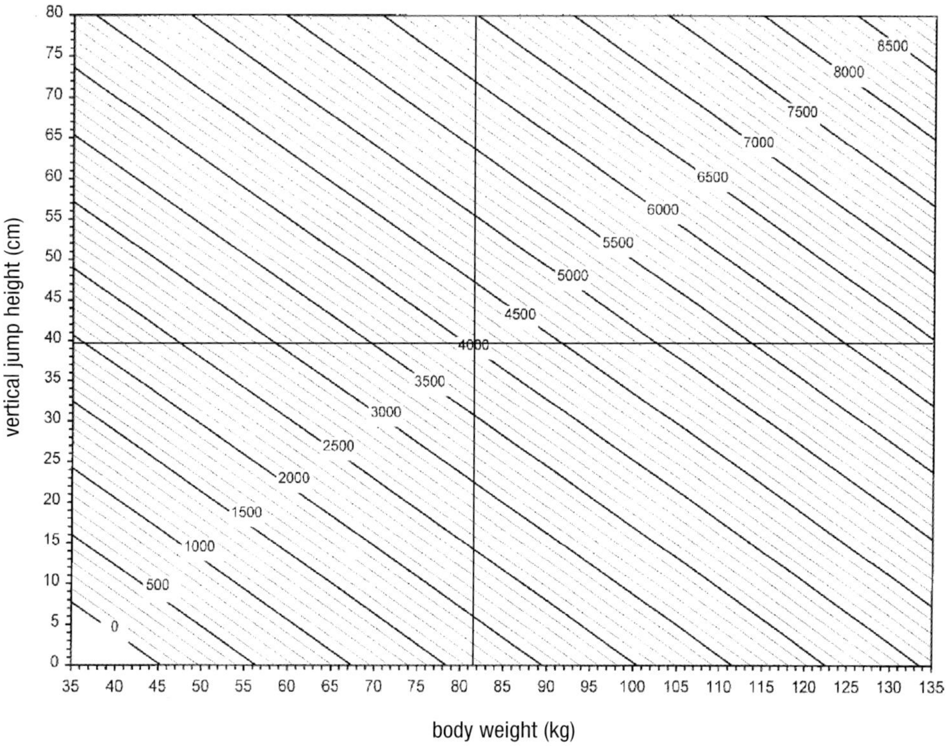

To estimate muscular power (watts) from the vertical jump height and body weight, first draw a vertical line upward from the X-axis at a point equal to the subject's body weight (kg). Next, draw a horizontal line to the right from the Y-axis at a level equal to the subject's best vertical jump height (cm). Find the muscular power value (expressed in watts) that is closest to the intersection of the two lines.[3] For example, based on the data provided in the sample calculations (body weight = 81.6 kg and best vertical jump height = 40 cm), the estimated muscular power is approximately 4050 watts.

worksheet 18.1 DETERMINATION OF VERTICAL JUMP HEIGHT AND MUSCULAR POWER

NAME ______________________________ DATE ______________

Gender: __________________

Age: __________________

Body weight: __________________ kg

Height: __________________ cm

Age: __________________

standing reach height __________________ cm

total jump height # 1 __________________ cm

total jump height – standing reach height = vertical jump height

__________________ cm – __________________ cm = __________________ cm

total jump height # 2 __________________ cm

total jump height – standing reach height = vertical jump height

__________________ cm – __________________ cm = __________________ cm

total jump height # 3 __________________ cm

total jump height – standing reach height = vertical jump height

__________________ cm – __________________ cm = __________________ cm

muscular power = (60.7 × _____________ cm) + (45.3 × _____________ kg) – 2055 = _____________ watts

estimated muscular power from the nomogram (see Figure L18.2) = _____________ watts

percentile rank based on muscular power (see Tables L18.1 and L18.2) _____________ watts

percentile rank based on vertical jump height (see Tables L18.3 and L18.4) _____________ cm

Nomogram for estimating muscular power in watts from vertical jump height and body weight.[3,5]

figure L18.2

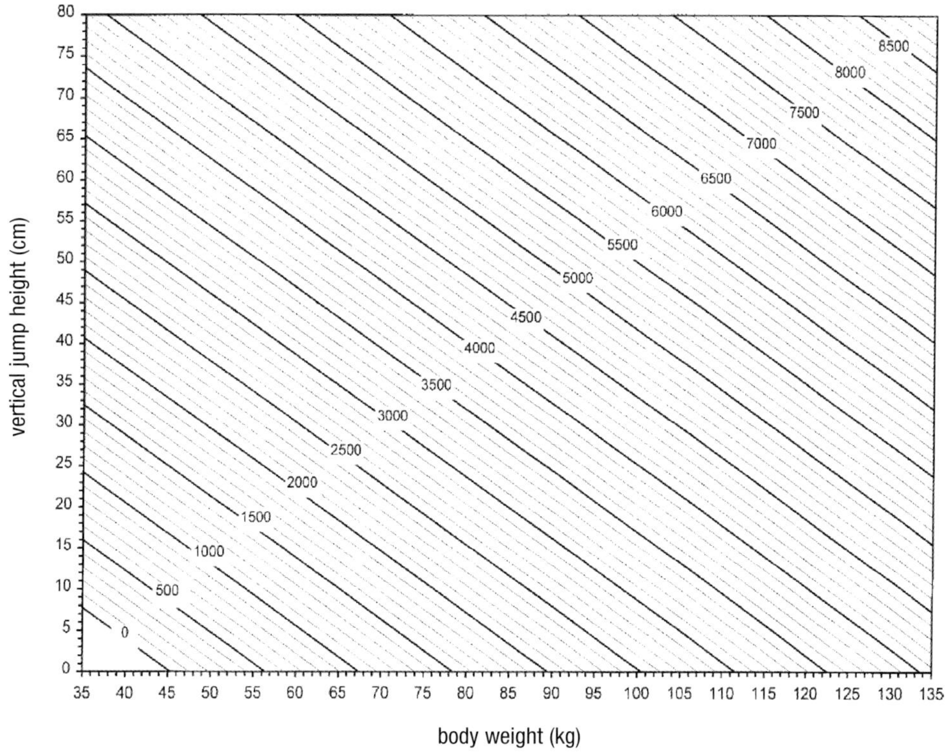

To estimate muscular power (watts) from the vertical jump height and body weight, first draw a vertical line upward from the X-axis at a point equal to the subject's body weight (kg). Next, draw a horizontal line to the right from the T-axis at a level equal to the subject's best vertical jump height (cm). Find the muscular power value (expressed in watts) that is closest to the intersection of the two lines.[3]

worksheet 18.2 EXTENSION ACTIVITIES

NAME ______________________________ DATE ______________________________

Gender: Female

Age: 26 years

Body weight: 54 kg

Vertical jump height: 30 cm

muscular power = (60.7 × ____________ cm) + (45.3 × ____________ kg) – 2055 = ____________ watts

estimated muscular power from the nomogram (see Figure L18.2) = ____________ watts

percentile rank based on muscular power (Table L18.2) ____________ watts

percentile rank based on vertical jump height (Table L18.4) ____________ cm

EXTENSION QUESTIONS

1. What are some common mistakes that may occur in administering this lab?

2. Identify possible sources of error in this lab.

3. Assess the practicality of using this lab in the field.

4. Research the reliability and/or validity of this lab using online resources, journal articles, and other credible sources.

REFERENCES

1. Bobbert, M. F., and Casius, J. R. Is the effect of a countermovement on jump height due to active state development? *Med. Sci. Sports Exerc.* 37: 440–446, 2005.
2. Burkett, L. N., Phillips, W. T., and Ziuraitis, J. The best warm up for the vertical jump in college-age athletic men. *J. Strength Cond. Res.* 19: 673–676, 2005.
3. Keir, P. J., Jamnik, V. K., and Gledhill, N. Technical-methodological report: A nomogram for peak leg power in the vertical jump. *J. Strength Cond. Res.* 17: 701–703, 2003.
4. Payne, N., Gledhill, N., Katzmarzyk, P. T., Jamnik, V. K., and Keir, J. P. Canadian musculoskeletal fitness norms. *Can. J. of Appl. Physiol.* 25: 430–442, 2000.
5. Sayers, S. P., Harackiewicz, D. V., Harman, E. A., Frykman, P. N., and Rosenstein, M. T. Cross validation of three jump power equations. *Med. Sci. Sports Exerc.* 31: 572–577, 1999.
6. Stockbrugger, B. A., and Haennel, R. G. Contributing factors to performance of a medicine ball explosive power test: A comparison between jump and nonjump athletes. *J. Strength Cond. Res.* 17: 768–774, 2003.

Aging and Exercise

19

As a result of reading this chapter you will:

Know the effects of aging on various aspects of physical performance and physiological functioning.

Understand how regular physical activity affects the rate of decline in physiological functioning.

Be able to describe the potential benefits of aerobic training in older adults.

Know the effects of resistance training in older adults.

key concepts

arteriosclerosis

force–velocity curve

thoracic wall compliance

Throughout the lifespan of humans, physical performance and physiological functioning improve rapidly from early childhood to a maximum somewhere between the late teens and about 30 years of age. Then, in most cases, a slow decline occurs during adulthood that becomes more rapid with increasing age. These declines in functioning are associated with age-related decreases in physical activity as well as the inevitable effects of aging. In general, however, the rates of decline in physical performance are more highly related to the decreased habitual activity than to age itself. Thus, regular physical activity throughout life can decrease the rate of decline in physiological functioning and physical performance.

Statistics on population trends for the United States indicate that we are becoming a nation of older people. The absolute number of older persons as well as the proportion of our older population segments are increasing rapidly.[2,14] In evaluating the effects of aging on human function, several problems arise. First, it is difficult to separate the effects of aging per se from those of concomitant disease processes (particularly cardiovascular problems) that become more numerous as age progresses. Second, the sedentary nature of adult life in the United States makes it very difficult to find older populations for comparisons with younger populations at equal activity levels. Third, very little work has been done on longitudinal studies of the same population over a long period of time.

Just as individuals age at different rates, various physiological functions have their own rates of decline with increasing age (see Figure 19.1). In general, the functions that involve the coordinated activity of more than one organ system (such as maximal oxygen consumption rate) decline most with age, and as might be expected, changes due to aging are most readily observed when the organism is stressed. Homeostatic readjustment following a stressor such as exercise is considerably slower with increasing age.

www

International Coalition for Aging and Physical Activity *www.humankinetics.com/ICAPA*

AGE-RELATED CHANGES IN PHYSIOLOGICAL FUNCTIONING

Muscle Function

Strength. Rapid improvement in strength accompanies the growth of children (see Chapter 18), and maximal strength occurs for most muscle groups in early adulthood. This increase in strength is closely associated with increased size of the muscle. During childhood and adolescence, differences due to age and gender are very small or nonexistent when strength is expressed per unit of muscle cross-sectional area (kilograms per square centimeter).

Strength decreases slowly during adulthood primarily due to a loss of muscle mass.[12] After the fifth decade, strength decreases at a greater rate, but even at age 60 the loss does not usually exceed 10 to 20 percent of the young adult level (see Figure 19.2). In older adults, there may also be a decrease in strength per unit of muscle cross-sectional area when compared with young adults due to fewer actin–myosin cross-bridges per unit of muscle or less average force produced per cross-bridge.[12]

Endurance. When expressed relative to maximal strength (i.e., 50% of maximal voluntary contraction [MVC]), there is little change with age in the rate of decline in force during a continuous, fatiguing task.[12] This is true for dynamic as well as isometric muscle actions. These findings may be explained by an increase in the proportion of slow-twitch (ST) fibers and loss of fast-twitch (FT) fibers in the muscles of older subjects,[12] although this concept is somewhat controversial.[5]

Functional variables with age. **figure 19.1**

Data have been collected from various subjects, including healthy men. For data on the same function, only one study has been consulted. The values for the 25-year-old subjects = 100 percent. For the older ages the mean values are expressed in percentage of the 25-year-old individuals' values. The values should not be considered normal values but values that illustrate the effect of aging. Note that heart rate and oxygen pulse at a given workload (100 W or 600 kgm • min^{-1}, oxygen uptake about 1.5 L • min^{-1}) are identical throughout the age range covered, but the maximal oxygen uptake, heart rate, cardiac output, etc., decline with age. The data on cardiac output and stroke volume are based on few observations and are therefore uncertain.

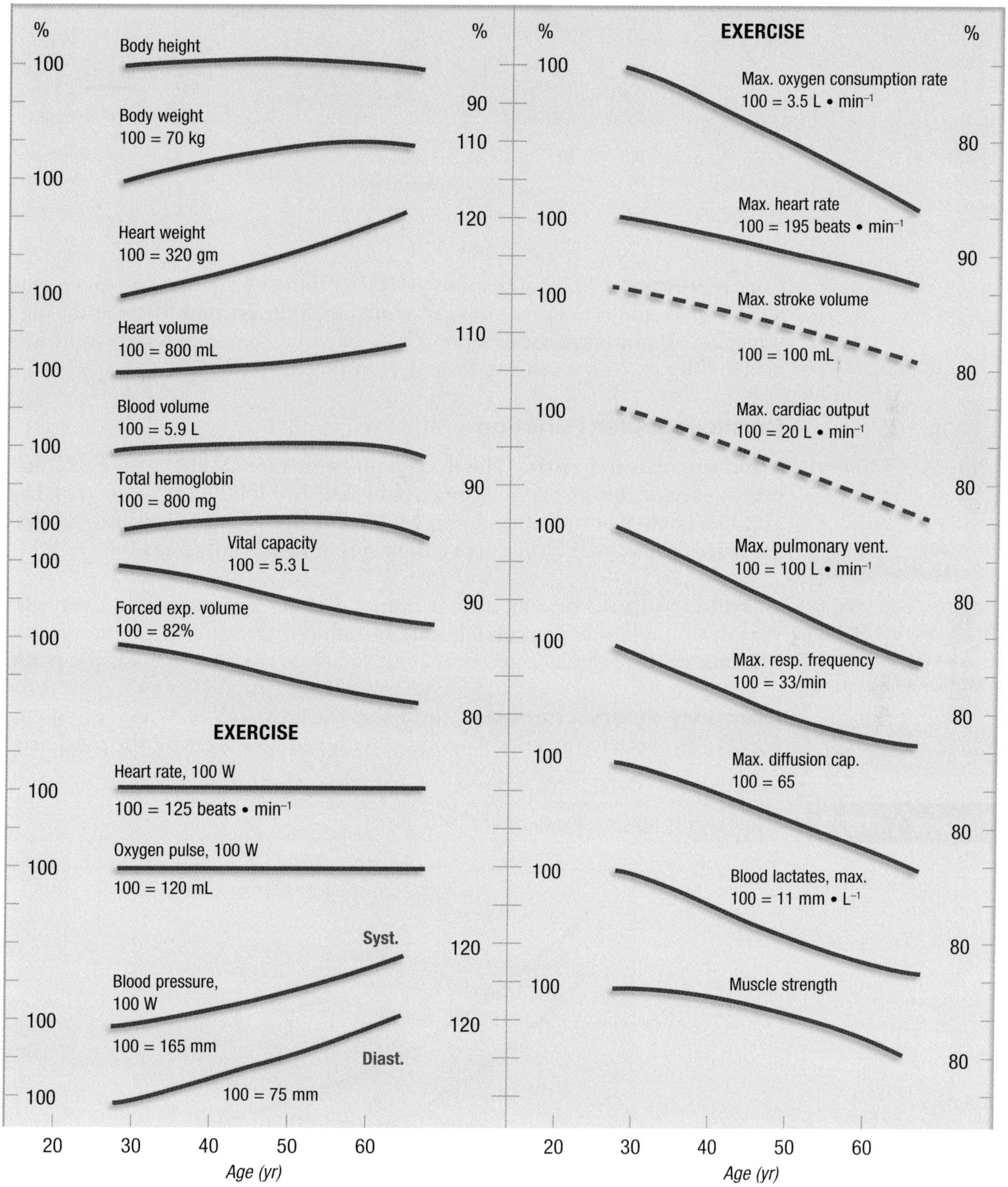

From P.O. Astrand and K. Rodahl, *Textbook of Work Physiology.* Copyright © 1977 McGraw-Hill Book Company. Used with permission.

figure 19.2 Age-related changes in muscular strength for males and females.

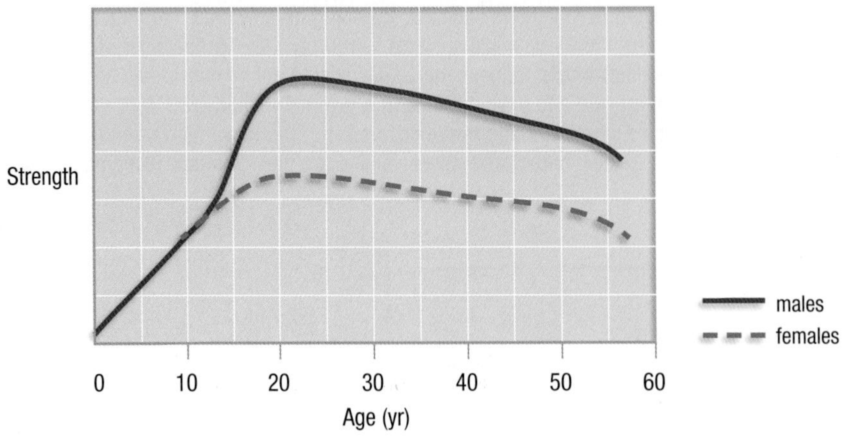

Force–velocity. The maximum velocity produced against any given mass is less for older adults than for younger adults, with the greatest losses at the highest velocities of movement (see Figure 19.3). Larsson[17] reported a 7 percent loss in maximal leg extension velocity from ages in the 20s to the 60s.

Cardiovascular Function

Maximum heart rate. The maximum heart rate (MHR) attainable during exercise decreases with age and can be estimated as: MHR = 220 – age (see Chapter 10). It is likely that the reduction in MHR with age is due to intrinsic changes in the myocardium itself rather than to changes in neural influences.[6]

WWW

Huffington Center on Aging: Geriatric Education and Research
www.bcm.edu/centers/huffington-center-on-aging/

Cardiac output. Resting cardiac output declines approximately 1 percent per year during adulthood, probably due to reduced strength of the myocardium. Maximal cardiac output decreases at a rate similar to that of resting cardiac output.[13]

Coronary artery changes. Normally, the cross-sectional area of the lumen (cavity) of coronary arteries is reduced with age. On average, the total arterial

figure 19.3 Force–velocity curves for younger and older adults.

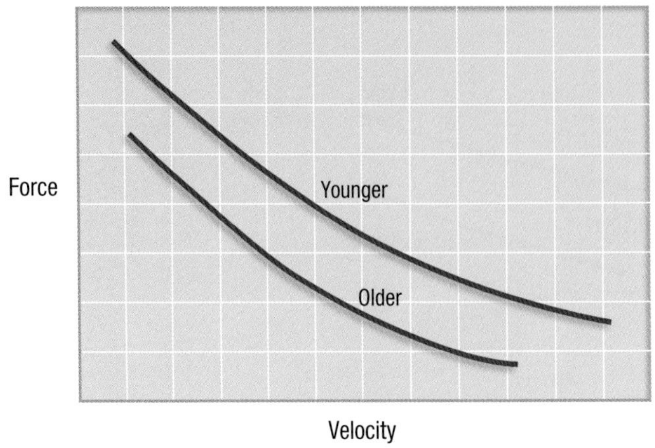

Type of exercise and osteoporosis

Osteoporosis, a progressive skeletal condition involving the deterioration of bone tissue and low bone mass, commonly occurs with aging and is a major public health problem. It is thought to affect approximately 200 million women worldwide. The incidence of osteoporosis is increasing due to an increase in women's life expectancy and the increasingly sedentary nature of older adults. The main concerns regarding osteoporosis are the increased susceptibility to fracture and the morbidity and mortality associated with these fractures. Mechanical loading appears to have positive side-effects on the skeleton, and many studies have shown that exercise can improve both muscle and bone mass, reducing the risk of falls and the fractures associated with them.

Basat et al.* were interested in determining the type of exercise training that had the greatest potential to reduce the incidence of osteoporosis. They examined 42 postmenopausal women who were assigned to one of three groups: strength exercise, high-impact exercise, or control. Bone mineral density of the lumbar spine and femoral neck, serum bone turnover markers, and quality of life were assessed before and after six months of each intervention. The subjects were asked to continue their normal activities throughout the study. The subjects in the control group were asked not to participate in any type of exercise training program. All of the subjects were given a daily supplement of calcium (1200 mg) and vitamin D (800 IU) to ensure an adequate intake. The subjects in the strength exercise training group performed 40 to 60 minutes of isometric strengthening exercises of the legs and abdomen three times per week for six months, while the subjects in the high-impact exercise training group participated in a progressive jump rope training program that started with 10 jumps per day^{-1} and progressed 5 jumps per day^{-1} to a maximum of 50 jumps per day^{-1}.

The bone mineral density in the lumbar spine and the femoral neck increased in both the strength exercise group and the high-impact exercise group. There was a decrease in the bone mineral density of the lumbar spine and femoral neck in the control group. Between-groups comparisons indicated that the only significant difference was between the high-impact and control groups. There was also a significant increase in bone formation markers in both the strength and high-impact exercise groups, but no significant increase in the control group. Between-groups comparisons revealed a significant difference between only the high-impact and control groups. In addition, quality of life, which was assessed using the Quality of Life Questionnaire of the European Foundation for Osteoporosis-41, indicated that both the strength and high-impact training groups improved their quality of life scores to a significantly greater degree than the control group. The results of this study indicate that six months of high-impact training can be effective in preventing bone loss and that both strength training and high-impact exercise training can play a role in improving the quality of life in postmenopausal women.

*Basat, H., Esmaeilzadeh, S., and Eskiyurt, N. The effects of strengthening and high-impact exercises on bone metabolism and quality of life in postmenopausal women: a randomized controlled trial. *J. Back and Musculoskeletal Rehab.* 26: 427–435, 2013.

cross-section that is open to blood flow decreases by about 30 percent from young adulthood to 60 years of age.

Circulatory changes. There appear to be no significant differences in the blood flow to the extremities at rest or in the vasomotor reflex responses to warming and cooling between healthy younger and older adults. Blood flow during exercise, however, is markedly less in the older than in the younger subjects,[28] although blood pressure shows a greater response in older adults than in younger subjects.[22] Lower flow with greater pressure is probably due to increased peripheral resistance.

WWW

Cardiovascular Response to Exercise

http://courses.washington.edu/conj/heart/exercise.htm

Maximal oxygen consumption rate ($\dot{V}O_2$ max). For adults of both genders, maximal oxygen consumption rate ($\dot{V}O_2$ max) declines gradually with age. On average, the rate of decline in $\dot{V}O_2$ max is approximately 9 to 15 percent per decade.[3,26] The decline in $\dot{V}O_2$ max with age is associated with decreases in maximal heart rate, cardiac output, and stroke volume as well as reduced oxygen extraction from the blood by working muscles.[26]

Pulmonary Function

Lung volumes and capacities. Vital capacity declines with age. There is no change in total lung capacity, however, and consequently residual volume increases with age. Thus, aging increases the ratio of residual volume to total lung capacity. In addition, anatomic dead space increases with age.

Thoracic wall compliance. Some tissues of the lungs and chest wall have the property of elasticity. Thus, in inspiration, the muscles must work against this elasticity, which then aids the expiration phase through elastic recoil. This relationship between force required (elastic force) per unit stretch of the thorax is called **thoracic wall compliance.** It is measured by the size of the ratio of volume change per unit pressure change and may be thought of as the elastic resistance to breathing. That is to say, the less compliant the tissues, the more elastic force must be overcome in breathing. Two tissues offer elastic resistance to breathing: the lung tissue itself and the wall of the thoracic cage. Lung compliance increases with age, but more importantly, thoracic wall compliance decreases.[25] Thus, older individuals do more elastic work at a given level of ventilation than their younger counterparts, and most of the additional work is performed in moving the chest wall.

thoracic wall compliance

Pulmonary diffusion. A significant decrease in the capacity for pulmonary diffusion both at rest and during exercise accompanies aging.

Ventilatory mechanics in exercise. The process of breathing becomes less efficient with age. Interestingly, there is a difference in the mechanics by which older subjects meet the increased ventilatory demand of exercise. Whereas the young first increase breathing frequency, older subjects tend to increase the volume of air inspired per breath or tidal volume.

Nervous System Function

Aging results in slowing of reaction time and speed of movement. Psychomotor slowing is probably an effect of the aging of the central nervous system, because the slowing is common to several sensory modalities and to several motor pathways.

Cerebral function is much more vulnerable to circulatory deficits than are most tissues. The brain must have a constant source of oxygen, and it cannot function anaerobically (as can muscle tissue, for instance). For this reason it is tempting to associate the effects of aging with a decreased cerebral blood flow and with the resulting hypoxia. However, when the effects of aging per se have been separated from the effects of **arteriosclerosis** (hardening of the arteries), which frequently accompanies the aging process, it appears to be arteriosclerosis that is at fault. Aging per se, in the absence of arteriosclerotic changes, probably does not result in circulatory or metabolic changes in cerebral function.

arteriosclerosis

Body Composition

It is typical for aging humans to increase their body weight and percent body fat, but to decrease fat-free weight.[3] To maintain a constant proportion of body fat as one ages, weight must not merely be maintained at a constant level, it must be decreased. It is conceivable, however, that the rate of loss in fat-free weight represents disuse atrophy of muscle tissue that can be reduced or avoided through vigorous activity.

Exercise frequency and bone, muscle, and cardiovascular risk factors

It is generally accepted that physical activity is associated with improved health and well-being throughout the life span. However, because most investigations into the effects of exercise on health in older adults focus on only one disease or risk factor, it is difficult to generalize regarding the impact of exercise on improving the overall health in this population. It is also difficult to determine how often exercise must be performed to achieve these health benefits. The primary general health issues affecting older adults are related to muscle mass, bone metabolism or falls risk, and cardiovascular events such as stroke and heart attack. A retrospective analysis that focused on the effects of a combination of aerobic, resistance, and balance exercise on various risk factors in older women indicated that an average exercise frequency of two to four sessions per week over 18 months had a favorable effect on a range of important risk factors and diseases of these women. The risk factors included those associated with both muscle and bone mass as well as coronary heart disease.[16]

Stature

On average, we grow shorter as we grow older. The average rate of loss in stature is about one-half inch per decade after age 40.[8]

PHYSICAL CONDITIONING AND AGE

The age-related changes in physiological functioning described thus far can only be said to accompany the aging process. Causal relationships have not been established. We can infer that changes in these various functional capacities with increasing age may result from a combination of at least three factors: (1) true aging phenomena, (2) unrecognized disease processes whose incidence and severity increase with age, and (3) disuse phenomena or the increasing sedentariness of our lifestyle as we grow older. We can do little to modify the first two factors, but the sedentary lifestyle can be modified through physical activity and conditioning.

It is clear that even a modest amount of physical activity can substantially improve the physical capabilities of most older adults. While improvement in physical capabilities may not add years to our life, it most certainly does add life to our years. The improvement of physical capabilities is tantamount to increasing the vigor of the older individual, and this can make a very important contribution to the later years of life, certainly in terms of lifestyle and possibly even in terms of health.[27]

The physiological bases for the improvement in physical capabilities in older adults with exercise training are still being studied. Clearly, however, older adults respond to training, and the capacity for improvement, as a percentage of current capabilities, is probably not greatly different from that of younger individuals. The capacity for maximum achievement is, of course, compromised since the older subject starts from a lower level. It is undeniable that some decline in physical capabilities accompanies advanced age, but it is equally as true that the decline can be slowed or ameliorated by a sensible program of physical activity. To this end, Hurley and Hagberg[14] have stated, "Perhaps the best concluding recommendation we can provide to older adults who want a program to optimize their current and future health is to initiate a well-rounded physical activity program, one that includes both AT [aerobic training] and ST [strength training] and probably also incorporates specific flexibility and balance exercises." Table 10.4 (p. 199) provides health-related physical activity guidelines for older adults (greater than or equal to 65 years of age).

WWW

Physical Fitness and Older Adults

www.cdc.gov/physicalactivity/basics/older_adults/index.htm

Aerobic Training for Older Adults

Aerobic training in older adults can have beneficial effects on health and physical performance. Table 19.1 lists some of the potential benefits. With regard to health, aerobic training can improve blood lipid profiles (circulating triglyceride and cholesterol levels), improve glucose tolerance, reduce body fatness, decrease hypertension, increase bone mineral density, and reduce the risk of falls. In addition, aerobic training in older adults can increase endurance capacity, reduce fatigue during daily living tasks, and increase vigor.

Older adults respond positively to aerobic training. An appropriately designed program of physical activity can be expected to result in an increase in $\dot{V}O_2$ max in older men and women. The Astrand–Rhyming Submaximal Cycle Ergometer Test (see **Chapter 19 Lab**) can be used to estimate changes in $\dot{V}O_2$ max. Furthermore, relative increases in $\dot{V}O_2$ max from aerobic training are similar in younger and older adults.[3] It is not necessary, however, for older adults to perform a highly structured, vigorous exercise training program to enjoy many of the health-related benefits associated with aerobic conditioning. For health-related benefits, they should be encouraged to meet the standards in Table 10.4 (p. 199).

Muscle-Strengthening and Resistance Training for Older Adults

Data from the Framingham Study indicate that 40 percent of women between ages 55 and 64, almost 45 percent of women age 65 to 74, and 65 percent of women between 75 and 84 years were unable to lift a 10-lb weight.[15] Of even greater concern is that studies of independent-living-aged persons show that though rising from a chair unassisted required only 50 percent of the knee extensor strength of a young adult, the task often exceeds 100 percent of the strength of an 80-year-old.[29] The ability to perform this and other daily living tasks such as housework, yard work, and self-care requires adequate muscle strength.

Older individuals respond favorably to muscle-strengthening activities.[2,3,10,11] Table 19.2 lists some of the potential benefits of muscle-strengthening activities in older adults. Resistance training results in considerable increases in muscle strength for these individuals. In fact, when expressed as percentage increases,

table 19.1 Potential benefits of aerobic training in older adults.

FACTOR	RESPONSE
Maximal oxygen consumption rate ($\dot{V}O_2$ max)	increase
Resting metabolic rate	increase
Triglycerides	decrease
High-density lipoprotein (HDL)	increase
HDL/total cholesterol ratio	increase
Glucose tolerance	improve
Blood pressure (in hypertensives)	decrease
Abdominal fat stores	decrease
Bone mineral density	increase or maintain
Risk of falls	decrease

Potential benefits of muscle-strengthening activities in older adults. **table 19.2**

FACTOR	RESPONSE
Isometric strength	increase
Dynamic constant external resistance (DCER) strength	increase
Isokinetic strength	increase
Muscle cross-sectional area	increase
Muscle fiber size (fast-twitch and slow-twitch)	increase
Bone mineral density	increase
Percent body fat	decrease
Abdominal fat stores	decrease
Daily living tasks	improve
Flexibility	increase or no change
Risk of falls	decrease
Resting metabolic rate	increase
Glucose tolerance	improve

younger and older subjects exhibit approximately the same increases in strength, even though the young make greater absolute gains.[3,21] Muscle-strengthening activities can be in the form of a structured resistance training program or activities of daily living (Table 10.4). Table 19.3 provides examples of muscle-strengthening and resistance training programs for older adults.

Resistance training also leads to increased muscle size in older adults. For many years it was believed that strength increases in young adults resulted from neural adaptations as well as hypertrophy, while in older adults, hypertrophy did not occur and training-induced increases in strength were due almost entirely to neural factors.[21] Recent studies using sensitive techniques such as computer tomography and magnetic resonance imaging, however, have found considerable hypertrophy in older men and women up to age 96.[4,7,9,11] It is also clear that resistance training can bring about hypertrophy of both fast-twitch and slow-twitch muscle fibers in these individuals.[18]

Musculoskeletal Injuries and Physical Activity in Older Adults

Despite the well-recognized benefits of physical conditioning discussed throughout this text, more and more exercise physiologists have become concerned about the incidence of injury, especially in older adults. Foot and ankle joint injuries are more common in this population, and the incidence of osteoarthritis is 2.5 times more common in older adults than in younger populations.[20] Pollock and colleagues[24] also urge caution in the use of strength testing and jogging for these individuals. Manfredi et al.[19] suggest that eccentric exercise is even more damaging to their muscles. Thus, for older adults it is important to have medical clearance before beginning an aerobic or strength training program, and the programs should progress slowly based on the subjects' tolerance levels.

table 19.3 Examples of muscle-strengthening and resistance training programs for older adults.[10]

BEGINNING HOME MUSCLE-STRENGTHENING PROGRAM
For upper body exercises, use soup cans or light resistance (2- to 5-lb hand dumbbells).
Perform 1 to 3 sets of 8 to 10 repetitions.
Take 1 to 2 minutes of rest between sets and exercises.
Concentrate on full range of motion movement and balance. A wall or solid chair can be used for help with balance in the beginning. Keep head up.
Exercises: Front shoulder raise, wall push-up, standing single knee lift, toe raise, arm curl, good morning exercise, side bend, standing knee curls, single arm shoulder press, 1/4 squat, single bent-over arm row, side shoulder raise, triceps extension
Program note: This is a light-resistance, calisthenic-type program to gain basic movement and range of motion abilities. Progression to heavier resistances, especially for the lower body musculature, is vital for optimal progression.
BEGINNING RESISTANCE TRAINING PROGRAM
Exercises: leg press, knee extension, knee curl, calf raise, chest press, seated row or lat pull-down, upright row, arm curl, trunk curl, triceps extension
Order of exercises: Large to small muscle group exercises, upper to lower or opposing muscle groups
Resistance used: 80% of 1 repetition maximum load (RM) or 10 to 15 RM
Number of sets: Start out with 1 and progress to 3 over a 12-week program.
Rest between sets and exercises: 1 to 3 minutes or until recovered.
PERIODIZED RESISTANCE TRAINING PROGRAM FOR LONG-TERM USE
Use a 12-week periodized cycle (e.g., Monday, Wednesday, Friday; see Chapter 11 for information on periodization), followed by an active rest of 2 weeks, and then repeat the cycle with appropriate variation in the program variables based on individual training goals and needs.
Exercises: Leg press or squat, knee extension, knee curl, calf raise, chest press, seated row, upright row, arm curl
Order of exercises: Large to small muscle group exercises
Resistance used: 8 to 10 RM (Mon.), 6 to 8 RM (Wed.), 12 to 15 RM (Fri.)
Number of sets: Start out with 1 and progress to 3 over the 12-week cycle.
Rest between sets and exercises: 1 to 2 minutes (Mon.), 2 to 3 minutes (Wed.), 1 to 2 minutes (Fri.).

Adapted from Fleck, S.J., and Kraemer, W.J. *Designing Resistance Training Programs,* 3rd edition. Champaign, IL: Human Kinetics, 2004, pp. 303–323.

summary

Older adults make up the fastest-growing proportion of the American population. Physiological functioning and physical performance tend to increase throughout childhood and adolescence, then decline during adulthood. Typically during adulthood there are decreases in strength, maximal heart rate, cardiac output, vital capacity, $\dot{V}O_2$ max, reaction time, speed of movement, stature, and muscle mass. These declines are associated with age-related decreases in physical activity and degenerative disease processes, as well as the aging process.

Regular physical activity can reduce the rate of decline in physical performance and physiological functioning that occurs with age. Older adults should be encouraged to initiate aerobic and muscle-strengthening programs.

Older adults respond favorably to both aerobic and resistance training. For example, aerobic training can be beneficial to health by improving blood lipid profiles and glucose tolerance, reducing body fatness and the risk of falls, and decreasing blood pressure in hypertensives. Physical performance may improve through increases in $\dot{V}O_2$ max and reduced fatigue.

Resistance training increases strength and muscle mass in older adults. In addition, resistance training can increase bone mineral density and resting metabolic rate while decreasing body fatness and the risk of falls.

questions for review

1. Discuss the physiological changes associated with aging. How can exercise slow this process?
2. Discuss the interrelationships among the aging process, a decline in physical activity with age, and degenerative disease processes.
3. What are the benefits of an aerobic training program for older adults?
4. As an exercise professional, what recommendations would you give to an older adult beginning an aerobic training program?
5. What are the benefits of resistance training for older adults?
6. Design a resistance training program for a sedentary 65-year-old. Include specific exercises, repetitions, sets, rest intervals, and frequency.
7. While exercise has many known health benefits, what factors may limit its potential to decrease disability among older adults?
8. What strategies would you recommend for optimizing bone mineral density in premenopausal women?

student companion website

For further review of this book's chapters and for test preparation, visit the book's website, **www.hhpcommunities.com/exercisephysiology**, to take practice quizzes, review the vocabulary terms, use the study guide, and view the digital image bank.

references

1. American College of Sports Medicine. *ACSM's Guidelines for Exercise Testing and Prescription,* 9th edition. Baltimore: Wolters Kluwer/Lippincott Williams & Wilkins, 2014.
2. American College of Sports Medicine Position Stand. Exercise and physical activity for older adults. *Med. Sci. Sports Exerc.* 41: 1510–1530, 2009.
3. American College of Sports Medicine Position Stand. The recommended quantity and quality of exercise for developing and maintaining cardiorespiratory and muscular fitness, and flexibility in healthy adults. *Med. Sci. Sports Exerc.* 30: 975–991, 1998.
4. Brown, A. B., McCartney, N., and Sale, D. G. Positive adaptations to weight-lifting training in the elderly. *J. Appl. Physiol.* 69: 1725–1733, 1990.
5. Cartee, G. D. Aging skeletal muscle: Response to exercise. In *Exercise and Sport Sciences Reviews*, ed. J. O. Holloszy. Baltimore: Williams & Wilkins, 1994, pp. 91–120.
6. Corre, K. A., Cho, H., and Barnard, R. J. Maximum exercise heart rate reduction with maturation in the rat. *J. Appl. Physiol.* 40: 741–744, 1976.
7. Craig, B. W., Brown, R., and Everhart, J. The effects of progressive resistance training on growth hormone and

testosterone levels in young and elderly subjects. *Mech. Aging Dev.* 49: 159–169, 1989.

8. DeQueker, J. V., Baeyens, J. P., and Claessens, J. The significance of stature as a clinical measurement of aging. *J. Am. Geriatr. Soci.* 17: 169–179, 1969.
9. Fiatarone, M. A., Marks, E. C., Ryan, N. D., Meredith, C. N., Lipsitz, L. A., and Evans, W. J. High intensity strength training in nonagenarians. *JAMA* 263: 3029–3034, 1990.
10. Fleck, S. J., and Kraemer, W. J. *Designing Resistance Training Programs,* 3rd edition. Champaign, IL: Human Kinetics, 2004, pp. 303–323.
11. Frontera, W. R., Meredith, C. N., O'Reilly, K. P., Knuttgen, H. G., and Evans, W. J. Strength conditioning in older men: Skeletal muscle hypertrophy and improved function. *J. Appl. Physiol.* 64: 1038–1044, 1988.
12. Grabiner, M. D., and Enoka, R. M. Changes in movement capabilities with aging. In *Exercise and Sport Sciences Review,* ed. J. O. Holloszy. Baltimore: Williams & Wilkins, 1995, pp. 65–104.
13. Hossack, K. F., and Bruce, R. A. Maximal cardiac function in sedentary normal men and women: Comparison of age-related changes. *J. Appl. Physiol.* 53: 799–804, 1982.
14. Hurley, B. F., and Hagberg, J. M. Optimizing health in older persons: Aerobic or strength training? In *Exercise and Sport Sciences Reviews,* ed. J. O. Holloszy. Baltimore: Williams & Wilkins, 1998, pp. 61–89.
15. Jette, A. M., and Branch, L. G. The Framingham Disability Study II: Physical disability in the aging. *Am. J. Public Health* 71: 1211–1216, 1981.
16. Kemmler, W., and von Stengel, S. Exercise frequency, health risk factors, and diseases of the elderly. *Arch. Phys. Med. Rehab.* 94: 2046–2053, 2013.
17. Larsson, L. Morphological and functional characteristics of aging skeletal muscle in man. *Acta Physiol. Scand. Suppl.* 457, 1978.
18. Larsson, L. Physical training effects on muscle morphology in sedentary males at different ages. *Med. Sci. Sports Exerc.* 14: 203–206, 1982.
19. Manfredi, G., Fielding, R. A., O'Reilly, K. P., Meredith, C. N., Lee, H. Y., and Evans, W. J. Plasma creatine kinase activity and exercise induced muscle damage in older men. *Med. Sci. Sports Exerc.* 23: 1028–1034, 1991.
20. Matheson, G. O., McIntyre, J. G., Taunton, J. E., Clement, D. B., and Lloyd-Smith, R. Musculoskeletal injuries associated with physical activity in older adults. *Med. Sci. Sports Exerc.* 21: 379–385, 1989.
21. Moritani, T., and deVries, H. A. Neural factors versus hypertrophy in the time course of muscle strength gain in young and old men. *J. Geront.* 36: 294–297, 1981.
22. Palmer, G. J., Ziegler, M. G., and Lake, C. R. Response of norepinephrine and blood pressure to stress increases with age. *J. Geront.* 33: 482–487, 1978.
23. Pate, R. R., Prat, M., Blair, S. N., et al. Physical activity and public health, a recommendation from the Centers for Disease Control and Prevention and the American College of Sports Medicine. *JAMA* 273: 402–407, 1995.
24. Pollock, M. L., Carroll, J. F., Graves, J. E., Leggett, S. H., Braith, R. W., Limacher, M., and Hagberg, J. M. Injuries and adherence to walk–jog and resistance training programs in the elderly. *Med. Sci. Sports Exerc.* 23: 1194–1200, 1991.
25. Rizzato, G., and Marazzini, L. Thoracoabdominal mechanics in elderly men. *J. Appl. Physiol.* 28: 457–460, 1970.
26. Spina, R.J. Cardiovascular adaptations to endurance exercise training in older men and women. In *Exercise and Sport Sciences Reviews,* ed. J. O. Holloszy. Philadelphia: Lippincott Williams & Wilkins, 1999, pp. 317–332.
27. Spirduso, W. W., and Cronin, D. L. Exercise dose–response effects on quality of life and independent living in older adults. *Med. Sci. Sports Exerc.* 33: S598–S608, 2001.
28. Wahren, J., Saltin, B., Jorfeldt, L., and Pernow, B. Influence of age on the local circulatory adaptation to leg exercise. *Scand. J. Clin. Lab. Invest.* 33: 79–86, 1974.
29. Young, A. Exercise physiology in geriatric practice. *Acta Med. Scand. Suppl.* 711: 227–232, 1987.

CHAPTER 19

lab

Astrand-Rhyming Submaximal Cycle Ergometer Test (Modified) to Estimate $\dot{V}O_2$ max

BACKGROUND

Endurance capabilities are reflected in one's ability to take in and utilize oxygen. Oxygen is a crucial factor in the operation of the electron transport system, where the production of large quantities of adenosine triphosphate (ATP) occurs as a result of oxidative metabolism. The ability to sustain moderate- to high-intensity exercise for appreciable lengths of time is based on the rate at which ATP can be produced by oxidative means. Consequently, this rate will be reflected by the rate at which oxygen is consumed (taken in and utilized): oxygen consumption rate or $\dot{V}O_2$. One means of describing the cardiorespiratory endurance fitness level of an individual is by determining maximal oxygen consumption rate ($\dot{V}O_2$ max).

As one performs heavier power outputs on a cycle ergometer, both oxygen consumption rate and heart rate (HR) increase. Oxygen consumption rate increases because the demands of the work require increased production of energy and increased HR to transport oxygen and fuels to the active muscle tissues and remove their metabolic waste products more rapidly. The relationship of power output to oxygen consumption rate remains fairly constant between individuals, as well as within an individual at different times. Therefore, when we know the power output, the corresponding oxygen consumption rate can be predicted with reasonable accuracy (± about 10%). However, the proportion to which HR increases in comparison to either power output or oxygen consumption rate will vary between individuals or within an individual based on level of fitness (endurance capability).

The ability to predict $\dot{V}O_2$ max is based on the fact that the heart pumps more efficiently and oxygen is more readily utilized for metabolism in individuals with higher maximal oxygen consumption capabilities. We can refer to this as increased cardiovascular efficiency, since the heart doesn't have to work as hard (HR is lower) to meet the metabolic demands of a task. Therefore, if two individuals are performing at the same power output (requiring the same rate of oxygen consumption), the individual with the higher $\dot{V}O_2$ max will tend to have a lower HR. The basis of the Astrand–Rhyming Test (named for the distinguished scientists who developed the test, the married couple P. O. Astrand and I. Rhyming) is to make use of this relationship.[2]

In essence, we would expect that if two individuals were to work such that similar HRs result (say 150 bpm), the individual with the higher $\dot{V}O_2$ max will actually be performing more physical work (again, this reflects cardiovascular efficiency). Therefore, the basic procedure of the test is to have an individual work at moderate intensity (HR = 120–170 bpm) and record both the HR and the power output. Using these two pieces of data, we can estimate $\dot{V}O_2$ max (± 10–15% error) from previously determined relationships available in Tables L19.1 and L19.2. The preliminary $\dot{V}O_2$ max value must then be corrected for age. This laboratory experience will help you become familiar with the procedures and supportive principles of this basic mode of fitness testing. In addition, you should be able to interpret the results of such testing in terms of fitness levels.

TERMS & ABBREVIATIONS

- kgm • min^{-1} = kilogram meters per minute
- HR = heart rate
- $\dot{V}O_2$ = oxygen consumption rate; an indirect measure of aerobic ATP production
- $\dot{V}O_2$ max = maximal oxygen consumption rate

PROCEDURES

1. Set the seat height on the Monark cycle ergometer (see photo 19.1) for near full extension of the subject's legs while pedaling.
2. Have the subject warm up at 50 revolutions per minute (rpm) for 3 to 5 minutes at zero resistance. A metronome or digital pedal cadence recorder should be used to ensure proper rate of pedaling (see photo 19.2).
3. Set the first power output at 600 to 900 kgm • min^{-1} (approximately 100–150 watts). Determine this by multiplying the pedal cadence (always 50 for this test) × 6 (distance in meters the flywheel on the Monark cycle ergometer travels in one revolution) × resistance setting (see photo 19.3). Thus, a resistance setting of 2 kg at 50 rpm is equal to 600 kgm • min^{-1} (2 kg × 50 rpm × 6 m).
4. Start the 6-minute test as soon as the correct pedaling cadence and power output are achieved (see photo 19.4).
5. Measure and record the 30-second HR for the last 30 seconds of each of minutes 2 through 6. Record data on Worksheet 19.1.
6. At the end of the third minute, adjust the power output (up or down) if it is not likely that the subject will be in the target HR zone (120–170 bpm) at the end of the 6-minute test.
7. If the subject has not reached a steady-state HR by the end of the 6 minutes, extend the test until the difference between consecutive minutes is less than 10 bpm. The last two HR values should be averaged to use in calculations.
8. Allow the subject to cool down (see photo 19.5).

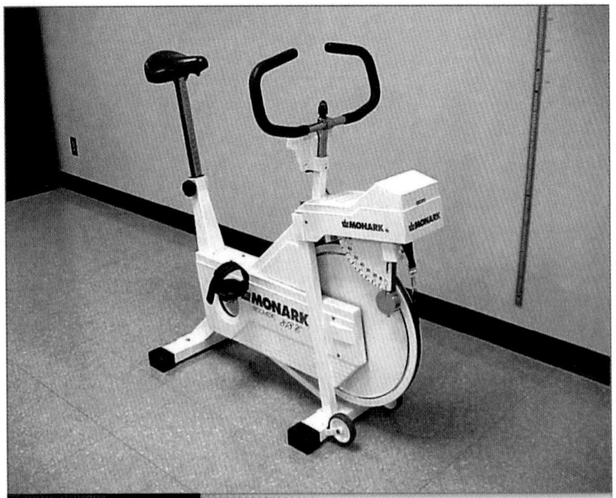

photo 19.1

Monark cycle ergometer.

photo 19.2

Have the subject warm up at 50 rpm for three to five minutes at zero resistance.

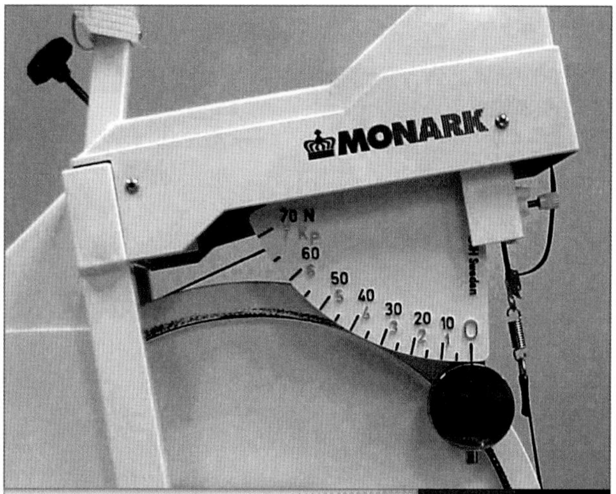

photo 19.3

Resistance setting on the Monark cycle ergometer.

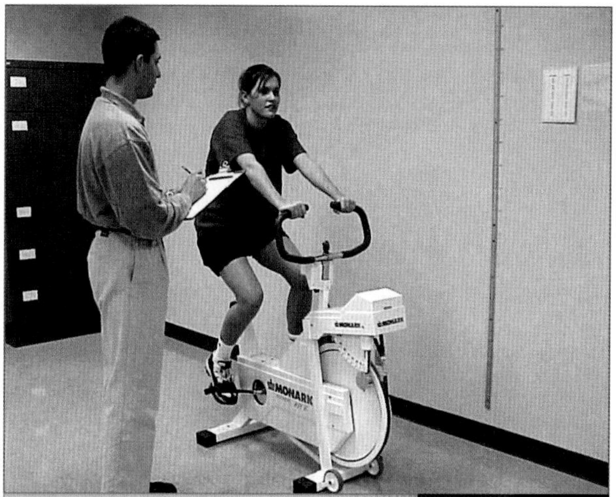

photo 19.4

Start the six-minute test as soon as the subject achieves the power output.

SAMPLE CALCULATIONS

If a 20-year-old, 154-pound male had an average HR of 150 bpm during the last 2 minutes of a 900 kgm • min^{-1} power output (3 kg resistance at 50 rpm), his values would be:

a. Preliminary $\dot{V}O_2$ max value from Table L19.1*
   = 3.2 L • min^{-1}

b. 3.2 × 1.07 (age correction factor, Table L19.3)
   = 3.425 L • min^{-1}

c. 3.425 L • min^{-1} × 1000 = 3425 mL • min^{-1}

d. $\dot{V}O_2$ max = (3425 mL • min^{-1}) / 70 kg
   = 48.9 mL • kg^{-1} • min^{-1} (body weight
   = 154 lbs / 2.2046 = 70 kg)

e. Fitness category (Table L19.4) = excellent

* Table L19.2 would be used if the subject were female.

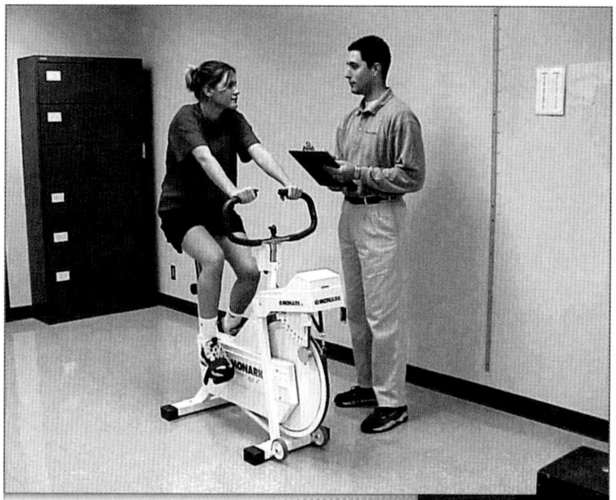

photo 19.5

Allow the subject to cool down.

table L19.1 Males' maximal oxygen consumption rate (L • min^{-1}) predicted from cycle ergometer test.[1]

	POWER OUTPUT (KGM • MIN^{-1})									
HR	150	300	450	600	750	900	1050	1200	1350	1500
120	1.6	2.2	2.8	3.5	4.1	4.8	5.6			
121	1.6	2.2	2.8	3.4	4.0	4.7	5.5			
122	1.6	2.2	2.8	3.4	4.0	4.6	5.4			
123		2.1	2.7	3.4	3.9	4.6	5.3			
124		2.1	2.7	3.3	3.9	4.5	5.2	6.0		
125		2.0	2.6	3.2	3.8	4.4	5.1	5.9		
126		2.0	2.6	3.2	3.8	4.4	5.1	5.8		
127		2.0	2.5	3.1	3.7	4.3	5.0	5.7		
128		2.0	2.5	3.1	3.6	4.2	4.9	5.6		
129		1.9	2.4	3.0	3.6	4.2	4.8	5.6		
130		1.9	2.4	3.0	3.5	4.1	4.8	5.5		
131		1.9	2.4	2.9	3.5	4.0	4.7	5.4		
132		1.8	2.3	2.9	3.4	4.0	4.6	5.3	6.0	
133		1.8	2.3	2.8	3.4	3.9	4.6	5.3	5.9	
134		1.8	2.3	2.8	3.3	3.9	4.5	5.2	5.8	
135		1.7	2.3	2.8	3.3	3.8	4.4	5.1	5.7	
136		1.7	2.2	2.7	3.2	3.8	4.4	5.0	5.6	
137		1.7	2.2	2.7	3.2	3.7	4.3	5.0	5.6	
138		1.6	2.2	2.7	3.2	3.7	4.3	4.9	5.5	
139		1.6	2.1	2.6	3.1	3.6	4.2	4.8	5.4	
140		1.6	2.1	2.6	3.1	3.6	4.2	4.8	5.4	6.0
141			2.1	2.6	3.0	3.5	4.1	4.7	5.3	5.9
142			2.1	2.5	3.0	3.5	4.1	4.6	5.2	5.8
143			2.0	2.5	2.9	3.4	4.0	4.6	5.2	5.7
144			2.0	2.5	2.9	3.4	4.0	4.5	5.1	5.7
145			2.0	2.4	2.9	3.4	3.9	4.5	5.0	5.6
146			2.0	2.4	2.8	3.3	3.9	4.4	5.0	5.6
147			2.0	2.4	2.8	3.3	3.8	4.4	4.9	5.5
148			1.9	2.4	2.8	3.2	3.8	4.3	4.9	5.4
149			1.9	2.3	2.7	3.2	3.7	4.3	4.8	5.4
150			1.9	2.3	2.7	3.2	3.7	4.2	4.8	5.3
151			1.9	2.3	2.7	3.1	3.7	4.2	4.7	5.2
152				2.3	2.7	3.1	3.6	4.1	4.6	5.2
153				2.2	2.6	3.0	3.6	4.1	4.6	5.1
154				2.2	2.6	3.0	3.5	4.0	4.5	5.1
155				2.2	2.6	3.0	3.5	4.0	4.5	5.0
156				2.2	2.5	2.9	3.4	4.0	4.4	5.0
157				2.1	2.5	2.9	3.4	3.9	4.4	4.9
158				2.1	2.5	2.9	3.4	3.9	4.3	4.9
159				2.1	2.4	2.8	3.3	3.8	4.3	4.8
160				2.1	2.4	2.8	3.3	3.8	4.3	4.8
161				2.0	2.4	2.8	3.2	3.7	4.2	4.7
162				2.0	2.4	2.8	3.2	3.7	4.2	4.6
163				2.0	2.4	2.8	3.2	3.7	4.2	4.6
164				2.0	2.3	2.7	3.1	3.6	4.1	4.5
165				2.0	2.3	2.7	3.1	3.6	4.1	4.5
166				1.9	2.3	2.7	3.1	3.6	4.1	4.5
167				1.9	2.2	2.6	3.0	3.5	4.0	4.4
168				1.9	2.2	2.6	3.0	3.5	4.0	4.4
169				1.9	2.2	2.6	3.0	3.5	3.9	4.3
170				1.8	2.2	2.6	3.0	3.4	3.9	4.3

Note: To convert kgm • min^{-1} to watts, divide by 6.12.

Females' maximal oxygen consumption rate ($L \bullet min^{-1}$) predicted from cycle ergometer test.[1] **table L19.2**

	POWER OUTPUT ($KGM \bullet MIN^{-1}$)					
HR	150	300	450	600	750	900
120	1.8	2.6	3.4	4.1	4.8	
121	1.7	2.5	3.3	4.0	4.8	
122	1.7	2.5	3.2	3.9	4.7	
123	1.7	2.4	3.1	3.9	4.6	
124	1.7	2.4	3.1	3.8	4.5	
125	1.6	2.3	3.0	3.7	4.4	
126	1.6	2.3	3.0	3.6	4.3	
127	1.6	2.2	2.9	3.5	4.2	
128	1.6	2.2	2.8	3.5	4.2	4.8
129	1.6	2.2	2.8	3.4	4.1	4.8
130		2.1	2.7	3.4	4.0	4.7
131		2.1	2.7	3.4	4.0	4.6
132		2.0	2.7	3.3	3.9	4.5
133		2.0	2.6	3.2	3.8	4.4
134		2.0	2.6	3.2	3.8	4.4
135		2.0	2.6	3.1	3.7	4.3
136		1.9	2.5	3.1	3.6	4.2
137		1.9	2.5	3.0	3.6	4.2
138		1.8	2.4	3.0	3.5	4.1
139		1.8	2.4	2.9	3.5	4.0
140		1.8	2.4	2.8	3.4	4.0
141		1.8	2.3	2.8	3.4	3.9
142		1.7	2.3	2.8	3.3	3.9
143		1.7	2.2	2.7	3.3	3.8
144		1.7	2.2	2.7	3.2	3.8
145		1.6	2.2	2.7	3.2	3.7
146		1.6	2.2	2.6	3.2	3.7
147		1.6	2.1	2.6	3.1	3.6
148		1.6	2.1	2.6	3.1	3.6
149			2.1	2.6	3.0	3.5
150			2.0	2.5	3.0	3.5
151			2.0	2.5	3.0	3.4
152			2.0	2.5	2.9	3.4
153			2.0	2.4	2.9	3.3
154			2.0	2.4	2.8	3.3
155			1.9	2.4	2.8	3.2
156			1.9	2.3	2.8	3.2
157			1.9	2.3	2.7	3.2
158			1.8	2.3	2.7	3.1
159			1.8	2.2	2.7	3.1
160			1.8	2.2	2.6	3.0
161			1.8	2.2	2.6	3.0
162			1.8	2.2	2.6	3.0
163			1.7	2.2	2.6	2.9
164			1.7	2.1	2.5	2.9
165			1.7	2.1	2.5	2.9
166			1.7	2.1	2.5	2.8
167			1.6	2.1	2.4	2.8
168			1.6	2.0	2.4	2.8
169			1.6	2.0	2.4	2.8
170			1.6	2.0	2.4	2.7

Note: To convert $kgm \bullet min^{-1}$ to watts, divide by 6.12.

table L19.3 Age correction factors for predicting maximal oxygen consumption rate.[1]

AGE (YRS)	CORRECTION FACTOR
20	1.07
25	1.00
35	0.87
45	0.78
55	0.71
65	0.65

From P. O. Astrand and K. Rodahl, *Textbook of Work Physiology*. Copyright © 1977 McGraw-Hill Book Company. Used with permission.

table L19.4 Men's and women's aerobic fitness classification.[3]

MEN		AGE (YEARS)					
Category	Measure	13-19	20-29	30-39	40-49	50-59	60+
I. Very Poor	$\dot{V}O_2$ max (mL • kg^{-1} • min^{-1})	<35.0	<33.0	<31.5	<30.2	<26.1	<20.5
II. Poor	$\dot{V}O_2$ max (mL • kg^{-1} • min^{-1})	35.0–38.3	33.0–36.4	31.5–35.4	30.2–33.5	26.1–30.9	20.5–26.0
III. Fair	$\dot{V}O_2$ max (mL • kg^{-1} • min^{-1})	38.4–45.1	36.5–42.4	35.5–40.9	33.6–38.9	31.0–35.7	26.1–32.2
IV. Good	$\dot{V}O_2$ max (mL • kg^{-1} • min^{-1})	45.2–50.9	42.5–46.4	41.0–44.9	39.0–43.7	35.8–40.9	32.3–36.4
V. Excellent	$\dot{V}O_2$ max (mL • kg^{-1} • min^{-1})	51.0–55.9	46.5–52.4	45.0–49.4	43.8–48.0	41.0–45.3	36.5–44.2
VI. Superior	$\dot{V}O_2$ max (mL • kg^{-1} • min^{-1})	>56.0	>52.5	>49.5	>48.1	>45.4	>44.3

WOMEN		AGE (YEARS)					
Category	Measure	13-19	20-29	30-39	40-49	50-59	60+
I. Very Poor	$\dot{V}O_2$ max (mL • kg^{-1} • min^{-1})	<25.0	<23.6	<22.8	<21.0	<20.2	<17.5
II. Poor	$\dot{V}O_2$ max (mL • kg^{-1} • min^{-1})	25.0–30.9	23.6–28.9	22.8–26.9	21.0–24.4	20.2–22.7	17.5–20.1
III. Fair	$\dot{V}O_2$ max (mL • kg^{-1} • min^{-1})	31.0–34.9	29.0–32.9	27.0–31.4	24.5–28.9	22.8–26.9	20.2–24.4
IV. Good	$\dot{V}O_2$ max (mL • kg^{-1} • min^{-1})	35.0–38.9	33.0–36.9	31.5–35.6	29.0–32.8	27.0–31.4	24.5–30.2
V. Excellent	$\dot{V}O_2$ max (mL • kg^{-1} • min^{-1})	39.0–41.9	37.0–40.9	35.7–40.0	32.9–36.9	31.5–35.7	30.3–31.4
VI. Superior	$\dot{V}O_2$ max (mL • kg^{-1} • min^{-1})	>42.0	>41.0	>40.1	>37.0	>35.8	>31.5

From Cooper, Kenneth H. *The Aerobics Way.* Toronto: Bantam Books, 1977, pp. 280–281. Printed with permission of Kenneth H. Cooper, MD, MPH, www.cooperaerobics.com.

ASTRAND-RHYMING TEST FORM worksheet 19.1

NAME ____________________ DATE ____________________

BODY WEIGHT ____________________ GENDER ____________________

Minute	Heart rate for last 30 seconds of the time interval	Power output
2	________________	________
3	________________	
4	________________	________
5	________________	
6	________________	
Use if needed		
7	________________	
8	________________	

Initial power output ____________

Adjusted power output (if applicable) ____________

Average HR for last 2 minutes of test ____________

a. Preliminary $\dot{V}O_2$ max value from Table L19.1 or L19.2: ____________ L • min^{-1}
b. Multiply preliminary $\dot{V}O_2$ max value by age correction factor (Table L19.3): ____________ L • min^{-1}
c. Multiply $\dot{V}O_2$ max in L • min^{-1} × 1000: ____________ mL • min^{-1}
d. Divide the age-corrected $\dot{V}O_2$ max (mL • min^{-1}) value by body weight in kg: ______ mL • kg^{-1} • min^{-1}
e. Fitness category (Table L19.4): ____________

worksheet **19.2** EXTENSION ACTIVITIES

NAME DATE

1. A 20-year-old male (175 lb) performed a submaximal cycle ergometer test. The following power outputs and heart rates were recorded. Using the blank graph below, predict this individual's maximal oxygen consumption rate ($\dot{V}O_2$ max). Assume a maximal HR of 200 bpm (220 – age = maximal HR) and express your answer relative to body weight (mL • kg^{-1} • min^{-1}). $\dot{V}O_2$ max = ____________ mL • kg^{-1} • min^{-1}

Power Output 1 (300 kgm • min^{-1}), HR = 100 bpm

Power Output 2 (900 kgm • min^{-1}), HR = 150 bpm

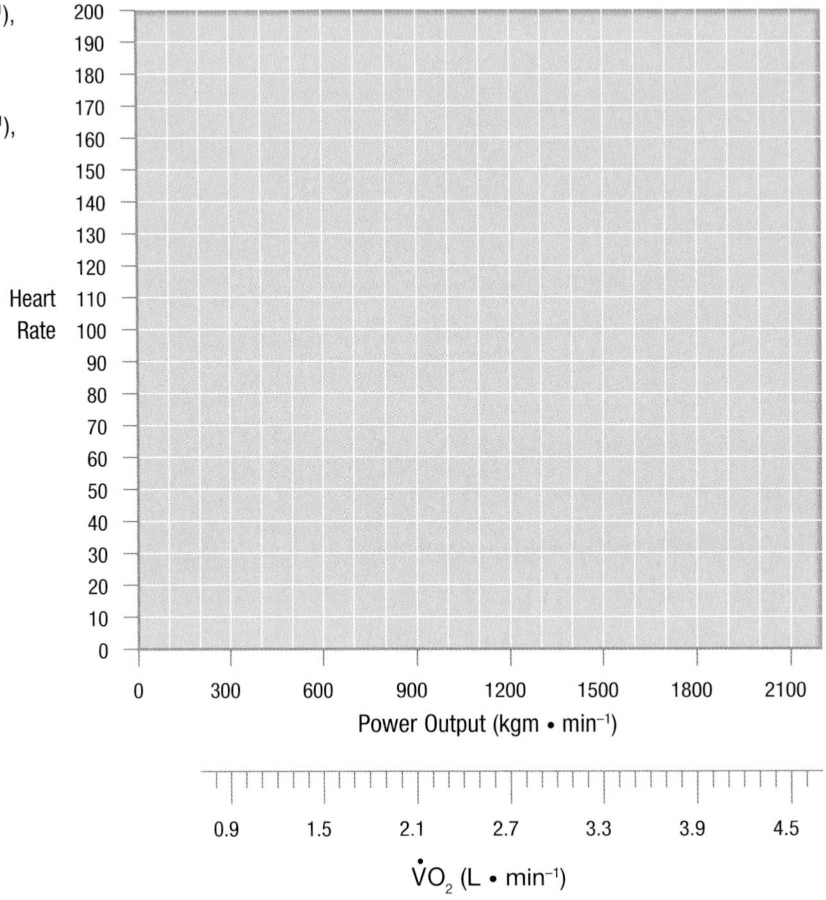

2. Activities such as weight training are not commonly used to estimate $\dot{V}O_2$ max. List at least one reason why this type of exercise would not accurately predict aerobic fitness.

3. Use your own data to calculate your estimated $\dot{V}O_2$ max (Table L19.1 or L19.2) relative to your body weight (mL • kg^{-1} • min^{-1}), multiply it by your age correction factor (Table L19.3), and determine your level of endurance fitness based on the classification from Table L19.4.

4. Use the following data to calculate the subject's estimated $\dot{V}O_2$ max relative to body weight (mL • kg^{-1} • min^{-1}) and determine her level of endurance fitness based on the classification from Table L19.4.

   a. Gender = female
   b. Age = 35 years
   c. Average HR during the last 2 minutes = 145 bpm
   d. Power output = 600 kgm • min^{-1}
   e. Body weight = 65 kg

   $\dot{V}O_2$ max = ______________ mL • kg • min^{-1}

   Classification = ______________ mL • kg • min^{-1}

EXTENSION QUESTIONS

1. What are some common mistakes that may occur in administering this lab?

2. Identify possible sources of error in this lab.

3. Assess the practicality of using this lab in the field.

4. Research the reliability and/or validity of this lab using online resources, journal articles, and other credible sources.

REFERENCES

1. Astrand, P. O., and Rodahl, K. *Textbook of Work Physiology*. New York: McGraw-Hill Book Company, 1977, pp. 350–352.
2. Astrand, P. O., and Rhyming, I. A nomogram for calculation of aerobic capacity (physical fitness) from pulse rate during submaximal work. *J. Appl. Physiol.* 7: 218–221, 1954.
3. Cooper, K. H. *The Aerobics Way*. Toronto: Bantam Books, 1977, pp. 280–281.

Units and Conversions

APPENDIX

DISTANCE
1 inch (in) = 2.54 centimeters (cm)
1 foot (ft) = 12 in = 30.48 cm = 0.3048 meters (m)
1 yard (yd) = 3 ft = 0.9144 m
1 mile (mi) = 5,280 ft = 1,760 yd = 1,609.35 m = 1.61 kilometers (km)
1 m = 39.37 in = 3.28 ft = 1.09 yd
1 km = 0.62 mi
1 m = 100 cm
1 cm = 10 millimeters (mm)

WEIGHTS
1 ounce (oz) = 0.0625 pounds (lb) = 28.35 grams (g) = 0.029 kilogram (kg)
1 lb = 16 oz = 454 g = 0.454 (kg)
1 g = 0.035 oz = 0.002205 lb
1 kg = 35.27 oz = 2.205 lb
1 kg = 1,000 g

VOLUME
1 oz = 29.57 milliliters (mL)
1 pint (pt) = 16 oz = 473.1 mL
1 quart (qt) = 32 oz = 2 pt = 0.9463 liters (L) = 946.3 mL
1 gallon (gal) = 128 oz = 8 pt = 4 qt = 3.785 L = 3785.2 mL
1 L = 1,000 mL = 1.057 qt

ENERGY
1 kilocalorie (kcal) = 1,000 calories (cal) = 4,184 joules (J) = 4.184 kilojoules (kJ)
1 L of oxygen (O_2) = 5.05 kcal = 21.139 kJ
1 kilogram meter (kg-m) = distance through which 1 kg is moved 1 m

POWER
Power = work / time
1 watt (W) = 0.0134 kcal • min^{-1} = 6.118 kg-m • min^{-1}
1 kg-m • min^{-1} = 0.1635 W
1 kcal • min^{-1} = 69.78 W
1 MET = 3.5 mL O_2 • kg^{-1} • min^{-1} = 0.01768 kcal • kg^{-1} • min^{-1}
VELOCITY
1 mile per hour (mph) = 88 ft • min^{-1} = 1.47 ft • s^{-1} = 0.45 m • s^{-1} = 26.8 m • min^{-1} = 1.61 kilometers per hour (kph)
1 kph = 16.7 m • min^{-1} = 0.28 m • s^{-1} = 0.91 ft • s^{-1} = 0.62 mph
TEMPERATURE
°Fahrenheit = 1.8 (°Celcius (C)) + 32
°Celcius (centigrade) = 0.555 (°F – 32)
°Kelvin = °C + 273
PRESSURE
1 atmosphere (atm) = 760 mm Hg

Glossary

1-RM: one-repetition maximum, a standard index to quantify muscle strength that refers to the maximum amount of weight that can be lifted one time

A band: the dark band seen as part of the striation effect of skeletal and cardiac muscle

acceleration: the act or process of speeding up

acceleration phase: the second phase of a sprinting event

accumulation hypothesis: an explanation of muscle fatigue in terms of the building up of metabolites such as lactate, hydrogen ions, inorganic phosphate, and ammonia, within muscle fibers

acetylcholine (ACH): a neurotransmitter widely distributed in body tissues with a primary function of mediating synaptic activity of the nervous system and skeletal muscles

acid: a compound that yields positively charged hydrogen ions in solution

acquired immune deficiency syndrome (AIDS): a disease state caused by the human immunodeficiency virus and characterized by a severe depletion of helper T cells and major complications such as cancer or opportunistic infection

actin: a type of contractile protein (myofilament)

action potential: an electrical impulse transmitted across the plasma membrane of a nerve fiber during the transmission of a nerve impulse and across the plasma membrane of a muscle fiber during contraction

acute musculoskeletal injury: injury resulting from trauma experienced during a single episode of training

adenosine diphosphate (ADP): a product of the hydrolysis of ATP

adenosine triphosphate (ATP): an energy-storing molecule in muscle that releases energy when it is hydrolyzed to adenosine diphosphate (ADP)

adenosine triphosphate–phosphocreatine (ATP–PC) system: the anaerobic metabolic pathway that utilizes adenosine triphosphate (ATP) and phosphocreatine (PC) to meet the energy demands of short-term, high-intensity exercise

adolescence: the period of development between the onset of puberty and adulthood, characterized by a growth spurt

ADP: adenosine diphosphate; a product of the hydrolysis of adenosine triphosphate (ATP)

adrenergic: norepinephrine secreting

aerobic: with oxygen

aerobic power: the maximal amount of oxygen that can be consumed per minute during maximal exercise; also known as *maximal oxygen consumption rate* and $\dot{V}O_2$ max

afferent neuron: a neuron that conducts impulses from the periphery to the central nervous system; also known as *sensory neuron*

agonist: the muscle causing a movement

alkaline reserve: the ability of the plasma bicarbonate system to buffer fixed acids such as lactic acid

allosteric inhibition: process in which the end product of a series of enzymatic steps inhibits the activity of the enzyme

all-or-none law: the fact that when a muscle fiber (or motor unit) responds to a single impulse at or above threshold value by contracting, the tension produced is independent of the intensity of the stimulus

alpha motor neuron: a motor neuron that transmits impulses from the central nervous system to the extrafusal skeletal muscle fibers

altitude acclimatization: the increased ability to perform at high altitudes; accomplished by various systems of physical conditioning at progressively higher altitudes or a progressive conditioning program at the competition altitude

alveolar duct: any of the small air passages in the lung that branch out from the bronchioles and lead to the alveoli

alveolar ventilation rate: the rate of air flow to the alveoli

alveolus: a small pouch in the lungs through which gas exchange between alveolar air and pulmonary capillary blood occurs (plural: alveoli)

amenorrhea: absence of menstrual flow

amphetamine: a sympathomimetic amine used in medicine as a central nervous system stimulant; sometimes used as an ergogenic aid

anabolic: growth promoting

anabolic steroid: a synthetically developed cholesterol-based drug that resembles naturally occurring hormones such as testosterone and has growth-promoting and masculinizing effects

anabolism: "to build up"; refers to metabolic processes in which structures are created

anaerobic: without oxygen

anaerobic glycolysis: the metabolism of glucose to lactate

anaerobic threshold: the intensity of exercise just below that at which metabolic acidosis and the associated changes in gas exchange occur

anatomical dead space: the volume of the conducting portion of the airways of the lungs where no gas exchange occurs

androgenic: masculinizing

androstenedione: a weakly androgenic steroid precursor; sometimes used as an ergogenic aid

aneurysm: a localized dilation of the wall of a blood vessel

angina pectoris: chest pain usually caused by myocardial anoxia as a result of atherosclerosis or coronary artery spasm

anorexia nervosa: an eating disorder characterized by emotional disturbance concerning body image, fear of becoming obese, and a prolonged refusal to eat, resulting in emaciation and amenorrhea

anovulation: suspension or cessation of the production and/or release of an ovum

antagonist: the muscle whose contraction opposes a movement

anthropometric: relating to the measurement of the size and proportions of the human body

anthropometry: the measurement of the size and proportions of the human body

antibody: a glycoprotein produced and secreted by plasma cells in response to bacteria, viruses, or other antigenic substances; also known as an *immunoglobulin*

antibody-dependent cell-mediated cytotoxicity (ADCC): the process of destroying cells by the binding of an antibody to an antigen on the cell surface and lysing those cells

antigen: any substance, usually a protein, that causes the formation of an antibody that reacts specifically with that substance

arginine: a semi-essential amino acid that is involved in a number of metabolic pathways and the production of biologically active compounds

arteriole: a muscular vessel that lies between an artery and a capillary

arteriosclerosis: hardening of the arteries

arteriovenous anastomose (AV shunt): short vascular connections between small arteries and veins, arterioles and venules, and metarterioles and venules

artery: an elastic vessel that carries blood away from the heart

asthma: a condition that involves chronic inflammation of the airways of the lungs and is characterized by obstruction of the flow of air due to bronchoconstriction, wheezing, coughing, shortness of breath, and tightness of the chest

atherosclerosis: an abnormal condition of the vascular system characterized by yellowish plaques of cholesterol, lipids, and cellular debris in the inner layer of the walls of large and medium-sized arteries

athletic menstrual cycle irregularities (AMI): disruption in the menstrual cycle as a result of high-intensity athletic training programs

ATP: adenosine triphosphate; an energy-storing molecule in muscles that releases energy when it is hydrolyzed to adenosine diphosphate (ADP)

ATP–PC (adenosine triphosphate–phosphocreatine) system: an anaerobic pathway that utilizes phosphagens for energy production

atrioventricular (AV) node: a specialized mass of conducting tissue located at the base of the atria in the interatrial septum

atrium: a chamber of the heart that receives blood from veins

atrophy: a gradual wasting away, or decrease in mass and size, of an organ or tissue

autonomic nervous system: the branch of the nervous system that regulates involuntary functions, including the activity of the cardiac muscle, smooth muscle, and glands

autorhythmicity: self-excitation, a property of cardiac muscle

axon: the portion of a neuron that conducts impulses away from the cell body

azoospermia: lack of sperm

B cell: a cell that resides in lymph nodes, spleen, and other lymphoid tissue and mediates humoral immunity

ballistic stretching: a method of muscle elongation (stretching) involving high-force, short-duration, jerky or bouncy movements

basal ganglia: paired masses of gray matter in each cerebral hemisphere

basal metabolic rate: the rate of metabolism required for basic body functions during rest

base: a compound that yields negatively charged hydroxyl ions in solution

beta-alanine: a nonproteogenic (not involved in protein synthesis) amino acid produced in the liver; the role of beta-alanine in exercise performance is related to its involvement in the synthesis of carnosine in skeletal muscle

beta-hydroxy-beta-methylbutyrate (HMB): a metabolite produced as a result of the breakdown of leucine; sometimes used as an ergogenic aid

beta oxidation: an aerobic metabolic process in which long chain fatty acids are broken into two carbon acetyl coenzyme A molecules to enter the Krebs cycle

Betz cells: large pyramidal cells in the motor area of the precentral gyrus of the cerebral cortex; also known as Bevan–Lewis cells

bicarbonate loading: sodium bicarbonate supplementation

bilateral deficit: a decrease in the strength of a muscle group when the contralateral limb is concurrently performing a maximal contraction

bilateral facilitation: an increase in bilateral strength compared to the sum of unilateral measurements

blood doping: a procedure involving the removal of blood 8 to 12 weeks prior to an athletic event, isolation and freezing of the red blood cells, and reinfusion of those cells during the week preceding the athletic event; also known as *erythrocythemia*

blood flow: the amount of blood flowing to the various organs each minute

blood pressure: the arterial pressure during systole over the arterial pressure during diastole

body building: a competitive sport in which the participant uses several resistance training methods to develop muscle size, symmetry, and definition

body mass index (BMI): body weight divided by height squared (kg/m^2)

Boyle's law: if temperature remains constant, the pressure of a gas varies inversely with its volume

bronchiole: one of the smaller subdivisions of the bronchial tubes, containing smooth muscle and elastic fibers, but no cartilage in its wall

bronchus: one of the primary subdivisions of the trachea; conveys air to and from the lungs (plural: bronchi)

buffer system: an acid and its conjugate base (salt) that, when present in a solution, reduce any change in pH that would otherwise occur in the solution when acid or alkali is added to it

bulimia nervosa: an eating disorder characterized by an insatiable craving for food, resulting in episodes of continuous eating often followed by purging, depression, and self-deprivation

caffeine: a central nervous system stimulant that increases sympathetic nervous system arousal and also acts as a diuretic; sometimes used as an ergogenic aid

capacitance vessels: thin-walled vessels, such as veins, that are important in altering the capacity, or storage function, of the postcapillary system

capillary: vessel with a single-cell layer wall that functions in gas exchange

carbohydrate loading: a method to produce the maximum possible glycogen storage in the muscles; sometimes used as an ergogenic aid; also known as *glycogen supercompensation*

carbohydrate sparing effect: the result of the preferential use of fatty acids for ATP production in endurance trained individuals

cardiac contractility: the ability of the heart to produce force per unit of time (power)

cardiac cycle: the cyclic pattern of contraction and relaxation of the heart

cardiac muscle: contractile tissue of the heart

cardiac output (CO): the amount of blood ejected by the heart each minute; heart rate times stroke volume

cardiac reserve: the heart rate reserve and the stroke volume reserve; the ability of the heart to increase its cardiac output

cardiovascular disease: an illness or disorder of the heart or blood vessels

cardiovascular system: the heart and blood vessels

carotid body: a chemoreceptor that is responsive to changes in the partial pressures of arterial oxygen, carbon dioxide, and pH, located at the bifurcation of the common carotid artery in the neck

catabolism: "to break down"; refers to metabolic processes of breaking down

catecholamine: a hormone secreted by the adrenal medulla that serves to increase the availability of fuel to the active muscles

cell-mediated immunity: the mechanism of acquired immunity characterized by T cell lymphocytes and involving resistance to infectious diseases caused by viruses and some bacteria; also known as *cellular immunity*

central command of breathing: the control of ventilation by the motor cortex

central fatigue: a decrease in motor performance due to mechanisms proximal to the motor neurons

central governor model: a model postulating that the central nervous system regulates exercise performance to ensure that physiological failure does not occur during normal exercise

central nervous system: the brain and spinal cord

chilblain: one of the most common nonfreezing cold injuries; typically less severe than trenchfoot and can occur with only one to five hours of exposure of bare skin to cold (<60°F) and wet conditions. The symptoms of chilblain include swollen, tender, itchy, and painful lesions on the fingers, ears, face, and other exposed skin areas. After rewarming, there are no long-lasting effects of chilblain.

childhood: the time between the first birthday and puberty, characterized by steady growth and maturation with particularly rapid progress in motor development

chilling: a sudden decrease in body temperature; often occurs when there are intermittent periods of activity and rest

cholestasis: arrest of bile flow

cholesterol: an animal lipid with the basic 4-ring steroid structure; facilitates the absorption and transport of fatty acids

cholinergic: acetylcholine secreting

chronic musculoskeletal injury: injury resulting from repeated microtrauma due to overuse

chronic obstructive pulmonary disease (COPD): Bronchitis and/or emphysema that is characterized by limited airflow to the lungs and is not fully reversible

chylomicron: a small droplet of lipoprotein synthesized in the gastrointestinal tract and transported through the lymph vessels into the plasma and eventually to the tissues for use

claudication: limping; usually refers to intermittent claudication

cluster designation (CD): a protein on the surface of an immune cell that is used to identify, classify, and study that cell

coefficient of oxygen utilization: the proportion of oxygen transported by the blood that is given off to the tissues

coenzyme: vitamin or vitamin derivative that transports hydrogen within the cell and affects the turnover rate of an enzyme in a metabolic pathway

cofactor: metal that affects the turnover rate of an enzyme in a metabolic pathway

cold acclimatization: the increased ability to withstand cold temperatures as a result of continued exposure to cold

collateral circulation: a redundant blood pathway developed through enlargement of secondary vessels after obstruction of a main channel

complement protein: any of nine proteins that are involved in the lysis of antibody-coated bacteria and other cells; stimulate phagocytosis and inflammation

complete protein: a protein that includes all of the essential amino acids

complex carbohydrate: a combination of three or more glucose molecules

compliance: the elastic force required per unit stretch of the thorax; a measure of the distensibility of the lung volume produced by a unit pressure change; sometimes referred to as the *elastic resistance to breathing*

concentric: muscle action that involves the production of force while the muscle is shortening

conduction: the transfer of heat between two objects that are in contact with one another

conductivity: the ability of muscle tissue to propagate a stimulus throughout any one fiber in skeletal muscle and from fiber to fiber in smooth and cardiac muscles

contractility: the ability of muscle tissue to contract

contraction phase: the period of muscle twitch during which the muscle shortens (also called *shortening period*)

contract–relax (CR): stretching technique of isometrically contracting the lengthened muscle, then relaxing and further passively lengthening the muscle

contract–relax with agonist-contraction (CRAC): stretching technique identical to contract–relax except that during the final stretching phase the muscle opposite the one stretched is concentrically contracted

controlled frequency of breathing (CFB): for swimmers, breathing is less than once per stroke cycle

convection: the transfer of heat through a gas or liquid by the circulation of heated particles

cooling down: low- to moderate-intensity activity performed after a physical activity

core temperature: the temperature of the central nervous system and internal organs; reflected by the rectal temperature

coronary heart disease (CHD): a condition causing reduced flow of oxygen and nutrients to the heart; formerly known as coronary artery disease

corpus striatum: a type of motor nucleus that serves as a relay station for the axons of the neurons of the premotor cortex to communicate with the lower motor neurons

creatine: a naturally occurring nitrogenous compound synthesized in the liver, kidneys, and pancreas; combined with phosphorus, it forms high-energy phosphate; sometimes used as an ergogenic aid

creatine loading: ingesting creatine monohydrate prior to a performance in order to increase muscle phosphocreatine stores

cross-bridge: the portion of the myosin protein that binds with the binding site on the actin protein; also known as *myosin head*

cross-bridge recycling: the process of a myosin cross-bridge swiveling inward, being released from the actin molecule, standing back up, rebinding to the actin molecule, and swiveling again; also called *cross-bridge recharging*

crossed extensor reflex: reflex extension of the contralateral (opposite) limb

cross-education effect: the phenomenon of strength increases in a contralateral (opposite) limb as a result of unilateral training; also known as the *cross-training effect*

cross-training effect: the phenomenon of strength increase in a contralateral (opposite) limb as a result of unilateral training; also known as the *cross-education effect*

cruise interval training: training performed at the lactate threshold, consisting of discontinuous work bouts lasting approximately 3 to 10 minutes with 1-minute rest intervals

CSA: cross-sectional area.

CT scan: computed tomography scan

cyclic AMP (cAMP): an activator of the enzyme phosphorylase kinase; formed from ATP by adenyl cyclase; also known as *adenosine 3',5'-cyclic phosphate* and *cyclic phosphate*

DCER: dynamic constant external resistance

deceleration: the act or process of slowing down

degenerative disease: any disease in which deterioration of a structure or function of tissue occurs; examples include cardiovascular disease, hypertension, and cancer

dehydroepiandrosterone (DHEA): a weakly androgenic steroid precursor; sometimes used as an ergogenic aid

dehydrogenase enzyme: an enzyme that transfers hydrogen ions

delayed onset muscle soreness (DOMS): the pain caused by microtrauma of the muscle felt 24 to 48 hours after an exercise bout

dendrite: the portion of a neuron that receives impulses

depletion hypothesis: a possible explanation of muscle fatigue; involves the concept of the depletion of glycogen, glucose, or phosphagen stores

detraining: the secession, or stopping, of a training program; usually accompanied by a decrease in fitness

development: 1. the differentiation of cells along specialized lines of function; 2. the evolution of competence in a variety of interrelated domains

diabetes mellitus: a metabolic disorder characterized by elevated blood glucose levels

diastole: the relaxation phase of the cardiac cycle

diastolic pressure: the arterial blood pressure during diastole

diffusion gradient: the rate of change of gas exchange; dependent upon the ease with which a gas can penetrate a membrane

disaccharide: simple carbohydrate made up of two simple sugar molecules

disordered eating: a disturbance in the behavior associated with taking in food; anorexia nervosa and bulimia nervosa are examples

drafting: a racing technique in which an athlete performs directly behind another athlete to reduce wind and air resistance

duration: how long exercise is performed each day

dynamic constant external resistance (DCER): a type of muscle action in which the external resistance remains constant throughout the movement; also known as *isotonic muscle action*

dynamic exercise: exercise, such as running or cycling, that involves rapid contractions alternating with relaxations

dynamic flexibility: a measurement of range of motion that reflects joint stiffness and resistance to limb movement

dynamometer: an instrument for measuring force

dyslipidemia: an elevation of LDL or triglycerides, or a reduction in HDL; a major, modifiable risk factor for CHD

dysmenorrhea: pain from uterine contractions or ischemia during menstruation

dyspnea: labored breathing; shortness of breath

eccentric: a muscle action that involves the production of force while the muscle is lengthening

economy of movement: the efficiency with which a movement is performed; may be determined by measuring the oxygen cost

edema: the abnormal accumulation of fluid in interstitial spaces of tissues; swelling

efferent neuron: a neuron that conducts impulses from the central nervous system to the muscles and other effectors; also known as *motor neuron*

elasticity: the ability of a tissue to regain its original size and shape after being stretched, squeezed, or otherwise deformed

electrocardiography: the recording of heart muscle action potentials (or their currents) during the cardiac cycle

electromyograph (EMG): the recording of muscle action potentials (or their currents)

electronic integrator: a tool that finds the average amplitude of summated muscle action potentials

electron transport system: an aerobic metabolic mechanism of oxidation and reduction, resulting in ATP production; also known as *respiratory chain*

embolus: a blood clot or other mass that circulates in the blood stream until it becomes lodged in a vessel

end diastolic volume (EDV): the amount of blood in each ventricle of the heart at the end of diastole

endocrine: pertaining to the system of ductless glands that secrete hormones into the blood and lymph

endolymph: the fluid in the semicircular canals of the inner ear

endomysium: the connective tissue sheath covering an individual muscle fiber

end systolic volume (ESV): the amount of blood in each ventricle of the heart at the end of systole

energy metabolism: the use of food to store energy in the form of ATP or to break down ATP for the purpose of doing work

enzyme: proteins that have specific properties and functions

ephaptic conduction: rapid transmission of an impulse from cell to cell

epidemiological studies: studies performed on human populations that attempt to link health effects to a cause; e.g., waist circumference and type 2 diabetes

epimysium: the connective tissue sheath covering a muscle

epinephrine: a hormone secreted by the adrenal medulla; serves to increase the availability of fuel to the active muscles

epiphyseal growth plate: a thin layer of cartilage between the epiphysis, a secondary bone forming center, and the bone shaft; new bone forms along the plate

ergogenic aid: a substance, such as a steroid, used by athletes with the expectation that it will provide a competitive edge

erythrocyte: red blood cell

erythrocythemia: a procedure involving the removal of blood 8 to 12 weeks prior to an athletic event, isolation and freezing of the red blood cells, and reinfusion of those cells during the week preceding the athletic event; also known as *blood doping*

erythropoiesis: the formation of red blood cells

erythropoietin: a naturally occurring hormone produced by the kidneys in response to low hemoglobin levels; stimulates bone marrow to produce red blood cells; sometimes used as an ergogenic aid

esophagus: the muscular tube in the neck, extending from the pharynx to the stomach; serves as a passageway for food

essential amino acid: an amino acid that cannot be synthesized by the body and therefore must be supplied by the diet

estrogen: a hormone secreted by the ovaries

eupnea: easy, free breathing as observed in the normal subject under resting conditions

evaporation: a change from liquid form into gas form; also known as *vaporization*

excised muscle: a muscle that has been removed from the body

exercise-induced asthma (EIA): bronchoconstriction caused by exercise

exercise-induced bronchospasm (EIB): a prolonged contraction of the involuntary muscles fibers of the walls of the bronchi and bronchioles during exercise

exercise intensity: the workload of an exercise, measured in foot-pounds or kilogram-meters per minute

exercise physiology: the study of the processes and functions of living organisms and their component parts during and after physical activity

exercise-related transient abdominal pain (ETAP): Pain that occurs in running or other repetitive movements that is felt in the lateral aspects of the mid abdomen, along the costal border and has been described as cramping, aching, or pulling when it is less intense, as well as sharp or stabbing, when the pain is more severe. Commonly referred to as *stitch in the side.*

exercise science: the study of how and why the body responds to physical activity

exertional heat exhaustion: The fatigue that develops during exercise in the heat; this fatigue may be caused by excess body heat and by dehydration

exertional heatstroke: A potentially fatal disorder that occasionally follows heat exhaustion; characterized by an elevated core body temperature greater than 104°F; loss of consciousness (coma) following exertion; and clinical symptoms of damage to the central nervous system, liver, and kidneys

exertional hyperthermia: An elevated core body temperature greater than 104°F that occurs during athletic or recreational activities; it is influenced by exercise intensity, environmental conditions, clothing, and equipment

exocrine: pertaining to glands that secrete their products through ducts

expiration phase: the process of breathing out

expiratory reserve volume: the maximal amount of gas that can be expired from the end-tidal expiratory level

external respiration: gas exchange in the lungs in which the blood in the lung capillaries takes up oxygen and gives up much of its carbon dioxide; also known as *pulmonary ventilation*

extrafusal muscle fiber: a typical skeletal muscle fiber

extrapyramidal system: the portion of the brainstem and spinal pathways that do not pass through the pyramids and are concerned with postural control

Fartlek training: training that consists of an easy, continuous pace alternating with short, high-intensity bursts

fascia: the fibrous connective tissue of the body

fasciculus: a bundle of muscle fibers (plural: fasciculi)

fast-twitch glycolytic (FG) fibers: fatigable muscle fibers that favor glycolytic (anaerobic) methods of energy production; also known as *type IIb fibers*

fast-twitch oxidative glycolytic (FOG) fibers: intermediately fatigue-resistant muscle fibers that utilize both oxidative (aerobic) and glycolytic (anaerobic) methods of energy production; also known as *type IIa fibers*

fat-free weight (FFW): the total weight of all of the tissues other than adipose (fat) in the body, i.e., the weight of the muscle, bone, and vital organs

fatigue: the state following a period of mental or bodily activity characterized by a lessened capacity for work and reduced efficiency of accomplishment, usually accompanied by a feeling of weariness, sleepiness, or irritability; may also supervene when, from any cause, energy expenditure outstrips restorative processes

fat weight (FW): the total weight of all of the adipose (fat) in the body

female athlete triad: a syndrome that affects extremely physically active females, characterized by disordered eating, amenorrhea, and osteoporosis

ferritin: a complex of iron and protein stored in the intestine, liver, spleen, and bone marrow

Fick method: an indirect method of estimating cardiac output by determining the rate at which oxygen is added to the blood as it flows through the lungs

FITT-VP: principle of aerobic exercise prescription focusing on six components: frequency of exercise, intensity of exercise, time (duration) of exercise, type (mode) of exercise, volume (amount) of exercise, and progression (advancement) or pattern of exercise

flexibility: the range of motion at a joint or a series of joints

flexion reflex: an involuntary flexion of a muscle in response to a stimulus; allows for the removal of the body part from the stimulus; a simple reflex

force–velocity curve: the relationship of the maximum force produced at any given velocity

frank anemia: the third and final stage of iron deficiency, characterized by inefficient cell metabolism and decreased oxygen transport

Frank–Starling law of the heart: the principle that contraction force during systole is dependent upon the length of the cardiac muscle fibers at the end of diastole

frequency: how often exercise is performed; usually, the number of times per week exercise is performed

frequency domain: the domain of the EMG signal that is the rate at which a wave form fluctuates above and below the baseline

frostbite: a damaging condition caused by the crystallization of fluids in the skin or subcutaneous tissues upon exposure to cold temperatures

functional murmur: a normal heart sound with no pathological significance that results from the turbulent flow that occurs as blood exits the heart and flows into the large vessels

functional residual capacity: the amount of gas remaining in the lungs at the resting expiratory level; includes the expiratory reserve volume and residual volume

gamma motor neuron: a motor neuron that transmits impulses from the central nervous system to the intrafusal fibers of a muscle spindle

gap junction: a small channel within an intercalated disk; allows for ion exchanges between the cytosol of adjacent cells

Gay–Lussac's law: if volume remains constant, the pressure of a gas increases directly in proportion to its absolute temperature

globin: the protein constituent of hemoglobin

glottis: a slitlike opening between the true vocal cords

glucagon: a hormone secreted by the pancreas that acts to raise blood glucose levels

gluconeogenesis: the formation of glucose from noncarbohydrate sources

glycogen: the storage form of glucose

glycogen depletion: the exhaustion or emptying of stored glucose (glycogen) as a result of long duration activities such as distance running or cycling

glycogenolysis: the conversion of glycogen to glucose

glycogen supercompensation: a procedure used to produce the maximum possible glycogen

glycogen synthetase: an enzyme that acts in the conversion of glucose to glycogen

glycolysis: an anaerobic pathway that utilizes glucose for energy production

Golgi tendon organ: a sensory receptor in the tendon of a muscle; it is sensitive to stretch and serves as a detector of tendon tension

gonads: the gamete-producing organs; testes in the male and ovaries in the female

gravid: pregnant

growth: an increase in the size of the body as a whole or the size attained by specific parts of the body

growth hormone: a naturally occurring polypeptide secreted by the anterior pituitary gland; promotes increases in muscle mass directly by increasing amino acid transport and protein synthesis in skeletal muscle and indirectly by stimulating the production of insulin-like growth factor

gynecomastia: excessive mammary gland development in males

heart murmur: a sound created by blood that is not flowing smoothly through the heart

heart rate reserve: the difference between maximum heart rate and resting heart rate; the ability of the heart to increase its rate of contraction; also known as *heart rate range*

heart sound: the noise heard when a cardiac valve closes

heat acclimatization: the increased ability to withstand hot temperatures as a result of continued exposure to heat

heat exhaustion: the fatigue that develops during exercise in the heat; characterized by weakness, dizziness, nausea, muscle cramps, and loss of consciousness

heat strain: the effect of heat stress on the body; the elevation of core temperature, skin temperature, and heart rate

heat stress: the sum of the metabolic and environmental heat loads; related to exercise intensity, environmental temperature, and evaporative potential of the environment

heat stroke: a potentially fatal disorder that occasionally follows heat exhaustion, resulting from failure of the temperature-regulating capacity of the body; characterized by loss of consciousness (coma)

heat syncope: dizziness associated with high environmental temperatures due to peripheral vasodilation, postural pooling of blood, diminished venous return, dehydration, reduced cardiac output, and/or cerebral ischemia; also known as *orthostatic dizziness*

helper T cell: a type of T cell that stimulates the cytotoxic action of killer T cells and increases antibody production by plasma cells

heme: the pigmented iron-containing, oxygen-carrying constituent of hemoglobin

hemochromatosis: a rare disease of iron metabolism, characterized by excess iron deposits throughout the body

hemodynamics: the principles governing blood flow

hemoglobin: a complex protein–iron compound of erythrocytes that carries oxygen from the lungs to the tissues and carbon dioxide from the tissues to the lungs

hemorrhagic stroke: an abnormal condition of the brain that occurs when a vessel ruptures in the brain, causing ischemia of the brain tissue

hemosiderin: a storage form of excess iron, over and above ferritin

Henry's law: the quantity of a gas that will dissolve in a liquid is directly proportional to its partial pressure, if temperature remains constant

hexokinase: the enzyme responsible for the phosphorylation of glucose, thereby creating glucose-6-phosphate

high-density lipoprotein (HDL): a plasma protein made in the liver and containing about 50 percent protein with cholesterol and triglycerides; transports cholesterol and other lipids to the liver for disposal

high risk: individuals with known cardiovascular, pulmonary, or metabolic disease or who exhibit certain symptoms

high velocity phase: the third phase of a sprinting event

hormone: a biological chemical that is secreted by an endocrine gland into the blood and lymph

human immunodeficiency virus (HIV): a retrovirus that causes acquired immune deficiency syndrome (AIDS); cripples the immune system by decreasing the number of helper T cells

humoral immunity: resistance to disease that exists in the blood and lymph

hunch: guess

hypercapnic training: a training method, such as controlled frequency breathing, in which ventilatory volume and partial pressure of oxygen decrease while the partial pressure of carbon dioxide increases

hyperextension: extension of a joint beyond the normal range of motion

hyperglycemia: elevated blood glucose levels

hyperlipidemia: elevated lipids in the blood

hyperplasia: an increase in the number of elements comprising a part (such as tissue cells)

hyperplastic obesity: a condition of excessive body fatness characterized by an increase in the number of fat cells

hypertension: elevated blood pressure; resting systolic blood pressure greater than 160 mm Hg or resting diastolic blood pressure greater than 95 mm Hg

hyperthermia: increased body temperature

hypertrophic obesity: a condition of excessive body fatness characterized by an increase in the size of the fat cells

hypertrophy: an increase in the size of existing parts (such as the size of the cells of a tissue)

hyperventilation: an increase in lung ventilation without a corresponding increase in metabolic rate

hypocapnia: abnormally low levels of carbon dioxide in the circulating blood

hypoglycemia: low blood glucose levels

hypothermia: severely reduced core body temperature

hypothesis: a tentative supposition (based on prior observations) provisionally adopted to explain certain facts and to guide investigations

hypoventilation: a reduction in lung ventilation without a corresponding decrease in metabolic rate

hypoxic training: a training method in which the partial pressure of oxygen is subnormal

H zone: a lighter area within the A band seen as part of the striation effect of skeletal and cardiac muscle

I band: a lighter area between the A bands seen as part of the striation effect of skeletal and cardiac muscle

immune: free from or resistant to an infectious disease

immunoglobulin: a glycoprotein produced and secreted by plasma cells in response to bacteria, viruses, or other antigenic substances; also known as *antibody*

indicator dilution method: an indirect method of estimating cardiac output by injecting dye (indicator) into a large vein or into the right atrium of the heart

infancy: the first year of life, characterized by rapid growth in almost all bodily functions and physical characteristics

infarction: necrosis or death of tissue

infectious disease: any communicable disease; a disease that can be transmitted from one human being to another or from animal to human by direct or indirect contact; examples include tuberculosis, diphtheria, and poliomyelitis

inspiration phase: the process of breathing in

inspiratory capacity: the maximal amount of gas that can be inspired from the resting expiratory level; includes the tidal volume and inspiratory reserve volume

inspiratory reserve volume: the maximal amount of gas that can be inspired from the end-tidal inspiratory level

insufficient heart valve: a heart valve that does not close completely; results in regurgitation, or backflow, of blood and a heart murmur

insulin: a hormone secreted by the pancreas that acts to reduce blood glucose levels

integration: the mathematical process of determining the area under a curve; used to find the mean amplitude of summated muscle action potentials

intensity: a term used to describe the degree of physiological strain or challenge of exercise

intercalated disk: a connective tissue structure located between adjacent cardiac muscle cells, allowing one cell to pull on the surrounding cells

interferon: a cellular protein produced by cells infected by viruses; act on neighboring cells to prevent infection

intermediate-density lipoprotein (IDL): a lipid–protein complex with a density between that of a low-density lipoprotein and a high-density lipoprotein

intermittent claudication: cramplike pains in the calves caused by ischemia of the muscles due to sclerosis with narrowing of the arteries and poor circulation to the leg muscles

internal respiration: gas exchange between the blood and cells; also known as *tissue respiration*

internuncial neuron: a neuron that lies in the gray matter of the spinal cord, between a sensory and a motor neuron

interval training: training consisting of short periods of work alternating with short rest intervals

intrafusal muscle fiber (IF): a small fiber located within the capsule of a muscle spindle

irritability: muscle tissue's responsiveness to stimuli

ischemia: insufficient blood flow

isocaloric state: state in which calories taken in equal calories expended

isokinetic: muscle action that has a constant velocity of movement

isometric: muscle action involving tension production without movement at the joint or shortening of the muscle fibers; also known as *static muscle action*

isotonic: muscle action in which the external resistance remains constant throughout the movement, also known as *dynamic constant external resistance (DCER)*

jet lag: the fatigue and sluggishness that travelers feel following long airplane flights across time zones

killer T cell: a type of T cell that defends against invading organisms by producing lymphotoxins, interferons, macrophage chemotactic factor, macrophage invading factor, and macrophage migration inhibiting factor

kinesiology: the study of the principles of mechanics and anatomy in relation to human movement

kinesthesis: The sense of movement and position of body parts in space

Krebs cycle: an aerobic metabolic process that utilizes acetyl coenzyme A molecules to produce ATP; also known as *citric acid cycle* or *tricarboxylic acid cycle*

lactate threshold: the measurement of the anaerobic threshold by blood lactate levels

lactic acid: a three-carbon acid resulting from anaerobic metabolism; also known as *lactate*

latent iron deficiency: the second stage of iron deficiency, characterized by an increased total iron binding capacity and reduced serum iron

latent period: the short delay between the application of a stimulus and the beginning of muscular contraction

law of energy balance: law describing the relationships between calories taken in and calories expended

Law of Mass Action: the ability of a reversible reaction to be driven from an area of high concentration to an area of low concentration

law of partial pressures: in a mixture of gases, each gas exerts a partial pressure, proportional to its concentration

leg extensors: the quadriceps, made up of the rectus femoris, vastus lateralis, vastus intermedius, and vastus medialis

leukocyte: white blood cell; any cell of the immune system

leukocytosis: an increase in the number of circulating white blood cells (leukocytes)

lipolysis: the breakdown of fat for use as an energy source

lipoprotein: a compound containing lipid (fat) and protein; the form lipids take as they travel in the blood

lock-and-key method: used to describe the specificity of fit involved in interactions such as those of antigen with antibody and hormone with receptor

long slow distance (LSD) training: training at approximately 65 to 70 percent of $\dot{V}O_2$ max to develop the cardiorespiratory system, circulatory blood supply to the active muscles, and enhance the metabolic characteristics of the muscles

low-density lipoprotein (LDL): a plasma protein that contains more cholesterol and triglyceride than protein

lower motor neuron: a neuron whose cell body is in the spinal cord

low risk: men under 45 and women under 55 who are asymptomatic and have no more than one risk factor

lung ventilation rate: volume of breathing per minute

lymphocyte: an agranular leukocyte formed in lymphoid tissue; includes T cells, B cells, and natural killer (NK) cells

lymphocytosis: an increase in the number of circulating lymphocytes

lymphokine: one of the chemical factors produced and released by T lymphocytes that attracts macrophages to a site of infection

lymphotoxin: a cytotoxic polypeptide produced by killer T cells

lysosome: a cytoplasmic, membrane-bound particle containing hydrolyzing enzymes

macrocycle: a training period of usually approximately one year in length, corresponding to the time from one competitive season to the next

macronutrient: carbohydrate, protein, or fat

macrophage: a large ameboid mononuclear phagocytic cell

macrophage activating factor: a lymphokine released from a sensitized leukocyte that stimulates phagocytosis by macrophages

macrophage chemotactic factor: a lymphokine released from a sensitized leukocyte that attracts macrophages to the site of an invasion by an antigen

macrophage migration inhibiting factor: a lymphokine released from leukocytes that immobilizes macrophages after contact with an antigen, thereby preventing the macrophages from exiting the area

making weight: the effort to reduce body weight in order to qualify for a particular weight class in competition

maturation: the tempo and timing of progress toward the mature (advanced) biological state

maximal effort vertical jump: total jump height

maximal oxygen consumption rate: the maximum amount of oxygen that can be consumed per minute during maximal exercise; also known as *aerobic power* and $\dot{V}O_2$ max

maximum heart rate (HR_{max}): the highest heart rate attainable during exercise; $HR_{max} = 220 - \text{age}$

maximum heart rate reserve: the difference between maximum heart rate and resting heart rate

mean power: the total work performed during a maximal 30-second cycle ergometer test; reflects the capacity of the glycolytic energy production pathway

memory B cell: a subclassification of B cell that recognizes and responds quickly to an antigen from a previous exposure

memory T cell: a type of T cell that recognizes and responds quickly to an antigen from a previous exposure

menarche: the first menstrual period or flow

mesocycle: a training period of usually approximately two to three months

metabolic equivalent (MET): $3.5 \cdot mL \cdot kg^{-1} \cdot min^{-1}$; average resting $\dot{V}O_2$; used to describe the intensity of an exercise as a multiple of the resting $\dot{V}O_2$, for example, 1 MET, 2 MET, etc.

metabolism: "to change"; includes the processes of anabolism and catabolism

metarteriole: a small blood vessel that lies between an arteriole and a true capillary

microcycle: a training period of approximately one week

mitochondrion: the organelle within the sarcoplasm that functions in aerobic energy metabolism and respiration (plural: mitochondria)

mode: a term used to describe the type of exercise

moderate risk: men over 45 and women over 55, or any person with more than one risk factor

monocyte: an agranular leukocyte normally found in lymph nodes, spleen, bone marrow, and loose connective tissue

monosaccharide: a six carbon atom sugar; glucose, fructose, and galactose

mortality: the death rate; the number of deaths per unit of population

motor cortex: the precentral gyrus of the frontal lobe of the cerebrum; contains nerve cell bodies whose axons form the descending pyramidal motor tracts

motor learning: the study of the acquisition and retention of motor skills

motor neuron: a neuron that conducts impulses from the central nervous system to the muscles and other effectors; also known as *efferent neuron*

motor unit: a motor neuron and all of the muscle fibers that it innervates

MRI: magnetic resonance imaging

multiple regression equation: a combination of a number of measurements that best predict a common variable

muscle action potential (MAP): the electrical charge that accompanies the contraction of muscle tissue

muscle atrophy: shrinking of a muscle

muscle (heat) cramps: acute, painful, and involuntary muscle contraction due to dehydration, electrolyte imbalances, and/or neuromuscular fatigue

muscle spindle: a sensory receptor within skeletal muscle, containing intrafusal muscle fibers enclosed in a fibrous sheath; it is sensitive to stretch and serves as a detector of muscle length

myocardial infarction: heart attack; death of heart tissue

myocardium: heart muscle

myofibrils: the slender column-like structures that run longitudinally within the sarcoplasm of a muscle fiber

myofilament: contractile protein

myoglobin: an iron-containing structure that transports oxygen from the sarcolemma to the mitochondria of the skeletal muscle fiber, where it is used for aerobic metabolism

myoneural junction: the intersection of a motor neuron and a muscle fiber; also known as *neuromuscular junction*

myosin: a type of contractile protein (myofilament)

myosin ATPase: an enzyme that breaks down ATP that is bound to the myosin cross-bridge, thereby liberating energy

myosin cross-bridge: the portion of the myosin protein that binds with the binding site on the actin protein; also known as *myosin head*

myotatic (stretch) reflex: a simple, two-neuron reflex in which the tapping (or stretching) of a tendon results in the contraction of that tendon's muscle

nasopharynx: the cavity of the nose and the nasal parts of the pharynx

natural killer (NK) cell: a non-T and non-B lymphocyte that is thought to be involved with immune surveillance against cancer by destroying certain cells before they can produce tumors

negative caloric balance: state in which calories expended exceed calories taken in

neuromuscular fatigue: a transient decrease in muscular performance usually seen as a failure to maintain or develop a certain expected force or power output

neuromuscular junction: the intersection of a motor neuron and a muscle fiber; also known as *myoneural junction*

neuron: a nerve cell

neutrophil: a granular leukocyte formed in the bone marrow and released into the bloodstream

nomogram: a graph that shows the relationship between variables and is used to predict a third variable

non-pathologic cardiac hypertrophy: an exercise-induced increase in the thickening of the heart walls (primarily the left heart) as well as an increase in the diameter of the left ventricle

norepinephrine: hormone secreted by the adrenal medulla and sympathetic nerve endings; serves to increase the availability of fuel to the active muscles

obesity: an abnormal increase of fat in the subcutaneous connective tissues

oligomenorrhea: irregular menstrual periods

oligospermia: reduced sperm count

orthopnea: an abnormal condition in which a person must sit or stand to breathe deeply or comfortably

orthostatic dizziness: dizziness associated with high environmental temperatures due to peripheral vasodilation, postural pooling of blood, diminished venous return, dehydration, reduced cardiac output, and/or cerebral ischemia; also known as *heat syncope*

osteoporosis: a disease characterized by low bone mass and microarchitectural deterioration of bone tissue

overload: a basic principle of resistance training, that in order to promote strength gains and hypertrophy, a resistance training program must demand more of a muscle or muscle group than it normally performs

overtraining: the adverse effects on health and performance that often result from increasing the total volume of training too quickly

oxygenation: the process of hemoglobin combining with oxygen

oxygen cost of breathing: the percentage of metabolism devoted to the muscular work required for breathing

oxygen dissociation curve: a graphic indication of the amount of oxygen released from hemoglobin as a result of changing carbon dioxide levels in the tissues

Pacinian corpuscle: a cutaneous sensory receptor that is sensitive to pressure

palpitation: a pounding or racing of the heart, associated with normal emotional responses or with heart disorders

parasympathetic branch: the division of the autonomic nervous system that originates in the brain and the sacral region of the spinal cord and is activated during times of inactivity and digestion of nutrients

parathyroid hormone (PTH): hormone secreted by the parathyroid gland, involved in calcium regulation

paroxysmal nocturnal dyspnea: a disorder characterized by sudden attacks of respiratory distress that awaken the person

pathologic cardiac hypertrophy: an increase in the thickness of the walls of the heart, usually caused by chronically high aortic pressure and not accompanied by an increase in ventricular chamber diameter

peak height velocity: the greatest rate of growth in height; used to assess the adolescent growth spurt

peak power: the greatest amount of work performed during a five-second period; reflects the efficiency of the phosphagen system (ATP and CP breakdown)

peak weight velocity: the greatest rate of increase in weight; used to assess the adolescent growth spurt

peliosis hepatis: blood-filled cysts

percent body fat: the proportion of the body that is composed of adipose (fat) tissue

percentile rank: a score that shows how the subject performed relative to others in the same group. A percentile rank of 70, for example, indicates that the subject's score is higher than 70% of the others in the same group and lower than 30% of the others in the same group

perimysium: the connective tissue sheath covering a fasciculus

periodization: periodic changes in a resistance training program to minimize boredom and facilitate adherence; a basic principle of resistance training

peripheral fatigue: a decrease in motor performance due to mechanisms in the motor units

peripheral nervous system: the nerves that lie outside the brain and spinal cord

peripheral vascular disease: any abnormal condition that affects the blood vessels outside the heart

phagocyte: a cell that is capable of ingesting bacteria, foreign particles, and other cells; there are two general types of phagocytes: microphages and macrophages

phagocytosis: the process by which unwanted particles are engulfed and destroyed by digestive enzymes

pharynx: throat

phenolic amine hormone: a hormone that contains a phenol group attached to an amine

phosphagen: the fuel source for the ATP–PC system of energy production

phosphagen depletion: the exhaustion or emptying of phosphocreatine (PC) stores and extensive reduction of adenosine triphosphate (ATP) as a result of very high intensity physical activity

phosphatase: the enzyme responsible for dephosphorylating glucose-6-phosphate, thereby creating glucose

phosphate loading: sodium phosphate supplementation

phosphocreatine (PC): a high energy bond containing phosphagen that is utilized for rapid ATP production during short-term, high-intensity exercise; also known as *creatine phosphate*

phosphofructokinase: the rate-limiting enzyme of glycolysis

physiology: the study of the processes and functions of living organisms and their component parts

physiology of exercise: the study of the processes and functions of living organisms and their component parts during and after physical activity

planimetry: the use of an engineering instrument to trace a curve and find the area under it

plasma cell: a subclassification of B cell that secretes, into circulation, antibodies that are specific to a particular antigen

plasticity: the capacity for being molded or altered

plyometrics: a type of training involving the stretching of a muscle through an eccentric (lengthening) phase followed by a forceful concentric (shortening) muscle action

polypeptide: several amino acids linked together

positive caloric balance: state in which calories taken in exceed calories expended

power: (force × distance) / time

power density spectrum (PDS): spectrum that describes the amount of power that exists in the EMG at each given frequency

power lifting: a competitive sport in which an athlete attempts to lift a maximal amount of weight in specific lifts (squat, dead lift, and bench press)

precapillary sphincter: a ring of smooth muscle that precedes a true capillary, controlling the amount of blood flowing through that capillary

prelatent iron deficiency: the earliest stage of iron deficiency, characterized by a decrease or absence of storage iron

premotor cortex: the portion of the brain that is rostral to the motor area and contains the nerve cell bodies of the extrapyramidal system

pressure gradient: the difference in pressure between two points

principle: a settled rule of action based on theories that are well supported by research findings

professional: a person who has "professed" or declared a commitment to a learned discipline with a well-defined body of knowledge

progesterone: a hormone secreted by the ovaries

progression: a basic principle of resistance training, that in order to maintain overload and continue to see adaptation from a resistance training program, it is necessary periodically to increase the volume of training

prohormone: refers to androstenedione and dehydroepiandrosterone, precursors to testosterone and estrogen; sometimes used as ergogenic aids

proprioception: feedback of sensory information regarding movement and body position

proprioceptive neuromuscular facilitation (PNF): a technique used for maintaining or increasing flexibility or restoring range of motion following injury

protein hormone: a hormone that is a chain of amino acids

pseudopod: a temporary protoplasmic projection put forth by an ameboid organism for the purpose of locomotion or prehension of food

puberty: the period of life during which the ability to reproduce begins or the time of sexual maturation

pulmonary vein: vessel that carries oxygenated blood from the lungs to the left heart

pulmonary ventilation: gas exchange in the lungs in which the blood in the lung capillaries takes up oxygen and gives up much of its carbon dioxide; also known as *external respiration*

Purkinje fibers: specialized conducting cells of the heart that conduct the cardiac impulse throughout the ventricular myocardium

pyramidal system: the corticospinal pathways that originate in large nerve cells that are shaped like pyramids and have axons that synapse with the motor neurons in the ventral horn of the spinal cord

pyramidal tracts: descending motor pathways that originate in cell bodies of the motor cortex and synapse with motor neurons in the ventral horn of the spinal cord

pyruvate: a metabolite of carbohydrate metabolism; sometimes used as an ergogenic aid

qualitative electromyography: electromyography concerned with the wave form of the muscle action potential from single discrete motor units

quantitative electromyography: electromyography concerned with the amount of electrical activity that is present in a given muscle under varying conditions

R: multiple correlation coefficient, a numerical measure of how well a dependent variable can be predicted from a combination of independent variables (a number between –1 and 1)

radiation: the transfer of heat between objects that are not in contact with one another, by means of electromagnetic waves

rate coding: the process of changing the firing frequency of motor units to produce varying amounts of tension in a muscle

rate-limiting enzyme: the enzyme within a metabolic pathway that has the lowest turnover rate

rating of perceived exertion (RPE): a 15-point scale used to quantify an individual's subjective opinion of exercise intensity

reactant: a substance acted on by an enzyme to create a product; also known as *substrate*

reciprocal inhibition: the neuromuscular function that serves to turn off one of a pair of muscles when its opponent is activated

recommended daily caloric intake: the quantity of daily calories suggested for the maintenance of good nutrition for healthy persons in the United States

recruitment: the calling into play of additional numbers, as in the additional motor units called into play in order to increase the tension production in a muscle

red nucleus: a type of motor nucleus that serves as a relay station for the axons of the neurons of the premotor cortex to communicate with the lower motor neurons

reflex: an involuntary motor response to a sensory stimulus

regurgitation: backflow

relaxation period: the lengthening period that follows the contraction phase of a muscle twitch

relaxin: a hormone secreted by the corpus luteum of the ovary and the placenta; involved with the relaxation of the pubic symphysis and dilation of the uterine cervix during pregnancy

repetition maximum (RM) load: the maximum amount of weight that can be lifted for a specific number of repetitions

repetition (REP) training: a type of training similar to interval training, but involving greater intensity, work bouts lasting approximately 30 to 90 seconds, and a work to recovery ratio of 1:5

reserve of heart rate: the ability of the heart rate to increase from the resting rate to the maximum rate

residual volume: the volume of gas remaining in the lungs after a maximal respiration

resistance: the sum of the forces that oppose blood flow, including blood viscosity, the length of the vessel, and the diameter of the vessel

resistance vessels: muscular vessels, such as the small arteries and arterioles, which dilate or constrict to control the resistance to blood flow

resorption: the loss of a substance by lysis

respiratory center: the nerve cells in the pons and medulla that are responsible for the automatic and rhythmic control of respiration

resting heart rate: the heart rate measured when the body is at rest

righting reflex: a series of reflex movements that cause a person or animal placed upside down to change to an upright position

Ruffini receptor: a subcutaneous sensory receptor located principally at the junction of the dermis and the subcutaneous tissue

runner's wall: fatigue experienced by long-distance runners at approximately 18 to 20 miles, probably caused by glycogen depletion in the quadriceps

running economy: the aerobic demand of submaximal running

sarcolemma: the cell membrane of a muscle fiber

sarcomere: the functional unit of the myofibril

sarcoplasm: the cytoplasm of a muscle fiber

sarcoplasmic reticulum: a network of tubules and sacs in skeletal muscle fibers that plays an important role in muscle contraction and relaxation by releasing and storing calcium ions; analogous to endoplasmic reticulum of other cells

saturated fat: a fat containing no double or triple bonds

second wind: the psychological and physical relief felt by an endurance athlete upon making the necessary metabolic adjustments to a heavy exercise intensity

SEE: standard error of estimate, a measure of the accuracy of predictions made using a regression equation

sensory neuron: a neuron that conducts impulses from the periphery to the central nervous system; also known as *afferent neuron*

Setchenov phenomenon: the fact that more work can be produced after a pause with diverting activity than after a passive rest pause

shortening period: the phase of muscle twitch in which the muscle shortens (also called *contraction phase*)

simple carbohydrate: one or two sugar molecules joined together

sinoatrial (SA) node: a specialized mass of cardiac tissue in the wall of the right atrium; initiates the cardiac cycle; also known as the *pacemaker of the heart*

size principle: the fact that the small motor neurons innervating slow twitch, oxidative fibers have the lowest threshold for activation and are therefore activated first during the recruitment of motor units for muscular contraction

skeletal muscle: contractile tissue attached to the skeleton

sliding filament model: the proposition that explains how protein filaments within the sarcomere move to cause muscle fiber contraction

slow-twitch oxidative (SO) fibers: fatigue-resistant muscle fibers that favor oxidative (aerobic) methods of energy production; also known as type I fibers

smooth muscle: contractile tissue found in the walls of the hollow viscera and blood vessels

sodium bicarbonate: a naturally occurring buffer in the blood; sometimes used as an ergogenic aid by athletes in an attempt to reduce lactic acid build-up during exercise

sodium phosphate: a granular crystalline salt sometimes used as an ergogenic aid

somatic nervous system: the branch of the nervous system that regulates voluntary functions

specificity: a basic principle of resistance training that suggests that the adaptations that occur as a result of a resistance training program will be specific to the characteristics of the program

specificity of speed: the fact that speed is not an overall characteristic of the individual but is specific to the limb and joint and direction of movement

speed: the result of applying force to a mass; implies constant movement

sphygmomanometer: a pressure cuff and mercury or anoid manometer used to measure blood pressure

spinal reflex: a two-neuron reflex in which a sensory neuron receives a stimulus and carries an impulse to the spinal cord, and the impulse is transmitted to another neuron, which carries the impulse to a muscle or gland

sports anemia: a decrease in blood hemoglobin levels that occurs in response to heavy endurance training in the absence of any recognizable disease process

spot reducing: exercising a specific area of the body to decrease fat stores at that location; this is ineffective

sprint-assisted training: a method of training that uses such techniques as assisted towing, downhill running, and high-speed treadmill running to improve sprint running performance

sprint-resisted training: a method of training that uses resistive exercises to improve sprint running performance

standard error of estimate (SEE): a measure of the accuracy of predictions made using a regression equation

start: the first phase of a sprinting event

state anxiety: the degree of a general feeling of impending danger or dread

static exercise: exercise that involves holding a position, such as isometric contractions

static flexibility: a measurement of the range of motion of a joint

static stretching: a method of muscle elongation (stretching) involving low-force, long-duration (30 to 60 seconds) movements

stenotic heart valve: a heart valve that does not open properly; results in restricted outflow of blood and thus a murmur

steroid hormone: a hormone that is derived from cholesterol and therefore exhibits a classic four-ring structure

stitch in the side: pain in the lower, lateral thoracic wall that occurs during exercise; may be caused by ischemia of the diaphragm or intercostal muscles

stretch reflex: the contraction of a muscle in response to being stretched

stretch–shortening cycle: an alternate term for plyometrics

stroke: an abnormal condition of the brain characterized by an embolus, thrombus, or hemorrhage, resulting in ischemia of the brain tissue

stroke volume (SV): the amount of blood ejected out of each ventricle of the heart with each cardiac contraction

stroke volume reserve: the ability of the heart to increase its contraction strength, its filling pressure, and the distensibility of its ventricles

substantia nigra: a type of motor nucleus that serves as a relay station for the axons of the neurons of the premotor cortex to communicate with the lower motor neurons

substrate: a substance acted on by an enzyme to create a product; also known as *reactant*

summation of twitches: the increase in tension produced in a muscle as a result of stimulation before the muscle is allowed to relax

suppressor T cell: a type of T cell that regulates the action of killer T cells and the development of B cells into plasma cells

sympathetic branch: the division of the autonomic nervous system that originates in the thoracic and lumbar regions of the spinal cord and is activated in emergency or stressful situations

synapse: the junction between two neurons or between a neuron and an effector organ

syncope: fainting; loss of consciousness

syncytium: a network of cells

systole: the contraction phase of the cardiac cycle

systolic pressure: the arterial blood pressure during systole

T cell: a class of lymphocyte that upon presentation of an antigen by a macrophage, enlarges and divides into four subclassifications (killer T cells, helper T cells, suppressor T cells, and memory T cells)

tachycardia: rapid heart rate; a condition in which the myocardium contracts at a rate greater than 100 beats/minute

Tanner scale: a commonly used technique that uses a 1 to 5 scale in assessing puberty, based on the level of development of secondary sex traits

target heart rate: the desired exercise heart rate for an exercise bout; usually obtained by multiplying the maximum heart rate reserve by a percentage within the range of 40 to 85 percent

target oxygen consumption rate: the desired oxygen consumption rate for an exercise bout; usually obtained by multiplying the maximum $\dot{V}O_2$ reserve by a percentage within the range of 40 to 85 percent

task-dependency model: a model that suggests the cause of neuromuscular fatigue is dependent upon the characteristics of the exercise task that is being performed

temperature regulatory center: the area of the hypothalamus that controls body temperature; receives sensory input regarding environmental and core temperatures and then activates and/or inhibits the body's heat production and conservation or heat loss mechanisms

tempo-pace training: training consisting of continuous work bouts of approximately 20 minutes duration

testosterone: a hormone secreted by the testes

tetanus: a sustained muscular contraction caused by a series of stimuli so frequent that the individual muscular responses are fused

theory: a position based on scientific evidence but insufficiently verified to be accepted as fact

thigh extensors: the gluteal muscles (gluteus maximus and gluteus medius) and the hamstrings (biceps femoris, semitendinosus, and semimembranosus)

thoracic wall compliance: the relationship between force required (elastic force) per unit strength of the thorax

thromboembolic stroke: an abnormal condition of the brain that occurs when a blood clot forms or an embolus breaks loose from somewhere in the body and blocks an artery in the brain, causing ischemia of the brain tissue

thrombus: a blood clot

tidal volume: the volume of gas inspired or expired during each respiratory cycle

time domain: the domain of the EMG signal that involves determining the amplitude (voltage) of electrical current that exists during a specific period of time

tissue respiration: gas exchange between the blood and cells; also known as *internal respiration*

torque: rotary force production

total lung capacity: the amount of gas in the lung after a maximal inspiration; includes the tidal volume, inspiratory reserve volume, expiratory reserve volume, and residual volume

trachea: the cartilaginous and membranous tube in the neck that extends from the larynx to the fifth thoracic vertebra, where it divides into two bronchi; serves as a passageway for air

trait anxiety: the degree of a feeling of impending danger or dread at the present time

transverse tubules (t-tubules): extensions of the sarcolemma that allow the action potential to move from the outside to the inside of a muscle fiber

trenchfoot: one of the most common nonfreezing cold injuries; typically develops after many hours (usually >12 hours) of exposure to cold, wet conditions when socks and shoes are worn continuously. Symptoms include swelling and numbness of the feet.

triglyceride: a fat compound consisting of glycerol and three molecules of fatty acid

tropomyosin: a type of contractile protein (myofilament) that changes shape upon calcium binding with troponin, allowing actin and myosin to bind

troponin: a type of contractile protein (myofilament) that binds calcium ions

turbinate: pertaining to the thin, bony plates within the nasal cavity

type 1 diabetes mellitus: a metabolic disorder characterized by elevated blood glucose levels, caused by the destruction of the beta cells of the pancreas and therefore a deficiency in the hormone insulin

type 2 diabetes mellitus: a metabolic disorder characterized by elevated blood glucose levels, caused by a decrease in insulin receptor number or sensitivity

unilateral imagined training: training that involves thinking about, but not actually performing, a resistance exercise with only one limb

upper motor neuron: a neuron whose cell body is in the brain

upper respiratory infection (URI): any infectious disease of the sinuses, tonsils, nose, pharynx, or larynx

vagus nerve: tenth cranial nerve; arises from the medulla oblongata and supplies the larynx, lungs, heart, esophagus, stomach, and most of the abdominal viscera

vascular resistance: the sum of the forces that oppose blood flow

$\dot{V}_E$: volume of gas expired per minute or minute ventilation

vein: a thin-walled vessel that carries blood toward the heart

ventilation equivalent: the number of liters of air breathed for every 100 mL of oxygen consumed

ventilatory threshold: the measurement of the anaerobic threshold by expired gas samples

ventricle: a chamber of the heart that pumps blood into arteries

venule: a small vessel that lies between a capillary and a vein

very low density lipoprotein (VLDL): a plasma protein that is primarily composed of triglycerides with small amounts of cholesterol, phospholipid, and protein

vestibular receptor: the portion of the inner ear that functions to provide a sense of equilibrium

viscosity: the stickiness and thickness of a fluid

vital capacity: the maximal amount of gas that can be expired with a forceful effort following a maximal inspiration; includes the tidal volume, inspiratory reserve volume, and expiratory reserve volume

$\dot{V}O_2$: oxygen consumption rate, an indirect measure of aerobic energy production

$\dot{V}O_2$ max: the maximal amount of oxygen that can be consumed per minute during maximal exercise; also known as aerobic power and maximal oxygen consumption rate

$\dot{V}O_2$ reserve: the difference between $\dot{V}O_2$ max and resting $\dot{V}O_2$

volume of exercise: the product of the frequency, intensity, and time of exercise (frequency × intensity × time), which reflects the total amount of physical activity performed

VT: ventilatory threshold, an estimation of the exercise intensity above which anaerobic ATP production must supplement aerobic metabolism

warming up: activities that increase general body temperature and the temperature of muscles involved in a physical activity, prior to the activity

weight lifting: a competitive sport in which an athlete attempts to lift a maximal amount of weight in specific lifts (clean and jerk and snatch)

weight training: the use of a variety of methods to increase muscular strength, endurance, and/or power for sports participation or fitness enhancement; also known as *strength training* and *resistance training*

wind chill factor: the effect of wind in reducing effective temperature

Z-line: the membrane that separates sarcomeres

Index